ENCYCLOPEDIA OF EDUCATION

SECOND EDITION

EDITORIAL BOARD

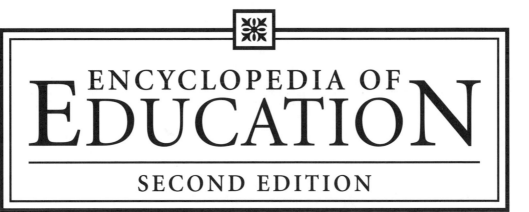

ENCYCLOPEDIA OF EDUCATION

SECOND EDITION

James W. Guthrie, Editor in Chief

VOLUME

5

Macdonald–Putnam

**MACMILLAN
REFERENCE
USA™**

New York • Detroit • San Diego • San Francisco • Cleveland • New Haven, Conn. • Waterville, Maine • London • Munich

Encyclopedia of Education, Second Edition

James W. Guthrie, Editor in Chief

For permission to use material from this product, submit your request via Web at http://www.gale-edit.com/permissions, or you may download our Permissions Request form and submit your request by fax or mail to:

Permissions Department
The Gale Group, Inc.
27500 Drake Road
Farmington Hills, MI 48331-3535
Permissions Hotline: 248-699-8006 or
800-877-4253 ext. 8006
Fax: 248-699-8074 or 800-762-4058

LIBRARY OF CONGRESS CATALOGING-IN-PUBLICATION DATA

Encyclopedia of education / edited by James W. Guthrie.—2nd ed.
    p. cm.
Includes bibliographical references and index.
    ISBN 0-02-865594-X (hardcover : set : alk. paper)
    1. Education—Encyclopedias. I. Guthrie, James W.
    LB15 .E47 2003
    370'.3—dc21   2002008205

ISBNs
Volume 1: 0-02-865595-8
Volume 2: 0-02-865596-6
Volume 3: 0-02-865597-4
Volume 4: 0-02-865598-2
Volume 5: 0-02-865599-0
Volume 6: 0-02-865600-8
Volume 7: 0-02-865601-6
Volume 8: 0-02-865602-4

Printed in the United States of America
10 9 8 7 6 5 4 3 2 1

M

MACDONALD, JAMES (1925–1983)

The work in curriculum theory of James Macdonald (1925–1983), Distinguished Professor of Education at the University of North Carolina at Greensboro, helped move the field beyond the traditional and scientific orientations of the 1950s and 1960s and toward an approach centered on human, ethical, and even spiritual considerations. Recognizing that schools were often dehumanizing and impersonal, Macdonald was a consistent critic of educational theory and practice that neglected the important work of helping students achieve their fullest potential as human beings in a democratic society.

Macdonald grew up in a small town in southern Wisconsin. First certified as a secondary school teacher in social studies, he briefly taught elementary school before enrolling in the doctoral program at the University of Wisconsin–Madison. There he studied under Virgil Herrick, a prominent professor of education whose analytic and conceptual work in curriculum theory would serve as a basis for Macdonald's own thought. Upon completing his doctoral degree, Macdonald taught at the University of Texas–Austin (1956–1957) and New York University (1957–1959) before returning to Wisconsin in 1959 as director of School Experimentation and Research at the University of Wisconsin–Milwaukee. In 1963 he moved to the University of Wisconsin–Madison as a professor in the Department of Curriculum and Instruction and the Department of Educational Policy. He returned to University of Wisconsin–Milwaukee in 1966 as a professor of Curriculum and Social and Philosophical Foundations of Education. In 1972 he accepted a position as Distinguished Professor of Education at the University

of North Carolina at Greensboro, where he remained until his death in 1983.

Throughout the course of its development, Macdonald's work reflected a systematic attempt to formulate a comprehensive curriculum theory that balanced the institutional, technocratic realities of schooling and educational research with human, ethical, and social ideals. He identified four stages through which his own thinking had evolved during the span of his career. The first stage was based on scientific theory and method and is reflected in Macdonald's work from the late 1950s and early 1960s. Taking his cue from Herrick, Macdonald's focus during this period was on building and explaining curriculum theory through scientific and empirical means.

Macdonald characterized the second stage of his thought as personalized humanism. During this time, Macdonald's work focused on understanding how schooling helped and hindered the development of students' self-concept. In his 1964 article, "An Image of Man: The Learner Himself," Macdonald extended humanist concepts popularized by psychologists like Carl Rogers and Abraham Maslow to processes of schooling. His concern was with human development, or becoming, and how schools and teachers could best facilitate the self-actualizing processes of their students.

By the late 1960s and early 1970s, Macdonald's thought had moved into a third stage, social humanism, which placed his earlier humanist concerns within a social and political context. His work of this period undertook an analytic critique of the social, bureaucratic, and institutional pressures on schooling and curriculum. His 1971 essay "The School as a Double Agent" took note of the conflict between the democratic ideals of schooling and the repressive realities of its organizational, procedural, and institutional demands. In the 1978 essay "Curriculum, Consciousness, and Social Change," Macdonald reiterated his belief that the curriculum work done in schools should liberate the spiritual, intellectual, and physical potentiality of students in the interest of realizing the ideals inherent to democratic society.

Macdonald called the fourth stage in the development of his thought transcendentalism. In this stage, Macdonald extended his personalized and social humanist concerns into the area of culture. He argued for the need to transcend normal patterns of cultural awareness in order to promote the fullest realization of a student's sense of what it is to be human. In his 1974 article "A Transcendental Developmental Ideology of Education," Macdonald critiqued four basic conceptual models, or ideologies, of education and found each inadequate with respect to the justification of its underlying values. As an alternative to these four models, he proposed a transcendental developmental ideology based in part on the notion of aesthetic rationality, a form of knowledge that is both rational and intuitive.

Although Macdonald never published a book-length manuscript, he was a prolific essayist whose work appeared in a variety of scholarly and professional journals, edited books, and monographs. He was a regular presenter at professional conferences and gatherings. His work is widely associated with the curriculum field's reconceptualization, a movement in 1970s that sought to broaden the means and aims of curriculum theorizing by borrowing insights and methods from the humanities.

See also: CURRICULUM, SCHOOL.

BIBLIOGRAPHY

BURKE, MELVA M. 1985. "The Personal and Professional Journey of James B. Macdonald." *The Journal of Curriculum Theorizing* 6:84–119.

MACDONALD, BRADLEY J., ed. 1995. *Theory as a Prayerful Act: The Collected Essays of James B. Macdonald.* New York: Lang.

MACDONALD, JAMES B., and ZARET, ESTHER, eds. 1975. *Schools in Search of Meaning.* Washington, DC: Association for Supervision and Curriculum Development.

PINAR, WILLIAM. 1995. "Introduction." In *Theory as a Prayerful Act: The Collected Essays of James B. Macdonald,* ed. Bradley J. Macdonald. New York: Lang.

SCHUBERT, WILLIAM H. 1992. "On Mentorship: Examples from J. Harlan Shores and Others through Lenses Provided by James B. Macdonald." *The Journal of Curriculum Theorizing* 9:47–69.

PATRICK A. ROBERTS
WILLIAM H. SCHUBERT

MAGNET SCHOOLS

Magnet schools are public K–12 schools, or programs within schools, developed around a particular theme to promote racial and ethnic diversity. Magnet schools are based on the premise that all students do not learn in the same ways, and that if educators find a unifying theme or a different organizational structure for students with similar interests, those students will be motivated to learn more in all areas. In addition, magnet schools provide public choice within school districts.

If a magnet school attracts students and teachers, its chance of succeeding is greatly improved because those in attendance want to be there—they will have chosen that school. When a parent chooses a school for his or her child, that school is more likely to succeed for that child than would one to which that child was randomly assigned. These tenets underlie the development of magnet schools in America.

History

In the United States during the 1960s some options to traditional public schools sprang up as a protest against racially segregated schools. These schools emphasized the basic subjects of reading, writing, and arithmetic, but they also included the study of the history of African Americans and the civil rights movement, and they were concerned with how schools could be tied to community needs. Some of these schools, called *street academies,* led to more permanent structures. Harlem Prep, for example, first funded by foundations, businesses, and industry, became one of the public schools of New York City.

The history of magnet schools is tied to the 1960s protest over school desegregation, and to the educational reform model of public choice as a way to address educational inequality. Until the early 1970s federal district courts had directed school systems to implement desegregation policies. In Detroit the courts did not impose a multiple-district solution to segregation, but did approve special enrichment programs intended to help overcome the effects of past discrimination. In the wake of this decision, nearly every court order mandating that schools desegregate also included a voluntary component, which became known as magnet schools. The courts learned that by using a carrot instead of a stick, more desegregation would occur, and quality of education would improve at the same time.

In the late 1960s school districts across America were being torn apart by resistance to forced desegregation of the schools. Many parents moved to a suburban district to keep from having their children bused to a school away from the neighborhood. Others chose private education for their children. School administrators and boards of education began to try to find a voluntary way to reduce racial isolation.

The highly publicized violence and protests, as well as the *white flight* from public schools, made public school choice a school segregation remedy. As Lauri Steele and Roger Levine noted, by making available a curricular alternative, magnet schools were intended to provide incentives to parents to remain in the public school system while sending their children to integrated schools.

The first public school designed to reduce racial isolation by offering a school choice to parents was McCarver Elementary School in Tacoma, Washington, which opened in 1968. In 1969 Trotter Elementary School, in Boston, Massachusetts, opened for the same reasons. Both of these first attempts offered a new organizational pattern. They guaranteed continuous-progress education, in which students would progress at their own rates. Neither of these schools was called a magnet; they were referred to as alternative schools.

In 1970, with the assistance of $6 million from the federal government, Minneapolis, Minnesota, mounted an alternative experiment in the southeast section of the city. This district opened four elementary schools and one high school with different organizational designs. Of the four elementary schools, the least structured was referred to as *free,* in which the students directed their own education. The sec-

ond type was called *open,* and had an informal classroom design. The third was a continuous-progress school, and the fourth used a traditional approach, which Minneapolis called *contemporary.*

Following the pattern established in Minneapolis, Haaren High School in New York City, with the assistance of the Urban Coalition, broke into smaller units with more personalized instruction. Berkeley, California, also following the pattern established in the Minneapolis elementary schools, embarked on a full-scale alternative schools program, featuring basic-skills centers, environmentally-oriented programs, independent contracting for curriculum delivery with businesses, and more. The word *magnet* was still not being used, although these programs looked much like schools that are called magnets in the early twenty-first century.

Dallas, Texas, opened the first *super* high school in 1971. Designed around the concept of career strands, Skyline High School attracted students of all kinds—rich, poor, Hispanic, African-American, Asian, white—from all over the city. It even offered adult classes in the evenings. In fact the school rarely closed its doors. Some students came for a full-day program, others came part-time, and still others came after school.

Magnet Schools

It was about this time that school administrators in Houston, Texas, in describing the effect of its Performing and Visual Arts School, said that it worked like a "magnet" in attracting students. The word appeared to catch on. By 1975 the term was being used to describe various types of fiscal assistance contemplated by the federal government.

In 1973 Cincinnati opened a wide range of school options, among them the first Montessori school in the public sector and the first foreign language school, both beginning in the primary grades. By 1980 most major cities had systems of magnets, but it was the federal courts, in ruling against school segregation, that caused the greatest surge in magnet education.

Magnet Schools in the Early Twenty-First Century

Magnet schools and magnet programs continue to be used to reduce racial isolation, but they are increasingly considered superior options within the public sector for all students, even in districts of primarily one race. School districts offer anywhere from one to more than one hundred *themes* to attract students, including fine and performing arts, communications, humanities, wellness and health, education, international studies, language arts, technology, foreign languages, and many others.

North Dade Center for Modern Languages in Miami, Florida, specializes in modern languages and multicultural education for elementary students. The school's "magnet" is instruction in Spanish and French. Students at North Dade have excelled in all areas of the Stanford Achievement Test, scoring well above the national median. The Carver Center for the Arts and Technology in Baltimore, Maryland, is a public school with students in the ninth through twelfth grades that attracts students from a 600-square-mile area. The students at Carver take ninety-minute block schedules that enable them to earn eleven additional credits beyond the Maryland state graduation requirements. Mabel Hoggard Magnet School is a K–5th grade school in Las Vegas, Nevada, that emphasizes math and science across the curriculum. The school has a partnership for student experience with the University of Nevada, Las Vegas, Engineering Department.

There are more than 4,000 magnet schools in the United States, and they are springing up in other countries, such as Canada and the Netherlands. The Dayton Accord, an agreement made to resolve the conflict in the former Yugoslavia, included a plan to develop a magnet school in Bosnia-Herzegovina. This school would promote cultural and ethnic diversity. Magnet schools in the United States come together to share their successes and struggles in a national non-profit membership organization: Magnet Schools of America (MSA).

Magnet Schools of America

MSA is a national organization representing more than 4,000 magnet schools. It was founded to promote and advance the cause of magnet-school education. According to former executive director Dr. Donald Waldrip, MSA had its beginning in 1977, in the Dallas Independent School District. The first MSA conference featured Dr. Mario Fantini, dean of the University of Massachusetts School of Education and an advocate of public school choice; Dr. John B. Davis Jr., former Superintendent of the Minneapolis Public Schools, which was the first school system to adopt magnet schools; U.S. Senator John Glenn, who sponsored the first funding bill for magnet schools; and the Honorable George Edwards, Chief Judge of the Sixth Circuit Court of Appeals and a voice for equity. Two more annual conferences were held—in 1978 in New Orleans and in 1979 in San Diego. Although Dr. Waldrip believed in 1979 that "everyone who was going to organize magnet schools had done so," after a seven-year hiatus the fourth conference was held in Milwaukee, and has been an annual event ever since. The conference offers staff development sessions, informational workshops, and opportunities to showcase magnet schools.

In 1991 Magnet Schools of America became a more formalized organization. At the tenth conference in Columbus, Ohio, a national board was elected, with Dr. Judith S. Stein serving as the first president. In 1994 MSA became a not-for-profit, 501(c)(3) corporation. For federally funded magnet schools (i.e., Magnet School Assistance Program grant recipients), MSA provides special technical assistance workshops on the development of new magnet schools, as well as programs for the improvement of existing schools.

Mission of Magnet Schools of America

MSA's mission is to (1) promote the goals of desegregation, equity, and excellence through the expansion and improvement of magnet schools; (2) encourage the passage of legislation at both the state and national levels that will promote the development and improvement of magnet schools, (3) explore and establish linkages with other professional groups with similar interests, and (4) promote networking among magnet schools. MSA seeks to encourage America's businesses to become actively involved in magnet schools by supporting them both conceptually and financially. It also provides information for parents and community members on the benefits of magnet schools as public schools of choice, and acts as a national clearinghouse for information dissemination on magnet schools.

The Federal Magnet Schools Assistance Program

The U.S. Department of Education has a competitive funding program for magnet schools, the Magnet School Assistance Program, which works in three-year cycles. Schools complete extensive applications based on a Request for Proposals from the federal government. Grant proposals can be quite extensive, sometimes running to several volumes. They include data on the community and school system, and require either a court-ordered or voluntary desegregation plan. The grant proposals are read by educators representing the various parts of the United States and the U.S. Department of Education and have a lengthy approval and encumbering process. The average grant is $2 million, but grants can range upwards to $4 million.

According to magnet school researchers Steele and Marion Eaton, the Magnet School Assistance Program was begun in 1984 to provide federal support for magnet schools that had desegregation plans, whether court-ordered or voluntary. The program provides funds to support the elimination, reduction, or prevention of minority isolation in elementary and secondary schools. Steel and Eaton note that federal support for magnet programs over the decade of the 1990s was substantial.

Research and Popular Press

The National Educational Longitudinal Survey (NELS) is a popular study that surveyed all types of schools in 1988. After examining the NELS study, Adam Gamoran stated that he "found that magnet schools are more effective than regular schools at raising the proficiency of students in science, reading, and social studies." Furthermore, "magnet schools are more likely to serve disadvantaged students than comprehensive schools, yet they rate at least as well in academic climate, social attachment, and course taking" (Brooks, Stein, Waldrip, and Hale, p. 37).

Texas and Florida have the most magnet schools. Miami, Florida, and Orlando, Florida, were each labeled in 2001 as one of the "10 best cities for families" by *Child* magazine, based upon the magnet schools in these cities. Miami-Dade County and Palm Beach County, Florida, both have extensive magnet school programs. According to *Working Mother* magazine the "only downside [to magnet schools] seems to be that there aren't enough of them to fill the demand, and not enough space in the ones that exist" (Hanson-Harding, pp. 67–68). Magnet schools can be located by contacting the local education agency or Magnet Schools of America.

See also: ALTERNATIVE SCHOOLING; MULTICULTURAL EDUCATION.

BIBLIOGRAPHY

BROOKS, ROBERT G.; STEIN, JUDITH S.; WALDRIP, DONALD R.; and HALE, PHALE D., eds. 1999. *De-finitive Studies of Magnet Schools: Voices of Public School Choice.* The Woodlands, TX: Magnet Schools of America.

CHILD MAGAZINE. 2001. "The 10 Best Cities for Families." *Child* 67.

HANSON-HARDING, BRIAN. 2001. "The New School Lingo." *Working Mother* March: 65, 67.

OLMSTEAD, PHYLLIS M., and STEIN, JUDITH S. 2001. *Directory of Magnet Mentors, 2001.* North Miami Beach, FL: Magnet Schools of America.

STEELE, L., and LEVINE, R. 1994. *Educational Innovation in Multiracial Contexts: The Growth of Magnet Schools in American Education.* Washington, DC: American Institutes for Research.

STEELE, LAURI, and EATON, MARION. 1996. *Reducing, Eliminating, and Preventing Minority Isolation in American Schools: Impact of MSAP, Executive Summary.* Washington, DC: American Institutes for Research.

STEIN, JUDITH S.; OLMSTEAD, PHYLLIS M.; BROOKS, ROBERT G.; and HALE, PHALE D. 2000. *Blueprint for Understanding and Operating Successful Magnet and Theme-Based Schools.* Pembroke Pines, FL: ROC EdTech.

WALDRIP, DONALD. 1998. "Executive Director's Column." *CHOICE* 8(4):2.

INTERNET RESOURCE

MAGNET SCHOOLS OF AMERICA. 2002. <www. magnet.edu>.

PHYLLIS M. OLMSTEAD
JUDITH S. STEIN
DONALD R. WALDRIP
JEAN WODE

MAINSTREAMING
See: SPECIAL EDUCATION.

MAJOR
See: ACADEMIC MAJOR, THE.

MANAGED CARE AND CHILDREN

Since the early 1980s the health care system in the United States has been radically transformed from one dominated by fee-for-service arrangements to one dominated by managed care. Between 1980 and 2000 the number of Americans enrolled in some form of managed care rose fourteenfold. By that year, an estimated 140 million people were enrolled in health maintenance organizations (HMOs), one form of managed care. Because many children are beneficiaries of employment-based insurance, they are increasingly enrolled in managed-care plans, along with their parents. It is estimated that as of 1996, half of all insured children were enrolled in managed-care plans. Children are also being enrolled in managed-care plans through the nationwide conversion of state Medicaid programs from fee-for-service to managed care, and through the adoption of the State Child Health Insurance Program (SCHIP), which was enacted by Congress in 1997 to extend health insurance to low-income children who are ineligible for Medicaid, but whose family incomes are too low to afford private insurance. By 2000 most states had implemented managed-care programs for Medicaid and SCHIP beneficiaries.

What Is Managed Care?

The term *managed care* refers to a variety of health care financing and delivery arrangements. The single unifying characteristic of these various approaches is that those enrolled are either encouraged or required to obtain care through a network of participating providers—providers that are selected by the managed-care organization and agree to abide by to the rules of that organization. This is in contrast to fee-for-service arrangements, in which patients typically may seek care from any licensed health care professional or organization, and providers may perform services based on their individual judgments about what care is appropriate or needed. Under fee-for-service, however, an insurer may decide after the fact not to reimburse the health care provider or the patient for certain services received.

The primary purposes of limiting the range of providers available to enrolled patients under managed care are twofold: to control the patient's access to services, and to control the behavior of the providers. A limited network of providers not only restricts utilization to those providers in the plan, but also permits the plan to control participating providers with respect to patient utilization. By controlling access and utilization, plans can better control costs.

The ways in which managed-care plans control access and utilization varies among the different managed-care models. Plans vary in terms of the degree of risk that is placed on the physicians (as opposed to the plan or the payer); the relationship among the physicians within the network; and the exclusivity of the relationship between the plan (or an intermediary) and the medical group.

HMO plans generally have two defining characteristics: providers are at direct or indirect financial risk for providing services, and enrollees usually have no coverage for out-of-network use. The types of HMO plans are distinguished from each other by the type of physicians organization that delivers the services, and by the exclusivity of the relationship between the plan or intermediary and large medical groups.

Preferred provider organization (PPO) plans have three defining characteristics. First, they do not capitate or put their network physician members at risk. (Capitation is defined as a single payment to a provider per member per month of service, regardless of patient encounters.) PPOs generally pay physicians on a fee-for-service basis, often at a discount from usual, customary, and reasonable charges. Second, enrollees in a PPO plan usually receive services from a network of solo or small-group physicians and a network of hospitals that have nonexclusive relationships with the PPO (though some PPO enrollees receive services from large group practices). Third, PPO enrollees receive some benefit coverage if they obtain health care services from a non-network provider.

Point-of-service (POS) plans may be thought of as HMOs with a PPO *wraparound*. They are defined by one typical characteristic. When services are needed (the *point-of-service*), enrollees can choose to obtain services out-of-network and still obtain some coverage for that service. POS-plan enrollees pay higher premiums than do those enrolled in traditional HMOs.

Trends in Managed Care among Children

Since 1973, when Congress enacted the Health Maintenance Organization Act to support the development of HMOs, managed care has rapidly taken hold. By 1995 nearly three-quarters of Americans who received their health insurance through an employer were enrolled in a managed-care plan, up from 51 percent just two years earlier. Total membership in insurer-sponsored managed care at the end of the 1990's approached $132 million. This widespread move toward managed care is largely a reflection of payers' interest in controlling their costs. Employers and government sponsors face increasing pressure to contain costs, including those related to health insurance for their employees. In some employer plans, as well as most Medicaid and SCHIP programs, consumers are no longer given the choice between managed care and open fee-for-service but are required to accept managed-care enrollment. Although both health insurance premium increases and Medicaid spending growth slowed in the late 1990s and into the twenty-first century, forecasters have predicted that managed care will continue to assume a greater proportion of the market.

The largest increases in managed-care enrollment have occurred in the private market. In 1996, 43 percent of insured persons were enrolled in HMOs. Managed care has also has taken over government insurance programs such as Medicaid. Since the early 1980s, when federal restrictions on managed-care enrollment were significantly relaxed, the number of Medicaid beneficiaries enrolled in managed care has risen. As a result, national enrollment rates in managed care grew fivefold during the 1990s. In California, where managed-care penetration is the greatest, half of all children with Medicaid coverage were enrolled in managed-care organizations in 1999. All states with SCHIP programs enroll participants in managed-care plans. Since Medicaid managed care involves mostly children, and SCHIP is exclusively for children, the adoption of managed care by these programs is significant. Indeed, managed care is becoming the norm for children. Nearly half of all insured children were enrolled in managed-care plans in 1996.

Is Managed Care Good or Bad for Children?

Most observers agree that the transition from fee-for service arrangements to managed care presents both challenges and opportunities in the provision of services to children. Managed care has the potential to affect access to health care, the quality of care received, and health care costs in countless ways. Advocates of managed care contend that it can result in improvements over fee-for-service through improved coordination and convenience of health services, an emphasis on prevention, and establishing a medical home or continuity in health care. Opponents of managed care argue the opposite, contend-

ing that it has the potential to create barriers for children through financial disincentives to provide quality care, limitations on providers and services, and other system-related obstacles to care, particularly specialty care. Which of these perspectives is correct remains an unresolved question.

Access, Quality, and Costs

Access. A major advantage of managed care over traditional fee-for-service delivery systems is that managed-care plans normally have more comprehensive information about their enrolled populations and can more effectively track service-use patterns. Managed-care plans can use data systems to develop strategies aimed at improving access to care and the quality of services received by children. A potential disadvantage is the strong incentive to control costs, which may limit needed medical services, particularly for vulnerable populations.

Despite these theoretical advantages and disadvantages, neither has been definitively proven. Studies assessing the impact of managed care on access to care among Medicaid-enrolled children in the early 1980s found that the use of routine preventive services was the same or slightly increased under Medicaid managed care compared to fee-for-service. However, compliance was below the recommended standards for check-ups set by the American Academy of Pediatrics and the federal Early Periodic Screening, Diagnostic, and Treatment (EPSDT) program, which is a component of Medicaid specifying benefits that must be made available to enrolled children. Several more recent studies confirm this general finding. Researchers who examined eighteen access indicators found that only three of them showed statistically significant differences between children enrolled in managed care and children enrolled in traditional health plans. Children enrolled in managed care were more likely to receive physician services, more likely to have access to office-based care during evening or weekend hours, and more likely to report being very satisfied with the overall quality of care. However, the analysis also revealed some problem areas, including challenges getting appointments and contacting medical providers by telephone. Lack of strong evidence of differences in access to care has been found in other recent studies, as well.

One exception to this general finding relates to access to specialty medical care. There is evidence that children in managed-care plans face greater difficulties than others in obtaining pediatric specialty services. This is especially problematic for children with special health care needs (such as disabilities and chronic health problems) who are enrolled in plans that are more restrictive in terms of parents' ability to self-refer their children for specialty care.

Among general populations of HMO enrollees, children get more primary and preventive care, but they also get less specialist care and experience more provider access and organizational barriers to care. HMO enrollees are more likely to report a regular source of care than those enrolled in other types of insurance, but they are more likely to report access problems related to the organization of care delivery.

Quality. Little is known about the quality of care children receive in managed-care settings. Detecting differences related to quality is impeded by imprecise definitions of quality, as well as the lack of uniform methods of measuring it. While measuring quality is problematic regardless of the population of interest or the type of plans within which the population is enrolled, the lack of consistent and reliable methods of assessing quality in managed-care settings (especially given its widespread and rapid adoption), is of concern to many.

Nonetheless, some studies have attempted to assess the quality of managed care for children. By and large, these studies rely on parents' reported satisfaction with care and other services within the plan. (To date, no studies have been published that examined clinical differences or other direct measures of health status.) In general, the results are mixed. One major study found that over 95 percent of families generally reported high levels of satisfaction with their children's care regardless of the type of plan in which they are enrolled. This study found no strong evidence of significant differences in satisfaction with care or quality of care between children enrolled in managed care and fee-for-service health plans. This is in contrast to another study, which found evidence that families and providers are sometimes less satisfied under managed care.

Such mixed findings are also found when examining the experience of children in Medicaid managed care. One major study found no significant differences in parents' ratings of the health care experience comparing those of children in Medicaid managed care versus fee-for-service, while another found that Medicaid managed-care enrollees were slightly more satisfied than their counterparts in fee-for-service plans. Interestingly, it appears that racial and ethnic minorities are generally less satisfied than their white counterparts. One study that found such differences concluded that language barriers largely account for the racial and ethnic disparities in satisfaction with care in Medicaid managed-care plans. These findings suggest the need for further research with diverse populations, such as African Americans, where language is not an issue in receiving care.

More research has been conducted on the impact of managed-care enrollment among general populations (rather than by age) and the majority of this work has focused on patient satisfaction. In general, these studies report that satisfaction with overall care was lower among HMOs, which also received fewer excellent ratings from enrollees regarding their visits with physicians. In addition, HMO enrollees were less confident that their physicians would refer them to needed specialty care than were consumers in non-HMO plans. All together, HMOs scored lower on eight out of nine satisfaction measures, with differences ranging from 3 to 7 percentage points, and enrollees reporting less satisfaction, lower levels of care, and less trust in their physicians.

Costs. Managed-care plans are nearly always designed to achieve some cost-savings. Despite this, few studies have examined the extent to which this promise is realized. Moreover, the bulk of pediatric research conducted thus far has focused on Medicaid populations. By and large, the research suggests that the extent to which managed care can lead to savings, at least among low-income children, is unclear. One major analysis of twelve evaluations of Medicaid managed-care programs for children found that seven studies reported a decrease in costs, two reported increased costs, and the remaining studies had mixed, unchanged, or unknown results. Other research has found savings up to 15 percent among children on welfare in managed care (compared with traditional fee-for-service Medicaid), while other experiments have produced little or no savings.

Among the general population, the findings are more certain. Compared to fee-for-service, enrollment in managed care has led to cost savings, particularly lower out-of-pocket costs for patients. Specifically, 10 percent of families enrolled in HMOs in one study paid more than $1,000 in out-of-pocket expenses, compared with 17 percent of families enrolled in other types of plans. Consequently, HMO enrollees were less likely to cite financial problems as a barrier to care. However, they were more likely to report administrative barriers to care. It appears, though, that future cost savings may be limited, largely because lower costs to patients have translated into reduced profits for the health plans. As plans attempt to recoup these profits, out-of-pocket costs, such as co-payments for services, may rise.

Conclusion

Because of the variability in managed-care plan organization and financing, much of the literature on managed care appears contradictory in its findings. In general, the research suggests that the extent to which managed care improves or impedes children's access to and utilization of quality care depends on the of type of managed care, the health status of children who are enrolled, and the circumstances under which they are enrolled (voluntary versus mandatory enrollment).

However, lack of more definitive data on access, quality, and costs, particularly among nonpoor children, suggests a need for more research on this subject. More and better information of the impact of managed-care enrollment on costs and quality are especially needed. These remain areas in which most information is anecdotal and largely speculative. Given that managed care is likely to remain a major, if not dominant, method of health care financing and delivery, it is critical that more is understood about its impact on children, so that any needed modifications in the design and organization can be made.

See also: HEALTH AND EDUCATION; HEALTH CARE AND CHILDREN.

BIBLIOGRAPHY

BERGMAN, DAVID A., and HOMER, CHARLES J. 1998. "Managed Care and the Quality of Children's Health Services." *The Future of Children.* 8(2):68–75.

CARTLAND, JENNIFER, and YUDKOWSKY, BETH. 1992. "Barriers to Pediatric Referral in Managed Care Systems." *Pediatrics* 89:183–188.

DEAL, LISA, and SHIONO, PATRICIA. 1998. "Medicaid Managed Care and Children: An Overview." *The Future of Children* 8(2):93–104.

DELIA, DEREK; CANTOR, JOEL C.; and SANDMAN, DAVID. 2001. "Medicaid Managed Care in New York City: Recent Performance and Coming Challenges." *American Journal of Public Health.* 91:458–460.

FOX, HARRIET B., and MCMANUS, MARGARET A. 1998. "Improving State Medicaid Contracts and Plan Practices for Children with Special Health Care Needs." *The Future of Children* 8(2):105–119.

FREUND, DEBORAH; ROSSITER, LOUIS F; FOX, PETER D; MEYER, JACK A; HURLEY, ROBERT E; CAREY, TIMOTHY S; and PAUL, JOHN R. 1989. "Evaluation of the Medicaid Competition Demonstrations." *Health Care Financing Review* 79:843–847.

GANZ, MICHAEL LEE, and SISK, JANE E. 2000. "Evaluation of Medicaid Managed Care for Children: Access and Satisfaction." *American Journal of Public Health* 2:1947–1948.

HEALTH INSURANCE ASSOCIATION OF AMERICA. 1999. *Source Book of Health Insurance Data, 1999–2000.* Washington, DC: Health Insurance Association of America.

HURLEY, ROBERT E.; FREUND, DEBORAH; and PAUL, JOHN R. 1993. *Managed Care in Medicaid: Lessons for Policy and Program Design.* Ann Arbor, MI: Health Administration Press.

JENSEN, GAIL A.; MORRISEY, MICHAEL A.; GAFFNEY, SHANNON; and LISTON, DEREK K. 1997. "The New Dominance of Managed Care: Insurance Trends in the 1990s." *Health Affairs* 16(1):125–136.

LESLIE, LAUREL K.; SARAH, REBECCA; and PALFREY, JUDITH S. 1998. "Child Health Care in Changing Times." *Pediatrics* 101(4):746–751.

LONG, SHARON K., and COUGHLIN, TERESA A. 2001. "Impacts of Medicaid Managed Care on Children." *Health Services Research* 36(1):7–23.

MAYNARD, CHARLES; RAMSEY, SCOTT; WICKIZER, THOMAS; and CONRAD, DOUGLAS A. 2000. "Healthcare Charges and Use in Commercially Insured Children Enrolled in Managed Care Health Plans in Washington State." *Maternal and Child Health Journal* 4(1):29–38.

MILLER, ROBERT, and LUFT, HAROLD. 1994. "Managed Care Plans: Characteristics, Growth and Premium Performance." *Annual Review of Public Health* 15:437–59.

NEWACHECK, PAUL W.; HUNG, YUN-YI; MARCHI, KRISTEN S.; HUGHES, DANA C.; PITTER, CHRIS-

TIAN; and STODDARD, JEFFREY J. 2001. "The Impact of Managed Care on Children's Access, Satisfaction, Use, and Quality of Care." *Health Services Research* 2:315–334.

ROCHA, CYNTHIA J., and KABALK, LIZ E. 1999. "A Comparison Study of Access to Health Care under a Medicaid Managed Care Program." *Health and Social Work.* 24(3):169–179.

ROSENBACH MARGO L.; IRVIN, CAROL; and COULAM, ROBERT F. 1999. "Access for Low-Income Children: Is Health Insurance Enough?"*Pediatrics* 103(6):1167–1174.

ROWLAND, DIANE, and LYONS, BARBARA. 1987. "Mandatory HMO's for Milwaukee's Poor." *Health Affairs.* 6:87–100.

SIMPSON, LISA, and FRASER, IRENE. 1999. "Children and Managed Care: What Research Can, Can't, and Should Tell Us about the Impact." *Medical Care Research and Review* 56(2):13–36.

SISK, JANE E.; GORMAN, SHELIA A.; REISINGER, ANNE L.; GLIED, SHERRY A.; DUMOUCHEL, WILLIAM H.; and HYNES, MARGARET M. 1996. "Evaluation of Medicaid Managed Care: Satisfaction, Access and Use." *Journal of the American Medical Association* 276(1):50–55.

WEECH-MALDONADO, R.; MORALES, LEO S.; SPRITZER, KAREN; ELLIOTT, MARC; and HAYES, RON D. 2001. "Racial and Ethnic Differences in Parents' Assessments of Pediatric Care in Medicaid Managed Care." *Health Services Research* 36(3):575–594.

DANA HUGHES
KAREN DUDERSTADT

MANN, HORACE (1796–1859)

Principal advocate of the nineteenth-century common school movement, Horace Mann became the catalyst for tuition-free public education and established the concept of state-sponsored free schools. The zeal with which Mann executed his plan for free schools was in keeping with the intellectual climate of Boston in the early days of the republic. The Mann contribution, state government sponsored education unfettered by sectarian control, made possible a democratic society rather than a government by elites. The atmosphere of early-nineteenth-century Boston stimulated keen minds to correct social disharmonies caused by ignorance, intemperance, and human bondage. Reform that emanated from the Lockean notion that human nature may be improved by the actions of government motivated these New Englanders, who shaped social and political thought for generations.

Horace Mann was born in Franklin, Massachusetts, to Thomas Mann and Rebecca Stanley Mann. His parents lacked the means to educate their children beyond rudimentary ciphering and elementary reading. Therefore Mann's education consisted of no more than eight or ten weeks a year of sitting in tight rows on slab benches, learning from a schoolmaster barely out of his teens. Of his early schooling, Mann recalled, "Of all our faculties, the memory for words was the only one specially appealed to." A small lending library in Franklin circulated such books as John Bunyan's *The Pilgrim's Progress*. School days were minimal as the majority of the year was spent in haying, planting, and plowing. When Horace's father died of tuberculosis in 1809, the farm was left to an older son, Stanley Mann. The modest sum of $200 was left to each child. Horace saved tuition by teaching his sister, Lydia, to read and write, instead of her attending school.

Education and Training

Part of the bequest of Thomas Mann to Horace was spent on his tuition at Barrett's school. Horace was twenty in 1816, and his education to that point amounted to several dozen weeks scattered over nine years. At Barrett School under an exacting but sometimes intemperate schoolmaster, Mann first conjugated Latin verbs.

A half year at Barrett School fitted Mann for admission to the sophomore class at Brown University, where penury remained a constant problem for Mann. Mann graduated first in his class (1819) two years after arriving at the university. His oration, entitled "The Gradual Advancement of the Human Species in Dignity and Happiness," linked the success of the American political experiment directly to the development of its educational system. No valedictory speech has ever been more prophetic. Brown University president Asa Messer honored Mann by making him an instructor soon after his graduation. From 1820 until 1822 he taught Latin classics. Nine years later, Mann married Messer's daughter, Charlotte.

Mann's ambition was to train in the law at Judge Tapping Reeve's prestigious law school in Litchfield, Connecticut. At the time there was no better preparation for legal and political careers than Reeve's plain, free-standing law library located in the yard of his stately home in Litchfield. Meanwhile, Mann clerked in the office of Judge Fiske for thirteen months to earn tuition money. Mann arrived in Litchfield in 1822 for the course of study that took a year and a half and cost $160. Then Mann became a clerk for Judge James Richardson in Dedham, Massachusetts, for several months until he was admitted to practice before the bar of the State of Massachusetts in 1823.

Career and Contribution

Intemperance and the humane treatment of criminals were topics debated in polite society around Dedham, and Mann championed reforms ranging from temperance to religious toleration. He realized that through proper educating of the public, lasting change could be effected.

The positions of trust Mann achieved in Dedham in the 1820s made him confident to offer for the legislature in Massachusetts. The same year he was elected to the Dedham School Commission, he was also elected to the state's general assembly. Mann added the title legal counsel to the state supreme court, as well as commissioner to the new mental hospital, to his growing list of responsibilities.

After the death of his wife Charlotte in 1832, Mann liquidated his estate and resigned all offices, including his seat in the legislature. To those around him, it was apparent he planned to immerse himself in his work. Taking lodging at a boarding house in Boston, Mann joined the law firm of his old friend, Edward Loring. Boarders there were Boston notables such as Elizabeth Peabody, social crusader, and Reverend William Ellery Channing, the voice of Unitarianism in Boston. Elizabeth Peabody's sister, Mary, was there as well.

Friends persuaded him that he should stand for the Massachusetts senate in 1834 as a Whig. Mann had never competed politically at this level, and campaigns for senate races brought vitriolic debates not seen in his career before. As he celebrated his forty-first birthday, he contemplated his newest responsibility, president of the Massachusetts senate. This honor as a junior senator typifies the trust and

respect colleagues placed in his judgment. One issue that the senate wrestled with for several years prior to Mann's election was how public education could better prepare people for citizenship in this expanding young republic. As senate president, Horace signed into law the bill creating the Massachusetts State Board of Education, unique for its time and designed to disseminate education information statewide and to improve curriculum, method, and facilities.

Educating the masses was also the concern of James G. Carter of Boston, and he published in 1825 the *Outline for an Institute for the Education of Teachers.* He wrote on the necessity of training teachers in the art of teaching. Normal schools were an outgrowth of this important early work in educational thought. Carter, a legislator, and Mann, president of the senate, maneuvered a revolutionary bill through both houses and to the desk of Governor Edward Everett.

The members of the board of the newly created State Department of Education selected Mann as its first secretary. Mann resigned his seat in the state senate. Mann, like many Bostonians, believed that the emphasis on public education held more promise than either government or religion for yielding lasting social reform. He accepted a 50 percent cut in pay, from $3,000 a year to $1,500. His personal journal records, "I have faith in the improvability of the race, in their accelerating improvability. . . ."

The struggle for common schools in Massachusetts defined the parameters of the free school movement for decades to come. Though Mann engaged in reforms such as temperance and the treatment of the insane, the perfection of the common school concept occupied his waking hours for the rest of his life. Mann argued that all citizens, regardless of race or economic status, should have equal access to a tuition-free, tax-supported public school system. Such a system must be responsive to all races and nonsectarian if society is to achieve the unshackled status of a true democracy.

Mann knew he had to convince the entire state that the common school system was desirable and worth the increased tax revenue. He conducted town meetings across the state, giving a speech "The Means and Objects of Common School Education." The obstacle was a populace that did not care whether more schooling was offered.

Mann's tour of the state's schools concluded with Salem, the town where Mary Peabody was teaching. Once more, he pleaded for a statewide system of tuition-free education that would, he claimed, break down the troubling hierarchy of class in American society. Mann had spent months on tour, and much of what he had encountered discouraged him. Revenue would have to be raised to build adequate schools and staff them with learned teachers. There was the problem of poor versus wealthy districts; and that of the poor counties' being able to offer an education comparable to that of wealthy counties. Inadequate instruction troubled Mann as much as broken-down school buildings. He contemplated teacher training academies, called *normal schools*, as a solution.

Required by state law to make an annual report to the legislature on the condition of the state's school districts and programs, Mann turned the legal mandate into a yearly treatise on educational philosophy and methods. His annual reports became his platform for launching new programs and educating the public on new ideas in pedagogy. He explored new ideas in school design and the teaching of reading by words rather than by alphabet letters. Simple instruction in daily hygiene was emphasized along with more interesting ways of teaching science. Mann saw education as the uniting force to bring understanding and toleration between factions of the populace, as well as between the various states themselves. One novel idea Mann put forth was that teachers should gather together periodically to share ideas.

Mann developed the special teacher training colleges that he called normal schools. Instruction expertise rose yearly because the normal schools graduated capable teachers and eliminated the unfit. With teaching skills garnered from the normal school programs, teachers looked forward to a higher pay scale. Horace Mann was certain that better schools coupled with compulsory education would cure the ills of society. Traditional education did not vanish quickly in Massachusetts, however. Many found that curriculum and instruction varied little from content and materials of their grandparents' time.

Mann recalled the small library he had known while growing up. He believed that every child should have that advantage, so he set up a library expansion program. Mann also liked the German kindergarten idea that his confidant, Mary Peabody, espoused. Horace married Mary Peabody in 1843 in the bookstore that her sister, Elizabeth, ran on West Street, a store that was a gathering place for William Ellery Channing, Ralph Waldo Emerson, Margaret Fuller, Nathaniel Hawthorne, and Henry David Thoreau. Mary's sister, Sophia, had wed Nathaniel Hawthorne there a few months earlier. Horace wished to take a trip to Europe to visit common schools, so they settled upon that idea as their honeymoon.

One person Mann wanted to meet in England was Charles Dickens, the social reformer and novelist. Dickens gave Mann and his wife a tour of London's wretched east side. The squalor was worse by far than anything Mann had seen in America. The English schools did not impress Mann, either. Recitation and Anglican dogma dulled the student's appetite for intellectual stimulation. He was amazed that teachers talked in monotone voices and stood transfixed during lecture. The Manns traveled widely in England and on the continent. While touring the University of Berlin, Horace learned that Alexander von Humboldt had implemented a state certification process and written examinations for teachers. Horace realized that this is what he must do in Massachusetts to eliminate the problem of incompetent teachers.

Mann's seventh annual report to the board was written partly on the voyage home. The comparisons he made with European schools, especially German schools, offended school administrators. Critics questioned Mann's credentials to lead school reform. Mann stood his ground for five more years and continued to bring uniformity to programs and quality of instruction.

Mann saw revenue for education rise precipitously over the twelve years of his tenure (1836–1848). He popularized the idea of a centralized bureaucracy to manage primary and secondary education. He advised the legislature on fiscal responsibility in implementing equal programs throughout the state. He standardized the requirements for the diploma.

When the eighth congressional seat became vacant due to the death of John Quincy Adams, Mann ran for the office and was successful in his first federal election. The two terms he spent in Washington were neither satisfactory nor productive. He had disagreements with his loyal political friends Daniel Webster and Charles Sumner. Against a backdrop of the rising tension over slavery, Horace sought a way out after his second term.

In 1852 Mann heard of a new college being built in Yellow Springs, Ohio, with support from a liberal Christian denomination. He decided that if the college presidency were offered, he would accept and resign from Congress. The post was offered, and Mann became the first president of Antioch College. The Ohio churchmen were so liberal in their doctrinal beliefs that they accepted Mann, a Unitarian. Antioch was a sectarian foundation and chapel attendance was not compulsory. Antioch College opened its doors to eight young men in 1850.

The Ohio frontier proved a different world from the East. Money was a problem from the start, grand illusions in the minds of the trustees never bore fruit, and paydays were missed regularly. Mann never compromised his expectations in scholarship. The financial problems at Antioch began before the buildings went up, and they steadily got worse.

The curriculum and methodology had all been Mann's development, and it was a creditable program. A preparatory school was added to accept the less qualified and was open to all no matter what race or gender. The mood of the populace, however, turned against Mann due to his Unitarian belief.

Mann turned his attention to the idea of publicly funded universities. He believed that church-sponsored colleges and universities undid the work of the free-school movement. The fight for the publicly funded university would be someone else's battle as Mann had developed a form of debilitating cancer. Mann's last educational act was to salvage the bankrupt Antioch College with a syndicate of New England investors. Mann died August 2, 1859. He could not have realized that he would become part of the legend of democracy built upon the foundation of a tuition-free public school system. Mann's last professional statement concluded the commencement address at Antioch College: "I beseech you to treasure up in your hearts these my parting words: Be ashamed to die until you have won some victory for humanity."

See also: COMMON SCHOOL MOVEMENT.

BIBLIOGRAPHY

CREMIN, LAWRENCE A. 1980. *American Education: The National Experience: 1783-1876.* New York: Harper and Row.

KENDELL, KATHLEEN EDGERTON. 1968. "Education as 'the Balance Wheel of Social Machinery': Horace Mann's Arguments and Proofs." *Quarterly Journal of Speech and Education* 54:13–21.

MANN, HORACE. 1891. *Life and Works of Horace Mann,* 5 vols. Boston: Lee and Shepard.

MANN, MARY PEABODY. 1891. *Life of Horace Mann.* Boston: Lee and Shepard.

MESSERLI, JONATHAN. 1972. *Horace Mann: A Biography.* New York: Knopf.

THARP, LOUISE HALL. 1950. *The Peabody Sisters of Salem.* Boston: Little, Brown.

TREICHLER, JESSIE. 1962. *Horace Mann.* Chicago: Encyclopaedia Britannica Press.

VINOVSKIS, MARIS A. 1970. "Horace Mann on the Economic Productivity of Education." *New England Quarterly* 43:550–571.

THOMAS B. HORTON

MASTER'S DEGREE, THE

The master's degree is awarded upon completion of one to two years of advanced graduate study beyond the bachelor's degree, with the length depending on the field of study and the conferring institution. It recognizes heightened expertise in an academic discipline or professional field of study, gained through intensive course work and, in most cases, the preparation of a culminating project, scholarly paper, thesis, or a comprehensive examination.

History

The master's degree has had somewhat a "checkered reputation" (Spencer, p. 5) in the United States. Since its debut in the 1850s at the University of Michigan, for instance, critics have questioned the academic legitimacy of the master's degree, dismissing it as a stepping-stone to the Ph.D. or as a consolation prize for those who failed to complete their doctoral studies.

Although historically viewed as ancillary to the doctorate, the changing nature of the U.S. workplace has contributed to a redefinition of the purpose and value of the master's degree in the latter quarter of the twentieth century. According to Eileen O'Brien, this "transformation occurred on an institution-by-institution basis, with the degree being adapted to offer an educational program focusing on specialization, professionalization, and career enhancement and development" (p. 4). Findings from the Council of Graduate Schools' sponsored National Study of Master's Degrees, outlined in Clifton F. Conrad et al.'s 1993 work, established that the master's degree is now frequently recognized as a significant—and often terminal—credential designating advanced preparation and training in a specialized area of study, most commonly for the purposes of entry into or advancement within the world of professional practice.

A Growing Demand

The popularity of the master's degree grew considerably during the last quarter of the twentieth century. Between 1970 and 1997, the number of master's degrees annually conferred almost doubled from 230,000 to just over 430,000. In 2001 master's degrees accounted for nearly one of every four degrees earned at the bachelor's level and above in the United States.

Student and employer demand for advanced education and certification within professional fields of study has sparked much of the growth in master's degree enrollments. These increases in demand have been spurred by broader global shifts toward a technology-driven, information-centered economy in which the need for highly trained, "expert" professionals in management, finance, information technology, and health care has skyrocketed. In 1970 for example, seven professional fields of study—business, computer and information science, education, engineering, health professions, library science, and public administration—accounted for slightly more than two-thirds of all master's degrees annually conferred. In 1997 these professional fields combined for slightly more than three-fourths of all master's degrees awarded. Particularly since the 1980s, it appears that the master's degree has, at least for employers outside of academe, taken on a new "gatekeeper" role, functioning as an important credential for managing entry into and advancement within the professions. In physical therapy and library science, for example, the master's is now generally regarded as an entry-level credential. In business, education, engineering, and nursing, the master's is almost always required for advancement into more financially lucrative specialty and leadership positions.

A Changing Clientele

As the reach of master's education has expanded, the population of students earning the degree has diversified. The percentage of women earning master's degrees increased steadily over the past three decades, growing from 41 percent of degree recipients in 1970 to 56 percent in 1996. During this same time frame, the proportion of part-time and older students enrolling in master's programs shifted considerably; by the mid-1990s, approximately three-fifths of all master's students were enrolled part-time, and more than one-half were thirty years of age or older.

Educators have developed various strategies for meeting the needs of this changing clientele. Especially during the 1980s, a large number of colleges and universities began to offer master's-level courses (and, in some cases, entire programs) in the evenings and on weekends. In the 1990s, the use of satellite-, videotape-, and web-based courses (and, again, entire programs) likewise became increasingly popular at the master's level.

The overwhelming majority of master's degree programs are course-work driven, but the number of required courses or credit hours varies by field of study and type of degree (for example, some master's programs may be completed in as few as twenty-four semester credit hours; other master's programs—including several in education—may require up to sixty semester credit hours). While approximately 70 percent of master's degrees no longer require the completion of a thesis, most still include a comprehensive examination, which tests students on foundational knowledge in their field of study. Since the mid-1980s, a rising number of programs have begun to offer students the option of completing a final—or culminating—master's project or paper as an alternative to a scholarly thesis. These projects or papers typically focus on applied problems, issues, or concerns relevant to the world of professional practice.

The growing practitioner orientation that has accompanied the increasing professionalization of the master's degree has led to several interesting curricular changes in master's programs. To begin with, the inclusion of part-time instructors who have extensive practitioner-based professional experience has become more commonplace. These practitioner faculty instructors are assumed to bring a real-world edge to the courses they teach, creating stronger linkages between theory and practice in the professions. Increasingly common as well is the inclusion of relevant professional work experience as a requirement for admission, particularly within the professional fields of business, education, and nursing. Finally, growing professionalization has also invited greater oversight by specialized accrediting bodies. In recent years several accrediting bodies that had traditionally focused largely on undergraduate education have begun to monitor the content and quality of master's degree programs in various fields, including business (Association to Advance Collegiate Schools of Business), education (National Council for Accreditation of Teacher Education), and nursing (National League for Nursing).

Unlike the National Research Council's *Survey of Earned Doctorates,* a national database is not maintained to study or track master's degree programs, students, or degree recipients. Other than the findings of a few scholars, there is comparatively little known about the general purposes, quality, and value of the master's degree and master's education in the United States.

See also: BUSINESS EDUCATION, *subentry on* COLLEGE AND GRADUATE STUDY; DOCTORAL DEGREE, THE; GRADUATE SCHOOL TRAINING.

BIBLIOGRAPHY

BERELSON, BERNARD. 1960. *Graduate Education in the United States.* New York: McGraw-Hill.

CONRAD, CLIFTON F.; HAWORTH, JENNIFER GRANT; and MILLAR, SUSAN BOLYARD. 1993. *A Silent Success: Master's Education in the United States.* Baltimore: Johns Hopkins University Press.

GLAZER, JUDITH S. 1986. *The Master's Degree: Tradition, Diversity, Innovation.* Washington, DC: Association for the Study of Higher Education.

HAWORTH, JENNIFER G., and CONRAD, CLIFTON F. 1997. *Emblems of Quality in Higher Education: Developing and Sustaining High-Quality Programs.* Needham Heights, MA: Allyn and Bacon.

NATIONAL CENTER FOR EDUCATION STATISTICS. 2000. *Digest of Education Statistics.* Washington, DC: U.S. Government Printing Office.

O'BRIEN, EILEEN M. 1992. "Master's Degree Students and Recipients: A Profile." *ACE Research Briefs* 3(1):1–14. Washington, DC: American Council on Education.

SPENCER, DONALD S. 1986. "The Master's Degree in Transition." *CGS Communicator* 19:1–3, 10, 12.

JENNIFER GRANT HAWORTH
CLIFTON F. CONRAD
ANDREA S. POLSTER

MATHEMATICS EDUCATION, TEACHER PREPARATION

Mathematics teachers are educated in diverse ways, depending to a great extent on the context in which the education occurs. Typically, pre-service teacher preparation occurs at the baccalaureate level, while in-service education occurs at the graduate level or is conducted by the local school systems in which the teacher is employed. There are, however, some pre-service programs in which participants acquire a masters' degree prior to beginning their teaching career.

In preparation for teaching at the elementary level, most undergraduate students take two mathematics courses that are either part of the institution's core liberal arts program or are designed specifically for elementary teaching majors. Additionally, it is likely that prospective elementary teachers will have one or two courses that deal specifically with the teaching of elementary school mathematics. Concerns that teachers at the elementary level need more background in mathematics have resulted in recent trends toward upgrading the mathematical education of prospective elementary teachers. Secondary teachers typically have a major in mathematics, or a closely related field, with an additional course (or courses) in mathematics education. Smaller programs are more likely to offer only a single course in mathematics education. The education of prospective middle school teachers is very dependent on the type of institution. In some schools, middle school teaching majors follow a program similar to the elementary majors, but with extra courses in mathematics; in others, they take a program for secondary school pre-service teachers specializing in mathematics, with one or more additional courses in middle school education. A few larger universities have programs designed specifically for the prospective middle school mathematics teacher. The following sections focus on the intent and foci of the different programs.

The Evolution of Mathematics Teacher Education

Before 1960 most teacher education programs for secondary school mathematics teachers consisted of training in mathematics, a methods course of some kind, and student teaching. Smaller programs at colleges or universities tended to have generic methods courses that addressed the needs of secondary teachers of all subjects. One can glean an understanding of the content-specific methods courses by considering the methods texts of that time. For example, the popular 1960 methods text by Charles Butler and Frank Wren (first published in 1941) consisted of two sections. The first section dealt with general issues such as planning for instruction. The second section was decidedly mathematical, with specific suggestions for teaching topics such as arithmetic, algebra, geometry, and trigonometry. There was a clear distinction between these two sections. Donovan Johnson and Gerald Rising's innovative 1967 text was based on what mathematics teachers do in the classroom. As such, it addressed issues specific to the teaching and learning of mathematics. A 1975 text by Thomas Cooney, Edward Davis, and Kenneth Henderson for secondary mathematics teachers also had a very distinct pedagogical orientation based on research on how teachers teach mathematics. Whereas the Johnson and Rising text was based primarily on teachers' daily responsibilities, the Cooney, Davis, and Henderson text was based on a theoretical analysis of teachers' verbal actions, called moves, and the way those moves were used to teach mathematical concepts, generalizations, and skills.

During the 1960s and 1970s educators began to see the value in studying the teaching and learning of mathematics more specifically. Out of this new focus on research grew an interest in developing a psychological basis for understanding why some students learned but others did not, and what kind of teaching methods and curricula could affect student learning. This growing knowledge base contributed to mathematics teacher education as well.

The Evolution of Mathematics Education as a Field of Inquiry

Prior to 1960 there was little research on how children learn mathematics and how teachers teach mathematics. The teacher's job was seen primarily as a matter of telling students the mathematics they were expected to learn. But as research in mathematics education matured, questions arose about how students understand mathematics. Consider, for example, the variation in understanding of mathematics conveyed in the responses of two students to the following questions:

> Are there any numbers between 440 and 450 that are divisible by 7? Why or why not?
>
> **Response of Student 1:** There must be a number because 7 is less than 10. So in every 10 numbers there has to be at least one that is divisible by 7. (Student elaborates for entire page.)
>
> **Response of Student 2:** There is no number because 440 and 450 is not divisible by 7—44 is not, 45 is not, and 0 is not.

The response of student 1 reveals a deep understanding of how numbers work, while the response of student 2 demonstrates some understanding of divisibility, since 44 and 45 are not divisible by 7, but fails to capture the mathematical essence of the question. If the interest of teacher educators in evaluating these two responses goes beyond one student having gotten it right and the other student not, then they can begin to ask how a teacher could enable the second student to better understand divisibility. Indeed, teacher education today focuses, in part, on enabling teachers to create and use such questions so that they can better analyze their students' understanding of mathematics. Simply put, the education of mathematics teachers entails a certain kind of knowledge that involves mathematics, psychology, and ways of teaching mathematics that are more effective than simply telling students what mathematics is and what the answers to various problems are. This knowledge base has grown substantially over the past decades because of the extensive research in mathematics education.

In-Service and Staff Development Programs

An appreciation of the complexity of teaching has led teacher educators to move toward programs in which teachers are provided with extensive training and support to implement new practices—such as problem-solving techniques or infusing technology into their teaching. There is mounting evidence that teachers need support and time if they are to reform their practice. For example, the successful professional development program by Raffaella Borasi, Judith Fonzi, Constance Smith, and Barbara Rose not only emphasizes having teachers interact with materials designed to foster student inquiry but also provides teachers with support as they use the materials in their classroom. Some in-service programs engage teachers in deep experiences with the mathematics they are teaching, thereby giving them new insights into their students' understanding of that mathematics. Programs that encourage teachers to reflect on the types of experiences they have and are providing to their students are becoming increasingly popular.

Trends, Issues, and Controversies

Perhaps the single most significant force affecting mathematics teacher education today has been the development of standards for school mathematics by the National Council of Teachers of Mathematics (NCTM). Through these standards, the NCTM has taken the view that mathematics is a subject suitable for inquiry and not just memorization, a subject that can be learned by all students and should be taught with an emphasis on processes such as problem solving, reasoning, communicating mathematically, and connecting mathematics to the real world. One way or another, most teacher education programs today embody the NCTM standards. Controversies about this approach stem from several questions, including: What constitutes mathematics? and, Should mathematics teacher education programs be about reform or about maintaining the status quo?

The Nature of Mathematics

Different segments of society possess different views about what constitutes mathematics. Some think of mathematics as a collection of rules and procedures to be learned and applied for basic living. From this perspective, the teaching of mathematics relies on those methods best suited to promote the acquisition of skills. Others see mathematics as a basis for developing critical thinking and problem-solving skills. From this second perspective, which is closely aligned to the NCTM Standards, teacher education encourages reflection and promotes attention to problem solving and critical thinking. How a community defines mathematics affects what, and how, mathematics gets taught in the local schools. It can also have an impact on how teachers are trained to teach in those schools.

The Intent of Teacher Education Programs

There is always a certain tension between the intellectual preparation of teachers and the practice of teaching as manifested in student teaching. Those from outside the field of mathematics education often take the position that teacher education should be modeled after an apprenticeship program. That is, one learns mathematics and then works in the schools to acquire the necessary pedagogical skills to be a successful teacher. This type of program tends to promote the status quo, as young teachers model those methods of teaching that they experienced as students. Teacher educators, however, usually take the position that a greater part of the program should be devoted to transforming the teaching of mathematics from a "teaching is telling" approach to an inquiry-based teaching style that is student centered. The notion of *constructivism* is often used to describe this latter kind of teaching; that is, children construct their own mathematical ideas, and teachers need to be aware of these constructions in order to effectively teach the children.

The preparation and education of mathematics teachers, like any educational endeavor, exists in a sociopolitical environment that ultimately shapes the enterprise. Conditions of the workplace also shape what transpires in classrooms. These circumstances affect mathematics teacher education programs as well. Schools today are run much as they were in yesteryear, thus perpetuating a certain conservatism with respect to reform. This approach strengthens the position of those who advocate an apprenticeship form of teacher education. Evidence suggests that the United States is experiencing, and will continue to experience, serious teacher shortages, particularly in mathematics. Such shortages usually preclude more extensive training in favor of short, intense programs that are less demanding on the schools' staffing resources.

On the other hand, reform-based teacher education programs enjoy the support of such national organizations as the NCTM and are rooted in the thinking of scholars such as John Dewey. Dewey's notion of *reflective thinking*, albeit adapted and modified, is part and parcel of most current teacher education programs. Indeed, if the position is taken that education is about educating young people to become thinking citizens in a democratic society, then the education of teachers to infuse problem solving, reasoning, and critical thinking into their teaching should be of paramount importance. In some sense, the notion of what constitutes a good teacher education program is dependent on what one values regarding society's education of its young people.

See also: MATHEMATICS LEARNING; NATIONAL COUNCIL OF TEACHERS OF MATHEMATICS.

BIBLIOGRAPHY

BORASI, RAFFAELLA; FONZI, JUDITH; SMITH, CONSTANCE F.; and ROSE, B. J. 1999. "Beginning the Process of Rethinking Mathematics Instruction: A Professional Development Program." *Journal of Mathematics Teacher Education* 2:49–78.

BUTLER, CHARLES H., and WREN, FRANK L. 1960. *The Teaching of Secondary School Mathematics.* New York: McGraw-Hill.

COONEY, THOMAS J. 1994. "Research and Teacher Education: In Search of Common Ground." *Journal for Research in Mathematics Education* 25:608–636.

COONEY, THOMAS J.; DAVIS, EDWARD J.; and HENDERSON, KENNETH B. 1975. *Dynamics of Teaching Secondary School Mathematics.* Boston: Houghton Mifflin.

DAVIS, PHILIP, and HERSH, REUBEN. 1981. *The Mathematical Experience.* Boston: Birkhauser.

DEWEY, JOHN. 1933. *How We Think: A Restatement of the Relation of Reflective Thinking to the Educative Process.* Boston: Heath.

DONOVAN, BRIAN F. 1990. "Cultural Power and the Defining of School Mathematics: A Case Study." In *Teaching and Learning Mathematics in the 1990s,* ed. Thomas J. Cooney and Christian R. Hirsch. Reston, VA: National Council of Teachers of Mathematics.

DOSSEY, JOHN A. 1992. "The Nature of Mathematics: Its Role and Its Influence." In *Handbook of Research on Mathematics Teaching and Learning,* ed. Douglas A. Grouws. New York: Macmillan.

JOHNSON, DONOVAN A., and RISING, GERALD R. 1967. *Guidelines for Teaching Mathematics.* Belmont, CA: Wadsworth.

NATIONAL COUNCIL OF TEACHERS OF MATHEMATICS. 1989. *Curriculum and Evaluation Standards for School Mathematics.* Reston, VA: National Council of Teachers of Mathematics.

NATIONAL COUNCIL OF TEACHERS OF MATHEMATICS. 1991. *Professional Standards for Teaching Mathematics.* Reston, VA: National Council of Teachers of Mathematics.

NATIONAL COUNCIL OF TEACHERS OF MATHEMATICS. 1995. *Assessment Standards for School Mathematics.* Reston, VA: National Council of Teachers of Mathematics.

NATIONAL COUNCIL OF TEACHERS OF MATHEMATICS. 2000. *Principles and Standards for School Mathematics.* Reston, VA: National Council of Teachers of Mathematics.

SCHIFTER, DEBORAH. 1998. "Learning Mathematics for Teaching: From a Teacher's Seminar to the Classroom." *Journal of Mathematics Teacher Education* 1:55–87.

SIMON, MARTIN A. 1997. "Developing New Models of Mathematics Teaching: An Imperative for Research on Mathematics Teacher Development. In *Mathematics Teachers in Transition,* ed. Elizabeth Fennema and Barbara Scott Nelson. Mahwah, NJ: Erlbaum.

THOMAS J. COONEY

MATHEMATICS LEARNING

ALGEBRA
  Mitchell J. Nathan
COMPLEX PROBLEM SOLVING
  Alan H. Schoenfeld
GEOMETRY
  Vera Kemeny
LEARNING TOOLS
  Susanne P. Lajoie
  Nancy C. Lavigne
MYTHS, MYSTERIES, AND REALITIES
  Michael T. Battista
NUMBER SENSE
  Chris Lowber
  Teruni Lamberg
NUMERACY AND CULTURE
  Yukari Okamoto
  Mary E. Brenner
  Reagan Curtis
WORD-PROBLEM SOLVING
  Lieven Verschaffel
  Brian Greer
  Erik De Corte

ALGEBRA

Algebraic reasoning is a major development (circa 800), both culturally and individually. Culturally, the invention of algebraic representations in graphical and symbolic form is viewed as central for the advancement of mathematics and science. Algebra provides a succinct notation for recording mathematical relationships and describing computational algorithms and scientific laws. Algebraic reasoning is viewed as a major conceptual advancement beyond arithmetic thinking. For individuals, algebra can serve as a *thinking tool,* or, more aptly, a toolkit, for describing relationships in terms of unknown quantities and modeling complex and dynamic situations. For many, algebra instruction is the sole source for the formal study of abstract representations and problem solving.

Algebra has also been identified as a societal gatekeeper for further development of mathematical and scientific instruction, and for wide-ranging economic opportunities. Consequently, at the beginning of the twenty-first century, there is a major shift in the United States to move algebra education into the middle and primary grades, and to reconceptualize instruction appropriately for these age groups. The utility of algebra is boundless. However, learning and teaching algebra, particularly algebra word problems, is often viewed as the bane of mathematics education.

What Is Algebra?

Abstract algebra refers to the use of formal mathematical structures and symbols, such as F (X), to represent relations between terms or objects. It includes the operations that operate on those structures, such as the inverse, F-1(X), and the identity, I(X). An especially important structure is the *function,* which specifies a one-to-many relationship (or mapping) between an independent variable (the *input*) and a set of dependent variables (the *output*).

School-based algebra is most commonly viewed as the generalization of arithmetic to include the use of literal symbols (such as the letters X and Y) and arbitrarily complex symbolic expressions. School algebra also includes the study of functions as well as the construction of abstract formalisms that inductively describe a pattern of instances, predict future instances, and characterize the general form of the pattern (e.g., linear).

Challenges of Learning Algebra

To encompass the multifaceted nature of school-based algebra, new concepts arise that contribute to its learning difficulties. The *variable* is expanded from being a place-holder (or box) in arithmetic, to representing an unknown value or set of values that stand in relation to (and may covary with) other values and expressions. Symbols that represent variables in algebra must denote the same thing everywhere in a problem, but generally take on new meanings with each new problem.

Detailed analyses of problem solving show that result-unknown problems, such as $25x4+8=?$, are solvable by direct application of the arithmetic operators, or by using counting objects to physically model the number sentence; whereas start-unknown problems, such as $25Y+8=108$, defy modeling and are considered to be algebraic. Both children and adults exhibit lower levels of performance with start-unknown than with result-unknown problems.

In algebra, the equal sign ($=$) takes on a relational or structural role, as when two sides of an equation are compared, such as $25Y=108$. This is in addition to its operational role in arithmetic where the equal sign signals one to perform a computation, as with $25x4=?$. Facility with and among multiple representations, including symbolic, tabular, graphical, and verbal formats, is an important aspect of algebraic reasoning, as is an understanding of the relative utility of each. Each representational format has unique advantages. However, in practice, equations receive far more attention that other representations, such as graphs.

The prototypical activities for school-based algebra are solving symbolic equations and word problems. Equation solving most typically involves applying legal rules of symbolic manipulation to isolate an unknown value (see Figure 1, part a). Legal rules typically entail performing the same symbolic calculations to both sides (such as subtracting 10 from both sides of Equation 1 in step 1) to maintain the relations specified in the original problem.

Novices often perform actions that violate the syntactic, hierarchically nested relationships contained in equations, and so inappropriately change their original meanings. For example, in Figure 1 it is algebraically illegal to combine 10 and 5 in step 1 because the original relation is no longer preserved. However, preconceptions from reading and arithmetic, where processing is done from left to right, can lead students to misstep.

Word-problem solving is the next most common activity in algebra education. Word problems can be in the form of a story (Figure 1, part b), or a word equation (Figure 1, part c). Although based on the same quantitative relations as Equation 1, students perform very differently on these three tasks. A misconception generally held by high school mathematics teachers is that high school students solve Equation 1 more easily than a matched story problem or word equation. Teachers justify this prediction by noting that a student must first write a symbolic equation that models the verbal statement, and that this invites other types of errors. While translation from words to mathematical expressions is error-ridden for novices, high school students typically circumvent this step when permitted. Instead, they use highly reliable informal methods, such as guess-and-test and working backwards, which produce higher levels of performance than equation solving.

FIGURE 1

> **Three forms of a start-unknown problem: (a) symbolic form, and the manipulation steps for solving the algebraic equation; (b) story problem; and (c) word equation**
>
> (a) Solve for X: 10+5X=30 (Equation 1)
>   1. 10+5X−10=30−10
>   2. (10−10)+5X=(30−10)
>   3. 0+5X=20
>   4. (5X)/5=20/5
>   5. (5/5)X=4
>   6. X=4
>
> (b) Story problem: Starting at the 10-mile mark, Robin walked 5 mph. How much time will it take her to travel 30 miles?
>
> (c) Word equation: If I multiply some number by 5 and then add 10, I get 30. What is the original number?
>
> SOURCE: Courtesy of author.

Curricular and Technological Advances in Algebra Education

Like many algebra teachers, traditional algebra textbooks take a largely *symbol precedence* view of the development of algebraic reasoning, introducing algebraic concepts through symbolic problem solving, and later applying them to verbal reasoning activities. In contrast, several alternative curricula have recently emerged that begin by eliciting students' invented strategies and representations for describing patterns and data, and developing from these inventions algebraic equations and graphs through a process called *progressive formalization*. These reform-based curricula typically draw on problem-based learning (PBL), which emphasizes complex, multi-day, collaborative problem solving. Three of these approaches, Mathematics in Context, Connected Mathematics, and The Adventures of Jasper Woodbury, have produced commercially available curricula that cover the major topics in middle grade mathematics, such as geometry and algebra.

Technology has also been effectively wedded to innovative curriculum designs. Graphing calculators have had a profound effect on the teaching of algebra using graphical, tabular, and programming forms. The Algebra Sketchbook supports the relationship between verbal descriptions and graphics. The Animate system helps students to construct situation-based meaning for equations. Jasper uses multimedia to present rich problem contexts and encourage production of Smart Tools, representations that support modeling, analysis, and comparison. The Pump Algebra Tutor provides individualized computer-based instruction by relying on adaptive cognitive models of individual students.

See also: MATHEMATICS EDUCATION, TEACHER PREPARATION; MATHEMATICS LEARNING, *subentries on* COMPLEX PROBLEM SOLVING, GEOMETRY, LEARNING TOOLS, WORD-PROBLEM SOLVING.

BIBLIOGRAPHY

THE COGNITION AND TECHNOLOGY GROUP AT VANDERBILT. 1997. *The Jasper Project: Lessons in Curriculum, Instruction, Assessment, and Professional Development.* Mahwah, NJ: Erlbaum.

ENGLISH, LYN, ed. 2002. *Handbook of International Research in Mathematics Education: Directions for the 21st Century.* Mahwah, NJ: Erlbaum.

KAPUT, JAMES J., 1999. "Teaching and Learning a New Algebra." In *Mathematics Classrooms that Promote Understanding,* ed. Elizabeth Fennema and Thomas A. Romberg. Mahwah, NJ: Erlbaum.

KIERAN, CAROLYN. 1992. "The Learning and Teaching of School Algebra." In *Handbook of Research on Mathematics Teaching and Learning,* ed. Douglas A. Grouws. New York: Macmillan.

KOEDINGER, KENNETH R.; ANDERSON, JOHN R.; HADLEY, WILLIAM H.; and MARK, MARY A. 1997. "Intelligent Tutoring Goes to School in the Big City." *International Journal of Artificial Intelligence in Education* 8:30–43.

LADSON-BILLINGS, GLORIA. 1997. "It Doesn't Add Up: African-American Students' Mathematics Achievement." *Journal for Research in Mathematics Education* 28(6):697–708.

LAPPAN GLENDA; FEY, JAMES T.; FITZGERALD, WILLIAM M.; FRIEL, SUSAN N.; and PHILLIPS, ELIZABETH D. 1998. *Connected Mathematics.* Palo Alto, CA: Dale Seymour.

LEHRER, RICHARD, and CHAZAN, DANIEL, eds. 1998. *Designing Learning Environments for Developing Understanding of Geometry and Space.* Mahwah, NJ: Erlbaum.

MAYER, RICHARD E. 1982. "Different Problem-Solving Strategies for Algebra Word and Equation Problems." *Journal of Experimental Psychology: Learning, Memory, and Cognition* 8:448–462.

NATHAN, MITCHELL J.; KINTSCH, WALTER; and YOUNG, EMILIE. 1992. "A Theory of Algebra Word Problem Comprehension and Its Implications for the Design of Computer Learning Environments." *Cognition and Instruction* 9(4):329–389.

NATHAN, MITCHELL J.; LONG, SCOTT D.; and ALIBALI, MARTHA W. 2002. "The Symbol Precedence View of Mathematical Development: An Analysis of the Rhetorical Structure of Algebra Textbooks." *Discourse Processes* 33(1):1–21.

NATIONAL CENTER FOR RESEARCH IN MATHEMATICAL SCIENCES EDUCATION, and FREUDENTHAL INSTITUTE, eds. 1997. *Mathematics in Context: A Connected Curriculum for Grades 5–8.* Chicago: Encyclopaedia Britannica Educational Corporation.

OWENS, S.; BISWAS, G.; NATHAN, MITCHELL J.; ZECH, L.; BRANSFORD, J. D.; and GOLDMAN, S. R. 1995. "Smart Tools: A Multi-Representational Approach to Teaching Function Relations." In *Proceedings of the Seventh World Conference on Artificial Intelligence in Education, AI-ED'95* (Washington, D.C.). Charlottesville, VA: Association for the Advancement of Computing in Education.

USISKIN, ZALMON. 1997. "Doing Algebra in Grades K–4." *Teaching Children Mathematics* 3:346–349.

MITCHELL J. NATHAN

COMPLEX PROBLEM SOLVING

In April 2000, the National Council of Teachers of Mathematics (NCTM) published *Principles and Standards for School Mathematics,* a document intended to serve as "a resource and a guide for all who make decisions that affect the mathematics education of students in prekindergarten through grade 12," and that represented the best understandings regarding mathematical thinking, learning, and problem solving of the mathematics education community at the dawn of the twenty-first century. It also reflected a radically different view from the perspective that dominated through much of the twentieth century.

Principles and Standards specifies five mathematical content domains as core aspects of the curriculum: number and operations, algebra, geometry, measurement, and data analysis and probability. These content areas reflect an evolution of the curriculum over the course of the twentieth century. The first four were present, to various degrees, in 1900. Almost all children studied number and measurement, which comprised the bulk of the elementary curriculum in 1900. Algebra and geometry were mainstays of the secondary curriculum, which was studied only by the elite; approximately 10 percent of the nation's fourteen-year-olds attended high school. Data analysis and probability were nowhere to be seen. Over the course of the twentieth century, the democratization of American education resulted in increasing numbers of students attending, and graduating from, high school.

Curriculum content evolved slowly, with once-advanced topics such as algebra and geometry becoming required of increasing numbers of students. The study of statistics and probability entered the curriculum in the 1980s, and by 2000 it was a central component of most mathematics curricula. This reflected an emphasis on the study of school mathematics for "real world" applications, as well as in preparation for mathematics at the collegiate level.

While content changes can thus be seen as evolutionary, perspectives on mathematical *processes* must be seen as representing a much more fundamental shift in perspective and curricular goals. Given equal weight with the five content areas in *Principles and Standards* are five process standards: problem solving, reasoning and proof, communication, connections, and representation. All of these are deeply intertwined, representing an integrated view of complex mathematical thinking and problem solving. Problem solving might be viewed as a "first among equals," in the sense that the ultimate goal of mathematics instruction can be seen as enabling students to confront and solve problems—not only problems that they have been taught to solve, but unfamiliar problems as well. However, as will be elaborated below, the ability to solve problems and to use one's mathematical knowledge effectively depends not only on content knowledge, but also on the process standards listed above.

Solving difficult problems has always been the concern of professional mathematicians. Early in the twentieth century, *problem books* were viewed as ways for advanced students to develop their mathematical understandings. Perhaps the best exemplar is George Pólya and Gabor Szegö's *Problems and Theorems in Analysis,* first published in 1924. The book offered a graded series of exercises. Readers who managed to solve all the problems would have learned a significant amount of mathematical content, and (although implicitly) a number of problem-solving strategies.

The idea that one could isolate and teach strategies for problem solving remained tacit until the publication of Pólya's *How to Solve It* in 1945. Pólya introduced the notion of *heuristic strategy*—a strategy that, while not guaranteed to work, might help one to better understand or solve a problem. Pólya illustrated the use of certain strategies, such as drawing diagrams; "working backwards" from the goal one wants to achieve; and decomposing a problem into parts, solving the parts, and recombining them to obtain a solution to the original problem. Pólya's ideas resonated within the mathematical community, but they were exceptionally difficult to implement in practice. For example, while it was clear that one should draw diagrams, it was not at all clear which diagrams should be drawn, or what properties those diagrams should have. A problem could be decomposed in many ways, but it was not certain which ways would turn out to be productive.

Means of addressing such issues became available in the 1970s and 1980s, as the field of artificial intelligence (AI) flourished. Researchers in AI wrote computer programs to solve problems, basing the programs on fine-grained observations of human problem solvers. Allen Newell and Herbert Simon's classic 1972 book *Human Problem Solving* showed how one could abstract regularities in the behavior of people playing chess or solving problems in symbolic logic—and codify that regularity in computer programs. Their work suggested that one might do the same for much more complex human problem-solving strategies, if one attended to fine matters of detail. Alan Schoenfeld's 1985 book *Mathematical Problem Solving* (and his subsequent work) showed that such work could be done successfully. Schoenfeld provided evidence that Pólya's heuristic strategies were too broadly defined to be teachable, but that when one specified them more narrowly, students could learn to use them. His book provided evidence that students could indeed learn to use problem-solving strategies—and use them to solve problems unlike the ones they had been taught to solve. It also indicated, however, along with other contemporary research, that problem solving involved more than the mastery of relevant knowledge and powerful problem-solving strategies.

One issue, which came to be known as *metacognition* or *self-regulation,* concerns the effectiveness with which problem solvers use the resources (including knowledge and time) potentially at their disposal. Research indicated that students often fail to solve problems that they might have solved because they waste a great deal of time and effort pursuing inappropriate directions. Schoenfeld's work indicated that students could learn to reflect on the state of their problem solving and become more effective at curtailing inappropriate pursuits. This, however, was still only one component of complex mathematical behavior.

Research at a variety of grade levels indicated that much student behavior in mathematics was shaped by students' beliefs about the mathematical enterprise. For example, having been assigned literally thousands of "problems" that could be solved in a few minutes each, students tended to believe that all mathematical problems could be solved in just a few minutes. Moreover, they believed that if they failed to solve a problem in short order, it was because they didn't understand the relevant method. This led them to give up working on problems that might well have yielded to further efforts. As Magdalene Lampert observed, "Commonly, mathematics is associated with certainty; knowing it, with being able to get the right answer, quickly. These cultural assumptions are shaped by school experience, in which *doing* mathematics means following the rules laid down by the teacher; *knowing* mathematics means remembering and applying the correct rule when the teacher asks a question; and mathematical *truth is determined* when the answer is ratified by the teacher. Beliefs about how to do mathematics and what it means to know it in school are acquired through years of watching, listening, and practicing" (p. 31).

Lampert argued that the very practices of schooling resulted in the development of inappropriate beliefs about the nature of mathematics, and that those beliefs resulted in students' poor mathematical performance. Given the link between students' experiences and their beliefs, the necessary remedy was to revise instructional practices—to create instructional contexts in which students could engage in mathematics as an act of sense-making, and thereby develop a more appropriate set of knowledge, beliefs, and understandings.

Research on mathematical thinking and problem solving conducted in the 1970s and 1980s established the underpinnings for the first major "reform" document, *Curriculum and Evaluation Standards for School Mathematics* (1989), also published by NCTM. The climate was right for change, for the nation was concerned about its students' mathematical performance. Reports such as *A Nation at Risk* (1983) had documented American students' weak mathematical performance in comparison to that of students from other nations, and there was a sense of national crisis regarding the nation's mathematical and scientific capacities. In the early 1990s the U. S. National Science Foundation began to support the development of curricular materials consistent with emerging research on mathematical thinking and learning. The first wave of curricula developed along these lines began to be adopted in the late 1990s.

Many of the new curricula call for students to work on complex problems over extended periods of time. In some cases, important mathematical ideas are introduced and developed through working on problems, rather than taught first and "applied" later. Either way, the fundamental idea is that students will need to have opportunities to develop both the content and process understandings described in *Principles and Standards.* As indicated above, this calls for changes in classroom practices. The best way for students to develop productive mathematical dispositions and knowledge is for them to be supported, in the classroom, in activities that involve meaningful mathematical problem solving. Given a complex problem, students can work together, under the guidance of a knowledgeable teacher, to begin to understand the task and the resources necessary to solve it. This can help them develop productive mathematical dispositions (i.e., the understanding that complex problems will yield to sustained, systematic efforts) and analytic skills. Complex problems may span mathematical areas or be drawn from real-world applications, thus helping students make mathematical connections.

Understanding and working through such problems calls for learning various representational tools—the symbolic and pictorial languages of mathematics. Tasks that call for explaining one's reasoning (i.e., asking students to make a choice between two options and to write a memo that justifies their choice on mathematical grounds) can help students develop their skills at mathematical argument. They also reinforce the idea that obtaining an answer is not enough; one must also be able to convince others of its correctness. Teachers can help students understand that there are standards for communicating mathematical ideas. The arguments students present should be coherent and logical, and ultimately, as students develop, formalizable as mathematical proofs. In these ways, complex problem solving becomes a curricular vehicle as well as a curricular goal.

See also: Mathematics Education, Teacher Preparation; Mathematics Learning, *subentries on* Learning Tools, Myths, Mysteries, and Realities, Number Sense, Word-Problem Solving.

BIBLIOGRAPHY

Brown, Ann L. 1978. "Knowing When, Where, and How to Remember: A Problem of Metacognition." In *Advances in Instructional Psychology,* Vol. 1, ed. Robert Glaser. Hillsdale, NJ: Erlbaum.

Henry, Nelson B., ed. 1951. *The Teaching of Arithmetic.* Chicago: University of Chicago Press.

Lampert, Magdalene. 1990. "When the Problem Is Not the Question and the Solution Is Not the Answer: Mathematical Knowing and Teaching." *American Educational Research Journal* 17:29–64.

Lester, Frank. 1994. "Musings about Mathematical Problem-Solving Research: 1970–1994." *Journal for Research in Mathematics Education* 25(6):660–675.

National Commission on Excellence in Education. 1983. *A Nation at Risk: The Imperative for Educational Reform.* Washington, DC: U.S. Government Printing Office.

National Council of Teachers of Mathematics. 1989. *Curriculum and Evaluation Standards for School Mathematics.* Reston, VA: National Council of Teachers of Mathematics.

National Council of Teachers of Mathematics. 2000. *Principles and Standards for School Mathematics.* Reston, VA: National Council of Teachers of Mathematics.

Newell, Allen, and Simon, Herbert A. 1972. *Human Problem Solving.* Englewood Cliffs, NJ: Prentice-Hall.

Pólya, George. 1945. *How to Solve It.* Princeton, NJ: Princeton University Press.

Pólya, George, and Szegö, Gabor. 1972. *Problems and Theorems in Analysis.* New York: Springer-Verlag.

Schoenfeld, Alan H. 1985. *Mathematical Problem Solving.* Orlando, FL: Academic Press.

Schoenfeld, Alan H. 1992. "Learning to Think Mathematically: Problem Solving, Metacognition, and Sense-Making in Mathematics." In *Handbook of Research on Mathematics Teaching and Learning,* ed. Douglas A. Grouws. New York: Macmillan.

Whipple, Guy M., ed. 1930. *Report of the Society's Committee on Arithmetic.* (The twenty-ninth yearbook of the National Society for the Study of Education.) Bloomington, IL: Public School Publishing Company.

Alan H. Schoenfeld

GEOMETRY

Geometry originated in the ancient practice of earth measurement used in agriculture, the building of pyramids, and the observation of the patterns in the movement of the stars applied in navigation. In spite of the very practical origin of geometry in the investigation of the world, geometry is also the subject area where the development of abstract reasoning began, culminating in the first systematic organization of mathematical knowledge by Euclid around 300 b.c.e. Euclid's deductive system, built on definitions, postulates, theorems, and proofs, has served as the blueprint for representing mathematical knowledge since its inception.

Tension between the experiential, empirical origins of geometry and its abstract deductive representation characterizes contemporary instructional practice and research. Critics of the traditional Euclidean approach to the teaching and learning of geometry argue that the severance of geometric knowledge from its foundation in an inherently geometric world is a pedagogical error.

Educators in the United States have been reluctant to introduce geometry in the primary grades. The traditional view of geometry as an exemplification of abstract reasoning and a fear of exposing students prematurely to formal thinking may be among the reasons for this reluctance. When primary grade teachers choose to spend a short instructional period on geometry, it is usually limited to having students recognize and recall the names of prototypical two-dimensional shapes like triangles, squares, and rectangles. This practice fails to take advantage of the host of informal geometric knowledge children bring to school.

Even before entering school, children develop intuitions about geometric shapes and their characteristics during their early explorations with their environment. For example, in exploring the objects around them, children experience that surfaces can be bumpy or smooth. Building with blocks or stacking other objects, children learn about differences in forms and sizes. Using boxes and other containers, they form intuitive ideas of space-filling or volume. As children walk around in their neighborhood they develop informal notions of spatial arrangements, distance, and directionality. The learning of geometry can be built on this naturally acquired spatial sense. Guiding children to reflect on the characteristics and regularities of their spatial experience can easily lead to the development of the basic concepts (abstractions) of geometry, such as straight and curved lines, points as intersections, planes, and planar and three-dimensional shapes. Uncultivated or ignored, however, children's natural spatial sense fades away, and it is difficult to retrieve it for use when students enroll in their first official geometry course in high school.

A programmatic document, the 1989 *Curriculum and Evaluation Standards for School Mathematics,* produced by the National Council of Teachers of Mathematics (NCTM) to guide reform in mathematics education, recommends that geometric topics be introduced and applied to real-world situations whenever possible. However, this does not imply that immersing children in real-world situations automatically leads to mathematical or geometrical understanding. Hands-on activities are a popular way to establish a connection between instruction and real life, but as instructional means they are only as good as the meanings derived from them. The challenge of geometry instruction is to elevate children's experience with real-world objects to the level of mathematics.

This happens in well-designed instructional tasks that promote reflection on the geometric features of real-life situations, leading to the development of geometric concepts and spatial reasoning. Children learn to generate geometric arguments by participating in carefully orchestrated conversations where they articulate, share, and discuss their ideas regarding spatial problems. Children develop skills of modeling spatial situations when they are invited to publicly display and discuss their visualizations in drawings. These drawings can then be turned into mathematical representations during revision cycles, in the course of which the geometrical features are accentuated while the mathematically irrelevant features (e.g., material, color, and other decorative elements) gradually fade away.

At the secondary level, the traditional Euclidean geometry curriculum that revolves around deductive proof procedures has been criticized because it separates geometry from its empirical, inductive foundation. Critics refer to the typical lack of student appreciation for the subject—often accompanied by low achievement. The deductive organization of the geometry course has been seen as a viable model to help introduce students to mathematical reasoning. However, this is a misrepresentation of the actual reasoning that goes on among expert mathematicians. The deductive logic applied in proofs constitutes only a subset of the rules, and it seldom accounts for the actual thought processes that contributed to the discovery communicated in a proof. Actual discovery usually follows an inductive line of reasoning that begins with empirical investigation and the observation of regularities. It continues with making conjectures based on the observed regularities, and then testing them on multiple examples. Attempts at explaining and generalizing the observed relationship with the help of proof come only after the long process of empirical exploration.

Alternatives to a traditional Euclidean secondary geometry curriculum have been offered based on this more grounded view of mathematical reasoning that incorporates exploration and induction. In the process of exploration, students learn to deconstruct geometric objects into their constitutive elements, and to rely on properties—such as the number and relative size of the sides of the objects, the measure of angles, and their relationships—rather than a prototypical or customary presentation of an image when they identify shapes. Ideally, students will learn to go beyond the appearance of an actual drawing of a shape and argue about generalized concepts of shapes as defined by their properties (for example, a rectangle is a quadrilateral with four right angles and with opposite sides equal and parallel). These skills serve as the foundation of geometrical understanding and need to be acquired—ideally in the primary grades—before students are exposed to proofs.

Some of the new secondary geometry curricula have been organized around technology tools, including geometry construction programs such as the Geometer's Sketchpad and the Geometric Super-Supposer. These programs provide an electronic environment for geometric explorations and allow the learner to generate multiple solutions of geometric construction problems, thus facilitating the generation and testing of hypotheses. Proofs gain a different meaning in this context, becoming the means of explaining why the conjectures developed by the students themselves hold beyond the examples created by the program. This has a motivating effect on the learner. Without such an inductive foundation, students see proofs as an unnecessary procedure to arrive at a simple truth that they already know and accept.

See also: MATHEMATICS EDUCATION, TEACHER PREPARATION; MATHEMATICS LEARNING, *subentries on* ALGEBRA, COMPLEX PROBLEM SOLVING, LEARNING TOOLS, WORD-PROBLEM SOLVING.

BIBLIOGRAPHY

CHAZAN, DANIEL, and YERUSHALMY, MICHAL. 1998. "Charting a Course for Secondary Geometry." In *Designing Learning Environments for Developing Understanding of Geometry and Space,* ed. Richard Lehrer and Daniel Chazan. Mahwah, NJ: Erlbaum.

LAKATOS, IMRE. 1976. *Proofs and Refutations: The Logic of Mathematical Discovery.* Cambridge, Eng.: Cambridge University Press.

LEHRER, RICHARD, and CHAZAN, DANIEL, eds. 1998. *Designing Learning Environments for Developing Understanding of Geometry and Space.* Mahwah, NJ: Erlbaum.

LEHRER, RICHARD; JACOBSON, CATHY; KEMENY, VERA; and STROM, DOLORES. 1999. "Building on Children's Intuitions to Develop Mathematical Understanding of Space." In *Mathematics Classrooms that Promote Understanding,* ed. Elizabeth Fennema and Thomas A. Romberg. Mahwah, NJ: Erlbaum.

NATIONAL COUNCIL OF TEACHERS OF MATHEMATICS. 1989. *Curriculum and Evaluation Standards for School Mathematics.* Reston, VA: National Council of Teachers of Mathematics.

NATIONAL COUNCIL OF TEACHERS OF MATHEMATICS. 2000. *Principles and Standards for School*

Mathematics. Reston, VA: National Council of Teachers of Mathematics.

SCHWARTZ, JUDAH L.; YERUSHALMY, MICHAL; and WILSON, BETH, eds. 1993. *The Geometric Supposer: What Is It a Case Of?* Hillsdale, NJ: Erlbaum.

SERRA, MICHAEL. 1989. *Discovering Geometry: An Inductive Approach.* Berkeley, CA: Key Curriculum Press.

VERA KEMENY

LEARNING TOOLS

The manner in which students learn mathematics influences how well they understand its concepts, principles, and practices. Many researchers have argued that to promote learning with understanding, mathematics educators must consider the tasks, problem-solving situations, and tools used to represent mathematical ideas. Mathematical tools foster learning at many levels—namely, the learning of facts, procedures, and concepts. Tools can also provide concrete models of abstract ideas, or, when dealing with complex problems, they can enable students to manipulate and think about ideas, thereby making mathematics accessible and more deeply understood.

Mathematical learning tools can be traditional, technological, or social. The most frequently employed tools are traditional, which include physical objects or manipulatives (e.g., cubes), visualization tools (e.g., function diagrams), and paper-and-pencil tasks (e.g., producing a table of values). Technological tools, such as calculators (i.e., algebraic and graphic) and computers (e.g., computation and multiple-representation software), have gained attention because they can extend learning in different ways. Social tools, such as small-group discussions where students interact with one another to share and challenge ideas, can be considered a third type of learning tool. These three tools can be used independently or conjointly, depending on the type of learning that is intended.

Learning Tools in Mathematics

A learning tool can be as simple as an image or as complex as a computer-based environment designed to improve mathematical understanding. The key characteristic of a learning tool is that it supports learners in some manner. For example, a tool can aid memory, help students to review their problem-solving processes, or allow students to compare their performance with that of others, thereby supporting self-assessment. Learning tools can represent mathematical ideas in multiple ways, providing flexible alternatives for individuals who differ in terms of learner characteristics. For example, learners who have difficulty understanding the statistical ideas of arithmetic mean (center) and variance (spread) may be assisted through interactive displays that change as data points are manipulated by the learner. A mathematical learning tool can scaffold the learner by performing computations, providing more time for students to test mathematical hypotheses that require reasoning. In the statistics example, learners can focus on why changes to certain parameters affect data—and in what ways, rather than spending all their time calculating measures.

Traditional Tools. Traditional tools are best suited for facilitating students' learning of basic knowledge and skills. Objects that can be manipulated, such as cubes, reduce the abstract nature of concepts, such as numbers, thereby making them real and tangible, particularly for younger children. Such tools support the development of children's understanding of arithmetic by serving as a foundation for learning more complex concepts. Visualization tools, such as graphs, can support data interpretation, while paper-and-pencil tools that provide practice of computational skills can support memory for procedures and an ability to manipulate symbols. Combining physical tools with visualization tools can substantively increase students' conceptual knowledge. Dice and spinners, for example, can be used to support elementary school students in creating graphs of probability distributions, helping them develop an understanding of central tendency.

Technological Tools. Technological tools are most effective in facilitating students' understanding of complex concepts and principles. Computations and graphs can be produced quickly, giving students more time to consider why a particular result was obtained. This support allows students to think more deeply about the mathematics they are learning. Electronic tools are necessary in mathematics because they support the following processes: (a) conjectures—which provide access to more examples and representational formats than is possible by hand; (b) visual reasoning—which provides access to powerful visual models that students often do not create for themselves; (c) conceptualization and modeling—which provide quick and efficient execution of procedures; and (d) flexible thinking—which support the presentation of multiple perspectives.

Spreadsheets, calculators, and dynamic environments are sophisticated learning tools. These tools support interpretation and the rapid testing of conjectures. Technology enables students to focus on the structure of the data and to think about what the data mean, thereby facilitating an overall understanding of a concept (e.g., function). The graphics calculator supports procedures involving functions and students' ability to translate and understand the relationship between numeric, algebraic, and graphical representations. Transforming graphical information in different ways focuses attention on scale changes and can help students see relationships if the appropriate viewing dimensions are used. Computers may remove the need for overlearning routine procedures since they can perform the task of computing the procedures. It is still debatable whether overlearning of facts helps or hinders deeper understanding and use of mathematics. Technology tools can also be designed to help students link critical steps in procedures with abstract symbols to representations that give them meaning.

Video is a dynamic and interactive learning tool. One advantage of video is that complex problems can be presented to students in a richer and more realistic way, compared to standard word problems. An example is The Adventures of Jasper Woodbury, developed by the Learning Technology Center at Vanderbilt University. Students are required to solve problems encountered by characters in the Woodbury video by taking many steps to find a solution. This tool supports students' ability to solve problems, specifically their ability to identify and formulate a problem, to generate subgoals that lead to the solution, and to find the solution. However, the information presented in a video cannot be directly manipulated in the same way that data can be changed in spreadsheets and calculators.

Learning tools that present the same information in several ways (e.g., verbal equation, tabular, graphic) are referred to as multiple-representation tools. The ability to interpret multiple representations is critical to mathematical learning. There is evidence to suggest that multiple representations can facilitate students' ability to understand and solve word problems in functions, and to translate words into tables and graphs. However, interpretation is not easy without some kind of support. One type of support involves highlighting common elements between the different representations to make the relationship between each explicit, thereby facilitating interpretation in both contexts. In some cases, this type of support is insufficient and students need to be explicitly taught to make the connections. Multiple representations can be a powerful learning tool for difficult problems—when students have acquired a strong knowledge base.

Additional research is needed to determine the exact benefits of multiple representational tools. It is important to emphasize that, as with any educational innovation, mathematical learning tools must be designed with a consideration of the teacher, curriculum, and student in mind. For example, with the help of curricular teams and teachers, complex computer environments that present students with multiple representation tools for learning algebra and geometry were successfully adopted in several school systems in the United States.

Social tools. Social tools are a fairly recent consideration. In the 1990s, small-group work where students share strategies for solving problems began to be used as a powerful learning tool. This tool facilitates students' ability to solve word problems and to understand arithmetic. Group collaboration while learning with technology can help students develop the perspectives and practices of mathematics, such as what constitutes acceptable mathematical evidence. Peers and computers can provide feedback that makes students aware of contradictions in their thinking. In this way, social tools can assist learning and transform understanding.

Issues for Further Consideration

Mathematical learning tools should be an important part of students' educational experience. However, a few issues must be addressed before their potential is fully realized. First, use of technological tools is fairly limited in classrooms, despite their potential in changing the nature of mathematical learning. Moreover, software used in schools is often geared towards the practice of computational skills. For example, there may be a potential misuse of the graphing calculator if it is not utilized in the context of sense-making activities. There is a fine line between using a tool for understanding and using it because problems cannot be solved without its use.

Second, learning tools should be an integral part of instructional activities and assessment tasks.

Learning tools should be a regular part of the mathematics experience at every educational level, and different tools should be used for various purposes. The question of ethics and equity is raised when technological tools that are used in instruction are not accessible in assessment situations.

Third, learning tools will only meet their promise through professional development. Teachers who understand the strengths and weaknesses of tools can have a strong impact on how they are used. Support is needed at all levels of education to ensure that sophisticated learning tools are available for use in every mathematics classroom. Learning tools are only as good as the activities that provide the mathematical experiences. The effectiveness of such tools is thus highly dependent on the purpose of the activity and the learning that is intended.

See also: MATHEMATICS LEARNING, *subentry on* COMPLEX PROBLEM SOLVING; SCIENCE LEARNING, *subentry on* TOOLS; TECHNOLOGY IN EDUCATION, *subentry on* CURRENT TRENDS.

BIBLIOGRAPHY

BURILL, GAIL. 1997. "Graphing Calculators and Their Potential for Teaching and Learning Statistics." In *Research on the Role of Technology in Teaching and Learning Statistics,* ed. Joan B. Garfield and Gail Burrill. Voorburg, Netherlands: International Statistical Institute.

COBB, PAUL. 1999. "Individual and Collective Mathematical Development: The Case of Statistical Data Analysis." *Mathematical Thinking and Learning* 1(1):5–43.

COGNITION AND TECHNOLOGY GROUP AT VANDERBILT. 1992. "The Jasper Series as an Example of Anchored Instruction: Theory, Program Description, and Assessment Data." *Educational Psychologist* 27(3):291–315.

FENNEMA, ELIZABETH, and ROMBERG, THOMAS, eds. 1999. *Mathematics Classrooms That Promote Understanding.* Mahwah, NJ: Erlbaum.

HORVATH, JEFFREY K., and LEHRER, RICHARD. 1998. "A Model-Based Perspective on the Development of Children's Understanding of Chance and Uncertainty." In *Reflections on Statistics: Learning, Teaching, and Assessment in Grades K–12,* ed. Susanne P. Lajoie. Mahwah, NJ: Erlbaum.

KAPUT, JAMES. 2000. "Teaching and Learning a New Algebra." In *Mathematics Classrooms That Promote Understanding,* ed. Elizabeth Fennema and Thomas A. Romberg. Mahwah, NJ: Erlbaum.

KOEDINGER, KENNETH, R.; ANDERSON, JOHN, R.; HADLEY, WILLIAM, H.; and MARK, MARY, A. 1997. "Intelligent Tutoring Goes to School in the Big City." *International Journal of Artificial Intelligence in Education* 8:30–43.

LAJOIE, SUSANNE P., ed. 2000. *Computers as Cognitive Tools: No More Walls,* Vol. 2. Mahwah, NJ: Erlbaum.

LESGOLD, ALAN. 2000. "What Are the Tools For? Revolutionary Change Does Not Follow the Usual Norms." In *Computers as Cognitive Tools,* Vol. 2, ed. Susanne P. Lajoie. Mahwah: Erlbaum.

NATIONAL COUNCIL OF TEACHERS OF MATHEMATICS. 2000. *Principles and Standards for School Mathematics.* Reston, VA: National Council of Teachers of Mathematics.

SUSANNE P. LAJOIE
NANCY C. LAVIGNE

MYTHS, MYSTERIES, AND REALITIES

According to the National Research Council, "Much of the failure in school mathematics is due to a tradition of teaching that is inappropriate to the way most students learn" (p. 6). Yet, despite the fact that numerous scientific studies have shown that traditional methods of teaching mathematics are ineffective, and despite professional recommendations for fundamental changes in mathematics curricula and teaching, traditional methods of teaching continue. Indeed, mathematics teaching in the United States has changed little since the mid–twenieth century—essentially, teachers demonstrate, while students memorize and imitate.

Realities

Although research indicates that learning that emphasizes sense-making and understanding produces a better transfer of learning to new situations, traditional classroom instruction emphasizes imitation and memorization. Even when traditional instruction attempts to promote understanding, most students fail to make sense of the ideas because classroom derivations and justifications are too formal and abstract. Though research indicates that mathematical knowledge is truly understood and usable only when it is organized around and interconnected with important core concepts, traditional mathematics curricula make it difficult for students to meaningfully organize knowledge. This is because such curricula provide little time for, or attention to, the type of sense-making activities that enable students to genuinely understand and organize mathematical knowledge. Indeed, the major finding that caused the authors of the Third International Mathematics and Science Study (TIMSS) to characterize the U.S. mathematics curricula as "a mile wide and inch deep" is that traditional curricula cover far too many topics, almost all superficially. As a result, though the same topics are retaught yearly, many are never learned, and few are truly understood.

Furthermore, because traditional instruction focuses so much on symbolic computation procedures, many students come to believe that mathematics is mainly a matter of following fixed and rigid procedures that have no connection to their thinking about realistic and meaningful situations. Instead of seeing mathematics as thoughtful, reflective reasoning, students see it as a matter of parroting procedures, as an academic ritual that has no genuine usefulness. Such ritualistic mathematics, stripped of its power to explain anything that matters and devoid of the interconnections that arise from sense-making, becomes a hodgepodge of memorized—and easily forgotten—rules. The National Research Council dubbed such knowledge "mindless mimicry mathematics."

The modern scientific view of mathematics learning. Almost all current major scientific theories describing how students learn mathematics with genuine understanding (instead of by rote) agree that: (a) mathematical ideas must be mentally constructed by students as they intentionally try to make personal sense of situations; (b) how students construct new ideas is heavily dependent on the cognitive structures students have previously developed; and (c) to be effective, mathematics teaching must carefully guide and support the processes by which students construct mathematical ideas. According to these *constructivist-based* theories, the way a student interprets, thinks about, and makes sense of newly encountered mathematical ideas is determined by the elements and the organization of the relevant mental structures that the student is currently using to process his or her mathematical world. Consequently, instruction that promotes understanding cannot ignore students' current ideas and ways of

reasoning, including their many informal, and even incorrect, ideas.

However, despite the value of the general notion that students must actively construct their own mathematical knowledge, a careful reading of research in mathematics education reveals that the power and usefulness of the these *constructivist* theories arise from: (a) their delineation of specific learning mechanisms, and (b) the detailed research they have spawned on students' mental construction of meaning for particular mathematical topics such as whole-number operations, fractions, and geometric shapes. It is this elaboration and particularization of the general constructivist theory to specific mathematical topics and classroom situations that make the theory and research genuinely relevant to teaching mathematics.

The modern view of mathematics teaching. Both research and professional recommendations suggest a type of mathematics instruction very different from that found in traditional classrooms. In the spirit of inquiry, problem solving, and sense-making, such instruction encourages students to invent, test, and refine their own ideas, rather than unquestioningly follow procedures given to them by others. This type of instruction guides and supports students' construction of personally meaningful ideas that are increasingly complex, abstract, and powerful, and that evolve into the important formal mathematical ideas of modern culture.

However, unlike instruction that focuses only on classroom inquiry, this type of instruction is based on detailed knowledge of students' construction of mathematical knowledge and reasoning. That is, this teaching is based on a deep understanding of: (a) the general stages that students pass through in acquiring the concepts and procedures for particular mathematical topics; (b) the strategies that students use to solve different problems at each stage; and (c) the mental processes and the nature of the knowledge that underlies these strategies. This teaching uses carefully selected sequences of problematic tasks to provoke appropriate perturbations and reformulations in students' thinking.

An abundance of research has shown that mathematics instruction that focuses on student inquiry, problem solving, and personal sense-making—especially that guided by research on students' construction of meaning for particular topics—produces powerful mathematical thinkers who not only can compute, but have strong mathematical conceptualizations and are skilled problem solvers.

Myths and Misunderstandings

Misunderstanding the nature of mathematics. One of the most critical aspects of effective mathematics learning is developing a proper understanding of the nature of mathematics. The chairperson of the commission that wrote the National Council of Teachers of Mathematics (NCTM) *Standards* stated, "The single most compelling issue in improving school mathematics is to change the epistemology of mathematics in schools, the sense on the part of teachers and students of what the mathematical enterprise is all about" (Romberg, p. 433).

Mathematics is first and foremost a form of reasoning. In the context of analytically reasoning about particular types of quantitative and spatial phenomena, mathematics consists of thinking in a logical manner, making sense of ideas, formulating and testing conjectures, and justifying claims. One does mathematics when one recognizes and describes patterns; constructs physical or conceptual models of phenomena; creates and uses symbol systems to represent, manipulate, and reflect on ideas; and invents procedures to solve problems. Unfortunately, most students see mathematics as memorizing and following little-understood rules for manipulating symbols.

To illustrate the difference between mathematics as reasoning and mathematics as rule-following, consider the question: "What is 2-1/2 divided by 1/4?" Traditionally taught students are trained to solve such problems by using the "invert and multiply" method: $2\text{-}1/2 \div 1/4 = 5/2 \times 4/1$. Students who are lucky enough to recall how to compute an answer can rarely explain or demonstrate why the answer is correct. Worse, most students do not know when the computation should be applied in real-world contexts.

In contrast, students who have made genuine sense of mathematics do not need a symbolic algorithm to compute an answer to this problem. They quickly reason that, since there are 4 fourths in each unit and 2 fourths in a half, there are 10 fourths in 2-1/2. Furthermore, such students quickly recognize when to apply such thinking in real-world situations.

Obviously, not all problems can be easily solved using such intuitive strategies. Students must also develop an understanding of, and facility with, symbolic manipulations. Nevertheless, students' use of symbols must never become disconnected from their powerful intuitive reasoning about actual quantities. For when it does, students become overwhelmed with trying to memorize countless rules.

The myth of coverage. One of the major components of traditional mathematics teaching is the almost universal belief in the myth of *coverage.* According to this myth, if mathematics is "covered" by instruction, students will learn it. This myth is so deeply embedded in traditional mathematics instruction that, at each grade level, teachers feel tremendous pressure to teach huge amounts of material at breakneck speeds. The myth has fostered a curriculum that is superficially broad, and it has encouraged acceleration rather than deep understanding. Belief in this myth causes teachers to criticize as inefficient curricula that emphasize depth of understanding because students in such curricula study far fewer topics at each grade level.

But research on learning debunks this myth. Based on scientific evidence, researchers John Bransford, Ann Brown, and Rodney Cocking explain that covering too many topics too quickly hinders learning because students acquire disorganized and disconnected facts and organizing principles that they cannot make meaningful. Indeed, in his article "Teaching for the Test," Alan Bell, from the Shell Centre for Mathematical Education at the University of Nottingham, presents research evidence showing the superiority of sense-making curricula. Consistent with Bell's claim, TIMSS data suggest that Japanese teachers, whose students significantly outperform U.S. students in mathematics, spend much more time than U.S. teachers having students delve deeply into mathematical ideas.

In summary, because students in traditional curricula learn ideas and procedures rotely, rather than meaningfully, they quickly forget them, so the ideas must be repeatedly retaught. In contrast, in curricula that focus on deep understanding and personal sense-making, because students naturally develop and interrelate new and rich conceptualizations, they accumulate an ever-increasing network of well-integrated and long-lasting mathematical knowledge. Thus, curricula that emphasize deep understanding may cover fewer topics at particular grade levels, but overall they enable students to learn more material because topics do not need to be repeatedly taught.

Putting skill before understanding. Many people, including teachers, believe that students, especially those in lower-level classes, should master mathematical procedures first, then later try to understand them. However, research indicates that if students have already rotely memorized procedures through extensive practice, it is very difficult for later instruction to get them to conceptually understand the procedures. For example, it has been found that fifth and sixth graders who had practiced rules for adding and subtracting decimals by lining up the decimal points were less likely than fourth graders with no such experience to acquire conceptual knowledge from meaning-based instruction.

Believing that bright students are doing fine. Although there is general agreement that most students have difficulty becoming genuinely competent with mathematics, many people take solace in the belief that bright students are doing fine. However, a closer look reveals that even the brightest American students are being detrimentally affected by traditional teaching. For instance, a bright eighth grader who was three weeks from completing a standard course in high school geometry applied the volume formula in a situation in which it was inappropriate, getting an incorrect answer:

> Observer: How do you know that is the right answer?
>
> Student: Because the equation for the volume of a box is length times width times height.
>
> Observer: Do you know why that equation works?
>
> Student: Because you are covering all three dimensions, I think. I'm not really sure. I just know the equation. (Battista, 1999)

This student did not understand that the mathematical formula she applied assumed a particular mathematical model of a real-world situation, one that was inappropriate for the problem she was presented. Although this bright student had learned many routine mathematical procedures, much of the learning she accomplished in her accelerated mathematics program was superficial, a finding that is all too common among bright students. Indeed, only 38 percent of the students in her geometry class answered the item correctly, despite the fact that all of them had scored at or above the ninety-fifth percentile in mathematics on a widely used standardized mathematics test in fifth grade. Similarly, in the suburbs of one major American city in which the median family income is 30 percent higher than the national average, and in which three-quarters of the students were found to be at or above the international standard for computation, only between one-fifth and one-third met the international standard for problem solving.

Misunderstanding inquiry-based teaching. Many educators and laypersons incorrectly conceive of the inquiry-based instruction suggested by modern research as a pedagogical paradigm entailing nonrigorous, intellectual anarchy that lets students pursue whatever interests them and invent and use any mathematical methods they wish, whether these methods are correct or not. Others see such instruction as equivalent to cooperative learning, teaching with manipulatives, or *discovery* teaching in which a teacher asks a series of questions in an effort to get students to discover a specific, formal mathematical concept. Although elements of the latter three conceptions are, in altered form, similar to components of the type of instruction recommended by research in mathematics education, none of these conceptions is equivalent to the modern view. What separates the new, research-based view of teaching from past views is: (a) the strong focus on, and carefully guided support of, students' construction of personal mathematical meaning, and (b) the use of research on students' learning of particular mathematical topics to guide the selection of instructional tasks, teaching strategies, and learning assessments.

To illustrate, consider the topic of finding the volume of a rectangular box. In traditional didactic teaching, students are simply shown the procedure of multiplying the length, width, and height. In classic discovery teaching, students might be given several boxes and asked to determine the boxes' dimensions and volumes using rulers and small cubes. The teacher would ask students to determine the relationship between the dimensions and the volumes, with the goal being for students to discover the "length times width times height" procedure. In contrast, research-based inquiry teaching might give students a sequence of problems in which students examine a picture of a rectangular array of cubes that fills a box, predict how many cubes are in the array, then make the box and fill it with cubes to check their prediction. The goal would be for each individual student to develop a prediction strategy that not only is correct but also makes sense to the student.

Research shows that the formula rarely makes sense to students, and that, if given appropriate opportunities, students generally develop some type of layering strategy, for instance, counting the cubes showing on the front face of an array and multiplying by the number of layers going back. Because the layering strategy is a natural curtailment of the concrete counting strategies students initially employ on these problems, it is far easier for students to make personal sense of layering than using the formula.

Modern research further guides inquiry teaching by describing the cognitive obstacles students face in learning and the cognitive processes needed to overcome these obstacles. For instance, research indicates that before being exposed to appropriate instruction, most students have an incorrect model of the array of cubes that fills a rectangular box. Because of a lack of coordination and synthesis of spatial information, students can neither picture where all the cubes are nor appropriately mentally organize the cubes. Instruction can support the development of personal meaning for procedures for finding volume only if it ensures that (a) students develop proper mental models of the cube arrays, and (b) students base their enumeration strategies on these mental models.

Forgetting the need for fluency. Because of mistaken beliefs about the type of instruction suggested by research and professional recommendations, low-fidelity implementations of reform curricula often focus so much on promoting class discussions and reasoning that they lose sight of the critical need to properly crystallize students' thinking into a sophisticated and fluent use of mathematics. Although modern approaches to instruction have rightly shifted the instructional focus from imitating procedures to understanding and personal sense-making, it is clearly insufficient to involve students only in sense-making, reasoning, and the construction of mathematical knowledge. Sound curricula must also assure that students become fluent in utilizing particularly useful mathematical concepts, ways of reasoning, and procedures. Students should be able to readily and correctly apply important mathematical strategies, procedures, and lines of reasoning in various situations, and they should possess knowledge that supports mathematical reasoning. For instance, students should know the *basic number facts,* because such knowledge is essential for mental computation,

estimation, performance of computational procedures, and problem solving.

Mysteries and Challenges

To inquire or not to inquire. Scientific research and professional standards recommend inquiry-based instruction because such instruction elicits classroom cultures that support students' genuine sense-making, and because such classrooms focus on the development of students' reasoning, not the disconnected rote acquisition of formal, ready-made ideas contained in textbooks. However, the critical ingredient in research-based teaching is the focus on fostering students' construction of personal mathematical meaning. This focus suggests that inquiry-based teaching that does not focus on students' construction of personally meaningful ideas is not completely consistent with research-based suggestions for teaching. It also suggests that demonstrations, and even lectures, might create meaningful learning if students are capable of, and intentionally focus on, personal sense-making and understanding. However, the question of whether, and when, lecture/demonstration—the most common mode of teaching found in American schools—can produce meaningful mathematics learning has not received much research attention. Research is needed that thoroughly investigates the role that this cherished traditional instructional tool can play in meaningful mathematics learning.

Scientific practice versus tradition. One of the major reasons that school mathematics programs in the U.S. are so ineffective is because they ignore modern scientific research on mathematics learning and teaching. For instance, many popular approaches to improving mathematics learning focus on getting students to "try harder" or take more rigorous courses. Or, in attempts to increase students' motivation, educators use gimmicks to try to make mathematics classes—but not mathematics itself—more interesting. But almost all of these approaches are rooted in a traditional perspective on mathematics learning; they ignore the cognitive processes that undergird mathematical sense-making. So even when these approaches are "successful," they produce only mimicry-based procedural knowledge of mathematics.

It is not that increasing motivation and effort are bad ideas. If students are unwilling to engage in intellectual activity in the mathematics classroom, there is little chance that mathematics instruction of any kind, no matter how sound, will induce or support their mathematics learning. However, students' motivation and effort to learn mathematics are strongly dependent on their beliefs about the value that mathematics, and school in general, has for their lives. The nature of these beliefs is determined partly by students' interaction with family, peers, schools, and community, but also by the quality of their mathematics instruction. Instruction that does not properly support students' mathematical sense-making builds counterproductive beliefs about mathematics learning.

Thus, because instructional approaches that are not based on modern scientific research on the learning process ignore the workings of the very process they are attempting to affect, they cannot support genuine mathematical sense-making or produce productive beliefs about learning mathematics. One of the greatest challenges is to determine how to get teachers, administrators, and policymakers to base their instructional practices and decisions on modern scientific research.

Assessment. Because commonly used assessments inadequately measure students' mathematics learning, there is a critical need for the creation and adoption of new assessment methods that more accurately portray student learning. Assessments are needed that not only determine *if* students have acquired particular mathematical knowledge, skills, and types of reasoning, but also determine precisely *what* students have learned. Such assessments must be firmly and explicitly linked to scientific research on students' mathematics learning, something that is sorely missing in traditional assessment paradigms. To be consistent with such research, assessment must focus on students' mathematical cognitions, not their overt behaviors.

See also: INSTRUCTIONAL STRATEGIES; MATHEMATICS EDUCATION, TEACHER PREPARATION.

BIBLIOGRAPHY

BATTISTA, MICHAEL T. 1999. "The Mathematical Miseducation of America's Youth: Ignoring Research and Scientific Study in Education." *Phi Delta Kappan* 80(6):424–433.

BELL, ALAN. 1989. "Teaching for the Test." *The Times Educational Supplement,* October 27.

BOALER, JO. 1998. "Open and Closed Mathematics: Student Experiences and Understandings." *Journal for Research in Mathematics Education* 29(1):41–62.

BRANSFORD, JOHN D.; BROWN, ANN L.; and COCKING, RODNEY R. 1999. *How People Learn: Brain, Mind, Experience, and School.* Washington, DC: National Research Council.

CARPENTER, THOMAS P.; FRANKE, MEGAN L.; JACOBS, VICTORIA R.; FENNEMA, ELIZABETH; and EMPSON, SUSAN B. 1998. "A Longitudinal Study of Invention and Understanding in Children's Multidigit Addition and Subtraction." *Journal for Research in Mathematics Education* 29(1):3–20.

COBB, PAUL; WOOD, TERRY; YACKEL, ERNA; NICHOLLS, JOHN; WHEATLEY, GRAYSON; TRIGATTI, BEATRIZ; and PERLWITZ, MARCELLA. 1991. "Assessment of a Problem-Centered Second-Grade Mathematics Project." *Journal for Research in Mathematics Education* 22(1):3–29.

DE CORTE, ERIK; GREER, BRIAN; and VERSCHAFFEL, LIEVEN. 1996. "Mathematics Teaching and Learning." In *Handbook of Educational Psychology,* ed. David C. Berliner and Robert C. Calfee. London: Simon and Schuster; New York: Macmillan.

FENNEMA, ELIZABETH; CARPENTER, THOMAS P.; FRANKE, MEGAN L.; LEVI, LINDA; JACOBS, VICTORIA R.; and EMPSON, SUSAN B. 1996. "A Longitudinal Study of Learning to Use Children's Thinking in Mathematics Instruction." *Journal for Research in Mathematics Education* 27(4):403–434.

GREENO, JAMES G.; COLLINS, ALLAN M.; and RESNICK, LAUREN. 1996. "Cognition and Learning." In *Handbook of Educational Psychology,* ed. David C. Berliner and Robert C. Calfee. London: Simon and Schuster; New York: Macmillan.

HIEBERT, JAMES. 1999. "Relationships between Research and the NCTM Standards." *Journal for Research in Mathematics Education* 30(1):3–19.

HIEBERT, JAMES, and CARPENTER, THOMAS P. 1992. "Learning and Teaching with Understanding." In *Handbook of Research on Mathematics Teaching,* ed. Douglas A. Grouws. Reston, VA: National Council of Teachers of Mathematics/ Macmillan.

HIEBERT, JAMES; CARPENTER, THOMAS P.; FENNEMA, ELIZABETH; FUSON, KAREN C.; WEARNE,

DIANA; MURRAY, HANLIE; OLIVIER, ALWYN; and HUMAN, PIET. 1997. *Making Sense: Teaching and Learning Mathematics with Understanding.* Portsmouth, NH: Heinemann.

MACK, NANCY K. 1990. "Learning Fractions with Understanding: Building on Informal Knowledge." *Journal for Research in Mathematics Education* 21(1):16–32.

MACLEOD, DOUGLAS B. 1992. "Research on Affect in Mathematics Education: A Reconceptualization." In *Handbook of Research on Mathematics Teaching,* ed. Douglas A. Grouws. Reston, VA: National Council of Teachers of Mathematics/ Macmillan.

NATIONAL CENTER FOR EDUCATION STATISTICS. 1996. *Pursuing Excellence: A Study of U.S. Eighth-Grade Mathematics and Science Teaching, Learning, Curriculum, and Achievement in International Context.* Washington, DC: National Center for Education Statistics.

NATIONAL COUNCIL OF TEACHERS OF MATHEMATICS. 1989. *Curriculum and Evaluation Standards for School Mathematics.* Reston, VA: National Council of Teachers of Mathematics.

NATIONAL COUNCIL OF TEACHERS OF MATHEMATICS. 2000. *Principles and Standards for School Mathematics.* Reston, VA: National Council of Teachers of Mathematics.

NATIONAL RESEARCH COUNCIL. 1989. *Everybody Counts.* Washington, DC: National Academy Press.

PESEK, DELORES D., and KIRSHNER, DAVID. 2000. "Interference of Instrumental Instruction in Subsequent Relational Learning." *Journal for Research in Mathematics Education* 31(5):524–540.

REESE, CLYDE M.; MILLER, KAREN E.; MAZZEO, JOHN; and DOSSEY, JOHN A. 1997. *NAEP 1996 Mathematics Report Card for the Nation and the States.* Washington, DC: National Center for Education Statistics.

RESNICK, LAUREN B. 1995. "Inventing Arithmetic: Making Children's Intuition Work in School." In *Basic and Applied Perspectives on Learning, Cognition, and Development,* ed. Charles A. Nelson. Mahwah, NJ: Erlbaum.

ROMBERG, THOMAS A. 1992. "Further Thoughts on the Standards: A Reaction to Apple." *Journal for Research in Mathematics Education* 23(5):432–437.

SCHMIDT, WILLIAM H.; McKNIGHT, CURTIS C.; and RAIZEN, SENTA A. 1997. *A Splintered Vision: An Investigation of U.S. Science and Mathematics Education.* Dordrecht, Netherlands: Kluwer Academic.

SILVER, EDWARD A.; and STEIN, MARY KAY. 1996. "The QUASAR Project: The 'Revolution of the Possible' in Mathematics Instructional Reform in Urban Middle Schools." *Urban Education* 30:476–521.

STEFFE, LESLIE P., and KIEREN, THOMAS. 1994. "Radical Constructivism and Mathematics Education." *Journal for Research in Mathematics Education* 25(6):711–733.

WOOD, TERRY, and SELLERS, PATRICIA. 1996. "Assessment of a Problem-Centered Mathematics Program: Third Grade." *Journal for Research in Mathematics Education* 27(3):337–353.

MICHAEL T. BATTISTA

NUMBER SENSE

What does it mean to suggest that an individual possesses good *number sense?* The ability to see patterns and relationships between numbers, to work flexibly with operations and procedures, to recognize order and relative quantities, and to utilize estimation and mental computation are all components of what is termed *number sense.* Individuals who quickly calculate a 15 percent gratuity at a restaurant, know that the seven-digit display 0.498732 is approximately 1/2, or recognize that calculating 48×12 will be less problematic than calculating 48×13 are said to manifest qualities associated with good number sense.

Most mathematics educators agree that developing number sense is important, yet there is no single definition that is unanimously accepted. Number sense is highly personalized and thought to develop gradually. It includes self-regulation, an ability to make connections in number patterns, and an intuition regarding numbers. Number sense "refers to a person's general understanding of number and operations along with the ability and inclination to use this understanding in flexible ways to make mathematical judgments and to develop useful strategies for handling numbers and operations" (McIntosh et al., p. 3).

Historical Background

Before the term *number sense* came into use, the word *numeracy* was coined in 1959 to denote those within the realm of mathematics who had a propensity to comprehend higher-level mathematical concepts. Yet the general public took numeracy to be the mathematical analogue of literacy, and therefore reduced its meaning to connote the propensity to comprehend basic arithmetic. A book by John Allen Paulos, *Innumeracy: Mathematical Illiteracy and Its Consequences* (1988), demonstrated the dangers of a population that lacks a basic understanding of mathematics and that views the subject as enigmatic due to poor education or psychological anxiety. Many of those involved with mathematics education felt that math pedagogy was in need of serious reform due to a superficial acquisition of knowledge based merely on a procedural understanding of mathematics (e.g., "just follow this algorithm").

In the late 1980s and the 1990s researchers and educators saw a heightened need to examine the role of computation as it related to elementary mathematics, reflecting on both the process and result of employing algorithmic strategies. It was during this period that the term *number sense* gained wide acceptance, epitomizing the desired outcome for the teaching and learning of mathematics. Yet due to its implicit nature, succinctly describing how number sense is revealed can be problematic. The mathematician Stanislas Dehaene, in his 1997 book *The Number Sense: How the Mind Creates Mathematics,* states, "Our number sense cannot be reduced to the formal definition provided by rules or axioms" (p. 240). In addition, James Greeno relates, "We recognize examples of number sense, even though we have no satisfactory definition that distinguishes its features" (p. 171).

Similar to the ambiguous implications of common sense, number sense is open to a variety of interpretations. The National Council of Teachers of Mathematics, in *Curriculum and Evaluation of Standards for School Mathematics* (1989), defines number sense as "an intuition about numbers that is drawn from all the varied meanings of number. It has five components: (1) having well-understood number meanings, (2) developing multiple relationships among numbers, (3) understanding the relative magnitudes of numbers, (4) developing intuitions about the relative effect of operating on numbers, (5) developing referents for measures of common objects" (pp. 39–40). However, others would argue

that such descriptors and boundaries for the nature of number sense do not characterize it in forms that guide instruction. Lauren Resnick and Judith Sowder categorize number sense as an open-ended form of reasoning that is nonalgorithmic, complex, and involves uncertainty. These multiple views are highlighted merely to show the somewhat amorphous nature of number sense and qualities ascribed to it.

Examples of Number Sense

Most often, number sense is recognized through example. One ascribed attribute is the ability to use numbers flexibly when mentally computing an abstract numerical operation. This flexibility evolves through infixing connections and relationships between numbers and their representations. By augmenting the number of connections to analogous situations, more flexibility and utility ensues. For example, a simple computation involving subtraction is the problem $7 - 4$. The ability to place this abstraction of symbols into multiple situations signifies a certain number sense, such as: (1) a set or group—seven cookies take away four cookies; (2) a distance—in order to move from space 4 to space 7 in a board game, 3 moves are required; (3) a temperature reading—to change from 7° C to 4° C, the temperature must drop 3° C. These mental models seem natural to most adults and children who have been guided to think with such models. With the simple transition of this problem, reversing the minuend and subtrahend mandates an ability to move into negative numbers: $4 - 7$ equals what? For a child who has only the group mental model (4 cookies take away 7 cookies), this operation seems problematic or impossible. A child who has multiple models can utilize the one that gives a more intuitive representation of the abstract operation—if the temperature is 4° C and then falls 7°C, then the new temperature would be negative (or minus) 3° C.

In addition, being able to compare the relative size of numbers would be a sign of number sense. Students should recognize that 4,562 is large compared to 400 but small compared to 400,000. There should also be emphasis placed on providing context to compare large numbers. For example, a million and a billion are ubiquitous quantities in many economies. Therefore, to recognize that it takes roughly eleven-and-a-half days for a million seconds to pass and nearly thirty-two years for a billion seconds to pass connotes a deeper appreciation for the relative magnitude of quantities.

Number sense extends beyond the set of whole numbers and integers. Consider a more frequent area of concern for many school children, fractions. Consider the following example: $2/3 + 1/4$. For conceptual understanding, fractions and ratios necessitate the skill of proportional reasoning in order to make sense of this abstract representation. Considering a part-to-a-whole relationship, the adroit student can recognize the necessity to compare equal size parts (and therefore find a common denominator) before total parts can be computed:

$$\frac{2}{3} + \frac{1}{4} = \frac{8}{12} + \frac{3}{12} = \frac{11}{12}$$

In contrast, a child who has no intuitive grasp for fractions will most likely commit the error of adding the numerators and adding the denominators. This algorithmic error might also be attributed to those who rely on a strictly procedural understanding, because this procedure is correct when it relates to multiplying fractions,

$$\left(\frac{2}{3} \times \frac{1}{4} \; does \; equal \; \frac{2 \times 1}{3 \times 4} = \frac{2}{12} \; or \; \frac{1}{6}\right)$$

and students often confuse these two rules. Furthermore, this nonconventional result for addition can be justified with concrete examples. If Barry Bonds plays in both games of a double-header, and he bats 2 for 3 in the first game and 1 for 4 in the second game, then his correct batting average for the day is 3 for 7, which, in terms of the traditional procedure for adding fractions, is not conventionally correct:

$$\frac{2}{3} + \frac{1}{4} = \frac{2+1}{3+4} = \frac{3}{7} \; or \; \approx 0.429$$

Therefore, number sense involves knowing *when* a specific model is applicable.

Sometimes, number sense can be grasped intuitively through visual clues as well. Some people have an affinity for understanding visual models, which they might then internalize and incorporate into their personal number sense. Figure 1 contains no symbolic representation of numerals; rather, actual quantities are depicted as the objects themselves. The question at hand is to compare the available cake for girls and for boys and determine in which of the two groups does an individual receive more cake. Students who are versed in strictly procedural understandings might set up ratios that symbolize

the situation, then try to rely on memorized algorithms to simplify the symbols:

$$\frac{3}{8} \; compared \; with \; \frac{1}{3}$$

$$assume \; equality \; \therefore \; \tfrac{3}{8} = \tfrac{1}{3}$$

$$cross \; multiply \; \rightarrow \; \frac{3}{8} = \frac{1}{3} = 3 \cdot 3 = 8 \cdot 1$$

$$\therefore \; 9 > 8 \; so \; \tfrac{3}{8} > \tfrac{1}{3}$$

Someone with a more flexible understanding might simply notice that for the boys there is one cake for a group of three; therefore, an equal ratio based on three cakes would be a group of nine girls. From this equivalency, they would deduce that since there are less than nine girls, then each girl must receive more cake than each boy.

Developing Number Sense

The acquisition of number sense is often considered to develop as stages along a continuum, rather than as a static object that is either possessed or not. Dehaene reports that most children enter preschool with a well-developed understanding of approximation and counting. Dehaene presents research from cognitive psychologists, such as Jean Piaget, Prentice Starkey, and Karen Wynn, suggesting contradictory results about what skills are innate, when skills are developed, and how they are acquired. Part of the complexity to succinctly describe a development of number sense stems both from the subtlety of multiple factors it encompasses and the lack of explicit demonstrability. For example, with the problem 18×5, someone demonstrating number sense might recognize the relationship of the quantity 5 compared to *10* is simply half, and knowing that, taking half of this result would give the desired result, 90. This sophisticated innovation may be entirely internal, with only the final solution given and no account of the process. Although we can recognize number sense when we see it, the question as to how one's cognitive process completes individual tasks is less certain. It is similar to mathematicians' demands for valid proofs to be *rigorous,* though they are unable to adequately describe what is meant by *rigor.*

There are several factors regarding the development of number sense that mathematics educators have come to agree upon from empirical research during the 1990s. Results from Paul Cobb et al., Judith Sowder, Sharon Griffin and Robbie Case, and

FIGURE 1

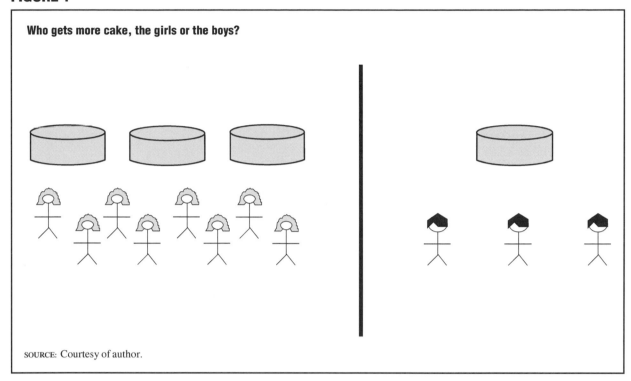

Who gets more cake, the girls or the boys?

SOURCE: Courtesy of author.

Eddie Gray and David Tall have provided a more clearly agreed upon framework regarding advantageous skills for building number sense. Sowder notes that computational estimation and mental computation are important links to building number sense. Both Cobb et al. and Greeno state that both the use of mental models and creating a conceptual environment are necessary facilitators to make these links. Educators see a necessity to incorporate rich examples that guide students toward conceptual understandings, instead of superficial procedures that are not considered malleable. Developing mental models and utilizing mental computation are increasingly considered vital skills in mathematics; however research about reasoning with mental models is in a preliminary state.

Current Trends and Their Effects on Mathematics Education

The twentieth century saw its share of reforms in mathematics pedagogy—from the algorithmic framework of connectionist theory attributed to Edward L. Thorndike to the axiomatic formalization of modern mathematics pursued by Bourbaki (a pseudonym taken by a group of French mathematicians) and Piaget's constructivist theory, which dominated the second half of the century and em-

phasized individuals as constructing their own knowledge through a process of abstraction, generalization, and concept formation. The concern in the 1990s surrounding a superficial (or merely procedural) understanding of mathematics with a lack of conceptual understanding was the catalyst that galvanized a push toward interpreting mathematics not as rote and memorization, but as problem solving, intuitive reasoning, and pattern recognition. The concept of number sense sprang forth from these shifts in philosophy regarding mathematics education. With this shift, a question arises: What significance does number sense have on mathematics education and pedagogy?

Another difficulty in encapsulating pedagogy that develops number sense stems from the fact that most mathematicians fail to recognize their own number sense and how they employ it. Their ability to move beyond procedures and definitions into the realm of concepts is rarely a conscious process. To a mathematician, the act is incorporated into their thinking process such that its nature becomes an involuntary action, like blinking or breathing. The mathematical paradox of striving for efficiency, both in notation and procedures, can oftentimes add to a lack of understanding for the student. To communicate efficiently, all those involved must be fluent in the language of mathematics.

Obviously, some students are successful in mathematics regardless of the pedagogical approach used. If this were not the case, the explosion within the new fields of mathematics that occurred after 1950 would not have occurred. Philip Davis and Reuben Hersh attest that more than half of all of mathematics was discovered after World War II. The question, then, is what percentage of those who completed traditional education were finding this success. Gray and Tall speculate that only 30 percent of students were able to develop an intuitive grasp of mathematics and higher-order thinking with previous pedagogies. So what about the other 70 percent? The research by Paul Cobb et al., Sharon Griffin and Robbie Case, and others consider this a central focus of current pedagogical issues.

This search for conceptual understanding seems to be the focus of research and pedagogy in the beginning of the twenty-first century. Empirical evidence supports a curriculum that stresses practical, intuitive, and rich real-world examples within mathematics. The Rightstart project, developed by Case and Griffin in 1997, is one such example. Their research focused on children living in urban, low-income communities who were lagging behind their peers in terms of age-level mathematics abilities. After participating in forty twenty-minute sessions that incorporated numerical games and concrete materials (using thermometers, board games, and number lines) these children were propelled to the top of their class, and they maintained this placement over a longitudinal study lasting several years. This success was achieved by focusing on two main goals: (1) to help students to develop a set of symbolic states and operations that are intimately tied to real-world quantities, and (2) to develop students' explicit knowledge of notational systems in conjunction with their implicit and intuitive knowledge, thus ensuring that these two types of knowledge act as natural companions to each other. Both of these goals coincide with the parameters of developing number sense.

The mathematician Warren McCulloch (1965) once observed, "What is a number, that a man may know it, and a man, that he may know a number?" The answer to this question, which has been posed in various forms since antiquity, changes with the understanding of mathematics. Since the 1990s, mathematics educators have been researching how number sense ameliorates students' understanding of mathematics. Mathematics educators have embraced this shift toward a pedagogy that strives to merge intuition, formal notation, and conceptual understanding. Number sense helps students eschew the notion that mathematics is merely a collection of rules to memorize. Number sense fosters students' ability to make judgments about the reasonableness of solutions and to build on their intuitions and insights. Number sense helps convince students that mathematics makes sense.

See also: MATHEMATICS EDUCATION, TEACHER PREPARATION; MATHEMATICS LEARNING, *subentries on* MYTHS, MYSTERIES, AND REALITIES, NUMERACY AND CULTURE.

BIBLIOGRAPHY

ANGHILERI, JULIA. 2000. *Teaching Number Sense.* London: Continuum.

COBB, PAUL; WOOD, TERRY; YACKEL, ERNA; NICHOLLS, JOHN; WHEATLEY, GRAYSON; TRIGATTI, BEATRIZ; and PERLWITZ, MARCELLA. 1991. "Assessment of a Problem-Centered Second Grade Mathematics Project." *Journal for Research in Mathematics Education* 22(1):3–29.

DAVIS, PHILIP, and HERSH, REUBEN. 1981. *The Mathematical Experience.* Boston: Mariner Books.

DEHAENE, STANISLAS. 1997. *The Number Sense: How the Mind Creates Mathematics.* New York: Oxford University Press.

GRAY, EDDIE, and TALL, DAVID. 1994. "Duality, Ambiguity, and Flexibility: A 'Proceptual' View of Simple Arithmetic." *Journal for Research in Mathematics Education* 25(2):116–140.

GREENO, JAMES G. 1991. "Number Sense as Situated Knowing in a Conceptual Domain." *Journal for Research in Mathematics Education* 22(3):170–218.

GRIFFIN, SHARON, and CASE, ROBBIE. 1997. "Rethinking the Primary School Math Curriculum: An Approach Based on Cognitive Science." *Issues in Education: Contributions from Educational Psychology* 3(1):1–50.

HIEBERT, JAMES; and LEFEVRE, PATRICIA. 1986. "Conceptual and Procedural Knowledge in Mathematics: An Introductory Analysis." In *Conceptual and Procedural Knowledge: The Case of Mathematics,* ed. James Hiebert. Hillsdale, NJ: Erlbaum.

MARKOVITS, ZVIA, and SOWDER, JUDITH. 1994. "Developing Number Sense: An Intervention Study in Grade 7." *Journal for Research in Mathematics Education* 25(1):4–30.

MCCULLOCH, WARREN. 1965. *Embodiments of Mind.* Cambridge, MA: MIT Press.

MCINTOSH, ALISTAIR; REYS, BARBARA J.; and REYS, ROBERT E. 1992. "A Proposed Framework for Examining Basic Number Sense." *For the Learning of Mathematics* 12(3): 2–8.

NATIONAL COUNCIL OF TEACHERS OF MATHEMATICS. 1989. *Curriculum and Evaluation of Standards for School Mathematics.* Reston, VA: National Council of Teachers of Mathematics.

PAULOS, JOHN ALLEN. 1988. *Innumeracy: Mathematical Illiteracy and Its Consequences.* New York: Vintage.

PIAGET, JEAN. 1965. *The Child's Conception of Number.* New York: Norton.

RESNICK, LAUREN B. 1989. "Defining, Assessing, and Teaching Number Sense." In *Establishing Foundations for Research on Number Sense and Related Topics: Report of a Conference,* ed. Judith T. Sowder and Bonnie P. Schappelle. San Diego, CA: San Diego State University Center for Research in Mathematics and Science Education.

SOWDER, JUDITH T. 1992. "Estimation and Number Sense." In *Handbook of Research on Mathematics Teaching and Learning: A Project of the National Council of Teachers of Mathematics,* ed. Douglas A. Grouws. New York: Macmillan.

SOWDER, JUDITH T. 1992. "Making Sense of Numbers in School Mathematics." In *Analysis of Arithmetic for Mathematics Education,* ed. Gaea Leinhardt, Ralph Putnam, and Rosemary Hattrup. Hillsdale, NJ: Erlbaum.

CHRIS LOWBER
TERUNI LAMBERG

NUMERACY AND CULTURE

In simple terms, *numeracy* can be defined as the ability to understand basic mathematical concepts and operations. Numeracy thus encompasses a wide range of topics, including formal symbolic mathematics, cultural practices, children's intuitions about mathematics, and everyday behaviors mediated by mathematics. There are different forms of numeracy, and their realization in various cultural contexts has commonly been called *ethnomathematics*. Researchers have explored how pedagogy can be changed to incorporate cultural practices related to numeracy.

Numeracy in Cultural Context

All cultures have developed various representational systems that provide ways of thinking about quantitative information. Different systems highlight different aspects of knowing. For example, the Oksapmin of Papua New Guinea have a counting system that uses body parts to express numbers from one to twenty-seven. Though no base is used in this system, it is adequate when trading goods using a one-to-one correspondence. It is inadequate, however, for computing or counting objects beyond twenty-seven. A contrasting example is the enumeration system of many Asian languages that is congruent to the structure of base ten. Asian children using this system tend to recite more number names in correct sequence and show earlier mastery of place-value concepts (i.e., relations among number words, multi-digit numerals, and quantities) than children using less regular base-ten systems.

In addition to enumeration systems, cultures have developed representational systems for locating (geometry, navigation), measuring, designing (form, shape, pattern), playing (rules, strategies), and explaining (abstraction). These representational systems entail beliefs and values associated with numeracy, and they support numeracy activities using tools such as abaci, clocks, and digital computers. A broad array of human activities to which mathematical thinking is applied is thus interwoven with cultural artifacts, social conventions, and social interactions.

Cultural variations in mathematical behavior are also seen in the ways people use mathematical representations in their everyday activities. For example, children working as street vendors in Brazil were found to use different computational strategies when selling than when doing school-like problems. While selling they used such strategies as oral computation, decomposition, and repeated groupings, whereas when given school-like problems they used standard algorithms. These children were found to be much more accurate in the context of selling than in the school setting. Research in other domains, such as measurement and proportional reasoning, further confirms that informal mathematics can be effective and does not depend upon schooling for its development.

Mathematics is used in everyday life in pursuit of goals that differ from the goals of academic mathematics found in schools and universities. This type of mathematics is often referred to as *informal,* or *naive,* mathematics. Representational systems and practices deriving from everyday activities are modified as new goals emerge. Thus, everyday mathematics is an adaptive system that can be used to creatively meet new challenges. For example, as the Oksapmin became more involved with the currency system, their body counting system described earlier began to change toward a base system. Although knowledge acquired through informal experiences are often distinguished from school mathematics, skills developed in the informal domain can be used to address goals and practices in the school setting. For example, the most successful elementary students in Liberian schools combine the strategies from their indigenous mathematics with school algorithms. Use of informal mathematics in school settings, therefore, may be an effective way to help children learn school mathematics. Several authors have argued for building bridges between informal and formal mathematics.

Although most research on numeracy and culture has been done outside of the United States, understanding informal and everyday mathematics is important for educators in the United States for a number of reasons. According to the census conducted in October 1999, about 2.5 million foreign-born children came to U.S. schools, bringing with them different mathematics representational systems and associated computational skills. In addition, everyday mathematical activities and language repertoires for American children of different ethnic groups have been shown to differ both across groups and when compared to the school curriculum. In the case of some groups, such as Native Americans, mathematical reasoning derived from cultural traditions is distinct from that of the schools, posing major conceptual problems for these children in the regular school curriculum.

Research on Curricular Change

A number of projects have attempted to make mathematics instruction more culturally relevant for groups of children who have traditionally underachieved in the U.S. school system. Mary Brenner has worked with teachers to improve mathematics

teaching for Native Hawaiian children. She interviewed parents and children and observed children in everyday settings to determine what kinds of numerical skills children brought with them to school. At the kindergarten level, adapting the existing curriculum consisted of reordering topics to begin with counting and computation (areas of student strength), more use of the students' nonstandard dialect in mathematics lessons, and more emphasis upon hands-on and game-like activities. At the higher grade levels, adaptations focused more on including activities, such as a school store, that enabled students to move from informal mathematical activities to more standard mathematical practices.

Ethnographic research has revealed many mathematically rich activities in everyday adult life. Luis Moll and James Greenberg have developed a culturally relevant pedagogy for Latino students by building classroom activities from the "funds of knowledge" that are present in their family networks. Teachers and researchers worked together to plan lessons based upon ethnographic data, and they also invited parents to teach. New mathematics units, such as one involving candy making, were developed as the contexts for teaching specific mathematical ideas.

In a different approach, Jerry Lipka and Ester Ilutsik, who work with the Yup'ik people in Alaska, advocate giving the community control over the process of curriculum development. The goal is to make the schools a local institution, rather than having schools act as representatives of the dominant society. Researchers, Yup'ik teachers, and tribal elders have worked together to translate Yup'ik mathematical knowledge into a form that can be utilized in classrooms. Like the Funds of Knowledge project, this group has analyzed everyday adult activities, such as fish camps, to understand the culturally relevant mathematics. In addition, they have worked to better understand the Yup'ik number system and how it can be used in the classroom. The goal is to create an entire mathematics curriculum based upon Yup'ik culture, rather than adapting existing curricula.

Gloria Ladson-Billings has conducted research on culturally relevant mathematics instruction for African-American children. This research has highlighted a variety of attitudinal changes that teachers must make in their teaching, including expecting higher academic standards for students, emphasizing cultural competence, and instilling critical consciousness in students.

Teaching and Cultural Context

Teaching is an inherently cultural activity; it is situated in a bed of routines, traditions, beliefs, expectations, and values of students, teachers, administrators, parents, and the public. Thus, the inclusion of cultural and everyday mathematical knowledge in school mathematics must take into account the school-based assumptions about the appropriate way to teach mathematics.

For example, cultural assumptions about effective ways to improve teaching in Japan include lifelong professional development activities carried out by ordinary teachers. Typically, a few teachers with similar goals and interests form a study group. They select a few lessons that need improvement and analyze what is and is not working in the current practice in terms of learning goals for students, students' misunderstandings, and use of activity. They gather information on the topics by reading about other teachers' ideas, as well as other sources of recommended practices. A revised lesson is then planned, and one of the teachers from the group implements it while the others observe and evaluate what is and is not working. This process of evaluation, planning, and implementation is repeated until a satisfactory lesson is crafted, and may consume an entire school year. This is in sharp contrast to the type of model lesson developed by expert teachers and handed down to ordinary teachers in the United States. This is also different from the "one-day, make-it-and-take-it" type professional development workshops often implemented in the United States—a practice whose long-term effectiveness is questionable.

Ideas for Teachers

The importance of raising awareness of cultural diversity among teachers has been extended to the teaching of mathematics in the United States. For example, in the mid-1990s a task force for the National Council of Teachers of Mathematics recommended the publication of a series, *Changing the Faces of Mathematics,* in order to help make the slogans of *Mathematics for All* and *Everybody Counts* real. Particular efforts were made to focus on education of ethnic and cultural minority students. Included in this series are volumes on African-American perspectives, Latino perspectives, and Asian-American and Pacific Islander perspectives.

Each of these volumes includes articles that discuss successful pedagogical strategies for culturally diverse groups of students. The volumes also feature articles that may help educators develop a deeper understanding of the cultural differences that influence classroom dynamics, behavior, and environment.

See also: MATHEMATICS EDUCATION, TEACHER PREPARATION; MATHEMATICS LEARNING, *subentries on* LEARNING TOOLS, MYTHS, MYSTERIES, AND REALITIES, NUMBER SENSE.

BIBLIOGRAPHY

BISHOP, ALAN. 1991. *Mathematical Enculturation: A Cultural Perspective on Mathematics Education.* Dordrecht, Netherlands: Kluwer.

BRENNER, MARY E. 1998. "Adding Cognition to the Formula for Culturally Relevant Instruction in Mathematics." *Anthropology and Education Quarterly* 29:214–244.

BRENNER, MARY E. 1998. "Meaning and Money." *Educational Studies in Mathematics* 36:123–155.

EDWARDS, CAROL A., ed. 1999. "Perspectives on Asian Americans and Pacific Islanders." In *Changing the Faces of Mathematics,* ed. Walter G. Secada. Reston, VA: National Council of Teachers of Mathematics.

GALLIMORE, RONALD. 1996. "Classrooms Are Just Another Cultural Activity." In *Research on Classroom Ecologies: Implications for Inclusion of Children with Learning Disabilities,* ed. Deborah L. Speece and Barbara K. Keogh. Mahwah, NJ: Lawrence Erlbaum.

GAY, JOHN, and COLE, MICHAEL. 1967. *The New Mathematics and an Old Culture.* New York: Holt, Rinehart and Winston.

HIEBERT, JAMES, and STIGLER, JAMES W. 2000. "A Proposal for Improving Classroom Teaching: Lessons from the TIMSS Video Study." *Elementary School Journal* 101:3–20.

LADSON-BILLINGS, GLORIA. 1995. "Making Mathematics Meaningful in Multicultural Contexts." In *New Directions for Equity in Mathematics Education,* ed. Walter G. Secada, Elizabeth Fennema, and Lisa Byrd Adajian. Cambridge, Eng.: Cambridge University Press.

LIPKA, JERRY, and ILUTSIK, ESTHER. 1995. "Negotiated Change: Yup'ik Perspectives on Indigenous

Schooling." *Bilingual Research Journal* 19:195–207.

MILLER, KEVIN F.; SMITH, CATHERINE M.; ZHU, JIANJUN; and ZHANG, HOUCAN. 1995. "Preschool Origins of Cross-National Differences in Mathematical Competence." *Psychological Science* 6:56–60.

MIURA, IRENE T.; OKAMOTO, YUKARI; KIM, CHUNG-SOON C.; STEERE, MARCIA; and FAYOL, MICHEL. 1993. "First Graders' Cognitive Representation of Number and Understanding of Place Value: Cross-National Comparisons: France, Japan, Korea, Sweden, and the United States." *Journal of Educational Psychology* 85:24–30.

MOLL, LUIS C., and GREENBERG, JAMES B. 1990. "Creating Zones of Possibilities: Combining Social Contexts." In *Vygotsky and Education: Instructional Implications and Applications of Sociohistorical Psychology,* ed. Luis C. Moll. Cambridge, Eng.: Cambridge University Press.

NUNES, TEREZINHA; SCHLIEMANN, ANALUCIA D.; and CARRAHER, DAVID. W. 1993. *Street Mathematics and School Mathematics.* Cambridge, Eng.: Cambridge University Press.

ORTIZ-FRANCO, LUIS; HERNANDEZ, NORMA G.; and DE LA CRUZ, YOLANDA, eds. 1999. "Perspectives on Latinos." In *Changing the Faces of Mathematics,* ed. Walter G. Secada. Reston, VA: National Council of Teachers of Mathematics.

PINXTEN, RIK. 1997. "Applications in the Teaching of Mathematics and the Sciences." In *Ethnomathematics,* ed. Arthur B. Powell and Marilyn Frankenstein. Albany, NY: State University of New York.

SAXE, GEOFFREY B. 1982. "Developing Forms of Arithmetic Operations among the Oksapmin of Papua New Guinea." *Developmental Psychology* 18:583–594.

SECADA, WALTER G. 1992. "Race, Ethnicity, Social Class, Language, and Achievement in Mathematics." In *Handbook of Research on Mathematics Teaching and Learning,* ed. Douglas A. Grouws. New York: Macmillan.

STRUTCHENS, MARILYN E.; JOHNSON, MARTIN L.; and TATE, WILLIAM F., eds. 2000. "Perspectives on African Americans." In *Changing the Faces of Mathematics,* ed. Walter G. Secada. Reston, VA: National Council of Teachers of Mathematics.

INTERNET RESOURCE

U.S. CENSUS BUREAU. 2001. "School Enrollment in the United States—Social and Economic Characteristics of Students." <www.census.gov/prod/2001pubs/p20-533.pdf>

YUKARI OKAMOTO
MARY E. BRENNER
REAGAN CURTIS

WORD-PROBLEM SOLVING

A *word problem* is a verbal description of a problem situation wherein one or more questions are posed, the answers to which can be obtained by the application of mathematical operations to information (usually numerical data) available in the text. In its most typical form, a word problem describes the essentials of some situation assumed to be familiar to the solver. Within the text, certain quantities are explicitly given, while others are not. The student is required to give a numerical answer to a stated question by making exclusive use of the quantities given—and of the mathematical relationships between these quantities. Simple examples include: "Pete wins 3 marbles in a game and now has 8 marbles. How many marbles did he have before the game?" and "One kilogram of coffee costs 12 euros. Susan buys 0.75 kilogram of coffee. How much does she have to pay?"

Despite its label, a word problem need not constitute a *problem* in the cognitive-psychological sense of the word—higher-order thinking going beyond the application of a familiar routine procedure is not necessarily required. Indeed, in typical elementary mathematics instruction, many word problems provide thinly disguised practice in adding, subtracting, multiplying, or dividing.

Structural Dimensions of Word Problems

Several structural dimensions can be distinguished in word problems that affect their difficulty and how they are solved:

- *Mathematical structure,* which includes the nature of the given and unknown quantities of the problem, and the mathematical operations by which the unknowns can be derived from the givens.

- *Semantic structure,* which includes the ways in which an interpretation of the text points to particular mathematical relationships. For example, addition or subtraction is indicated when the text implies a combination of disjoint subsets into a superset, a change from an initial quantity to a subsequent quantity by addition or subtraction, or the additive comparison between two collections.

- *Context*, meaning the nature of the situation described. For example, an additive problem involving combination of disjoint sets might deal with physically combining collections of objects or with conceptually combining collections of people in two locations.

- *The format*, meaning how the problem is formulated and presented. Format involves such factors as the placement of the question, the complexity of the lexical and grammatical structures, the presence of superfluous information, and so on.

Over several decades, numerous studies have analyzed the role of these task variables on the difficulty of problems, on the kind of strategies students use to solve these problems, and on the nature of their errors, particularly for simple word problems involving addition and subtraction or multiplication and division.

Roles of Word Problems

Why does school mathematics include word problems? Perhaps simply because they are there, and have been for many centuries. Indeed, their role in mathematics education dates back to antiquity; the oldest known being in Egyptian papyri dating from 2000 B.C.E., with strikingly similar examples in ancient Chinese and Indian manuscripts. The following example is from the first printed mathematical textbook, a Treviso arithmetic of 1478: "If 17 men build 2 houses in 9 days, how many days will it take 20 men to build 5 houses?"

Despite this striking continuity across time and cultures, until recently there was little explicit discussion of why word problems should be such a prominent part of the curriculum, or of the variety of purposes behind their inclusion. Some have a puzzle-like nature and act as "mental manipulatives" (Toom, p. 36) to guide thinking within mathematical structures. Such problems are intended to train students to think creatively and develop problem-solving abilities. By contrast, the type mainly used educationally consists of a text representing (at least putatively) a real-world situation in which the derived answer would "work." Ostensible goals for the use of this type include offering practice for the situations of everyday life in which the mathematics learned will be needed, thereby showing students that the mathematics they are learning will be useful.

Apparent Suspension of Sense-Making

In recent years, the characteristics, use, and rationale of word problems have been critically analyzed from multiple perspectives, including linguistic, cultural, and sociological perspectives. In particular, it has been argued by many mathematics educators that the stereotyped and artificial nature of word problems typically represented in mathematics textbooks, and the discourse and activity around these problems in traditional mathematics lessons, have detrimental effects. Many observations have led to the conclusion that children answer word problems without taking into account realistic considerations about the situations described in the text, or even whether the question and the answer make sense. The most dramatic example comes from French researchers who posed children nonsensical questions such as: "There are 26 sheep and 10 goats on a ship. How old is the captain?" It was found that the majority of students were prepared to offer an answer to such questions. In another study, thirteen-year-old students in the United States were asked the following question: "An army bus holds 36 soldiers. If 1,128 soldiers are being bussed to their training site, how many buses are needed?" The division was correctly computed by 70 percent of the students to get a quotient of 31 and remainder 12—but only 23 percent gave the appropriate answer, "32 buses." Nineteen percent gave the answer as "31 buses" and 29 percent gave the answer as "31, remainder 12."

To explain the abundant observations of this "suspension of sense-making" when doing word problems, it has been suggested by Erik De Corte and Lieven Verschaffel that the practice surrounding word problems is controlled by a set of (largely implicit) rules that constitute the "word-problem game." These rules including the following assumptions: (1) every problem presented by the teacher or in a textbook is solvable and makes sense; (2) there is only one exact numerical correct answer to every word problem; and (3) the answer must be obtained by performing basic arithmetical operations on all numbers stated in the problem.

Reconceptualizing Word Problems as Modeling Exercises

One reaction to criticisms of traditional practice surrounding word problems in schools is to undermine the approach that allows students to succeed using superficial strategies based on the "rules." This is done by breaking up the stereotypical nature of the problems posed. For example, by including problems that do not make sense or contain superfluous or insufficient data, students can be guided to interpret word problems critically.

A more radical suggestion is to treat word problems as exercises in mathematical modeling. The application of mathematics to solve problem situations in the real world, termed *mathematical modeling,* is a complex process involving several phases, including understanding the situation described; constructing a mathematical model that describes the essence of the relevant elements embedded in the situation; working through the mathematical model to identify what follows from it; interpreting the computational work to arrive at a solution to the problem; evaluating that interpreted outcome in relation to the original situation; and communicating the interpreted results.

This schema can be used to describe the process of solving mathematical word problems as application problems. In the simplest cases, situations may be directly modeled by addition, subtraction, multiplication, or division, and children need to learn the variety of prototypical situations that fit unproblematically onto these operations. In other cases, the modeling is not so straightforward if serious attention is given to the reality of the situation described. In the example from the Treviso arithmetic, attention would be drawn to the assumptions that underpin an answer based on direct proportionality—and to the fact that the answer thus derived would at best provide a rough approximation in the real situation. In the bus problem, the "raw" result of the computation has to be appropriately refined in the context of the situation described.

Reforming the Teaching of Word Problems

In line with the above criticisms and recommendations with respect to the traditional practice surrounding word problems in schools, researchers have set up design studies to develop, implement, and evaluate experimental programs aimed at the enhancement of strategies and attitudes about solving mathematical word problems. In these studies, positive outcomes have been obtained in terms of both outcomes (test scores) and underlying processes (beliefs, strategies, attitudes). Characteristics common to such experimental programs include:

- The use of more realistic and challenging tasks than traditional textbook problems.
- A variety of teaching methods and learner activities, including expert modeling of the strategic aspects of the competent solution process, small-group work, and whole-class discussions.
- The creation of a classroom climate that is conducive to the development in pupils of an elaborated view of mathematical modeling, and of the accompanying beliefs and attitudes.

To some extent, these characteristics of a new approach to word-problem solving are beginning to be implemented in mathematical frameworks, curricula, textbooks, and tests in many countries. Much remains to be done, however, to align the teaching of word problems with widely accepted principles that children should make connections between mathematics and their lived experience—and that mathematics should make sense to them.

See also: MATHEMATICS EDUCATION, TEACHER PREPARATION; MATHEMATICS LEARNING, *subentries on* COMPLEX PROBLEM SOLVING, LEARNING TOOLS, MYTHS, MYSTERIES, AND REALITIES, NUMBER SENSE.

BIBLIOGRAPHY

CARPENTER, THOMAS P.; LINDQUIST, MARY M.; MATTHEWS, WALTER; and SILVER, EDWARD A. 1983. "Results of the Third NAEP Mathematics Assessment: Secondary School." *Mathematics Teacher* 76:652–659.

COGNITION AND TECHNOLOGY GROUP AT VANDERBILT. 1997. *The Jasper Project: Lessons in Curriculum, Instruction, Assessment, and Professional Development.* Mahwah, NJ: Erlbaum.

DE CORTE, ERIK, and VERSCHAFFEL, LIEVEN. 1985. "Beginning First Graders' Initial Representation of Arithmetic Word Problems." *Journal of Mathematical Behavior* 4:3–21.

FUSON, KAREN. 1992. "Research on Whole-Number Addition and Subtraction." In *Handbook of Research on Mathematics Teaching and Learning,* ed. Douglas A. Grouws. New York: Macmillan.

GREER, BRIAN. 1992. "Multiplication and Division as Models of Situations." In *Handbook of Research on Mathematics Teaching and Learning,* ed. Douglas A. Grouws. New York: Macmillan.

LAVE, JEAN. 1992. "Word Problems: A Microcosm of Theories of Learning." In *Context and Cognition: Ways of Learning and Knowing,* ed. Paul Light and George Butterworth. New York: Harvester Wheatsheaf.

NESHER, PEARLA. 1980. "The Stereotyped Nature of School Word Problems." *For the Learning of Mathematics* 1:41–48.

REUSSER, KURT. 1988. "Problem Solving Beyond the Logic of Things: Contextual Effects on Understanding and Solving Word Problems." *Instructional Science* 17:309–338.

SCHOENFELD, ALLEN H. 1991. "On Mathematics as Sense-Making: An Informal Attack on the Unfortunate Divorce of Formal and Informal Mathematics." In *Informal Reasoning and Education,* ed. James F. Voss, David N. Perkins, and Judith W. Segal. Hillsdale, NJ: Lawrence Erlbaum.

TOOM, ANDRÉ. 1999. "Word Problems: Applications or Mental Manipulatives." *For the Learning of Mathematics* 19(1):36–38.

VERSCHAFFEL, LIEVEN; DE CORTE, ERIK; LASURE, SABINE; VAN VAERENBERGH, GRIET; BOGAERTS, HEDWIG; and RATINCKX, ELIE. 1999. "Design and Evaluation of a Learning Environment for Mathematical Modeling and Problem Solving in Upper Elementary School Children." *Mathematical Thinking and Learning* 1:195–229.

VERSCHAFFEL, LIEVEN; GREER, BRIAN; and DE CORTE, ERIK. 2000. *Making Sense of Word Problems.* Lisse, Netherlands: Swets and Zeitlinger.

LIEVEN VERSCHAFFEL
BRIAN GREER
ERIK DE CORTE

MATHEMATICS, TEACHING OF

See: MATHEMATICS EDUCATION, *subentry on* TEACHER PREPARATION; MATHEMATICS LEARNING.

MAYS, BENJAMIN (1895–1984)

Benjamin Elijah Mays was born to former slaves Hezekiah and Louvenia (Carter) Mays in Epworth, Greenwood County, South Carolina. The youngest of eight children, he became a theologian, theoretician, orator, author, college president, civil rights activist, and school board president. Casting himself as a "rebel," he greatly influenced the country and the world with his ideals and activities.

The Formative Years

The 1890s was an especially difficult period for blacks as whites in the South were angry in the aftermath of Reconstruction: lynchings and violence were common. Born on an isolated cotton farm, Mays's earliest recollections were of the Phoenix Riots in Greenwood County during November 1898 in which several black people were lynched. He wrote in his autobiography, "That mob is my earliest memory" (p. 1). Mays's intellectual prowess became known in church and school. He, however, attended the Brickhouse School only from November to February as he was needed to help his sharecropping family bring in the harvest. In 1911 he abandoned the farm to enroll in the High School Department of South Carolina State College, graduating as valedictorian at age twenty-one in 1916.

Following one year of study at Virginia Union University, Mays tired of the bitter racial climate in the South, and gained admission to Bates College in Lewiston, Maine. He worked as a Pullman porter before winning scholarships. Encouraged by the relatively liberal racial climate of New England, Mays flourished. He graduated from Bates with honors in 1920 and became committed to a life of teaching and learning. After one year of sampling assorted graduate courses at the University of Chicago, Mays taught psychology, math, and religion at Morehouse College in Atlanta from 1921 to 1923. While in Atlanta, he was ordained a Baptist minister in 1922. He returned to the University of Chicago's School of Religion and completed a master's degree in New Testament Studies in 1925.

Mays returned to teach English at South Carolina State College for a year. Hoping to make a difference in the lives of deprived black people, he then moved, with his new wife Sadie Gray, to the Urban League in Tampa, Florida for two years. Working with his wife, a case worker, his title at the Urban League was executive secretary of the Family Service

Association. After two years, he accepted a position as student secretary of the YMCA in Atlanta, where he hoped to once again influence the larger community.

In 1930, the Institute of Social and Religious Research, funded by the Rockefeller family, embarked on the most ambitious study to date on the black church and its influence on the African-American population. Mays and Joseph W. Nicholson, a minister in the Colored Methodist Episcopal (CME) Church, conducted a fourteen-month study of 691 churches in 12 large cities. That study would establish Mays as an important scholar and "rebel" theoretician.

Early Religious Scholarship

The result of the Mays/Nicholson collaboration was published in 1933 as the iconoclastic work *The Negro's Church*, which was premised upon the church's importance at the center of black culture and social life. The authors argued that the church belonged to the Negro and provided a place of refuge, expression, democracy, fellowship, and freedom surrounded by the lack of all those things elsewhere. They spoke of the "genius" of the black church. Mays (and Nicholson), however, also found that it possessed significant constraints.

Throughout the work, the authors explored sensitive and rarely addressed issues such as denominational rivalry, misplaced ministerial ambition, poor theological training, irrelevant sermon content, unnecessary emotionalism, appeals to fear, and finally the "overchurching" of the Negro. The provocative work concluded that "analysis reveals that the status of the Negro church is in part the result of the failure of American Christianity in the realm of race-relation" (p. 278).

This critique, followed by a companion book, *The Negro's God: As Reflected in His Literature* (1938), catapulted Mays to a new level of scholarship.

The Howard Years

In 1932 Mays had returned to the University of Chicago to complete his doctorate in three years. One year before completing the doctorate, Mordecai Johnson, the respected president of Howard University in Washington, D.C., persuaded Mays to assume the deanship at Howard's School of Religion. From 1934 to 1940 Mays worked to elevate that department to one of national prominence. Increased enrollment, enriched curriculum, a better-credentialed faculty, higher revenues, and improvements to the physical plant and library gained the department a Class "A" rating from the American Association of Theological Schools and national attention for Mays.

During the Howard years, Mays traveled widely, expanding his network of colleagues and friends, working to strengthen other black colleges, and most importantly developing his version of a liberation theology. Mid-1930s visits to Europe, China, North Africa, the Middle East, Asia, and the Indian subcontinent provided Mays with a startling look at poverty, hatred, oppression, racism, and caste. His personal audience with Mahatma Gandhi, whom he already admired, reinforced his belief in nonviolence as an "active force" for social change. Mays emerged from these experiences as one of the most influential black men in the South. In early 1940, banker and Morehouse trustee John Wheeler was dispatched by the Board of Trustees to recruit Mays for the presidency of the school. Reluctant to leave Howard, Mays spent months seeking the advice of leading educators. With the blessing of Mordecai Johnson he became president of Morehouse on August 1, 1940.

Morehouse College

Benjamin Mays became the sixth president of Morehouse College, which would be his home base for the next twenty-seven years. A man of great faith and vision, Mays was also politically astute. He understood that the plight of black people had always been at the center of the social, political, economic, and cultural life of the South and the nation. He sensed that Morehouse College could and would play an important role in the lives of black America, and ultimately the country. Although its student body was relatively small and resources meager, the school was situated in an important place at an important time.

By 1940 Morehouse College was well established among the nation's historically black colleges. The notion of an intellectually capable "Morehouse Man" was emergent. Morale problems had, however, surfaced as the school was seen by students and alumni as falling behind the other black colleges of Atlanta. Between 1930 and 1940 the faculty at Atlanta University increased by 220 percent and the faculty at Spelman increased by 78 percent, while Morehouse's faculty had decreased by 16 percent. Morehouse students were taught by Atlanta University and Spelman faculty. In addition, uncollected tuition and a feeble endowment inhibited expansion.

As president, Mays immediately began exhorting alumni to increase contributions. Secondly, he appealed for contributions from philanthropic foundations and friends of the college. Most importantly, he began aggressively collecting the considerable tuition arrears from students. Students were not allowed to register for classes, obtain transcripts, or graduate until debts were cleared. Those efforts earned Mays the nickname "Buck Benny" around the campus. His obsession with quality faculty, previously noted during his years at Howard, quickly became evident at Morehouse.

He searched widely for faculty with doctorates. Despite social and residential problems in rigidly segregated Atlanta, white professors were welcomed by Mays. Where high-quality professors could not be hired, Mays offered existing faculty financial support to seek higher degrees.

During Mays's presidency, the campus land area increased from 10.7 to 20.2 acres. New buildings included five small dormitories housing 115 men, a large dormitory housing 120 men, a physical educational and health building, an infirmary, a dining hall, a small academic building, a meditation chapel, a dormitory for students enrolled in the Morehouse School of Religion, a music studio, and three faculty apartments.

The Morehouse Mentor

Beyond those accomplishments, Benjamin Mays is far better known for his spiritual guidance and intellectual leadership. Reared in an environment of hatred, Mays could talk of uplift because he lived it. The testimony of former students and public figures such as Martin Luther King Jr., Julian Bond, Lerone Bennett and many others suggests that his students listened to his exhortations.

Leadership and the pursuit of further education became watchwords at Morehouse. Its students became distinguished by their accomplishments after graduation. By the mid-1960s more that half the school's graduates had entered graduate or professional schools; of its graduates, 118 had earned Ph.D.s, and by 1967, more than 300 Morehouse graduates earned M.D. and D.D.S. degrees. By that time Morehouse graduates held teaching or administrative positions at 58 black and 22 white institutions of higher learning. Twenty-one institutions of higher learning had Morehouse graduates as president. Between 1945 and 1967 Morehouse ranked second among Georgia institutions in the production of Woodrow Wilson Fellows. Mays's figures also reveal a large number of Morehouse graduates occupying high administrative positions in school districts scattered around the country.

Mays was particularly proud of the School of Religion, where he invested significant personal attention. Several of its graduates, including Martin Luther King Jr., Howard Thurman, Dillard H. Brown, Thomas Kilgore, and George Kelsey, have been singled out for high honors and distinction.

With great pride, Mays identified the group of Morehouse graduates who occupied high profile positions in the world of politics, law, and business. Widely known scholars and writers such as Lerone Bennett Jr., James Birnie, Benjamin Brawley, Michael Lomax, and Ira Reid inspired Mays to petition for the establishment a Phi Beta Kappa chapter at the college which was granted in 1967.

No discussion of Mays at Morehouse would be complete without mention of chapel. Chapel was a longstanding tradition at Morehouse, where students were required to attend every day except Saturday. Mays used chapel to build community and expand learning outside the classroom. Martin Luther King Jr. recalled chapel and Mays' motivational talks as among his most inspirational college experiences.

Philosopher and Liberation Theologian

Mays developed a religious philosophy of morality, justice, and humanity rooted in the quest for freedom. While the term *liberation theology* perhaps belongs to a later time period, it is nevertheless applicable to Mays's views.

Beyond an individual morality, Mays reflected on the wider role of the black church in the lives of its people, concluding that the church must go beyond providing comfort, freedom of expression, and socializing. It must engage a social consciousness offering visions of freedom, empowerment, and equality. It must go beyond the personal and into the political.

Stephen Preskill (1996) sees Mays' views as the ideological antecedent of the liberatory views of Cornel West, a contemporary African-American scholar-activist and social critic. He examines three propositions advanced by West: (1) human discernment, or understanding the present from a social analysis of the past, more specifically understanding how to practice democracy in a racist society; (2) human connection, embracing the lived concrete realities of oppressed people; and (3) human hypocrisy, exposing the contradictions between deeds and words. In all cases Preskill traces West's three propositions to Mays' affirmation of the common people's right to make change.

Mays's nascent liberation theology is outlined in his little-known work *The Negro's God: As Reflected in His Literature* (1938). In this study Mays explores portrayals of God in a wide variety of biblical, classical, political, and sociological literature. He identifies salient themes recurring in the literature, arguing that these themes resonate with and contribute to the prevailing culture of African Americans. Mays clusters and describes Negro views about God into three categories: traditional biblical themes; justice and equality; and social change.

Mays retired from Morehouse in 1967. By then the modern civil rights movement was well under way. Mays remained a quiet mentor, staying in touch and offering advice to his former students who were leading the movement. Additionally, he sat on many committees and commissions, including the Ford Foundation and the Department of Health, Education, and Welfare, advising presidents, governors, and policymakers on civil rights matters.

Upon the assassination of Dr. Martin Luther King, Mays concluded his eulogy for his former student and long-standing friend by saying, "If physical death was the price he had to pay to rid America of prejudice and injustice, nothing could be more redemptive."

His last great task was to serve the city he always saw as crucial in American race relations. He joined the Atlanta School Board of Education, becoming its first black president, from 1969 through 1981. In his last years, Mays continued to advise leaders from politics and business on matters of race. He served as an adviser to President Jimmy Carter, and received forty-three honorary degrees (including honorary doctorates from Harvard and Brandeis), the Dorie Miller Medal of Honor, and the Older Citizen Award.

See also: HISTORICALLY BLACK COLLEGES AND UNIVERSITIES; MULTICULTURAL EDUCATION.

BIBLIOGRAPHY

COLSTON, FREDDIE C. 1993. "Dr. Benjamin E. Mays: His Impact as Spiritual and Intellectual Mentor of Martin Luther King Jr." *The Black Scholar* 23(2):6–15.

LOGAN, RAYFORD W. 1965. *The Betrayal of the Negro: From Rutherford B. Hayes to Woodrow Wilson.* New York: Macmillan.

MAYS, BENJAMIN E. 1971. *Born to Rebel: An Autobiography.* Athens: University of Georgia Press.

MAYS, BENJAMIN E. 1968. *The Negro's God: As Reflected in His Literature* (1938). New York: Atheneum.

MAYS, BENJAMIN E., and NICHOLSON, JOSEPH WILLIAM. 1969. *The Negro's Church* (1933). New York: Negro Universities Press.

PRESKILL, STEPHEN. 1996. "Combative Sprirituality and the Life of Benjamin E. Mays." *Biography: An Interdisciplinary Quarterly* 19(4):404–416.

WILLIAM H. WATKINS

MCCALL, WILLIAM A. (1891–1982)

Professor of educational psychology, William Anderson McCall was an expert in the construction of tests and measurements to evaluate student learning and achievement. Born in Wellsville, Tennessee, McCall received his early education in a one-room schoolhouse, near Red Ash, Kentucky. Reared in a family of limited means, he spent up to half of each calendar year, from the time he was nine years old through his teenage years, working as a coal digger in the mines in Red Ash and neighboring Jellico, Tennessee. Encouraged by local educators who recognized his intellectual abilities, McCall continued his education at Cumberland College in Kentucky, where he received an A.B. degree in 1911, and at Lincoln Memorial University, in Tennessee, where he taught psychology and earned a second undergraduate degree in 1913. In the same year he enrolled at Teachers College, Columbia University, where he earned a Ph.D. in 1916, under the reputed behavioral psychologist, Edward L. Thorndike.

McCall began his graduate studies at Teachers College at the height of the Progressive educational reform movement, which began in the 1890s and stretched into the early decades of the twentieth century. No other university-affiliated school of education rivaled Teachers College in terms of its influence in shaping the Progressive educational agenda, which among other objectives aimed to establish a scientific basis for the study and practice of education and to ensure greater order, accountability, and economy in school management. Over the course of his forty-year professorship at Teachers College, Thorndike generated in collaboration with his students—McCall counting prominently among them—a body of quantitative knowledge in the field of mental measurements that was a central, supporting element of these overlapping goals.

Standard measures of educational objectives and statistical analyses of learning and achievement favored by Thorndike and his students formed the basis, among other new administrative practices, for the homogenous grouping of students by intellectual ability and became cornerstones of the efficiently managed schools that educational reformers envisioned.

As McCall remembered, he first attracted the attention and respect of Thorndike, who he grew to revere, based on the proficiency he demonstrated, in his first year at Teachers College, at navigating a series of mazes with which Thorndike challenged a class of students. By any measure, McCall's professional career advanced quickly at Teachers College. In the same year he completed his doctoral studies, he was appointed an instructor in elementary education and published the results of experimental work he conducted with Thorndike, measuring the relationship between different conditions of air ventilation and mental functioning. In 1919 he was appointed an assistant professor of elementary education, and in 1927 he became professor of measurement, research, and statistics.

In the intervening years, McCall published two of his most noteworthy books, *How to Measure in Education* and *How to Experiment in Education*. Both volumes, which are in effect practical guides for educators to the field of mental measurements, address the need for precise means of quantifying student intelligence and for experimental projects to test the validity of educational theory and the effectiveness of classroom practice. Building on Thorndike's well-known maxim that "whatever exists at all, exists in some amount" (p. 16), McCall reasons in *How to Measure* that "there is never a quantity that does not measure some existing quality, and never an existing

quality that is non-quantitative" (1923a, p. 4). In response to contemporary educational critics, who framed educational questions in philosophical and qualitative terms, or who otherwise questioned the true limits of quantification, McCall insists that "all the abilities and virtues for which education is consciously striving can be measured and be measured better than they ever have been. The measurement of initiative, judgment of relative values, leadership, appreciation of good literature and the like," he asserts, "is entirely possible"(1923b, p. 4).

In keeping with his view of educational reform, McCall wrote extensively over the course of his career about the technical aspects of constructing, implementing, scaling, and scoring tests to evaluate intellectual competency and achievement. In addition, he was the author or coauthor of numerous tests and courses of instruction in the fields of reading, arithmetic and spelling, including the *Thorndike-McCall Reading Scale,* the *Multi-Mental Scale,* the *McCall Speller, Woody-McCall Mixed Fundamentals in Arithmetic Language,* and *McCall-Crabbs Standard Test Lessons in Reading.*

McCall's expertise in mental measurements was not limited to the reform of American education. On leave from Teachers College, McCall spent the 1922–1923 academic year in China, where he served as director of psychological research for the Chinese National Association for the Advancement of Education. The enrollment of Chinese students at Teachers College, beginning in 1910, paved the way during a period of educational modernization in China for intellectual exchange between Teachers College faculty and leading Chinese educators. McCall traveled to China, following visits there by Paul Monroe, who was a professor of history and education, and the philosopher John Dewey, who taught courses in education at Teachers College. Eager to encourage the scientific study of education in China, McCall worked diligently, overseeing the construction of educational tests and measurements and their use in Chinese schools nationwide. He was firmly committed to realizing the same objectives in China that shaped his work to improve education in the United States. In a 1923 report, *Scientific Measurement and Related Studies in Chinese Education,* which outlines his work in China, McCall notes that "to test all things and hold fast that which is good is as prerequisite to progress in education as it has been to the correction of our practical philosophy, or the improvement of every form of life upon the earth" (1923b, p. 19).

Although McCall had hoped to spend an additional year in China to further the work he had begun, his request for another leave of absence was denied by Teachers College. He resumed his teaching duties there until 1927, when he contracted tuberculosis and was forced to abandon his professional responsibilities to convalesce. He returned to Teachers College sometime around 1930. He never fully recovered from his illness though and left active duty with the faculty in 1941. He moved with his wife, Gretchen Schweizer McCall, to the Smoky Mountains in North Carolina. McCall continued to be active professionally, revising and constructing new tests and courses of reading instruction, and consulting on various educational projects. In 1952 he published the results of a study, *Measurement of Teacher Merit,* that he conducted for the North Carolina State Education Commission, which measured the effectiveness of classroom teachers in relationship to pupil progress and growth. In 1975 he published *I Thunk Me a Thaut,* a compilation of the diary entries he wrote in Appalachian dialect, beginning when he was eight years old, about his boyhood. McCall eventually made his home in Coral Cables, Florida, where he died.

See also: EDUCATIONAL PSYCHOLOGY; THORNDIKE, EDWARD L.

BIBLIOGRAPHY

MCCALL, WILLIAM ANDERSON. 1922. *How to Measure in Education.* New York: Macmillan.

MCCALL, WILLIAM ANDERSON. 1923a. *How to Experiment in Education.* New York: Macmillan.

MCCALL, WILLIAM ANDERSON. 1923b. *Scientific Measurement and Related Studies in Chinese Education.* Peking: Chinese National Association for the Advancement of Education.

MCCALL, WILLIAM ANDERSON. 1934. "My Philosophy of Life and Education," parts 1–3. *Teachers College Record* 35:560–572; 36:303–316, 409–418; 37:50–59.

MCCALL, WILLIAM ANDERSON. 1952. *Measurement of Teacher Merit.* Raleigh, NC: State Superintendent of Public Instruction.

MCCALL, WILLIAM ANDERSON. 1975. *I Thunk Me a Thaut.* New York: Teachers College Press, Columbia University.

BETTE WENECK

MCMURRY, CHARLES (1857–1929)

The principal disseminator of Herbartian pedagogical ideas in the United States, Charles Alexander McMurry formulated the concept of interdisciplinary curriculum. He grew up in rural Illinois and took the classical high school course in the training school of the Illinois State Normal University (ISNU), followed by two years of classical study at the University of Michigan. He then taught in Illinois country schools for two years and in Colorado for two years. He returned to Illinois and in 1882 was persuaded by a colleague to go to Halle, Germany, to study Christian theology. Through conversations with Charles DeGarmo, he became interested in the pedagogical ideas being disseminated by the German Herbartians, who believed that the development of moral character in the elementary school was achieved by a structured academic curriculum. McMurry returned to Halle in 1886, accompanied by his younger brother Frank, who was also interested in finding a theoretical grounding for teaching. After completing his Ph.D. in 1887, Charles joined his brother in the newly established Herbartian pedagogical seminar of Professor Wilhelm Rein at the University of Jena. There, teacher preparation and practice teaching were carried out according to a full interpretation of Herbartian psychology and pedagogy. It was this experience with the integration of theory and practice that led the brothers to launch American Herbartianism in the 1890s.

Convinced of the potential value of the Herbartian approach for American teachers, by the time McMurry arrived home in 1888 he had a complete ten-year writing plan to bring those ideas to teachers, and he began testing them in practice as a principal in Evanston, Illinois, and then as head of the training school at the Winona State Normal School in Minnesota in 1889. He and Frank published a translation from Wilhelm Rein's work as *The Method of the Recitation* in 1890. In 1892 Charles published *The Elements of General Method Based on the Principles of Herbart,* the same year that he returned to Illinois to become assistant in the training school at ISNU. He soon became its director and over the next seven years produced the first volumes in his series of special methods books that carried Herbartian ideas into normal schools all over the country. In spring of 1892 the McMurry brothers and Charles DeGarmo spearheaded the formation of a National Herbart Club, modeled on the German *Verein der wissenschaftliche Pädagogik,* which disseminated Herbartian ideas through local discussion clubs.

Through the interest of such national figures as Francis W. Parker, the Herbartian notion of correlated curriculum gained sufficient attention to prompt calls in the National Education Association's Committee of Ten report for more correlation, and the establishment of a special subcommittee to report on the efficacy of correlation as a guiding principle for elementary school curriculum. That 1895 report, written by U.S. Commissioner of Education William Torrey Harris, in effect ignored the Herbartian notion, provoking vociferous objections and prompting the McMurrys, DeGarmo, and others to found and publicize the National Herbart Society for the Scientific Study of Education (NHS) in 1895 as a forum for open discussion of new educational ideas. McMurry served as its secretary and yearbook editor for eight years, carrying it through its transition to the National Society for the Study of Education (NSSE) in 1902 and actively recruiting members for local clubs. Harris's resistance to Herbartianism on philosophical grounds was overridden; most educators believed in the pedagogical utility of Herbartian ideas and in particular by the semiscientific nature of their expression. McMurry disseminated Herbartianism through book production and through summer school teaching at the universities of Minnesota, Chicago, Illinois, Columbia, and Cornell, and through his work as secretary of both the NHS and the Illinois Society for Child Study.

In 1899 McMurry established the teacher education program at the new Northern Illinois State Normal School at DeKalb along Herbartian lines. In 1906 to 1907 he served as acting president of the California State Normal School of Pennsylvania. He returned to DeKalb to begin a process of integrating the city schools into the teacher education program, becoming superintendent in 1911. During this period he wrote extensively, revising his special methods books in history, geography, literature, arithmetic, natural science, and language, and reworked his translation and adaptation of the Herbartian eight-year course of study. He gave particular emphasis to the development of "type studies," units that examined a "typical" phenomenon (such as a forest community) in depth in order to develop a thorough understanding of principles that could then be applied to the study of other phenomena. In 1915 he became professor of elementary education at the newly reorganized Peabody College of Education at Vanderbilt University. He died in 1929, remembered by his colleagues and students as a master teacher at all levels.

See also: EDUCATIONAL PSYCHOLOGY; EIGHT-YEAR STUDY; HERBART, JOHANN.

BIBLIOGRAPHY

McMurry, Charles A. 1903. *Special Method in History; A Complete Outline of a Course of Study in History for the Grades below the High School.* New York: Macmillan.

McMurry, Charles A. 1904a. *The Elements of General Method Based on the Principles of Herbart.* New York: Macmillan.

McMurry, Charles A. 1904b. *Type Studies from the Geography of the United States.* New York: Macmillan.

McMurry, Charles A. 1906. *Course of Study in the Eight Grades.* New York: Macmillan.

McMurry, Frank, and McMurry, Charles A. 1890. *How to Conduct the Recitation, and the Principles Underlying Methods of Teaching in Classes.* New York: Kellogg.

Tyler, Kenneth. 1982. "The Educational Life and Work of Charles A. McMurry: 1872–1929." Ph.D. diss., Northern Illinois University.

KATHLEEN CRUIKSHANK

MEDIA AND LEARNING

Educators have examined the impact of media on learning since at least 1912, when the American psychologist Edward L. Thorndike recommended pictures as a labor saving device for instruction. Five questions about media and learning will be briefly examined. The first section will define media and summarize the results of research on learning from media, the relative cost of media use, and the impact of media on access to education. The second section describes new research on the economic benefits of instructional media, including suggestions for "cognitive efficiency" studies. The third section presents new information about learning problems caused by poor design of instructional media "displays." The fourth part will examine claims that new media enhance student's motivation to learn. The final section will describe work on technology integration that focuses on learning how to solve problems.

Definitions and Summary of Research

Media are generally defined as the means by which information is conveyed from one place to another. In the past century, various forms of media have been used to convey instruction and to support learning. Examples of instructional media include traditional means of delivering instruction (chalkboards, textbooks, overhead projectors, and teachers), mass media used for education (newspapers, movies, radio, and television), and the newer "electronic" instructional media (computers, interactive video, and multimedia systems). All instruction requires the selection and use of at least one medium to deliver instruction. Many alternative media and mixtures of media may be chosen for any given learning goal and group of students. Thus, research questions have compared the learning benefits of various media and mixes of media for different types of learning goals and students at different ages and aptitude levels. Thousands of studies have been and continue to be conducted.

Do some media produce more learning than others? In his 2001 book *Learning from Media,* Richard E. Clark concluded that there are no learning benefits from any specific medium or mix of media. He summarized the research on this issue in an analogy that is often repeated: "The best . . . evidence is that media are mere vehicles that deliver instruction but do not influence student achievement any more than the truck that delivers our groceries causes changes in our nutrition. Basically, the choice of vehicle might influence the cost or extent of distributing instruction, but only the content of the vehicle can influence achievement" (p. 13). While some media will not convey certain types of information necessary for learning (for example, newspapers cannot transmit sound or "real-time" visual events), any necessary information can be conveyed by a number of media (sound and visual events can be conveyed by many media other than newspapers). A more positive way to state this conclusion is that educators

can expect similar levels of learning from a great variety of media provided that essential instructional methods are used. When more than one medium can provide the instructional method needed for learning, the choice of medium is based on expected economic benefits such as the per-student cost of instruction, not learning benefits. An alternative view was expressed in 1994 by Robert B. Kozma, who contended that media and method should not be separated.

Media and method. The key issue here is that when media are used for instruction, they may often be confused with the instructional methods and information they convey. For example, computer-based instruction is often thought to be highly "interactive" because computers permit high levels of exchange between student and computer-delivered instructional programs. Yet most media permit interaction, although some media do so more quickly and economically.

Any medium seems to be able to increase learning provided that the information content and instructional methods they convey are adequate to support student learning. The existing research suggests that when learning is influenced by external events, those events must support the use of mental processes that are required for learning goals by students who are unable or unwilling to provide them for themselves. The specification for these external events is what Clark called an "instructional method." Instances of common instructional methods are learning plans, examples, and practice exercises with interactive, corrective feedback. Since a variety of media will present any of the common instructional methods required to learn, the benefits of media are not in their impact on learning but instead in their economic impact and their capacity to increase access to educational information and instructional programs.

Do Media Influence the Cost and Access to Instruction?

It appears that media can significantly influence the cost of learning and the ease and cost of access to instruction by students. Determining the per-student cost of instruction and access to information requires careful analysis. In 2000 Brenda Sugrue and Clark reviewed the research and practice in media selection and cost analysis. They described different methods of performing cost analysis prior to selecting media for instruction or training.

Cognitive efficiencies from media. A twist in the discussion about the economic benefits of media came from a suggestion made by Thomas Cobb in a 1997 article. He argued that some media and symbol systems lead to quicker and/or less demanding learning results than other media or symbolic modes for some students. Cobb's suggestion opens an area of research where there are at least two possibilities: First, any medium or representational mode used for presenting an instructional method (for instance, an example presented in either pictorial or verbal modes) might help some individuals to learn easier and/or faster (for instance, high visual but low verbal ability learners may learn faster from pictures than from narrative descriptions of examples). Second, the cost of learning is, after all, one of the most important issues for those concerned with the application of research to solving practical problems. The expectation that currently guides research in this area could be stated as: Whenever a given instructional method is necessary for learning, different media or symbolic modes will have different learning efficiencies for learners with different aptitudes.

Visual and aural learning aids. Compelling examples of possible cognitive efficiencies can be found in several studies, including a 1995 study by Samual Mousavi and colleagues, and a 1997 study by Richard E. Mayer. These researchers provided evidence that presenting novel and difficult science concepts to learners in both auditory and visual symbolic modes results in more efficient (quicker, easier) learning than information presented in either mode alone for high visual ability and low prior knowledge learners. The researchers' explanation for their findings is that the conscious human mind is supported by both auditory and visual "buffers" that specialize in storing different symbolic representations of information to be learned. These buffers permit instructional information to be stored in both visual and aural (sound) forms. Conscious consideration of information to be learned or used in problem solving can be held in the mind only briefly (approximately six to eight seconds) unless the person repeats it or elaborates it somehow. Imagine a person who is trying to remember a new telephone number someone gave them verbally as they walk a long distance to find a telephone. Unless the person repeats the information or writes it down, he or she will tend to forget it before reaching the telephone. Giving information content in two different modalities (visual and auditory) apparently results in storage by two

different, sensory-based memory buffers, which increases the duration and quality of information available to learners while they mentally process the information. Thus, providing key instructional information in both pictorial and auditory (narrative) forms might extend the duration of "thinking time" during learning for some learners. It is critical to note that in their 2000 article Roxana Moreno and Mayer limited this "learning efficiency" impact of both visual and aural modes of instruction to a small group of learners. The increased efficiency was primarily useful for students who had a very low prior knowledge and very high visual ability. One might wonder what percentage of students received a significantly enhanced efficiency from both visual and aural forms of instruction.

Media Display Problems

There is increasing evidence that the "busy" screen designs that are typical in computer-based and multimedia learning environments often cause learning problems. Many media designers are tempted toward instructional presentations that include active animated figures, music, sounds, and other visually and aurally exciting displays. While most people welcome the visual and aural entertainment, the best evidence suggests that learners are often overloaded by these "seductive details" and their learning is reduced. Screen designs that separate visual and text-based explanations or demonstrations, and/or are heavily text laden, seem to damage learning because they overload a person's thinking while she is trying to learn. Mayer and his students recommend the spatial (visual) and temporal (time) integration of verbal and visual information. They also recommend the use of narration rather than large bodies of text. This line of research provides important guidance for screen design. It strongly indicates that instructional designers and teachers must focus learners constantly on learning goals and resist the temptation to offer enticing and aesthetically pleasing but irrelevant formats and features.

Do Some Media Motivate Learning More than Other Media?

While many advocates of new forms of instructional media have argued for motivational benefits, existing evidence suggests that important components of motivation may actually be decreased by common features of, for example, computer or multimedia instruction. In a 1984 article Gavriel Salomon presented evidence that students who express strong preferences for any medium or mix of media tend to expect that it will be a less demanding way to learn. This expectation results in the investment of lower levels of mental effort and lower achievement levels when compared to instructional conditions that are perceived as more demanding. Yet, it is likely that other motivational benefits might exist with newer media. For example, students may be more enthusiastic about enrolling in instruction presented by newer media because of optimistic expectations about ease of access and flexibility of scheduling. Delays in finishing online courses and rumors about high "drop-out" rates suggest the need for more research on whether students persist in courses offered using new media.

Not much is known about the direct impact of new media on mental effort (aside from Salomon's cautions), but the early research is not promising. Some studies indicate that many instructional strategies and complex screen displays risk overloading working memory and causing "automated" cognitive defaults where mental effort is both reduced and directed to nonlearning goals. Educators are thus faced with an ironic contradiction where students are attracted to media qualities that are known to reduce their learning. Complicating this finding is strong evidence that learners are not aware when they become overloaded by too much visual and/or verbal information.

Technology Integration

This discussion of media has thus far focused on media as a delivery device. Educators have typically viewed media in two ways. First, media are viewed as a means to amplify the teacher's message, such as with the use of an overhead projector or a video projector. Second, media are viewed as a way to deliver instruction using computer-based instruction or television. For example, Alfred Bork suggested that computer-based instruction would revolutionize schools and change the way students would learn. Yet, by the beginning of the twenty-first century the computer-based instruction revolution had yet to materialize.

Subsequent efforts shifted attention away from using computers to deliver instruction through a tutorial or drill-and-practice instructional method toward using computers as a tool that is integrated into other classroom activities to facilitate problem solving and learning. In their 2002 book *Integrating Computer Technology into the Classroom*, Gary R. Morrison and Deborah L. Lowther described technology integration as the process of using application software (for example, spreadsheets, databases, and web browsers) as tools to help students learn problem solving. An example of technology integration is the NteQ (Integrating Technology for Inquiry) model. This model provides teachers with a ten-step approach for developing problem-based instructional units that integrate technology. Students use computers to gather, manipulate, and present information related to solving academic problems. The emphasis at this level is on the use of the computer as a tool in the same way that scientists and business professionals use computers in their work.

This shift in focus from using computers and other media to deliver instruction to one of using computers as an integrated problem-solving tool places a greater emphasis on the development of media-based instructional methods. The emphasis of the research also shifts from comparing two media conditions (e.g., classrooms with and without computers) to one of investigating the effectiveness of the media-based instructional strategies employed in the classroom. An extensive description of a classroom-based example of technology integration can be found in an online article from 2000, written by Steven M. Ross, Morrison, Lowther, and Robert T. Plants, that investigated a school district's pilot of an Anytime Anywhere Learning project focused on writing achievement. Teachers in the pilot project, where the students had laptop computers, were more likely to use problem-based learning, cooperative learning, facilitation, and sustained writing than teachers in traditional classrooms. Similarly, students in the pilot project had significantly higher scores on a writing sample collected at the end of the year. These differences were attributed to the student-centered environment created by the teachers rather than the computer technology.

See also: LITERACY, *subentry on* LEARNING FROM MULTIMEDIA SOURCES; TECHNOLOGY IN EDUCATION, *subentry on* CURRENT TRENDS.

BIBLIOGRAPHY

BORK, ALFRED. 1987. *Learning with Personal Computers.* New York: Harper and Row.

CLARK, RICHARD E. 2001. *Learning from Media.* Greenwich, CT: Information Age Publishers.

COBB, THOMAS. 1997. "Cognitive Efficiency: Toward a Revised Theory of Media." *Educational Technology Research and Development* 45(4):21–35.

DAVIES, IVOR K. 1964. *Competency Based Learning: Technology, Management, and Design.* New York: McGraw-Hill.

GIMINO, AMY. 2000. "Factors that Influence Students' Investment of Mental Effort in Academic Tasks: A Validation and Exploratory Study." Ph.D. diss., University of Southern California.

KOZMA, ROBERT B. 1994. "The Influence of Media on Learning: The Debate Continues." *School Library Media Quarterly* 22(4):233–239.

MAYER, RICHARD. 1997. "Multimedia Learning: Are We Asking the Right Questions?" *Educational Psychologist* 32(1):1–19.

MORRISON, GARY R., and LOWTHER, DEBORAH L. 2002. "Information Management Tools for Learning." In *Developing Minds*, 3rd edition, ed. Arthur L. Costa. Alexandria, VA: Association for Supervision and Curriculum Development.

MORRISON, GARY R., and LOWTHER, DEBORAH L. 2002. *Integrating Computer Technology into the Classroom.* Columbus, OH: Merrill Prentice-Hall.

MOUSAVI, SAMUAL Y.; LOW, ROBERT; and SWELLER, JOHN. 1995. "Reducing Cognitive Load by Mixing Auditory and Visual Presentation Modes." *Journal of Educational Psychology* 87:319–334.

REISER, ROBERT A., and DICK, WALTER. 1996. *Instructional Planning: A Guide for Teachers.* Needham Heights, MA: Allyn and Bacon.

SALOMON, GAVRIEL. 1984. "Television Is 'Easy' and Print Is 'Tough': The Differential Investment of Mental Effort in Learning as a Function of Perceptions and Attributions." *Journal of Educational Psychology* 76:774–786.

SUGRUE, BRENDA, and CLARK, RICHARD E. 2000. "Media Selection for Training." In *Training Handbook*, ed. Sigmund Tobias and Dexter Fletcher. New York: Macmillan.

THORNDIKE, EDWARD L. 1912. *Education.* New York: Macmillan.

INTERNET RESOURCES

MORENO, ROXANA, and MAYER, RICHARD E. 2000. "A Learner-Centered Approach to Multimedia Explanations: Deriving Instructional Design Principles from Cognitive Theory." *Interactive Multimedia Electronic Journal of Computer-Enhanced Learning.* <http://imej.wfu.edu/articles/2000/2/05/printver.asp>.

ROSS, STEVEN M.; MORRISON, GARY R.; LOWTHER, DEBORAH L.; and PLANTS, ROBERT T. 2000. "Anytime, Anywhere Learning: Final Evaluation Report of the Laptop Program." <www.nteq.com/Research/Year1.pdf>.

RICHARD E. CLARK
GARY R. MORRISON

MEDIA CENTERS, SCHOOL

See: SCHOOL LIBRARIES.

MEDIA, INFLUENCE ON CHILDREN

According to the American Academy of Pediatrics (AAP), "Children are influenced by media—they learn by observing, imitating, and making behaviors their own" (2001, p.1224). The influence of media on children has been the subject of increased attention among parents, educators, and health care professionals. The significance of this issue becomes obvious when one notes the diversity of Americans who share this concern. Included in this group of concerned citizens are those, most notably politicians, who typically stand in opposition to one another on many issues, but who stand together in agreement on this one.

Media influence on children has steadily increased as new and more sophisticated types of media have been developed and made available to the American public. Availability, as well as greater affordability for American families, has provided easier access to media for children. Beneficial effects include early readiness for learning, educational enrichment, opportunities to view or participate in discussions of social issues, exposure to the arts through music and performance, and entertainment. Harmful effects may result from sensationalization of violent behavior, exposure to subtle or explicit sexual content, promotion of unrealistic body images, presentation of poor health habits as desirable practices, and exposure to persuasive advertising targeting children.

In the following discussion, some attention will be given to the beneficial effects of media on children, but the primary focus will be on negative influences, which have been more widely researched.

History of Media for Children

The twentieth century was a time of phenomenal growth and development of new kinds of media. In the early twentieth century, film, radio, and newspapers were the media forms to which children had access, though limited. Beginning in the early 1940s and continuing through the end of the century, children's media experiences expanded to include television, recorded music, videotapes, electronic games, interactive computer software, and the Internet. Print media, such as comic books and children's magazines, also expanded during this period, though not at the same accelerated rate as the visual electronic media.

Commercial television made its debut in 1941, initiating a new era of media influence. One of the earliest documented examples of the effect of advertising in the media was the introduction in 1952 of television ads for Mr. Potato Head, a toy manufactured by Hasbro. Gross sales were more than $4 million in its first year of television advertising. At that time, more than two-thirds of television sets were owned by families with children under twelve years of age.

Educational programming, offered primarily on public television stations, was the next milestone in television's early influences on children. In the larger discussion of media influence on children, educational programming is without question the source of the most significant and long-lasting positive effects.

A pioneer in educational programming was the Children's Television Workshop, founded in 1968 by Joan Ganz Cooney, Lloyd Morrisett, Gerald Lesser, and others. The creation of a television production company dedicated to children's educational programming was a result of Cooney's study of television for preschool children for the Carnegie Corporation of New York. The project that evolved was a research-based collaboration by educators, psychologists, child development experts, writers and musicians. *Sesame Street* was the first program produced, making its televised debut in 1969. *Sesame Street* was designed to combine education with entertainment and to target children of preschool age.

The development of *Sesame Street* was research-driven to ensure that the most effective strategies for early learning through media were employed. Other children's programs subsequently developed by the Children's Television Workshop included *3-2-1 Contact, The Best of Families, The Electric Company,* and *Feeling Good.* Programming produced by the Children's Television Workshop was innovative, was well received by the public, and became a model for other programs, both in the media and as in school settings, for providing effective early learning experiences to prepare young children to enter school. The positive influence of the Children's Television Workshop on American children was widespread.

During the 1980s and 1990s, unprecedented growth occurred in the field of computer technology, resulting in the increased availability of computers to children, both in their homes and schools. Improved access for children resulted in expanded media influence on children, with a new interactive element that was not previously seen in media.

During this same period, media content underwent a transformation that was characterized by increased use of sexual themes and violent behavior. This change was evident in movies, television programming, music lyrics, video games, cartoons, and magazines. There was an outcry from parents and concerned adults who objected to children's exposure to content that was age inappropriate and who were troubled by the probable negative effects of such exposure. In an attempt to inform adults who were monitoring children's media exposure, ratings systems were developed that identified content categories and frequency or intensity of specific incidents. Rating codes were used to label movies, television programs, and music lyrics. Although rating systems served their purpose of informing the public, it is questionable to what extent children were actually affected by their implementation.

General Considerations

There are two important factors that must be included in the discussion of media influence on children. One factor, called *media literacy,* was addressed by Renee Hobbs. Hobbs contended that:

> Just because our students can use media and technology doesn't mean they are effective at critically analyzing and evaluating the messages they receive. Students need a set of skills to ask important questions

about what they watch, see, listen to and read. Often called media literacy, these skills include the ability to critically analyze media messages and the ability to use different kinds of communication technologies for self-expression and communication.

A child who is media illiterate is more vulnerable to being influenced by messages in all kinds of media.

The second factor that can affect how children are influenced by media is the amount of parental involvement in supervising media exposure of children. The U.S. Department of Education's Office of Educational Research and Improvement published guidelines in 1994 that said:

> Parental monitoring is a key factor, since the research studies show that increasing guidance from parents is at least as important as simply reducing media violence. Children may learn negative behavior patterns and values from many other experiences as well as TV programs, and parental guidance is needed to help children sort out these influences and develop the ability to make sound decisions on their own.

An important media literacy skill, which can be developed through parental guidance, is a child's ability to distinguish between reality and fantasy in media messages. Children may not be capable of making this distinction without an adult's help, resulting in a child's confused perception of fantasy as reality. But with proper adult guidance, they can learn to critique what they view and become more discriminating consumers of media.

Studies of Media Influence

Media violence and its effects on children was the first area in which extensive scientific research was done. In 1972 the Office of the Surgeon General conducted studies on media violence and its effects on children who viewed it. The conclusions of these studies were confirmed and extended by studies performed at the National Institute of Mental Health in 1982. Three years later, the American Psychological Association (APA) published a report that reaffirmed the previous studies. A landmark report of media influence on children was published by the AAP in 1999. The study was done by the Committee on Public Education, and presented in their policy statement of August 1999. In July 2000, at a Congressional Public Health Summit, the AAP, the

American Medical Association, the American Academy of Child and Adolescent Psychiatry, and the APA issued an unprecedented "Joint Statement on the Impact of Entertainment Violence on Children." Speaking for members of the national public-health community, the statement presented a consensus opinion on the effects of violence in the media on children. The joint statement, however, included an interesting and important distinction that addressed the context of violence in the media, stating: "It is not violence itself but the context in which it is portrayed that can make the difference between learning about violence and learning to be violent." With the important caveat in mind, the overwhelming consensus of the aforementioned studies was that there is substantial evidence that exposure to violence in the media has harmful effects on children and has been linked to children's aggressive behavior.

Violence in interactive media forms (Internet, computer and video games) as opposed to passive media forms (television, movies, videos) may have even stronger effects on children and, as a result, has become a focus of new research. According to the Office of the Surgeon General, "children are theoretically more susceptible to behavioral influences when they are active participants than when they are observers." To further legitimize these concerns, the AAP reported that initial studies of interactive media show that the element of child-initiated virtual violence may result in even more significant effects than those of passive media. Because research has already shown that passive media violence has significant influence on children, the implications of increased effects from interactive media are troublesome.

Despite the research reports, there was debate between television broadcasters and scientists regarding the harmful effects of television violence on children. Broadcasters asserted that there was not enough evidence to link viewing television violence to children's aggressive behavior. Scientists, nevertheless, stood by their research findings.

Domains of Influence

Research studies have identified the following domains of influence in which media content has been shown to have negative effects on children: violence and aggressive behavior, sexual content, body image and self-esteem, and physical health and school performance. Information on media violence has been taken from the following primary sources: the 2002 APA study titled "Violence on Television" and the

1999 and 2001 policy statements of the Committee on Public Education of the AAP. The 2001 policy statement is recommended as a comprehensive source of information on the topic of media violence. Other studies were referenced for information on sexual content, body image, and health issues.

Violence and aggressive behavior. The question of violence in the media and its influence on children is probably the most widely researched domain of media influence. Studies over a span of three decades, beginning in the early 1970s, have shown that significant exposure to media violence increases the risk of aggressive behavior in certain children and adolescents. Other effects on children include desensitization to others' pain and suffering and the tendency to be fearful of the world around them, viewing it as a dangerous place. Research has also shown that news reports of violent crimes can traumatize young children.

Sexual content. Increased attention has been given to the second domain, sexual content in the media. The sexualization of American media has become the focus of widespread discussion and criticism by children's advocates. According to studies commissioned by the Kaiser Family Foundation collectively labeled "Sex, Kids, and the Family Hour," there was a 400 percent increase from 1976 to 1996 in sexual references during the evening television viewing time period commonly referred to as "family hour." It was determined that by 1996 children were exposed to about eight sexual references per hour during this time slot. In *Media, Children, and the Family*, Jennings Bryant and Steven Rockwell reported the results of their studies that investigated the effects of exposure to sexual content on television. They found that such exposure affected adolescents' moral judgment. They qualified the results, however, by saying that parental discussion and clear expression of personal values mitigated the effects on adolescents.

Body image and self-esteem. The third domain, body image and self-esteem, is widely affected by advertising in the media. Researchers have suggested that media may influence the development of self-esteem in adolescents through messages about body image. Television, movies, magazines, and advertisements present images that promote unrealistic expectations of beauty, body weight, and acceptable physical appearance. Efforts to sell an image that adheres to certain standards of body weight and size may be a catalyst for eating disorders suffered by some adolescents. And, when adolescents fall short of their own expectations based on media images, self-esteem can suffer. Media theorists and researchers have determined that the effects of this trend are being seen in both boys and girls, with negative psychological affects. Advertisement of appealing, but often financially unaffordable, clothing and promotion of negative gender stereotypes are other areas of concern. Further research on the connections among media messages, body image, and self-esteem is warranted.

Physical health and school performance. The fourth domain involves the amount of time that children spend engaged with media activities. The average American child or adolescent spends more than twenty hours per week viewing television. Additional time is often spent watching movies, listening to music, watching music videos, playing video or computer games, or spending computer time on the Internet. This increase in time spent by children using media for recreation has been shown to be a significant factor in childhood obesity due to associated physical inactivity. School achievement may also be affected as a result of decreased time spent on homework or school assignments. And parents often unintentionally contribute to this negative influence by using the television as a way to occupy their children's attention—as a babysitter of sorts. Educators have expressed concerns that the passive nature of media exposure undermines the ability of students to be active learners. Conversely, there have been concerns that overstimulation due to excessive media use might be related to attention deficit disorder or hyperactivity. There has been no research to date that indicates a clear relationship.

Increasingly, tobacco, alcohol, and illicit drugs have been glamorized in the media. Tobacco manufacturers spend $6 billion per year and alcohol manufacturers $2 billion per year in advertising that appeals to children. Movies and television programs often show the lead character or likeable characters using and enjoying tobacco and alcohol products. On the other hand, media also provide factual information and venues for discussion, typically through public service announcements or through public programming, informing children and warning them of the dangers of addictions to these substances. These educational messages, however, are on a much smaller scale and are much less appealing in their presentation.

Recommendations

The AAP, the Office of the Surgeon General, and the APA have offered recommendations to address the issues of media influence on children. Included in these recommendations are suggestions for parents, educators, and health care professionals to advocate for a safer media environment for children through media literacy. They urge media producers to be more responsible in their portrayal of violence. They advocate for more useful and effective media ratings.

A consistent recommendation in studies, however, is proactive parental involvement in children's media experiences. By monitoring what children hear and see, discussing issues that emerge, and sharing media time with their children, parents can moderate the negative influences as well as increase the positive effects of media in the lives of their children.

See also: LITERACY, *subentry on* MULTIMEDIA LITERACY; MEDIA AND LEARNING; OUT-OF-SCHOOL INFLUENCES AND ACADEMIC SUCCESS; TECHNOLOGY IN EDUCATION, *subentry on* CURRENT TRENDS.

BIBLIOGRAPHY

AMERICAN ACADEMY OF PEDIATRICS. 2001. "Media Violence." *Pediatrics* 108:1222–1226.

FIELD, ALISON E. 2000. "Media Influence on Self-Image: The Real Fashion Emergency." *Healthy Weight Journal* 14(6).

FIELD, ALISON E.; CAMARGO, CARLOS A., JR.; TAYLOR, C. BARR; and BERKEY, CATHERINE S. 2001. "Peer, Parent, and Media Influences on the Development of Weight Concerns and Frequent Dieting among Preadolescent and Adolescent Girls and Boys." *Pediatrics* 107:54–60.

HOFFNER, CYNTHIA. 1996. "Media, Children, and the Family: Social Scientific, Psychodynamic, and Clinical Perspectives." *Journal of Broadcasting and Electronic Media* 40(1):389–402.

HUSTON, ALETHA C.; DONNERSTEIN, EDWARD; FAIRCHILD, HALFORD; FESHBACH, NORMAN D.; KATZ, PHYLLIS A.; MURRAY, JOHN P.; RUBINSTEIN, ELI A.; WILCOX, BRIAN L.; and ZUCKERMAN, DIANA. 1992. *Big World, Small Screen: The Role of Television in American Society.* Lincoln: University of Nebraska Press.

LIEBERT, ROBERT M., and SPREFKIN, JOYCE N. 1988. *The Early Window: Effects of Television on Children and Youth.* New York: Pergamon.

NATIONAL INSTITUTE OF MENTAL HEALTH. 1982. "Television and Behavior: Ten Years of Scientific Progress and Implications for the Eighties." Rockville, MD: U.S. Department of Health and Human Services.

POLCE-LYNCH, MARY; MYERS, BARBARA J.; KLIEWER, WENDY; and KILMARTIN, CHRISTOPHER. 2001. "Adolescent Self-Esteem and Gender: Exploring Relations to Sexual Harassment, Body Image, Media Influence, and Emotional Expression." *Journal of Youth and Adolescence* 30:225–244.

INTERNET RESOURCES

AMERICAN ACADEMY OF PEDIATRICS, AMERICAN MEDICAL ASSOCIATION, AMERICAN ACADEMY OF CHILD AND ADOLESCENT PSYCHIATRY, and AMERICAN PSYCHOLOGICAL ASSOCIATION. 2000. "Joint Statement on the Impact of Entertainment Violence on Children—Congressional Public Health Summit." <www.aap.org/advocacy/releases/jstmtevc.htm>.

AMERICAN PSYCHOLOGICAL ASSOCIATION. 2002. "Violence on Television." <www.apa.org/pubinfo/violence.html>.

CHILDREN NOW. 1996. "New Study Finds Increase in Sexual Content on TV's Family Hour." <www.childrennow.org/newsroom/news-96/pr-96-12-11.html>.

HOBBS, RENEE. 2001. "Media Literacy in the Classroom." *Newsweek* <http://school.newsweek.com/pages/extra_media_literacy.htm>.

MEDIA HISTORY PROJECT. 1996. "Film History." <mediahistory.umn.edu/movies.html>.

OFFICE OF THE SURGEON GENERAL. 2001. "Youth Violence: A Report of the Surgeon General." <www.surgeongeneral.gov/library/youthviolence/>.

TVHISTORY.TV. 2002. "Television History: The First Seventy-Five Years." <www.tvhistory.tv/>.

UNIVERSITY OF MARYLAND LIBRARIES. 2001. "Children's Television Workshop." <www.lib.umd.edu/NPBA/subinfo/ctw.html>.

U.S. DEPARTMENT OF EDUCATION. OFFICE OF EDUCATIONAL RESEARCH AND IMPROVEMENT. 1994. "TV Viewing and Parental Guidance." <www.ed.gov/pubs/OR/ConsumerGuides/tv.html>.

LAURA BLACKWELL CLARK

MEDICAL COLLEGE ADMISSION TEST (MCAT)

The Medical College Admission Test (MCAT) is the standardized test required of all applicants to allopathic (M.D.), osteopathic (D.O.), and podiatric medical schools. It is also accepted as an option for some veterinary and allied health schools. The MCAT tests the mastery of basic biology, chemistry, and physics concepts, problem solving requiring the integration of these disciplines, critical thinking, and writing skills. The test consists of four sections. The Verbal Reasoning section contains multiple-choice questions based on reading selections drawn from a multitude of sources, many outside of the sciences. The intent of this section is to test reading comprehension, evaluation of ideas, analysis of data, and the application of new information. The Physical Sciences section contains multiple-choice questions involving basic knowledge in physics and general chemistry as well as the ability to apply that knowledge and interpret new information. The Writing Sample requires two brief essays written in response to a brief topic statement and assesses the presentation and development of an idea as well as the technical writing skills of the writer. The Biological Sciences section involves multiple-choice questions about basic concepts in biology and organic chemistry as well as the application of that knowledge and interpretation of new information.

The MCAT is a five and three-quarters hour test and is offered in April and August of each year. The Verbal Reasoning, Physical Science, and Biological Science scores are reported on a scale from 1 (low) to 15 (high). The Writing Sample is reported on a scale from J (low) to T (high), representing the sum of the two essay scores. Although there is no limit to the number of times the test may be taken, special permission must be obtained after the third time. Registration for the MCAT is done online by accessing the website of Association of American Medical Colleges (AAMC). Five practice tests have been released by the AAMC.

The MCAT plays a substantial role in the medical school admissions process. How much emphasis is placed on MCAT scores varies from school to school. Other factors that are considered include: grades (overall and science), the interview, letters of recommendation, research, activities, experience in medicine, application essays, and state of residence. The two most important factors, however, are grades and MCAT scores. High grades and test scores, though, will not guarantee acceptance. If an applicant with strong grade and test credentials has poor interpersonal skills, poor references, or no experience in medicine, gaining acceptance is very unlikely. On the other hand, a very personable individual with a great deal of medical experience is very unlikely to gain acceptance if MCAT scores or grades are low. It may be useful to think of MCAT scores and grades as threshold criteria. Once the threshold is reached, the other factors become more significant. It is important to note that scores in individual sections of the MCAT may be considered as important as the overall score. For example, an applicant with 10s in each section of the test would probably be considered more favorably than an applicant with scores of 12, 12, and 6. Both total scores are 30, but the former shows consistency and the latter indicates one rather weak area.

The MCAT scores are required for several reasons. First, they validate an applicant's grades. They help the medical school admissions committee compare applicants from many different schools of varying rigor. MCAT scores are particularly useful when considering an applicant from a school that is not well known to the admissions committee. A second reason for the reliance on MCAT scores is that they are predictive of an applicant's success in the academic course work generally taken during the first two years of medical school. Finally, MCAT scores are evidence of an applicant's test-taking ability. This is relevant because successful applicants will face at least three additional major standardized tests that must be passed before they can obtain a license to practice medicine.

Work is underway in 2002 to revise and update the MCAT, although it is likely to be several years before any changes are actually made. One thing is certain, though: the MCAT will continue to play an important role in evaluating applicants for medical school.

See also: MEDICAL EDUCATION.

BIBLIOGRAPHY

CORDER, BRICE W., ed. 1998. *Medical Professions Admission Guide: Strategy for Success,* 4th edition. Champaign, IL: National Association of Advisors for the Health Professions.

MCAT Student Manual. 1995. Washington, DC: Association of American Medical Colleges.

INTERNET RESOURCE

ASSOCIATION OF AMERICAN MEDICAL COLLEGES. 2002. <www.aamc.org>.

KIRSTEN A. PETERSON

MEDICAL EDUCATION

The path to a career in medicine in the United States is well defined. Aspiring physicians must earn an undergraduate degree, complete four years of medical school, participate in a minimum of three years of graduate medical training, and pass three national examinations for licensure. Becoming a physician also demands a desire to work with people; intellectual, emotional, and physical stamina; and an ability to think critically to solve complex problems.

Preparation for one of the world's most highly respected careers often starts in high school by taking courses in biology, chemistry, and physics. Preparation continues during college, with particular attention to the courses needed for admission to medical school. Although the specific number of credits required for admission to medical school varies, the minimum college course requirements include one year of biology, two years of chemistry (one year of general/inorganic chemistry and one year of organic chemistry), and one year of physics, all with adequate laboratory experiences. Medical schools may require or strongly recommend taking mathematics and computer science courses in college, though only a small number demand a specific sequence of mathematics courses. Candidates for admission to medical schools are also expected to have a solid background in English, the humanities, and the social sciences.

There is an expectation that aspiring physicians will participate in health-oriented research and in volunteer activities to demonstrate their commitment to the profession. These types of extracurricular activities provide opportunities to explore ones' motivations, specific interests, and aptitude for a career in medicine.

Typically, the process of applying to medical school begins during the junior year of undergraduate study. One of the first steps is to take the Medical College Admission Test (MCAT) in the spring of the junior year. The MCAT is a standardized test designed to measure knowledge in the biological and physical sciences, the ability to read and interpret information, and communication skills. Students indicate which medical schools they want to receive their MCAT scores.

The American Medical College Application Service (AMCAS) facilitates applying to medical school by centralizing the submission of information and supporting materials. Of the 125 medical schools in the United States, 114 participate in AMCAS. Students submit one set of application materials and one official transcript to AMCAS, which in turn distributes the information to participating institutions as designated by the applicant. Deadlines for receiving applications are determined by the individual medical schools. Applications to non-AMCAS medical schools are submitted directly to those institutions in accordance with their individual requirements and deadlines.

Admission committees, composed of faculty members from the basic and clinical sciences departments, screen and prioritize the applications. Academic ability and personal qualities are used to discern applicants' qualifications for medical school. Academic ability is measured in terms of grades on undergraduate courses (with emphasis on the required science courses) and MCAT scores. College grades and MCAT scores are considered the most important predictors of medical school performance during the first two years. Most students admitted to medical school have above average (3.0 and higher) undergraduate grade point averages. An undergraduate major in the sciences is not a mandatory requirement for admission to medical school. Most admission committees look for well-rounded individuals and strive to admit a diversified class. The importance of MCAT scores to admission decisions varies by institution.

Admission committees also look for evidence of maturity, self-discipline, commitment to helping others, and leadership qualities. Candidates' personal statements, letters of evaluation, and the breadth and variety of extracurricular activities in health-related settings are used as indicators of personal attributes. Many medical schools have specific programs for recruiting and enrolling minority students to help increase the number of underrepresented minorities who practice medicine. Interviews with faculty members also provide information about the applicant's personal background and motivation to become a doctor.

Each medical school decides the number of students that will be admitted each year. Some medical schools accept high school graduates into combined bachelor's and medical degree programs, or combined medical and graduate degree programs.

Medical school applicants are urged to submit applications for financial assistance in conjunction with applications for admission. Loans, primarily sponsored by the federal government, are the major source of financial aid for medical school. Some schools offer academic scholarships.

For the 1998–1999 academic year, the American Association of Medical Colleges (AAMC) reported that 41,004 individuals applied to medical school. AMCAS participants applied to an average of 11.5 AMCAS-participating schools. Among first-time applicants, 45.9 percent (27,525) were accepted to a medical school. AAMC data further indicates that 6,353 candidates were accepted to two or more medical schools in 1998. Medical schools start issuing acceptances to the entering class by March 15 each year.

Medical schools typically provide four years of medical education, with the goal of preparing students to enter three- to seven-year programs of graduate medical training, which are referred to as residency programs. Medical school programs leading to the medical degree (M.D.) generally consist of two years of study in the basic sciences and two years in the clinical sciences. The basic sciences include anatomy, biochemistry, physiology, microbiology, pharmacology, pathology, and behavioral sciences. Clinical education begins in the third year with required clinical clerkships in internal medicine, pediatrics, family medicine, obstetrics and gynecology, surgery, and psychiatry. During six- to twelve-week rotations, students learn how to take a medical history, conduct a physical examination, and recognize familiar disease patterns. Students are allowed to shape their own course of study during the fourth year with elective courses in the clinical specialties or research. Most medical schools strive to integrate basic science and clinical science instruction throughout the four-year curriculum.

In addition to written examinations and direct observations of performance, Step 1 and Step 2 of the United States Medical Licensing Examination (USMLE) are also used to measure the acquisition of medical knowledge. Medical students take Step 1, which measures understanding and ability to apply key concepts in the basic sciences, after completion of the second year of medical school. Passing Step 1 is a requirement for graduation at the majority of medical schools. Step 2, which is taken at the beginning of the senior year, evaluates medical knowledge and understanding of the clinical sciences. More than half of all American medical schools require passing Step 2 as a condition for graduation.

The Liaison Committee on Medical Education (LCME) monitors the quality of education that is provided by American medical schools that award the medical degree. Similar accrediting bodies exist for schools of osteopathic medicine and schools of podiatry.

Students apply to graduate medical programs through the Electronic Residency Application Service (ERAS), a centralized computer-based service that transmits applications, personal statements, medical school transcripts, and Dean's Letters to residency program directors. Students register their first, second, and third choices for residency placements through the National Resident Matching Program (NRMP). The NRMP provides an impartial venue for matching applicants and programs. The "match" facilitates placements by establishing a uniform procedure for communication between students and residency directors, and for announcing residency selections. Matches are usually announced in March of the senior year of medical school.

Graduate medical education programs (residencies) provide extensive, direct patient-care experiences in recognized medical specialties. Three-year residencies in family practice, emergency medicine, pediatrics, and internal medicine are typical. Several other specialties require one year of general practice followed by three to five years of advanced training. Participation in an accredited residency program and passing the USMLE Step 3 are requirements for licensure in most states.

See also: MEDICAL COLLEGE ADMISSION TEST.

BIBLIOGRAPHY

ASSOCIATION OF AMERICAN MEDICAL COLLEGES. 1999. *Medical School Admission Requirements: United States and Canada, 2000–2001,* 50th edition. Washington, DC: Association of American Medical Colleges.

CRAWFORD, JANE D. 1994. *The Premedical Planning Guide,* 3rd edition. Baltimore, MD: Williams and Wilkins.

INTERNET RESOURCES

AMERICAN ASSOCIATION OF MEDICAL COLLEGES. 2000. "AAMC: Medical College Admission Test (MCAT)." <www.aamc.org/students/mcat/>.

ASSOCIATION OF AMERICAN MEDICAL COLLEGES. 2000. "Getting into Medical School." <www.aamc.org/students/considering/gettingin.htm>.

NATIONAL RESIDENT MATCHING PROGRAM. 2000. "About the NRMP." <www.nrmp.org/about_nrmp>.

NATIONAL RESIDENT MATCHING PROGRAM. 2000. "About Residency." <www.nrmp.org/res_match/about_res>.

JUANITA F. BUFORD

MEIKLEJOHN, ALEXANDER (1872–1964)

The youngest of eight sons, Alexander Meiklejohn (1872–1964) was born in Rochdale, England, of Scottish parents. His family moved to Rhode Island when he was eight, and he later attended nearby Brown University where he earned his baccalaureate and master's degrees in philosophy. He followed his graduate adviser and close friend James Seth to Cornell University to pursue his doctorate. A few years later, Meiklejohn married his first wife, Nannine, and they began a family.

Upon receiving his doctorate, Meiklejohn returned to Brown as an assistant professor of logic and metaphysics. He attained the rank of professor after nine years, having earned the respect of his colleagues and the admiration of his students. In 1901 Meiklejohn was named dean at Brown (his title was later changed to dean of undergraduates). His most distinctive act as dean was to disqualify Brown's championship baseball team over questions of sportsmanship and honesty. Brown's trustees supported this action and the students accepted it, but the alumni were outraged.

Even as he was establishing himself at his alma mater, Amherst College sought Meiklejohn as a new president who could bring energy and innovation to a college facing declining admissions and sagging academic standards. Inaugurated as president of Amherst in October 1912, Meiklejohn quickly set to work to institute his educational ideals. Almost as quickly, his policies created enemies among the faculty, trustees, and alumni. He opposed the newly popular elective system, believing that students could better understand human culture and the natural world if they were not educated in narrowly specialized classes. He proposed a variety of options for a required curriculum, none of which the faculty accepted.

Turning his attention to other passions, Meiklejohn set up college extension classes in local mills and factories where students taught and interacted with laborers. He hired many new faculty members, terminated many older professors, and chose to ignore those whose tenure was beyond challenge. He irritated additional alumni by refusing to emphasize athletics and by maintaining the tradition of part-time basketball and football coaches. Even within the local community, Meiklejohn was unpopular: Neither he nor his wife were active in the predominant Congregationalist church, and she wrote children's books, traveled to Europe alone, and smoked cigarettes. Meiklejohn himself was known as a socialist, although he never affiliated himself with the Socialist Party. His outspoken opposition to the World War I eroded further the base of supporters of his presidency at Amherst. Nevertheless, he persevered.

By 1923 Meiklejohn was accused by his enemies of financial mismanagement, and the board of trustees asked for his resignation. In protest, twelve graduating seniors refused their diplomas, and eight faculty members resigned their positions. Though he resigned from Amherst, Meiklejohn capitalized on the media controversy surrounding his departure. He toured the country and delivered speeches to promote his first two books: *The Liberal College*, published in 1920, and *Freedom and the College* released in 1923.

President Glenn Frank offered Meiklejohn a professorship at the University of Wisconsin in Madison, but struggling with the death of his wife Nannine, he refused the appointment. The next year, however, Frank asked Meiklejohn to create an experimental college within the university, for which he would be given free reign to institute many of the reforms that he had advocated at Amherst and in his books and speeches. Meiklejohn took the post in March, 1926.

The Experimental College at the University of Wisconsin opened in 1927 with an incoming class of

119 men, who signed up for the two-year prescribed program of study. During the first year, students studied Athens in the fifth century B.C.E.; in their second year they traced the history of America through the nineteenth and twentieth centuries. Between academic years, students were expected to write an anthropological report on the region where they grew up. Faculty members (called advisers to defuse traditional expectations) met with students throughout each week in full-class meetings, but also held regular sessions with subgroups of twelve and engaged in many personal discussions with students.

External opposition to the program mounted quickly. University faculty criticized its independent governance and eclectic curriculum, and newspaper editorials and press reports lambasted its egalitarian pedagogy and Meiklejohn's arrogant style. Responding to these threats and to the economic problems of the Great Depression, the university administration proposed significant changes in the Experimental College in the 1930–1931 academic year. Standardized testing was to be introduced, and curriculum modifications made. Meiklejohn and the faculty refused to comply, and the university senate and administration closed the program in the spring of 1932. The short-lived experiment, however, gave birth to a long-lived legacy: Over the next half-century, the Experimental College inspired scores of innovative undergraduate programs across the United States.

Following the closure of his college, Meiklejohn and his second wife, Helen, moved to Berkeley, California, where they helped found the San Francisco School for Social Studies. The school was open and free to all applicants—from traditional students to housewives, laborers, and retired persons. Beginning with the first class of 300 students in 1934, readings and discussions centered on classical social thinkers and contemporary social problems. By 1942, when the school closed due to economic pressures from World War II, more than 1,700 students were enrolling each year. Meiklejohn pursued his interests in constitutional rights to free speech, protesting against the permanent installation of the House Un-American Affairs Committee and loyalty oaths. He published *Free Speech and its Relation to Self Government* in 1948, and received honors from the American Civil Liberties Union and the Socialist League for Industrial Democracy. He served as vice president of the league for almost forty years. Alexander Meiklejohn died at the age of ninety-two.

Alexander Meiklejohn's influence is still felt in higher education. Scott Buchanan and Stringfellow Barr rebuilt St. John's College based on Meiklejohn's Experimental College in Wisconsin and Robert M. Hutchins' reforms at the University of Chicago. In Meiklejohn's later years, he was a "sympathetic observer" and senior guide for Joseph Tussman and others who founded the Experimental College at the University of California, Berkeley. Tussman described himself in those years as a "direct spiritual descendent" of Alexander Meiklejohn.

See also: HIGHER EDUCATION IN THE UNITED STATES, *subentry on* HISTORICAL DEVELOPMENT; LIBERAL ARTS COLLEGES.

BIBLIOGRAPHY

BROWN, CYNTHIA STOKES. 1981. *Alexander Meiklejohn: Teacher of Freedom.* Berkeley, CA: Meiklejohn Civil Liberties Institute.

TUSSMAN, JOSEPH. 1969. *Experiment at Berkeley.* New York: Oxford University Press.

L. JACKSON NEWELL
PADRAIC MACLEISH

MEMORY

AUTOBIOGRAPHICAL MEMORY
 Charles P. Thompson
DEVELOPMENT OF
 Patricia J. Bauer
 Rebecca M. Starr
GRAPHICS, DIAGRAMS, AND VIDEOS
 Priti Shah
IMPLICIT MEMORY
 Henry L. Roediger III
 Lisa Geraci
MENTAL MODELS
 Gabriel A. Radvansky
 David E. Copeland
METAMEMORY
 Gregory Schraw
 John Nietfeld
MYTHS, MYSTERIES, AND REALITIES
 Elizabeth J. Marsh
STRUCTURES AND FUNCTIONS
 Peter E. Morris

AUTOBIOGRAPHICAL MEMORY

In the early twenty-first century there is general agreement among memory researchers that memory consists of a number of distinctly different types of memory rather than one single memory. A brief overview of the major divisions in memory will help put autobiographical memory in context. Philosophers have long made a distinction between *knowing how* (e.g., knowing how to ride a bicycle) and *knowing what* (e.g., knowing what a bicycle is). Modern research has verified the distinction between these two types of memory, and they are currently called procedural or implicit memory (knowing how) and declarative or explicit memory (knowing what). In 1972 Endel Tulving divided declarative memory into semantic and episodic memory. Semantic memory, because it contains general information such as facts, names, and important historical dates, could be described as a person's knowledge of the world. Episodic memory refers to a person's memory of events.

Autobiographical memory is a large and important subset of episodic memory containing those events that constitute the story of one's life. In the words of Katherine Nelson, autobiographical memory is "specific, personal, long-lasting, and (usually) of significance to the self-system. Phenomenally, it forms one's personal life history" (p. 8). If the first meeting with a loved one involves going to a movie, that event stands a good chance of becoming part of autobiographical memory. Other occasions on which movies are attended, however, will be remembered for a short time but probably will not become part of autobiographical memory. Instead, those events will contribute to generic memory. Generic memory contains memory for frequently occurring events such as brushing teeth or going to a movie. When asked about such events, it is unlikely that a specific instance of toothbrushing or going to a movie will be remembered.

The Organization of Autobiographical Memory

Autobiographical memory is organized as nested clusters of events that are all highly interconnected. Take the memory of a lawyer as a hypothetical example. Under the topic of school, that person would find events for elementary school, secondary school, college, and law school. Nested under each of those categories would be the events for each year (e.g., sophomore in college). Under the category of sophomore in college would be the events for each semester, which, in turn, would be grouped in categories such as academic events (e.g., classes), jobs, and friends. All these autobiographical events would be accessible in a number of ways. A particular event might involve a certain year in college, a particular job, and certain friends. That event could be accessed when thinking about school, friends, or jobs.

The topic of school is just one example of the many topics that have many subcategories. Other such topics include marriage, jobs, and military service. Just like the clusters of events nested under topics, the topics also are highly interconnected. The end result is a memory system that has the ability to retrieve the memory of a particular event from a large number of starting points. The most obvious example of the power of autobiographical memory to retrieve events is involuntary memory—memories that just pop into mind. In a 1998 article Dorthe Berntsen described her studies of involuntary memories, which showed that people average six to eight such memories every day.

Memory for Autobiographical Events

Remembering an autobiographical event usually involves both retrieving the content of the event (remembering what) and placing it in time (remembering when). Of course, memory for both fades over time. Autobiographical memory can be either reproductive or reconstructive. When it is reproductive, virtually all the details are retrieved from memory. When it is reconstructive, a few major points are retrieved from memory and the rest is constructed from generic memory. People are very good at reconstructing memory from generic events, and they are usually not aware that they are doing so. One of the consequences is that memory for old events is often wrong. Sometimes the error is minor and sometimes it is not.

Memory researchers have shown that memory for the content of the event gradually changes from being almost entirely reproductive to being, after about a year, almost entirely reconstructive. By contrast, memory for when an event occurred is almost always entirely reconstructive.

There are three additional distinctive characteristics of memory for autobiographical events. First, as time passes, the number of events that can be recalled drops off rapidly at first and then more slowly—a negatively decelerating curve. Second, older people show what David C. Rubin and his colleagues called a "reminiscence bump." Older people recall more events for the period when they were in their twenties than predicted by the negatively decelerating memory curve. Typically, many important life events (such as college graduation, marriage, and children) occur when people are in their twenties. Research has shown that the reminiscence bump can be attributed to these important life events. Third, almost all people show infantile amnesia. When people are asked to recall events from their childhood, they usually cannot recall events prior to age three. Not only are they unable to recall memories before age three, but the number of memories retrieved between ages three and six is also markedly below the number available after that period. Infantile amnesia is an intriguing puzzle because researchers have shown that children under age three can report details of isolated specific events and, most important, can remember them for up to two years. There is a growing consensus that the answer to the puzzle may lie in the development of autobiographical memory.

The Development of Autobiographical Memory

By the early twenty-first century there was considerable evidence that children learn how to talk about memories with others. They learn how to tell their life stories as a narrative. This is the social interaction view of autobiographical memory. This view proposes that infantile amnesia is overcome when children learn how to retain their memories in a recoverable form by turning them into narratives.

One strong source of support for the social interaction view has been the investigation of mother-child discussions of past events. These discussions can be classified as narrative or pragmatic. The narrative conversations focused on what happened when, where, and with whom. The pragmatic conversations used memory to retrieve specific information such as "Where did you put your book?" Children of mothers who used the narrative type of discussion remember more about the events than children of mothers who used the pragmatic type of discussion.

Autobiographical Memory as an Expert System: Implications for Learning

Experts learn new material in their field much faster than novices, and they retain that material much better as well. The reason for their outstanding performance in learning and memory is that they have a highly organized and detailed memory for their area of expertise. This allows them to relate new material to one or more pieces of information that they already know. Metaphorically speaking, they have many potential pegs on which they can hang new in-

formation. When they have to retrieve the new information, they can follow a well-beaten path to that information.

Autobiographical memory is also a highly organized and detailed memory. When it is possible to relate new information to life events, autobiographical memory functions in the same way as an expert system. The new information will be learned faster and remembered better than information that cannot be related to life events (or to another expert system).

Life Is Pleasant—and Autobiographical Memory Makes It Better

In studies of subjective well-being conducted around the world, people generally report that they are happy with their life. In the United States, this positive feeling is found in people with physical disabilities, people with mental illness, low-income people, minorities—in short, it is found for virtually all categories. Research on autobiographical memory shows two sources for this positive feeling of well-being. First, life events are generally pleasant with positive events occurring roughly twice as often as negative events. This is true for childhood memories, involuntary memories, and adult memories.

Second, the general level of pleasantness typically is enhanced when remembering life events. That occurs because the emotion attached to the events fades over time but the emotion for unpleasant events fades much faster than the emotion for pleasant events. Thus, the overall emotional tone becomes more pleasant for autobiographical memory. The mechanism responsible for this change appears to be the rehearsal (thinking about or talking about) of pleasant events.

For most people, autobiographical memory is a very positive and useful part of memory. It is equivalent to an expert system and therefore can be very helpful in learning new material. Most important, it holds the story of one's life. That story is typically very pleasant and, because negative emotions fade rapidly, becomes more pleasant as time passes. People's lives would be much reduced without their access to autobiographical memory.

See also: MEMORY, *subentries on* DEVELOPMENT OF, MYTHS, MYSTERIES, AND REALITIES.

BIBLIOGRAPHY

BERNTSEN, DORTHE. 1998. "Voluntary and Involuntary Access to Autobiographical Memory." *Memory* 6:113–141.

DIENER, ED, and DIENER, CAROL. 1996. "Most People Are Happy." *Psychological Science* 7:181–185.

FIVUSH, ROBYN; HADEN, CATHERINE; and REESE, ELAINE. 1995. "Remembering, Recounting, and Reminiscing: The Development of Autobiographical Memory in Social Context." In *Constructing Our Past: An Overview of Autobiographical Memory,* ed. David C. Rubin. New York: Cambridge University Press.

HUDSON, JUDITH A. 1990. "The Emergence of Autobiographic Memory in Mother-Child Conversation." In *Knowing and Remembering in Young Children,* ed. Robyn Fivush and Judith A. Hudson. New York: Cambridge University Press.

NELSON, KATHERINE. 1993. "The Psychological and Social Origins of Autobiographical Memory." *Psychological Science* 4:7–14.

RUBIN, DAVID C.; RAHHAL, TAMARA A.; and POON, LEONARD W. 1998. "Things Learned in Early Adulthood Are Remembered Best." *Memory and Cognition* 26:3–19.

THOMPSON, CHARLES P.; SKOWRONSKI, JOHN J.; LARSEN, STEEN; and BETZ, ANDREW. 1996. *Autobiographical Memory: Remembering What and Remembering When.* New York: Erlbaum.

TULVING, ENDEL. 1972. "Episodic and Semantic Memory." In *Organization of Memory,* ed. Endel Tulving and Wayne Donaldson. New York: Academic Press.

WALDFOGEL, SAMUEL. 1949. "The Frequency and Affective Character of Childhood Memories." *Psychological Monographs* 62 (whole no. 291).

WALKER, W. RICHARD; VOGL, RODNEY J.; and THOMPSON, CHARLES P. 1997. "Autobiographical Memory: Unpleasantness Fades Faster than Pleasantness over Time." *Applied Cognitive Psychology* 11:399–413.

CHARLES P. THOMPSON

DEVELOPMENT OF

Traditionally, the construct of memory has been divided into a number of different types, defined largely in terms of the length of time over which information is retained or stored. For example, memory is divided into a very brief (on the order of milliseconds) sensory store for visual or acoustic properties of a stimulus; short-term or working memory, in which information can be stored and manipulated for about twenty seconds; and long-term memory, in which information can be stored virtually permanently. Long-term memory can be further divided into storage of procedures or skills, such as how to tie a shoe, and storage of explicit or declarative memories, such as memories of personal events or of general knowledge about the world. The study of the development of each of these systems can aid in understanding the cognitive abilities of both children and adults. Because working memory has important implications for learning and education, it is the focus of this entry.

Defining and Measuring Working Memory

Whereas short-term memory refers to the storage of information over brief delays, working memory refers to the capacity to store information for brief periods and to manipulate it during storage. A prominent model of working memory suggests that it is a multicomponent resource consisting of a limited-capacity central executive or "work space," where processing takes place, and two storage components, one for verbal information and one for spatial information. Working memory underlies a variety of complex cognitive tasks, including reading comprehension and mental arithmetic. For example, mentally adding the numbers 12 and 49 requires that both numbers be held in mind as the operation of addition is performed. Because conscious manipulation of information depends on working memory, one must examine its development in order to understand the abilities of different aged children to comprehend, learn, and remember the information taught to them.

Unlike the capacity for long-term memory, which is considered to be virtually unlimited, the capacity for working memory is limited to a few items. Indeed, the increase in the number of items that can be stored and manipulated at a time (referred to as the working memory "span") is a major source of age-related change in working memory. Moreover, at any given age, there are differences among individuals in their working memory spans. Measures of working memory span thus are integral to the study of working memory. Methods of assessing working memory include the reading span task, the A-not-B task, and the imitation task.

The reading span task. A classic measure of working memory in adults is the reading span task. Reading span is assessed by having adults read a series of sentences and then recall the final word of each of the sentences in the order that they read them. The reading span task requires both the storage and manipulation of information: The reader must store the last word of each sentence while reading subsequent words and sentences. Measures have also been developed to assess working memory throughout childhood, and these measures reveal systematic increases in working memory capacity across age.

The A-not-B task. In the second half of the first year of life, working memory most frequently is assessed by the A-not-B task. In the A-not-B task, a small toy is hidden in one of two identical wells (Well A) in full view of the infant. After a brief delay, the infant is allowed to reach into Well A to find the toy. Following several "A" trials, the toy is hidden in the second well (Well B). Even though the infants watch as the toy is hidden in Well B, they often reach to Well A again, making the "A-not-B error." Overcoming the A-not-B error, and thus, successfully searching in Well B, requires that infants (1) remember where they saw the toy hidden (requiring storage of information) and (2) inhibit the learned tendency to reach to Well A (requiring processing of information). As working memory ability increases, infants are able to withstand longer delays without making the A-not-B error. The delay that infants are able to tolerate without making the error increases about two seconds per month between the ages of seven to twelve months.

The imitation task. In the second year of life, working memory can be assessed using imitation. In a standard imitation task designed to assess short-term or long-term memory, props are used to produce a sequence of actions (e.g., making a rattle by putting a ball into a nesting cup [step 1], covering it with another cup [step 2], and shaking the cups to make a rattle [step 3]). The child then is allowed to imitate the sequence either immediately (as a measure of short-term memory) or after a delay (as a measure of long-term memory). To assess working memory, the steps of several sequences are presented in interleaved order. That is, rather than the steps of a single event in sequence (A-1, A-2, A-3, with the alphabetic character referring to the sequence and the number referring to a step in the sequence), the child sees, for example, A-1, B-1, C-1, A-2, B-2, C-2, A-3, B-3, C-3. The child is then provided with the materials for each of the sequences in turn (e.g., all of the materials for sequence A) and is encouraged to produce the sequences. The interleaving of the sequences during presentation requires that the child not only store the information for each individual step but also attend to subsequent steps and integrate the steps into their respective sequences. Researchers have used the imitation task with seventeen- and twenty-month-old children, finding increases in performance, and therefore in working memory, with age.

Tasks for assessing older children. Working memory may be assessed in older children with an adaptation of the reading span task and with a similar task using numbers. Both tasks indicate increases in working memory across the age range of seven to thirteen years. In addition, children with reading disabilities perform at lower levels on both tasks than do their normal age-mates, and children with arithmetic disabilities have trouble with the number task. Thus, working memory plays an important role in the development of reading and number skills during middle childhood. Adult levels of performance on working memory tasks are reached by the high school years.

Factors Affecting Developmental Changes in Working Memory

Developmental changes in working memory may be due to several factors, including brain maturation, increases in the speed of information processing, increases in knowledge, better use of strategies, and more effective management of attention. For example, the processes involved in working memory are largely dependent on the prefrontal cortex of the brain. The prefrontal cortex matures late relative to other brain regions, such as those involved in sensory and motor processes, and does not reach full maturity until adolescence or even early adulthood. Thus, the time courses of development of the functions of working memory and of the brain regions thought to support them are closely linked. Brain maturation also involves a process called myelination, in which a fatty substance surrounds the nerve cells and aids in the conduction of brain impulses. Myelination may increase the speed of processing, thereby increasing working memory abilities as children mature: Faster processing allows for the storage of more information before it decays from working memory.

Other factors that may affect the development of working memory include increased knowledge, strategy use, and management of the focus of attention. Breadth of knowledge affects working memory to the extent that new information can be linked to existing knowledge. For example, it is easier to store nine letters that form three words that are already stored in long-term memory (e.g., p-e-n, d-o-g, h-a-t) than to store a list of nine random letters in working memory (e.g., p-o-h-e-d-t-n-g-a). The learning of and increased efficiency in the use of strategies also aids working memory. For example, as children reach the late grade-school years, they begin to spontaneously use rehearsal (the strategy of repeating the information mentally) when they attempt to remember something new. Working memory also develops with age as children gain increasing control over the focus of their attention. This permits them to attend to more information, switch the focus of attention as needed, and inhibit attention to irrelevant information. All three of these factors—increased knowledge, strategy use, and management of attention—likely play a role in the development of working memory throughout childhood.

Summary

Working memory involves the conscious storage and manipulation of information that is integral to the performance of complex cognitive tasks. It is clear that working memory develops throughout childhood, as children are able to hold increasingly more information "online" even as they perform a greater number of mental manipulations on the information. Because working memory underlies so much of mental functioning, it is important to understand its development, as well as the sources and implications of individual differences in it.

See also: MEMORY, *subentry on* MYTHS, MYSTERIES, AND REALITIES.

BIBLIOGRAPHY

BADDELEY, ALAN. 1981. "The Concept of Working Memory: A View of Its Current State and Probable Future Development." *Cognition* 10:17–23.

BADDELEY, ALAN, and HITCH, GRAHAM. 1974. "Working Memory." In *The Psychology of Learning and Motivation,* ed. Gordon A. Bower. New York: Academic Press.

BAUER, PATRICIA J.; VAN ABBEMA, DANA L.; and DE HAAN, MICHELLE. 1999. "In for the Short Haul: Immediate and Short-Term Remembering and Forgetting by Twenty-Month-Old Children." *Infant Behavior and Development* 22:321–343.

BAUER, PATRICIA J.; WENNER, JENNIFER A.; DROPIK, PATRICIA L.; and WEWERKA, SANDI S. 2000. "Parameters of Remembering and Forgetting in the Transition from Infancy to Early Childhood." *Monograph of the Society for Research in Child Development* 65(4).

CASE, ROBBIE D.; KURLAND, MIDIAN; and GOLDBERG, JILL. 1982. "Operational Efficiency and the Growth of Short-Term Memory Span." *Journal of Experimental Child Psychology* 33:386–404.

COWAN, NELSON. 1997. "The Development of Working Memory." In *The Development of Memory in Childhood,* ed. Nelson Cowan. Hove, East Sussex, Eng.: Psychology Press.

DANEMAN, MEREDYTH, and CARPENTER, PATRICIA. 1980. "Individual Differences in Working Memory and Reading." *Journal of Verbal Learning and Verbal Behavior* 19:450–466.

DIAMOND, ADELE. 1985. "Development of the Ability to Use Recall to Guide Action, as Indicated by Infants' Performance on A not B." *Child Development* 56:868–883.

GATHERCOLE, SUSAN. 1998. "The Development of Memory." *Journal of Child Psychology and Psychiatry* 39:3–27.

LUCIANA, MONICA, and NELSON, CHARLES A. 1998. "The Functional Emergence of Prefrontally-Guided Working Memory Systems in Four- to Eight-Year-Old Children." *Neuropsychologia* 36:273–293.

SIEGAL, LINDA S., and RYAN, ELLEN B. 1989. "The Development of Working Memory in Normally Achieving and Subtypes of Learning Disabled Children." *Child Development* 60:973–980.

STARR, REBECCA M.; DE HAAN, MICHELLE; and BAUER, PATRICIA J. 2001. "Piecing It Together: Assessing Working Memory in Preverbal Children." Paper presented at the biennial meeting of the Society for Research in Child Development, Minneapolis, MN.

PATRICIA J. BAUER
REBECCA M. STARR

GRAPHICS, DIAGRAMS, AND VIDEOS

Graphics, diagrams, and videos are frequently used to enhance learning of verbal material. Indeed, as much as half of the space in K–12 textbooks is devoted to graphics and diagrams, and videos are frequently presented in classrooms. Furthermore, recent technological advances have made possible the use of additional, primarily visual, materials for instruction, such as animation and hypertext.

Presumably, graphics, diagrams, video, and other visual materials are used to make information accessible and memorable. But how might such visual materials be exploited to facilitate learning and memory? When are such displays actually beneficial for learning, and when are they simply decorative or even distracting? This brief review begins with a discussion of general research on how visual media displays aid comprehension and enhance memory for verbal material, and the circumstances in which visual materials are distracting and perhaps even reduce comprehension memory of verbal material. This discussion incorporates guidelines for the design of visual displays for effectively enhancing memory in the context of specific commonly used displays such as graphic organizers, graphs, diagrams, and videos.

Main Benefits of Graphics, Diagrams, and Videos

Visual displays and videos play a number of important roles in learning. Perhaps the most cited cognitive explanation for the benefits of presenting information both visually and verbally is Allan Paivio's dual-coding theory. In classic memory studies, Paivio and his colleagues demonstrated that people were better at remembering lists of words coded visually and verbally, rather than merely verbally. One explanation for the superiority of dual-coding is that by encoding information to be learned in two modalities rather than a single modality, people have multiple retrieval cues that help them access information, thus enhancing memory.

A second general benefit of visuo-spatial displays is that they are visually appealing. Viewers' attention is attracted to these displays, and viewers are more likely to study them for longer periods of time. This, in turn, can lead to enhancement of memory for information depicted in them. For example, one study of memory for materials taught in introductory psychology courses found that students recalled ideas and examples presented in videos and in-class demonstrations better than information presented in the text alone.

In addition to directly enhancing memory for information, diagrams, graphics, and videos can also make complex information easier to comprehend. Specifically, visual representation can make complex information "visually obvious" and thus require less cognitive effort to understand than text-based descriptions of the same information. Better comprehension, along with more cognitive resources that can be allocated to learning and memory, will together enhance memory for the information to be learned.

Concepts that Visual Displays Are Most Useful in Communicating

Visual displays are particularly beneficial to the comprehension of some classes of concepts that often involve specialized types of displays. First, visual displays are useful for communicating cause-and-effect information. For example, a diagram can help illustrate how turning a key can unlock a door. When such displays are designed to highlight the cause-and-effect sequence (e.g., by animating one portion at a time or by using a sequence of arrows), viewers' comprehension and memory for the cause-and-effect information is enhanced.

Second, visual displays are frequently useful for representing relationships amongst elements (e.g., a Venn diagram, a text-based graphic organizer, a scientific model). One benefit of such representations is that they can facilitate problem solving. Another benefit is that they provide concrete representation of key concepts or elements and their relationships. Graphic organizers, for example, are often used to represent relationships among the main ideas in a text. For example, information in a text can be summarized in matrix form such that similar concepts are closer together along one or more dimensions. Research has suggested that representations that group relevant concepts, such as matrices, can significantly enhance memory for text compared to representations that simply summarize materials, such as outlines. Indeed a general principle that is relevant for any diagram intended to represent relationship elements, including graphic organizers but also including graphs, flowcharts, and so on, is that information that is closely related be placed close together on a page or related visually (e.g., via Gestalt principles of grouping).

Third, visual displays are useful for communicating information that is intrinsically visuospatial. For example, visual displays of a map of a building or a drawing of how different parts of a car engine fit together communicate information that is difficult to describe verbally. Not all intrinsically visuospatial displays, however, are equally beneficial. One general guideline is to design displays that facilitate integrating relevant information (placing text and graphics together) to reduce working memory load and allow viewers to focus on learning relevant content. A 2001 book by Richard Mayer on multimedia learning includes a number of guidelines for the design of such displays.

Fourth, visual displays provide natural mappings to quantitative information (e.g., more is higher) and thus increase comprehension and memory for quantitative information. One difficulty associated with graphs is that students often make interpretation errors and therefore remember erroneous data. In a 2002 article, Priti Shah and James Hoeffner discuss a set of guidelines for teachers and other graph designers who need to depict data for students. These guidelines include making relevant trends visually salient in the graph and writing text to be compatible with information in the graph.

Additional Benefits of Visual Displays

In addition to making some concepts easier to understand, diagrams, graphics, and videos tend to focus viewers' or readers' attention and thus highlight important information. Displays or videos can guide a viewer's attention from one step to the next in a description of causal information or in instructions. For example, a sequence of arrows might highlight how a mechanical device, such as a bicycle pump or a toilet, works, or a sequence of panels might instruct someone how to bake cookies. Such displays, by highlighting information or key elements in a sequence, help students learn and remember relevant information.

In addition to the cognitive aspects of how they influence memory, visual displays and videos serve a social function beneficial to memory. In particular, visual displays and videos provide a common motivating experience for students. In "anchored instruction," students view movies with built-in problems that serve as a reference point for lessons on a wide variety of topics such as solving mathematical problems, discussing social issues, and understanding physics concepts. The common anchor may provide a social and personal context for information to be learned.

The use of graphics, diagrams, and videos includes not just presenting such visual information to students but also asking them to create them. Creating visual artifacts or inscriptions appears to be motivating to students, especially when they share their products with fellow students. Furthermore, developing them forces students to consider the important elements and relationships and also to identify what information they understand and what they do not. Thus, the creation of graphics, diagrams, and videos can be used to enhance comprehension and memory for to-be-learned information.

Drawbacks of Displays and Videos

Despite the benefits of graphics, diagrams, and videos for helping students comprehend and remember important information, there are some cases in which displays and videos can be harmful. Specifically, because graphics, diagrams, and videos attract attention, it is possible that in many cases such visual presentations serve as seductive details detracting attention from important information and thus impair rather than enhance learning. A concrete example of a display that may serve as a seductive detail is a picture, in a scientific text about how lightning is formed, of someone who was struck by lightning. Although the intention of such a picture might be to interest the students in the content of the text, research has found that, in fact, displays such as these are actually distracting and reduce the quality of readers' understanding of the scientific content of the text. Videos, also, can serve as or include seductive details detracting viewers from the main message of a particular lesson.

In summary, this general discussion of visual displays suggests that diagrams, graphics, and videos can help users comprehend relevant information and enhance memory for that information. The content and format of the information, however, should be consistent with the goals of communication. When the content is not consistent with the goals of communication, students may remember irrelevant or inaccurate information.

See also: LITERACY, *subentry on* LEARNING FROM MULTIMEDIA SOURCES; MEDIA AND LEARNING; READING, *subentry on* CONTENT AREAS.

BIBLIOGRAPHY

CLARK, JAMES M., and PAIVIO, ALLAN. 1991. "Dual Coding Theory and Education." *Educational Psychology Review* 3:149–210.

LARKIN, JILL H., and SIMON, HERBERT A. 1987. "Why a Diagram Is (Sometimes) Worth Ten Thousand Words." *Cognitive Science* 11:65–99.

MAYER, RICHARD E. 1993. "Illustrations that Instruct." In *Advances in Instructional Psychology,* ed. Robert Glaser. Hillsdale, NJ: Erlbaum.

MAYER, RICHARD E. 2001. *Multimedia Learning.* New York: Cambridge University Press.

MAYER, RICHARD E.; HEISER, JULIE; and LONN, STEVE. 2001. "Cognitive Constraints on Multimedia Learning: When Presenting More Material Results in Less Understanding." *Journal of Educational Psychology* 93:187–198.

MICHAS, IRENE C., and BERRY, DIANNE C. 2001. "Learning a Procedural Task: Effectiveness of Multimedia Presentations." *Applied Cognitive Psychology* 14:555–575.

OESTERMEIER, UWE, and HESSE, FRIEDRICH W. 2000. "Verbal and Visual Causal Arguments." *Cognition* 75:65–104.

ROBINSON, DANIEL H. 2002. *Educational Psychology Review* 14 (Special issue on text adjuncts).

ROBINSON, DANIEL H., and SKINNER, CHRISTOPHER H. 1996. "Why Graphic Organizers Facilitate Search Processes: Fewer Words or Computationally Efficient Indexing?" *Contemporary Educational Psychology* 21:166–180.

SHAH, PRITI, and HOEFFNER, JAMES. 2002. "Review of Graph Comprehension Research: Implications for Instruction." *Educational Psychology Review* 14:47–49.

VANDERBILT UNIVERSITY. THE COGNITION AND TECHNOLOGY GROUP AT VANDERBILT. 1997. *The Jasper Project: Lessons in Curriculum, Instruction, Assessment, and Professional Development.* Mahwah, NJ: Erlbaum.

VANDERSTOEP, SCOTT W.; FAGERLIN, ANGELA; and FEENSTRA, JENNIFER S. 2000. "What Do Students Remember from Introductory Psychology?" *Teaching of Psychology* 27:89–92.

PRITI SHAH

IMPLICIT MEMORY

Implicit memory refers to the expression of past events on current behavior when people are not trying to retrieve these past events and when they are usually not even aware of the events' influence. This process is different from explicit memory, which refers to conscious attempts to retrieve memories of past events; in implicit memory tests there is no conscious effort to retrieve. The customary use of the terms *memory* or *remembering* refers to explicit, conscious recollection during which people attempt to travel back in time to mentally relive or reexperience past events. Many behaviors people perform, however, reflect past learning even when they are not consciously attempting to retrieve; therefore, these behaviors reflect the manifestation of implicit memory. Some of these behaviors involve motor skills. When people tie their shoes or ride a bicycle or walk, they need not consciously retrieve their first attempts to learn these skills. The same is true of other types of learning. It is much easier to read a passage of text that one has read before, even if not consciously trying to remember the original time the passage was read. As these examples indicate, implicit learning is sometimes referred to as occurring rather automatically or at least to having an automatic component.

As a Reflection of Conscious Learning

Implicit memory measures are sometimes said to reflect unconscious learning because densely amnesic brain-damaged patients typically show intact uses of implicit memory. The data in Figure 1 are from a 1984 experiment by Peter Graf, Larry Squire, and George Mandler. They compared brain-damaged participants who displayed serious impairments on explicit memory tests such as recall and recognition to age- and education-matched control participants. In one test condition, both groups of participants studied lists of words and attempted to recall them in any order (free recall). As can be noted on the left of the graph in Figure 1, the patients recalled the words much worse than did the controls. This pattern reflects the patients' deficit on an explicit memory test, in which they were asked to consciously retrieve past events.

In the implicit test, both groups studied the lists of words but were tested by being shown three-letter stems of words with the instruction to produce the first word that came to mind in response to each stem clue. So, if the word *chair* had been in the list, participants would get *cha* and be asked to say the first word that came to mind (*chain, chapter, challenge* and so on—each stem had at least ten possible

FIGURE 1

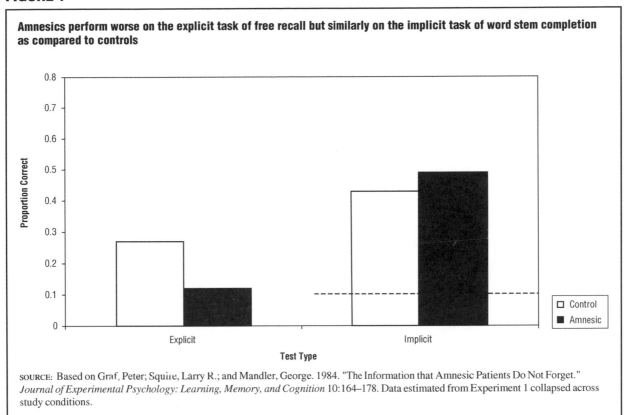

Amnesics perform worse on the explicit task of free recall but similarly on the implicit task of word stem completion as compared to controls

SOURCE: Based on Graf, Peter; Squire, Larry R.; and Mandler, George. 1984. "The Information that Amnesic Patients Do Not Forget." *Journal of Experimental Psychology: Learning, Memory, and Cognition* 10:164–178. Data estimated from Experiment 1 collapsed across study conditions.

completions). If *chair* had not been presented in the list, people in both groups produced it about 10 percent of the time (the dashed line on the right side of Figure 1). However, if *chai* had been presented in the list, both patients and the control participants produced the word about 45 percent of the time. The fact that both groups completed the word so much above the base rate reflects priming, the basic measure of implicit memory tests. Priming is defined as the difference between performance on a test when the relevant information has been presented and performance when the relevant information has not been recently presented. Therefore, the amount of priming reflected in the data in Figure 1 was about 35 percent (45% in the primed condition minus the 10% base rate). Although the participants were told to produce any word that came to mind, the presentation of chair in the list primed them to produce that word rather than another on the test.

This priming effect reflects a use of memory, but not a conscious or intentional use of memory. Because the patients were densely amnesic and probably did not remember even studying the list of words, the priming may be said to be unconscious

(in this sense). The amnesic patients produced just as much priming as did control participants. Because the patients had suffered brain damage that impaired their use of explicit memory processes, it appears that the brain mechanisms and processes that underlie explicit and implicit memory tests are quite different. Put another way, the results show that memory is not a unitary entity; people with certain types of brain damage can be severely impaired on one type of memory test and unaffected on other types of tests.

Implicit Memory Tests

The study of implicit memory began in psychology in the early 1980s and in the early twenty-first century there is a large amount of literature on the topic. There seem to be at least two distinct types of implicit memory tests, perceptual and conceptual.

Perceptual memory tests. Perceptual implicit memory tests challenge the perceptual system by presenting impoverished test stimuli to which participants respond. The word stem completion test already described (*cha*) is one such test. Others are word identification (presenting words very briefly and having participants guess what they are), and word fragment completion (naming words from fragments such as l_p_a_t. (That fragment is hard if not recently primed [with word *elephant*].) If pictures are used as study materials, then the test can involve giving fragmented forms of pictures or having them be gradually clarified through a series of successively fuller fragments until the participant can identify the picture. Again, the measure in all cases is priming—as reflected by more accurate or faster completion of the target when it has been studied relative to when it has not been studied.

Factors that greatly affect priming on perceptual implicit memory tests are often quite different from those that affect performance on most explicit memory tests in both patients and in healthy control participants, indicating further that these two types of tests seem to be measuring different processes. For example, modality of presentation of words strongly affects performance on perceptual implicit tests. Visual presentation of words enhances priming on visual tests, whereas auditory presentation enhances priming on auditory implicit tests (e.g., presenting words describing noise with auditory cues for identification). Modality generally matters little in tests of explicit memory. On the other hand, factors that can have a great effect on explicit memory tests can have little or no effect on priming on implicit tests. For example, when participants read pairs of words (*hot* and *cold*) or generate the second word from a clue such as "opposite of cold," they scored better on an explicit test of recognition for the words they generated, but exhibited more priming for the words they just read on an implicit test, in which they had to quickly identify the word. The data are shown in Figure 2.

The results described above can be explained, at a general level, by the theory of transfer appropriate processing. This principle states that performance on memory tests will be enhanced if there is a match between the conditions of study and test, which will permit the study experience to transfer better to the test. For example, if the test involves deciphering a fragmented or briefly presented word given visually (classified as a perceptual test), then performance on this test should benefit from prior visual presentation more than from a prior auditory presentation or from generating the word, as is indeed the case. Practice reading a visual word (versus hearing or generating it) transfers better to a test that also involves reading words.

Conceptually driven tests. Whereas most implicit tests depend on perceptual processing, most explicit memory tests depend heavily on the meaning of the concepts or events that are being remembered. These tests are called conceptually driven tests because, when people are trying to retrieve past events, it is the meaning of the events that is important. Generating a word involves more attention to meaning than simply reading it, and so generating produced greater explicit recognition in results shown in Figure 2. Again, this finding is in accord with the transfer appropriate processing theory. The transfer appropriate processing theory can account for a large body of findings although some problems remain.

Although explicit memory tests are usually driven by meaning or by conceptual information, there is a class of implicit memory tests that is also conceptually driven. These tests are probably the most relevant for education, but they have not yet been studied as much as perceptual implicit tests. One class of conceptual implicit memory tests that has been studied is the general knowledge test. "What animal did Hannibal use to help him cross the Alps in his attack on Rome?" and "What is the name of the ship that carried the pilgrims to America in 1620?" are examples of questions on general knowledge tests. Prior exposure to the words *elephant* or *Mayflower* before the questions are asked increases correct answers to these questions, which reflects priming of concepts. Free association tests ("say the first word that you think of to the stimulus word *tusk*") and category association tests ("list as many African animals as you can in thirty seconds") are other examples of conceptually driven implicit memory tests. These priming effects again seem to be indicative of implicit retrieval because they also appear in brain-damaged patients with severe difficulties in explicit expressions of memory.

In some sense, much of education is intended to permit people the automatic, unconscious retrieval of facts, routines, and principles when they need them. Education is meant to provide learning experiences that will, at least in some cases, last a lifetime. Of course, not all facts and principles will be remembered for that long. Much information learned in the classroom will be forgotten (at least when explicit tests are given). The hope is that one's general knowledge and skills (writing, thinking logically)

FIGURE 2

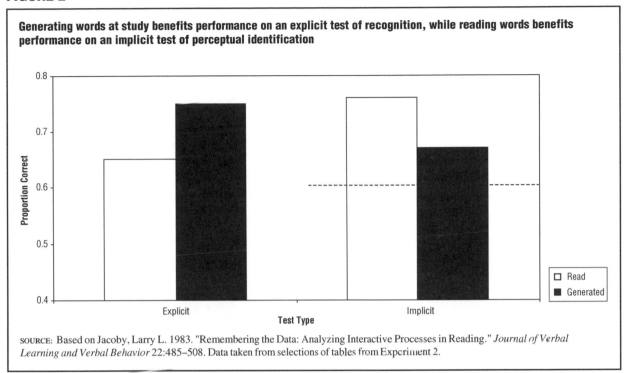

Generating words at study benefits performance on an explicit test of recognition, while reading words benefits performance on an implicit test of perceptual identification

SOURCE: Based on Jacoby, Larry L. 1983. "Remembering the Data: Analyzing Interactive Processes in Reading." *Journal of Verbal Learning and Verbal Behavior* 22:485–508. Data taken from selections of tables from Experiment 2.

will survive. There are no studies of residual, implicit retention of formal education but such studies will surely come in the future.

See also: MEMORY, *subentries on* MYTHS, MYSTERIES, AND REALITIES, STRUCTURES AND FUNCTIONS.

BIBLIOGRAPHY

BLAXTON, TERESA A. 1989. "Investigating Dissociations among Memory Measures: Support for a Transfer-Appropriate Processing Framework." *Journal of Experimental Psychology: Learning, Memory, and Cognition* 15:657–668.

GARDINER, HOWARD; BOLLER, FRANCOIS; MOREINES, JUDITH; and BUTTERS, NELSON. 1973. "Retrieving Information from Korsakoff Patients: Effects of Categorical Cues and Reference to the Task." *Cortex* 9:165–175.

GRAF, PETER; SQUIRE, LARRY R.; and MANDLER, GEORGE. 1984. "The Information that Amnesic Patients Do Not Forget." *Journal of Experimental Psychology: Learning, Memory, and Cognition* 10:164–178.

JACOBY, LARRY L. 1983. "Remembering the Data: Analyzing Interactive Processes in Reading." *Journal of Verbal Learning and Verbal Behavior* 22:485–508.

JACOBY, LARRY L., and DALLAS, MARK. 1981. "On the Relationship between Autobiographical Memory and Perceptual Learning." *Journal of Experimental Psychology: General* 110:306–340.

MCDERMOTT, KATHLEEN B., and ROEDIGER, HENRY L. 1996. "Exact and Conceptual Repetition Dissociates Conceptual Memory Tests: Problems for Transfer Appropriate Processing Theory." *Canadian Journal of Experimental Psychology* 50:57–71.

ROEDIGER, HENRY L. 1990. "Implicit Memory: Retention without Remembering." *American Psychologist* 45:1043–1056.

ROEDIGER, HENRY L., and MCDERMOTT, KATHLEEN B. 1993. "Implicit Memory in Normal Human Subjects." In *Handbook of Neuropsychology,* ed. François Boller and Jordan Grafman. Amsterdam: Elsevier.

SCHACTER, DANIEL L. 1987. "Implicit Memory: History And Current Status." *Journal of Experimental Psychology: Learning, Memory, and Cognition* 13:501–518.

SQUIRE, LARRY R. 1987. *Memory and the Brain.* New York: Oxford University Press.

TULVING, ENDEL. 1985. "How Many Memory Systems Are There?" *American Psychologist* 40:385–398.

VAIDYA, CHANDAN J.; GABRIELI, JOHN D. E.; KEANE, MARGARET M.; and MONTI, LAURA A. 1995. "Perceptual and Conceptual Memory Processes in Global Amnesia." *Neuropsychology* 9:580–591.

HENRY L. ROEDIGER III
LISA GERACI

MENTAL MODELS

Mental models, also called situation models, are mental representations of the state of affairs in a real or possible world. They serve as mental simulations of events. For reading, a mental model represents the situation described by the text rather than the text itself. The creation of a coherent mental model is the goal of comprehension.

Mental models are complex representations that contain many different types of information. This includes a spatial-temporal framework about the spatial context in which an event occurred and the time period in which the event transpired (i.e., where and when it occurred). They also contain tokens to represent entities, such as people, animals, objects, and ideas. These tokens might have properties associated with them, such as physical characteristics, emotions, or names. Within a framework there may be structural relations that define the event. This can include spatial relations (e.g., the umpire is behind home plate), ownership relations (e.g., the players are using the shortstop's ball), social relations (e.g., the two teams are bitter rivals), and so forth. Finally, because events are dynamic, several frameworks can be joined by linking relations that contain temporal order and causal information.

The Role of Experience

Mental model creation involves integrating prior knowledge with what has been given. This allows inferences to be drawn for information that has not been provided. Of course, the more knowledge a person has, the more likely it is that an adequate mental model will be constructed. For example, when watching a baseball game, a person with a lot of baseball knowledge will better understand the structure of the game, the causal and goal-related relations among the players, and the sequence of events.

The structure of one's experience influences the creation of mental models. Suppose a person reads a text on a topic that the reader has a fair amount of knowledge of, such as going to a baseball game. In this case, there is a certain sequence in which the events occur (e.g., buying a ticket before finding one's seat). Even if two events are adjacent in the text, reading times increase as the distance between them in the standard sequence increases. So when building mental models, people consult their knowledge systematically. It is as if they are scanning sequentially through their knowledge to assess where the current events fit. The greater the distance, the longer the scanning process and the more that needs to be inferred.

Mental models are essentially an amalgam of the given information that can be acquired through a film, book, lecture, discussion, and so forth, along with prior knowledge that a person has in long-term memory. The use of mental models is found in a wide variety of circumstances, including language comprehension and memory.

Comprehension

Mental models are critical for understanding. When people comprehend language, they create three types of mental representations. The simplest is a verbatim representation of what was heard or read. This is forgotten very quickly unless there is something important about the exact wording, as with a joke. At a more abstract level is the propositional textbase. This is a representation of the idea units that were expressed. For example, the sentences "The ball was hit by the batter" and "The batter hit the ball" would correspond to the same propositional representation. This representation is forgotten less rapidly. Finally, at the most abstract and highest level is the mental model. This is a referential representation of the described events. The mental model is a representation of what the message is about. In contrast, the verbatim and textbase levels are representations of the message itself but may serve as scaffolding from which to build a mental model.

While the goal of comprehension is to construct a mental model, its organization and function can influence comprehension itself. During reading, people keep track of what is going on in the described situation. For example, readers may keep track of the spatial location of a protagonist in a story. When that person moves from one location to another, knowledge about people or objects in the old location become less available. Switching from one spatial framework to another influences what information is readily available during comprehension. Moreover, the further the protagonist moves from the original location, the less available the information becomes. A similar thing occurs for temporal frameworks. Short time periods are more likely to be part of the same time frame, whereas long time periods are more likely to include a shift to a new time frame, and hence a new situation. Information that was relevant to the original situation is less available after a large time shift. Finally, people also monitor a protagonist's goals. Information that is relevant to current, unsatisfied goals is more available than information relating to goals that were successfully completed. The prior goal information is no longer maintained in the current mental model.

When the structure of the situation changes, reading times increase, as if readers are monitoring the described events. This includes changes in space, time, entities, causality, or the goals of the protagonist. When a major change in the described situation occurs, people update their mental models. In addition to monitoring event changes, people may also notice inconsistencies with what has been described before. Such inconsistencies result in increased reading times as the reader tries to resolve what they know of the situation with the current information.

One of the most important dimensions that people monitor is causality. Information varies in the degree of its causal importance. Information that plays an active role in the described situation is causally more important. Such information is typically read more quickly. Presumably, this is because it can be more easily integrated into the current mental model.

Memory

Mental models are also involved in memory. At very long periods of time, this is the representation that will dominate a person's recollections. Many of the influences during comprehension carry over into memory. For example, shifts in a situation during comprehension result in the memory being organized around those shifts. Also, causally important parts of an event are better remembered than less important parts. It should be noted that the ease

with which information is integrated into a mental model has an influence on the ability to identify that situation later. Continuous and consistent descriptions are remembered better than discontinuous, inconsistent descriptions.

Mental models include both given information and inferences a person generates. With the passage of time, it becomes difficult to disentangle these two. People often mistakenly identify information as having been encountered before if it is consistent with the previously described situation, even when that information is new.

How information refers to the world is important for how it is represented in mental models. This has important consequences for memory. When given a large set of related information, a person can integrate this information into one mental model if the information can be interpreted as being consistent with a single situation in the world. Otherwise, it may be stored in separate mental models. When a person needs to remember one piece of information, if there are related mental models containing related but irrelevant information, this will produce interference, causing the memory retrieval to be slower and more error prone. If, however, the information is integrated into a single model, there is no such cost to memory.

While these findings suggest that a mental model can influence memory retrieval, it is also possible to remove these influences to a certain degree. As mentioned earlier, people create multiple representations during comprehension, including verbatim, propositional, and mental model representations. The mental model will contain many inferences and will also capture the perspective of the comprehender. If the mental model is discredited in some way, such as asking a person to take a different perspective on the text that was read, then the person will rely less on the mental model and more on the propositional representation. For example, people reading a description of a baseball game might originally be told that the home team was going to make the playoffs. Then when the person is asked to recall the story, they could be told that the story was about a team that ended up in last place. This shift in perspective will cause a decrease in the number of inferences a person reports and also increase memory for those previously unremembered propositions that are consistent with the new perspective. Thus, the person has disregarded their mental model during memory retrieval.

Summary

Mental models are mental representations of specific states of affairs in the world. They are created using the knowledge a person has at hand, along with prior knowledge. The organization and extensiveness of this prior knowledge is of great importance. People use mental models during comprehension as the basis for their understanding. Changes in the described situations cause people to update their mental models, which has a tangible effect on the comprehension process itself. Finally, mental models appear to be the form of mental representation that is stored in memory for long periods of time. The ability of a person to remember information in part reflects the organization and structuring of information into mental models.

See also: LEARNING, *subentry on* KNOWLEDGE ACQUISITION, REPRESENTATION, AND ORGANIZATION; READING, *subentry on* COMPREHENSION.

BIBLIOGRAPHY

ALBRECHT, JASON E., and O'BRIEN, EDWARD J. 1995. "Goal Processing and the Maintenance of Global Coherence." In *Sources of Coherence in Reading,* ed. Robert F. Lorch and Edward J. O'Brien. Hillsdale, NJ: Erlbaum.

BOWER, GORDON H.; BLACK, JOHN B.; and TURNER, TERRENCE J. 1979. "Scripts in Memory for Text." *Cognitive Psychology* 11:177–220.

GARNHAM, ALAN. 1982. "Situation Models as Representations of Text." *Memory and Cognition* 9:560–565.

HASHER, LYNN, and GRIFFIN, MARY. 1978. "Reconstructive and Reproductive Processing in Memory." *Journal of Experimental Psychology: Human Learning and Memory* 4:318–330.

JOHNSON-LAIRD, PHILIP N. 1983. *Mental Models: Towards a Cognitive Science of Language, Inference, and Consciousness.* Cambridge, MA: Harvard University Press.

MORROW, DANIEL G.; GREENSPAN, STEVEN L.; and BOWER, GORDON H. 1987. "Accessibility and Situation Models in Narrative Comprehension." *Journal of Memory and Language* 26:165–187.

RADVANSKY, GABRIEL A., and COPELAND, DAVID E. 2000. "Functionality and Spatial Relations in Situation Models." *Memory and Cognition* 28:987–992.

RADVANSKY, GABRIEL A., and ZACKS, ROSE T. 1991. "Mental Models and the Fan Effect." *Journal of Experimental Psychology: Learning, Memory, and Cognition* 17:940–953.

SUH, SOO Y., and TRABASSO, THOMAS. 1993. "Inferences during Reading: Converging Evidence from Discourse Analysis, Talk-Aloud Protocols, and Recognition Priming." *Journal of Memory and Language* 32:279–300.

VAN DIJK, TIEN A., and KINTSCH, WALTER. 1983. *Strategies in Discourse Comprehension.* New York: Academic Press.

ZWAAN, ROLF A. 1996. "Processing Narrative Time Shifts." *Journal of Experimental Psychology: Learning, Memory, and Cognition* 22:1,196–1,207.

ZWAAN, ROLF A.; MAGLIANO, JOSEPH P.; and GRAESSER, ARTHUR C. 1995. "Dimensions of Situation Model Construction in Narrative Comprehension." *Journal of Experimental Psychology: Learning, Memory, and Cognition* 21:386–397.

ZWAAN, ROLF A., and RADVANSKY, GABRIEL A. 1998. "Situation Models in Language Comprehension and Memory." *Psychological Bulletin* 123:162–185.

GABRIEL A. RADVANSKY
DAVID E. COPELAND

METAMEMORY

Metamemory refers to a person's knowledge about the contents and regulation of memory. The term originally derives from the work of John H. Flavell in the early 1970s. Metamemory enables a person to reflect on and monitor her memory. In addition, metamemorial knowledge plays an important role in planning, allocation of cognitive resources, strategy selection, comprehension monitoring, and evaluation of performance.

This entry begins with a description of the two main structural components of metamemory—declarative knowledge, which enables a person to evaluate the contents of memory, and procedural knowledge, which enables a person to monitor and regulate memory performance. It next summarizes important developmental trends in metamemory, then discusses several important educational implications of metamemory research, including the relationships among metamemory, strategy instruction, and self-regulation.

Declarative and Procedural Aspects of Metamemory

Most theorists distinguish between declarative and procedural components of metamemory. The declarative component corresponds to statable knowledge about the contents and contexts of memory use and includes knowledge of memory's contents, knowledge of essential intellectual tasks such as reading and problem solving, and conditional knowledge about why and when strategies are most effective. The procedural component includes knowledge about procedural skills necessary to manage memory efficiently, including control processes such as planning and evaluating and monitoring processes such as judgments of learning. Some theorists, but especially those interested in the relationship between metamemory and social cognition, have proposed a third component, usually referred to as a beliefs component, that regulates affect, social cognition, and efficacy judgments of memory performance. The focus here, however, is on the declarative and procedural components.

The declarative component includes at least three distinct subcomponents: knowledge of contents and capacity, knowledge of tasks, and conditional knowledge about optimal memory performance. The content subcomponent enables a person to assess whether he possesses enough knowledge to meet task demands. The task subcomponent allows a person to determine whether he fully understands task demands and possesses adequate resources to perform the task. The conditional knowledge subcomponent, which many view as the most important of the three, helps a person determine why, when, and where to use a particular strategy or under what conditions he is most likely to achieve optimal performance. Conditional knowledge plays an especially important role in self-regulation.

The procedural component includes control and monitoring subcomponents. The control subcomponent includes regulatory processes such as planning, selection of relevant information, resource allocation decisions, selection of relevant strategies, and inferencing. The monitoring subcomponent includes a variety of self-assessment strategies such as ease-of-learning judgments, judgments of learning prior to beginning a task, feeling-of-knowing judg-

ments made during learning, and comprehension-monitoring judgments made during or after a task. Most theories of metamemory assume that control processes directly regulate cognition and performance, whereas monitoring processes inform the precision of control decisions. Thus, control processes are at a higher level than monitoring processes, even though both reciprocally inform one another.

Development of Metamemory

A number of researchers have studied the development of metamemory, and four main conclusions can be drawn from this research. The first conclusion is that metamemory awareness is rather poor in children until the age of ten or older. Younger children frequently find it difficult to monitor the contents of memory, estimate the resources needed to complete a task, select appropriate strategies for a task, and monitor their learning. As a consequence, self-regulation is quite poor among children younger than ten years of age. Even among adults, however, metamemory awareness is poor, sometimes leading to overconfidence and illusions of knowing.

A second conclusion is that metamemory development is incremental and continuous. Development appears to be linear in nature with a steady increase in metamemory awareness, control, and monitoring from preschool through early puberty. Research generally does not reveal significant breaks or jumps in metamemory ability, suggesting continuous development over a ten-year period from early childhood through adolescence. It is less clear whether metamemory awareness continues to develop in adults, although most research indicates that awareness increases within specific domains as expertise develops.

A third conclusion is that metamemorial knowledge is self-constructed in nature through individual and interactive problem solving, as well as explicit strategy instruction and monitoring training. One essential element of the construction process is self-generated and other-generated feedback that increases knowledge of the contents of memory and tasks. A second essential element is modeling, in which an individual has the opportunity to observe and emulate skilled models. Thus far, researchers have failed to detect a strong link between metamemory and either intellectual ability or traditional measures of working memory speed and capacity. This suggests that metamemory awareness develops independent of other individual differences in memory.

The final conclusion is that metamemory facilitates strategy use and performance. For example, correlations between metamemory and memory performance typically range from .30 to .50, even in younger children between the ages of five and ten years. The correlation may be even stronger in adults and experts. Knowledge about the contents of one's memory as well as tasks clearly should affect performance. In addition, declarative knowledge appears to be correlated with regulatory awareness. The more one knows about memory, the better able one is to regulate one's performance.

Metamemory and Learning

Metamemory affects learning in many ways but especially with respect to the efficient use of limited cognitive resources, strategy use, and comprehension monitoring. Children and adults often experience difficulty learning because of cognitive overload—that is, too much mental work to do and too few cognitive resources at their disposal. Research reveals that declarative and procedural knowledge enables learners to use available resources more efficiently because they are better able to plan, sequence, and monitor learning tasks.

A second way that metamemory improves learning is through the flexible use of cognitive learning strategies. Research indicates that self-regulated learners use a diverse repertoire of strategies that are controlled using conditional knowledge in metamemory. Strategy use is highly correlated with skilled problem solving. Research also suggests that strategy training increases metamemory awareness, provided that conditional knowledge about the strategies is embedded within the instruction. In 1999 Roger Bruning, Gregg Schraw, and Royce Ronning provided a step-by-step summary of cognitive strategy instruction that includes feedback and modeling from peers, tutors, and teachers. Strategy instruction is especially effective for helping students develop conditional knowledge that enables them to select the most appropriate strategy and monitor its usefulness.

A third way that metamemory improves learning is comprehension monitoring. Unfortunately, many children and adults do not monitor with a high degree of accuracy. Monitoring training helps learners monitor more successfully and also im-

proves performance. Strategy instruction also improves monitoring even when monitoring instruction is not included as part of the instruction. Thus, either strategy instruction or monitoring training improve monitoring accuracy. Combining strategy instruction and monitoring training within the same intervention helps learners construct the control and monitoring subcomponents of regulatory knowledge described above.

Classroom Implications

Metamemory research has not had a major impact on classroom instruction. The research suggests, however, that children acquire and construct metamemory knowledge in three distinct ways. One way is hands-on experience that provides declarative knowledge about tasks as well as procedural knowledge about optimal performance. A second way is through skilled models who provide detailed feedback—especially conditional feedback—that enables the student to distinguish between effective and less-effective strategies. A third way is through self-reflection and group reflection in which students explicitly discuss the effectiveness of different strategies and ways to improve performance in the future. Thus, there are many ways to improve metamemory awareness through classroom activities.

Several learning interventions have been developed that promote metamemory development and awareness. For example, in 1984 Annemarie S. Palincsar and Ann L. Brown described a program of reciprocal teaching that promotes the self-regulation of metamemory strategies. The program involves the teacher gradually handing over control of reading processes to the student in a small-group format. The teacher first models effective strategies (e.g., finding the main idea of a passage) then provides scaffolding to the students as they attempt to do the same while receiving feedback from their peers regarding the strategies they employ.

Summary

Metamemory is knowledge about memory. Metamemory awareness develops late and incrementally yet has an important impact on memory and cognitive performance. Metamemory is not linked strongly to other cognitive factors such as intelligence and memory capacity. Rather, it develops as a function of experience, guided modeling and feedback, and individual and group reflection.

See also: LEARNING TO LEARN AND METACOGNITION; READING, *subentry on* COMPREHENSION.

BIBLIOGRAPHY

ALEXANDER, JOYCE M.; CARR, MARTHA; and SCHWANENFLUGEL, PAULA J. 1995. "Development of Metacognition in Gifted Children: Directions for Future Research." *Developmental Review* 15:1–37.

BRUNING, ROGER H.; SCHRAW, GREGG; and RONNING, ROYCE R. 1999. *Cognitive Psychology and Instruction,* 3rd edition. Upper Saddle River, NJ: Prentice Hall.

BUTLER, DEBORAH L., and WINNE, PHILIP H. 1995. "Feedback and Self-Regulated Learning: A Theoretical Synthesis." *Review of Educational Research* 65:245–282.

DIXON, ROGER A. 2000. "The Concept of Metamemory: Cognitive, Developmental, and Clinical Issues." In *Memory Disorders in Psychiatric Practice,* ed. German E. Berrios and John R. Hodges. New York: Cambridge University Press.

FLAVELL, JOHN H. 1971. "First Discussant's Comments: What Is Memory Development the Development Of?" *Human Development* 14:272–278.

METCALFE, JANET. 2000. "Metamemory: Theory and Data." In *The Oxford Handbook of Memory,* ed. Endel Tulving and Fergus Craik. New York: Oxford University Press.

NELSON, THOMAS O., and NARENS, LOUIS. 1994. "Why Investigate Metacognition?" In *Metacognition: Knowing about Knowing,* ed. Janet Metcalfe and Arthur P. Shimamura. Cambridge, MA: MIT Press.

PALINCSAR, ANNEMARIE S., and BROWN, ANN L. 1984. "Reciprocal Teaching of Comprehension-Fostering and Comprehension-Monitoring Activities." *Cognition and Instruction* 1:117–175.

SCHNEIDER, WOLFGANG. 1999. "The Development of Metamemory in Children." In *Attention and Performance XVII: Cognitive Regulation of Performance,* ed. Daniel Gopher and Asher Koriat. Cambridge, MA: MIT Press.

SCHNEIDER, WOLFGANG, and PRESSLEY, MICHAEL. 1997. *Memory Development between Two and Twenty,* 2nd edition. Mahwah, NJ: Erlbaum.

SCHRAW, GREGG. 2001. "Promoting General Metacognitive Awareness." In *Metacognition in Learning and Instruction,* ed. Hope J. Hartman. Norwell, MA: Kluwer.

SCHRAW, GREGG, and MOSHMAN, DAVID. 1995. "Metacognitive Theories." *Educational Psychology Review* 7:351–372.

STONE, N. J. 2000. "Exploring the Relationship between Calibration and Self-Regulated Learning." *Educational Psychology Review* 12:437–476.

SWELLER, JOHN; VAN MERRIENBOER, JEROEN J.; and PAAS, FRED G. 1998. "Cognitive Architecture and Instructional Design." *Educational Psychology Review* 10:251–296.

GREGORY SCHRAW
JOHN NIETFELD

MYTHS, MYSTERIES, AND REALITIES

Why is it that people remember some things and forget others? How long do people remember things? What kinds of cues are likely to help a person remember a forgotten item? These are just a few of the many questions of interest to memory researchers. This entry reviews some of the important questions in the field of memory research and describes how psychologists use experimental methods to answer these questions. It also describes some of the major findings and rebuts some of the common myths about memory. This discussion is structured around the three stages of memory: encoding, storage, and retrieval.

Encoding refers to the intake of information and creation of a memory trace. In a typical memory experiment, the encoding phase involves presentation of the to-be-remembered stimuli, such as nonsense syllables, words, pictures, stories, films, or staged events. In real life, encoding includes all forms of perception, from watching a movie to having a conversation. Encoding may be *intentional* in that subjects are forewarned to memorize the items or *incidental* in that subjects learn the to-be-remembered material through performance of another task such as making a category judgment. In educational settings, encoding is intentional when students deliberately study the meanings of vocabulary words, learn facts for a test, or memorize a famous speech. In everyday life, however, most things are learned incidentally. Examples in the education domain include students learning about a historical period by watching films, role-playing, and reading memoirs.

Storage or *retention* refers to the maintenance of the memory trace over time. In most laboratory experiments, the retention interval is quite short and the subject does an unrelated task during that time. In the education domain, there may be a retention interval of several weeks between learning and testing; students may continue to practice the target information during the retention interval.

Retrieval involves later accessing that memory trace. There are many different ways to test memory. *Explicit tests* require subjects to consciously remember events from the study phase. Most educational tests are explicit; students know they are being tested and that they should remember facts from class and textbooks. Explicit educational tests include essay, short-answer, multiple-choice, and true-false tests; these roughly correspond to the laboratory tests of free recall, cued recall, forced choice, and old-new recognition. *Implicit tests* measure the effect of previous experience on a task that does not require the subject to consciously refer back to the study phase. In education, pure implicit tests are rare although many explicit tests may tap a student's implicit knowledge (e.g., essay tests implicitly test a student's knowledge of grammar). In the laboratory, there are many different implicit tests. For example, a subject who had recently seen a list that included the word *octopus* would complete the word stem "oct___" with "octopus" at a higher rate than subjects who had not seen the list.

In the following sections, some of the facts and myths associated with each of the three stages of memory are described.

Encoding

Key questions about encoding include what kinds of things are easily memorized and what study strategies can be employed to ensure later memory.

Not all materials are remembered equally well. Pictures are remembered better than words, and in general memory is better for distinctive items. Likewise, concrete words are better remembered than abstract words. Good teachers often apply this finding by using concrete analogies to explain abstract phenomena or theories, such as when the movement of gas molecules is compared to the movement of billiard balls on a pool table.

Not all study strategies are equal. In general, elaborative encoding yields the best memory. Elaboration involves going beyond the stimulus at hand

to create a richer memory trace. For example, rather than simply repeating a to-be-memorized vocabulary word, a student might think of other words similar in sound and meaning, draw a picture that somehow represents the word and its definition, or write sentences using the word in context. In perhaps the most famous laboratory demonstration of this, Fergus I. M. Craik and Endel Tulving looked at subjects' memory for words after perceptual, phonemic, or semantic processing in a 1975 study. For example, if all subjects studied the word *EAGLE,* one group decided if the word was in uppercase letters (perceptual), the second group decided if it rhymed with legal (phonemic), and the third group decided if it was an animal (semantic). All of these questions would have been answered affirmatively, but memory was best following semantic processing, next best with phonemic processing, and worst after perceptual processing. This is the classic levels of processing effect. The educational implication is that incidental study can be just as effective as intentional memorization. If students are studying via a semantic or other elaborative task, the resulting memory can be just as strong even if they are not forewarned about the upcoming memory test.

Encoding is not like taking pictures with a camera; not everything is recorded. Instead, encoding is selective. The levels of processing effect is an example of this; depending on the instructions, subjects directed their attention to different features of the target word. More generally, what students encode will be a function of what they already know and how well they can understand and link the incoming information to their prior knowledge. A *schema* is the term for a person's knowledge representation of a concept or domain. Without a schema, the understanding and interpretation of incoming information is difficult. For example, in a 1977 study by D. James Dooling and Robert E. Christiaansen, subjects had poor memories for such passages as "With hocked gems financing him / our hero bravely defied all scornful laughter that tried to defy his scheme / Your eyes deceive, he said—an egg not a table correctly typifies this unexplored planet." Good memory required knowledge that the upcoming passage would be about Christopher Columbus. Schemas also serve to direct a subject's attention to particular schema-relevant details and to allow for inferences. For example, according to a 1977 study conducted by James Pichert and Richard Anderson, students who read a story about two boys playing hooky and spending the day at home remembered different things depending on which of two perspectives had been instantiated at encoding: home buyer or burglar. Subjects who read the story with the perspective of a burglar attended to and remembered better such details as that the house's side door was unlocked, a fact unlikely to be relevant to a home buyer.

Another fact about encoding is that more is not necessarily better; massed study is not a good idea. While many students choose to cram for exams the night before, the data clearly suggest that spaced study opportunities are preferable. The same holds true for rehearsal of to-be-remembered information, which is described in the next section on activities during the retention interval.

Storage

Encoding is a necessary but not sufficient condition for later memory. As time passes, it becomes less and less likely that a person will be able to retrieve the target event. In 1985 Herman Ebbinghaus first documented the now classic forgetting function; he taught himself series of consonant-vowel-consonant trigams and tested his memory after varying time lags. Memory dropped off quickly at first, but eventually forgetting leveled out over time to a fairly stable level. Most laboratory studies involve fairly short retention intervals; in 1984, however, Harry P. Bahrick examined knowledge of Spanish following retention intervals of up to fifty years (participants reported very little use of Spanish during that time). Again, there was a sharp drop in knowledge by three to six years poststudy, but after that initial drop, knowledge was surprisingly stable over the next twenty-five years. Bahrick termed this long-term retention the *permastore.*

Rehearsal during the retention interval aids memory; not all forms of rehearsal, however, are equal. Simply repeating a to-be-remembered item will not necessarily lead to enhanced memory. A student who writes a fact over and over will not remember that fact as well as a student who takes a more active approach to rehearsal. One of the best strategies is that of expanding rehearsal combined with self-testing. For example, the student who wants to learn a vocabulary word should not simply stare at the word paired with its definition. Rather, she should test herself and produce the definition of the word from memory; after a short delay she should repeat the process, and so on, incrementally increas-

ing the delay until the retention interval is at the desired length.

Memories do not lie dormant during the retention interval but are affected by the new information that continues to enter the system. In one classic demonstration of *interference,* subjects saw a slide show of a traffic accident involving a car passing a stop sign. In the next phase of the experiment, subjects in the experimental condition read a narrative description of the slide show that included a misleading reference to a yield sign. Control subjects also read a narrative, but it did not contain the misinformation. All subjects were later asked whether they had seen a stop sign or a yield sign. Subjects who had been exposed to the misleading post-event information were more likely to mistakenly say they had seen a yield sign than the control group. Although the exact mechanisms underlying the misinformation effect are still under debate, in at least some circumstances the misinformation works to block or interfere with access to the original memory.

Retrieval

No single test of memory is perfect. No one test yields an absolute measure of what is in memory; rather, one can ascertain what is accessible only under a particular set of test conditions. The failure to recall part of a list is not necessarily synonymous with forgetting those words. Rather, they may be *available* in memory but not *accessible* given the current retrieval cues. When asked to write down all the words from a studied list, a subject may not be able to recall studying the word *robin.* This allegedly forgotten word, however, may be recalled in response to the category cue "birds" or correctly labeled as "old" on a test that re-presents the word *robin* for an old-new decision. Similarly, a student who is unable to produce an answer on an essay test may recognize it on a multiple-choice test.

Conclusions about memory may vary across tests. Take, for example, the effects of word frequency on memory. Following study of a word list, words that occur with high frequency in the language (e.g., *tree*) are recalled with a higher probability than are words that occur with low frequency in the language (e.g., *ecru*). The opposite result, however, is obtained on recognition memory tests. When subjects are asked to label words as "old" or "new," they do a better job with low frequency than high frequency words. This paradox is one that continues to interest researchers.

So, how then to get the best performance possible on a memory test? The general rule is that the test should match study as much as possible. Returning to the levels of processing effect described earlier, semantic processing leads to better memory in part because most memory tests are semantic in nature. When subjects are given a phonological test (e.g., did you study a word that rhymes with *beagle*?), performance is better when words are encoded as rhymes than when they are categorized. Effects of test expectancy are nicely explained within this framework. Performance on an open-ended (essay or free recall) test suffers if students are incorrectly led to expect a multiple-choice test. Depending on which test is expected, students study differently. Students expecting a multiple-choice test focus less on relations between items and spend less time preparing than do students expecting a more open-ended test. The way students study for multiple-choice tests does not match the demands of the recall test; hence, performance suffers when students are surprised with the unexpected version of the test. A good educator will make clear the test demands early in a course so that students will tailor their study strategies appropriately.

Memory is not like a tape that can be played back perfectly at test. Rather, memory is reconstructive. In one example of this, from the 1977 study of Dooling and Christiansen, subjects read a paragraph that began "Carol Harris was a problem child from birth. She was wild, stubborn and violent." Right before the test phase, some of the subjects were told that Carol Harris was really Helen Keller. These informed subjects were much more likely to incorrectly identify the statement "She was deaf, dumb, and blind" as having been in the original paragraph than subjects who were not informed of Harris's true identity. Subjects made use of their knowledge at test to reconstruct what they read during the first part of the experiment. Schemas are as active during test taking as they are during encoding, and they provide retrieval cues and allow for reconstruction.

Conclusions

There are two very general requirements for effective memory: quality encoding and appropriate retrieval cues. These principles are exemplified in a classic study method, the SQ3R method, which Francis P. Robinson described in 1970. SQ3R stands for: sur-

vey, *question*, *read*, *rehearse*, and *review*. Students begin by surveying the textbook chapter before reading it, to become familiar with its organization. As they read the chapter, they form questions that they then answer. Finally, they rehearse and test themselves on what they have just read, and review all the material repeatedly. Each of these activities links to basic memory processes. The initial survey of the chapter leads students to set up a schema for the chapter that guides both encoding and later retrieval. The questions students create serve as retrieval cues later on. Answering these questions, repeated rehearsing, self-testing, and reviewing the material are all forms of retrieval practice that will aid memory. Studying a textbook chapter need not be a mystery to students.

See also: MEMORY, *subentries on* AUTOBIOGRAPHICAL MEMORY, IMPLICIT MEMORY, METAMEMORY, STRUCTURES AND FUNCTIONS.

BIBLIOGRAPHY

AYERS, MICHAEL S., and REDER, LYNNE M. 1998. "A Theoretical Review of the Misinformation Effect: Predictions from an Activation-Based Memory Model." *Psychonomic Bulletin and Review* 5:1–21.

BAHRICK, HARRY P. 1984. "Semantic Memory Content in Permastore: Fifty Years of Memory for Spanish Learned in School." *Journal of Experimental Psychology: General* 113:1–29.

CRAIK, FERGUS I. M., and LOCKHART, ROBERT S. 1972. "Levels of Processing: A Framework for Memory Research." *Journal of Verbal Learning and Verbal Behavior* 11:671–684.

CRAIK, FERGUS I. M., and TULVING, ENDEL. 1975. "Depth of Processing and the Retention of Words in Episodic Memory." *Journal of Experimental Psychology: General* 104:268–294.

DEMPSTER, FRANK N. 1988. "The Spacing Effect: A Case Study in the Failure to Apply the Results of Psychological Research." *American Psychologist* 43:627–634.

DOOLING, D. JAMES, and CHRISTIANSEN, ROBERT E. 1977. "Episodic and Semantic Aspects of Memory for Prose." *Journal of Experimental Psychology: Human Learning and Memory* 3:428–436.

HALL, JOHN F. 1954. "Learning as a Function of Word Frequency." *American Journal of Psychology* 67:138–140.

HYDE, THOMAS S., and JENKINS, JAMES J. 1969. "Differential Effects of Incidental Tasks on the Organization of Recall of a List of Highly Associated Words." *Journal of Experimental Psychology* 82:472–481.

KINSBOURNE, MARCEL, and GEORGE, JAMES. 1974. "The Mechanism of the Word-Frequency Effect on Recognition Memory." *Journal of Verbal Learning and Verbal Behavior* 13:63–69.

LOFTUS, ELIZABETH F.; MILLER, DAVID G.; and BURNS, HELEN J. 1978. "Semantic Integration of Verbal Information into a Visual Memory." *Journal of Experimental Psychology: Human Learning and Memory* 4:19–31.

MORRIS, C. DONALD; BRANSFORD, JOHN D.; and FRANKS, JEFFREY J. 1977. "Levels of Processing versus Transfer Appropriate Processing." *Journal of Verbal Learning and Verbal Behavior* 16:519–533.

PICHERT, JAMES W., and ANDERSON, RICHARD C. 1977. "Taking Different Perspectives on a Story." *Journal of Educational Psychology* 69:309–315.

ROBINSON, FRANCIS PLEASANT. 1970. *Effective Study.* New York: Harper and Row.

RUNDUS, DEWEY. 1977. "Maintenance Rehearsal and Single-Level Processing." *Journal of Verbal Learning and Verbal Behavior* 16:665–681.

SCHMIDT, STEPHEN R. 1991. "Can We Have a Distinctive Theory of Memory?" *Memory and Cognition* 19:523–542.

TULVING, ENDEL, and PEARLSTONE, ZENA. 1966. "Availability versus Accessibility of Information in Memory for Words." *Journal of Verbal Learning and Verbal Behavior* 5:381–391.

TULVING, ENDEL, and THOMSON, DONALD M. 1973. "Encoding Specificity and Retrieval Processes in Episodic Memory." *Psychological Review* 80:359–380.

TVERSKY, BARBARA. 1973. "Encoding Processes in Recognition and Recall." *Cognitive Psychology* 5:275–287.

WHITTEN, WILLIAM B., and BJORK, ROBERT A. 1977. "Learning from Tests: Effects of Spacing." *Journal of Verbal Learning and Verbal Behavior* 16:465–478.

ELIZABETH J. MARSH

STRUCTURES AND FUNCTIONS

In the study of memory there have been many metaphors adopted in the search for an explanation of the memory process. The fourth century B.C.E. Greek philosopher Aristotle compared memorizing to making impressions in wax, and the idea that memories are copies of reality that a person stores and later retrieves has been widespread. This is sometimes called the storehouse metaphor, and many of the ways in which people talk about memory (searching for memories, bringing them back from the recesses of one's mind) assume such a metaphor. The computer metaphor that has been popular with psychologists researching memory is a version of the storehouse view. It conceptualizes the stages involved in remembering in terms of encoding, storage, and retrieval in which information is entered into memory, retained, and then found again at a later time. Thinking about remembering in this way can be valuable, but it can lead to the incorrect assumption that what is remembered is a simple copy of what was originally experienced. In reality, much that is remembered captures the gist rather than the details of the original experience, and remembering is often a process of reconstruction. Examples of constructive remembering can be found in research on false memories. Elaborate and detailed false memories of events from an individual's past can be easily created. More mundanely, hearing a list of close associates to a particular word leads to recall of the word itself even though it was not presented. One alternative to the storehouse metaphor is the correspondence metaphor that emphasizes the deviation between the memory and the original experience.

Memory Structure

Researchers who study memory use a number of terms to subdivide the enormous field. One major distinction is that between explicit and implicit memory. Explicit memory refers to the conscious recall of information. Conscious awareness of past experiences involves explicit memories. Often, however, people are influenced by experiences that are not consciously recallable. For example, the ease and speed with which a person solves the anagram *rbocoilc* depends upon how recently the person has encountered the word *broccoli.* This facilitation reflects implicit memory. Processing of new information is primed by past experiences without conscious awareness. The distinction between explicit and implicit memory may reflect different underlying memory systems. Quite different timescales and sensitivities have been demonstrated for some explicit and implicit memory tasks. The differences may arise, however, from the processing requirements of the tasks rather than from different memory systems.

A distinction that overlaps with explicit and implicit memory is that between episodic and semantic memory. This distinction, associated with Endel Tulving, is between memory for events and memory for facts. Episodic memory is for events that people can remember happening, whereas semantic memory is for facts that people know about the world without necessarily retaining any recollection of the situation in which they learned the information. One's memory for eating breakfast on a particular morning is an episodic one, whereas one's memory that Coca-Cola is a drink is a semantic one. One area of episodic memory is autobiographical memory—memory for personal events in one's own life. Autobiographical memories from the first two years of life are very rare, while memories from the late teens and early twenties are more frequently held than the average. Certain autobiographical memories seem to be so distinct and full of the apparently irrelevant details from the original event that they have been called flashbulb memories because the nature of the memory is similar to a photograph of the moment. Archetypal examples of flashbulb memories are associated with hearing or seeing particularly dramatic events such as the assassination of a famous person or a major accident.

Submemories. One approach to understanding the structure of memory has been to seek separate submemories that are responsible for retaining information over differing time periods. In 1968 Richard Atkinson and Richard Shiffrin proposed a model with three types of memory: a sensory store, a short-term store, and a long-term memory. Visual information, for example, is believed to be retained for about one second in a sensory store while perceptual processing takes place. Similar sensory memories aid in the processing of acoustic and other inputs. Beyond the perceptually based sensory memories is the short-term memory, which retains information for a few seconds before selected elements of that information are transferred to a long-term memory. Atkinson and Shiffrin recognized that there were control processes in short-term memory that influence what is attended to and processed. The Atkinson and Shiffrin model has been elaborated into the working memory system, which has been particularly investigated by Alan Baddeley and his colleagues. Baddeley has subdivided the working memory into several subcomponents, the most heavily researched of which are the phonological loop, the visuo-spatial sketchpad, and the central executive. The phonological loop holds a couple of seconds of speech sounds and plays a role in reading. The visuo-spatial sketchpad is used in the creation of mental images and in the solution of visual and spatial problems. The central executive is a controlling attentional system that supervises and coordinates current cognitive processing.

Formal models of memory. A number of formal models of memory that can be run as computer simulations have been developed. Among the most influential of these are Jerome Raaijmaker's and Richard Shiffrin's 1981 SAM model, James McClelland, David Rumelhart, and Geoffrey Hinton's 1986 PDP model, and John Anderson's 1993 ACT model.

SAM (Search of Associative Memory) is a mathematical model based upon items and the strength of associations between them. It is particularly appropriate to the learning of lists of words. Each word has a memory strength as a result of it being studied, and each word has an associate strength with the other words in the studied list. The memory strength is combined with the association between the word and the context in which it was learned to produce a strength that is the basis of recognition or retrieval. The model can account for many of the memory phenomena associated with the learning of lists, but it shares with the other two formal models described here the difficulty that many of its assumptions are not based on observations and are difficult to test.

The PDP (Parallel Distributed Processing) model is a neural network model inspired by the analogy of neural circuits in the brain. The network consists of units that are connected to form a network. The strengths of the connections (weights) are adjusted as the network is trained to produce correct responses. Activation spreads through the network and the weightings direct that spread. A response is selected when it achieves a sufficient level of activation. One feature of neural network models is that memory is not located in one place but is captured by particular patterns of activation over many units and links. The neural network models are attractive in apparently simulating the structure of the brain. The choice of the particular structure of units and their interconnections, however, turns out to be important for each simulation of human memory. A general representation that is applicable to many types of remembering has yet to be developed.

The ACT framework is a production system theory for both memory of facts and skills. Anderson has developed several versions of ACT including ACT-R (Adaptive Control of Thought-Rational). Production rules are condition-action rules of the form: *If* this is the condition, *then* execute that action. Within the system, units of information are linked by associations, with the association strength being increased through use. The ACT models were developed to account for problem solving and skill acquisition as well as memory. As with the other formal models discussed here, there are many assumptions that make a model difficult to evaluate.

Memory Functions

What is remembered of a particular event depends upon the way in which it is processed. Elaborate processing that emphasizes meaning and associations that are familiar leads to good recall. So, for example, the word *albatross* would be remembered poorly if only the font in which it was printed was noticed and little thought was given to its meaning. It is much more likely to be remembered, however, if at the time the word is read the reader thinks about how albatrosses are white seabirds living in southern oceans. On the other hand, if what is encountered is difficult to understand, then not only will it be poorly remembered but what is remembered may be distorted by an effort to comprehend the meaning.

The processing of new information draws very heavily upon memory of past experience. Schemas have been developed for often-encountered familiar situations such as going to a supermarket or eating at a restaurant. These schemas guide understanding and memory of the new events but may also lead to memory errors by adding expected events that did not actually occur. Information that is organized on the basis of one's existing knowledge is much easier to learn and remember than is disorganized information. So, for example, a list of the names of animals is much easier to memorize if it is categorized according to type of animals (domestic, farm, wild) and if the categories are laid out in a structured way. Experts in an area memorize new information within their area of expertise much more quickly than do novices. So, soccer fans easily learn new soccer scores

and chess masters memorize real board configurations easily.

When material is restudied to strengthen the memory of it, the shorter the interval between the first and second study periods, the less the improvement in recall. This spacing effect is large, so that studying in two spaced sessions can produce twice as much recall as a single session of equal length. The rereading of factual material makes only a small contribution to the further learning of it. Testing oneself by retrieving studied material, however, is a particularly effective technique for improving memory.

What is remembered depends upon the information that is available to cue recall when it is retrieved. In 1983 Tulving summarized much research in the encoding specificity principle. This principle asserts that retrieval is successful to the extent that the cues available at retrieval match those that were processed by the learner at the study phase. The retrieval cues may be aspects of the material that was studied, but they also include environmental cues and the mood and mental state of the learner.

The learning of information that is similar creates a problem for retrieval. There is interference from similar material learned earlier (proactive interference) and from material encountered since the original learning (retroactive interference), and these reduce recall. More insidious are misinformation effects. These occur when misleading information is presented, for example, to eyewitnesses during questioning. The misleading information is then frequently recalled, and the original information becomes very difficult to retrieve.

When tested across time, forgetting follows a logarithmic curve—information loss is rapid initially but then information is lost more slowly. Nevertheless, the fate of information that has been initially very well learned is rather different. Where facts, names, or foreign-language vocabulary have been used repeatedly but are no longer regularly recalled, the pattern of their forgetting is an initial loss over a three-year period, after which recall may be equally good with delays of one or twenty-five years.

See also: MEMORY, *subentry on* MYTHS, MYSTERIES, AND REALITIES.

BIBLIOGRAPHY

ANDERSON, JOHN R. 1993. *Rules of the Mind.* Hillsdale, NJ: Erlbaum.

BADDELEY, ALAN D. 1997. *Human Memory: Theory and Practice.* Hove, Eng.: Psychology Press.

BAHRICK, HARRY P. 1984. "Semantic Memory Content in Permastore: Fifty Years of Memory for Spanish Learned in School." *Journal of Experimental Psychology: General* 113:1–29.

BARTLETT, FREDERICK C. 1932. *Remembering.* Cambridge, Eng.: Cambridge University Press.

BOWER, GORDEN H.; BLACK, JOHN B.; and TURNER, TERRENCE J. 1979. "Scripts in Memory for Text." *Cognitive Psychology* 11:177–220.

BOWER, GORDEN H.; CLARK, MICAL C.; LESGOLD, ALAN M.; and WINZENZ, DAVID. 1969. "Hierarchical Retrieval Schemes in Recall of Categorised Word Lists." *Journal of Verbal Learning and Verbal Behavior* 8:323–343.

BRANSFORD, JOHN D., and JOHNSON, MARCIA K. 1972. "Contextual Prerequisites for Understanding: Some Investigations of Comprehension and Recall." *Journal of Verbal Learning and Verbal Behavior* 11:717–726.

CARRIER, MARK, and PASHLER, HAROLD. 1992. "The Influence of Retrieval on Retention." *Memory and Cognition* 20:633–642.

CHASE, WILLIAM G., and SIMON, HERBERT A. 1973. "The Mind's Eye in Chess." In *Visual Information Processing,* ed. William G. Chase. New York: Academic Press.

CONWAY, MARTIN A. 1996. "Autobiographical Memory." In *Memory,* ed. Elizabeth L. Bjork and Robert A. Bjork. San Diego, CA: Academic Press.

CRAIK, FERGUS I. M., and TULVING, ENDEL. 1975. "Depth of Processing and the Retention of Words in Episodic Memory." *Journal of Experimental Psychology: General* 104:268–294.

DEMPSTER, FRANK N. 1996. "Distributing and Managing the Conditions of Encoding and Practice." In *Memory,* ed. Elizabeth L. Bjork and Robert A. Bjork. San Diego, CA: Academic Press.

EICH, ERIC, and METCALFE, JANET. 1989. "Mood Dependent Memory for Internal versus External Events." *Journal of Experimental Psychology: Learning, Memory, and Cognition* 15:443–455.

FRITZ, CATHERINE O.; MORRIS, PETER E.; BJORK, ROBERT A.; GELMAN, ROCHEL; and WICKENS, THOMAS D. 2000. "When Further Learning Fails: Stability and Change following Repeated Presentation of Text." *British Journal of Psychology* 91:493–511.

HABERLANDT, KARL. 1999. *Human Memory: Explorations and Application.* Boston: Allyn and Bacon.

JACOBY, LARRY L. 1983. "Remembering the Data: Analyzing Interactive Processes in Reading." *Journal of Verbal Learning and Verbal Behavior* 22:485–508.

KORIAT, ASHER, and GOLDSMITH, MORRIS. 1996. "Memory Metaphors and the Real Life/Laboratory Controversy: Correspondence versus Storehouse Conceptions of Memory." *Behavioural and Brain Sciences* 19:167–228.

LOFTUS, ELIZABETH F., and LOFTUS, GEOFFREY R. 1980. "On the Permanence of Stored Information in the Human Brain." *American Psychologist* 35:585–589.

MCCLELLAND, JAMES L.; RUMELHART, DAVID E.; and HINTON, GEOFFREY E. 1986. "The Appeal of Parallel Distributed Processing." In *Parallel Distributed Processing: Explorations in the Microstructure of Cognition,* ed. David E. Rumelhart, James L. McClelland, and the PDP Group. Cambridge, MA: MIT Press.

MORRIS, PETER E.; TWEEDY, MARGARET; and GRUNEBERG, MICHAEL M. 1985. "Interest, Knowledge, and the Memorising of Soccer Scores." *British Journal of Psychology* 76:415–425.

RAAIJMAKERS, JEROME G., and SHIFFRIN, RICHARD M. 1981. "SAM: Search of Associative Memory." *Psychological Review* 88:93–134.

ROEDIGER, HENRY L., III, and MCDERMOTT, KATHLEEN B. 1999. "Distortions of Memory." In *The Oxford Handbook of Memory,* ed. Endel Tulving and Fergus I. M. Craik. Oxford: Oxford University Press.

ROEDIGER, HENRY L., III; WELDON, MARY S.; and CHALLIS, BRADFORD H. 1989. "Explaining Associations between Implicit and Explicit Measures of Retention: A Processing Account." In *Varieties of Memory and Consciousness: Essays in Honour of Endel Tulving,* ed. Henry L. Roediger and Fergus I. M. Craik. Hillsdale, NJ: Erlbaum.

RUBIN, DAVID C., and WENZEL, AMY E. 1996. "100 Years of Forgetting: A Quantitative Description of Retention." *Psychological Review* 103:734–760.

TULVING, ENDEL. 1983. *Elements of Episodic Memory.* Oxford, Eng.: Oxford University Press.

TULVING, ENDEL, and SCHACTER, DANIEL L. 1990. "Priming and Human Memory Systems." *Science* 247:301–306.

PETER E. MORRIS

MENTAL HEALTH SERVICES AND CHILDREN

It is estimated that the percentage of children and adolescents in the United States who are in need of mental health services is between 15 and 20 percent. This means that more than 10 million children in the country suffer from some mental disorder. It is also estimated that 3 to 8 percent have a serious mental illness. More children suffer from psychiatric illness than from leukemia, diabetes, and AIDS combined. There are also both short-term and long-term financial and emotional costs associated with these disorders.

Determining which children need mental health services is a complex undertaking. In most cases, a youth has to receive a mental health diagnosis from a qualified clinician. The American Psychiatric Association, in their Diagnostic and Statistical Manual (DSM), has codified diagnostic categories. Researchers may use a structured clinical interview, such as the Diagnostic Interview Schedule for Children (DISC), to obtain a diagnosis, but these rigorous instruments are rarely used in clinical practice, and there is little agreement among clinicians in their use as a diagnostic tool. In addition to meeting the criteria for a diagnosis, federal regulations now require that for a child to be classified as having a *serious emotional disturbance* (SED) the child must have a functional impairment in two or more areas. These areas include home, school, and work (where relevant).

Who Receives Mental Health Services?

Children can receive mental health services from several sources, including schools; mental health institutions such as hospitals; community mental health centers; mental health services provided through child welfare; services from juvenile justice; and primary care physicians. Estimates of use of mental health services by children range from 1.9 to 6 percent in any given year for the general population. Most children receive services from schools.

There are several factors that are related to an increase in the probability in accessing mental health services. In two studies comparing a system of care that offered a full range of services with the more typical community services, such as those provided by community mental health centers, children were more likely to receive services, and to receive more services, in a system of care. (A system of care includes a continuum of services from outpatient to hospitalization, coordination or management of these services, and, usually, the involvement of multiple child-serving agencies.) However, the provision of services in a system of care was more expensive and was not any more effective than the usual services available in the community.

Use of Services

Patterns of service use are not well understood, but it is generally agreed that services are underutilized by youth. There are several possible reasons for this, including the stigma associated with such services and parental dissatisfaction with services. Most children do not enter services willingly, and it should be recognized that specialized children's mental health services alone will never be sufficient to meet the need for mental health services. More services will have to be provided by other systems, such as schools and the juvenile justice system.

There is a high dropout rate of children from services, although estimates vary considerably. Some studies have found that 40 to 60 percent of children who begin treatment terminate it before the therapist recommends they should terminate. It is believed that the majority of children attend outpatient treatment for only one or two sessions. It is not clear why the dropout rate is so high, but it is suspected that referral to services are often made by others, such as schools, and not the parent or adolescent.

Where Do Children Receive Mental Health Services?

School systems. Schools usually identify children with mental health problems only after the problems have not been successfully dealt with by their classroom teacher or their parents. However, once identified, students are much more likely to use the services in the schools than in the community. Schools usually try informal interventions before referring a child to special education. A federal law, the Individuals with Disabilities Education Act (IDEA), requires that such children be evaluated and, if eligible, placed in a special classroom or provided with special assistance in their regular classrooms.

There is a strong relationship between SED and several measures of school performance. Students with SED have lower grades, are retained more often in grade, and fail more courses than other students with disabilities. Less than half (42%) of children with SED graduate high school, as compared to 56 percent of students with other disabilities and 71 percent of all students. The rates of identification of youth with SED vary across racial, gender, and socioeconomic lines, with Hispanics and Asian Americans receiving proportionally the least amount of services. Research also suggests that students from low socioeconomic backgrounds and males are overrepresented among those identified with SED.

Schools are not good at identifying children with mental health problems. There are several reasons for this difficulty, including the avoidance of stigma, lack of training in recognizing mental health problems, and the desire of the system to avoid the costs of mental health services. There is not a substantial amount of evidence that schools are successful in treating children with mental health problems. Comprehensive support systems and training for teachers and administrators are not typically found in school systems.

Recent trends in SED lead to one of three possibilities: (1) the number of children with SED is increasing, (2) schools are recognizing more children with SED, or (3) both of these are occurring. Since 1976 there has been an increase of more than 118,000 students with SED (a 48% increase) receiving services under the Chapter 1 Handicapped program of the Elementary and Secondary Education Act (ESEA) and IDEA Part B programs. However, this program ended in 1994.

As in other service sectors, there are a significant number of children who are not receiving needed services in the schools. In addition, little is known about the quality, appropriateness, or effectiveness of the services delivered to children and adolescents in schools.

Primary care. Pediatricians and primary-care physicians prescribe most of the psychotropic drugs prescribed for children. They may also counsel families, but some studies indicate that families do not interpret this counseling as mental health services. For preschool children such visits may be their only contact with a health delivery system. Studies have shown that physicians often fail to identify children with mental health problems. Moreover, parents often fail to mention that their child has a problem. There are several barriers to proper identification and the delivery of effective services—physicians are not trained to deal with mental health problems, the service may not be reimbursed at an attractive level, and the average visit to the doctor is only eleven to fifteen minutes long.

Juvenile justice. The magnitude of mental-health-service needs far exceeds current resources in the juvenile justice system. It also appears that children of low socioeconomic status populate the juvenile justice system, and thus are less likely to receive mental health services because they are in the juvenile justice system. Findings show that mental health placements are rarely used relative to other court outcomes (i.e., dismissal, probation, or other types of placements), and that gender and race significantly influence whether a child will receive a mental health service. Females are more likely to receive mental health services than males, and white delinquents are more likely to be placed in a mental health setting than black offenders, regardless of gender.

The Effectiveness of Mental Health Services

Providing ineffective services to children and adolescents would clearly not be good public policy. It would simply waste resources and not result in any improvement in child outcomes. Moreover, it would provide the illusion that society is intervening in a positive manner and thus inhibit change. For this reason, determining the effectiveness of services is a key goal in this field. A distinction should be made between the *efficacy* of an intervention and its *effectiveness*. Efficacy studies examine a treatment under optimal situations. These studies are likely to take place in a university-based laboratory using well-trained and supervised clinicians and children who are selected to meet the needs of the study. For example, a study of the treatment of depression would screen out all children who had depression *and* other comorbid mental health disorders; only children with depression alone would be studied.

Standing in stark contrast to efficacy research, effectiveness studies evaluate the effects of treatment in typical conditions. Studies of effectiveness are conducted in community mental health centers and in real-world settings such as schools. In these studies the investigator does not have the same level of influence on which types of children get into the study, how the therapists are trained and supervised, and how carefully they follow the treatment approach. The distinction between efficacy and effectiveness is important because each type of study tells a different story about how beneficial mental health services for children and adolescents are.

Although efficacy research is important in establishing the potential utility of treatments, these studies are not very informative about how the intervention will operate in the real world. While there are hundreds of efficacy studies of psychological child and adult treatments, there are only a handful of effectiveness studies. Meta-analytic studies of treatment (mostly psychotherapy) show that, on average, mental health treatment is very powerful when studied under laboratory-like conditions. However, the picture is different for effectiveness studies.

Most effectiveness research has been done on such system-level constructs as service coordination and access. There have been few studies of the child and family outcomes of mental health treatment. These studies have not found that treatment makes a difference in child and family outcomes. For example, the Fort Bragg Evaluation Project, the largest study of mental health systems of care, found that children in a system of care had increased access to services compared to children receiving treatment as usual in the comparison sites. However, both groups improved over time and the clinical and family outcomes did not differ between the two groups. Unfortunately, the system of care was much more expensive and thus could not be justified. Research in this area is in its infancy; only more research in the real world will lead to an understanding of the conditions under which mental health treatment is effective.

The contrast in findings between efficacy and effectiveness studies is dramatic. It is suspected that a major reason for the weak effects found in the community is that practitioners are not using effective treatments. To encourage the use of effective treatments, several professional groups are identifying what they describe as evidence-based treatments. These treatments typically have sufficient efficacy results to warrant their use. Some organizations, such as the American Pediatric Association and the American Academy of Adolescent and Child Psychiatry, have developed diagnosis and treatment guidelines that are less specific than evidence-based treatments

that are spelled out in treatment manuals. However, just informing practitioners about the existence of evidence-based treatments is not sufficient for practitioners to adopt those practices. It is not clear that these techniques can be transferred to the real world, or that practitioners will use them. It is also uncertain if the guidelines are specific enough to make a difference in outcomes.

There are several reasons why these efficacious treatments are not being used in clinical practice. First, there is no agency in the behavioral field similar to the Food and Drug Administration that certifies medications as safe and effective. This means that there is no central authority that approves the several hundred existing behavioral treatments. There are few advantages for the already overworked clinicians to make significant changes in their practices and to incur the costs of additional training in evidence-based treatments. New research is focusing on how to encourage service providers to use new treatments.

Medication

Progress has been made in the use of medication to treat several disorders, including attention deficit hyperactivity disorder (ADHD), obsessive-compulsive disorder (OCD), and childhood anxiety disorders. In addition, studies are underway to test the effectiveness of medication for major depression. Clinical trials are also being started for bipolar disorder, autism, and several other mental disorders.

A major study on ADHD found that medication was more effective than behavior therapy for symptom reduction. However, combining medication and behavior therapy was more effective for children who had co-occurring disorders such as anxiety and ADHD. Furthermore, this study found that medication was more effective when managed by the study investigators than when medication was managed by physicians in routine community care. The investigators think that the greater effectiveness under the more controlled conditions was related to the higher frequency of office visits, their longer duration, and the more carefully controlled dosage.

One of the problems in using medications for the treatment of mental disorders in children is that the Food and Drug Administration (FDA) has not specifically approved most psychotropic drugs for use with children. While it is legal and ethical to use medications tested on adults on children, this "off-label" use means that physicians do not have research findings to guide their treatment decisions for the majority of psychiatric problems. An additional problem with medication treatment is that many severely ill children are treated with multiple drugs simultaneously. There are no systematic studies of the effects of polypharmacy, and thus the effects of combinations of medications are not known.

See also: HEALTH CARE AND CHILDREN; HEALTH SERVICES, *subentry on* SCHOOL.

BIBLIOGRAPHY

BICKMAN, LEONARD. 1996. "A Continuum of Care: More Is Not Always Better." *American Psychologist* 51(7):689–701.

DOUGLAS-KELLEY, SUSAN M.; NIXON, CAROL T.; and BICKMAN, LEONARD. 2000. "Evaluating Mental Health Services for Children and Adolescents." In *Handbook for Research Methods in Pediatric and Clinical Child Psychology,* ed. Dennis Drotar. New York: Kluwer Academic/Plenum.

WEISZ, JOHN R., and JENSEN, PETER S. 1999. "Efficacy and Effectiveness of Psychotherapy and Pharmacotherapy with Children and Adolescents." *Mental Health Services Research* 1(3):125–157.

INTERNET RESOURCE

SURGEON GENERAL OF THE UNITED STATES. 2002. "Mental Health: A Report of the Surgeon General." <www.surgeongeneral.gov/library/mental health/home.html>.

LEONARD BICKMAN

MENTAL RETARDATION, EDUCATION OF INDIVIDUALS WITH

Throughout history, the definition, diagnosis, terminology, and etiology of mental retardation have changed, influencing services, policy, education, and prevalence.

Definition and Prevalence of Mental Retardation

Mental retardation is a condition of substantial limitations in intellectual functioning that impacts performance in daily life. Its diagnosis includes three criteria: concurrent, significant limitations in both intelligence and adaptive skills that begin in childhood (birth to age eighteen). The American Association on Mental Retardation's (AAMR's) 1992 definition specifies limitations of two or more standard deviations in intelligence (IQ of 70 to 75 or less) with coexisting deficiencies in two or more of ten adaptive skills: communication, self-care, home living, social skills, community use, self-direction, health and safety, functional academics, leisure, and work. These individuals range broadly in functioning, depending in part on the degree of limitations but also on the services and support received. Individuals with severe and multiple disabilities are considered a small subset of this population. Most persons with mental retardation are capable of achieving self-sufficiency. A 1998 study indicates that prevalence estimates cluster around 1 percent, with a high of 2 percent.

Brief History of Education

Prior to the 1700s, those with mental retardation suffered greatly. In the 1700s to the late 1800s, they entered an optimistic period when French educational methods spread to other Western countries. These methods derived mainly from Edward Seguin and less so from his predecessor Jean-Marc Itard in the first half of the nineteenth century. Seguin called his educational methods *physiological education,* which consisted of three components: muscular or physical education, education of the senses, and moral treatment. The goal of Seguin's method was independence grounded in relationships with other citizens, not isolation from society. These educational methods produced uneven results and were followed by disillusionment.

In the late 1800s to the 1960s there was widespread building of institutions to house individuals with mental retardation. Intelligence tests, developed in the early 1900s, became the tools of the eugenic movement—a period when many people with low intelligence were sterilized under the assumption that the population would be improved. Starting in the 1970s the institutional population in the United States was gradually reduced, primarily because of a reduction in admissions. Many former residents were relocated to smaller community-based settings, but others remained in their natural homes with services and supports provided. Of those remaining in state institutions at the end of the twentieth century, persons over forty with profound mental retardation and multiple disabilities dominated the population.

Schools' Responses and Goals and Methods of Teaching

Before 1975 when the Education of All Handicapped Children Act was passed (Pub. L. 94-142) and special education was required, some students with milder mental retardation attended school until they failed or quit, but others with greater support needs attended parent-operated schools or remained at home. The number of individuals with mental retardation in institutions reached its peak in the mid-1960s, where educational services of widely varying quality sometimes existed. According to the U.S. Department of Education's statistics, at the end of the twentieth century students with labels of mental retardation who were enrolled in U.S. public schools constituted 11 percent of all students with disabilities. The number of students classified as having mental retardation declined substantially since the 1970s, in part because of the label's stigma and recognition of intelligence test inaccuracy. Minority children were overrepresented in school programs serving those with mental retardation, a fact often accounted for by inaccurate testing.

The primary goal of education for this group is to increase self-sufficiency by teaching functional academics and other skills needed in everyday life across home, community, work, and leisure domains. Depending on the student's abilities (conceptual, social, and practical), needs for support (intermittent to pervasive), and school placement, the educational focus and methods will vary. The socioeconomic level of the community influences the quality of special education and the amount of support an individual receives in school and during adult life.

Trends, Issues, and Controversies

Although the label of mental retardation brings services, it also brings stigma and low expectations. The reduction in students labeled as mentally retarded (with a corresponding increase in those with learning disabilities) from the 1970s to the 1990s serves as evidence. Parents and educators have grappled with this issue. Some believe the label should be reserved for those with organic etiologies, assuming the smaller group would be more homogeneous. Others propose a change in the label and improved education of the public.

Current law requires education in the least restrictive environment with appropriate services and support. Students with mental retardation have a poor record for being served in general education classrooms: 46 percent of all students with disabilities are so served compared with 12 percent of those with mental retardation. Many believe that educators need to understand better how to serve these students in the mainstream and also equip them for the transition to adult life.

See also: COUNCIL FOR EXCEPTIONAL CHILDREN; SPECIAL EDUCATION, *subentries on* CURRENT TRENDS, HISTORY OF.

BIBLIOGRAPHY

ANDERSON, LYNDA L., et al. 1998. "State Institutions: Thirty Years of Depopulation and Closure." *Mental Retardation* 36:431–443.

BEIRNE-SMITH, MARY; ITTENBACK, RICHARD F.; and PATTON, JAMES R. 1998. *Mental Retardation,* 5th edition. Upper Saddle River, NJ: Merrill/Prentice-Hall.

Education of All Handicapped Children Act of 1975. U.S. Public Law 94-142. *U.S. Code.* Vol. 20, secs. 1401 et seq.

GRESHAM, FRANK M.; MACMILLAN, DONALD L.; and SIPERSTEIN, GARY N. 1995. "Critical Analysis of the 1992 AAMR Definition: Implications for School Psychology." *School Psychology Quarterly* 10:1–19.

Individuals with Disabilities Education Act Amendments of 1997. U.S. Public Law 105-12. *U.S. Code.* Vol. 20, secs. 1400 et seq.

LUCKASSON, RUTH, et al. 1992. *Mental Retardation: Definition, Classification and Systems of Supports,* 9th edition. Washington, DC: American Association on Mental Retardation.

TRENT, JAMES W., JR. 1994. *Inventing the Feeble Mind: A History of Mental Retardation in the United States.* Berkeley: University of California Press.

U.S. DEPARTMENT OF EDUCATION. 2000. *Twenty-Second Annual Report to Congress on the Implementation of the Individuals with Disabilities Education Act.* Washington, DC: Office of Special Education Programs, U.S. Department of Education.

MARTHA E. SNELL

MENTORING

Schools that provide mentoring programs assign a veteran teacher to act as adviser, teacher, and coach to beginning teachers within their schools. Some have defined mentoring as "a formalized relationship between a beginning teacher and a master teacher (mentor) that provides support and assesses teaching skills" (Education Commission of the States website). Others use the terms *buddy, coach,* and *master teacher* to describe the person who helps the beginning teacher develop into a seasoned veteran.

Often mentoring programs are just one strategy of full induction programs designed to ease the transition of the new teacher into the profession of teaching. Within an induction program, schools develop structured activities to help orient new teachers to the system and assume the roles and responsibilities of practicing teachers. Induction programs are typically comprehensive programs that guide new teachers through their beginning years in the school. Induction programs are often seen as a process lasting from one to three years. Within the induction program, the mentorship puts the focus on the relationship between the new teacher and mentor; the mentor is charged with assisting and supporting the new teacher as he or she transitions from student teacher to teacher of students. Many believe mentoring to be an essential component of the induction program.

The roles and responsibilities undertaken by the mentor vary from program to program. In all cases, however, it is the mentor who plays an essential role in achieving the goals of the induction program. Using strategies such as consultation, demonstration, and observation, the mentor can act as the primary source of assistance for the new teachers.

A mentor is defined as simply a veteran teacher assigned to a new teacher. *Veteran* means that the teacher is not in his or her first year of teaching; however, the number of years of experience is not necessarily specified. Typically, mentors have at least three years of experience in their school district or division that allows the mentor to develop an expertise and understanding about the school system and to become skilled and comfortable within the classroom. Mentors may or may not have classroom teaching responsibilities at the same time that they act as mentors. In some cases, mentors may have been relieved of teaching assignments and act solely as mentors. Occasionally schools entice retired teachers back into the schools to act as mentors.

Mentors assist their new teachers in a variety of ways. It is the school district's duty to define the roles and responsibilities of mentors. One way is to assist neophyte teachers to become acquainted with their new environment. Mentors might provide a tour of the facilities, introduce the new teacher to staff and faculty, describe procedures and policies of the division, explain grading philosophies, and offer suggestions for lessons and classroom management. In the work of Sharon Feiman-Nemser and Michelle Parker, mentors who assume these duties are called local guides.

Others envision the responsibilities of the mentor as going beyond those acclimation duties. In such cases, the mentor fulfills the necessary orientation responsibilities and then moves the conversations to the next level. These mentors talk with their new teachers about instructional issues and their effect on student learning. They help the new teachers reflect on their performances and decisions so that improved student learning is the outcome. A label applied to mentors fulfilling these roles is *educational companion.*

Finally, Feiman-Nemser and Parker have identified another role that mentors can adopt: that of change agent. Mentors as change agents seek to establish a new culture within a school—one of collaboration and commitment to continual professional development. This role transcends the typical role of assisting new teachers. In this case mentors attempt to break the traditional "closed-door" culture within schools and affect change throughout a system. Regardless of the role, how mentors assist new teachers is the prerogative of the school district.

Rationale for Mentoring

School districts are faced with a myriad of problems. Not the least of those problems is ensuring that all children are taught by competent and qualified teachers. This is a growing concern in the early twenty-first century. It is anticipated that over two million new teachers will be required to fill the classrooms of America by 2012 because of mushrooming enrollments, teacher attrition, and massive retirements among the aging population of current teachers. The job of a teacher is not an easy one. Districts and divisions are looking for ways to acknowledge the demands of the job and offer support to those who accept the challenge. Mentor programs, a promise of support, are one benefit that school districts can offer.

Filling the demand is not the sole issue, however. Even if school districts could find the sheer numbers of teachers needed, retention of these new hires becomes a problem. It is estimated that 30 percent of new teachers do not return to the classroom after their first year. Over the first five years, 40 percent leave the profession. In many cases, those leaving are the most academically talented teachers. Furthermore, new teachers are more apt to leave schools with the greatest need, leaving children to experience a succession of new teachers. Such high-need schools include those in urban settings and the rural countryside.

Many new teachers cite the feelings of isolation and lack of support as critical determinants in their decision to leave. Teaching is one of the few professions whereby a new graduate is expected to perform as fully as a seasoned professional does. Other professions such as medicine offer supervised internships and residencies that allow the new graduate an opportunity to practice with guidance from a veteran. Education, to date, rarely provides such experiences. The educational tradition of "sink or swim" that often leaves the new teachers on their own to discover what works and what doesn't is no longer a viable option for schools.

Extensiveness of Mentoring Programs

Information about the role of mentoring programs that support new teachers during their first years is not well documented. In 1996 the National Center for Educational Statistics published data regarding the participation of new teachers in induction programs. Although specific information about mentoring programs is absent, some encouraging trends are seen. For the 1993 to 1994 school year more than half (56.4%) of all public schools teachers with three or fewer years of experience were involved in induction programs. This is an increase of 39 percent from new teachers involved in induction programs of the 1980s. The National Center for Educational statistics for 1999 to 2001 data are expected to indicate that more new teachers were involved in induction programs.

In fact, induction programs are blossoming all over the country as one strategy to support teachers in their transition from student teacher to professional teacher. Data released in 2001 indicates that thirty-three states have written beginning teacher induction statutes; twenty-two of the states mandate and fund the programs. In addition, assigning mentors to assist the new teachers is often a component of induction programs. Twenty-nine states include mentorships as part of the induction process according to data published by the American Federation of Teachers in 2001.

Issues and Controversies

As mentoring programs develop to help new teachers transition from student teacher to classroom teacher, questions, issues, and debates begin to surface as well. One such issue centers on the question of purpose; a second issue focuses on effectiveness.

For many years mentoring programs were defined as vehicles to support and assist new teachers as they began their teaching careers. This assistance and support was based on the trusting relationship that developed between the mentor and new teacher. Much of the trust came from the defined role that mentors were there only to assist and support, not assess. New teachers felt comfortable exposing their concerns and problems to the mentor because the mentor was there to help. The argument was that if mentors evaluated the new teachers, then the new teachers would not come to the mentors with problems and concerns. Trust would be violated and the purpose of the mentoring programs defeated.

In the early twenty-first century some are questioning the separation of assistance and assessment. Given the intimate role mentors play in the lives of new teachers, mentors may possess critical information about the quality of the new teachers' skills and knowledge. Such information should not be absent from a comprehensive evaluation of the new teachers. The ultimate purpose of mentoring programs is to ensure quality teachers for every child; therefore, the argument is that mentors should provide evaluative data that are used in the decision of continued employment.

The general feeling, however, is that most mentoring programs embrace the concepts of assistance and support, leaving evaluation to those outside the mentor role. A small number of programs are combining assistance and assessment, however, so the verdict is still out as to which approach works best.

A second issue being explored is the effectiveness of mentoring programs. How should mentoring programs be evaluated to determine their effectiveness? During the last wave of mentoring programs in the early 1990s, the effectiveness of mentoring programs was usually framed around the perceived benefits to the participants. New teachers felt the mentors were helpful; mentors perceived their roles as effective. What is needed and being pursued are more empirical data that indicate mentoring programs are responsible for the goals they strive to achieve. Typically mentoring programs identify one or more of five common goals: (1) to improve the skills of new teachers, (2) to acclimate the new teacher to the culture of the school and community, (3) to provide emotional support, (4) to retain quality teachers, and (5) to meet state mandates and requirements for licensure. Data need to be collected that identify the ways in which mentoring programs' features and practices achieve these goals. Specific correlations between what mentoring programs do and what goals are achieved would allow schools to incorporate practices and features designed to succeed. These are the avenues for future research.

See also: TEACHER; TEACHING, *subentry on* LEARNING TO TEACH.

BIBLIOGRAPHY

FEIMAN-NEMSER, SHARON, and PARKER, MICHELLE B. 1992. *Los Angeles Mentors: Local Guides or Educational Companions?* East Lansing, MI: National Center for Research on Teacher Learning.

FIDELER, ELIZABETH F., and HASELKORN, DAVID. 1999. *Learning the Ropes: Urban Teacher Induction Programs and Practices in the United States.* Belmont, MA: Recruiting New Teachers.

NATIONAL COMMISSION ON TEACHING AND AMERICA'S FUTURE. 1996. *What Matters Most: Teaching for America's Future.* New York: National Commission on Teaching and America's Future.

ODELL, SANDRA, and FERRARO, DOUGLAS. 1992. "Teacher Mentoring and Teacher Retention." *Journal of Teacher Education* 43(3):200–204.

SERPELL, ZEWELANJI. 2000. *Beginning Teacher Induction: A Review of the Literature.* Washington, DC: American Association of Colleges for Teacher Education.

SERPELL, ZEWELANJI, and BOZEMAN, LESLIE. 1999. *Beginning Teacher Education: A Report on Beginning Teacher Effectiveness and Retention.* Washington, DC: National Partnership for Excellence and Accountability in Teaching.

INTERNET RESOURCES

AMERICAN FEDERATION OF TEACHERS. 2001. "Beginning Teacher Induction: The Essential Bridge." <www.aft.org/edissues/downloads/NEW_TEACH_INDUCT.pdf>.

EDUCATION COMMISSION OF THE STATES. 1999. "Beginning Teacher Mentoring Programs." <www.ecs.org/clearinghouse/13/15/1315.doc>.

NATIONAL CENTER FOR EDUCATIONAL STATISTICS. 2002. "Schools and Staffing Survey." <www.nces.ed.gov/surveys/sass/>.

NATIONAL CENTER FOR RESEARCH ON TEACHER LEARNING. 2001. "NCRTL Explores Learning from Mentors: A Study Update." <http://nctrl.msu.edu>.

SOUTHWEST EDUCATIONAL DEVELOPMENT LABORATORY. 2002. "Mentoring Beginning Teachers: Lessons from the Experiences in Texas." <http://emissary.ots.utexas.edu/wings/mentoring>.

MICHELLE HUGHES

METACOGNITION

See: LEARNING TO LEARN AND METACOGNITION.

MICROTEACHING

Microteaching is a scaled-down, simulated teaching encounter designed for the training of both preservice or in-service teachers. It has been used worldwide since its invention at Stanford University in the late 1950s by Dwight W. Allen, Robert Bush, and Kim Romney. Its purpose is to provide teachers with the opportunity for the safe practice of an enlarged cluster of teaching skills while learning how to develop simple, single-concept lessons in any teaching subject. Microteaching helps teachers improve both content and methods of teaching and develop specific teaching skills such as questioning, the use of examples and simple artifacts to make lessons more interesting, effective reinforcement techniques, and introducing and closing lessons effectively. Immediate, focused feedback and encouragement, combined with the opportunity to practice the suggested improvements in the same training session, are the foundations of the microteaching protocol.

Over the years microteaching has taken many forms. Its early configurations were very formal and complex. Real students (typically four or five) were placed in a rotation of teaching stations in a microteaching clinic. Teachers would teach an initial five to ten minute, single element lesson that was critiqued by a supervisor. The teacher would have a brief time to revise the lesson and then reteach the same lesson to a different group. In later years these sessions were videotaped. Videotaping microteaching lessons became the optimal practice because it allowed teachers to view their own performance.

Microteaching soon spread to more than half of the teacher preparation programs in the United States, and to other parts of the world. Though successful, its complexity overwhelmed its effectiveness as a training device and its use declined over the following decades.

The New Microteaching: Simplified

In the late 1980s and 1990s microteaching was reinvigorated with a completely new format developed in southern Africa and later in China. Because of the lack of available technology in developing countries, microteaching's format had to be made less technology dependent in order to be useful. Early modifications were made in Malawi, but it was in Namibia and China where microteaching was completely transformed.

Twenty-first-century microteaching increases training effectiveness using an even more scaled-down teaching simulation environment. The new microteaching format was primarily shaped as a response to in-service teacher education needs in Namibia, where the vast majority of teachers were uncertified and there were few resources with which to train them. In China it became part of a national effort to modernize teaching practice. Three important new concepts were incorporated:

1. Self-study groups. Teachers rotate between the roles of teacher and student, building on earlier versions of "peer microteaching." Self-study groups of four or five teachers have become the norm.

2. The 2 + 2 evaluation protocol. In earlier versions of microteaching, rather elaborate observation protocols had been developed to evaluate performance for each teaching skill. In the new microteaching, each new skill is introduced to trainees in varied combinations of face-to-face training sessions, multimedia presentations, and printed materials. These training materials give cued behaviors to watch for and comment on in the accompanying microteaching lesson. After a microteaching lesson is taught, each of the teachers playing a student role provides peer evaluation of the teaching episode using the 2 + 2 protocol—two compliments and two suggestions. Compliments and suggestions are focused on the specific skill being emphasized, but may relate to other aspects of the lesson as well.

3. Peer supervision. Originally the microteaching protocol required the presence of a trained supervisor during each lesson. However, with minimal training the compliments and suggestions of peers can become powerful training forces. Trainees feel empowered by the practice of encouraging them to evaluate the compliments and suggestions they receive from their peers (and supervisors, when present), allowing them the discretion to accept or reject any or all suggestions. On average, about two-thirds of the suggestions are considered worthwhile and suggestions from peers and trained supervisors are about equally valued.

The new, simplified format—widely used in the United States as well as abroad in the early twenty-first century—also makes it easier to incorporate the full, recommended protocol of teaching and reteaching each lesson for each student. The microteaching experience goes well beyond the formal, narrow training agenda. The gestalt experience of planning and executing a brief lesson that is closely monitored and scrutinized and the offering and receipt of feedback from respected peers is an integral part of the experience. In the present format students often have three or four complete microteaching cycles in a single course. More cycles tend not to be well received by students, as the training format seems to break down after about four cycles. Some in-service training programs have received enthusiastic reception from students for periodic microteaching sessions (one session each term or semester) over an extended period of time.

The flexibility of allowing each microteaching self-study group to make its own schedule, find its own location, and organize its own training and feedback procedures becomes an important part of the training experience. This leads to substantial savings of resources and allows the number of scheduled sessions to be determined by academic merit, not resource limitations.

Variants of Microteaching

Over the years many microteaching clinics have made modifications in the basic training protocol that detract from the effectiveness of microteaching training, but are thought necessary, given the constraint of resources. Some of the most frequent of these modifications includes greatly increasing the size of the microteaching class. Sometimes an entire class of twenty to thirty-five students is used as the microteaching class. This is necessary for scheduling reasons and because of the lack of facilities and staff for multiple, simultaneous sessions. This adaptation requires students to be passive learners for large numbers of lessons as each trainee has a turn to teach. The number of students in each class means that students teach very infrequently, often only once, and usually have no opportunity to reteach.

Another adaptation is the use of longer lessons, often fifteen or twenty minutes in length, because it is difficult to fit some lesson concepts into a five-minute lesson. This difficulty results from a lack of understanding of a single lesson element. A typical lesson will combine multiple concepts within the same topic, yet teachers often are not trained to break down their lessons into individual concepts. Identifying single concepts and planning a single concept lesson is itself an important skill. Microteaching is well suited to help teachers identify single concepts and learn how to create learning modules from which longer lessons can easily be constructed. Longer lessons in microteaching greatly increase the complexity and duration of training sessions, reduce the number of sessions possible for each individual trainee (unless the length of training is increased), and tend to cause the training sessions to lose focus. Microteaching research at Stanford University repeatedly showed that a five minute lesson is sufficient for the practice of many useful teaching skills in all subject areas.

The development of elaborate microteaching facilities, sometimes with permanent installation of multiple cameras, one-way glass partitions, and even audio capability at each student desk, has been another development. Though very well intentioned, such clinic facilities have not proven cost-effective for the widespread use of microteaching. These facilities are even more personnel intensive. Often special technicians are assigned along with a supervisor/proctor. These facilities would be more effective if the videotaping capacity was entrusted to students, thereby reducing the cost. The ideal would be for one out of every three or four sessions to be videotaped with a simple, one-camera setup with the opportunity to view the lesson immediately. When videotaping is not available and lessons are not taped, the training results have been found to be quite acceptable, though not optimal.

Microteaching Models of Teaching Skills

Microteaching can be an effective tool for the development of teacher training materials. When training protocols are being created to demonstrate new teaching skills, microteaching sessions can be developed and taped giving instances and non-instances of the skill. Asking trainees to view these tapes together is an effective way to highlight and demonstrate the essential aspects of the skill being taught.

Microteaching Courses

Microteaching has been developed as a course in many teacher-training institutions around the world. It readily combines theory with practice. When one considers that teacher trainees in many training programs do their practice teaching under inadequate supervision with no student feedback, the relative merits and economy of microteaching become more and more apparent. Microteaching offers the advantages of both a controlled laboratory environment and realistic practical experience. It is hardly a substitute for teaching practice, but it offers advantages such as close supervision, manageable objectives established according to individual trainee needs and progress, continuous feedback, an unprecedented opportunity for self-evaluation, immediate guidance in areas of demonstrated deficiency, and the opportunity to repeat a lesson whenever desired. When these advantages are combined with the economy of resources required to obtain them, microteaching becomes a valuable training method under many conditions throughout the world.

See also: ELEMENTARY EDUCATION, *subentry on* PREPARATION OF TEACHERS; SECONDARY EDUCA-

TION, *subentry on* PREPARATION OF TEACHERS; TEACHER EDUCATION, *subentry on* INTERNATIONAL PERSPECTIVE.

BIBLIOGRAPHY

ALLEN, DWIGHT, and RYAN, KEVIN. 1969. *Microteaching.* Reading, MA: Addison-Wesley.

ALLEN, DWIGHT, and WANG, WEIPING. 1996. *Microteaching.* Beijing, China: Xinhua Press.

ALLEN, MARY E., and BELZER, JOHN A. 1997. "The Use of Microteaching to Facilitate Teaching Skills of Practitioners Who Work with Older Adults." *Gerontology and Geriatrics Education* 18(2):77.

BORG, WALTER R.; KELLEY, MARJORIE L.; LANGER, PHILIP; and GALL, MEREDITH D. 1970. *The Mini Course: A Microteaching Approach to Teacher Education.* Beverly Hills, CA: Macmillan.

BRENT, REBECCA; WHEATLEY, ELIZABETH; and THOMSON, W. SCOTT. 1996. "Videotaped Microteaching: Bridging the Gap from the University to the Classroom." *The Teacher Educator* 31(3):238.

BROWN, GEORGE A. 1975. *Microteaching: A Program of Teaching Skills.* London: Methuen.

GREGORY, THOMAS B. 1972. *Encounters with Teaching: A Microteaching Manual.* Englewood Cliffs, NJ: Prentice-Hall.

McGARVEY, BRIAN, and SWALLOW, DEREK. 1986. *Microteaching in Teacher Education and Training.* Dover, NH: Croom Helm.

McINTYRE, DONALD; MACLEOD, GORDON; and GRIFFITHS, ROY. 1977. *Investigations of Microteaching.* London: Croom Helm.

TURNEY, CLIFF; CAIRNS L.; WILLIAMS, G.; and HATTON, N. 1975. *Sydney Micro Skills.* Sydney: Sydney University Press.

TURNEY, CLIFF; CLIFT, JOHN C.; DUNKIN, MICHAEL J.; and TRAILL, RONALD D. 1973. *Microteaching: Research, Theory and Practice.* Sydney: Sydney University Press.

VARE, JONATHAN W. 1994. "Partnership Contrasts: Microteaching Activity as Two Apprenticeships in Thinking." *Journal of Teacher Education* 45(3):209.

WAHBA, ESSAM HANNA. 1999. "Microteaching." *Forum: A Journal for the Teacher of English outside the United States* 37(4):23.

WILKINSON, GAYLE A. 1996. "Enhancing Microteaching through Additional Feedback from Preservice Administrators." *Teaching and Teacher Education* 12(2):211.

DWIGHT W. ALLEN
WEIPING WANG

MIDDLE EAST AND NORTH AFRICA

This entry provides an overview of the status of education in the Middle East and North Africa (MENA) region. It contains both statistically based assessments of individual countries as well as a discussion of the overall factors that are currently affecting the level of and accessibility to primary, secondary, and tertiary education. Current and future systemic challenges are also exposed, and possible solutions from similar case studies are advanced.

Regional Background

Depending upon the scope, origin, and purpose of study, the MENA region can include the countries of Algeria, Bahrain, Djibouti, Egypt, Iran, Iraq, Jordan, Kuwait, Lebanon, Libya, Malta, Mauritania, Morocco, Oman, Qatar, Saudi Arabia, Sudan, Syria, Tunisia, the United Arab Emirates (UAE), Yemen, and West Bank-Gaza. (While the State of Israel is geographically located within this region, this article focuses on those countries that are classified as Arab through their common usage of and reliance on the Arabic language [except Iran, where Farsi is predominant].) For the purposes of this article, MENA includes all of the above, except Malta, Djibouti, Mauritania, and Sudan. Although the region is bound, to a large extent, by the prevalence of the Islamic religion and the commonality of Arabic as a language, it is diverse in ethnicity, tradition, history, and spoken Arabic. As a region it has a population of more than 295 million that reflects diversities in social stratification and economic development ranging from the high-income, oil-rich countries of Kuwait, Qatar, and UAE to the low-income countries of Egypt and Morocco.

Owing to rising oil revenues in the 1970s, oil-producing countries underwent a major economic boom that resulted in a tremendous expansion in social services, construction, and basic infrastructure.

Non-oil-producing countries such as Jordan, Morocco, and Tunisia also benefited from the influx of capital by exporting their human capital in the form of professional and lay labor. According to the World Bank, from the early 1970s to the late 1990s, MENA grew faster than any other region except East Asia.

Because of the emphasis placed on upstream and downstream oil production, revenues from these activities continue to be the dominant generator of funds throughout MENA, and the central government became both the storehouse and distributor of these funds. As such, governmental social ministries were created to disperse, invest, and manage these appropriations as it deemed fit, with little or no initial studies and a deficit of long-term planning and analysis. In part, this is due to the general receptivity of centralized planning and manpower forecasting that was dominant in the 1950s. Manpower forecasting makes the assumption that a nation can reasonably predict its human capital requirement based on its potential growth rate and its developing infrastructure. While this method may provide viable predictions for a country that has a measured growth rate from a diverse and sustainable resource base, it is less reliable for single-resource-based economies, especially those that experience tremendous revenue variations from the single main resource. Given these conditions, governments in the MENA region initiated and managed revenue streams that fed into industry, agriculture, and social services.

Because of these factors, the countries of MENA continue to experience fluctuations in economic performance (see Figure 1), resulting in a region that exhibits an overall low economic growth rate, rising populations, sporadic civil unrest, and a lack of regional transparency and cooperation in many governmental areas, not excluding education. Governments that in boom years had ingested most of its graduates in swelling public-service sectors, find themselves each year with a growing number of graduates who expect their government to offer them an encompassing position in perpetuity—not only a job, but a lifelong career. While there are movements throughout MENA to "nationalize" positions that once were held by expatriates, it is logical to predict that the public sector will eventually build to capacity and the private sector will need to alleviate this influx of human capital.

Oman, for example, employs most of its workforce in public service, but the state can no longer offer positions for the nearly 30,000 Omanis who enter the workforce annually. As a result, the state mandated that financial and banking corporations begin hiring from the national base. The swelling numbers mean that other private sectors will also need to be included. It is also important to note that if an educational system were training its workforce at submarket levels, a rapid nationalization would have a negative effect, resulting in falling productivity, output, and national income. Although some of the questions concerning nationalization of public and private enterprise are beginning to find answers, the deeper question remains: How are the state-driven educational systems going to enable the workforce to compete on national, regional, and global levels? (See Figure 2.)

Educational Perspective

To understand the scope of the problem, it is important to study some of the weak points in the implementing of the educational system.

Access, literacy, and equity. In a regional comparison, MENA accounts for only 0.1 percent of the global expenditure on research and development, which is lower than that of every other region except Sub-Saharan Africa. While there is a considerable lack of regional cooperation, there is also a weak communication network that impedes the transfer and flow of knowledge, with fewer than fifteen main telephone lines per 100 people in urban settings and fewer than five lines per 100 people in rural environments (see Figure 3). This is less than 65 percent that of the Europe and Central Asia region and less than 25 percent that of the nations of the Organisation for Economic Co-operation and Development.

Because all countries operate from a fixed budget and most countries have several ministries that serve the different levels of education, there is competition between ministries for prominence and funding (see Table 1). This leads to a number of questions, including: If funding for primary education is increased, which ministry is willing to suffer a reduced budget and by what amount? Within the continuous cycle of education, how is it feasible to diminish one level of education without compromising the remaining levels? Furthermore, with the inherent nature of the accelerating and steep learning curve of the technology in the global market, how will educational ministries be able to secure

FIGURE 1

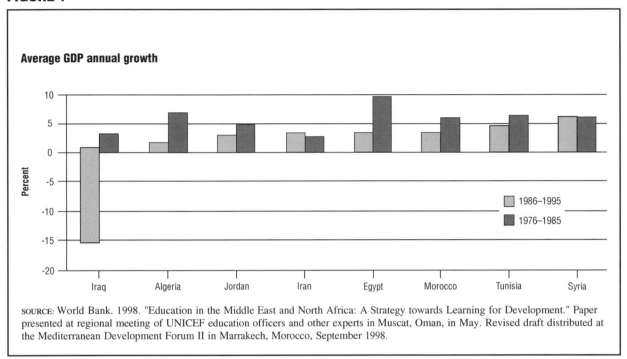

Average GDP annual growth

SOURCE: World Bank. 1998. "Education in the Middle East and North Africa: A Strategy towards Learning for Development." Paper presented at regional meeting of UNICEF education officers and other experts in Muscat, Oman, in May. Revised draft distributed at the Mediterranean Development Forum II in Marrakech, Morocco, September 1998.

higher funding within countries whose economies are already strapped?

In 1960 a large percentage of the population in the MENA countries were illiterate; by 1995 literacy rates had doubled. While overall literacy increased more than in any other region, countries with a significant rural population, such as Egypt, Morocco, and Yemen, reported a lower literacy increase than those with high urban populations. Also, countries with high rural populations exhibit the lowest literacy rates among women. Women in rural Morocco and Yemen have the least educational opportunity, with literacy rates of less than 10 percent.

Equity among educational systems is not encouraging, with 5 million children aged six to ten and 4 million children aged eleven to fifteen out of a regular school program, in 1995. By 2015 it is estimated that this number will grow by 40 percent, resulting in projected figures of 7.5 million and 5.6 million, respectively (see also Figure 4). While all countries offer compulsory education, there is limited ability to track student progression, and retention rates from the early 1990s do not indicate a strong success factor. Nearly 30 percent of primary students in Tunisia fail to complete the seven-year cycle, and in Yemen female school retention falls from 31 percent in first grade to only 25 percent in sixth grade.

Although the formal language or language of instruction (especially with regard to religious education) may be Arabic, formal and written Arabic is grammatically different from the vernacular of the spoken dialect. This can constitute a disadvantage especially to those of rural backgrounds with little or no formal exposure to a grammatical understanding of Arabic. Even at the level of the dialect, there are differences that are evident enough to distinguish rural from urban students, differences that can highlight class division rather than encourage educational unity.

In addition to language obstacles, there is also an opportunity compromise mentality that exists, especially within disadvantaged communities. With the lack of child labor laws and a financially struggling economic class, what is the financial incentive for retaining a child in the educational system versus the lost wage opportunity of a working child if there is no foreseeable cost–benefit factor? While this effect may be dominant within rural cultures, it is not uncommon in urban society either because of strong perceptions that the educational systems are misguided and dysfunctional. It is not surprising that there is a generational continuance of poor retention rates in public schools in such countries as Egypt, Morocco, and Yemen.

FIGURE 2

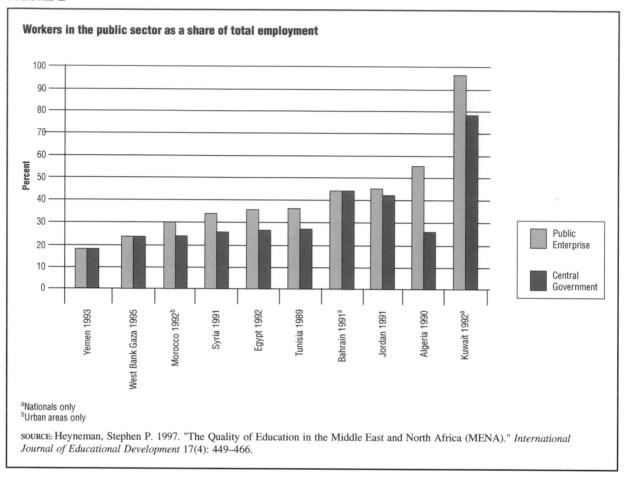

Workers in the public sector as a share of total employment

[a]Nationals only
[b]Urban areas only

SOURCE: Heyneman, Stephen P. 1997. "The Quality of Education in the Middle East and North Africa (MENA)." *International Journal of Educational Development* 17(4): 449–466.

Quality of teaching. It is difficult to gauge the quality of education administered throughout the region because only two middle-income countries have participated in objective international assessments: Iran (in the Third International Mathematics and Science Study of 1995) and Jordan (in the International Assessment of Educational Progress of 1991). Other countries, however, have already indicated a willingness to participate in similar future studies. Once it becomes evident that such studies not only provide a baseline of national educational strengths and weaknesses but also suggest methods and directions for systemic improvement, there will be more of an incentive for regional cooperation and participation.

A more complex issue, however, centers around the method of teaching, the relevancy of the material, and the students' ability to manipulate and apply knowledge and data in a manner that will lead to effective problem solving, as well as theory and analysis. Data from 1995 indicate that although the number of secondary education teachers rose, the percentage of teachers with university degrees fell from 85 percent to 77 percent, and this was accompanied by an average decline in salary expenditure. This reveals a system that is not only reticent about placing an emphasis upon creating a progressive learning environment but that also fails to recognize educational programs as less than a formulation of inputs and outputs. As a consequence of this lack of consistent commitment to faculty and staff, there exists an unbalance in teacher–student ratios.

In addition, there is regional deterioration of the infrastructure of the learning environment. There is not a correlating commitment to libraries, laboratories, and technology workshops for the influx of students, and those facilities that do exist are overburdened and in need of repair.

Quality of educational materials. Because the central government continues to play such a dominant role in the management of national education, the quality of educational materials tends to reflect a sys-

FIGURE 3

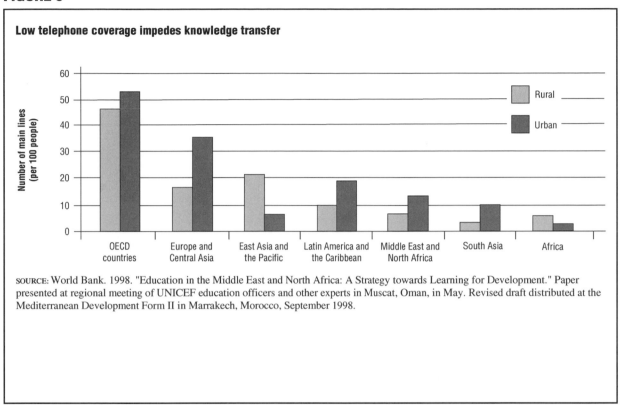

Low telephone coverage impedes knowledge transfer

SOURCE: World Bank. 1998. "Education in the Middle East and North Africa: A Strategy towards Learning for Development." Paper presented at regional meeting of UNICEF education officers and other experts in Muscat, Oman, in May. Revised draft distributed at the Mediterranean Development Form II in Marrakech, Morocco, September 1998.

tem plagued by micromanagement and misapplication. Educational ministries obtain their educational materials through a centrally funded governmental appropriation that is contracted out to either a governmental printing agency or a private agency that relies heavily upon such business. All content, nature, scope, and graphics for educational materials (print and computer-based) are decided from within the hierarchy of the ministry of education, without field study analysis of the needs of the ministry's constituencies. Because this process must be one that stresses cost-effectiveness, texts are a homogenized production that are not able to reflect issues in an authoritatively complete manner, nor are they specifically targeted at different constituent populations. This process, if left unchecked, has the potential to further isolate national student populations from the global market by insulating them from both the technology and the ideas that underpin international commerce. (See Figure 5.)

Cultural aspects of education. In their dogmatic mode of planning and their uniform approach to sector problem solving, the central governments of the MENA region are similar to the centrally planned regimes of the former Eastern bloc coun-

tries. In contrast to the nonreligious Eastern bloc regimes, however, the MENA governments have a very strong religious component that permeates the social and political culture. With the rise of state wealth based on oil reserves came the governmental drive to create educational institutions that were governed by Islamic law—new institutions that were in addition to the public establishments. Because of the prominence afforded to Islamic thought, however, all of the educational institutions took on an aspect of Islamic doctrine that was incorporated into religious studies, the study of Arabic, or both. Being forced to respond to many masters is not a unique position in the educational field, especially with the emphasis upon creating the diverse revenue streams of institutional planning and advancement. Nevertheless, because the educational institutions of the countries of MENA are public establishments and rely upon single-source revenues, they must carefully negotiate several powerful relationships within that revenue stream. This results in institutions that are by and large politically, economically, and directionally powerless.

Accompanying the rise of the central government was the creation of the welfare state. Prior to

TABLE 1

Education indicators

	Ministries with education authority	Years of compulsory education	Percent of children 6–10 in school, mid-1990s	Adult's mean years of schooling, 1990	Primary general enrollment ratio, 1995	Secondary general enrollment ratio, 1995	Tertiary general enrollment ratio, 1995
Algeria	4	9	95	4.0	107	62	11
Egypt*	4	8	84	4.3	100	74	18
Iran*	4	12	97	3.9	99	69	15
Iraq	2	6	79	4.0	90	44	–
Jordan	4	10	100	6.0	94	65	18
Lebanon*	3	6	96	–	109	76	29
Morocco***	3	6	54	2.5	83	39	11
Syria	3	6	91	5.1	101	44	18
Tunisia	3	–	97	3.9	116	61	13
West Bank Gaza**	2	10	–	8.0	92	66	–
Yemen	2	9	50	1.5	60	27	10

* Egyptian tertiary general enrollment ratio and all Iranian general enrollment ratios are 1994 data; Lebanese secondary and tertiary general enrollment ratios are 1993 data.
** West Bank Gaza years of schooling for 1992. General enrollment ratios are arithmetic averages for females and males.
*** In Morocco basic education starts at age seven.

SOURCE: Based on data from UNESCO 1997, Barro and Lee 1996, World Bank 1997, Palestinian Authority 1996, National Center for Human Resources Development <www.hcrd.gov.jo>, World Bank 1998, World Bank staff calculation using data from FAFO 1993 and 1996.

the oil boom, the work ethic was closely affiliated with local indigenous industries that remained largely unchanged for generations. With the rapid influx of funds, populations began to rely upon the state to provide for their basic needs, including major sectors of education, health, and employment. This has greatly enhanced the general perception of the responsibilities of the state while diminishing the need for social responsibility and achievement. It is not surprising that vocational training is unpopular, as are blue-collar jobs in comparison with white-collar positions. This attitude of a state-reliant labor force and the general popular disinclination toward bottom-to-top corporate ladder climbing puts the educational system into a distinct role: that of educating a workforce that is focused solely upon receiving prominent state-sponsored positions. In this position, the educational system is blamed both for not adequately preparing the workforce to create new jobs and for not adequately training the workers to be able to participate in the economy. Because of this, there is little curricular incentive to emphasize the importance of acquiring and honing the managerial, operational, and technical skills that are basic to the formation of a progressive, evolving, and adapting society.

Under the pressures of central control, religious persuasion, and the micromanaged process that largely characterizes public education, the system will continue to flounder and be directionless. Such a state of affairs has the potential to further discourage the population from participation if, at some point, the system cannot demonstrate its efficacy in producing national, regional, and international leaders.

Future Challenges and Direction

Without a doubt, the leadership of the MENA countries will have to develop an acute awareness of the strengths and weaknesses of their educational systems. Based upon this awareness, they will need to design plans and solutions that are both realistic and practical.

Testing, benchmarking, and information exchange. If educational systems in MENA are to succeed and effectively integrate with the global community, education must return to its primary goal: "learning should be understanding concepts and principles in order to make inferences from that knowledge and to apply it in daily life" (Heyneman 1990, p. 187). Usage of regional testing of these concepts can and needs to be employed. Creating a "national assessment" that is provided at regular intervals will enable both national progress and overall regional standing to be determined and to be tracked over time. This should not necessarily encourage partisanship among countries, because comprehensive regional progress will become a reality with only interregional cooperation. Although initially countries may be hesitant to divulge such previously "sensitive" information, it will become apparent that the introduction to and full participation in the global environment will necessitate such transparency.

Financing strategies. Although the state may remain the organizational and licensing body of education, providers and consumers of education need to understand the ineffectiveness of a state-sponsored educational system. While this does not indicate a total financial withdrawal of the government from the educational arena, it does suggest a reevaluation of the government's ability to simultaneously finance a growing population and an improvement in the educational services that are provided. It should be determined to what position the state could be expected to recede, but such a transformation should be implemented incrementally over at least one generational period.

Along similar lines, as sectors within the educational ministry are privatized, the state should encourage and initially subsidize private sources of funding. This will result in a competitive environment within the educational industries, encouraging lean costs, higher quality, product accountability, and enhanced consumer choice.

The method of government-controlled educational materials must also be privatized, with the central government operating as "quality control" in the general sense, without overt religious overtones and control. Governments will need to provide subsidy incentives to jump-start this private industry, but as in other countries this will encourage competition and a healthy environment.

The encouragement of compulsory education. In encouraging compulsory education, there must be an intention to provide a framework for students that will encourage both the completion of the track and the ability to choose a direction upon completion. This implies a need to abandon the rigid prerequisites during compulsory education that are commonly associated with elite institutions. Teachers will need to be held accountable for their performance in results-oriented evaluations, rather than through strict adherence to a curriculum.

FIGURE 4

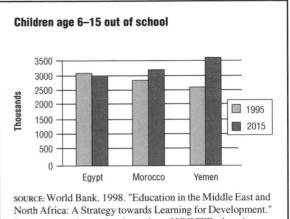

SOURCE: World Bank. 1998. "Education in the Middle East and North Africa: A Strategy towards Learning for Development." Paper presented at regional meeting of UNICEF education officers and other experts in Muscat, Oman, in May. Revised draft distributed at the Mediterranean Development Forum II in Marrakech. Morocco, September 1998.

Conclusion

Within the countries of the MENA region, there exist systems of education that are anachronistic in character and dysfunctional with regard to adapting for the world of the future. It is imperative that if MENA is to become an active, tradable partner within the global community, it will need to ready its workforce for the market of today and the market of tomorrow. This implies the need for a self-directed, systematic, and objective look at each country from the method of governance and finance to the manner in which education is presented to the various populations. As painful, costly, and labor intensive as this may be, however, it is only the harbinger of a future in which those countries that are poised to react and adapt will prevail at the expense of countries saddled with unwilling and nonintrospective forms of government.

See also: INTERNATIONAL ASSESSMENTS; ISLAM.

BIBLIOGRAPHY

BAHGAT, GAWDAT. 1999. "Education in the Gulf Monarchies: Retrospect and Prospect." *International Review of Education* 45(2):127–136.

HEYNEMAN, STEPHEN P. 1987. "Uses of Examinations in Developing Countries: Selection, Research, and Education Sector Management." *International Journal of Educational Development* 7(4):251–263.

FIGURE 5

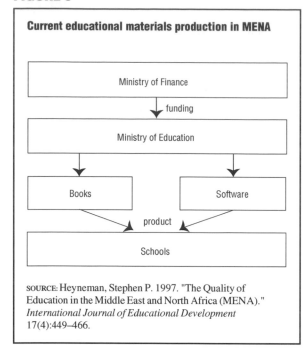

Current educational materials production in MENA

SOURCE: Heyneman, Stephen P. 1997. "The Quality of Education in the Middle East and North Africa (MENA)." *International Journal of Educational Development* 17(4):449–466.

HEYNEMAN, STEPHEN P. 1990. "Using Examinations and Testing to Improve Educational Quality." *Educational Policy* 4(3):177–192.

HEYNEMAN, STEPHEN P. 1997. "The Quality of Education in the Middle East and North Africa (MENA)." *International Journal of Educational Development* 17(4):449–466.

LANCASTER, PAT, and SIDDIQI, MOIN A. 2001. "Meeting the Twenty-First Century Challenges." *Middle East* 317:23–31.

MOJAB, SHAHRZAD. 1998. "The State, University, and the Construction of Civil Society in the Middle East." *Futures* 30:657–667.

SHAW, K. E. 1993. "Development Tasks for Arab Gulf Universities." *Arab Studies Quarterly* 15(4):83–91.

TANSEL, AYSIT, and KAZEMI, ABBAS. 2000. "Educational Expenditure in the Middle East and North Africa." *Middle Eastern Studies* 36(4):75–101.

WORLD BANK. 1998. "Education in the Middle East and North Africa: A Strategy towards Learning for Development." Paper presented at regional meeting of UNICEF education officers and other experts in Muscat, Oman, in May. Revised draft distributed at the Mediterranean Development Forum II in Marrakech, Morocco, September 1998.

ERIC HILGENDORF

MIDDLE SCHOOLS

In 1888 Harvard University president Charles Eliot launched an effort to reorganize primary and secondary schooling. At that time, as state after state enacted compulsory attendance laws, eight-year elementary schools and four-year high schools were the most common types of institutions. But Eliot and his colleagues on the National Education Association's Committee of Ten on Secondary School Studies argued that young adolescents wasted time in the last years of elementary school and should be introduced to college preparatory courses such as algebra and Latin at an earlier age. The committee recommended reducing elementary schools to six grade levels (1–6) and increasing secondary grades to six grade levels (7–12). They also recommended that the new secondary schools be designed to allow talented, college-bound students to be promoted quickly so that they could complete the six years of secondary school in as few as four years.

As grades seven and eight began to be considered *junior* or *introductory* high school grades rather than elementary grades, intermediate schools (grades 7–8), junior high schools (grades 7–9), and junior-senior high schools (grades 7–12) began to appear. These new secondary schools were seen as a way of offering young adolescents a curriculum that was more substantial and more differentiated than that offered in elementary schools, while also addressing common practical problems such as the overcrowding of K–8 elementary schools and high rates of students leaving school after grade eight. In addition to giving college-bound youths earlier access to college preparatory work, educators in these schools sought to entice greater numbers of non-college-bound youths to stay in school at least through grade nine by offering them commercial, domestic, and vocational curricula. By 1920 the number of junior high schools in the United States had grown to 883. By the 1940s more than half of the nation's young adolescents attended a junior high school, and by 1960 four out of five did so.

The enduring contributions of junior high schools to middle-level education in America are many. These schools introduced a broader range of exploratory, *tryout* courses and activities in order to assist young adolescents to discover and develop their interests and abilities. Junior high schools were also the source of other educational innovations, including homeroom and teacher-adviser programs, extracurricular activities, and core curriculum approaches emphasizing the correlation of subject areas and the integration of learning across disciplinary boundaries.

The Emergence of Middle Schools

Despite the innovations and successes of junior high schools, these schools became the target of increasing criticism for tending to adopt the curricula, grading systems, large size, schedules, regimentation, and impersonal climate of senior high schools. Ironically, some of the key organizational changes that the early promoters of junior high schools believed would meet the special needs of young adolescents—departmentalization, teacher specialization, and tracking—had been taken to the extreme and were now being challenged as inappropriate for junior high school students. Similarly, many began to have second thoughts about having ninth-grade educational programs in the same school buildings as seventh- and eighth-grade programs. The ninth-grade program and curriculum were constrained by Carnegie unit requirements for high school graduation and college entrance. Because these requirements affected scheduling and staffing decisions, they often strongly influenced the educational programs offered to seventh and eighth graders in junior high schools as well.

Fifty years after the first junior high schools were established, educators began to call for middle schools—new schools that had a different grade organization and a more developmentally responsive program—in order to provide a more gradual and appropriate transition between the elementary and high school years. In the 1950s Alvin Howard became one of the first to advocate the creation of a 6–8 school that would remove the limitations imposed by Carnegie units, have a more stable school climate than a 7–8 school, and would recognize the earlier onset of puberty of young adolescents in the second half of the twentieth century. William Alexander and Emmett Williams, in 1965, recommended the creation of 5–8 middle schools featuring interdisciplinary teaming, small learning communities, a teacher advisory program, and special learning cen-

ters where students could catch up on needed skills or branch out into further exploration. For example, Alexander and Williams suggested the creation of *wing units* (interdisciplinary teams of teachers to jointly plan curriculum and deliver instruction to 100 students). Each wing unit would join with wing units from the other grade levels in the school to form a "school within the school." The special learning centers would be open during the school day, after school, and on Saturday, and would include a library, a reading laboratory, a home arts center, a typing and writing laboratory, a foreign language laboratory, an arts and hobby center, a music room, and a physical education/recreation center.

In 1966 Donald Eichorn, a school district superintendent, wrote the first full book promoting the creation of 6–8 middle schools. The book attempted to apply Piaget's theories regarding early adolescent development in designing a suitable educational program. For example, Eichorn proposed that middle schools offer frequent opportunities for active learning and interaction with peers. He suggested eliminating activities that might embarrass late maturers or place them at a competitive disadvantage (e.g., interscholastic athletics and prom queen contests) and replacing them with less competitive activities that welcome and affirm all students regardless of their current level of physical or cognitive development (intramural athletics and physical education programs and flexible self-selected projects that allow all students to pursue personal interests and develop further interests while making frequent use of a well-equipped resource center). He proposed flexible scheduling to allow for extended learning opportunities and flexible groupings of middle school students for instruction (e.g., by current cognitive functioning or interests) rather than just by chronological age or grade level. He called for a curriculum that featured frequent use of interdisciplinary thematic units that reflected the interrelated nature of different content areas and that balanced traditional academic subjects with cultural studies, physical education, fine arts, and practical arts.

By 1970 a small group of educators founded the Midwest Middle School Association, amid much debate and confrontation between advocates of 6–8 middle schools and 7–9 junior high schools. Three years later its name was changed to the National Middle School Association to acknowledge the national scope of the growing middle school movement. The writings of key educators in this movement displayed increasingly widespread agreement on practices that they believed were especially appropriate for young adolescents, including interdisciplinary team teaching, discovery and inquiry methods, teacher-adviser plans, flexible scheduling, exploratory courses, and ungraded programs.

Growth and Maturation of the Middle School Movement

In 1965 only 5 percent of middle-grades schools in the United States were 6–8 or 5–8 middle schools, and 67 percent were 7–9 junior high schools. By the year 2000 these percentages were reversed: only 5 percent of middle-grades schools were 7–9 junior highs and 69 percent were 6–8 or 5–8 middle schools. The number of middle schools grew rapidly—from 1,434 (23%) in 1971 to 4,094 (33%) in 1981; 6,168 (51%) in 1991; and 9,750 (69%) in 2000.

Although the number of middle schools grew quickly during the 1960s and 1970s, according to William Alexander, writing in 1978, most of these new schools displayed "limited progress toward the objectives of the middle school movement" (p. 19). In fact, John Lounsbury noted in 1991 that the first comparative studies of the new middle schools and the old junior high schools revealed that the schools "were surprisingly alike in actual practice" (p. 68). Changes were restricted largely to the names of schools and the grades they contained.

One reason for the lack of progress in implementing a set of distinct practices was that many middle schools were established for reasons of expediency. For example, the new grade arrangements helped some districts reduce overcrowding in elementary schools, poor utilization of buildings, or racial segregation. Through the 1970s little empirical research was conducted on the consequences of implementing or ignoring the lists of recommended practices. Thus, there was no scientific evidence to persuade educators to change their programs and practices.

By the 1980s the debates between educators about the best grade structures for young adolescents began to die out, as both middle school and junior high school advocates realized that the typical middle-grades school, regardless of grade organization, was still failing to meet the needs of its students. "Junior high and middle school proponents and practitioners began to coalesce into a single cause—the cause of improving early adolescent edu-

cation" (Lounsbury, p. 67). This new unity of purpose and vision was also fueled by the emergence of a strong and respected literature on the characteristics of early adolescents, and by research indicating that the transition to middle-grades schools was associated with declines in academic motivation and performance.

Research also indicated that students perceived their middle-grades teachers as more remote and impersonal than their elementary teachers, and that they were less certain that their middle-grades teachers cared about them or knew them well. Furthermore, student work completed in the first year of the middle grades was often less demanding than in the last year of elementary school, academic expectations in middle-grades schools were generally low, and students had few opportunities to learn important new concepts and apply them to real-world problems. This research along with case studies and empirical analyses of the effects of recommended practices on the quality of school programs and on the learning, motivation, and development of young adolescents all gave further impetus to the calls for the reform of middle-grades schools.

As practitioners, researchers, and scholars began speaking with one voice about the continuing shortcomings of middle-grades education in the United States, middle-grades reform began receiving unprecedented national attention. That is, at the end of the 1980s, states and foundations that had been focusing their educational reform initiatives on preschool and early elementary education or on high school improvement and dropout prevention, began to recognize that the middle grades might be central to helping more students succeed and stay in school. California was one of the first states to produce a task-force report calling for middle-grades reform. California's 1987 report, *Caught in the Middle*, was followed by a long line of reports from Florida, Maryland, Louisiana, and at least fifteen other states. At about the same time, foundations such as the Lilly Endowment, the Carnegie Corporation of New York, the Edna McConnell Clark Foundation, and the W. K. Kellogg Foundation began advocating and funding middle-grades reform initiatives.

These efforts helped solidify the consensus on the kinds of supportive structures and responsive practices needed by students in the middle grades (e.g., the eight principles outlined in 1989 by the Carnegie Council on Adolescent Development in *Turning Points*). At this time, research in the middle grades by a wide variety of researchers began to show that schools serving early adolescents, especially middle schools, were increasingly implementing educational programs that were based on these recommended practices for the middle grades. Fewer schools were middle schools only in name.

Accomplishments of the Middle School Movement

Anthony Jackson and Gayle Davis noted in 2000 that "structural changes in middle-grades education—how students and teachers are organized for learning—have been fairly widespread and have produced good results" (p. 5). Changes in practice that ensure each student in a middle-grades school has more support from (and more meaningful relationships with) caring adults at the school have reduced the negative shifts in students' motivational beliefs during the middle grades. Schools-within-schools, looping (assigning teachers to the same students for two or three years), semidepartmentalization (assigning a teacher to teach two subjects to three class sections rather than one subject to six class sections), and interdisciplinary teaming with a common planning period for the teachers on a team are examples of structural reforms that have been made in many middle-grades schools. Such reforms have been found to increase students' well-being and perceptions that their teacher cares about them and their learning, and to strengthen teacher–student relationships. In turn, when middle-grades students perceive their teachers care about them and their learning, they are more likely to report that they try to do what their teachers ask them to do and give their best effort in class, and they are less likely to engage in risky behaviors.

In sum, many middle-grades schools have succeeded in changing their climates and structures to become what Joan Lipsitz and colleagues, in 1997, called "warmer, happier, and more peaceful places for students and adults"(p. 535). However, as David Hamburg noted in 2000, changes in climates and structures "are necessary but not sufficient for major improvement in academic achievement" (p. xii). That is, while modest achievement gains may result from changes in school organization—such as semidepartmentalization, team teaching, or creating smaller learning environments—major achievement gains are obtained only in schools that have implemented both changes in school organization and in curriculum, instruction, and professional development changes that assist teachers to "transmit a core of common, substantial knowledge to all students in ways that foster curiosity, problem solving, and critical thinking" (Hamburg, p. x). For example, in a 1997 study by Robert Felner and colleagues of a group of thirty-one Illinois middle schools, those schools that had made both structural and instructional changes that were consistent with *Turning Points* recommendations achieved substantially better and displayed larger achievement gains over a two-year period than did similar schools that had implemented at least some of the key structural changes outlined in *Turning Points,* but not changes in curriculum and instruction. Another study suggesting the critical importance of going beyond just structural changes in improving achievement was conducted by Steven Mertens, Nancy Flowers, and Peter Mulhall in 1998, and involved 155 middle-grades schools in Michigan. When these researchers analyzed outcomes in schools that had one of the key structural changes in place (interdisciplinary teams that were given high levels of common planning time), they found that achievement gains were much higher among the subset of these schools that had a received a grant from the Kellogg Foundation that made it possible for their teachers to engage more regularly in staff development activities focused on curriculum and instruction. In fact there is even evidence from this study that staff development may be more important than common planning time in facilitating achievement gains. Schools whose teams had inadequate common planning (but had a grant that made frequent professional development possible) showed more achievement gains than did schools without grants, even those whose teams had high levels of planning time.

Unfortunately, high-performing middle schools are still rare, because "relatively little has changed at the core of most students' school experience: curriculum, assessment, and instruction" (Jackson and Davis, p. 5). Although structures and practices that are in keeping with the best of the middle-grades reform documents are an essential foundation for middle-grade reform, dramatic and sustained improvements in student performance occur only if teachers also provide all students with markedly better learning opportunities every day.

Enduring Problems

One particularly vexing problem that plagued junior high schools and continues to plague middle schools is what Samuel H. Popper termed being "a school without teachers" (p. 57). Because of the lack of teacher education programs and licensure that focus on the middle school level, the majority of young adolescents are taught by teachers who prepared for a career as an elementary or high school teacher. Fewer than one in four middle-grades teachers have received specialized training to teach at the middle level before they begin their careers. As a result, teachers who wind up teaching in middle schools, even those who discover that they enjoy teaching middle school students, find themselves woefully unprepared to work with this age group. Thomas Dickinson commented in 2001 that these instructors enter middle schools "unschooled in appropriate curriculum and instruction for young adolescents, and ignorant of the place and purpose of middle school organizational practices and the complex role of the middle school teacher" (p. 7). This is clearly one reason why curriculum and instruction in the middle grades continues to show little improvement over time.

There is a growing consensus to support specialized teacher preparation at the middle-grades level. Numerous studies show that middle-grades teachers and principals favor specialized teacher preparation of middle-grades teachers. Similarly, the National Middle School Association, The National Association for Secondary School Principals, and the National Forum to Accelerate Middle Grades Reform have all called for the specialized preparation of middle-grades teachers. Perhaps the only solution to this enduring problem is for states to establish mandatory requirements for middle-level licensure that do not overlap significantly with licensure for elementary school or high school teachers. This will serve as an incentive for colleges and universities to establish specialized programs that prepare practicing and future teachers to work effectively with middle school students, curricula, and instructional practices, and also as an incentive to teachers to pursue this specialized training.

Unfortunately, there is also a lack of middle-school principal preparation. "Preparation to lead a school based on the tenets of the middle school concept is even more rare than middle school teacher preparation programs. The same can be said for the licensure of middle school principals" (Dickinson, p. 7).

The National Forum to Accelerate Middle Grades Reform declared in 2000 that high-performing middle schools are "academically excellent, developmentally responsive, and socially equitable" (p. K7). If such middle schools are going to become the norm rather than the exception, both middle school teachers and principals need more specialized preparation and continuing professional development to support and sustain their trajectory toward excellence.

See also: CURRICULUM, SCHOOL; EDUCATIONAL LEADERSHIP; LOOPING; SECONDARY EDUCATION.

BIBLIOGRAPHY

ALEXANDER, WILLIAM M. 1978. "How Fares the Middle School Movement?" *Middle School Journal* 9(3):319–321.

ALEXANDER, WILLIAM M., and MCEWIN, C. KENNETH. 1989. *Schools in the Middle: Status and Progress.* Columbus, OH: National Middle School Association.

ALEXANDER, WILLIAM M., and WILLIAMS, EMMETT L. 1965. "Schools for the Middle Years." *Educational Leadership* 23(3):217–223.

CALIFORNIA STATE DEPARTMENT OF EDUCATION. 1987. *Caught in the Middle: Educational Reform for Young Adolescents in California Public Schools.* Sacramento, CA: State Department of Education.

CARNEGIE COUNCIL ON ADOLESCENT DEVELOPMENT. 1989. *Turning Points: Preparing American Youth for the 21st Century.* New York: Carnegie Corporation of New York.

DICKINSON, THOMAS S. 2001. "Reinventing the Middle School: A Proposal to Counter Arrested Development." In *Reinventing the Middle School,* ed. Thomas S. Dickinson. New York: Routledge Falmer.

ECCLES, JACQUELYNNE S., and MIDGLEY, CAROL. 1989. "Stage-Environment Fit: Developmentally Appropriate Classrooms for Young Adolescents." In *Research on Motivation in Education,* Vol. 3: *Goals and Cognitions,* ed. Russell E. Ames and Carole Ames. Orlando, FL: Academic Press.

EICHORN, DONALD H. 1966. *The Middle School.* New York: Center for Applied Research in Education.

EPSTEIN, JOYCE L. 1981. "Patterns of Classroom Participation, Student Attitudes, and Achievement." In *The Quality of School Life,* ed. Joyce L. Epstein. Lexington, MA: Lexington Books.

EPSTEIN, JOYCE L., and MAC IVER, DOUGLAS J. 1990. *Education in the Middle Grades: National Practices and Trends.* Columbus, OH: National Middle School Association.

FELNER, ROBERT D.; JACKSON, ANTHONY W.; KASAK, DEBORAH; MULHALL, PETER; BRAND, SALLY; and FLOWERS, NANCY. 1997. "The Impact of School Reform for the Middle Years: Longitudinal Study of a Network Engaged in Turning Points-Based Comprehensive School Transformation." *Phi Delta Kappan* 78: 528–532, 541–550.

HAMBURG, DAVID A. 2000. "Foreword." In *Turning Points 2000: Educating Adolescents in the 21st Century,* ed. Anthony W. Jackson and Gayle A. Davis. New York: Teachers College Press.

HOWARD, ALVIN W. 1956. "The Carnegie Unit." *Clearing House* 39:135–129.

JACKSON, ANTHONY W., and DAVIS, GAYLE A. 2000. *Turning Points 2000: Educating Adolescents in the 21st Century.* New York: Teachers College Press.

LIPSITZ, JOAN; MIZELL, M. HAYES; JACKSON, ANTHONY W.; and AUSTIN, LEAH M. 1997. "Speaking with One Voice: A Manifesto for Middle-Grades Reform." *Phi Delta Kappan* 78:533–540.

LOUNSBURY, JOHN H. 1991. *As I See It.* Columbus, OH: National Middle School Association.

MAC IVER, DOUGLAS J.; YOUNG, ESTELLE; BALFANZ, ROBERT; SHAW, ALTA; GARRIOTT, MARIA; and COHEN, AMY. 2001. "High-Quality Learning Opportunities in High Poverty Middle Schools: Moving from Rhetoric to Reality." In *Reinventing the Middle School,* ed. Thomas S. Dickinson. New York: Routledge Falmer.

MAC IVER, DOUGLAS J.; YOUNG, ESTELLE M.; and WASHBURN, BENJAMIN. 2002. "Instructional Practices and Motivation During Middle School (with Special Attention to Science)." In *Development of Achievement Motivation,* ed. Allan Wigfield and Jacquelynne S. Eccles. San Diego: Academic Press.

McEWIN, C. KENNETH; DICKINSON, THOMAS S.; and JENKINS, DORIS M. 1996. *America's Middle Schools: A 25-Year Perspective.* Columbus, OH: National Middle School Association.

MELTON, GEORGE E. 1984. "The Junior High School: Successes and Failures." In *Perspectives: Middle School Education,* ed. John H. Lounsbury. Columbus, OH: National Middle School Association.

MERTENS, STEVEN B.; FLOWERS, NANCY; and MULHALL, PETER F. 1998. *The Middle Start Initiative, Phase 1: A Longitudinal Analysis of Michigan Middle-Level Schools.* Champaign: University of Illinois, Center for Prevention Research and Development.

NATIONAL EDUCATION ASSOCIATION. 1894. *Report of the Committee of Ten on Secondary School Studies.* New York: American Book Company.

NATIONAL FORUM TO ACCELERATE MIDDLE GRADES REFORM. 2001. "The Vision." *Phi Delta Kappan* 81:K7.

POPPER, SAMUEL H. 1967. *The American Middle School: An Organizational Analysis.* Waltham, MA: Blaisdell.

VALENTINE, JERRY W.; CLARK, DONALD C.; NICKERSON, JR. NEAL C.; and KEEFE, JAMES W. 1981. *The Middle Level Principalship: A Survey of Middle Level Principals and Programs.* Reston, VA: National Association of Secondary School Principals.

VALENTINE, JERRY W.; CLARK, DONALD C.; HACKMANN, DONALD G.; and PETZKO, VICKI N. 2002. *Leadership in Middle Level Schools,* Vol. I: *A National Study of Middle Level Leaders and School Programs.* Reston, VA: National Association of Secondary School Principals.

WIGFIELD, ALLAN; ECCLES, JACQUELYNNE S.; MAC IVER, DOUGLAS; REUMAN, DAVID A.; and MIDGLEY, CAROL. 1991. "Transitions During Early Adolescence: Changes in Children's Self-Esteem Across the Transition to Junior High School." *Developmental Psychology* 27:552–565.

INTERNET RESOURCE

VALENTINE, JERRY W. 2000. "United States Middle Level Grade Organizational Trends." <www.mllc.org/docs/USMLTrends.pdf>.

DOUGLAS MAC IVER
ALLEN RUBY

MIEL, ALICE (1906–1998)

A nationally prominent social educator, Alice Miel was also a curriculum development scholar and practitioner.

Career

Miel, born on a small farm in rural Michigan, eventually studied to become a teacher during the height of the Progressive movement in education, which emerges as the strong undercurrent in Miel's life. Her formative years as an educator were spent at the University of Michigan and at Tappan Junior High School in Ann Arbor, Michigan, where she taught social studies and Latin in the early 1930s. There her benefited from an educational environment in which local school faculty and students could practice democratic skills of deliberation and decision-making. In particular, Miel's participation in collaborative curriculum development projects reflected her growing concern about the effects of the Great Depression on society and the schools. Incorporating the ideas of John Dewey, as well as those of leading progressive educators such as Harold Rugg, Ann Shumaker, and William Heard Kilpatrick, Miel and her colleagues demonstrated their conviction that the school curriculum must be modified to emphasize the study of contemporary social problems. Another early landmark experience for Miel was a 1936 study session at Ohio State University with Laura Zirbes, a prominent figure in the field of elementary education. Miel left this meeting with a commitment to understanding children, not just content, and to providing for their individual differences.

The "child-centered" Progressive education movement of the late 1930s had become the conventional wisdom in American educational thought and practice, and Miel moved into this company in the early years of her career in education, even as the Progressive movement began to fracture because of both internal divisions and external attacks. At this time of transition, the locus of Miel's story began to shift to Teachers College, Columbia University, where it would remain for the next three decades. Miel became the doctoral student of Hollis L. Caswell, then chair of the newly organized Department of Curriculum and Teaching at Teachers College. Caswell had already enhanced the visibility of the curriculum field, developed the idea of method in curriculum making, focused attention on the process by which a variety of people interacted in order to make curriculum, tried to reduce the gap between theory and practice by defining curriculum as actual experiences undergone by learners under the direction of the school, and provided a curriculum design that helped teachers to apply concepts from organized knowledge to the solution of social problems.

Caswell helped Miel to formulate the problem of curriculum change as a social process for her dissertation, which was later published as *Changing the Curriculum: A Social Process* (1946). Miel went on to serve as a professor at Teachers College from 1944 through 1971; she chaired the Department of Curriculum and Teaching at Teachers College from 1960 through 1967.

Miel became more deeply involved in Progressive ideas, even as the movement itself began to wane. Her career at Teachers College spanned the later years of the college's preeminence as the intellectual crossroads of the Progressive education movement. Her tenure there also spanned the movement's alleged decline and disarray in the 1950s as the main target of conservatives who attacked Progressive philosophy and demanded a return to the "basics" of schooling. In the 1960s, Miel's last decade at Teachers College, the national mood shifted again as Charles Silberman and other humanist educators decried conformity and rigidity in school curricula and wanted to return the focus of education to the needs of individual learners.

Miel made substantial efforts to promote democratic leadership and decision-making among educators and to enhance the capacity of schools for change and self-renewal. Her ideas and activities in this regard are instructive for current policymakers. Miel developed a knowledge base of factors that affect schools' capacity for change, established collaborative relationships with educational institutions and associations that shared the value underlying this goal, used cooperative action research to help school systems plan and implement research-based instructional innovations, worked to influence and involve a variety of community members in decisions affecting their schools, and developed exemplary models of school change in her curriculum development research.

Contribution

Several significant themes emerge from Miel's body of work. First, Miel advocated the development of democratic behavior as the ultimate goal of schooling. More importantly, she was one of the first curriculum scholars to apply social learning theories and democratic principles and processes to various aspects of curriculum development and school administration. She emphasized that curricular change is a complex social process that involves an array of participants in individual schools and communities.

Also, she strongly advocated that educators develop curriculum at the school level because of her belief that the teacher was the most important factor in curriculum change and that reform efforts would fail if they did not include the people who would have to carry them out. Through these ideas, Miel addressed the gap that long existed between educational theory and practice, implying that the involvement of various participants in the curriculum development process creates a relationship between theory and practice and allows that relationship to flourish.

Furthermore, Miel focused on the democratic social learning environment of children in schools. Miel believed that the school was democracy's proving ground because it had a large share of the responsibility for socializing the nation's young people into participation in democracy. Although some critics may have questioned whether democratic lessons could be gained from an institution that mandated participation, Miel viewed the school as society in microcosm, where people from many backgrounds learned about freedom and responsibility, individuality and cooperation—all with an eye toward citizenship. Furthermore, throughout her own life, Miel continued to develop a keen sense of the historical context of social problems that, for her, raised acute concerns for the future of a democratic society: postwar reconstruction, the cold war and Red Scare, the social tensions between "haves" and "have nots," and the Watergate scandal. In particular, she was deeply affected by the state of race relations and civil rights in American society. Through these experiences, Miel sought to move beyond the outmoded notion of racial tolerance, which, for her, connoted "putting up" with people who were different, to a more active, broader notion of intercultural understanding and appreciation. In this area, one of Miel's research accomplishments during her tenure at Teachers College merits particular attention: her 1967 book with Edwin Kiester, *The Shortchanged Children of Suburbia,* an award-winning study that has been characterized as a "groundbreaker" in its emphasis on what suburban schools were failing to teach about human differences and cultural diversity. Miel also sought to refute the claims of back-to-basics school reformers of the 1970s, arguing that the "basics" also extended to the "moral-ethical-social realm," and that they should be given a prominent place in the school curriculum. She returned to these themes in 1986 in the context of the "educational excellence" movement, manifested in reports such as *A Nation at Risk: The Imperative for Educational Reform* (1983). For Miel, the overarching responsibility in democracy was to know how democracy worked and how to maintain it through changing conditions.

Several factors likely limited the widespread acceptance of Miel's conceptions of social learning and social studies. First, Miel believed that social learning should be taught throughout the school day and not compartmentalized into one particular academic subject area. This view may have posed problems for teachers and curriculum workers, who increasingly tended to think in terms of discrete subject areas. Second, the circulation of Miel's ideas was restricted by the publication of her book *More Than Social Studies* (1957) during the conservative, subject-centered reform movements of the late 1950s. The book's publication unfortunately coincided with increasing public criticism of the perceived academic "softness" of American schools and growing demands that mathematics and science receive priority in education. The *Sputnik*-inspired National Defense Education Act (1958), linking federal support for schools with national policy objectives, ensured that social studies would be deemphasized and that traditional academic history likely would prevail in new federal guidelines for education. Third, Miel lacked affiliation with social studies traditionalists and was not considered an "expert" or specialist in any of the social sciences. Nor did Miel become deeply involved in the "new social studies" movements of the 1960s, particularly because they often resulted in written courses of study that she eschewed—for example, Man: A Course of Study (MACOS), which she criticized because of its lack of emphasis on modern man and his problems.

Finally, in terms of other accomplishments, Miel was one of the early presidents of the Association for Supervision and Curriculum Development (1953–1954). In the 1970s, she became a guiding influence in the founding of the World Council on Curriculum and Instruction (WCCI). The establishment of the WCCI was a natural outgrowth of her interest in improved curricula for all children and her work with doctoral students from all over the world. One of the distinguishing features of her career was her advocacy of global understanding through cooperation in international educational activities. Through these activities, and through her supervision of more than 140 doctoral dissertations, Miel's influence was indeed widespread.

See also: CURRICULUM, SCHOOL; PROGRESSIVE EDUCATION; ZIRBES, LAURA.

BIBLIOGRAPHY

MIEL, ALICE. 1946. *Changing the Curriculum: A Social Process.* New York: Appleton-Century.

MIEL, ALICE. 1981. "Social Studies for Understanding, Caring, Acting." In *Strategies for Educational Change: Recognizing the Gifts and Talents of All Children,* ed. Walter L. Marks and Raphael O. Nystrand. New York: Macmillan.

MIEL, ALICE, and BROGAN, PEGGY. 1957. *More than Social Studies: A View of Social Learning in the Elementary School.* Englewood Cliffs, NJ: Prentice-Hall.

MIEL, ALICE, and KIESTER, EDWIN. 1967. *The Shortchanged Children of Suburbia.* New York: Institute of Human Relations Press, The American Jewish Committee.

YEAGER, ELIZABETH ANNE. 1997. "Curriculum Change as a Social Process: An Historical Perspective on the Curriculum Ideas of Alice Miel." *Journal of Curriculum and Supervision* 13:30–55.

YEAGER, ELIZABETH ANNE. 1998. "Democracy, Social Studies, and Diversity in the Elementary School Classroom: The Progressive Ideas of Alice Miel." *Theory and Research in Social Education* 26:198–225.

YEAGER, ELIZABETH ANNE. 1999. "Alice Miel: Progressive Advocate of Democratic Social Learning for Children." In *Bending the Future to Their Will: Civic Women, Social Education, and Democracy,* ed. Margaret Smith Crocco and Orzo Luke Davis Jr. Lanham, MD: Rowman and Littlefield.

ELIZABETH ANNE YEAGER

MIGRANTS, EDUCATION OF

Anyone who has marveled at the amazing variety of fresh produce and canned and frozen foods in most U.S. supermarkets can thank a migrant farm worker for this bounty. In spite of increased mechanization of agricultural work, seasonal labor continues to be required for the cultivation and harvest of fruits and vegetables. The dairy and fishing industries are also reliant on seasonal migrant labor.

Unfortunately the children of migrant agricultural workers are among the most educationally disadvantaged children in the United States. The conditions associated with their migratory lifestyle, such as discontinuity in education, social and cultural isolation, strenuous work outside of school, extreme poverty, and poor health, impose multiple obstacles to educational success. Limited proficiency in English may be an additional educational burden. Schools coping with temporary seasonal increases in enrollment can face significant challenges in addressing the migrant students' unique educational needs. Many schools serving migrant students are small schools located in rural areas, often with limited staff and resources.

Migrant students reside in all states, the District of Columbia, and Puerto Rico. It is difficult to know the exact number of migrant children in a state at a given point in time, since migrant farmworkers and their families often move across state and national boundaries. In 2000 the U.S. Department of Education counted approximately 800,000 migrant children in U.S. schools. Close to half of these children attend schools in California and Texas; and ten other states—Arizona, Colorado, Florida, Kentucky, Michigan, North Carolina, Oregon, Pennsylvania, Puerto Rico, and Washington—account for nearly one-third of migrant students.

Migrant Families

The life of migrating families is in many ways distinct from mainstream America. Each year migrant families travel to remote parts of the country seeking employment in highly uncertain labor markets to work under strenuous and often hazardous conditions. Most migrant workers were born outside the United States, and many have difficulty speaking English. Due to the extreme economic conditions of migrant life, children often must take on work and family responsibilities at a young age, sometimes to the detriment of school attendance. In addition working in the fields exposes migrant students to a variety of health risks, such as accidental injury or exposure to pesticides.

About two-thirds of migrant students come from families where earnings are below the poverty level. The cost of migrating is high, and it is common for migrants to arrive at a new destination with little or no money or food. Living conditions are cramped and substandard—camp housing units often consist of one small room for each family that serves for cooking, eating, and sleeping. Many migrant students suffer educational disadvantages stemming from poverty and poverty-related health problems that can directly affect school performance, such as malnutrition, parasitic infections, and chronic illness.

The typical migrant adult has received less than seven years of formal schooling. Most were schooled in their home country, and are unfamiliar with the American educational system. As in many homes where the adult literacy level is low, children are less likely to be exposed to books, magazines, and other print media that promote early literacy and school readiness. Nonetheless, migrant parents, like all parents, see education as a path to a better life and place a high value on their children's education.

While migrant families may consider school quality, among other factors, when moving, decisions about where and when to relocate are ultimately based on economic necessity. Migrants must weigh such factors as the length of seasons, changes in crop conditions, demand for labor, wages, and housing availability. Migrants tend to follow the crops from south to north in the spring and then back south in the fall. Since the pattern of enrollment for migrant children is generally one of late entry in the fall and early withdrawal in the spring, migrant students are often unable to complete a school term.

In terms of ethnicity, the population of agricultural workers is overwhelmingly of Hispanic origin. More than three-quarters of workers are Mexican-born. Not surprisingly, the great majority (84%) of migrant workers are native Spanish speakers; only 12 percent are native English speakers. About 80 percent of migrant children are likely to live in a home where no English is spoken, so many arrive in schools unable to comprehend the language of instruction.

School Programs for Migrant Students

While the specific services available to migrant students in schools can vary widely, all programs address the identification and recruitment of migrant students, their assessment and placement, and the coordination of services.

School services for migrant students start with their identification or recruitment. *Identification* is the process by which children already enrolled in school are identified by staff as migratory, and therefore eligible for supplementary services. *Recruitment* refers to the process of bringing nonenrolled school-age migrant children into the school system. Migrant specialists hired by the school district or state usually perform student recruitment. Recruiters also act as ambassadors, welcoming students into the school system and serving as a conduit of information between migrant parents and schools.

Once a migrant student is enrolled, the school must determine if the regular school program will be sufficient, or if additional services are required. In many cases formal assessments must be administered to determine language proficiency, grade-level placement, and the need for special education services. School staff, or a migrant liaison, will communicate with the family about the child's educational and health history. If the students' prior school and medical records are available, this greatly expedites the placement process and avoids needless educational delays and interruptions. For secondary students, the consequences of delayed placement can be particularly high, as they may fail to accrue the credits needed for graduation.

In states and districts with a predictably high migrant population, schools may offer well-coordinated programs and services that target their specific needs. In other areas, service coordination and academic programs may be deficient or lacking entirely. Students migrating during the academic year might experience both environments. Quality programs for migrant students generally include a number of features to help them overcome educational disruption, cultural and language barriers, social isolation, and health-related problems. These features include:

- Enhanced reading and math instruction.
- English as a Second Language (ESL) and/or bilingual instruction.
- Tutoring.
- Classroom aides.
- Summer programs.
- Guidance and counseling.
- Parent outreach.
- Social work.
- Clothing.

- Nutrition.
- Transportation.
- Dental and medical services.
- Accommodations for enrollment, credit accrual, and transfer.

Transitional centers, sometimes called Newcomer Centers, may exist in districts with high numbers of immigrant and migrant students. Aimed at secondary students, these centers undertake a comprehensive assessment of incoming student needs and offer specialized classes designed to facilitate transition to regular classrooms. Most newcomer programs are set apart from the regular schools and focus on providing intensive English language instruction and developing basic literacy for students with limited formal schooling. The centers also help students develop study skills, and they familiarize new students and their families with the schools' expectations and protocols.

Another type of comprehensive program is known as a *schoolwide,* or *whole-school,* program. Rather than separate students out for specialized instruction, schools with schoolwide programs have reformed their entire regular educational program and incorporated a variety of health and other services to improve achievement for all students. Approximately 20 percent of migrant students are served in schoolwide programs.

When the small numbers of migrants or limited resources may prevent the implementation of a comprehensive program, many schools concentrate available resources on a few of the program features listed above. Programs may focus on supplementary and remedial instruction, generally in reading, math, or ESL, through specialized classes either during the school day or after school. Other schools may rely on bilingual aides to help students keep up in the regular classroom, or on migrant advocates/liaisons to help migrant families understand and access the services available to them. In several states most or all of the special educational services for migrant students are provided through summer educational programs.

In the Classroom

Services for migrants may be provided by specialized personnel such as bilingual instructors, remedial instructors, counselors, or summer school teachers, but regular classroom teachers play a critical role in helping migrant students thrive. The literature on migrant education repeatedly emphasizes the importance of: (1) building on the strengths and experiences migrant students bring to the classroom, (2) establishing a positive learning environment where the diversity among students is acknowledged and celebrated, and (3) allowing students to demonstrate their knowledge in a variety of ways.

It is important for teachers and aides to have an open communication with migrant students about their prior educational and life experiences so they can build on what the student already knows. For example, students who have worked in the fields will have knowledge of nature and agriculture, which can be a starting point for learning in science. If the student has been learning in his or her home language, a teacher can capitalize on that skill; either by using the native language or by locating supplementary native language materials to reinforce material presented in English.

Easing the transition of migrant students to a new school is crucial, especially when the student is a late starter. A student who feels disoriented or unwelcome will have difficulty learning. Teachers can reduce anxieties and avoid difficulties by clearly explaining the everyday routines and policies within the school. Students new to U.S. schools may be completely unfamiliar with elements of school that seem commonplace to most American school kids, such as hall passes, school bells, changing classes, gym, cafeterias and lunch lines, lockers, holidays, and disciplinary methods. Using cooperative groups or assigning classroom "buddies" for new students can help the students to adapt and begin to feel more at home. Teachers of migrant students need to be attentive to warning signs. When new students are withdrawn, aggressive, or over-talkative, these may be indicative of adjustment problems rather than general behavior problems.

Teachers may also take advantage of professional development opportunities to enhance classroom techniques for working with diverse learners. Effective schooling research suggests strategies to promote excellence for *all* students. These include maintaining high expectations, personalized contact and smaller classroom size, and providing opportunities for students to demonstrate initiative, competence, and responsibility.

National and State Programs

Most programs for migrant students receive funding through the U.S. Department of Education's Migrant Education Program (MEP). Federal MEP funds are allocated to states based on the number of migrant students and the state's average per-pupil expenditure. Since its inception in 1966, the MEP has supported school-based supplementary educational programs, tutoring services, school- and community-based health services, parent involvement and family literacy programs, summer enrichment programs, and professional development for teachers. The MEP also maintains a toll-free nationwide Migrant Education Hotline that families can use to reach the nearest migrant program.

Funding from several smaller federal grant programs also reaches many migrant students. Migrant Head Start (MHS) provides comprehensive preschool and daycare programs. The Migrant Education Even Start (MEES) program helps migrant families break the cycles of poverty and illiteracy through programs for early childhood education, adult basic education, and parent education. The High School Equivalency Program (HEP) provides grants to colleges, universities, and community organizations to help migrants obtain a General Educational Development Diploma (GED) and prepare them for college or the workplace. College Assistance Migrant Program (CAMP) grants help colleges and universities provide financial and academic assistance to migrant students in their first year.

In the absence of a national system to transfer migrant student records between schools, states have developed intrastate and regional interstate databases to track and transfer student records, and also to share curriculum materials. By facilitating timely identification and appropriate placement of students, these information-sharing consortia play a critical role in reducing the educational disruption experienced by migrant youth. Many states share student information, as well as teachers and textbooks, with schools in Mexico though the Binational Migrant Education Program. Multistate programs, such as the Portable Assisted Study Sequence (PASS), which is used in thirty-one states, help secondary migrant students meet graduation requirements by allowing students to complete their coursework semi-independently through correspondence study. Newer state and regional programs have adapted the PASS model to enable mobile students to complete coursework though the Internet.

Issues and Trends

Many millions of migrant children have benefited from the work of federal agencies, states, and schools to expand educational opportunities and open the way for a better future. Still, very little is known about how well these programs and services are working. Due to the high mobility of the population, different record-keeping among the states, and the absence of a national tracking system, program administrators have limited means of determining the impact of a program or a schedule of services on a particular migrant child. Establishing a workable, efficient, secure, nationwide system of tracking migrant student records and progress remains the central challenge for the migrant education community. A centralized information system would help minimize disruptions caused by placement delays, and would also permit meaningful assessment of educational outcomes. The No Child Left Behind Act, signed into law in January 2002, calls for an expanded federal role in the development of a national system of records transfer.

Since the early 1990s, education reform has tended to focus on the setting of high education standards and the development of standards-based curricula and assessments. As more and more states are requiring that all students be included in statewide assessments, it is likely that more data on migrant student achievement will become available. Students migrating within a state may benefit from having consistent curricula and clearly defined goals and improved documentation of their progress.

While instruction by video and correspondence remain widely used distance-education tools in migrant programs, the benefits of Internet technology are also beginning to reach migrant students. Some programs allow students to complete coursework online and take advantage of Internet-based distance learning. Migrant educators are creating innovative ways of using new technologies to enhance the continuity of learning; for example, the Estrella program, based in Texas, provides students with laptop computers and modems to help them keep up with course work while away from their home district.

Helping migrant students overcome multiple barriers to success poses a tremendous challenge to teachers, migrant advocates, schools, and families. The mission for all members of the migrant education community is to ensure that students' cumulative educational experiences—in spite of obstacles, moves, and changes—lead them toward success.

See also: BILINGUALISM, SECOND LANGUAGE LEARN-
ING, AND ENGLISH AS A SECOND LANGUAGE; POVER-
TY AND EDUCATION; RURAL EDUCATION.

BIBLIOGRAPHY

DI CERBO, PATRICIA A. 2001. *Why Migrant Education Matters.* Washington, DC: National Clearinghouse for Bilingual Education.

LEBLANC FLORES J., ed. 1997. *Children of la Frontera:
Binational Efforts to Serve Mexican Migrant and
Immigrant Students.* Charleston, WV: ERIC
Clearinghouse on Rural Education and Small
Schools.

MEHTA, KALA, et al. 2000. *Findings from the National
Agricultural Workers Survey (NAWS) 1997–
1998: A Demographic and Employment Portrait
of United States Farm Workers.* Washington,
DC: U.S. Department of Labor.

PERRY, JOHN D. 1997. *Migrant Education: Thirty
Years of Success, but Challenges Remain.* Provi-
dence, RI: The Education Alliance.

PREWITT-DIAZ, JOSEPH O.; TROTTER, ROBERT T.;
and RIVERA, VIDAL A. 1989. *The Effects of Migration on Children: An Ethnographic Study.*
Harrisburg: Pennsylvania Department of Education, Division of Migrant Education.

ROMO, HARRIET D. 1999. *Reaching Out: Best Prac-
tices for Educating Mexican-Origin Children and
Youth.* Charleston, WV: ERIC Clearinghouse on
Rural Education and Small Schools.

U.S. DEPARTMENT OF EDUCATION. 1999. *Meeting the
Needs of Migrant Students in Schoolwide Programs.* Rockville, MD: Westat.

INTERNET RESOURCES

EASTERN STREAM CENTER ON RESOURCES AND
TRAINING. 1998. "Help! They Don't Speak English Starter Kit for Primary Teachers."
<www.escort.org/products/helpkit.html>.

ERIC CLEARINGHOUSE ON RURAL EDUCATION AND
SMALL SCHOOLS. 2002. <www.ael.org/eric/
migrant.htm>.

MARTÍNEZ, YOLANDA G., and VELÁZQUEZ, JOSÉ A.
2000. "Involving Migrant Families in Education." *ERIC Digest.* <www.ael.org/eric/digests/
edorc004.htm>.

MENCHACA, VELMA, and RUIZ-ESCALANTE, JOSÉ.
1995. "Instructional Strategies for Migrant Students." *ERIC Digest.* <http://gopher.ael.org/
eric/digests/edorc9510.htm>.

MORSE, SUSAN C. 1997. "Unschooled Migrant
Youth: Characteristics and Strategies to Serve
Them." *ERIC Digest.* <www.ael.org/eric/digests/
edorc972.htm>.

U.S. DEPARTMENT OF EDUCATION, OFFICE OF MI-
GRANT EDUCATION. <www.ed.gov/offices/
OESE/MEP>.

U.S. GENERAL ACCOUNTING OFFICE. 1999. "Migrant
Children: Education and HHS Need to Improve
the Exchange of Participant Information."
<www.ncbe.gwu.edu/miscpubs/gao/
nehs004migrant.pdf>.

WRIGLEY, PAMELA. 2001. "The Help! Kit: A Resource Guide for Secondary Teachers of Migrant English Language Learners."
<www.escort.org/products/
secondaryhelpkit.html>.

ANNEKA L. KINDLER

MILITARY ACADEMIES

U.S. AIR FORCE ACADEMY
　John Sherfesee
U.S. COAST GUARD ACADEMY
　Thomas J. Haas
U.S. MERCHANT MARINE ACADEMY
　Lee C. Deighton
U.S. MILITARY ACADEMY
　Dean W. Meyerson
U.S. NAVAL ACADEMY
　U.S. Naval Academy Publications Office

U.S. AIR FORCE ACADEMY

The mission of the U.S. Air Force Academy, the nation's newest federal service academy, is to "inspire
and develop outstanding young men and women to
become Air Force officers with knowledge, character, and discipline; motivated to lead the world's
greatest aerospace force in service to the nation."
The academy is located just north of the city of Colorado Springs, Colorado. Its 18,000 acres border the
eastern slopes of the Colorado Rocky Mountains.
Since its establishment in 1954, the academy has
graduated more than 34,000 cadets to serve in all of
the U.S. military services. It is accredited by the
North Central Association of Colleges and Schools,
Commission on Institutions of Higher Education,
and the chemistry, computer science, engineering,
and management programs are accredited by their
respective accrediting organizations.

The first class of 207 graduated in June 1959, while the first class to include women graduated in June 1980. Since then, the academy has had more than 2,600 women graduates. Congressional legislation limits enrollment to a maximum of 4,000 students as of the early twenty-first century. Cadets are appointed from all fifty states and from the U.S. territories, and must be between seventeen and twenty-two years of age on July 1 of the year of admission. Each must be a U.S. citizen, unmarried, and have no dependent children. They must be qualified academically, physically, and medically, and be nominated by a legal source as authorized in Title 10 of the U.S. Code. Those sources include a candidate's U.S. Representatives, U.S. Senators, the President of the United States, the Vice President of the United States, and several military-related sources for eligible individuals. To graduate, cadets must complete the entire four-year program.

The faculty comprises 560 full-time military and civilian members. Approximately 55 percent possess doctoral degrees. Fifteen percent of the faculty are women. Career Air Force officers provide most of the instruction, complemented by officers from the other services, officers from several allied nations, permanent civilian faculty, visiting professors from civilian institutions, and representatives from several federal governmental agencies. Many of the military faculty and some of the civilian faculty are academy graduates.

Legal Status

Since its inception, the academy's overall mission, goals, and objectives have not appreciably changed. That singularity of purpose—to graduate second lieutenants who are motivated and prepared for military careers in service to their country—has been a unifying force across the institution's history and structure. Various sections under Title 10 of the U.S. Code establish the basic guidelines for the functioning of the academy to include the instruction and preparation of the cadets for military service, the four-year course of study, and civilian oversight through its Board of Visitors.

Governance

The superintendent reports directly to the chief of staff of the U.S. Air Force. Through the chief of staff, the academy also responds to the secretary of the Air Force. The superintendent has the clear responsibility and authority to make decisions affecting the re-

sources and functional integrity of the academy. The principal internal governing body is the academy board. The superintendent, through the board, exercises institutional decision-making authority. Board members are both experienced educators and senior officers in positions to institute changes in policies or practices across the academy.

Each fall, a conference, attended by the most senior Air Force general officers and the secretary of the Air Force, is held at the academy. This conference presents a unique opportunity to formally present and advocate specific programs to Air Force leaders. It also gives these leaders an opportunity to provide guidance or recommendations to the academy on its programs or practices.

Although not a formal governing body, the presidentially and congressionally appointed Board of Visitors is the academy's primary external review group. This board, which reports directly to the president of the United States, is chartered to review policies and protect the integrity of the institution, including its resources. The inclusion of two professional educators on this board, which also contains academy graduates, ensures a well-informed basis for institutional oversight and advocacy.

Academics

The academy offers a four-year undergraduate curriculum of academic, leadership, and military training; physical education; athletics; and aviation courses. The total academic curriculum provides cadets with a solid foundation appropriate to an Air Force career and the activities of a responsible American citizen. A core curriculum provides the common body of knowledge that prepares all cadets for the Air Force profession. The academic core consists of courses in basic sciences, engineering, humanities, and social sciences. Other core requirements include military strategic studies and physical education courses.

The academy offers thirty academic majors: aeronautical engineering, astronautical engineering, basic sciences, behavioral sciences, biology, chemistry, civil engineering, computer engineering, computer science, economics, electrical engineering, English, engineering mechanics, environmental engineering, foreign area studies, general engineering, geography, history, humanities, legal studies, management, mathematical sciences, mechanical engineering, meteorology, military strategic studies, operations research, physics, political science, space operations, and social sciences. Minors in foreign language and philosophy are also offered. All cadets must have a major and may choose their courses from the more than 500 offered each year.

The Air Force Academy ranked second in the United States in the 2001 *U.S. News and World Report* ranking of top aeronautics and astronautics programs, behind Embry Riddle Aeronautical University. It tied for sixth place in the 2001 *U.S. News and World Report* ranking of best undergraduate engineering programs in schools without Ph.D. programs, and it was ranked the fourth-best overall academic experience for undergraduates by *Princeton Review*'s 2001 "Best 331 Ranking," placing just behind Princeton, Amherst, and Harvard. The academy was also named a Truman Scholarship Honor Institution for 2001. Only four or five colleges and universities are selected for this honor each year, and only thirty have been selected in the history of the award, which is based upon academics, leadership qualities, public service, and positive influence upon the changing face of higher education.

Other honors include being named one of sixteen Leadership Institutions by the American Association of Colleges and Universities' Greater Expectations Initiative Consortium on Quality Education, and the receipt of a Pioneer Award at the Fourth Annual Conference on Ubiquitous Computing, sponsored by Educause. The Pioneer Award was presented to seven higher education institutions that made early commitments toward offering students access to technology.

Cadet Development

The academy program of cadet development rests on four conceptual pillars: professional military training, academics, athletics, and character development. The military training program develops the techniques and attributes of successful leadership. The goal of this multidimensional program is to develop the knowledge, skills, values, and behavior patterns required to be an effective Air Force officer. The academic program is designed to provide cadets with a broad, high-quality education at the undergraduate level. Since the academy's origin, it has sought to produce graduates with the breadth and ʾility to represent the Air Force in academic set-ʒs and with the general public.

ʾhe objective of the physical development proʾs to develop good physical conditioning, as well as to foster traits of teamwork, courage, aggressiveness, self-confidence, and an intense desire to win—all of which are essential to a military officer. While at the academy, every cadet takes at least six semester hours of physical education courses. In addition, cadets must participate in intramural or intercollegiate sports throughout the academic year.

While good character is important in most professions, it is vital to the military officer. Character includes ethical behavior, respect for human dignity, and a sense of honor that transcends self-interest. The character development program fosters development of these characteristics and ensures they also are reflected in the other pillars. This program focuses on the academy's core values of "Integrity First, Service Before Self, and Excellence in All We Do." The balanced emphasis on the four pillars of cadet development sets the academy apart from most of the approximately 3,800 institutions of higher education in the United States.

Upon graduation, a cadet receives a bachelor of science degree and a reserve commission as an active-duty second lieutenant. Graduates are required to serve at least five years in the Air Force or, for a very few graduates, in one of the other armed services. The excellent education graduates receive is reflected in the number of prestigious postgraduate scholarships and fellowships they have been awarded. Cadets have won more than 1,900 of these prestigious awards (as of 2001), including thirty-two Rhodes scholarships, nine Truman scholarships, and five Marshall scholarships.

To further motivate academic excellence, the academy has a graduate program that annually allows approximately twenty selected cadets to attend advanced degree programs immediately after graduation at schools around the country. This program prepares them for a possible future assignment as a faculty member. Additionally, the National Competitive Scholarship Program allows approximately twenty cadets to attend prestigious international and national graduate schools for advanced educational opportunities, and up to 3 percent of each graduating class are allowed to attend medical school, .5 percent are allowed to attend dental school, and .5 percent are allowed to attend nursing school.

See also: MILITARY ACADEMIES, *subentries on* U.S. COAST GUARD ACADEMY, U.S. MERCHANT MARINE ACADEMY, U.S. MILITARY ACADEMY, U.S. NAVAL

ACADEMY; MILITARY PROFESSIONAL EDUCATION
SYSTEM.

INTERNET RESOURCE

U.S. AIR FORCE ACADEMY. 2002. <www.
usafa.af.mil>.

JOHN SHERFESEE

U.S. COAST GUARD ACADEMY

The Coast Guard's ability to effectively serve as a viable maritime, military, multimission organization hinges on its leaders' ability to think, learn, and act effectively and ethically. Thus, the Coast Guard Academy (CGA), as an institution of higher learning and the primary source of the Coast Guard's leaders, is critical in enabling the Coast Guard to perform its duties and fulfill its mission.

The mantra of developing leaders of character is firmly embedded in CGA's institutional mission: "The Coast Guard Academy is committed to strengthening the nation's future by educating, training, and developing leaders of character who are ethically, intellectually, professionally, and physically prepared to serve their country."

History

The U.S. Coast Guard fulfills unique roles in support of the nation's military and economic security. These roles go directly back to visionary, nation-building initiatives of Alexander Hamilton, George Washington, and the first Congress. In 1790 Alexander Hamilton, the nation's first treasury secretary, developed fiscal plans and economic policies for the United States. Central to his vision for a self-sufficient and strong nation was the creation of the Revenue Cutter Service. In 1915 the Life-Saving Service and the Revenue Cutter Service were combined to create the present-day U.S. Coast Guard, which is now an agency in the Department of Transportation.

Congress chartered the Coast Guard Academy in 1876. At first it was simply a school ship—the academy's first home was the Revenue Cutter *Dobbin*. Nine cadets were selected by competitive examinations, and appointments of CGA cadets today continue on a merit basis. The early cadets learned at sea under a single professor, studying a blend of liberal arts and professional subjects. In the early 1900s the curriculum grew to three years, gaining emphasis on engineering and science. In 1910 the Academy came ashore to makeshift facilities at Fort Trumbull in New London, Connecticut, and in 1932 moved to its modern, purpose-built campus, also in New London. In 1939 the academy's general engineering program was accredited by the Engineer's Council for Professional Development (ECPD). In 1940, after also being accredited by the Association of American Universities, it was given the authority to grant the bachelor of science degree. In 1946 the USCG Barque *Eagle,* a prize of war, was commissioned into the U.S. Coast Guard and stationed at the academy for sail training.

The academy became accredited by the New England Association of Schools and Colleges (NEASC) in 1952. In 1973 electrical, marine, and ocean engineering programs were accredited by ECPD, and in 1978 the civil engineering major was accredited as well. In 1980 ECPD was renamed ABET (Accreditation Board for Engineering and Technology), and in 1996 the academy was fully accredited in mechanical engineering. The management major was admitted into candidacy in 1998 by AACSB International— The Association to Advance Collegiate Schools of Business. The CGA also offers majors in government, marine and environmental sciences, and operations research and computer analysis.

Over the years, the Coast Guard Academy matured into a learning environment that (1) fosters a high sense of honor, loyalty, and dedication to service and humanity; (2) provides a sound undergraduate education in fields of interest to the Coast Guard; and (3) trains future officers in professional and military skills required for career service. Cocurricular activities in professional development and athletics add to the ability of CGA to fulfill its mission. Commissioned graduates from the undergraduate program have served with distinction in peace and war and they make up the majority of the officer corps of the modern Coast Guard.

Other noteworthy milestones include the admission of women cadets into the Academy in 1976, with the first women graduates in 1980. In 1998 the Academy established the Leadership Development Center (LDC), a center for leadership education, training, and development that focuses on the career needs for a diverse population of Coast Guard adult learners (military and civilian members associated with the Coast Guard and a limited number of international students from other maritime countries).

Organizational Structure

Since 1994 governance of the academy has been provided by a board of trustees, comprising Coast Guard senior managers and other distinguished individuals with strong ties to education. Their general purpose is to oversee all programs at the academy and provide guidance and advice to the superintendent of the academy, the Coast Guard chief of staff, and the commandant of the Coast Guard. It was this newly chartered board that endorsed the LDC and supported a substantive mission change, which was accepted by the NEASC in 1997. The undergraduate program and LDC complement each other, and both support the institutional mission. In 1999 the courses offered through the LDC were evaluated and granted American of Council of Education (ACE) course credit recommendations.

Other governance is provided by a congressional Board of Visitors, composed of three senators and five congressmen, which is authorized to review the academy's programs, curricula, and facilities. The superintendent is aided by the senior management team (SMT), comprising the dean, the commandant of cadets, and other senior staff members. Together they provide for the strategic management of the academy as well as the day-to-day administration.

The dean administers the academy's academic division, encompassing more than 100 full-time faculty and a number of staff. The commandant of cadets serves as a dean of students and has a central role in maintaining commissioning standards. The athletic director oversees student physical development and the National Collegiate Athletic Association Division III sports programs. Other senior leaders manage admissions and business processes. Several boards advise the superintendent. They include the Academic Council, Faculty Senate, Curriculum Committee, Credentials Committee, Resources Allocation Board, Cadet Academic Advisory Board, and others.

Admission

The Coast Guard Academy is one of the most selective schools in the nation, enrolling about 300 young men and women, who are selected from more than 6,000 applicants. The 900 cadets who make up the corps are competitively selected from across the country, as well as twenty from foreign countries. The LDC serves about 3,000 adult learners per year through short courses or programs. The faculty supporting the LDC and the cadets are both military and civilian.

The Coast Guard Academy is committed, as proclaimed in its vision statement, to be the "wellspring of leadership and character for the United States Coast Guard. In serving the American public, the Academy is recognized as an exemplary institution and valued national asset. To earn that recognition and inspire life-long learners, CGA excels in education and military training, and leadership development."

See also: MILITARY ACADEMIES, *subentries on* U.S. AIR FORCE ACADEMY, U.S. MERCHANT MARINE ACADEMY, U.S. MILITARY ACADEMY, U.S. NAVAL ACADEMY.

INTERNET RESOURCE

U.S. COAST GUARD ACADEMY. 2002. <www.cga.edu>.

THOMAS J. HAAS

U.S. MERCHANT MARINE ACADEMY

The U.S. Merchant Marine Academy is one of five federal service academies. It is operated by the Maritime Administration, an agency of the U.S. Department of Transportation. The Merchant Marine Academy is located on an eighty-two-acre waterside campus in Kings Point, New York, about twenty miles from New York City on the north shore of Long Island. The academy is commonly referred to as *Kings Point.* It offers a four-year program leading to a bachelor of science degree and is accredited by the Middle States Association of Colleges and Schools. The academy includes the Global Maritime and Transportation School, which was established in 1994 to meet the continuing education and training needs of professionals from the commercial and military maritime transportation industry.

Each graduate of the academy is awarded a license as a third mate or third assistant engineer in the U.S. Merchant Marines; academy graduates are also commissioned as ensigns in the U.S. Naval Reserve. In 2001 the student body numbered about 950, with approximately 750 in residence at Kings Point and the rest in training aboard ships at sea. The academy was established to prepare young

American men, and later women, for careers as deck or engineering officers aboard ships of the U.S. Merchant Marine. One of the conditions for admission is the signing of an agreement to serve as a licensed officer in the U.S. Merchant Marine for at least five consecutive years after graduation.

The U.S. Merchant Marine consists of all commercial U.S. flag vessels and crews engaged in the foreign and domestic transport of cargo and passengers. Although the ships are owned and operated by private shipping companies, they provide logistics support to the U.S. military services in times of emergency; accordingly, the U.S. Merchant Marine is often called the "fourth arm of national defense."

Each Kings Point graduate joins a ship as a fully qualified junior officer and immediately takes charge of a watch on the bridge or in the engine room. Deck officers are responsible for navigation, cargo handling, vessel maintenance, and shipboard safety. Engineering officers are responsible for maintaining and operating all the ship's machinery, including propulsion, auxiliary, refrigeration, and deck equipment.

Curriculum

The educational program of the U.S. Merchant Marine Academy consists of three years ashore at Kings Point and one year spent at sea aboard merchant ships. Each academic year is eleven months in duration, with a rigorous program of study in order that professional and degree requirements may be met within the three-year period ashore. The academy's academic year is divided into three trimesters.

Students at the Merchant Marine Academy are called *midshipmen,* a term that applies to both men and women. Midshipmen can select one of seven major programs of study: marine transportation, marine operations and technology, logistics and intermodal transportation, marine engineering, marine engineering systems, marine engineering and shipboard management, or dual license. Each program leads to a bachelor of science degree. The challenging dual-license program, available only to top students, combines marine engineering and marine transportation studies and leads to licensing in both specialties. This program was pioneered by the academy in 1965, in anticipation of technological changes in the industry that would call for highly trained officers possessing both deck and engineering proficiency.

At the end of their fourth year of study, all midshipmen must pass a comprehensive written examination, after which they are licensed as either deck officers or engineering officers, depending on their major. In addition to the attainment of maritime professional excellence, midshipmen are provided with mathematical and scientific knowledge and a basic general education that includes the study of history, English, business, economics, and humanities. Such a broad education prepares midshipmen for executive positions when they move ashore after careers at sea.

Students majoring in marine transportation, logistics and intermodal transportation, or maritime operations and technology study a curriculum that includes such professional subjects as seamanship, communications, navigation, naval architecture, meteorology, safety of life at sea, cargo handling, gyrocompass principles, electronics, international law of the sea, and marine transportation. Students in one of the three engineering majors study such technical subjects as machine shop, engineering graphics, marine machinery repair, statics, dynamics, thermodynamics, strength of materials, hydraulics, internal combustion engines, marine refrigeration and air conditioning, electrical engineering, and marine engineering. Each curriculum also includes a certain number of hours in mathematics, physics, chemistry, English, history, foreign languages or comparative culture, business and economics, maritime law, labor relations, marine insurance, ship's medicine, physical education, and naval science. Each curriculum is composed primarily of required courses, though a midshipman with the necessary academic standing may add one elective course each trimester.

Transfer credit may be awarded for any course completed at another college that is equivalent to a course offered at the academy. Validation credit may also be awarded in certain subjects upon passing an examination administered at the academy. A student may then substitute courses from the list of electives to complete the academic program.

Because the U.S. Merchant Marine operates with the U.S. Navy in time of war, an understanding of naval procedures by its officers is essential to successful cooperation. Candidates for admission to the Merchant Marine Academy must meet the qualifications for naval reserve midshipmen. All midshipmen take a prescribed program of naval science courses, taught by naval officers, which leads to a commission, upon graduation, as an ensign in the Merchant Marine Reserve/U.S. Naval Reserve. The graduate is then under obligation to remain in the naval reserve for eight years and to maintain his status by completing correspondence courses and undergoing training duty.

Sea Year

After one year at the academy, during which midshipmen take introductory courses in all areas of study, they are assigned to several different types of U.S. flag merchant vessels for three nonconsecutive trimesters during their second and third year of training. Midshipmen who are interested in a naval career may also train aboard U.S. Navy ships. This is a unique work-study situation in which the ship serves as a laboratory. Midshipman are introduced to life at sea, and they become familiar with the work done aboard ocean vessels. In addition, they are issued a sea project manual containing assignments that they must complete and forward to the academy for grading. Midshipmen also receive voluntary instruction from ships' officers while observing and performing some of the duties of a junior officer. Academy training representatives in New York, New Orleans, and San Francisco assign midshipmen to the ships and oversee their progress.

Regimental Life

The academy is military in character, and midshipmen are organized into a regiment. The regimental program provides an opportunity to practice leadership as midshipmen officers, a system of strict discipline in which infractions of regulations incur demerits and punishment, and the standing of watches. Regimental life is considered essential to the development of leadership ability, self-discipline, a sense of responsibility, and the ability to adapt to the rigorous life at sea.

In addition to participation in the military routine of the regiment, the Kings Pointer may take part in student government and such extracurricular activities as publications, musical groups, special interest and hobby clubs, debates, and social affairs. An arts and world affairs series brings a program of cultural activities to the campus throughout the year. Participation in religious activities and attendance at services in the Merchant Marine Memorial Chapel are voluntary. In addition, there are intramural athletic programs and scheduled intercollegiate competitions. Liberty is granted as a matter of privilege.

Admission

The academy selects 266 men and women for admission annually. Candidates for admission must be U.S. citizens between the ages of seventeen and twenty-five. Appointment to the academy begins with an application to the appropriate nominating authority, usually a U.S. senator or representative from the candidate's home state, who officially requests that the applicant's name be submitted in nomination to become a candidate for admission. A candidate must meet general and scholastic requirements, including high school graduation or its equivalent and qualifying ACT Assessment or SAT scores.

Candidates are ranked in order of merit by an objective evaluation of all credentials. They are then competitively selected to fill academy vacancies through a quota system based on each state's representation in Congress. The candidate must then pass a physical examination conducted by the U.S. Navy for appointment as a midshipman in the U.S. Naval Reserve, and must also meet security requirements. The academy also admits up to thirty students from Latin America and certain other foreign countries.

The U.S. government bears the major portion of academy costs, including tuition, quarters and subsistence, and medical and dental care. While at the academy, each midshipman receives a yearly allowance for required uniforms and textbooks. During the sea year, a monthly salary is paid by the shipping companies.

History

The U.S. Merchant Marine Academy was developed from a program of merchant-marine officer training that began in 1891 when the federal government authorized the assignment of cadets aboard ships receiving mail. When the handling of training by shipping companies proved unsatisfactory, the federal government passed the Merchant Marine Act of 1936, which provided for the establishment in 1938 of the U.S. Merchant Marine Cadet Corps. The training program was conducted solely aboard ship at first, but temporary shore facilities were soon established. Construction of a permanent academy was begun in January 1942 at the Walter P. Chrysler estate, whose thirteen acres form the nucleus of the present campus. The academy was dedicated on September 30, 1943. In his dedicatory message, President Franklin D. Roosevelt summed up the purpose of the academy: "This academy serves the Merchant Marine as West Point serves the Army and Annapolis serves the Navy."

During World War II, the academy berthed at one time as many as 2,700 cadets taking an abbreviated curriculum that included training aboard ships in combat zones. The academy graduated 6,634 officers during the war. The four-year course was instituted with the class entering in September 1945, and authorization to grant a bachelor of science degree was granted by Congress in 1949. A 1956 act of Congress made the academy a permanent institution.

The academy accelerated training to supply officers during the Korean War and the Vietnam War. The academy was also involved in training officers for the country's first nuclear-powered merchant ship, the *Savannah*. In 1974 the Merchant Marine Academy became the first federal service school to admit women. Before and during the 1991 Persian Gulf conflict, academy graduates and midshipmen aided the extensive sea-lift of troops and military supplies to the Middle East. Academy midshipmen and graduates also provided support for military actions in Somalia and Haiti during the 1990s.

See also: MILITARY ACADEMIES, *subentries on* U.S. AIR FORCE ACADEMY, U.S. COAST GUARD ACADEMY, U.S. MILITARY ACADEMY, U.S. NAVAL ACADEMY.

BIBLIOGRAPHY

BUTLER, JOHN A. 1997. *Sailing on Friday: The Perilous Voyage of America's Merchant Marine.* Dulles, VA: Brassey's.

KAPLAN, PHILIP, and CURRIE, JACK. 2000. *Convoy: Merchant Sailors at War, 1939–1945.* Annapolis, MD: Naval Institute Press.

INTERNET RESOURCE

U.S. MERCHANT MARINE ACADEMY. 2002. <www.usmma.edu>.

LEE C. DEIGHTON
Revised by
JUDITH J. CULLIGAN

U.S. MILITARY ACADEMY

The U.S. Military Academy, located in West Point, New York, is a postsecondary educational institution operated under the general direction and supervision of the U.S. Army. The academy, usually referred to as *West Point,* occupies a 2,500-acre campus, which is augmented by about 15,000 acres of adjacent government-owned land. The mission of the academy is to train selected young men and women for careers as officers in the regular army of the United States. Successful completion of the four-year course leads to a bachelor of science degree and a commission as a second lieutenant in the U.S. Army. The academy has an enrollment of about 4,000 students; approximately 15 percent of whom are women.

Curriculum

The West Point curriculum includes a combination of academic, military, and physical training. The core academic curriculum, which focused largely on engineering in the past, now includes a balance of arts and sciences. Although most of the curriculum is prescribed, there is some flexibility that permits cadets to pursue particular interests and aptitudes. Class size is small, usually numbering between fourteen to eighteen students.

Every cadet must complete thirty-one courses that make up the academy's core curriculum. Cadets must also complete at least nine elective courses, chosen to support a major or a field of study. In 2001 the academy offered twenty-five fields of study and twenty-two majors, most of which were related to engineering, foreign area and foreign language studies, or modern history and political science. Cadets choose a major (which requires ten to thirteen elective courses) or field of study (which requires only nine electives) at the end of their second year.

The total curriculum is designed to develop the qualities of character, intellect, and physical competence needed by army officers, who at various stages of their careers must be prepared to lead the smallest combat unit or to advise the highest governmental official. In order to achieve this goal, the curriculum is rounded out by military and physical training, in addition to the academic stress on science and the humanities. The total program provides a sound foundation for both graduate education and professional development.

Military training at West Point is designed to provide a comprehensive knowledge of military fundamentals and doctrine, as well as proficiency in basic military skills. The student body is organized as a *brigade* under the command of a brigadier general known as the Commandant of Cadets. The brigade is lead by a professional officer and a cadet chain of command. By serving in various positions of responsibility within the corps of cadets, cadets are given opportunities to apply their knowledge and to improve their leadership abilities. This portion of a cadet's training, including both practical military training and military-science instruction, is the foundation for more specialized postgraduate training in armor, infantry, engineering, signal corps, field artillery, air defense artillery, military intelligence, or another of the various branches of military science.

Most of the academy's military training occurs during the summer months. New cadets (called *plebes*) undergo Cadet Basic Training during their first six weeks at the academy. Sophomores (*yearlings*) complete eight weeks of intensive field training at Camp Buckner, located near West Point. Juniors (*cows*) engage in specialized military training, such as airborne, air assault, northern warfare, or mountain warfare at various locations and military bases around the world. Seniors (*firsties*) learn military leadership skills by helping direct military training for plebes and yearlings.

The academy's rigorous physical training program continues throughout the entire year. Each cadet participates every season in either intramural or intercollegiate athletics. Formal instruction includes courses in coaching techniques, which provide the basis for another valuable dimension of leadership.

As part of their military and physical curriculum, cadets undergo training in ethics and morals. Such training supports the West Point Honor Code: "A cadet will not lie, cheat, steal, or tolerate those who do." Moral and ethical training is also buttressed by formal instruction in important military values, voluntary religious programs, and a guest speaker program.

Admission and Military Obligation

All men and women who meet academic and physical requirements may apply to West Point, but admission is extremely competitive. Above-average high school records, demonstrated leadership skills, strong performance on the ACT Assessment or SAT college entrance examinations, physical aptitude tests, and medical tests are prerequisites. In addition, an applicant must be between the ages of seventeen and twenty-two, neither married nor pregnant nor carrying the legal obligation to support a child, and a citizen of the United States. Naturalized American citizens must provide proper documentation to be considered for admission. A small number of foreign students may be nominated by formal agreement between the U.S. government and another country.

Procedures for admission to the academy differ in several respects from those of civilian educational institutions. A prospective candidate cannot apply directly to the academy for admission, but must first secure a nomination from an authorized source, usually a United States representative or senator from the candidate's home state, or the secretary of the army. By law, these officials are authorized to nominate up to ten young people to compete for vacancies at the military academy each year. After nomination, candidates receive permission to undertake the examinations for appointment, which determine their academic, medical, and physical qualifications. Classes enter the academy in July of each year. Every cadet enters as a plebe. Transfer credit is not given for college work completed prior to entry into West Point.

Upon entering the academy, a cadet takes an oath committing to a military obligation of six years, the first five on active duty. Upon graduation and appointment as a second lieutenant in the regular army, the West Point graduate serves the five-year active-service commitment. If a cadet is separated after he or she has started the first academic term of the second class year (except for physical disqualification, unfitness, or unsuitability), he or she is subject to transfer to the reserve or ordered to active duty in an enlisted status.

Cadet Life

The daily life of a cadet, apart from academic instruction, is centered on the cadet's company in the corps of cadets. Cadets live in barracks, stand formation, and participate in intramural athletics as a member of this company. There are approximately 110 cadets in a company, with equal membership from all four classes. A cadet company commander, subordinate cadet officers, and noncommissioned officers are responsible for the military formations and many of the daily administrative matters. Every company is assigned a tactical officer who is specially selected on the basis of his or her commissioned service in the regular army and proven leadership ability to counsel and advise cadets.

An integral part of daily life within the corps of cadets is the honor system. The system and the honor code upon which it is based are fundamental to the stress placed upon personal integrity. Every day, cadets see their work or signature accepted as final proof for authorized absences, for compliance with instructions, and as certification of accuracy.

No tuition is charged for attendance at the academy. Cadets are considered members of the regular army and receive stipends of about $600 per month, enabling them to buy uniforms, books, and supplies. In effect, each cadet receives a full scholarship.

History

The U.S. Military Academy is the oldest service academy in the nation. Troops were first garrisoned at West Point during the Revolutionary War, and the military academy was established there in 1802. George Washington was among the revolutionary leaders who strongly felt that a national military academy was needed to eliminate reliance on foreigners for training Americans in artillery, engineering, and other military skills. Initially, the corps of engineers operated the academy and was responsible for training officers in all branches of the service. Because provisions were made for the study of many branches of science, the U.S. Military Academy became the first national center for scientific engineering.

After the War of 1812 came a period of academic pioneering that laid the foundation for the methods and standards that still exist at West Point. Colonel Sylvanus Thayer, superintendent from 1817 to 1833, made courses in civil engineering the academic center of the curriculum. In his endeavor to produce trained leaders, Thayer strove for excellence in personal qualities that went beyond the sound practical knowledge his program of instruction imparted. The subsequent impact of the graduates he trained upon the internal communications of the fledgling nation was widely recognized. The construction of canals, railroads, and harbors under the leadership of men schooled at West Point greatly accelerated the emergence of the United States as a unified country.

Although the primary purpose of the academy was to provide professionally trained officers, its secondary role as a national school of civil engineering

continued until after the Civil War, when academy graduates served in both the Union and Confederate armies. In 1877 Henry O. Flipper, a native of Georgia, becomes the first African American to graduate from the academy. During the post–Civil War period, the proliferation of civilian engineering and technical schools created alternate means of training the engineers needed throughout the United States. In response, West Point shifted its academic emphasis from civil engineering to a pattern of courses affording a broader education. In 1889 Antonio Barrios became the first Hispanic to graduate from West Point; Barrios later served in the Guatemalan army, where he rose to the rank of general.

The emphasis on a broad, general education was maintained in subsequent revisions of the curriculum after World War I, World War II, and the Korean conflict. The expansion of the army's role in international affairs provided additional reasons for increased attention to the academic disciplines of history, geography, economics, and the social sciences. In 1964 President Lyndon Johnson signed legislation permitting the academy to accept nearly 2,000 additional cadets each year, and a major project to expand facilities ensued. During the 1970s and 1980s the curriculum was revised to permit cadets more academic options, including the choice to major in a wide range of disciplines. Women cadets were first admitted to the academy in 1976. During the 1980s and 1990s an increasing number of woman and minorities were admitted.

Notable West Point graduates include Ulysses S. Grant (1843), Jefferson Davis (1828), Robert E. Lee (1829), George Meade (1835), William Tecumseh Sherman (1840), Thomas J. "Stonewall" Jackson (1846), John J. Pershing (1886), Douglas MacArthur (1903), George S. Patton (1909), Omar Bradley (1915), Dwight D. Eisenhower (1915), Brent Scowcroft (1947), Edwin E. "Buzz" Aldrin (1951), and H. Norman Schwarzkopf (1956).

See also: MILITARY ACADEMIES, *subentries on* U.S. AIR FORCE ACADEMY, U.S. COAST GUARD ACADEMY, U.S. MERCHANT MARINE ACADEMY, U.S. NAVAL ACADEMY.

BIBLIOGRAPHY

AMBROSE, STEPHEN E. 1999. *Duty, Honor, Country: A History of West Point.* Baltimore, MD: Johns Hopkins University Press.

RUGGERO, ED. 2001. *Duty First: West Point and the Making of American Leaders.* New York: Harper-Collins.

STEWART, ROBERT. 1996. *The Corps of Cadets: A Year at West Point.* Annapolis, MD: Naval Institute Press.

INTERNET RESOURCE

U.S. MILITARY ACADEMY. 2002. <www.usma.edu>.

DEAN W. MEYERSON
Revised by
JUDITH J. CULLIGAN

U.S. NAVAL ACADEMY

As the undergraduate college of the U.S. Naval Service, the Naval Academy prepares young men and women to become professional officers in the U.S. Navy and the U.S. Marine Corps. Naval Academy students are midshipmen on active duty in the U.S. Navy. They attend the academy for four years, graduating with bachelor of science degrees and reserve commissions as either ensigns in the Navy or second lieutenants in the Marine Corps. Naval Academy graduates serve at least five years as Navy or Marine Corps officers.

The scenic Naval Academy campus, known as the "Yard," is located in historic Annapolis, Maryland, where the Severn River flows into the Chesapeake Bay. With its combination of early twentieth-century and modern buildings, the Naval Academy is a blend of tradition and state-of-the-art technology that exemplifies the Navy and Marine Corps in the early twenty-first century. Throughout the Yard, tree-shaded monuments commemorate the bravery and heroism that are an inherent part of the academy's heritage. Buildings and walkways are named for Naval Academy graduates who have contributed to naval history and their nation.

The Naval Academy is also the final resting place of Revolutionary War naval hero John Paul Jones. A National Historic Site, the Naval Academy hosts more than 1 million tourists every year from the United States and around the world.

History

Founded in 1845 by Secretary of the Navy George Bancroft, the academy started as the Naval School on ten acres of old Fort Severn in Annapolis. Since then, the development of the Naval Academy has reflected the history of the United States. In 1850 the Naval School became the U.S. Naval Academy. A new curriculum went into effect requiring midshipmen to study at the academy for four years and to train aboard ships each summer. That format is the basis of what has evolved into a far more advanced and sophisticated curriculum at the Naval Academy. As the U.S. Navy grew over the years, the academy expanded. The campus of ten acres increased to 338. The original student body of fifty-five midshipmen grew to a brigade of 4,000, and modern granite buildings replaced the old wooden structures of Fort Severn and the Naval School.

Congress authorized the Naval Academy to begin awarding bachelor of science degrees in 1933. The academy later replaced a fixed curriculum taken by all midshipmen with a core curriculum plus eighteen major fields of study, a wide variety of elective courses, and advanced study and research opportunities.

Mission and Program

The Naval Academy's official mission is "to develop midshipmen morally, mentally and physically and to imbue them with the highest ideals of duty, honor and loyalty in order to provide graduates who are dedicated to a career of naval service and have potential for future development in mind and character to assume the highest responsibilities of command, citizenship and government" (U.S. Naval Academy). This gives everyone—faculty, staff, and midshipmen—the same focus. It also encourages a sense of spirit and pride found at few other schools.

The moral, mental, and physical elements of the Naval Academy program are equally important, all contributing to the qualities of an outstanding naval officer. Each midshipman's academic program begins with a core curriculum that includes courses in engineering, science, mathematics, humanities, and the social sciences. This is designed to give a broad-based education that will qualify midshipmen for practically any career field in the Navy or Marine Corps. At the same time, the majors program provides students the opportunity to develop a particular area of academic interest. For especially capable and highly motivated students, the academy offers a challenging honors programs and an opportunity to begin a postgraduate degree while still at the academy.

After four years at the Naval Academy, the life and customs of naval service become second nature. First, a student learns to take orders from practically everyone, but before long, students acquire the responsibility for making decisions that can affect hundreds of other midshipmen. Professional classroom studies are backed by many hours of practical experience in leadership and naval operations, including assignments with Navy and Marine Corps units during the summer months.

Moral and ethical development is a fundamental element of all aspects of the Naval Academy experience. As future officers in the Navy or Marine Corps, midshipmen will someday be responsible for the lives of many men and women and multimillion-dollar equipment. From "Plebe Summer" through graduation, the Naval Academy's Character Development Program is a four-year integrated continuum that focuses on the attributes of integrity, honor, and mutual respect. One of the goals of this program is to develop midshipmen who possess a clearer sense of their own moral beliefs and the ability to articulate them. Honor is emphasized through the Honor Concept of the Brigade of Midshipmen—a system that was originally formulated in 1951 and states: "Midshipmen are persons of integrity: they stand for that which is right." These Naval Academy "words to live by" are based on the moral values of respect for human dignity, respect for honesty, and respect for the property of others. Brigade Honor Committees composed of elected upperclass midshipmen are responsible for education and training in the Honor Concept. Midshipmen found in violation of the Honor Concept by their peers may be separated from the Naval Academy.

The Naval Academy teaches the importance of being physically fit and prepared for stress because the duties of Navy and Marine Corps officers often require long, strenuous hours in difficult situations. The physical requirements of Plebe Summer training, four years of physical education, and year-round athletics also develop pride, teamwork, and leadership.

Profile of Midshipmen

It takes a special kind of young man or woman to handle the Naval Academy's demanding program, but that doesn't mean all midshipmen are alike. Midshipmen come from all fifty states, from U.S. territories, and from several foreign countries. They have roots in cities and suburbs, farms and ranches, small towns and military bases. Midshipmen are good students, leaders in their high schools and communities, and participants in competitive sports. The young men and women who choose the Naval Academy are looking for more than a college degree, however—they like the idea of being challenged morally, mentally, and physically.

See also: MILITARY ACADEMIES, *subentries on* U.S. AIR FORCE ACADEMY, U.S. COAST GUARD ACADEMY, U.S. MERCHANT MARINE ACADEMY, U.S. MILITARY ACADEMY.

INTERNET RESOURCE

U.S. NAVAL ACADEMY. 2002. <www.nadn. navy.mil>.

U.S. NAVAL ACADEMY PUBLICATIONS OFFICE

MILITARY PROFESSIONAL EDUCATION SYSTEM

Career military officers and noncommissioned officers (NCOs) of the Armed Forces of the United States are the beneficiaries of sequential, regularly scheduled periods of professional education. Military leaders return full-time to the "schoolhouse" every three to five years during a twenty-plus year career. Each of these in-residence educational experiences lasts from two months to a year or longer. When coupled with advanced civil schooling, self-study, and on-the-job learning, these courses provide the officer or NCO with the theoretical and practical knowledge needed for duties of increasing complexity and scope as she or he advances in rank. For the sake of brevity, the U.S. Army's Officer Professional Military Education (OPME) and Noncommissioned Officers Education System (NCOES) will be used here as examples.

Professional military education focuses on leadership, management theory and practices, military history and operational doctrine, national defense policy, planning and decision-making, legal responsibilities, and professional ethics. Academic evaluations are primarily performance-oriented, with criteria and learning conditions prescribed for each task. Frequent informal feedback and periodic in-depth performance evaluations are provided. Emphasis is on enhancing the ability to function effectively as a leader and team member, and in staff positions of combined arms and joint service organizations.

For the majority of commissioned officers, professional education begins with the precommissioning phase, which is completed at one of the service academies (U.S. Military Academy, Naval Academy, Air Force Academy, or Coast Guard Academy) or through a Reserve Officers Training Corps (ROTC) program at a participating college or university. Officer Candidate Schools provide opportunities for selected enlisted members of the various services to complete the requirements for commissioning. These educational programs prepare young men and women to assume the responsibilities of junior officers (second lieutenants in the Army, Air Force, and Marines and ensigns in the Navy and Coast Guard) in active-duty (full-time), Reserve, or National Guard units.

For enlisted members of the Armed Services, professional education begins with basic training, or boot camp, followed by advanced technical training in one of the many occupational and vocational fields required by increasingly complex and technologically advanced organizations. Members receive a Military Occupational Specialty (MOS) designation upon successful completion of this training. The military-skill training component of precommissioning programs has much in common with basic training. Following an initial tour of duty, selected Army enlisted members attend the NCOES Basic Course, which focuses on small-unit leadership.

The second phase of OPME focuses on the technical and tactical duties of junior officers specific to each branch and service. Army lieutenants attend the Officers Basic Course for their initial branch assignment, such as the Armor Officers Basic Course at Fort Knox, Kentucky. Marine Corps officers attend their infantry-oriented basic course at Quantico, Virginia, and then may attend a specialty course such as the Army's Artillery School at Fort Sill, Oklahoma. Naval ensigns selected for Surface Warfare or Submarine Service attend basic courses in their specialty. Officers selected for flight training attend flight school. Some officers attend special qualification courses such as the U.S. Army Ranger School, material maintenance programs, nuclear propulsion, or language school prior to their first unit assignments. Officers Basic Courses provide the functional equivalent of enlisted MOS certification

and the tactical leadership training provided during the Basic NCO Course.

After completing three to five years of service with troop units, Army officers attend a two-phased Captains Career Course. Phase one is a branch-specific advanced course that prepares attendees for command of companies, batteries, or troops (military units ranging in size from 60 to 200 soldiers), and for technical and staff responsibilities at battalion and brigade levels. Experiential, case-based interactive learning with extensive use of simulation devices and practical field applications predominate the instructional methodologies.

Immediately following completion of phase one, Army officers attend phase two, the six-week Staff Process Course at the Combined Arms and Services Staff School (CAS3). CAS3 employs small-group instruction techniques designed to improve an officer's ability to analyze and solve problems, communicate orally and in writing, interact effectively as a key member of a military staff, and to apply operational doctrine and procedures in the field. Each staff group is composed of twelve students from combat, combat support, combat service support, and specialty branches in order to encourage interdisciplinary thinking and combined arms doctrine. Naval officers attend similar courses to prepare them for duty as divisional officers on board ships and submarines, and for staff positions. In preparation for assuming duties as platoon sergeants, staff specialists, and first sergeants, noncommissioned officers attend the installation-based Advanced Noncommissioned Officer Course (ANCOC).

Selected Army officers receive education in non-branch-related functional areas—such as Systems Automation, Army Acquisition Corps, and Foreign Area Specialties at residential military schools—through the Advanced Civil Schooling program, which includes the Technological Enhancement Program, or through Training With Industry. Most midcareer officers complete advanced academic degrees through government-funded programs on duty time or personally financed off-duty study, while many noncommissioned officers complete associate and bachelor's degrees while off duty. Today, the American military is unique among the armies of the world in its high percentage of officers with master's degrees and Ph.D.s.

The fourth stage of OPME is the Command and General Staff College (CGSC). Attendance at resident CGSC is selective and prepares officers for command at battalion and brigade levels and for senior staff positions. Nonresident/distance learning CGSC courses are also offered for active-duty, Reserve, and National Guard officers.

Selected officers attend a *sister service* CGSC level course (i.e., Air Command and Staff College) or an allied national institution such as the British Staff College. Emphasis is placed on planning and direction of joint (multiservice) and combined (multinational) operations, in accordance with the congressionally mandated Phase I of the Joint Professional Military Education Program (DOD Reorganization Act of 1986). Selected officers attend the Joint Forces Staff College as Phase II of this program. A small group of officers is chosen to participate in a second year of intensive study at the School of Advanced Military Studies at Fort Leavenworth, Kansas, focusing on military history and the art of war, computerized war games, research, and doctrinal writing.

Army officers selected for command at battalion and higher levels attend pre-command courses in preparation for these demanding assignments. The Noncommissioned Officer Education System equivalent of CGSC and pre-command courses is the Sergeants Major Academy. This final stage of NCOES prepares highly qualified senior NCOs for service as Command Sergeants Major and as senior staff assistants.

Attendance at one of the Senior Service Colleges is the final stage of OPME. Emphasis is on strategic planning, policy, national security decision-making, and joint and combined military operations. Some officers pursue Senior Service College Fellowship studies at leading universities such as Harvard and Georgetown, at the NATO Defense College, and at interdepartmental courses such as the Advanced Operational Studies program, the Defense Systems Management College, or the Center for Strategic and International Studies.

See also: MILITARY ACADEMIES.

BIBLIOGRAPHY

BONN, KEITH E. 1999. *Army Officer's Guide,* 48th edition. Harrisburg, PA: Stackpole.

CARROLL, JOHN M., and BAXTER, COLIN F., eds. 1993. *The American Military Tradition: From Colonial Time to the Present.* Wilmington, DE: Scholarly Resources.

GORMAN, PAUL F. 1994. *The Secret of Future Victories.* Fort Leavenworth, KS: U.S. Army Command and General Staff College Press.

PERRET, GEOFFREY. 1989. *A Country Made by War.* New York: Random House.

U.S. DEPARTMENT OF THE ARMY. 1995. *Pamphlet 600-3 Commissioned Officer Development and Career Management.* Washington, DC: U.S. Department of the Army.

BRUCE T. CAINE

MILITARY TRAINING DOCTRINE, PHILOSOPHY AND PRACTICE

The training of armies as a systematic educational practice has ancient roots. While other trades, crafts, and vocations are often individual pursuits, organized warfare requires the common training of vast numbers to produce synchronized efforts and predictable responses under stress. The evolution of military training doctrine and professional education in the United States provides a model of experimentation, advances, and rediscoveries in pedagogical practices and learning theory. As in the case of research and practical applications in medicine, engineering, technology, management, and organizational leadership, military professional education and training have been a proving ground for innovations. For the sake of brevity, the training doctrine of the U.S. Army will serve here as the primary example.

Doctrinal debates abound in the history of military training. Military educators have assessed the relative efficacy of rote memory and static knowledge, as opposed to creativity and dynamic knowledge. They have struggled with the choice between a single proven solution and situational initiative; that is, between rigid routine and fixed practice and standardized yet flexible techniques. They have appraised lecture/discussion-based learning and, for many skills, found experiential and case-based learning preferable. Simulations (war games), service learning, internships, and apprenticeships are longstanding practices. And in the evolving relationship between teacher and student, military trainers have moved away from an authoritarian, directive mode to a more participative colearner model of shared expertise.

History of Military Training in the United States

Friedrich von Steuben, a Prussian volunteer serving as George Washington's inspector general during the Revolutionary War, composed the first uniquely American training doctrine. Steuben brought his organizational energy and negotiation skills to the struggling Continental army at Valley Forge during the winter of 1777–1778. His ability as a teacher and trainer were anchored in his genuine concern for individuals, his personal integrity and sense of humor, and a keen perception of the character of Americans. He earned the trust of both Washington and the common soldier.

Steuben saw the Continentals as real soldiers, but of a new type—quick learners, likely to respond favorably to participative, practical, caring, and adaptive leadership, and to the discipline of a trained team. He instituted three essential reforms. First, he put commissioned officers in charge of training, insisting that they lead their men in training as they would in battle. He also advised that officers care for their soldiers. In his drill regulations, published in 1779, Steuben wrote: "A captain can not be too careful of the company the State has committed to his charge. He must pay the greatest attention to the health of his men, their discipline, arms, accouterments, clothes and necessaries" (Moss, p. 259). This dual focus enhanced the proficiency of both leader and those being led, while reinforcing the bond between them—a view reflected in the modern principle "mission first, soldiers always."

Second, Steuben prescribed an overhaul of army discipline, supply accountability, and manpower utilization. Soldiers scattered on various fatigue details and serving as officers' servants were returned to tactical units for training—a principle reflected in the current practice of priority training periods. He understood more clearly than Washington that European methods of discipline could not be imposed on the American army. Initiative, self-reliance, and a desire to know the *why* behind an order or a procedure were foundations of the American character. Steuben believed training for collective action had to be built on these entrepreneurial characteristics, and not designed to eliminate them.

Finally, Steuben standardized and simplified battle formations, tactics, and drills. He developed a manual of arms that reduced the steps in loading and firing muskets, taught the practical use of the bayonet, and trained the army to march in columns of four rather than in long, rambling single file. His teaching methods were insightful. He recruited 100 men of robust constitution for a demonstration guard company. With the assistance of carefully selected sub-inspectors, Steuben personally trained one squad in the new manual of arms and movement techniques, then supervised the drilling of other squads by the sub-inspectors. Once the squads were trained, he drilled them as a company, starting each day with squad drills and ending with company exercises—the beginnings of what now is called multi-echelon, progressive, or integrated training.

Many officers and soldiers came to watch Steuben's "parades" and were impressed. Washington directed that unit commanders adopt Steuben's model and appointed training inspectors coached by Steuben to oversee training throughout the Continental army. In a sense, these inspectors became the master teachers of their day—Steuben's concepts of teaching and learning have much in common with those of the twentieth-century educational philosopher John Dewey.

Steuben's innovations ran counter to a trend all too common in military history. Rigid adherence to outdated concepts of operational doctrine, including tactics and training methods that do not reflect the changing nature of military weapons and of warfare itself, has repeatedly proven costly, both in terms of military objectives and the lives of soldiers. Experience yields valuable lessons to those willing to learn. Unfortunately, many lessons are forgotten, only to be relearned by later generations.

One excellent example is that of Emory Upton, an 1861 graduate of West Point who rose to the rank of brevet major general in the Union army. Upton solved the problem of assaulting entrenchments defended by men with rifled muskets. In contrast to massed formations of soldiers marching shoulder to shoulder in the open, Upton employed four-man assault teams that moved independently, in short rushes, while other teams engaged the enemy—a technique today called *fire and movement.*

Trained to work together, taking advantage of cover and concealment and relying more on speed, surprise, and teamwork than on firepower, Upton's four-man team was the precursor of the modern infantry squad and an early model of the self-managed learning and production teams of today. European armies ignored Upton's lesson until the last year of World War I, when, in response to lethal battlefield conditions, both German and American assault troops devised innovative infiltration tactics employing interdependent teams.

The Post-Vietnam Era

The post-Vietnam era was a time of deep reflection for military professionals. The persistent threat of the cold war, however, did not allow for near-total demobilization and a return to isolationism, as had repeatedly occurred in the past. In the 1970s, the challenge facing military leaders was to train a force that would be fully prepared to fight in a "come as you are" war—one without a lengthy mobilization period.

A method had to be found to institutionalize experiential learning. The practical classroom of combat repeatedly reveals the strengths and deficiencies of military training. Standardized training schedules and techniques, fixed tactical solutions, and common doctrine—efficient in teaching the "book solution" and easy to evaluate—are often not effective in preparing leaders or soldiers to deal with new missions, unique environmental conditions, and the uncertainties of combat.

To meet this challenge, operational doctrine, recruiting methods, and training techniques required major revisions. The U.S. Army's Training and Doctrine Command (TRADOC) was established in 1973 as the single proponent for training reforms, doctrine revision, leader development, and the modernization of organizational structure, weapons, and equipment. William DePuy, the first Commanding General of TRADOC, recognized that the United States must be able to fight and win the "first battle of the next war." The Arab-Israeli War of 1973 provided a vivid example of modern warfare's speed and lethality, and its sudden onset allowed no time for the shallow seasoning (learning) curve of earlier wars.

DePuy's World War II and Vietnam experiences convinced him that the root cause of first-battle failures was combat training "by the numbers," where "learning and relevance were secondary to scheduling" (Scales, p. 11) and leadership development lacked demands for realistic combined-arms synchronization in the uncertainty of the battlefield. He initiated doctrinal changes that focused on a systems approach of "training to task, not to time" that educated leaders to optimize the advances in weapons and mobility, seeking to steepen the prewar seasoning curve. A parallel civil education reform is the shift from accumulating Carnegie units (number of hours per subject) to block scheduling and interdisciplinary, across-the-curriculum learning.

In the mid-1970s, Army Training and Evaluation Programs (ARTEP) and soldier's manuals replaced earlier training schedules. Each individual and unit task was analyzed, specified, and defined by measurable performance standards and the conditions under which it would be performed. Evaluations stressed actual performance under field conditions. Skills mastered at each level contributed to effectiveness at higher levels. Doctrinal innovations reflecting the realities of modern warfare were integrated into a series of *how to fight* and *training the force* manuals used to guide learning and actual operations.

Under the new doctrine, individual and unit training takes full advantage of techniques that are gaining acceptance in civilian schools and organizational settings. Internship experiences are provided to cadets and midshipmen. Initial tours of duty have a strong apprenticeship focus, while service learning (that is, learning from practical experience in an applied setting under the guidance or coaching of a trainer or teacher) is the norm. Theory and principles taught in the classroom are habitually applied and evaluated in field settings under expert supervision. Computer-assisted instruction and simulations, as well as distance learning organized under corresponding studies programs, are used extensively. Annual performance evaluations for leaders are anchored in individually prepared professional development plans. Across disciplines education is mandated by combined arms and joint operations doctrine.

The slogan "train as you will fight" gained credence with the adoption the Multiple Integrated Laser Engagement System (MILES) for tactical training. Eye-safe laser projectors were developed to match weapons from rifles to tank cannons; laser sensitive target arrays were rigged to soldiers' field gear and to vehicles; and computers recorded hits and near misses. MILES allowed, for the first time, force-on-force exercises that realistically simulated combat.

Evaluation of Training Methods

Inspired by the Navy's Top Gun program, the Army began tactical unit training evaluations at Fort

Irwin's National Training Center (NTC) in the early 1980s. MILES-equipped companies and battalions, linked into a computerized Core Instrumentation System supported by video cameras, radio monitors, and experienced controllers, engaged a numerically superior opposing force (OPFOR) in a "no-holds-barred battle" that tested individual and unit tactical skills and the real-time decision-making skills of commanders and their staffs.

The learning value of the NTC and other similarly equipped centers results from the direct experience of no-nonsense combat simulations and the cumulative effects of candid and detailed After Action Reviews (AARs). During an AAR, leaders' decisions, and their consequences, are evaluated using automated records of actions, controllers' observations and, significantly, the memories of unit participants. AARs are professional, collective reflections, and can be very humbling experiences. No other army exposes commanders to such a skilled opposing force and then reveals the results of the field exercise to that commander's subordinates and peers. Each NTC experience produces lessons learned that are actively shared.

As a key tool for learning from experience, the AAR technique is also applied to computer-assisted free-play simulations called Battle Command Training Programs (BCTPs), which are used to evaluate commanding generals and their staffs. To deal with the highly sensitive issue of such public assessments of senior officers, each BCTP simulation and its AAR is supervised by three retired four-star generals.

Evaluation and professional reflection are not limited to the NTC and BCTP. Mission-essential tasks, defined in each unit's ARTEP, are evaluated against measurable standards during AARs conducted after each training event. This commitment to honest feedback has instilled an institutional obsession to train realistically for combat and to learn from the experience. As vividly demonstrated by the Persian Gulf war and operations throughout the 1990s, units realistically trained prior to actual combat suffered remarkably low losses compared to first engagements in earlier wars. Well-prepared leaders made the right choices and soldiers performed with confidence grown from their repeated exposure to evaluated training experiences. Realism in training reinforced by professional reflection and shared lessons learned saves lives.

The military forces of the early twenty-first century face complex missions and diverse challenges, demanding training not just for combat but also for operations short of war, such as peacekeeping, humanitarian aid, counter-terrorism, and nation building. Soldiers must be prepared to shift rapidly from one operational mode to another, often with radically different rules of engagement. Current training practices emphasize this adaptability. Self-discipline and initiative, a shared understanding of the mission and the commander's vision, skillful application of technology, battlefield mobility and firepower, and a belief in both individual uniqueness and in skilled teams remain, as in Steuben's day, the foundations of organizational effectiveness. Military service is a calling and a vocation, linked throughout America's history by a remarkable faith in professional education and training.

See also: MILITARY PROFESSIONAL EDUCATION SYSTEM.

BIBLIOGRAPHY

CARROLL, JOHN M., and BAXTER, COLIN F., eds. 1993. *The American Military Tradition: From Colonial Time to the Present.* Wilmington, DE: Scholarly Resources.

CLARY, DAVID A., and WHITEHORNE, JOSEPH W. A. 1987. *The Inspectors General of the United States Army, 1777–1903.* Washington, DC: U.S. Government Printing Office.

GORMAN, PAUL F. 1994. *The Secret of Future Victories.* Fort Leavenworth, KS: U.S. Army Command and General Staff College Press.

MOSS, JAMES A. 1941. *Officers' Manual.* Menasha, WI: George Banta

SCALES, ROBERT H., JR. 1994. *Certain Victory: The U.S. Army in the Gulf War.* McLean, VA: Brassey's.

U.S. ARMY HEADQUARTERS, TRAINING AND DOCTRINE COMMAND. 1988. *Field Manual 25-100: Training the Force.* Washington, DC: Department of the Army.

U.S. ARMY HEADQUARTERS, TRAINING AND DOCTRINE COMMAND. 1990. *Field Manual 25-101: Training the Force: Battle Focused Training.* Washington, DC: Department of the Army.

BRUCE T. CAINE

MISCONDUCT IN EDUCATION

The definition of education corruption includes both its existence and the perception of its existence. According to Transparency International, for instance, Romania ranks 69 out of 91 countries in terms of corruption perception. Uzbekistan ranks 71 and the Russian Federation ranks 79. The definition of education corruption derives from the more general set of corruption issues. As in other areas, it includes the abuse of authority for material gain. But because education is an important public good, its professional standards include more than just material goods; hence the definition of education corruption includes the abuse of authority for personal as well as material gain.

Why Is It Important for a Nation to Be Free of Education Corruption?

Since the time of Plato, it has generally been understood that a key ingredient in the making of a nation-state is how it chooses its technical, commercial, and political leaders. In general it is agreed that no modern nation can long survive if leaders are chosen on the basis of ascriptive characteristics, that is, the characteristics with which they are born: race, gender, social status. On the other hand it is common for families to try to protect and otherwise advantage their own children and relatives. All parents wish for the success of their own children; every group wishes to see the success of children from their particular group. This is normal.

Schooling provides the mechanism through which these opposing influences can be carefully managed. It is a common instrument employed by nations to "refresh" the sources of its leadership. Economists have tried to estimate the sacrifice in economic growth if there is a serious bias in the selection of leaders. It has been estimated that developing nations could improve their gross national product per capita by 5 percent if they were to base their leadership upon merit rather than on gender or social status. In fact by some estimates, the economic benefit to developing countries of choosing leaders on the basis of merit would be three times more than the benefit accruing from a reduction in Organisation for Economic Co-operation and Development (OECD) trade restrictions on imports.

Success in one's schooling is one of the few background characteristics seen as necessary for modern leadership. Although it is possible for leaders to emerge through experience or just good fortune, getting ahead in schooling is seen as essential.

But what if schooling itself is not fair? What if the public comes to believe that the provision of schooling favors one social group? What if the public does not trust the teachers to judge student performance? What would happen if the process of schooling had been corrupted?

The fact is that in a democracy, the public takes a very active interest in the fairness of its education system. If the public does not trust the education system to be fair or effective, more may be sacrificed than economic growth. It might be said that current leaders, whether in commerce, science, or politics, had acquired their positions through privilege rather than achievement. If the school system cannot be trusted, it may detract from a nation's sense of social cohesion, the principal ingredient of all successful modern societies.

The Characteristics of an Education System Free of Corruption

A school system that is free of corruption is characterized by the following:

- Equality of access to educational opportunity
- Fairness in the distribution of educational curricula and materials
- Fairness and transparency in the criteria for selection to higher and more specialized training
- Fairness in accreditation in which all institutions are judged by professional standards equally applied and open to public scrutiny
- Fairness in the acquisition of educational goods and services
- Maintenance of professional standards of conduct by those who administer education institutions and who teach in them, whether public or private

Categories of Educational Corruption

Some refer to corruption as though it were a unitary concept or a problem with a single dimension. It is more complex than many realize. So frequent is corruption in education that it cannot be well understood without first differentiating one type from another.

Corruption in selection. There is no nation in which the proportion of the age cohort attending at the end of the system is as large as it is at the beginning. Educational opportunity is shaped not like a rectangle, but like a pyramid. If one defines *elite* as meaning only those who are able to enter, then all nations have education systems that have elite characteristics. Therefore, the question is not whether a system selects a few to proceed, because all nations must select. Rather, the question is how that selection is made.

Educators sometimes argue that certain kinds of selection tests and techniques are "better" than others. For instance, some might argue that essay questions or oral examinations are better than multiple-choice questions. This kind of discussion, when divorced from context, is spurious.

Three principles help determine the choice of appropriate selection techniques: (1) available resources, (2) logistical challenges, and (3) the level of public accountability. Maintaining the same standard of reliability, cost differences in grading an essay versus a multiple-choice question can be as much as 10:1. Moreover, as test-taking populations expand, the differences in costs expand as well. The cost difference between grading an oral and a multiple-choice exam may be 10:1 if the number of test takers is 1,000. But if the number of test takers is 1 million, the cost difference may be 100:1.

The appropriate system in Sweden might be to have each teacher individually design and grade selection examinations. But with about 1 percent of Sweden's education resources, about 100 times the number of university applicants, and a extensive geographical challenge, the appropriate system in China must be more standardized and machine gradable.

A key difference among nations is not the kind of test used, but whether whatever technique is chosen can be corrupted. How selection is managed is deeply important for maintaining the equality of education opportunity. Since World War II the technology of administering examinations has changed radically in OECD countries, but in many parts of the former Soviet Union and other parts of the world, the technologies have not kept pace. Often, each faculty within each higher education institution administers examinations independently. Many examinations are delivered orally. And many can be taken only at the university where they are designed. This system of selection is unfair, inefficient, and low quality. It is *unfair* because examinations have to be taken where they are designed, meaning that those who cannot easily travel have less opportunity. The effect of this is to limit access to higher education to students who can afford to travel. It is *inefficient* because students must take a new examination for each institution to which they apply, and given that they cannot do this at a single sitting, they must wait for a new test-taking occasion. This may delay their entry by a year or more. It is of *low quality* because questions are designed by faculty who are isolated from modern labor markets. They use skills that are out of date, and they design tests whose administration cannot be standardized. But the key issue is corruption.

Tests that are centrally scored can still be corrupted by leaks. In some parts of South Asia, questions are privately sold to high-paying candidates before the test is administered. Being more subjective and administered in private, oral examinations are even more open to corruption. As faculty salaries decline in value, and higher education institutions require alternative sources of income, bribery surrounding the admissions process can become a matter of routine. Candidates may even know how much a "pass" will cost and be expected to bring the cash ahead of time. This may be the case, for instance, in the Russian Federation.

Consequences of a corrupt selection system. The process of academic selection is the linchpin of any education system and of overall national cohesion. It represents the essence of the public good. If the system is corrupt or widely believed to be corrupt, little else in the education system can be successful. Inattention to corruption in selection places all other aspects of a nation's economic and social ambitions at risk.

How to avoid corruption in selection. Designing selection examinations is technically complex. It requires a high degree of professionalism, modern equipment, and staff with scarce technical skills who are able to garner high salaries in the private sector. Unless they are in very wealthy countries, few government ministries are able to perform selection functions well. The alternative is to create an autonomous agency, staffed with internationally recognized experts and guided by public education standards and policies, but financed by modest examination fees.

Corruption in accreditation. The way in which institutions of higher education are publicly "recognized" is through a system of accreditation. When all institutions were state owned and administered, the system was managed within the central ministries. In the 1990s two things happened that corrupted many systems of accreditation. First, because of the openness to new economic systems and new labor markets, higher education institutions responded with the introduction of a number of new degree programs. All of them need to be recognized. Second, the number of private institutions blossomed, with many of these claiming to be as high in quality as the older, more established public institutions.

Both of these tendencies are positive and should be encouraged. The problem is not that there is private education. The problem is that the system of accreditation has not sufficiently changed in response to the new programs and institutions. In many instances accreditation committees remain in the hands of rectors of public institutions who may have an interest in preventing competition.

The higher education system of accreditation is often corrupt because the connection between higher education and the system of "licensing" or "certifying" professionals has not been reformed. (A license allows a person to practice a given profession, such as medicine; certification allows a person to practice a specific specialization, such as surgery.) Whenever higher education institutions are associated with licensure and/or certification, the stakes for accreditation are high. The price for accreditation on the corrupted market is therefore high as well.

Institutions that seek recognition of new programs, or private institutions that seek institutional recognition, often have to pay a bribe. This places the nation at risk because an institution of low quality may be licensing individuals who may not be of sufficient professional standard. There are many instances of corrupted accreditation leading to poor medical schools, law schools, and programs of business and accounting. On the other hand, the correct response should not be to confine a nation to only old programs and traditional institutions. All nations need innovation in higher education in response to social and labor market challenges.

How to avoid corruption in accreditation. How can a nation encourage educational innovation and, at the same time, protect itself from poor quality higher education programs? The answer is twofold. First, the process of accreditation must be liberalized. It should be simple and inexpensive for a new program and for new institutions to operate. Control over quality should not be made at the stage of accreditation. In nations that have a wide variety among accredited institutions, the function of accrediting changes. Instead of creating institutions of identical quality, it creates institutions with identical transparency in public accounting of their purposes, staffing, and results. The public is then free to choose a wide range of educational quality at different prices.

Second, the process by which individuals leave higher education and apply to practice or be certified in their professions should be separated from the higher education institutions themselves. No matter how excellent, no university should provide a license to practice medicine. In many parts of the world, such as the United States, where significant portions of higher education is in private hands, the process of licensing and certification is separate from universities. A law degree from the University of Chicago or Yale will not permit someone to practice law. For that they, and all others, must sit for the external examination. It is the law examination that weeds out potentially low quality lawyers, not the law schools. This lowers the risk of bribery in the process of accreditation. The license to practice medicine should be governed by a board of medical examiners that manages a system of testing to which all medical applicants must pass. Similar systems must be established for law, accounting, and other fields. Key to this new system is to allow many new higher education institutions to compete with one another. This will allow both low- and high-quality institutions to operate freely and at different prices. Having a variety of quality allows some low-quality institutions to attract new students, to innovate, and to improve. Open competition may allow some institutions of high quality to slip in status and competitiveness. At the same time as this variation in quality occurs, the public is protected from malpractice by the rigor of the licensing and certification examinations. And because accreditation is no longer associated with a license to practice, the process of accreditation can be more liberal. Furthermore, having a more open system of accreditation takes the pressure off it. The effect of this will be to eliminate graft and corruption in the process of accreditation.

Corruption in supplies. It is rarely recognized that, in fact, education is a big "business." In North America, the education and training sector accounts for 10 percent of gross domestic product. Education

FIGURE 1

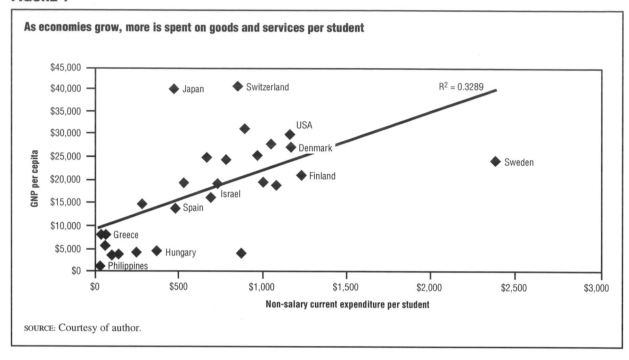

As economies grow, more is spent on goods and services per student

$R^2 = 0.3289$

GNP per cepita (y-axis): $0, $5,000, $10,000, $15,000, $20,000, $25,000, $30,000, $35,000, $40,000, $45,000

Non-salary current expenditure per student (x-axis): $0, $500, $1,000, $1,500, $2,000, $2,500, $3,000

Japan, Switzerland, USA, Denmark, Sweden, Finland, Israel, Spain, Greece, Hungary, Philippines

SOURCE: Courtesy of author.

and training is the economy's largest sector after health care, and the fastest in growth. In considering only compulsory education for a moment, expenditures can be divided first into capital and recurrent categories, then into salary and nonsalary categories. In terms of nonsalary expenditures there is wide variation from one country to another, with Sweden spending about U.S. $2,394 per pupil and India spending less than U.S. $1.00 per pupil. Nevertheless, as countries develop economically, more resources are allocated to support educational quality (see Figure 1).

This process of development raises the size of the education markets around the world, particularly in countries with healthy rates of economic growth. Across the world, public education expenditures doubled between 1980 and 1994. In North America they grew by 103 percent; in Western Europe by 135 percent. But in East Asia and the Pacific, they grew by more than 200 percent during the same period (see Table 1).

First it might be noted that corruption in school supplies can be found in countries at all levels of economic development, from Kenya and Uganda to the United States and other more well-endowed nations. To understand the problem of corruption in educational supplies, one must divide the supply process into three distinct parts: (1) design (such as with

pedagogical materials and textbooks), (2) manufacturing (printing), and (3) distribution. The source of problem may be different with each category.

The corruption of the design process usually occurs when a public agency, such as a ministry of education, contracts for designs (such as the writing of textbooks) among a short list of privileged authors or providers. Sometimes these authors or companies provide educational officials with a gift or bribe for the privilege of designing educational materials. If an author receives a proportion of the sales, the level of illegal earnings can be significant. In terms of book sales in North America, for instance, two-thirds of publishing profits come from educational publishing. Hence, the receipt of contracts for textbook design can bring an automatic benefit to the authors.

In the manufacturing process, the hazard of corruption is similar. Benefits will accrue to the firms that are given contracts for printing or making the materials, and because of the guaranteed nature of educational sales, the profits are often high.

Most corruption in school supplies stems from the use of "protection." Protection is a well-known notion in other fields, such as the manufacturing of automobiles, furniture, glass, and steel. If a country sets up trade barriers targeting imports, these barriers have an economic cost. Governments may be-

TABLE 1

Large growth of education expenditures per region

Continents, major areas, and groups of countries	Public expenditures on education per inhabitant (in dollars)				Percent change 1980–1994
	1980	1985	1990	1994	
World total	126	124	202	252	100
Africa (North and Sub-Saharan Africa)	48	40	41	41	-15
America	307	375	521	623	103
Asia	37	39	66	93	151
Europe	418	340	741	982	135
Oceania	467	439	715	878	88
Industrializing countries	31	28	40	48	55
Sub-Saharan Africa	41	26	29	32	-22
Arab States	109	122	110	110	1
Latin America and the Caribbean	93	70	102	153	65
East Asia and the Pacific	12	14	20	36	200
South Asia	13	14	30	14	1
Poorest countries	9	7	9	9	0
Industrialized countries	487	520	914	1,211	149

SOURCE: Based on data from *UNESCO Statistical Yearbook,* 1998.

lieve that the costs are worth it and that protection is justified on the basis of five common arguments:

- National interest, image, and pride. To appear strong, some believe it necessary to "protect oneself" from foreign products. This argument is very common in education. All nations believe they have the right to educate their citizens in the way they choose. What may not be well understood is that to do this well, curriculum, supplies, and materials need not be a public sector monopoly.

- Safeguard of local jobs. This is rarely made in education by comparison, say, to textiles, but it can be used when other arguments appear weak.

- Grace period for "infant industries." This refers to the argument that a new business is likely to be more vulnerable to competition than a more mature business. Sometimes those responsible for a new business may argue for tariff protection against foreign competition on grounds that they are inexperienced and that the protection is needed for a "short period of time," until they are more prepared for the competition. This interim period is known as the grace period and the new industry is referred to as an "infant industry." This is commonly heard with respect to local textbook publishers and providers of tests and standardized examinations.

- Saving foreign exchange. This is an argument typical of very low-income countries with artificial restrictions on foreign exchange. The prob-

lem with this argument is that the cost in local exchange may be considerably higher than an imported product.

- Unavailable supply from nongovernment sources. In education this is the most common argument heard, particularly with respect to textbooks. This argument is common in countries where the language of instruction is local. It is argued that because no local suppliers exist, the government must therefore manufacture the nation's textbooks. The argument rests on the assumption that the "supply response" would be near zero if open competitive bidding were allowed—that, in essence, there would be market failure. In many instances this assumption rests on the experience of there being no fair or open competition in the past. It also must be remembered that, given market principles, international suppliers—such as Oxford University Press, Microsoft, and World Book Encyclopedia—are usually quite happy to produce the products in whatever language is required and are also quite prepared to lease copyrighted materials to local publishers and manufacturers.

How to avoid corruption in supplies. Corruption risk can be minimized by following three distinct steps. First is to treat the educational procurement process in the same way as the procurement of all other goods and services. Educational supplies should not be singled out as distinct in any way. This first step will bring the procurement process in education in line with the procurement process in other areas, such as pharmaceuticals for the health care system, office supplies, and vehicles. Second is to establish bidding procedures in which there are no hidden "wires." Specifications should not be written that would in any way benefit a single group of manufacturers. Third is to open up the bidding process in parallel with the new guidelines on education services circulated by the World Trade Organization.

Strong resistance to open and competitive bidding often emerges from the education community. It might be noted that protection in educational manufacturing—whether software or computer hardware, furniture, textbooks, or even testing items—has the same cost as protection of any industrial product. It raises the real price, it constrains the quality, and it lowers the effectiveness. Most industrialized nations have come to realize that the natural public responsibility for education is to establish the curriculum principles and objectives of education. It is then a public responsibility to establish professional specification for the delivery of products and services to meet important national goals. The rest should be in the hands of private entities, competing against one another. The more limited the role of the government in the manufacturing process, the lower the chance for corruption in the process of educational supply.

Professional misconduct. Because education is a public good, education corruption must include an element broader than illicit material gain for personal use; it must include an element of professional misconduct. Misconduct can be found in other professions—the law, architecture, accounting, engineering, and so on. But when misconduct affects children and youth—citizens who are not adults or who are young adults—the implications are more serious and the safeguards must be more stringent.

Elements of professional misconduct in education include:

- Accepting material gifts or rewards in exchange for positive grades or assessments or for selection to specialized programs
- Assigning grades or assessments that are biased by a student's race, culture, social class, ethnicity, or other ascriptive attributes
- Insisting on a student's adoption of the instructor's personal values and philosophy
- Disclosing confidential information regarding a student

- Exploiting, harassing, or discriminating against particular students
- Adopting an inadequate textbook or inferior educational materials because of a manufacturer's gifts or incentives
- Forcing students to purchase materials that are copyrighted by the instructor
- Ignoring the inadequate teaching of colleagues, the unequal treatment of students, or the misconduct of fellow professionals
- Using school property for private commercial purposes

Definitions of faculty misconduct may differ from one country to another. For example, if a faculty member were to assign reading only from his own book, this would be interpreted as misconduct in higher education institutions in the United States but not in all parts of the world. Nevertheless, no nation can long ignore the existence of significant misconduct. In some countries it is common for teachers to accept payment for allowing students to proceed to the next grade. In some countries it is common for teachers to offer after-school tutoring for a price and to suggest that students might fail if they do not pay for after-school tutoring. In some countries, faculty may operate a "private" school in the after-school hours, hence using public property for private gain. In other instances, a school administrator or university rector may rent school property or use it for manufacturing or agricultural commerce and not report the income.

In some instances, the misconduct constitutes a criminal offense. Theft or misuse of public property for personal gain is a crime. With the installation of new tuition and fees, it is common for them to be used for private profit rather than for the benefit of the school or university. In these instances, misconduct needs to be judged by the criminal court system. In other instances, such as a teacher's bias against a certain category of student, the misconduct may be limited to professional ethics. In these cases, strong professional boards with the authority to fine and dismiss should be encouraged. The public needs to feel protected from faculty misconduct, and the effectiveness of the professional review boards may be an essential ingredient in their protection.

Corruption in educational property and taxes. Educational facilities often occupy prime locations in urban areas. These can be rented or leased for both educational and other purposes. Almost all higher education institutions, and also many institutions in compulsory education, must supplement public with other resources. But how should educational property be considered: as a private or public income? And how should alternative sources of income be taxed, or should they be taxed at all? And if there is reason not to tax educational institutions, or to tax them at a different rate than commercial businesses, should one treat all educational institutions the same? Should income to public education institutions from nontraditional sources be taxed the same as nontraditional income in private educational institutions? Should equity-owned private educational institutions (which share profits among the owners) be treated the same as a nonprofit institution, which reinvests all profits back into the institution?

One reason why corruption is so common in education is because the answers to these questions have never been adequately sorted out. From the time that government ministries "owned" all property in the Soviet Union to the present, it has never been quite clear which portion of government had ownership of educational property. Take the illustration of a local vocational school: Would it be owned by the enterprise on whose land it might sit? By the local municipality? By the region? By the national sector ministry? Take a technical university, previously under the ministry of industry: Does the land still belong to that ministry? Does land at all higher education institutions now belong to the ministry of education? Does it belong to the local municipality? Does it belong to the rectors council? Or would different authorities "own" different elements? Would the state-owned enterprise own the equipment, the ministry of education own the building, and the local municipality own the land?

How to avoid corruption in property and taxes. In the area of educational property and taxes, the single most important factor in reducing the risk of corruption is to clarify the situation of the land and the tax obligations. Recommendations include the following:

- Higher education land should belong to the board of trust of the higher education institutions themselves. This board of trust may be government appointed and would guide the long-term institutional interests.
- Profit-making educational institutions that are equity-owned should pay the same taxes as all commercial businesses.

- As long as they are not commercial (i.e., equity owned), neither public nor private educational institutions should pay tax on income.
- Information about gifts from individuals and from corporations should be made public, and such tax should be tax deductible.

What Can Be Done about Educational Corruption?

In some respect, solving the problem of educational corruption is not significantly different from solving the problem of corruption in other sectors. Such behaviors as misappropriation of public property or bribery in conjunction with public procurement—whether in education, housing, or some other area—are governed by similar rules and regulations. If the rules and regulations fail to deter the corruption in these other sectors, they will be similarly ineffective in education.

On the other hand, there are certain preventive measures specific to education corruption. These fall into four categories: (1) structural reforms necessary to reduce the opportunity for corruption, (2) improvements in adjudication and management to help anticipate questions of definition and interpretation, (3) measures necessary to actually prevent corruption practice, and (4) sanctions required to demote or punish when infractions do occur (see Table 2).

Summary

It has not been common to focus attention on corruption in education. There were many other pressing problems in business, banking, the judicial and legal system, manufacturing, and agriculture. In the early twenty-first century, however, such a focus may be necessary. Collapsing public expenditures have driven all institutions to generate their own resources, for which there is no precedent, and no regulatory structure is in place to give them guidance. One thing is abundantly clear: Whenever rules and regulations are confusing, one must expect a high level of corruption.

The burgeoning profit-making and not-for-profit enterprises within private education, and the entrance of public institutions into private education, have blurred the lines between what is public and what is private. Few within the public may understand what is in the private interest and should be taxed, or what is in the public interest and should

TABLE 2

Deterring education corruption

Structure Reform	Adjudication and Management	Prevention	Sanction
Autonomous examination agency	Professional boards	Blue-ribbon committee evaluations	Clear penalties for economic and professional corruption
Autonomous accreditation agency	Boards of trustees for each higher education institution	Annual reports on educational corruption	
Licensing and certification process separated from higher education	School boards		
Land ownership by educational institution			
Tax differentiation between profit-making and noncommercial education institutions			
Income generated by nonprofit educational institutions not subject to taxation			

SOURCE: Courtesy of author.

not be taxed. Confusion reigns over issues of educational property. Who actually owns these institutions? And without clear ownership of its land, no higher education institution can successfully approach the private capital markets for a development loan. In essence, no higher education institution can invest in its future until the principles of land ownership are sorted out.

Because of the lack of modern methods and technologies, the systems for selecting entrants into higher education are riddled with bribery. Because the structures are outdated, corruption is common in the accreditation process, the licensing process, and the certification process. Textbooks and supplies often remain under monopolies of the state; foreign suppliers are often prohibited from participating in the bidding process; and designers are chosen on the basis of unprofessional specification and through personal connections. Because of these corruptions and distortions, the education received by young people suffers in quality and in efficiency.

Lastly, because of the inadequate instruments of management and sanctions, professional misconduct is common. It is common for teachers to misuse their professional positions, to accept favors for normal services, and to accept bribes for looking with favor on certain students. And it is common for tuition and fees to be used for private profit.

These practices would be serious no matter what sector they occurred in. But the fact that they occur with frequency in education poses a particular problem. This is because education is the linchpin of a nation's social cohesion, and once the public comes to believe that the education system is corrupt, they will also believe that the future of their nation has been unfairly determined against them and their interests. If this occurs, a nation will not be able to establish a partnership with other democracies.

See also: ETHICS; HIGHER EDUCATION, INTERNATIONAL ISSUES; INTERNATIONAL EDUCATION; INTERNATIONAL TRADE IN EDUCATION PROGRAMS, GOODS, AND SERVICES.

BIBLIOGRAPHY

ANECHIARICO, FRANK, and JACOBS, JAMES B. 1996. *The Pursuit of Absolute Integrity: How Corruption Control Makes Government Ineffective.* Chicago: University of Chicago Press.

BELLAMY, CLAYTON. 2002. "Teacher Too Tough on Cheaters to Suit School Board." *Nashville Tennessean* February 7.

BOGDANOV, ALBERT. 2001. "Education Too Costly, Says Kyrgyz Minister." *BBC Monitoring* January 30.

BRAXTON, JOHN M., and BAYER, ALLEN E. 1999. *Faculty Misconduct in Collegiate Teaching.* Baltimore: Johns Hopkins University Press.

HEYNEMAN, STEPHEN P. 1975. "Changes in Efficiency and in Equity Accruing from Government Involvement in Ugandan Primary Education." *African Studies Review* (April):51–60.

HEYNEMAN, STEPHEN P. 1983. "Education during a Period of Austerity: Uganda, 1971–1981." *Comparative Education Review* 27:403–413.

HEYNEMAN, STEPHEN P. 1984. "Educational Investment and Economic Productivity: The Evidence from Malawi." *International Journal of Education Development* 4:9–15.

HEYNEMAN, STEPHEN P. 1987. "Uses of Examinations in Developing Countries: Selection, Research, and Education Sector Management." *International Journal of Educational Development* 7:251–263.

HEYNEMAN, STEPHEN P. 1990. "Protection of the Textbook Industry in Developing Countries." *Book Research Quarterly* 5(4):3–11.

HEYNEMAN, STEPHEN P. 1997. "Education and Social Stabilization in Russia." *Compare* 27(1):5–18.

HEYNEMAN, STEPHEN P. 1998. "Transition from the Party/State to Open Democracy: The Role of Education." *International Journal of Educational Development* 18(1):21–40.

HEYNEMAN, STEPHEN P. 2000. "Educational Qualifications: The Economic and Trade Issues." *Assessment in Education: Principles, Policy, and Practice* 7:417–439.

HEYNEMAN, STEPHEN P. 2000. "From the Party/State to Multi-ethnic Democracy: Education and Social Cohesion in the Europe and Central Asia Region." *Educational Evaluation and Policy Analysis* 22(2):173–191.

HEYNEMAN, STEPHEN P. 2001. "The Growing International Market for Education Goods and Services." *International Journal of Educational Development* 21:345–361.

HEYNEMAN, STEPHEN P., and FAGERLIND, INGEMAR, eds. 1988. *University Examinations and Standardized Testing.* Washington, DC: World Bank.

KALNINS, VALTS. 2001. *Latvia's Anti-corruption Policy: Problems and Prospects.* Riga, Latvia: Soros Foundation.

KIGOTHO, WACHIRA. 2002. "Kenyan Authorities Arrest Twenty-One Accused of Running Fake-Diploma Ring at Ministry of Education." *Chronicle of Higher Education* February 4.

KIRMANI, NAHEED. 1986. *The Effects of Increased Market Access on Exports of Developing Countries.* Washington, DC: International Monetary Fund.

KLITGAARD, ROBERT E. 1986. *Elitism and Meritocracy in Developing Countries.* Baltimore: Johns Hopkins University Press.

LINDEN, GLENN M., and BECK, WILLIAM W. 1981. "White Collar Crime in the Dallas Public Schools." *Phi Delta Kappan* 62:574–577.

PINERA, SEBASTIAN, and SELOWSKY, MARCELO. 1981. "The Optimal Ability: Education Mix and the Misallocation of Resources within Education." *Journal of Development Economics* 8:111–131.

PLOMP, TJEERD, and VOOGT, JOKE. 1995. "Curriculum Standards and Assessment in Modern Russian Education." In *Reflections on Education in Russia,* ed. Ferdinand J. H. Mertens. Leuven, Belgium: Acco.

ROCHE, GEORGE C. 1994. *The Fall of the Ivory Tower: Government Funding, Corruption, and the Bankrupting of American Higher Education.* Lanham, MD: National Book Network.

SADLAK, JAN. 1994. "The Emergence of a Diversified System: The State/Private Predicament in Transforming Higher Education in Romania." *European Journal of Education* 29(1):13–23.

SEGAL, LYDIA. 1997. "The Pitfalls of Political Decentralization and Proposals for Reform: The Case of New York City Public Schools." *Public Administration Review* 57:141–149.

SENTER, R. J. 1996. "Economic Development and the University: A Case Study of a Failed Program." *Research in Higher Education* 37:367–387.

WORLD BANK. 1995. *Russia: Education in the Transition.* Washington, DC: World Bank.

XUEQUIN, JIANG. 2001. "Corrupt Admissions Alleged in China." *Chronicle of Higher Education* September 14.

INTERNET RESOURCE

CENTER FOR QUALITY ASSURANCE IN INTERNATIONAL EDUCATION. 2002. <www.inqaahe.nl>.

STEPHEN P. HEYNEMAN

MISSISSIPPI FREEDOM SCHOOLS

The Mississippi freedom schools were an important project of the Student Nonviolent Coordinating Committee (SNCC) designed to promote freedom, self-determination, and participatory activism aimed at African-American youth in the improvement of local communities and state organizations.

Project Planning

In November 1963 the Council of Federated Organizations (COFO) and the SNCC conceived a major civil rights incursion into Mississippi during the summer of 1964. This incursion, spearheaded largely by SNCC and officially known as the Mississippi Summer Project, would promote African-American equality and basic democratic rights through a number of social action projects. One of those projects was the creation of a summer school program aimed at high school–age African-American students, providing them with a richer school experience than they were able to have in their own schools and, it was hoped, committing these students to become a force for social change in Mississippi. This educational endeavor became known as the Mississippi freedom schools.

Charles Cobb, field secretary for SNCC, proposed the idea of freedom schools as a war against academic poverty. He claimed the Mississippi school system and the African-American schools were meant to "squash intellectual curiosity." Cobb wanted young African-American students to have an education related directly to the everyday experiences and problems of these students. Freedom schools would "offer young black Mississippians an education that public schools would not supply, one that both provided intellectual stimulation and linked learning to participation in the movement to transform the South's segregated society" (Chilcoat and Ligon 1994, p. 132).

Implementation

To effect the idea of freedom schools, a curriculum conference was held in New York in March 1964. Approximately fifty people with varied backgrounds in education and civil rights work attended the conference. The major focus of the conference and the core of the freedom school curriculum was the formulating of a civic curriculum. The civic curriculum was to be composed of: (1) fourteen problem-solving case studies dealing with the political, economic, and social forces relating to the direct experiences of the students; (2) a *Citizenship Curriculum* facilitating student discussion as a means of achieving a new society; (3) a *Guide to Negro History* providing a comprehensive survey of African-American history; and (4) an emphasis on teachers extrapolating directly from students those personal experiences in which they lived each day in a hostile, repressive, dominantly white society. Also because of the lack of other academic opportunities offered to African-American students in their public schools, the conference included in the freedom schools a reading and writing remediation curriculum, a humanities curriculum emphasizing English, foreign languages, art, and creative writing, and a general science and mathematics curriculum. Coupled with the curriculum, the conference recommended a variety of progressive democratic teaching techniques emphasizing self-discovery and self-expression that were to stimulate the act of questioning.

In June 1964 two one-week orientation meetings were held on the campus of Western College for Women at Oxford, Ohio, for most of the freedom school summer volunteers. The second-week orientation involved the freedom school teachers. The orientation workshops were training courses in pedagogical techniques and in the use of the core civic curriculum developed at the curriculum conference. Upon completing the orientation, the volunteers traveled to their freedom school locations in Mississippi to begin their six-week stay. The original expectation was the creation of twenty schools with a desired student population of 1,000. However, freedom schools became a far greater success than the project had planned, with forty-one schools in twenty communities and 2,165 students.

As the Summer Project ended, it was hoped that freedom schools would continue. Although some of the schools did continue to operate, few could sustain either learning or activism. The schools were never projected as permanent institutions but rather, according to most of the original planners, as a tactic for immediate change. However, for many students and teachers, the freedom schools in those short six weeks had a substantial impact on their lives.

> The Freedom Schools showed that there can be a situation where learning is not forced upon youth. This was a type of education which gave individuals a personal interest in social relationships, a personal interest that made learning something to be sought after . . . . The Freedom Schools met the challenge of changing the social order through the educative process. They showed that this is not an additional burden that must be met through education, but a necessity if we are to have truth, justice, and equality in society. (Chilcoat and Ligon 1995, p. 6)

See also: COMMUNITY-BASED ORGANIZATIONS, AGENCIES, AND GROUPS; MULTICULTURAL EDUCATION.

BIBLIOGRAPHY

CHILCOAT, GEORGE W., and LIGON, JERRY A. 1994. "Developing Democratic Citizens: The Mississippi Freedom Schools as a Model for Social Studies Instruction." *Theory and Research in Social Education* 22:128–175.

CHILCOAT, GEORGE. W., and LIGON, JERRY A. 1995. "We Will Teach What Democracy Really Means by Living Democratically Within Our Own Schools: Lessons from the Personal Experiences of Teachers Who Taught in the Mississippi Freedom Schools." *Education and Culture* 11:1–19.

CHILCOAT, GEORGE. W., and LIGON, JERRY A. 1999. "Helping to Make Democracy a Living Reality: The Curriculum Conference of the Mississippi Freedom Schools." *Journal of Curriculum Supervision* 15:43–68.

GEORGE W. CHILCOAT
JERRY A. LIGON

MNEMONIC STRATEGIES AND TECHNIQUES

Mnemonic ("nee-moh-nick") techniques, also referred to as mnemonic strategies, mnemonic devices, or simply mnemonics, are systematic procedures designed to improve one's memory. The word *mnemonic* derives from the Greek goddess of memory, Mnemosyne, and means "memory enhancing." The most comprehensive treatise on the historical development of mnemonic techniques may be found in Robert Alan Hrees's 1986 doctoral dissertation, in which it is noted that in preliterate cultures "history is preserved orally and the poets, like Homer, tell that history in their rich poetry, 'recited by heart.' [The ancient] Greeks prefaced such performances with a call to Mnemosyne, requesting her aid for a flowing and accurate recitation" (p. 1).

Since the mid-1970s, mnemonic techniques have been the subject of extensive research attention by psychological scientists. This attention has been directed at both analyzing the presumed components of mnemonic techniques and evaluating their effectiveness in numerous applied and academic contexts. As will be seen, mnemonic techniques come in different varieties and combinations. Moreover, the "accurate recitation" goal of the ancient Greeks notwithstanding, mnemonic techniques have been shown to serve a wide range of memory-related functions.

Components of Mnemonic Techniques

Mnemonic techniques work because they provide meaningful connections between informational items that are typically novel or unfamiliar and, therefore, are difficult to remember. Suppose, for example, that an eleventh-grade student has just encountered the word *philatelist* for the first time and wants to remember the textbook definition that accompanies it ("a person who collects stamps"). Applying Joel Levin's (1983) "three R's" of associative mnemonic techniques—recoding, relating, and retrieving—the student would first engage in recoding the unfamiliar word *philatelist* into a familiar proxy, or "keyword"—a salient part of the unfamiliar word's sound or spelling that, ideally, is picturable. Thus, for *philatelist,* a reasonable keyword might be *Philistine* (represented by, say, the Biblical giant, Goliath), *Philadelphia, pilot, plate,* or *flat.* For present purposes, *Philistine* will be used.

The second "R" component of the mnemonic process involves relating the keyword to the to-be-remembered definition in the context of some integrated scene or episode. Here, for example, the student might imagine Goliath, the Philistine, being smitten by an object from little David's sling. In this constructed scene, however, the object is not a stone, but rather a colorful postage stamp that has been left ("collected"?) on Goliath's forehead.

Thus, with the unfamiliar word effectively recoded and related, the third "R" represents the systematic path that has been constructed for retrieving the definition from memory when the unfamiliar word is re-encountered. Here, when the student attempts to remember the meaning of the word *philatelist,* the keyword *Philistine* should come to mind, which in turn should re-evoke the picture of Goliath with the colorful postage stamp collected on his forehead, which in turn should elicit the "person who collects stamps" definition.

Comments on the mnemonic process. Four related comments are in order. First, authors of many popular books in which mnemonic techniques are promoted assert that the focal information in the integrated scene (i.e., the keyword related to the associated information) needs to be greatly exaggerated or be in some way "bizarre." Yet, scientific research on mnemonic techniques has indicated that such an assertion is without empirical foundation. Rather than exaggeration or bizarreness, what seem to be critical for mnemonic techniques to work are: (1) the effort and attention devoted by the learner to the task at hand, namely the selection/use of an effective keyword; and (2) the formation of a vivid (clear) image of the integrated keyword-information scene. Thus, for the *philatelist* example, a bizarre or exaggerated postage stamp is not a necessity, but selecting an effective keyword cue (one that resembles a salient part of *philatelist,* such as *Philistine*) and creating a vivid image of Goliath with a postage stamp on his forehead are likely to be.

Second, and also based on considerable scientific research, mnemonic techniques work whether their two principal ingredients (recoded keywords and relating scenes) are produced either *by* or *for* a learner. For individuals with adequate cognitive skills (e.g., older students and adults) and with to-be-learned information that is relatively straightforward to identify, recode, and relate, creating one's own keywords and integrated scenes can be expected to yield memory benefits. On the other hand, for less cognitively capable individuals (e.g., young children or handicapped learners) and with less straightforward to-be-learned information, providing already-constructed keywords and integrated scenes is typically more effective.

Third, such keywords and scenes can be represented either pictorially (in the form of actual illustrations or visual images) or verbally (in the form of sentences or phrases, such as "Somehow, the forehead of Goliath the Philistine had collected a colorful postage stamp on it."). Fourth and finally, through the introduction of conventional concrete symbols, mnemonic techniques are easily adapted to associating "abstract" (not easily pictured) items. For example, "justice" can be pictorially represented by the scales of justice, "democracy" by a voting booth, "technology" by an electronic computer, "wealth" by a stack of dollar bills, and so on.

Varieties and Uses of Mnemonic Techniques

The keyword method (which goes under many other names by writers of popular memory-improvement books) is designed to strengthen associations between two or more items. Such items frequently consist of one or more pieces of information that a learner has not previously integrated as a unit (e.g., the definitions of unfamiliar words, the contributions of various famous people, the natural habitats of unfamiliar animals, the capitals of the fifty U.S. states). In each of these cases, less familiar, less meaningful terms (vocabulary words and the names of famous people, animals, or capitals/states) are recoded into something more familiar and picturable (i.e., keywords) and then related to the to-be-associated information (for vocabulary words, to their definitions; for famous people, to their associated contributions; for animals, to their associated habitats; for state and capital names, to each other). It should be noted that the state-capital example is actually a dual-keyword variation of the original keyword method, in that both of the to-be-associated items are recoded as picturable keywords (e.g., *Kansas* as *cans* and its capital, *Topeka,* as a *top*) and then related to one another in an integrated scene (e.g., a spinning top knocking over a bunch of tin cans).

Verbal-pictorial associations. In each of the examples in the previous paragraph, the initial form of the two pieces of information to be associated is verbal in nature (i.e., verbal terms and associated verbal information). A variation of the keyword method, for which an item that is pictorial in nature (e.g., a person's face, an animal's appearance, an artist's painting) is to be associated with verbal information (e.g., an unfamiliar name), is known as the face-name mnemonic technique. With this method, the "keyworded" unfamiliar name is related to a prominent feature of the physical or pictorial representation. For example, when being introduced to a new person with the unfamiliar surname *Lectka,* one could recode the name as the more familiar word *lecture.* Carefully examining the appearance of the person, one might notice the mouth as a prominent characteristic. Then, focusing on that mouth, one could imagine the person delivering a highly technical lecture. When subsequently encountering the person (either at the same gathering or in the future), and with one's attention drawn to the prominent mouth, it is hoped that the lecture emanating from it would come to mind, which in turn would be helpful in retrieving the surname *Lectka.*

Ordered associations. In contrast to the function of the keyword method and its variations (namely, associating unfamiliar, or arbitrary, paired items), the major function of the earliest mnemonic techniques—as applied by Mnemosyne's protégés—was to remember a list or group of numerically or chronologically ordered information (i.e., to associate each item of a list with a specific number, or to remember the items in a specific order). Chief among such mnemonic techniques was the method of loci, through which ordered items in a list (including the order of topics or points to be covered in a lengthy oration) were associated with a familiar sequence of objects, such as specific landmarks along a well-traveled route—or as has been developed in recent research investigations, familiar holidays to symbolize the numerically coded calendar months.

Two other common mnemonic techniques for remembering ordered information are the first-letter mnemonic and the link method (also known as the chain or story method). With the first-letter mnemonic, the first letter of each to-be-remembered list item is successively linked, either as an acronym (e.g., HOMES to represent the five Great Lakes: *H*uron, *O*ntario, *M*ichigan, *E*rie, and *S*uperior) or as a constructed phrase or sentence consisting of words beginning with those letters, to cue the list items themselves. For example, to remember the increasing distances of the first five planets from the sun (Mercury, Venus, Earth, Mars, Jupiter) using the first-letter mnemonic, one could focus on the letter sequence MVEMJ and construct a little "story" such as: "*Murray's Very Elderly Mother Jumped.*" (*Murray* was intentionally selected here to resemble *Mercury* in order to help distinguish it from another planet starting with the same letter, *Mars.*) With the

link method, an association is connected between each successive item in a to-be-remembered list through a sequentially constructed "house that Jack built"–type story or imagined episode. Associated links (e.g., between successive planet names) can be similarly constructed through the introduction of rhyme and meter.

Two mnemonic techniques that are suitable for remembering either ordered or numerically identified information are the pegword method and the digit-symbol method (also known as the digit-consonant method). With the simpler-to-master pegword method, the numbers from 1 to 10 (or 1 to 20) are recoded as familiar rhyming pegwords (for example, 1 = *bun,* 2 = *shoe,* 3 = *tree,* 4 = *door,* 5 = *hive,* etc.). Then, each numbered item in a list is related to the pegword in an integrated scene. For example, if the fifth item in a 20-item list had something to do with sailboats, then one could construct a scene in which bees from a *hive* (for 5) were swarming all over the skipper of a *sailboat.* To later remember the fifth item of the list, one systematically retrieves *sailboat* from the *hive* pegword for 5. To reconstruct the complete list or to order the items in the list, one would need to retrieve the information associated with each of the 20 ordered pegwords.

With the more-complex-to-master digit-symbol method, each digit from 1 through 9 (plus 0) is first recoded as a previously established consonant sound (for example, in one standard system, 1 becomes a *t* or *d* sound, 2 an *n* sound, 3 an *m* sound, 4 an *r* sound, 5 an *l* sound, . . . , 0 an *s* or *z* sound). Either single recoded letters (for up to 10 items) or combined recoded letters (for more than 10 items) are additionally recoded as words that include just those consonant sounds (vowels and silent consonants are ignored in this system). For example, the number 5, recoded as an *l* sound, would additionally be recoded as the words *lie, lye, oil, aisle,* and so on. In contrast, the number 15, recoded as a *t* or *d* sound plus an *l* sound, would additionally be recoded as the words *tail, tile, doll, dial, deli,* and so on. Returning to the sailboat example: If *sailboat* were the fifth item in a list, it would be associated with a recoded 5, such as *oil,* and then related to *sailboat* as, say, an imagined scene in which the skipper is oiling the sailboat's steering mechanism. On the other hand, if *sailboat* were the fifteenth item in a list, it would be associated with a recoded 15, such as *tile,* and related to *sailboat* as, say, an imagined scene in which the skipper is covering the main deck of his sailboat with tile. The digit-symbol method is also commonly applied to remembering numbers per se, as, for example, telephone numbers, zip codes, and institution-assigned security numbers. For example, to remember a bank-assigned ATM machine personal identification number of 5131, one could apply the digit-symbol method as follows: l (5) + d (1) + m (3) + d (1) = *old maid*. When approaching the ATM machine, one would simply think of the process as starting to play the card game called Old Maid.

Educational Applications of Mnemonic Techniques

Joel R. Levin, in his contribution to the 1996 book *The Enlightened Educator: Research Adventures in the Schools,* documented numerous successful educational applications of mnemonic techniques, based on both individual and combined adaptations. Such mnemonic adaptations, several of which have been alluded to throughout this discussion, have been shown to improve students' memory for such educational content as: the meanings of unfamiliar vocabulary words (including foreign-language vocabulary); mathematics facts, concepts, and operations; the states and their capitals; the U.S. presidents; artists and their paintings; people and dates associated with various inventions; and scientific facts, relationships, and processes. In addition, mnemonic techniques have helped students organize and remember both narrative and expository information presented in text passages, with benefits observed on both tests of simple factual recall and those requiring higher-order thinking (e.g., essay production, inferential thinking, and problem solving). From an educational standpoint, mnemonic techniques may not be ideally suited for *all* students in *all* instructional contexts. Such techniques nonetheless provide widespread versatility in their potential for enabling students to grasp basic information efficiently and confidently, thereby freeing them to move on to more cognitively demanding tasks. Continuing mnemonic research is helping teachers and students realize the limits of that educational potential.

See also: MEMORY, *subentry on* METAMEMORY.

BIBLIOGRAPHY

ATKINSON, RICHARD C. 1975. "Mnemotechnics in Second-Language Learning." *American Psychologist* 30:821–828.

HIGBEE, KENNETH L. 1993. *Your Memory: How It Works and How to Improve It,* 3rd edition. New York: Prentice Hall.

HREES, ROBERT A. 1986. "An Edited History of Mnemonics from Antiquity to 1985: Establishing a Foundation for Mnemonic-Based Pedagogy with Particular Emphasis on Mathematics." Ph.D. diss., Indiana University.

HWANG, YOOYEUN; RENANDYA, WILLY A.; LEVIN, JOEL R.; LEVIN, MARY E.; GLASMAN, LYNETTE D.; and CARNEY, RUSSELL N. 1999. "A Pictorial Mnemonic Numeric System for Improving Students' Factual Memory." *Journal of Mental Imagery* 23:45–69.

LEVIN, JOEL R. 1982. "Pictures as Prose-Learning Devices." In *Discourse Processing,* ed. August Flammer and Walter Kintsch. Amsterdam: North-Holland.

LEVIN, JOEL R. 1983. "Pictorial Strategies for School Learning: Practical Illustrations." In *Cognitive Strategy Research: Educational Applications,* ed. Michael Pressley and Joel R. Levin. New York: Springer-Verlag.

LEVIN, JOEL R. 1996. "Stalking the Wild Mnemos: Research That's Easy to Remember." *The Enlightened Educator: Research Adventures in the Schools,* ed. Gary G. Brannigan. New York: McGraw-Hill.

MCCARTY, DAVID L. 1980. "Investigation of a Visual Imagery Mnemonic Device for Acquiring Face-Name Associations." *Journal of Experimental Psychology: Human Learning and Memory* 6:145–155.

JOEL R. LEVIN

MODERN LANGUAGE ASSOCIATION OF AMERICA

Founded in 1883, the Modern Language Association (MLA) of America is the largest society of humanists in the United States. Its mission is to promote study, criticism, and research in the modern languages and their literatures and to further the common interests of teachers of these subjects.

Programs and Publications

The MLA's programs are designed to serve the scholarly and professional interests of its members.

The association publishes two journals: *PMLA*, a distinguished scholarly journal, appears six times per year; *Profession* is an annual that carries committee reports, association surveys, and articles on a range of professional topics. Established in 1922, the *MLA International Bibliography* provides an annual classified listing and subject index of more than 50,000 books and articles about film, folklore, language, linguistics, and literature that are published worldwide. It is available in print and electronic formats. The reference work began to cover publications about rhetoric and composition and the teaching of language and literature with the 2000 edition. The MLA's book publication program meets the needs of students, teachers, and scholars through several series: *Approaches to Teaching World Literature, Texts and Translations, Introductions to Older Languages, Options for Teaching,* and *Teaching Languages, Literatures, and Cultures.* Well-known to students are the *MLA Handbook for Writers of Research Papers, A Research Guide for Undergraduate Students,* and the *Literary Research Guide.* The *Job Information List,* which is available in print and electronic formats, offers up-to-date descriptions of employment opportunities in postsecondary English and foreign language departments.

The MLA convention, which takes place each year from December 27 through 30 and attracts between 8,000 and 9,000 participants, gives members opportunities for scholarly exchange on a wide range of topics. The association is also committed to collecting statistical information about the field. Recent studies examine enrollment trends in foreign languages, the use of part-time faculty members in English and foreign language departments, employment opportunities for new Ph.D.s, and the characteristics of successful college and university foreign language programs.

The MLA houses the Association of Departments of English (ADE) and the Association of Departments of Foreign Languages (ADFL). These organizations arrange summer seminars for chairs of English and foreign language departments, develop standards for the field, and publish the *ADE Bulletin* and *ADFL Bulletin,* which serve departmental administrators.

In 1997 the MLA introduced *What's the Word?,* a 29-minute weekly radio series that was available by 2001 on 125 National Public Radio stations and through Armed Forces Radio. The series showcases scholars in the field. Its purpose is to demonstrate how the study of languages and literature enriches people's lives. Sample topics include "Literature of the Sea," "Shakespeare Then and Now," "Film Couples," "Post-Apartheid South African Literature," "The Blues as Literature," and "Sermon Traditions."

Organizational Structure

Seventeen MLA members are elected to serve on the executive council, which has fiduciary responsibility for the association and selects the executive director, approves the annual budget, and appoints committees. A larger elected body, the delegate assembly, meets at the annual convention and considers a range of issues affecting the profession and the association. The assembly recommends actions to the executive council. MLA committees and staff members develop and implement the association's programs.

The MLA is a constituent society of the American Council of Learned Societies and an associate member of the American Council on Education. The MLA maintains membership in two advocacy coalitions—the National Humanities Alliance and the Joint National Committee for Languages. It is also a member of the Fédération Internationale des Langues et Littératures Modernes.

Membership and Financial Support

Membership in the MLA is open to any individual interested in advancing the goals of the association. The association has 30,000 members and supports its programs through publication revenue, library subscriptions, annual dues, and registration fees for the annual meeting. An endowment fund is valued at $1.1 million.

History and Development

The MLA was established in 1883 by forty college teachers who wished to encourage the study of the modern languages in U.S. colleges and universities at a time when the role of the classical languages was beginning to decline. Initially, MLA members established a journal for the publication of research in the field and organized an annual meeting to discuss scholarly and pedagogical issues. As the study of the modern languages grew increasingly important in both higher education and the schools, the MLA also grew.

INTERNET RESOURCE

MODERN LANGUAGE ASSOCIATION. 2002. <www.mla.org>.

PHYLLIS FRANKLIN

MODERN RED SCHOOLHOUSE

The Modern Red Schoolhouse (MRSh) is part of a larger effort in the United States to design schools for the twenty-first century—schools where all students can achieve world-class academic standards. In the early 1990s, during its design and pilot phase, MRSh was housed at the Hudson Institute, a public policy research organization in Indianapolis, Indiana. The institute was awarded a competitive five-year contract from the New American Schools Development Corporation to develop the design, pilot it, and provide training and support to schools that chose to adopt it.

The Modern Red Schoolhouse design for twenty-first-century schools evolved around a central premise: All students can master high academic standards, but they vary in the ways that they learn best and in the time that they need to learn. While simple in concept, this premise constitutes a stark contrast to the ways in which public schooling evolved during the twentieth century in the United States—when expectations for learning varied by the presumed ability and interest of a given student, yet the pedagogy and time to learn was the same for all students. The MRSh premise is built from research in sociology and psychology showing that: (a) intelligence is heavily influenced by a learner's effort and opportunity to learn, rather than simply inherited, and (b) instructional methods that make effective links to students' prior experiences and learning are essential to learning.

The MRSh design seeks to structure a school environment that allows students to vary their level of effort to meet academic standards and enables teachers to use a variety of pedagogies and adapt instructional strategies to meet the needs of students. High academic standards are the same for all students. The MRSh design assumes that schools are accountable for student outcomes, but proposes giving schools considerable freedom in selecting strategies to achieve student outcomes in terms of staffing, instructional design, and the use of time. Community and parent involvement focuses on activities that support student learning—whether it be assisting teachers in establishing links between disciplinary knowledge and concrete problems in industry and communities, or by providing students with additional opportunities to advance their understanding or mastery of standards outside the regular school day.

This design views assessment as an ongoing activity embedded in the instructional process. Remedial courses should not be necessary; rather, extra time or varying approaches are available as needed in any given week. Formal assessments in the original design include *capstone units* that, taken collectively, address all academic standards through interdisciplinary performance assessments. Capstone units are interdisciplinary units that have a cumulating performance assessment intended to allow students to demonstrate mastery of a number of academic standards. As part of a larger assessment system, they provide teachers with data regarding a student's readiness to take one or more subject exams to confirm their mastery. A more traditional set of subject exams, common to all schools, verifies that students have met the necessary level of mastery required of all MRSh students. Extending the services already available to students with special needs, the design expects teachers to work with students and their parents to develop an Individual Education Compact, which is an ongoing plan for student learning that specifies the responsibility of each party (student, parent, and teacher). As students mature, they take increasing responsibility for proposing the compact, constrained only by the standards they are ultimately required to master. Technology is not only used for instructional activities, but is an essential tool for communication within the school community and for management of classroom instruction.

In developing training to support wider adoption of the design among existing schools, MRSh sought to enable schools to complete substantial portions of implementation within a three-year period with twenty to thirty days of technical assistance a year. The structure and content of the assistance assumes that schools are at different starting points along a continuum of implementation—thus the need to customize the time and methods of implementation at each school. Similarly, the MRSh design calls for developing the actual plan of instruction at each school to reflect the state or district academic standards and the prior cultural and academic experiences of the students attending the school.

In 1998 federal funding became available that allowed schools with economically disadvantaged students to adopt a Comprehensive School Reform Design, which would enable them to effect substantial improvements in student achievement over a three-year period. In this massive scale-up, MRSh Institute—which had been established as an independent organization in 1997—adapted the original model to serve these schools. In general, the formal assessment system in the original design was replaced by that of the relevant state or district, and the technology acquisition was adapted to meet the various exigencies of urban school districts. The MRSh Institute's essential contribution to school reform has been to operationalize the notion of a standards-driven school and classroom and, as such, many districts rely upon its services to assist schools in reframing their work to match district or state standards. From 1993 to 2002 the Modern Red Schoolhouse Institute had served 130 schools in fifty-six districts and provided district-wide services in five metropolitan areas.

See also: ACCELERATED SCHOOLS; ALTERNATIVE SCHOOLING; GRADING SYSTEMS.

INTERNET RESOURCE

MODERN RED SCHOOLHOUSE INSTITUTE. 2002. <www.mrsh.org>.

SALLY B. KILGORE

MONTESSORI, MARIA
(1870–1952)

Physician Maria Montessori is recognized as one of the pioneers in the development of early childhood education. She is also credited with promoting a substantial number of important educational reforms that have worked their way over the course of the twentieth century into the mainstream of education. These include the recognition of multiple pathways to learning, the importance of concrete or hands-on learning, the stages of cognitive development in children, and the link between children's emotional development and their ability to learn at an optimal rate. Her ideas about the importance of the first six years of life and the boundless potential of children—regardless of race, gender, or social class—made a significant contribution to human rights as societies around the world began to redefine the rights and roles of women and children.

Biography

Montessori was born in 1870 to an educated middle-class family in Ancona, Italy. Growing up in a country that was, at the time, very conservative in its attitude toward and treatment of women, Montessori pursued a medical and scientific education. In 1896, despite many years of opposition from her father, teachers, and male fellow students, she graduated with highest honors from the Medical School of the University of Rome, becoming the first woman physician in Italy.

Work with Disabled Children

As a physician, Montessori specialized in pediatrics and the newly evolving field of psychiatry. Her approach was that of a well-trained scientist, rather than the familiar philosophical exploration and intuitive approach followed by many of the educational innovators who came before and after. Montessori found it ironic that she became best known for her contributions in education, a field that she had been unwilling to enter as it was one of the three traditional roles open to women at the time: working with children, homemaking, or the convent.

Montessori taught at the medical school of the University of Rome, and through its free clinics she came into frequent contact with the children of the working class and poor. Her experience with the children of poverty convinced Montessori that intelligence is not rare, although it seemed to present itself in many forms other than those recognized by traditional schools.

In 1900 Montessori was appointed director of the new Orthophrenic School attached to the University of Rome, formerly a municipal asylum for the "deficient and insane" children of the city, most of whom would be diagnosed in the twenty-first century as autistic or mentally disabled. She and her colleagues initiated a wave of reform in an institution that formerly had merely confined these mentally challenged youngsters in barren settings. Recognizing her young patients' need for stimulation, purposeful activity, and self-esteem, Montessori dismissed the caretakers who treated the inmates with contempt. Facing a desperate lack of staff to care for so many children in a residential setting, she set out to teach as many as possible of the less-disturbed children to care for themselves and their fellow inmates.

Links to Itard and Séguin

From 1900 to 1901, Montessori combed the medical libraries of western Europe seeking successful work previously done with the education of children with disabilities. Her studies led Montessori to the work of two almost forgotten French physicians of the eighteenth and nineteenth centuries: Jean-Marc-Gaspard Itard and Édouard Séguin. Itard is well known in the twenty-first century for his work with the "Wild Boy of Aveyron," a youth who had been found wandering naked in the forest, presumably abandoned as a very young child and thus spending many years living alone. The boy could not speak and lacked almost all of the skills of everyday life. Here apparently was a "natural" man, a human being who had grown up outside of human society without the influence of interaction with his own kind. Itard hoped from this study to shed some light on the age-old debate about what proportion of human intelligence and personality is hereditary and what proportion stems from learned behavior.

This experiment was a limited success, although it captured the attention and imagination of many of his contemporaries. Itard found his wild boy uncooperative and unwilling or unable to learn most things. This led him to postulate the existence of developmental periods in normal human growth. He formed the hypothesis that, during these "sensitive periods," a child must experience stimulation to develop normally, or grow up, forever lacking the skills and intellectual concepts not developed at the stage when nature expects them to be readily absorbed.

Although Itard's efforts to teach the wild boy were barely successful, he followed a methodical approach in designing the process, arguing that all education would benefit from the use of careful observation and experimentation. This idea had tremendous appeal to the scientifically trained Montessori, and later became the cornerstone of her method.

From the work of Édouard Séguin, a French psychologist who studied with Itard and carried on his research, Montessori drew further confirmation of Itard's ideas, along with a far more specific and organized system for applying it to the everyday education of children with disabilities. Working primarily with the blind, Séguin developed a methodical approach to breaking skills down into small steps, and was highly successful with a carefully developed collection of hands-on educational materials. In the early twenty-first century, Séguin is recognized as the founder of the modern approach to special education.

The Orthophrenic School

From these two predecessors, Montessori took the idea of a scientific approach to education, based on observation and experimentation. She belongs to the child study school of thought and pursued her work with the careful training and objectivity of the biologist studying the natural behavior of an animal in the forest. Montessori studied her mentally disabled patients, listening and carefully noting their response to her attempts to implement Séguin's educational methods, as well as their progress in becoming increasingly independent and verbal.

Slowly the children learned to perform most of the everyday tasks involved in preparing the meals and maintaining the environment of the residential school. Her success with these mentally disabled children received international attention when, after two years, many of Montessori's such adolescents were able to pass the standard exams given by the Italian public schools.

Acclaimed for this miracle, Montessori responded by suggesting that newborn human beings normally enter the world with an intellectual potential that was barely being developed by schools in the early years of the twentieth century. She challenged that if she could attain such results with children who were disabled, schools should be able to get dramatically better results with normal children.

Montessori's work reinforced her humanistic ideals, and she actively supported various social reform movements. She was a highly regarded guest speaker throughout Europe on behalf of children's rights, the women's movement, peace education, and the importance of a league of nations. Montessori become well known and highly regarded throughout Europe, which contributed to the publicity that surrounded her schools.

The Children's House

Unfortunately, the Italian Ministry of Education did not welcome Montessori's ideas, and she was denied access to school-aged children. Frustrated in her efforts to conduct the experiment with public school students, in 1907 she welcomed the opportunity to serve as the medical director for a day-care center that was being organized for working-class children who were too young to attend public school.

This first Casa dei Bambini (Children's House) was located in the worst slum district of Rome, and the conditions Montessori faced were appalling. Her first class consisted of fifty children, from two through five years of age, taught by one untrained caregiver. The children remained at the center from dawn to dusk while their parents worked, and had to be fed two meals per day, bathed regularly, and given a program of medical care. The children themselves were typical of extreme inner-city poverty conditions. They entered the Children's House on the first day crying and pushing, exhibiting generally aggressive and impatient behavior. Montessori, not knowing whether her experiment would work under such conditions, began by teaching the older children how to help out with the everyday tasks that needed to be done. She also introduced the manipulative perceptual discrimination and puzzles and eye-hand manipulative exercises that she had used with mentally disabled children.

The results surprised her, for unlike her mentally disabled children who had to be prodded to use her apparatus, these very small children were drawn to the work she introduced. Children who had wandered aimlessly the week before began to settle down to long periods of constructive activity. They were fascinated with the puzzles and perceptual training devices.

To Montessori's amazement, children three and four years old took the greatest delight in learning practical everyday living skills that reinforced their independence and self-respect. Each day they begged her to show them more, even applauding with delight when Montessori taught them the correct use of a handkerchief to blow one's own nose. Soon the older children were taking care of the school, assisting their teacher with the preparation and serving of meals and the maintenance of a spotless environment. Their behavior as a group changed dramatically from that of street urchins running wild to models of grace and courtesy. It was little wonder that the press found such a human-interest story appealing and promptly broadcast it to the world.

Montessori education is sometimes criticized for being too structured and academically demanding of young children. Montessori would have laughed at this suggestion. She often said, "I followed these children, studying them, studied them closely, and they taught me how to teach them."

Montessori made a practice of paying close attention to the children's spontaneous behavior, arguing that only in this way could a teacher know how to teach. Traditionally schools at this time paid little attention to children as individuals, other than to demand that they adapt to external standards. Montessori argued that the educator's job is to serve the child, determining what each student needs to make the greatest progress. To her, a child who fails in school should not be blamed, any more than a doctor should blame a patient who does not get well fast enough. Just as it is the job of the physician to help people find the way to cure themselves, it is the educator's job to facilitate the natural process of learning.

Montessori's children exploded into academics. Too young to go to public school, they begged to be taught how to read and write. They learned to do so quickly and enthusiastically, using special manipulative materials that Montessori designed for maximum appeal and effectiveness. The children were fascinated by numbers. To respond to their interest, the mathematically inclined doctor developed a series of concrete math learning materials that still fascinates many mathematicians and educators to this day. Soon her four- and five-year-olds were adding and subtracting four-digit numbers, soon progressing on to multiplication, division, skip counting, and increasingly advanced and abstract concepts.

Their interests blossomed in other areas as well, compelling the overworked physician to spend night after night designing new materials to keep pace with the children in geometry, geography, history, and natural science. Further proof of the children's academic interests came shortly after her first school opened, when a group of well-intentioned women gave the children a collection of lovely and expensive toys. The new gifts held the children's attention for a few days, but they soon returned to the more interesting learning materials. To Montessori's surprise, she found that children who had experienced both generally preferred work over play, at least during the school day. Of the early twenty-first century classroom, Montessori would probably add: "Children read and do advanced mathematics in Montessori schools not because we push them, but because this is what they do when given the correct setting and opportunity. To deny them the right to learn because we, as adults, think that they should not is illogical and typical of the way schools have been run before."

Montessori evolved her method through trial and error, making educated guesses about the underlying meaning of the children's actions. She was quick to pick up on their cues, and constantly experimented with the class. For example, Montessori tells of the morning when the teacher arrived late, only to find that the children had crawled through a window and gone right to work. At the beginning, the learning materials, having cost so much to make, were locked away in a tall cabinet. Only the teacher had a key and would open it and hand the materials to the children upon request. In this instance the teacher had neglected to lock the cabinet the night before. Finding it open, the children had selected one material apiece and were working quietly. As Montessori arrived the teacher was scolding the children for taking them out without permission. She recognized that the children's behavior showed that they were capable of selecting their own work, and removed the cabinet and replaced it with low open shelves on which the activities were always available to the children. This may sound like a minor change, but it contradicted all educational practice and theory of that period.

The Discovery of the Child

One discovery followed another, giving Montessori an increasingly clear view of the inner mind of the child. She found that little children were capable of long periods of quiet concentration, even though they rarely show signs of it in everyday settings. Although they are often careless and sloppy, they respond positively to an atmosphere of calm and order.

Montessori noticed that the logical extension of the young child's love for a consistent and often repeated routine is an environment in which everything has a place. Her children took tremendous delight in carefully carrying their work to and from the shelves, taking great pains not to bump into anything or spill the smallest piece. They walked carefully through the rooms, instead of running wildly as they did on the streets.

Montessori discovered that the environment itself was all-important in obtaining the results that she had observed. Not wanting to use heavy school desks, she had carpenters build child-sized tables and chairs. She was the first to do so, recognizing the frustration that a little child experiences in an adult-sized world. Eventually she learned to design entire schools around the size of the children. She had miniature pitchers and bowls prepared and found knives that fit a child's tiny hand. The tables were lightweight, allowing two children to move them alone. The children learned to control their movements, disliking the way the calm atmosphere was disturbed when they knocked into the furniture. Montessori studied the traffic pattern of the rooms, arranging the furnishings and the activity area to minimize congestion and tripping. The children loved to sit on the floor, so she bought little rugs to define their work areas and the children quickly learned to walk around work that other children had laid out on their rugs.

Montessori carried this environmental engineering throughout the entire school building and outside environment, designing child-sized toilets and low sinks, windows low to the ground, low shelves, and miniature hand and garden tools of all sorts. Many of these ideas were eventually adapted by the larger educational community, particularly at the nursery and kindergarten levels. Many of the puzzles and educational devices in use at the preschool and elementary levels in the early twenty-first century are direct copies of Montessori's original ideas. However, there is far more of her work that never entered the mainstream, and twenty-first-century educators who are searching for new, more effective answers are finding the accumulated experience of the Montessori community to be of great interest.

Worldwide Response

Maria Montessori's first Children's House received overnight attention, and thousands of visitors came away amazed and enthusiastic. Worldwide interest surged as she duplicated her first school in other settings with the same results. Montessori captured the interest and imagination of leaders and scientists around the world. In America, leading figures such as Woodrow Wilson, Alexander Graham Bell, Thomas Edison, and Henry Ford enthusiastically supported her. Through books and countless articles written about and by Montessori, she also became a well-known authority to parents and teachers.

As an internationally respected scientist, Montessori had a rare credibility in a field where many others had promoted opinions, philosophies, and models that have not been readily duplicated. The Montessori method offers a systematic approach that translates very well to new settings. In the first thirty years of the twentieth century, the Montessori method seemed to offer something for everyone. Conservatives appreciated the calm, responsible behavior of the little children, along with their love for work. Liberals applauded the freedom and spontaneity. Many political leaders saw it as a practical way to reform the outmoded school systems of Europe, North America, and Asia, as well as an approach that they hoped would lead to a more productive and law-abiding populace. Scientists of all disciplines heralded its empirical foundation, along with the accelerated achievement of the little children. Montessori rode a wave of enthusiastic support that many felt should have changed the face of education far more dramatically than it did.

The Decline and Resurgence of Interest in Montessori Education in America

By 1925 there were more than 1,000 Montessori schools in the United States and many tens of thousands more around the world. But by 1940 the movement had virtually disappeared from the American scene. Only a handful of schools remained that openly advertised that they followed the Montessori approach, although many continued to operate without using the name. Education textbooks failed to mention her at all except as an obscure footnote, and her work was virtually forgotten until it was "rediscovered" and brought back to North America in the 1960s by Dr. Nancy McCormick Rambush and the newly formed and rapidly expanding American Montessori Society. During this period, Montessori schools continued to expand in most of the rest of the world.

The question is often asked about what led to the decline of Montessori education in the United States. Several reasons can be reasonably postulated, including the disruption in trans-Atlantic travel during and after World War I and World War II. Many would agree that a highly influential book published in 1922 by Professor William Kilpatrick of Columbia University, *Montessori Reexamined*, may have led many American educators to dismiss Montessori unfairly as being an intellectual holdover from the outdated and no longer accepted theories of faculty psychology. Kilpatrick pronounced that Montessori was rigid, outdated, and mistaken in her attempt to educate the senses, suggesting that she was under the misapprehension that the brain and senses could be strengthened, like a muscle, by exercises in sensory training and memorization. Unfortunately, this and many other criticisms were unfounded, primarily based on a lack of accurate information and understanding, along with perhaps some bias against Montessori's popularity as she was a doctor and not a trained educator. Others have suggested that her being a highly articulate and outspoken woman who was openly critical of the schools of her day may have also played a substantial role.

In the early twenty-first century there are almost six thousand Montessori schools in the United States, and their number continues to expand in virtually every country around the world. In America, most Montessori schools are nonpublic and primarily serve early childhood students between the age of two and six. However, the number of public school districts implementing the Montessori approach has grown substantially since the 1980s, with more than 300 districts running more than 500 magnet Montessori schools. As charter schools have developed, Montessori schools are among the most popular and successful models.

Also since the 1980s, Montessori schools have tended to expand in both enrollment and the age levels served, with the majority of schools offering elementary programs as well as early childhood. Secondary Montessori programs are less common, but are beginning to appear in substantial numbers, initially as middle school programs and gradually as high school programs as well.

The largest professional society in the United States is the American Montessori Society in New York City. It accredits Montessori schools and more than fifty university-sponsored and independent Montessori teacher education centers around the United States. Several dozen smaller professional Montessori associations can also be found in the United States. They include the Association Montessori Internationale (AMI), the society founded by Montessori herself in 1929, which has its headquarters in the Netherlands and a national office in Rochester, New York; and the more recently founded umbrella organization for Montessori schools, the International Montessori Council (IMC), which has its American offices in Rockville, Maryland, and Sarasota, Florida. The Montessori Accreditation Council for Teacher Education (MACTE) also accredits Montessori teacher education programs and is recognized by the United States Department of Education.

Montessori's prime productive period lasted from the opening of the first Children's House in 1907 until the 1930s. During this time, she continued her study of children, and developed a vastly expanded curriculum and methodology for the elementary level as well. Montessori schools were set up throughout Europe and North America, and Montessori gave up her medical practice to devote all of her energies to advocating the rights and intellectual potential of all children.

During her lifetime, Montessori was acknowledged as one of the world's leading educators. As with all innovators, the educational community moved on beyond Montessori, adapting many elements of her work that fit into existing theories and methods. It can be fairly suggested that every classroom in America reflects Montessori's ideas to a fairly substantial degree. Certainly the contemporary attitudes about multiple intelligences, the importance of mental health and emotional literacy, the attractiveness of the modern classroom, the use of manipulative materials in instruction, cooperative learning, authentic assessment, and multiage classrooms as a desirable model for classroom groupings are just a few examples of ideas generally attributed to Maria Montessori.

Ironically, schools are beginning to recognize that the Montessori approach has much more to offer, primarily because to obtain the results that Montessori made world famous, schools must implement her model as a complete restructuring of the school and the teacher's role, rather than as a series of piecemeal reforms.

As understanding of child development has grown, many contemporary American educators and those who would reform education have rediscovered how clear and sensible her insight was. In the early twenty-first century, there is a growing consensus among many psychologists and developmental educators that her ideas and educational model were decades ahead of their time. As the movement gains support and continues to spread into the American public school sector, one can readily say that Montessori, begun at the dawn of the twentieth century, is a remarkably modern approach.

See also: EARLY CHILDHOOD EDUCATION; INSTRUCTIONAL STRATEGIES.

BIBLIOGRAPHY

KRAMER, RITA MARIA. 1988. *Maria Montessori: A Biography.* Reading, MA: Addison-Wesley.

LILLARD, PAULA. 1972. *Montessori, a Modern Approach.* New York: Schocken.

MONTESSORI, MARIA. 1992. *The Secret of Childhood* (1940). London: Sangam.

MONTESSORI, MARIA. 1995. *The Absorbent Mind* (1949). New York: Holt.

MONTESSORI, MARIA. 2002. *The Montessori Method* (1912). Mineola, NY: Dover.

STANDING, E. MORMITER. 1998. *Maria Montessori: Her Life and Work.* New York: Plume.

TIMOTHY DAVID SELDIN

MORAL DEVELOPMENT

The Swiss psychologist Jean Piaget, author of the 1932 book *The Moral Judgment of the Child,* is among the first psychologists whose work remains directly relevant to contemporary theories of moral development and education. From his observations and interviews of children, Piaget concluded that children begin in a "heteronomous" stage of moral reasoning, characterized by a strict adherence to rules and duties and obedience to authority. This heteronomy results from two factors. The first factor is the young child's cognitive structure. According to Piaget, the thinking of young children is characterized by egocentrism. Young children are unable to simultaneously take into account their own view of things with the perspective of someone else. This egocentrism leads children to project their own thoughts and wishes onto others. It is also associated with the unidirectional view of rules and power associated with heteronomous moral thought and with various forms of "moral realism." Moral realism is associated with "objective responsibility," which is valuing the letter of the law above the purpose of the law. This is why young children are more concerned about the outcomes of actions rather than the intentions of the person doing the act. Moral realism is also associated with the young child's belief in "immanent justice." This is the expectation that punishments automatically follow acts of wrongdoing.

The second major contributor to young children's heteronomous moral thinking is their relative social relationship with adults. In the natural authority relationship between adults and children, power is handed down from above. The relative powerlessness of young children, coupled with childhood egocentrism, feeds into a heteronomous moral orientation. Nevertheless, through interactions with other children in which the group seeks to play together in a way all find fair, children find this strict heteronomous adherence to rules sometimes problematic. As children consider these situations, they develop towards an "autonomous" stage of moral reasoning, characterized by the ability to consider rules critically and to selectively apply these rules based on a goal of mutual respect and cooperation. The ability to act from a sense of reciprocity and mutual respect is associated with a shift in the child's cognitive structure from egocentrism to perspective taking. Coordinating one's own perspective with that of others means that what is right needs to be based on solutions that meet the requirements of fair reciprocity.

Piaget concluded from this work that schools should emphasize cooperative decision-making and problem solving, nurturing moral development by requiring students to work out common rules based on fairness. He believed individuals define morality individually through their struggles to arrive at fair solutions. Given this view, Piaget suggested that classroom teachers should provide students with opportunities for personal discovery through problem solving, rather than indoctrinating students with norms.

Lawrence Kohlberg's Theory of Moral Development and Education

The American psychologist Lawrence Kohlberg modified and elaborated Piaget's work and determined that the process of attaining moral maturity took longer and was more gradual than Piaget had proposed. On the basis of his research, Kohlberg identified six stages of moral reasoning grouped into three major levels. At the first, *preconventional* level, a person's moral judgments are characterized by a concrete, individual perspective. Within this level, a Stage 1 heteronomous orientation focuses on avoiding breaking rules that are backed by punishment, obedience for its own sake, and avoiding the physical consequences of an action. At Stage 2 a moral orientation emerges that focuses on the instrumental, pragmatic values of actions. Reciprocity is of the form: "you scratch my back and I'll scratch yours."

Individuals at the second, *conventional*, level reason about moral situations with an understanding that norms and conventions are necessary to uphold society. Within this level, individuals at Stage 3 define what is right in terms of what is expected by people close to them and in terms of the stereotypic roles that define being good—for example, a good brother, mother, teacher. Stage 4 marks the shift from defining what is right in terms of local norms and role expectations to defining right in terms of the laws and norms established by the larger social system. This is the "member of society" perspective in which one is moral by fulfilling the actual duties defining one's social responsibilities.

Finally, the *postconventional* level is characterized by reasoning based on principles, using a "prior to society" perspective. These individuals reason on the basis of principles that underlie rules and norms. While two stages have been presented within the theory, only one, Stage 5, has received substantial empirical support. Stage 6 remains a theoretical endpoint that rationally follows from the preceding five stages. In essence this last level of moral judgment entails reasoning rooted in the ethical fairness principles from which moral laws would be devised. Laws are evaluated in terms of their coherence with basic principles of fairness rather than upheld simply on the basis of their place within an existing social order.

Kohlberg used findings from his research to reject traditional character education practices that are premised in the idea that virtues and vices are the basis to moral behavior, or that moral character is comprised of a "bag of virtues," such as honesty, kindness, patience, and strength. Kohlberg believed a better approach to affecting moral behavior would focus on stages of moral development. Initial educational efforts employing Kohlberg's theory sought to engage students in classroom discussions of moral dilemmas that would lead to an awareness of contradictions inherent in students' present level of moral reasoning and to shifts toward the next stage of moral judgment. Kohlberg and his colleagues eventually developed the "just community" schools approach toward promoting moral development, described in the 1989 book *Lawrence Kohlberg's Approach to Moral Education*. These schools seek to enhance moral development by offering students the chance to participate in community discussions to arrive at consensual resolutions of the actual moral problems and issues students face as members of the school community.

Domain Theory: Distinguishing Morality and Convention

In the early 1970s, longitudinal studies conducted by the Kohlberg research group began to reveal anomalies in the stage sequence. One of the most productive lines of research to come out of that period has been the domain theory advanced by Elliot Turiel and his colleagues. Within domain theory a distinction is drawn between the child's developing concepts of morality and other domains of social knowledge, such as social convention. According to domain theory, the child's concepts of morality and social convention emerge out of the child's attempts to account for qualitatively differing forms of social experience associated with these two classes of social events. Actions within the moral domain, such as unprovoked hitting of someone, have intrinsic effects (i.e., the harm that is caused) on the welfare of another person. Such intrinsic effects occur regardless of the nature of social rules that may or may not be in place regarding the action. Because of this, the core features of moral cognition are centered around considerations of the effects that actions have upon the well-being of persons. Morality is structured by concepts of harm, welfare, and fairness. In contrast, actions that are matters of social convention have no intrinsic interpersonal consequences. For example, there is nothing intrinsic to forms of address that makes calling a college teacher "professor" better or worse than calling the person Ms. or simply using her given name. What makes one form of address better than another is the existence of socially agreed-upon rules. These conventions, while arbitrary, are nonetheless important to the smooth functioning of any social group. Conventions provide a way for members of the group to coordinate their social exchanges through a set of agreed-upon and predictable modes of conduct. Concepts of convention, then, are structured by the child's understandings of social organization. These hypothesized distinctions have been sustained through studies since the mid-1970s that have included interviews with children, adolescents, and adults; observations of child-child and adult-child social interactions; cross-cultural studies; and longitudinal studies examining the changes in children's thinking as they grow older.

Educational research from within domain theory has resulted in a set of recommendations for what is termed "domain appropriate" values education. This approach entails the teacher's analysis and identification of the moral or conventional nature of social values issues to be employed in lessons. Such an analysis contributes to the likelihood that the issues discussed are concordant with the domain of the values dimension they are intended to affect. Teachers are also better enabled to lead students through consideration of more complex issues that contain elements from more than one domain.

Carol Gilligan and the Morality of Care

Carol Gilligan, in a 1982 book titled *In a Different Voice: Psychological Theory and Women's Development,* suggested that a morality of care can serve in the place of the morality of justice and rights espoused by Kohlberg. A way to look at how these differ is to view these two moralities as providing two distinct injunctions—the injunction not to treat others unfairly (justice) and the injunction not to turn away from someone in need (care). She presents these moralities as distinct, although potentially connected. In her initial work, Gilligan emphasized the gender differences thought to be associated with these two orientations. Further research has suggested, however, that moral reasoning does not follow the distinct gender lines that Gilligan originally reported. The preponderance of evidence is that both males and females reason based on justice and care. While this gender debate is unsettled, Gilligan's work has contributed to an increased awareness that care is an integral component of moral reasoning. Educational approaches based on Gilligan's work have emphasized efforts to foster empathy and care responses in students.

Persisting Controversies

Three primary controversies persist in the field of moral development research. First, there is disagreement over whether morality has universal elements or is cross-cultural. Second, there is disagreement over whether morality develops in stages or levels. Finally, there are unresolved issues regarding the connections between moral judgments and action. The latter is of greatest concern to educators because one of the primary goals of education is to produce citizens who will lead moral lives. The most promising line of work attempting to deal with this issue is exploring the development of what is referred to as the "moral self." This approach assumes that people act on the basis of their moral judgments if being moral is a central part of their sense of personal identity.

See also: CHARACTER DEVELOPMENT; KOHLBERG, LAWRENCE; MORAL EDUCATION; PIAGET, JEAN.

BIBLIOGRAPHY

DEVRIES, RHETA, and ZAN, BETTY. 1994. *Moral Classrooms, Moral Children: Creating a Constructivist Atmosphere in Early Education.* New York: Teachers College Press.

GILLIGAN, CAROL. 1982. *In a Different Voice: Psychological Theory and Women's Development.* Cambridge, MA: Harvard University Press.

KELLER, MONIKA, and EDELSTEIN, WOLFGANG. 1993. "The Development of the Moral Self from Childhood to Adolescence." In *The Moral Self,* ed. Gill G. Noam and Thomas E. Wren. Cambridge, MA: MIT Press.

KOHLBERG, LAWRENCE. 1969. "Stage and Sequence: The Cognitive-Developmental Approach to Socialization." In *The Handbook of Socialization Theory and Research,* ed. David A. Goslin. Chicago: Rand McNally.

NODDINGS, NEL. 1992. *The Challenge to Care in Schools.* New York: Teachers College Press.

NUCCI, LARRY P. 2001. *Education in the Moral Domain.* Cambridge, Eng.: Cambridge University Press.

PIAGET, JEAN. 1932. *The Moral Judgment of the Child.* New York: Free Press.

POWER, F. CLARK; HIGGINS, ANN; and KOHLBERG, LAWRENCE. 1989. *Lawrence Kohlberg's Approach to Moral Education.* New York: Columbia University Press.

LARRY NUCCI

MORAL EDUCATION

Only a handful of educational theorists hold the view that if only the adult world would get out of the way, children would ripen into fully realized people. Most thinkers, educational practitioners, and parents acknowledge that children are born helpless and need the care and guidance of adults into their teens and often beyond. More specifically, children need to learn how to live harmoniously in society. Historically, the mission of schools has been to develop in the young both the intellectual and the moral virtues. Concern for the moral virtues, such as honesty, responsibility, and respect for others, is the domain of moral education.

Moral education, then, refers to helping children acquire those virtues or moral habits that will help them individually live good lives and at the same time become productive, contributing members of their communities. In this view, moral education should contribute not only to the students as individuals, but also to the social cohesion of a community. The word *moral* comes from a Latin root (*mos, moris*) and means the code or customs of a people, the social glue that defines how individuals should live together.

A Brief History of Moral Education

Every enduring community has a moral code and it is the responsibility and the concern of its adults to instill this code in the hearts and minds of its young. Since the advent of schooling, adults have expected the schools to contribute positively to the moral education of children. When the first common schools were founded in the New World, moral education was the prime concern. New England Puritans believed the moral code resided in the Bible. Therefore, it was imperative that children be taught to read, thus having access to its grounding wisdom. As early as 1642 the colony of Massachusetts passed a law requiring parents to educate their children. In 1647 the famous Old Deluder Satan Act strengthened the law. Without the ability to read the Scriptures, children would be prey to the snares of Satan.

The colonial period. As common school spread throughout the colonies, the moral education of children was taken for granted. Formal education had a distinctly moral and religion emphasis. Harvard College was founded to prepare clergy for their work. Those men who carved out the United States from the British crown risked their fortunes, their families, and their very lives with their seditious rebellion. Most of them were classically educated in philosophy, theology, and political science, so they had learned that history's great thinkers held democracy in low regard. They knew that democracy contained within itself the seeds of its own destruction and could degenerate into mobocracy with the many preying on the few and with political leaders pandering to the citizenry's hunger for bread and circuses.

The founders' writings, particularly those of Thomas Jefferson, James Madison, John and Abigail Adams, and Benjamin Franklin, are filled with admonitions that their new country make education a high priority. While the early leaders saw economic reasons for more and longer schooling, they were convinced that the form of government they were adopting was, at heart, a moral compact among people.

Nineteenth century. As the young republic took shape, schooling was promoted for both secular and moral reasons. In 1832, a time when some of the Founding Fathers were still alive, Abraham Lincoln wrote, in his first political announcement (March 9, 1832), "I desire to see a time when education, and by its means, morality, sobriety, enterprise and industry, shall become much more general than at present." Horace Mann, the nineteenth-century champion of the common schools, strongly advocated for moral education. He and his followers were worried by the widespread drunkenness, crime, and poverty during the Jacksonian period in which they lived. Of concern, too, were the waves of immigrants flooding into cities, unprepared for urban life and particularly unprepared to participate in democratic civic life. Mann and his supporters saw free public schools as the ethical leaven of society. In 1849, in his twelfth and final report to the Massachusetts Board of Education, he wrote that if children age four to sixteen could experience "the elevating influences of good schools, the dark host of private vices and public crimes, which now embitter domestic peace and stain the civilization of the age, might, in 99 cases in every 100, be banished from the world" (p. 96).

In the nineteenth century, teachers were hired and trained with the clear expectation that they would advance the moral mission of the school and attend to character formation. Literature, biography, and history were taught with the explicit intention of infusing children with high moral standards and good examples to guide their lives. Students' copybook headings offered morally uplifting thoughts: "Quarrelsome persons are always dangerous companions" and "Praise follows exertion." The most successful textbooks during the nineteenth and early twentieth centuries were the famed McGuffey readers, which were filled with moral stories, urgings, and lessons. During this period of our evolution as a nation, moral education was deep in the very fabric of our schools.

There was, however, something else in the fabric of moral education that caused it to become problematic: religion. In the United States, as a group of colonies and later as a new nation, the overwhelming dominant religion was Protestantism. While not as prominent as during the Puritan era, the King James Bible was, nevertheless, a staple of U.S. public schools. The root of the moral code was seen as residing there. However, as waves of immigrants from Ireland, Germany, and Italy came to the country from the mid-nineteenth century forward, the pan-Protestant tone and orthodoxy of the schools came under scrutiny and a reaction set in. Concerned that their children would be weaned from their faith, Catholics developed their own school system. Later in the twentieth century, other religious groups, such as Jews, Muslims, and even various Protestant denominations, formed their own schools. Each group desired, and continues to desire, that its moral education be rooted in its respective faith or code.

Twentieth century. During this same late-nineteenth-century and twentieth-century period, there was also a growing reaction against organized religion and the belief in a spiritual dimension of human existence. Intellectual leaders and writers were deeply influenced by the ideas of the English naturalist Charles Darwin, the German political philosopher Karl Marx, the Austrian neurologist and founder of psychoanalysis Sigmund Freud, and the German philosopher and poet Friedrich Nietzsche, and by a growing strict interpretation of the separation of church and state doctrine. This trend increased after World War II and was further intensified by what appeared to be the large cracks in the nation's moral consensus in the late 1960s. Since for so many Americans the strongest roots of moral truths reside in their religious beliefs, educators and others became wary of using the schools for moral education. More and more this was seen to be the province of the family and the church. Some educators became proponents of "value-free" schooling, ignoring the fact that it is impossible to create a school devoid of ethical issues, lessons, and controversies.

During the last quarter of the twentieth century, as many schools attempted to ignore the moral dimension of schooling, three things happened: Achievement scores began to decline, discipline and behavior problems increased, and voices were raised accusing the schools of teaching secular humanism. As the same time, educators were encouraged to address the moral concerns of students using two approaches: values clarification and cognitive developmental moral education.

The first, *values clarification,* rests on little theory other than the assumption that students need practice choosing among moral alternatives and that teachers should be facilitators of the clarification process rather than indoctrinators of particular moral ideas or value choices. This approach, although widely practiced, came under strong criticism for, among other things, promoting moral relativism among students. While currently few educators confidently advocate values clarification, its residue of teacher neutrality and hesitance to actively address ethical issues and the moral domain persists.

The second approach, *cognitive developmental moral education,* sprang from the work of the Swiss psychologist Jean Piaget and was further developed by Lawrence Kohlberg. In contrast to values clarification, cognitive moral development is heavy on theory and light on classroom applications. In its most popular form, Kohlberg posited six sequential stages of moral development, which potentially individuals could achieve. Each stage represents a distinctive way an individual thinks about a moral situation or problem. Teachers are encouraged to engage students from an early age and throughout their schooling in discussion of moral issues and dilemmas. In the later years of his life, Kohlberg was urging educators to transform their schools into "just communities," environments within which students' moral stage development would accelerate.

The Return of Character Education

In the early 1980s, amid the widespread concern over students' poor academic achievements and behavior, educators rediscovered the word *character.* Moral education had a religious tinge, which made many uneasy. Character with its emphasis on forming good habits and eliminating poor habits struck a popular and traditional chord. The word *character* has a Greek root, coming from the verb "to engrave." Thus character speaks to the active process of making marks or signs (i.e., good habits) on one's person. The early formation of good habits is widely acknowledged to be in the best interests of both the individual and society.

In addition, character formation is recognized as something that parents begin early, but the work is hardly completed when a child goes to school. Im-

plicit in the concept of character is the recognition that adults begin the engraving process of habituation to consideration of others, self-control, and responsibility, then teachers and others contribute to the work, but eventually the young person takes over the engraving or formation of his own character. Clearly, though, with their learning demands and taxing events, children's school years are a prime opportunity for positive and negative (i.e., virtues and vices) character formation.

The impetus and energy behind the return of character education to American schools did not come from within the educational community. It has been fueled, first, by parental desire for orderly schools where standards of behavior and good habits are stressed, and, second, by state and national politicians who responded to these anxious concerns of parents. During his presidency, William Clinton hosted five conferences on character education. President George W. Bush expanded on the programs of the previous administration and made character education a major focus of his educational reform agenda. One of the politically appealing aspects of character education, as opposed to moral education with its religious overtones, is that character education speaks more to the formation of a good citizen. A widely repeated definition (i.e., character education is helping a child to know the good, to desire the good, and to do the good) straddles this issue. For some people the internal focus of character education comfortably can be both religious and civic and for others the focus can be strictly civic, dealing exclusively on the formation of the good citizen.

Current Approaches to Moral Education

The overwhelming percentage of efforts within public education to address the moral domain currently march under the flag of character education. Further, since these conscious efforts at addressing issues of character formation are relatively recent, they are often called *character education programs.* The term *program* suggests, however, discrete initiatives that replace an activity or that are added to the school's curriculum (e.g., a new reading program or mathematics program). And, although there are character education programs available, commercially and otherwise, most advocates urge the public schools to take an infusion approach to educating for character.

The infusion approach. In general, an *infusion approach* to character education aims to restore the formation of students' characters to a central place in schooling. Rather than simply adding on character formation to the other responsibilities of schools, such as numeracy, literacy, career education, health education, and other goals, a focus on good character permeates the entire school experience. In essence, character education joins intellectual development as the overarching goals of the school. Further, character education is seen, not in competition with or ancillary to knowledge- and skill-acquisition goals, but as an important contributor to these goals. To create a healthy learning environment, students need to develop the virtues of responsibility and respect for others. They must eliminate habits of laziness and sloppiness and acquire habits of self-control and diligence. The infusion approach is based on the view that the good habits that contribute to the formation of character in turn contribute directly to the academic goals of schooling.

A mainstay of the infusion approach is the recovery, recasting, or creating of a school's mission statement, one that reflects the priority placed on the development of good character. Such a statement legitimizes the attention of adults and students alike to this educational goal. It tells administrators that teachers and staff should be hired with good character as a criterion; it tells teachers that not only should character be stressed to students but also their own characters are on display; it tells coaches that athletics should be seen through the lens of sportsmanship rather than winning and losing; and it tells students that their efforts and difficulties, their successes and disappointments are all part of a larger process, the formation of their characters.

Critical to the infusion approach is using the curriculum as a source of character education. This is particularly true of the language arts, social studies, and history curricula. The primary focus of these subjects is the study of human beings, real and fictitious. Our great narrative tales carry moral lessons. They convey to the young vivid images of the kinds of people our culture admires and wants them to emulate. These subjects also show them how lives can be wasted, or worse, how people can betray themselves and their communities. Learning about the heroism of former slave Sojourner Truth, who became an evangelist and reformer, and the treachery of Benedict Arnold, the American army officer who betrayed his country to the British, is more than picking up historical information. Encountering these lives fires the student's moral imagination and deepens his understanding of what constitutes a life of character. Other subjects, such as mathematics and science, can teach students the necessity of intellectual honesty. The curricula of our schools not only contain the core knowledge of our culture but also our moral heritage.

In addition to the formal or overt curriculum, schools and classrooms also have a hidden or covert curriculum. A school's rituals, traditions, rules, and procedures have an impact on students' sense of what is right and wrong and what is desired and undesired behavior. So, too, does the school's student culture. What goes on in the lunchroom, the bathrooms, the locker rooms, and on the bus conveys powerful messages to students. This ethos or moral climate of a school is difficult to observe and neatly categorize. Nevertheless, it is the focus of serious attention by educators committed to an infusion approach.

An important element of the infusion approach is the language with which a school community addresses issues of character and the moral domain. Teachers and administrators committed to an infusion approach use the language of virtues and speak of good and poor behavior and of right and wrong. Words such as responsibility, respect, honesty, and perseverance are part of the working vocabulary of adults and students alike.

Other approaches. One of the most popular approaches to character education is service learning. Sometimes called community service, this approach is a conscious effort to give students opportunities, guidance, and practice at being moral actors. Based on the Greek philosopher Aristotle's concept of character formation (e.g., a man becomes virtuous by performing virtuous deeds; brave by doing brave deeds), many schools and school districts have comprehensive programs of service learning. Starting in kindergarten, children are given small chores such as feeding the classroom's gerbil or straightening the desks and chairs. They later move on to tutoring younger students and eventually work up to more demanding service activities in the final years of high school. Typically, these high-school level service-learning activities are off-campus at a home for the blind, a hospital, or a day-care center. Besides placement, the school provides training, guidance, and problem-solving support to students as they encounter problems and difficulties.

In recent years, schools across the country have adopted the virtue (or value) of the month approach, where the entire school community gives particular attention to a quality such as cooperation or kindness. Consideration of the virtue for that particular month is reflected in the curriculum, in special assemblies, in hallway and classroom displays, and in school-home newsletters. Related to this are schoolwide programs, such as no put-downs projects, where attention is focused on the destructive and hurtful effects of sarcasm and insulting language and students are taught to replace put-downs with civil forms of communication.

There are several skill-development and classroom strategies that are often related to character formation. Among the more widespread are teaching mediation and conflict-resolution skills, where students are given direct teaching in how to deal with disagreements and potential fights among fellow students. Many advocates of cooperative learning assert that instructing students using this instructional process has the added benefit of teaching students habits of helping others and forming friendships among students with whom they otherwise would not mix.

Issues and Controversies

The moral education of children is a matter of deep concern to everyone from parents to civic and religious leaders. It is no accident, then, that this subject has been a matter of apprehension and controversy throughout the history of American schools. Issues of morality touch an individual's most fundamental beliefs. Since Americans are by international standards both quite religiously observant and quite religiously diverse, it is not surprising that moral and character education controversies often have a religious source. Particularly after a period when moral education was not on the agenda of most public schools, its return is unsettling to some citizens. Many who are hostile to religion see this renewed interest in moral education as bringing religious perspectives back into the school "through the back door." On the other hand, many religious people are suspicious of its return because they perceive it to be an attempt to undermine their family's religious-based training with a state-sponsored secular humanism. As of the beginning of the twenty-first cen-

tury, however, the renewed attention to this area has been relatively free of controversy.

Contributing to the positive climate is the use of the term *character* rather than *moral.* While *moral* carries religious overtones for many, the word *character* speaks to good habits and the civic virtues, which hold a community together and allow us to live together in harmony.

A second issue relates to the level of schools and the age of students. The revival of character education in our schools has been evident to a much greater degree in elementary schools. Here schools can concentrate on the moral basics for which there is wide public consensus. The same is true, but to a somewhat lesser degree, for middle and junior high schools. And although there are many positive examples of secondary schools that have implemented broad and effective character education programs, secondary school faculties are hesitant to embrace character education. Part of it is the departmental structures and the time demands of the curriculum; part of it is the age and sophistication of their students; and part of it is that few secondary school teachers believe they have a clear mandate to deal with issues of morality and character.

A third issue relates to the education of teachers. Whereas once teachers in training took philosophy and history of education—courses that introduced them to the American school's traditional involvement with moral and character education—now few states require these courses. At the beginning of the twenty-first century, the American schools are seeing the large-scale retirement of career teachers and their replacement with large numbers of new teachers. These young teachers tend to be products of elementary and secondary schools where teachers gave little or no direct attention to moral and character education. In addition, a 1999 study by the Character Education Partnership of half of the nation's teacher education institutions showed that although over 90 percent of the leaders of these programs thought character education ought to be a priority in the preparation of teachers, only 13 percent were satisfied with their institution's efforts.

Evaluation of Moral and Character Education

There are a few character education programs with encouraging evaluation results. The Character Development Project (CDP) has more than 18 years of involvement in several K–6 schools, and in those schools where teachers received staff development and on-site support over 52 percent of the student outcome variables showed significant differences. The Boy Scouts of America developed the Learning For Life Curriculum in the early 1990s for elementary schools. This commercially available, stand-alone curriculum teaches core moral values, such as honesty and responsibility. In a large-scale controlled experiment involving fifty-nine schools, students exposed to the Learning For Life materials showed significant gains on their understanding of the curriculum's core values, but they were also judged by their teachers to have gained greater self-discipline and ability to stay on a task.

Still, evaluation and assessment in character and moral education is best described as a work in progress. The field is held back by the lack of an accepted battery of reliable instruments, a lack of wide agreement on individual or schoolwide outcomes, and by the short-term nature of most of the existent studies. Complicating these limitations is a larger one: the lack of theoretical agreement of what character is. Human character is one of those overarching entities that is the subject of disciples from philosophy to theology, from psychology to sociology. Further, even within these disciplines there are competing and conflicting theories and understandings of the nature of human character. But although the evaluation challenges are daunting, they are dwarfed by the magnitude of the adult community's desire to see that our children possess a moral compass and the good habits basic to sound character.

See also: CHARACTER DEVELOPMENT; ELEMENTARY EDUCATION, *subentries on* CURRENT TRENDS, HISTORY OF; ETHICS, *subentry on* SCHOOL TEACHING; SCHOOL REFORM; SECONDARY EDUCATION, *subentries on* CURRENT TRENDS, HISTORY OF.

BIBLIOGRAPHY

BERKOWITZ, MARVIN W., and OSER, FRITZ, eds. 1985. *Moral Education: Theory and Application.* Hillsdale, NJ: Lawrence Erlbaum.

CHAZAN, BARRY. 1985. *Contemporary Approaches to Moral Education: Analyzing Alternative Theories.* New York: Teachers College Press.

COLES, ROBERT. 1989. *The Call of Stories.* Boston: Houghton Mifflin.

DAMON, WILLIAM. 1995. *Greater Expectations: Overcoming the Culture of Indulgence in Our Homes and Schools.* New York: Free Press.

EBERLY, DON E., ed. 1995. *America's Character: Recovering Civic Virtue.* Lanham, MD: Madison.

HIMMELFARB, GERTRUDE. 1995. *The De-Moralization of Society: From Victorian Virtues to Modern Values.* New York: Knopf.

KILPATRICK, WILLIAM K. 1992. *Why Johnny Can't Tell Right from Wrong: Moral Literacy and the Case for Character Education.* New York: Simon and Schuster.

KREEFT, PETER. 1986. *Back to Virtue.* San Francisco: Ignatius.

LEWIS, CLIVE S. 1947. *The Abolition of Man.* New York: Macmillian.

LICKONA, THOMAS. 1991. *Educating for Character: How Our Schools Can Teach Respect and Responsibility.* New York: Bantam.

MACINTYRE, ALASDAIR. 1981. *After Virtue.* Notre Dame, IN: Notre Dame University Press.

MANN, HORACE. 1849. *Twelfth Annual Report of the Board of Education together with the Twelfth Annual Report of the Secretary of the Board of Education.* Boston: Dutton and Wentworth.

NUCCI, LARRY P., ed. 1989. *Moral Development and Character Education: A Dialogue.* Berkeley, CA: McCutchan.

POWER, F. CLARK; HIGGINS, ANN; and KOHLBERG, LAWRENCE. 1989. *Lawrence Kohlberg's Approach to Moral Education.* New York: Columbia University Press.

PRITCHARD, IVOR. 1998. *Good Education: The Virtues of Learning.* Norwalk, CT: Judd.

RYAN, KEVIN, and BOHLIN, KAREN. 1999. *Building Character in Schools: Practical Ways to Bring Moral Instruction to Life.* San Francisco: Jossey-Bass.

WILSON, JAMES Q. 1993. *The Moral Sense.* New York: Free Press.

WRIGHT, ROBERT. 1994. *The Moral Animal: Why We Are the Way We Are.* New York: Pantheon.

KEVIN RYAN

MORRISON, HENRY C. (1871–1945)

New Hampshire state superintendent of public instruction, superintendent of the Laboratory Schools of the University of Chicago, professor, and author, Henry Clinton Morrison developed an approach to learning in which material is organized into units students must master in order to progress to the next level. His five-step general pattern for the instructional process became well known as the Morrison Plan (also called the Morrison Method). Morrison's conception of mastery learning served as precursor to the "individualized instruction" and "mastery learning" educational movements of the 1970s and 1980s.

Morrison was born the son of John and Mary Louise (Ham) Morrison in Oldtown, Maine, a rugged fishing and lumber town in the middle of the Penobscot River. He worked in the lumber camps, but his own and his parents' earnings from the general merchandise store they ran could not finance his college education. Because Morrison had distinguished himself in his preparatory work for college, a local banker and the selectmen of the town raised money to finance his education at Dartmouth College. Morrison chose the college's classical course, with a concentration in philosophy. Robert Frost was a classmate. Morrison was graduated from Dartmouth with a Bachelor of Arts degree in 1895, one of two students to graduate magna cum laude.

Morrison served as a teaching principal at the consolidated high school in Milford, New Hampshire, from 1895 through 1899. Although he taught mathematics, history, Latin, and the sciences, he quickly became known for his abilities to organize and manage unruly students. The reputation Morrison built for Milford as a well-disciplined school earned him, at age twenty-eight, an appointment as superintendent of schools for Portsmouth, New Hampshire. He served in this position from 1899 to 1904. In 1902 he married Marion Locke; the couple had three sons.

In 1904 Morrison was appointed commissioner of public instruction for the state of New Hampshire. He served in this role as state superintendent until 1917 and during this time Morrison examined and approved all schools within the state, served on the state medical board, conducted teachers' examinations, and supervised attendance and child labor laws. In addition, during the summer of 1905, Morrison lectured on school administration at Dartmouth. In 1908 he was elected president of the American Institute of Instruction. In 1912 Morrison was invited by Charles Hubbard Judd, dean of the School of Education at the University of Chicago, to

be guest lecturer for the summer session at Chicago; Morrison thus strengthened initial ties with Judd, whom he had first met in 1911, that were to be most important later in his educational career. Morrison concluded his service as state superintendent of New Hampshire abruptly in 1917. From 1917 to 1919 Morrison lived in Connecticut and served as the assistant secretary of the State Board of Education.

In 1919 the position of superintendent of the Laboratory Schools of the University of Chicago became vacant. By then, Judd was well acquainted with Morrison's educational accomplishments and administrative expertise. On July 1, 1919, Morrison became professor of School Administration and superintendent of the Laboratory Schools, a position that he held until 1928.

In Morrison's educational career up to 1919, he had "insider" knowledge, as both teacher and administrator, of problems that plagued public education in the United States. From 1919 through 1928, he conceptualized theories for approaching these problems, tested tentative solutions within laboratory school contexts, and conducted a vast amount of empirical observation.

From Morrison's studies, he posited that genuine learning consisted of the student adapting or responding to a situation. Rejecting the notion that learning referred only to the acquisition of subject matter, Morrison instead concentrated on actual change in the behavior of the learner, what he called an adaptation. The unit was the procedure used for the teaching of an adaptation based on a stimulus-response psychology. This concept stems, in part, from Morrison's categorization of learning into a cycle of three phases: stimulus, assimilation, and reaction.

Morrison configured the secondary school curriculum into units of five types: science, appreciation, practical arts, language arts, and pure-practice. Acknowledging that instruction would vary among the different types of units, Morrison nonetheless identified a five-step instructional pattern. Morrison's general pattern for the instructional process (his plan or method) involves the following sequential steps: (1) pretest, (2) teaching, (3) testing the result of instruction, (4) changing the instruction procedure, and (5) teaching and testing again until the unit has been completely mastered by the student. In developing his concept of mastery learning, Morrison distinguished between learning and performance. Mastery, according to Morrison, is when students focus on learning a skill and acquire a fundamental grasp of subject matter. Once students have achieved a certain level of learning, they attempt to apply the skill; this application is called performance. The next step achieved is adaptation, the stage at which students become able to apply their learning to any situation.

Morrison's landmark publication, *The Practice of Teaching in the Secondary Schools* (1926), was the synthesis of his teaching, administrative, and research experiences. His book is widely regarded as one of the best known and most widely used systems of teaching from the late 1920s through the early 1940s. In this book, Morrison also drew a distinction between curriculum and instruction, thus marking the beginning of a major conceptual distinction between these two areas in the field of education.

Although Morrison's historical significance stems primarily from *The Practice of Teaching in the Secondary Schools,* he also brought important empirical analyses to the areas of school finance and organization, and administration of schools. Toward the end of school term in 1928, Morrison requested that he be transferred to the Department of Education and relieved of his position as superintendent of the Laboratory Schools. On July 1, 1937, Morrison retired from the University of Chicago; on March 19, 1945, he suffered a heart attack in the garden of his Hyde Park residence and died.

See also: CURRICULUM, SCHOOL; INSTRUCTIONAL STRATEGIES; SECONDARY EDUCATION, *subentry on* HISTORY OF; UNIVERSITY OF CHICAGO.

BIBLIOGRAPHY

BAYLES, ERNEST E. 1934. "The Objectives of Teaching with Special Reference to the Morrison Theory." *Educational Administration and Supervision* 20:561–568.

BECK, HUGO E. 1962. "The Contributions of Henry Clinton Morrison: An Educational Administrator at Work." Ph.D diss., The University of Chicago.

BROWN, HARRY A. 1945. "Henry C. Morrison and His Contributions to American Education." *School and Society* 61:380–382.

HENRY, NELSON B. 1937. "Mr. Morrison's Contributions to the Study of School Finance." *Zeta News of Phi Delta Kappa* 22:6–12.

MORRISON, HENRY C. 1924. *The Teaching Technique of the Secondary School.* Ann Arbor, MI: Edwards Brothers.

MORRISON, HENRY C. 1926. *The Practice of Teaching in the Secondary School.* Chicago: The University of Chicago Press.

MORRISON, HENRY C. 1932. *The Management of School Money.* Chicago: The University of Chicago Press.

MORRISON, HENRY C. 1943. *American Schools: A Critical Study of Our School System.* Chicago: The University of Chicago Press.

JANET L. MILLER

MOTIVATION

OVERVIEW
  Sandra Graham
INSTRUCTION
  Mark R. Lepper
  Jennifer Henderlong
SELF-REGULATED LEARNING
  Paul R. Pintrich

OVERVIEW

Motivation is the study of why people think and behave as they do. In an achievement setting, someone would be concerned with motivation if he were to ask, for example, why some students persist to task completion despite enormous difficulty, while others give up at the slightest provocation; or why some students set such unrealistically high goals for themselves that failure is bound to occur.

Motivation is also the study of what pushes or pulls an individual to start, direct, sustain, and finally end an activity. Consider, for example, an achievement activity such as studying for an exam. Motivation researchers would want to examine what the person is doing: the choice of behavior; how long it takes that person to get started. Or they wish to see the latency of behavior: how hard the individual actually works at the activity (the intensity of behavior); how long that individual is willing to remain at the activity (the persistence of behavior); and what the person is thinking or feeling while engaged in the activity, or the cognitions and emotional reactions that accompany behavior. Note that this focus on the "why" of achievement is quite different from the study of achievement itself. Educators sometimes confuse the topics of researchers who study motivation with the topics of researchers who study achievement and learning.

Early Theories

The scientific study of motivation as a discipline separate from learning began in the 1930s. Early motivation researchers were primarily interested in the factors that aroused behavior, or that got it started in the first place. It was widely believed at the time that the optimal state of an organism, both animal and human, was one of balance and equilibrium, where all needs were satisfied. The process of keeping the organism at this optimal level is known as homeostasis. Homeostatic balance was also thought to be satisfying, which was compatible with the belief that organisms were primarily motivated by hedonism, or the desire to maximize pleasure and minimize pain. Theories of motivation that emerged in the 1930s were based on the ideas of homeostasis and hedonism as fundamental principles.

Drive theory. The best known of these early conceptions was Clark Hull's drive theory. According to Hull, behavior is a function of drive and habit. Drives in the Hullian framework are unsatisfied needs, such as the need for food (hunger) or the need for water (thirst). The drive to satisfy one's needs is what arouses or energizes behavior. Habits, in turn, provide a direction for behavior. Habits are stimulus response bonds that are built up over time as a result of prior learning. For example, if someone's need to achieve has been satisfied in the past by studying hard for exams, then deficits in that need (arousal) should be satisfied by renewed study behavior. Thus behavior can be explained by both a motivation component (the drive that energizes behavior) and a learning component (the habit that provides direction or indicates what particular behavior will be initiated).

Simple yet elegant, drive theory generated a vast amount of motivation research from the 1930s through the 1950s. Of most relevance to education were studies on anxiety and learning conducted by Kenneth Spence, who was a student of Hull's. According to Spence, anxiety is a drive and it therefore arouses behavior, in this case the speed with which one learns simple versus complex tasks. On simple tasks where there is already a strong habit strength, anxiety will facilitate the speed of learning. With complex tasks, on the other hand, where there are

weak stimulus-response bonds, high anxiety should interfere with learning, because high anxiety activates incorrect stimulus-response bonds (habits) that compete with correct responses. In support of this analysis, many studies reveal that high anxiety is neither uniformly adaptive or maladaptive across all learning contexts.

Expectancy-value theory. Drive theory was very mechanistic. There was no role for complex cognitive processes such as how a person interprets an arousal cue or whether their expectations for success might energize behavior. With the cognitive revolution of the 1960s, motivation researchers became much more interested in how thoughts as well as unsatisfied needs and habits influenced behavior. The impact of drives as an organizing construct therefore waned. Furthermore, it became accepted that organisms are always active and the field of motivation shifted from the study of what turns organisms "on" and "off" to an interest in the direction of behavior, including choice and persistence.

The interest in cognition resulted in what is known as expectancy-value theory in motivation. The basic assumptions of expectancy-value theory are in accord with commonsense thinking about motivated behavior. Behavioral choice is determined by the perceived likelihood that the behavior will lead to a goal and how much that goal is desired or wanted. In the 1950s and 1960s, John Atkinson developed a theory of achievement motivation that perhaps best illustrates an expectancy-value framework. In its simplest form, Atkinson's theory states that the tendency to approach as achievement activity (T_s) is a function of three factors: the motive for success (M_s), the probability that one will be successful at the activity (P_s), and the incentive value of success (I_s). The factors are related multiplicatively, such that: $T_s = M_s \times P_s \times I_s$.

In this equation, M_s is the achievement motive, a relatively enduring personality trait presumed to be learned early in life. P_s, or the probability of success, takes on a numerical value from 0 to 1, with high numbers (e.g., $P_s = 0.8$) indicating greater likelihood of success, that is, an easy task. Finally, incentive value (I_s) represents an affective state, labeled pride in accomplishment, and it was assumed to be inversely related to expectancy ($1 - P_s$). That relationship captured the notion that easier tasks, where the probability of success was high, would elicit less pride and would therefore be less motivating.

Atkinson's theory was very popular from 1960 to 1980 and it generated many intriguing hypotheses about motivation. The theory predicted that high achievement oriented people prefer tasks of intermediate difficulty ($P_s = 0.5$) because such tasks elicited the most pride following success. People who were low in the achievement motive would be more motivated when tasks were very easy or very difficult. Atkinson was among the first theorists to point out that adaptive motivation was not necessarily associated with persisting at the hardest tasks where the probability of success is low. Indeed, the hallmark of a high achievement-oriented person is that they are able to gauge their efforts in response to their perceived expectancy, always striving toward intermediate difficulty.

Contemporary Theories of Motivation

Atkinson's theory gradually declined in the 1980s as motivation researchers turned their attention to a broader array of cognitions and to motivational traits other than the achievement motive. In general, contemporary motivation theories are dominated by three separate but interrelated constructs: expectancy, value, and achievement goals. As defined in the early twenty-first century, expectancy has to do with beliefs about ability (Can I do it?). Values are concerned with preferences and desires (Do I want it?). And goals capture purpose or the reasons for engaging in achievement activities (Why am I doing this?).

Beliefs about ability: Attribution theory. Three theories have addressed beliefs about ability. The first is attribution theory as developed by Bernard Weiner. Attributions are inferences about the causes of success and failure. (e.g., "Why did I get a poor grade on the exam?" or "Why did I get the highest grade?") Among the most prevalent inferred causes of success and failure are ability (aptitude), effort, task difficulty or ease, luck, mood, and help or hindrance from others. According to Weiner, these causes have certain underlying characteristics, which are known as causal dimensions. Causes differ in locus, or whether the cause is internal or external to the person; stability, which designates as cause as constant or varying over time; and in controllability, or the extent to which a cause is subject to volitional alteration. For example, low aptitude as a cause for failure is considered to be internal to the actor, stable over time, and uncontrollable, whereas lack of effort is judged as internal, but variable over time and subject to volitional control.

Each of these causal dimensions is linked to particular consequences that have motivational significance. For example, the stability dimension is related to expectancy for future success. When failure is attributed to a stable cause such as low ability, one is more likely to expect the same outcome to occur again than when the cause of failure is due to an unstable factor such as lack of effort. Thus the failing student who believes that he or she did not try hard enough can be bolstered by the expectation that failure need not recur again. Guided by these known linkages between causal stability and expectancy, attribution retraining programs have been developed that teach students to attribute failure to lack of effort rather than lack of ability. Many successful programs have been reported in which retrained students show greater persistence when they encounter challenging tasks, more confidence, and more positive attitudes toward school work.

The controllability dimension is related to a number of interpersonal affects, such as pity and anger. Pity and sympathy are experienced toward others whose failures are caused by uncontrollable factors (think of the teacher's reactions to the retarded child who continually experiences academic difficulty). In contrast, anger is elicited when others' failures are due to causes within their control (imagine that same teacher's affect toward the gifted student who never completes assignments). These emotional reactions also can serve as indirect attributional cues (i.e., they provide information about the cause of achievement). If a teacher expresses pity and sympathy following student failure, that student tends to make a low ability attribution. Hence, pity from others can undermine beliefs about ability.

Beliefs about ability: Self-efficacy theory. Popularized by Albert Bandura, self-efficacy refers to individuals' beliefs about their capabilities to perform well. When confronted with a challenging task, a person would be enlisting an efficacy belief if they asked themselves: "Do I have the requisite skills to master this task?" Unlike causal beliefs in attribution theory, which are explanations for past events, efficacy percepts are future oriented. They resemble expectations for personal mastery of subsequent achievement tasks. Also unlike attribution theory, which focuses on the perceived stability of causes as a determinant of expectancy, efficacy theorists have articulated a much more extensive set of antecedents, including prior accomplishments, modeling, persuasion, and emotional arousal. For example, physiological symptoms signaling anxiety, such as rapid heart beat or sweaty palms, might function as cues to the individual that he or she lacks the requisite skills to successfully complete a task.

According to Bandura, perceived efficacy determines how much effort a person is willing to put into an activity as well as how long they will persevere in the face of obstacles. Many studies have documented the adaptive consequences of high self-efficacy. For example, it is known that high self-efficacy and improved performance result when students: (1) adopt short-term over long-term goals, inasmuch as progress is easier to judge in the former case; (2) are taught to use specific learning strategies, such as outlining and summarizing, both of which increase attention to the task; and (3) receive performance-contingent rewards as opposed to reinforcement for just engaging in a task, because only in the former case does reward signal task mastery. All these instructional manipulations are assumed to increase the belief that "I can do it," which then increases both effort and achievement. Efficacy beliefs have been related to the acquisition of new skills and to the performance of previously learned skills at a level of specificity not found in any other contemporary theory of motivation.

Beliefs about ability: Learned helplessness theory. Whereas self-efficacy captures lay understanding of "I can," helplessness beliefs symbolize shared understanding about the meaning of "I cannot." According to this theory, a state of helplessness exists when failures are perceived as insurmountable, or more technically, when noncontingent reinforcement results in the belief that events are uncontrollable. That belief often is accompanied by passivity, loss of motivation, depressed affect, and performance deterioration. Martin Seligman, a main proponent of the theory, has argued that helplessness becomes a learned phenomenon when individuals inappropriately generalize from an experience with noncontingency in one situation to subsequent situations where control is possible. A prototypical example is the successful student who unexpectedly fails despite high effort and then becomes virtually incapable of completing work that was easily mastered prior to failure.

Helplessness theory has a decidedly attributional focus in that Seligman and others maintain that when individuals encounter failure, they ask, "Why?" How people characteristically answer this question is known as explanatory style. Some people typically explain bad events by pointing to factors that are internal, stable, and global. (e.g., "I'm always a failure no matter what I do"). These individuals are believed to have a pessimistic explanatory style. Other people interpret bad events by evoking momentary and specific causes (e.g., "I just happened to be in the wrong place at the wrong time"). Such individuals are characterized as having an optimistic explanatory style. A pessimistic explanatory style in the achievement domain has been related to poor school grades, reluctance to seek help, diminished aspirations, and ineffective use of learning strategies.

The research of Carol Dweck has focused particularly on individual differences the motivational patterns of children who may be vulnerable to helplessness beliefs. In response to challenging tasks where failure is possible, some children have a mastery-oriented motivational system: they believe that ability is incremental (e.g., "smartness is something you can increase as much as you want"), they focus on the task rather than their abilities, they enjoy challenge, and they can generate solution-oriented strategies that lead to performance enhancement. At the other end of the continuum are children who display a helpless motivational pattern: they believe that ability is fixed (e.g., "how smart you are pretty much stays the same"); they focus on personal inadequacies; express negative affect, including boredom and anxiety; and they show marked deterioration in actual performance. In other words, they display the classic symptoms associated with learned helplessness.

In summary, the dominant theme in contemporary motivation research revolves around beliefs about ability as represented by attribution theory, self-efficacy theory, and learned helplessness theory. Attribution theory has its origins in social psychology and is therefore especially concerned with the situational determinants of motivation and with both self-perception and the perception of others. Self-efficacy theory has emerged from a social learning perspective and therefore has close ties with behavioral change. Learned helplessness theory reflects the influence of clinical and personality psychology with its focus on coping with failure and individual differences in a presumed motivational trait.

Achievement values. There is a much smaller literature on achievement values, the other broad construct in expectancy-value approaches to motivation. Unlike expectancy, which focuses on beliefs about ability, values are more directly concerned with the perceived importance, attractiveness, or usefulness of achievement activities. Values also are rooted in the moral constructs of "ought" and "should," as illustrated by the belief that one should try hard in school regardless of his or her perceived abilities.

The most extensive research on achievement values has been conducted by Jacque Eccles and Allan Wigfield. These researchers define achievement tasks in terms of their attainment value (the perceived importance of doing well), intrinsic value (how much enjoyment the individual derives from engaging in the task), utility value (how the tasks relates to future goals), and costs (the undesirable consequences of engaging in the task). Most of the research guided by this conception has selected specific subject matter domains to examine whether task value predicts different consequences, such as course grades and enrollment decisions, or the extent to which value and expectancy are positively or negatively related (according to Atkinson's theory, these two constructs, I_s and P_s, should be inversely related). The findings of Eccles and Wigfield reveal that how much students value a particular domain influences choice behavior (i.e., their intention to enroll in particular courses and their actual enrollment). Task values, however, have little direct impact on actual course grades. Value and expectancy also appear to be positively correlated: individuals judge the tasks that they perceive themselves to be good at as more important, enjoyable, and useful. An unanswered question in this research is the issue of causal sequence. It is unclear whether individuals come to value what they are good at (expectancy $\rightarrow$ value), or whether individuals develop more confidence over time in the tasks that are most important (value $\rightarrow$ expectancy).

Achievement goals. Achievement goals capture the reasons why a person engages in achievement behavior, and two broad types have been identified. Students who pursue mastery goals are oriented toward acquiring new skills or improving their level of competence. In contrast, students who adopt performance goals are motivated by the intent to demonstrate that they have adequate ability and avoid displaying signs that they have low ability. According to this analysis, individuals can therefore decide to engage in achievement activities for two very different reasons: They may strive to develop competence by learning as much as they can, or they may

strive to publicly display their competence by trying to outperform others.

A vast number of studies suggest that mastery goals increase motivation more than do performance goals. The general thinking is that mastery oriented individuals seek out challenge and escalate their efforts when tasks become difficult, whereas performance-oriented individuals see their ability as threatened in challenging situations, which they tend to avoid. More recent research, however, suggests that adopting performance goals in some situations may enhance motivation. At times the two goal orientations may go hand in hand (people can strive to attain mastery and outperform others) or the pursuit of performance goals (i.e., comparing one's self to others) can provide cues that the person is competent and will therefore enhance motivation. It also appears that when performance goals are differentiated by approach (demonstrating ability) and avoidance (concealing low ability) tendencies, it is mainly the avoidance component that compromises sustained achievement strivings.

A related body of research, labeled self-determination theory by Edward Deci and Richard Ryan, conceptualizes achievement goal pursuits in terms of whether they fulfill the individual's basic needs for competence, autonomy, and relatedness to other people. Goals that satisfy these needs enhance intrinsic motivation. The pioneering research of Deci and Ryan has alerted many educators to the fact that extrinsic rewards, such as grades, gold stars, or even money, can undermine intrinsic motivation if they jeopardize people's sense of competence and feelings of personal control.

Future Challenges

Motivation is a rich and changing field that has enjoyed much progress in its relatively brief history. In more than six decades following Hull's insights, there have been major upheavals in the field (the shift from behaviorism to cognition); new theories and concepts have been introduced, and novel research directions have been pursued (such as the finding that reward can decrease motivation). Principles of motivation have been described that can become the basis for intervention. Quite a bit is known, for example, about the positive motivational consequences of attributing failure to lack of effort rather than low ability, of selecting tasks of intermediate difficulty, and of focusing on mastery rather than outperforming others. All these principles have good theoretical and empirical grounding. The challenge for the future will be to study motivation in context. Examining achievement expectancy, values, and goals and how they get expressed in the broader context of social and cultural influences might provide important clues for understanding the academic challenges faced by many ethnic minority youth. Addressing such issues will be a useful step toward promoting the field of motivation in education research and assuring its continued vitality.

See also: MOTIVATION, *subentries on* INSTRUCTION, SELF-REGULATED LEARNING.

BIBLIOGRAPHY

BANDURA, ALBERT. 1997. *Self-Efficacy: The Exercise of Control.* New York: Freeman.

DWECK, CAROL. 1999. *Self-Theories: Their Role in Motivation, Personality, and Development.* Philadelphia: Taylor and Francis.

GRAHAM, SANDRA, and WEINER, BERNARD. 1996. "Theories and Principles of Motivation." In *Handbook of Educational Psychology,* ed. David C. Berliner and Robert C. Calfee. New York: Macmillan.

PETERSON, CHRISTOPHER; MAIER, STEVEN; and SELIGMAN, MARTIN. 1993. *Learned Helplessness: A Theory for the Age of Personal Control.* New York: Oxford University Press.

PINTRICH, PAUL, and SCHUNK, DALE. 1996. *Motivation in Education: Theory, Research, and Applications.* Englewood Cliffs, NJ: Prentice-Hall.

WEINER, BERNARD. 1992. *Human Motivation: Metaphors, Theories, and Research.* Newbury Park, CA: Sage.

SANDRA GRAHAM

INSTRUCTION

The study of motivation has its roots in reinforcement theory, which focuses on the ways behaviors can be shaped by their consequences. In this model, the probability of a given response being repeated in the future is strengthened when it is followed by reward and weakened when it is not—a phenomenon the American psychologist Edward L. Thorndike, author of the 1911 book *Animal Intelligence,* termed the "law of effect." Reinforcement theory, as elaborated by American psychologist B. F. Skinner, examined the ways in which arbitrary responses could be elicited or eliminated through the use of systematic reinforcement and punishment. Rewards and punishments were thought to affect behavior automatically, without complex cognitive processes. Indeed, most early research was conducted with rats and pigeons, although the underlying principles and processes were thought to operate similarly in people.

Extrinsic Reformers

Until the 1960s, educators interested in enhancing student motivation were primarily instructed in the use of extrinsic reinforcers to control behavior. Such behavior modification programs, which remain in widespread use in the early twenty-first century, make desired consequences (e.g., rewards, praise, good grades, teacher attention) contingent upon performing specified behaviors (e.g., completing homework, paying attention, remaining quiet). One popular behavior modification technique is the token economy—a system in which students receive tokens each time they exhibit specified behaviors and in which these tokens can be subsequently exchanged for desired goods. Token economies can be extremely effective in producing immediate behavioral changes, and continue to be important techniques for classroom management. At the same time, these techniques have been less effective in producing persistence and generalization of desired behaviors when tangible rewards are no longer available. Thus, despite the obvious benefits of tangible extrinsic reinforcers, several weaknesses of this approach—especially as applied to education—became apparent.

First, although extrinsic contingencies often enhance classroom motivation, this approach ignores the mediating cognitive processes, such as the person's expectations, knowledge, and beliefs, that are essential for understanding when such changes will persist or generalize. Second, *extrinsic* constraints may sometimes conflict directly with children's *intrinsic* motivation to learn, subsequently causing as much harm as good. Third, this approach neglects other significant motivational variables, such as interests, values, and social relationships. Since the 1960s, these limitations of reinforcement theory have served as the impetus for the three broad classes of research reviewed below.

Mediating Cognitive Processes

Beginning in the 1960s, motivational researchers adopted a more cognitive approach. Rather than studying only the direct effects of rewards and punishments, researchers became concerned with people's subjective interpretations of these external consequences. Do they expect to be rewarded? Do they expect to succeed? Do they believe their actions will make a difference? Modern researchers believe that people, unlike rats and pigeons, consider whether they are capable of achieving a given goal before they attempt it.

One of the earliest approaches that included these mediating factors was the expectancy-value theory of motivation. This model, which viewed motivation as the multiplicative product of a person's expected probability of success and the expected value of success to that person, proved a significant turning point. Indeed, contemporary theories of motivation consider competence beliefs central to achievement motivation. Researchers have also examined more domain-specific expectancies, such as self-efficacy beliefs—in other words, beliefs that one can achieve specific goals in particular situations—which can promote effort expenditure, persistence in the face of setbacks, and academic performance. People's general theories about the mutability (capacity for change) of intelligence are also important. Compared to theories that intelligence is fixed, theories that intelligence is malleable produce more adaptive behaviors in academic contexts, such as persistence following setbacks and a focus on learning rather than performance.

Expectations for success also depend on attributions regarding past successes and failures. According to attribution theory, individuals characterize causes for success and failure along three dimensions: internal versus external locus (which affects feelings of self-esteem), stability over time (which affects expectations for success in the future), and controllability (which affects emotions such as guilt and shame). These causal attributions are particularly significant when individuals experience failure, and research suggests that attributions of failure to internal, unstable, and controllable causes—such as low effort or a poor strategy—are the most adaptive. Conversely, individuals who attribute failures to stable and uncontrollable causes, such as a lack of aptitude, tend to become helpless and give up, even when they could later easily succeed. Regardless of the presence of rewards, individuals are not motivated to engage in a behavior if they believe they cannot succeed.

Students' beliefs about their abilities and their expectations for success in school can be significantly influenced by teachers' instructional practices. Studies have shown that self-efficacy can be enhanced through direct success experiences, observed successes of a model, and verbal persuasion. One particularly effective procedure is to train students to set proximal (near-term) rather than distal (far-term) goals, which produces both self-efficacy and achievement gains. Teacher expectations can also influence student learning, even when these expectations have no basis in reality, suggesting that teachers convey subtle cues to students that have important consequences for motivation and achievement. Even seemingly innocuous behaviors, such as high praise for easy tasks or unsolicited help giving, can signify that teachers have low expectations and may adversely affect students' beliefs about their own abilities. Students can also be explicitly taught to focus on controllable and unstable causes for failure, such as a lack of effort or a poor strategy. Thus, effective instructional practices should communicate high but realistic expectations for success to students.

Intrinsic versus Extrinsic Motives

Also in the 1960s, researchers began to contrast extrinsic motivation with intrinsic motivation—the desire to engage in activities because they are inherently pleasurable, regardless of external contingencies. Given this contrast, it soon became apparent that extrinsic motivators have the potential to decrease students' subsequent intrinsic motivation when rewards are no longer available. That is, individuals must feel that their behavior is self-determined in order to experience motivation in the absence of extrinsic constraints. Studies have demonstrated that individuals who feel more in control of their own behavior also show more active learning, greater perceived competence, and higher academic achievement.

Conversely, the use of unnecessarily powerful extrinsic rewards can lead individuals to discount their intrinsic motivation. In many studies, students promised and given tangible rewards for engaging in initially intrinsically interesting activities showed less subsequent desire to perform those activities than students given no reward or the same reward unexpectedly. Thus, contracting to perform an activity in order to receive an extrinsic reward may undermine students' intrinsic motivation. Rewards do not always negatively impact intrinsic motivation, though, and much research has been devoted to understanding when rewards have beneficial versus detrimental effects. For example, rewards tend to enhance motivation when they are unexpected, intangible, and competence enhancing, and when there is little initial interest in an activity. Some controversy remains, however, regarding the specific conditions under which rewards negatively impact motivation.

The overuse of extrinsic incentives may also induce a performance orientation, as opposed to mastery orientation. Individuals with performance goals focus on appearing competent, even at the expense of further learning, whereas individuals with mastery goals focus on learning and understanding, even if their performance temporarily suffers. Research has shown that mastery goals are often associated with many positive achievement behaviors, such as persistence, effort, and effective strategy use. Nonetheless, performance goals may also sometimes be adaptive, and they may even correlate positively with mastery goals. As with intrinsic versus extrinsic motivation, sharp distinctions may be unwarranted.

Teachers can promote intrinsic motivation and foster mastery orientations. When students are encouraged to plan ahead, take personal responsibility, and set individual learning goals, they experience a greater sense of control and show gains in motivation and achievement. Personalizing learning activities or providing individuals with explicit choices can also boost motivation and enhance learning. The judicious use of extrinsic rewards and punishments, just sufficient to elicit compliance, will similarly have particularly positive effects on later intrinsic motivation. A classroom climate that supports mastery orientations—by minimizing public evaluation and normative comparisons, providing opportunities for improvement, and recognizing student effort—should also be beneficial. Instructional practices, therefore, should promote autonomy and minimize unnecessary extrinsic constraints, to foster intrinsic motivation and lifelong learning.

Additional Important Factors

Classic reinforcement theory also neglects other important factors, such as values, interests, and relationships. Values have more recently been viewed as having several components: attainment value (i.e., importance of doing well), interest value (i.e., task enjoyment), utility value (i.e., future usefulness), and cost (i.e., effort). Studies have shown that personal value of an academic domain can influence course enrollment, effort, persistence, and critical thinking. Closely related to value is interest, which has long been considered an important source of intrinsic motivation. The study of interest has recently received renewed attention, as researchers have sought to understand its relationship to self-regulation and to determine how different forms of interest are related to achievement outcomes.

Relationships are also not addressed by the extrinsic approach, although, much like competence and autonomy, they may be central to intrinsic motivation. Indeed, positive and secure relationships between students and teachers lead to greater classroom engagement, better emotional adjustment to school, and higher valuing of academic activities. It is not only beliefs, but also the more emotional factors of values, interests, and relationships, that can determine students' motivation.

Teachers can support values, interests, and relationships through a variety of instructional practices. Placing curriculum activities in interesting, perhaps even imaginary, contexts (e.g., learning math equations through a computerized space adventure) can produce gains in motivation and learning—provided that the context supports rather than distracts from the curriculum. Another strategy is to select or develop tasks centered on students' existing interests and concerns. This concept has been successfully implemented, both in small cooperative learning groups and in programs designed to create classroom "communities of learners" invested in working together to achieve common goals. Finally, research suggests that positive relationships are fostered when teachers provide appropriate structure and autonomy for their students and show them affection and respect.

Individual Differences

Many of these motivational variables may interact with individual differences, such as need for achievement, locus of control, explanatory styles, and self-theories. For example, stable individual beliefs about whether events are caused by internal versus external factors affect a host of achievement cognitions and behaviors, and different instructional practices may be more appropriate for internals versus externals. Researchers have also examined individual differences in general self-schemas or conceptual frameworks. For example, the extent to which individuals have a theory of intelligence as a malleable quality versus a fixed entity is thought to account for differences in achievement beliefs, goals, behaviors, and emotions. While it is unrealistic to assume that classroom practices can be perfectly matched to the needs of every individual student, at least given the current structure of most schools, differences in individuals' beliefs and behaviors must be considered, whenever possible.

Finally, motivational theories must include a developmental perspective, particularly when complex cognitive processes are involved. Studies suggest that there are developmental changes in children's beliefs about the relationship between ability and effort and the role that natural ability plays in achievement. Additionally, striking developmental decreases in children's intrinsic motivation and personal valuation of academic activities have been repeatedly documented. Clearly, these findings suggest that current practices have not been fully successful at promoting students' motivation as they progress through school.

See also: MOTIVATION, *subentries on* OVERVIEW, SELF-REGULATED LEARNING.

BIBLIOGRAPHY

ATKINSON, JOHN W. 1964. *An Introduction to Motivation.* Princeton, NJ: Van Nostrand.

BANDURA, ALBERT. 1969. *Principles of Behavior Modification.* New York: Holt, Rinehart and Winston.

BANDURA, ALBERT. 1997. *Self-Efficacy: The Exercise of Control.* New York: W. H. Freeman.

BERLYNE, DANIEL E. 1960. *Conflict, Arousal, and Curiosity.* New York: McGraw-Hill.

DECI, EDWARD L., and RYAN, RICHARD M. 1985. *Intrinsic Motivation and Self-Determination in Human Behavior.* New York: Plenum Press.

DWECK, CAROL S. 1999. *Self-Theories: Their Role in Motivation, Personality, and Development.* Philadelphia: Psychology Press.

HUNT, J. McVICKER. 1961. *Intelligence and Experience.* New York: Ronald Press.

KAZDIN, ALAN E. 1977. *The Token Economy.* New York: Plenum Press.

LEPPER, MARK R., and GREENE, DAVID, eds. 1978. *The Hidden Costs of Reward.* Hillsdale, NJ: Erlbaum.

McCLELLAND, DAVID C.; ATKINSON, JOHN W.; CLARK, RUSSELL A; and LOWELL, EDGAR J. 1953.
The Achievement Motive. New York: Appleton-Century-Crofts.

O'LEARY, K. DANIEL, and O'LEARY, SUSAN G. 1977. *Classroom Management: The Successful Use of Behavior Modification,* 2nd edition. New York: Pergamon Press.

SANSONE, CAROL, and HARACKIEWICZ, JUDITH M., eds. 2000. *Intrinsic and Extrinsic Motivation: The Search for Optimal Motivation and Performance.* San Diego, CA: Academic Press.

SKINNER, B. F. 1938. *The Behavior of Organisms: An Experimental Analysis.* New York: Appleton-Century-Crofts.

SKINNER, B. F. 1953. *Science and Human Behavior.* New York: Macmillan.

WEINER, BERNARD. 1986. *An Attributional Theory of Motivation and Emotion.* New York: Springer-Verlag.

MARK R. LEPPER
JENNIFER HENDERLONG

SELF-REGULATED LEARNING

Self-regulated learning refers to the processes by which individual learners attempt to monitor and control their own learning. There are many different models of self-regulated learning that propose different constructs and processes, but they do share some basic assumptions about learning and regulation.

Assumptions

One common assumption might be called the active, constructive assumption that follows from a general cognitive perspective. That is, all the models view learners as active constructive participants in the learning process. A second, but related, assumption is the potential for control assumption. All the models assume that learners can potentially monitor, control, and regulate certain aspects of their own cognition, motivation, and behavior as well as some features of their environments. This assumption does not mean that individuals will or can monitor and control their cognition, motivation, or behavior at all times or in all contexts, rather just that some monitoring, control, and regulation is possible. All of the models recognize that there are biological, developmental, contextual, and individual difference constraints that can impede or interfere with individual efforts at regulation.

A third general assumption that is made in these models of self-regulated learning is the goal, criterion, or standard assumption. All models of regulation assume that there is some type of criterion or standard (also called goals) against which comparisons are made in order to assess whether the process should continue as is or if some type of change is necessary. The commonsense example is the thermostat operation for the heating and cooling of a house. Once a desired temperature is set (the goal, criterion, or standard), the thermostat monitors the temperature of the house (monitoring process) and then turns on or off the heating or air conditioning units (control and regulation processes) in order to reach and maintain the standard. In a parallel manner, the general example for learning assumes that individuals can set standards or goals to strive for in their learning, monitor their progress toward these goals, and then adapt and regulate their cognition, motivation, and behavior in order to reach their goals.

A fourth general assumption of most of the models of self-regulated learning is that self-regulatory activities are mediators between personal and contextual characteristics and actual achievement or performance. That is, it is not just individuals' cultural, demographic, or personality characteristics that influence achievement and learning directly, nor just the contextual characteristics of the classroom environment that shape achievement, but the individuals' self-regulation processes that mediate the relations between the person, context, and eventual achievement. Most models of self-regulation assume that self-regulatory activities are directly linked to outcomes such as achievement and performance, although much of the research examines self-regulatory processes as outcomes in their own right.

Domains of Self-Regulation

Given these assumptions, a general working definition of self-regulated learning is that it is an active, constructive process whereby learners set goals for their learning and then attempt to monitor, regulate, and control their cognition, motivation, and behavior, guided and constrained by their goals and the contextual features in the environment. Following this general definition, research on models of self-regulated learning have delineated four general domains that learners can try to self-regulate: (1) cognition, (2) motivation, (3) behavior, and (4) the environment.

The cognitive domain includes the various cognitive strategies that learners can use to help them remember, understand, reason, and problem solve. Much of the work in this domain has focused on the learning strategies that students can use in academic contexts to comprehend text, to learn from lectures, to take notes, to solve math problems, to write papers, (e.g., testing their comprehension as they read a text). In addition, research has focused on metacognitive strategies that learners can use to plan, monitor, and control their own cognition. In many ways, metacognition is now seen as one part of the more general construct of self-regulated learning. In general, good self-regulating learners use a number of different strategies to control their cognition in ways that help them reach their goals.

The motivation and affective domain includes the various strategies that individuals can use to try to control and regulate their own motivation and emotions. This can include strategies for boosting their self-confidence or self-efficacy such as positive self-talk ("I know I can do this task") as well as strategies to try to control their interest (e.g., making the task more interesting by making a game out of it). Other strategies can be aimed at controlling negative emotions such as anxiety that can interfere with learning. In some research, these motivational and emotional control strategies are called volitional control strategies, but they can also be seen as part of the larger construct of self-regulated learning. As with cognition, good self-regulating learners do attempt to control their motivation and emotions in order to facilitate attainment of their goals.

The third domain includes actual attempts to control overt behavior, not just internal cognitions or motivational beliefs and emotions. This could involve increasing or decreasing effort on a task, as well as persisting on a task or giving up. Help-seeking behavior is another important self-regulatory behavior. Good self-regulators would adjust their effort levels to the task and their goals; they know when to persist, when to ask for help, and when to stop doing the task.

Finally, self-regulated learners can attempt to monitor and control the environment. Of course, they will not have as much control over the general classroom context or academic tasks as they do over their own cognition, motivation, and behavior, but there are some aspects of the context that can be controlled. For example, good self-regulated learners will try to control distractions by asking others to be quiet or by moving to another location. Good self-regulators also try to understand the task demands and the classroom norms and then try to adjust their learning to fit these demands. In other words, they are sensitive to the contextual demands and constraints that are operating in the classroom and attempt to cope with them in an adaptive manner.

The Development of Self-Regulation

There are a host of factors that can influence the development of self-regulation; three are noted here: cognitive development, motivation, and classroom contexts. Given the complexity of self-regulated learning, it is a phenomenon that emerges later in a child's life. There are clear developmental and maturational constraints on self-regulated learning. Although there are obviously aspects of self-regulation in place by the time a young child reaches school, the development of self-regulation for academic tasks takes place over the course of K–12 education. There is not as much research on the development of self-regulated learning as there is on how it operates, but it is probably not until the middle to late elementary school grades (third grade to sixth grade) that students begin to develop some of the important self-regulation strategies. In fact, it is likely that much of the development of self-regulated learning takes place in adolescence, given general cognitive developmental changes as well as the changes in the classroom context in middle schools and high schools. At the same time, there are many students who do not develop self-regulated strategies at all, even some of those more successful ones who go on to college. Accordingly, there is a need to develop explicit instructional strategies and programs to help students learn about self-regulation and develop expertise in regulating their learning.

Self-regulated learning is also time-consuming and quite difficult for some students, even when provided with explicit instruction in self-regulation. Accordingly, it is important that students are motivated to be self-regulating. Research of Paul R. Pintrich (1999) on the role of motivation in self-regulated learning has suggested three important generalizations about the relations between motivation and self-regulated learning. First, students must feel self-efficacious or confident that they can do the tasks. If they feel they can accomplish the academic tasks, then they are much more likely to use various self-regulation strategies. Second, students must be interested in and value the classroom tasks. Students

who are bored or do not find the tasks useful or worthwhile are much less likely to be self-regulating than those who are interested and find the tasks important. Finally, students who are focused on goals of learning, understanding, and self-improvement are much more likely to be self-regulating than students who are pursuing other goals such as trying to look smarter than others, or trying not to look stupid. These generalizations have been found in a large number of studies and seem to be fairly robust, but of course there is a need for more research on the role of motivation in self-regulated learning.

Finally, besides developmental and motivational factors, there are contextual factors that play a role in the development of self-regulation. One of the most important is that individuals actually have the opportunity to try to take control of their own learning and are given the chance to try tasks on their own. Of course, it is important that tasks are not too challenging or too easy, but in the students' range of competence. In addition, the modeling and demonstration of various self-regulatory strategies by parents, teachers, and peers can help students learn these strategies. Students also need the opportunity to have guided practice with the use of these strategies, with support and guidance from knowledgeable others, whether they be parents, teachers, or peers. Finally, there should be incentives in the context for the use of these strategies, such that students who are successful in using the strategies are rewarded in terms of praise or more tangible rewards such as better learning and achievement.

Importance of Self-Regulated Learning

In summary, self-regulated learning is an important aspect of learning and achievement in academic contexts. Students who are self-regulating are much more likely to be successful in school, to learn more, and to achieve at higher levels. Accordingly, it is important for schools and classrooms to attempt to foster the development of expertise in self-regulated learning. Of course, there are developmental, motivational, and contextual factors that can facilitate or constrain self-regulated learning, but there are implicit and explicit ways to help foster self-regulated learning. In the twenty-first century and as the explosion of information and multiple ways of learning increase, it will become even more important that individuals know how to self-regulate their learning and that fostering self-regulated learning becomes an important goal for all educational systems.

See also: LEARNING TO LEARN AND METACOGNITION; MOTIVATION, *subentries on* OVERVIEW, INSTRUCTION.

BIBLIOGRAPHY

BOEKAERTS, MONIQUE; PINTRICH, PAUL R.; and ZEIDNER, MOSHE, eds. 2000. *Handbook of Self-Regulation.* San Diego, CA: Academic Press.

PINTRICH, PAUL R. 1999. "The Role of Motivation in Promoting and Sustaining Self-Regulated Learning." *International Journal of Educational Research* 31:459–470.

PINTRICH, PAUL R. 2000. "The Role of Goal Orientation in Self-Regulated Learning." In *Handbook of Self-Regulation,* ed. Monique Boekaerts, Paul R. Pintrich, and Moshe Zeidner. San Diego, CA: Academic Press.

RANDI, JUDI, and CORNO, LYN. 2000. "Teacher Innovations in Self-Regulated Learning." In *Handbook of Self-Regulation,* ed. Monique Boekaerts, Paul R. Pintrich, and Moshe Zeidner. San Diego, CA: Academic Press.

SCHUNK, DALE, and ERTMER, PEGGY. 2000. "Self-Regulation and Academic Learning: Self-Efficacy Enhancing Interventions." In *Handbook of Self-Regulation,* ed. Monique Boekaerts, Paul R. Pintrich, and Moshe Zeidner. San Diego, CA: Academic Press.

WEINSTEIN, CLAIRE ELLEN; HUSMAN, JENEFER; and DIERKING, DOUGLAS. 2000. "Self-Regulation Interventions with a Focus on Learning Strategies." In *Handbook of Self-Regulation,* ed. Monique Boekaerts, Paul R. Pintrich, and Moshe Zeidner. San Diego, CA: Academic Press.

PAUL R. PINTRICH

MOTOR LEARNING

Human beings use movement to learn about their world, to function in the world as they grow and mature, and to maintain healthy bodies. Individuals must learn to move and at the same time move to learn. Children explore their worlds through movement and make fundamental links between action and reality through movement.

The scientific study and principles that undergird motor learning provide the guidance and an un-

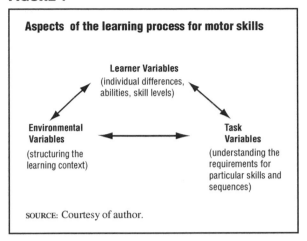

FIGURE 1

Aspects of the learning process for motor skills

SOURCE: Courtesy of author.

derlying framework for (1) curricula of physical education programs within schools; (2) the co-curricular sport programs; (3) the pedagogical principles applied by physical education teachers and coaches; and (4) the clinical interventions of occupational and physical therapists for individuals of all ages. Professionals who understand how children and youth acquire motor skills, whether building with blocks, learning to write or draw, effectively moving through space, or developing skills for sport or leisure activities, enhance their capacity to provide optimal learning experiences.

Understanding how individuals learn motor skills (motor learning) requires an appreciation for the following factors.

- Motor Development: how the capacity of children to produce motor skills naturally matures
- Motor Control: how the human neurological system controls movement
- Sport Psychology: how to motivate individuals to want to learn motor skills and participate in sport and exercise
- Pedagogy for Physical Education: how the learning environment can be organized to optimize the acquisition of motor skills

Motor learning focuses on the most effective ways to facilitate the acquisition of skills by understanding or manipulating three aspects of the learning process for motor skills, as illustrated in Figure 1.

Motor learning research has held a predominant place in both physical education and psychology for more than 100 years. The early work of Robert Woodworth (1899) examined the conditions that affect movement accuracy and began a long history of research in this area. In the early twenty-first century, two fundamental approaches (models) describe the acquisition of motor skills and the challenges that face the learner. The information-processing focus is grounded by the work of such researchers as James Adams (1971), Steven Keele (1968) and Richard Schmidt (1975). An alternative explanation of motor skill acquisition comes from a dynamical systems approach followed by Karl Newell (1991) and Walter, Lee, and Sternad (1998). This approach emphasizes self-organization as a function of specific control parameters and environmental conditions as a way to understanding motor behavior.

Motor Learning Research Informs Professional Practice

Research from motor learning focuses on understanding how individuals acquire and perform motor skills, and serves as the basis for informed practice in such professional fields as physical education, occupation therapy, sports medicine, and physical therapy. In order to illustrate the contributions of motor learning to professional practice, three examples have been selected.

Providing effective models/demonstrations. Historically it was believed that providing ideal models was the best way to transmit information to learners. This assumption suggested that teachers or professional models should provide demonstrations to facilitate the acquisition of motor skills. By the early twenty-first century, research had shown that providing "learning models" who are similar to the peer learners, and who are shown modifying their skills, are more effective than the traditional perfect model. In practice, this suggests that models who are individuals, similar to the learner, should be shown trying to learn a motor skill, receiving feedback, and improving as a result of this feedback. Teachers should therefore focus on selecting classmate children to model, and to provide feedback that allows the models to improve during the process of providing the demonstration.

Practice variability (contextual interference). Learning environments that provide reinforcement for the immediate performance of desired skills has often been the focus of physical education programs. The short-term benefits of practice that result do not take into account the need to consider the long-term benefits of various practice strategies.

For example, if students are to learn three tennis skills (forehand, backhand, and serve), they typically practice in a blocked fashion, focusing exclusively on each skill until it is learned (often to the 80 percent proficiency level). In contrast, early-twenty-first-century motor learning research has shown that practicing such skills in an interleaved or random fashion produces better long-term retention. This principle is referred to as *contextual interference* since practicing each of the three skills together produces some short-term interference (degradation of performance) compared to blocked practice, though eventually learners will be able to retain each skill at a level higher than those individuals who practice in a blocked schedule.

Brain gym. The provision of physical education in K-12 schools, and work in allied health professions (physical therapy, sports medicine, etc.) has relied on the scientific bases from a variety of disciplines (e.g., kinesiology, neurology, physical education, physical therapy, and psychology). By the twenty-first century, a resurgence of interest occurred in the neurological foundations of motor performance and in how the neurological system integrates cognitive and motor skills. One predominant influence has been the neuro-physiological bases of motor skill acquisition, and a curricular interpretation referred to as *brain gym*. The work of Paul Dennison and Gail Dennison (1994) has focused on the importance of inter-hemispheric activation, systematic challenges, and the use of cognitive resources in the production of motor skills.

In summary, the field of motor learning provides the understanding of the psychological and physiological features that enhance motor skill acquisition. It informs professional practice for both classroom and physical education teachers, and for allied health professionals, and impacts the quality of life for all individuals (birth through death).

See also: BRAIN-BASED EDUCATION; PHYSICAL EDUCATION; SPORTS, SCHOOL.

BIBLIOGRAPHY

ADAMS, JAMES A. 1971. "A Closed-Loop Theory of Motor Learning." *Journal of Motor Behavior* 3:111–150.

BUNKER, LINDA K.; NAIR, MURAH; and MARCOS, N. 2000. *The Contextual Interference Effect in Elementary Children Learning a Field Hockey Skill.*

Paper presented at American Alliance for Health, Physical Education Recreation, and Dance (AAHPERD) National Convention, Orlando, FL.

DENNISON, PAUL E., and DENNISON, GAIL E. 1994. *Brain Gym.* New York: New York Educational Kinesthetics.

GREEN, D. PENELOPE; WHITEHEAD, JEAN; and SUGDEN, DAVID A. 1995. "Practice Variability and Transfer of a Racket Skill." *Perceptual and Motor Skills* 81:1275–1281.

LAGUNA, PATRICIA L. 2000. "The Effect of Model Observation versus Physical Practice during Motor Skill Acquisition and Performance." *Journal of Human Movement Studies* 39:171–191.

KEELE, STEVEN W. 1968. "Movement Control in Skilled Motor Performance." *Psychological Bulletin* 70:387–403.

McCULLAGH, PENNY, and MEYERS, KORINNE N. 1997. "Learning versus Correct Models: Influence of Model Type on the Learning of a Free-Weight Squat Lift." *Research Quarterly for Exercise and Sport* 68:56–61.

McCULLAGH, PENNY; WEISS, MAUREEN R.; and ROSS, DIANE. 1989. "Modeling Considerations in Motor Skill Acquisition and Performance: An Integrated Approach." *Exercise and Sport Science Reviews* 17:475–513.

NEWELL, KARL M. 1991. "Motor Skill Acquisition." *Annual Review of Psychology* 42:213–237.

SCHMIDT, RICHARD A. 1975. "A Schema Theory of Discrete Motor Skill Learning." *Psychological Review* 82:225–260.

WALTER, C.; LEE, T. D.; and STERNAD, D. 1998. "Hot Topics in Motor Control and Learning: Promises, Potential Limitations, and Future Directions." *Research Quarterly for Exercise and Sport* 69:316–319.

WOODWORTH, ROBERT S. 1899. "The Accuracy of Voluntary Movement." *Psychological Review* 3:1–114.

LINDA K. BUNKER

MULTICULTURAL EDUCATION

Multicultural education is an idea, an approach to school reform, and a movement for equity, social justice, and democracy. Specialists within multicultural education emphasize different components and cultural groups. However, a significant degree of consensus exists within the field regarding its major principles, concepts, and goals. A major goal of multicultural education is to restructure schools so that all students acquire the knowledge, attitudes, and skills needed to function in an ethnically and racially diverse nation and world. Multicultural education seeks to ensure educational equity for members of diverse racial, ethnic, cultural, and socioeconomic groups, and to facilitate their participation as critical and reflective citizens in an inclusive national civic culture.

Multicultural education tries to provide students with educational experiences that enable them to maintain commitments to their community cultures as well as acquire the knowledge, skills, and cultural capital needed to function in the national civic culture and community. Multicultural theorists view academic knowledge and skills as necessary but not sufficient for functioning in a diverse nation and world. They regard skills in democratic living and the ability to function effectively within and across diverse groups as essential goals of schooling.

Multicultural education is highly consistent with the ideals embodied in the U.S. Constitution, the Declaration of Independence, and the Bill of Rights. It seeks to extend the rights and privileges granted to the nation's founding elites—the ideals of freedom, equality, justice, and democracy—to all social, cultural and language groups. Multicultural education addresses deep and persistent social divisions across various groups, and seeks to create an inclusive and transformed mainstream society. Multicultural educators view cultural difference as a national strength and resource rather than as a problem to be overcome through assimilation.

History

Multicultural education emerged during the civil rights movement of the 1960s and 1970s. It grew out of the demands of ethnic groups for inclusion in the curricula of schools, colleges, and universities. Although multicultural education is an outgrowth of the ethnic studies movement of the 1960s, it has deep historical roots in the African-American ethnic studies movement that emerged in the late nineteenth and early twentieth centuries.

Initiated by scholars such as George Washington Williams, Carter G. Woodson, W. E. B. DuBois, and Charles H. Wesley, the primary goal of the early ethnic studies movement was to challenge the negative images and stereotypes of African Americans prevalent in mainstream scholarship by creating accurate descriptions of the life, history, and contributions of African Americans. These scholars had a personal, professional, and enduring commitment to the uplift of African Americans. They believed that creating positive self-images of African Americans was essential to their collective identity and liberation. They also believed that stereotypes and negative beliefs about African Americans could be effectively challenged by objective historical research that was also capable of transforming mainstream academic knowledge.

Carter G. Woodson—one of the leading scholars of the early ethnic studies movement—helped found the Association for the Study of Negro (now Afro-American) Life and History in 1915. The association played a key role in the production and dissemination of African-American historical scholarship. In addition to writing numerous scholarly works and editing the association's publications, Woodson initiated Negro History Week (now Black History Month) to focus attention in the nation's schools on the life and history of African Americans.

In 1922 Woodson published a college textbook, *The Negro in Our History,* which was used in many African-American schools and colleges. In response to public demand for classroom materials, he wrote an elementary textbook, *Negro Makers of History,* followed by *The Story of the Negro Retold* for senior high schools. Woodson also wrote, edited, and published African-American children's literature. In 1937 he began publication of *The Negro History Bulletin,* a monthly magazine for teachers and students featuring stories about exemplary teachers and curriculum projects, historical narratives, and biographical sketches.

When the ethnic studies movement was revived in the 1960s, African Americans and other marginalized ethnic groups refused assimilationist demands to renounce their cultural identity and heritage. They insisted that their lives and histories be included in the curriculum of schools, colleges, and universities. In challenging the dominant paradigms and concepts taught in the schools and colleges, multicultural educators sought to transform the Eurocentric perspective and incorporate multiple perspectives into the curriculum.

By the late 1980s multicultural theorists recognized that ethnic studies was insufficient to bring about school reforms capable of responding to the academic needs of students of color. They consequently shifted their focus from the mere inclusion of ethnic content to deep structural changes in schools. During these years, multicultural educators also expanded from a primary focus on ethnic groups of color to other group categories, such as social class, language and gender. Although conceptually distinct, the key social categories of multicultural education—race, class, gender, and culture—are interrelated. Multicultural theorists are concerned with how these social variables interact in identity formation, and about the consequences of multiple and contextual identities for teaching and learning.

During the 1970s a number of professional organizations—such as the National Council for Social Studies, the National Council of Teachers of English, and the American Association of Colleges for Teacher Education—issued policy statements and publications that encouraged the integration of ethnic content into the school and teacher education curriculum. In 1973 the title of the forty-third yearbook of the National Council for the Social Studies (NCSS) was *Teaching Ethnic Studies: Concepts and Strategies.* NCSS published *Curriculum Guidelines for Multiethnic Education* in 1976, which was revised and reissued in 1992 as *Curriculum Guidelines for Multicultural Education.* A turning point in the development of multicultural education occurred in 1977 when the National Council for the Accreditation of Teacher Education (NCATE) issued standards for the accreditation of teacher education. The standards required all NCATE member institutions (about 80% of the teacher education programs in the United States) to implement components, courses, and programs in multicultural education.

Over the past two decades more ethnic content has appeared in the textbooks used in elementary and secondary schools in the United States. An increasing number of teachers are using anthologies in literature programs that include selections written by women and authors of color. In addition, the market for books dealing with multicultural education has gown substantially, and some of the nation's leading colleges and universities, including the University of California at Berkeley and the University of Minnesota, have either revised their core curriculum to include ethnic content or have established ethnic studies course requirements.

The Dimensions of Multicultural Education

James A. Banks's *Dimensions of Multicultural Education* is used widely by school districts to conceptualize and develop courses, programs, and projects in multicultural education. The five dimensions are: (1) content integration; (2) the knowledge construction process; (3) prejudice reduction; (4) an equity pedagogy; and (5) an empowering school culture and social structure. Although each dimension is conceptually distinct, in practice they overlap and are interrelated.

Content integration. Content integration deals with the extent to which teachers use examples and content from a variety of cultures and groups to illustrate key concepts, principles, generalizations, and theories in their subject area or discipline. The infusion of ethnic and cultural content into a subject area is logical and not contrived when this dimension is implemented properly.

More opportunities exist for the integration of ethnic and cultural content in some subject areas than in others. There are frequent and ample opportunities for teachers to use ethnic and cultural content to illustrate concepts, themes, and principles in the social studies, the language arts, and in music. Opportunities also exist to integrate multicultural content into math and science. However, they are less ample than they are in social studies and the language arts. Content integration is frequently mistaken by school practitioners as comprising the whole of multicultural education, and is thus viewed as irrelevant to instruction in disciplines such as math and science.

The knowledge construction process. The knowledge construction process describes teaching activities that help students to understand, investigate, and determine how the implicit cultural assumptions, frames of references, perspectives, and biases of researchers and textbook writers influence the ways in which knowledge is constructed.

Multicultural teaching involves not only infusing ethnic content into the school curriculum, but changing the structure and organization of school knowledge. It also includes changing the ways in which teachers and students view and interact with knowledge, helping them to become knowledge producers, not merely the consumers of knowledge produced by others.

The knowledge construction process helps teachers and students to understand why the cultural identities and social positions of researchers need to be taken into account when assessing the validity of knowledge claims. Multicultural theories assert that the values, personal histories, attitudes, and beliefs of researchers cannot be separated from the knowledge they create. They consequently reject positivist claims of disinterested and distancing knowledge production. They also reject the possibility of creating knowledge that is not influenced by the cultural assumptions and social position of the knowledge producer.

In multicultural teaching and learning, paradigms, themes, and concepts that exclude or distort the life experiences, histories, and contributions of marginalized groups are challenged. Multicultural pedagogy seeks to reconceptualize and expand the Western canon, to make it more representative and inclusive of the nation's diversity, and to reshape the frames of references, perspectives, and concepts that make up school knowledge.

Prejudice reduction. The prejudice reduction dimension of multicultural education seeks to help students develop positive and democratic racial attitudes. It also helps students to understand how ethnic identity is influenced by the context of schooling and the attitudes and beliefs of dominant social groups. The theory developed by Gordon Allport (1954) has significantly influenced research and theory in intergroup relations. He hypothesized that prejudice can be reduced by interracial contact if the contact situations have these characteristics: (1) they are cooperative rather than competitive; (2) the individuals experience equal status; and (3) the contact is sanctioned by authorities such as parents, principals and teachers.

An equity pedagogy. An equity pedagogy exists when teachers modify their teaching in ways that will facilitate the academic achievement of students from diverse racial, cultural, socioeconomic, and language groups. This includes using a variety of teaching styles and approaches that are consistent with the range of learning styles within various cultural and ethnic groups, such as being demanding but highly personalized when working with American Indian and Native Alaskan students. It also includes using cooperative learning techniques in math and science instruction to enhance the academic achievement of students of color.

An equity pedagogy rejects the cultural deprivation paradigm that was developed in the early 1960s.

This paradigm posited that the socialization experiences in the home and community of low-income students prevented them from attaining the knowledge, skills, and attitudes needed for academic success. Because the cultural practices of low-income students were viewed as inadequate and inferior, cultural deprivation theorists focused on changing student behavior so that it aligned more closely with mainstream school culture. An equity pedagogy assumes that students from diverse cultures and groups come to school with many strengths.

Multicultural theorists describe how cultural identity, communicative styles, and the social expectations of students from marginalized ethnic and racial groups often conflict with the values, beliefs, and cultural assumptions of teachers. The middle-class mainstream culture of the schools creates a cultural dissonance and disconnect that privileges students who have internalized the school's cultural codes and communication styles.

Teachers practice culturally responsive teaching when an equity pedagogy is implemented. They use instructional materials and practices that incorporate important aspects of the family and community culture of their students. Culturally responsive teachers also use the "cultural knowledge, prior experiences, frames of reference, and performance styles of ethnically diverse students to make learning encounters more relevant to and effective for them" (Gay, p. 29).

An empowering school culture. This dimension involves restructuring the culture and organization of the school so that students from diverse racial, ethnic, socioeconomic, and language groups experience equality. Members of the school staff examine and change the culture and social structure of the school. Grouping and labeling practices, sports participation, gaps in achievement among groups, different rates of enrollment in gifted and special education programs among groups, and the interaction of the staff and students across ethnic and racial lines are important variables that are examined and reformed.

An empowering school structure requires the creation of qualitatively different relationships among various groups within schools. Relationships are based on mutual and reciprocal respect for cultural differences that are reflected in school-wide goals, norms, and cultural practices. An empowering school structure facilitates the practice of multicultural education by providing teachers with opportunities for collective planning and instruction, and by creating democratic structures that give teachers, parents, and school staff shared responsibility for school governance.

Evidence of the Effectiveness of Multicultural Education

The Handbook of Research of Multicultural Education comprehensively reviews the research on multicultural education and the effectiveness of various kinds of multicultural curricular interventions. At least three categories of research that describe the effectiveness of multicultural education can be identified: (1) research that describes the effectiveness of multicultural curriculum interventions such as Banks's 2001 research review; (2) research on the effects of cooperative learning and interracial contact, such as Robert Slavin's 2001 research review; and (3) research on how culturally responsive teaching influences student learning, such as Carol Lee's 1993 study and Gloria Ladson-Billings's 2001 work. An extended discussion of studies in the first genre is presented in this entry. Research reviews of the other two genres are found in the *Handbook of Research on Multicultural Education.*

Slavin's 2001 research review and Cohen and Lotan's 1995 research on cooperative learning and interracial contact activities indicate that these interventions—if they are consistent with Allport's theory of intergroup contact—help students to develop more positive racial attitudes, to make more cross-racial friendships, and have positive effects on the academic achievement of Latino and African-American students. Lee's 1993 research on culturally responsive teaching indicates that when teachers use the cultural characteristics of students in their teaching the academic achievement of students from diverse groups can be enhanced.

Research on curriculum materials and interventions. Research indicates that the use of multicultural textbooks, other teaching materials, television, and simulations can help students from different racial and ethnic groups to develop more democratic racial attitudes and perceptions of other groups. Since the 1940s a number of curriculum interventions studies have been conducted to determine the effects of teaching units and lessons, multicultural textbooks and materials, role playing, and simulation on the racial attitudes and perceptions of students.

These studies provide guidelines that can help teachers to improve intergroup relations in their classrooms and schools. One of the earliest curriculum studies was conducted by Helen Trager and Marion Yarrow (1952). They found that a democratic, multicultural curriculum had positive effects on the racial attitudes of teachers and on those of first- and second-grade students. John Litcher and David Johnson (1969) found that white, second-grade children developed more positive racial attitudes after using multiethnic readers. Gerry Bogatz and Samuel Ball (1971) found that *Sesame Street,* PBS's multicultural television program, had a positive effect on the racial attitudes of children who watched it for long periods. In a study by Michael Weiner and Frances Wright (1973), children who themselves experienced discrimination in a simulation developed less prejudiced beliefs and attitudes toward others. Multicultural social studies materials and related experiences had a positive effect on the racial attitudes of African-American four-year-old children in a study conducted by Thomas Yawkey and Jacqueline Blackwell (1974).

Research indicates that curriculum interventions such as plays, folk dances, music, role playing, and simulations can have positive effects on the racial attitudes of students. A curriculum intervention that consisted of folk dances, music, crafts, and role playing positively influenced the racial attitudes of elementary students in a study conducted by M. Ahmed Ijaz and I. Helene Ijaz (1981). Four plays about African Americans, Chinese Americans, Jews, and Puerto Ricans increased racial acceptance and cultural knowledge among fourth-, fifth-, and sixth-grade students in a study conducted by Beverly Gimmestad and Edith DeChiara (1982).

Jossette McGregor (1993) used meta-analysis to integrate findings and to examine the effects of role playing and antiracist teaching on reducing prejudice in students. Twenty-six studies were located and examined. McGregor concluded that role playing and antiracist teaching "significantly reduce racial prejudice, and do not differ from each other in their effectiveness" (p. 215).

Demographic Trends and Issues

The ethnic, cultural, and language diversity within the United States and its schools is increasing. The U.S. Bureau of the Census projects that 47 percent of the U.S. population will consist of ethnic groups of color by 2050. Between 1991 and 1998, 7.6 million immigrants entered the United States, mostly from nations in Asia and Latin America. The U.S. Census estimates that more than one million immigrants will enter the United States every year for the foreseeable future. Thirty-five percent of students enrolled in U.S. schools in 1995 were students of color. If current demographic trends continue, students of color will comprise approximately 46 percent of the student population in 2020. The increasing ethnic and cultural diversity of the U.S. student population stands in sharp contrast to a teaching force that was 90.7 percent white, middle-class, and three-fourths female in 1996. Many of the students entering U.S. schools speak a first language other than English. The 1990 census indicated that 14 percent of the nation's school-age youth lived in homes where the primary language was not English.

In addition to increasing ethnic, language, and cultural diversity, a significant and growing percentage of children in the United States, especially children of color, are being raised in poverty. The number of children living in poverty rose from 16.2 percent in 1979 to 18.7 percent in 1998. According to the U.S. Census Bureau, of the 12.7 percent of the United States population living in poverty in 1997, 8.6 percent were non-Hispanic whites, 26.0 percent African Americans, and 27.1 percent Hispanics.

Multicultural education theorists believe that the nation's schools should respond to its increasing racial, ethnic, and language diversity. However, they have different views about how to define the field's boundaries and about which social groups should be included under its umbrella. Some theorists are concerned that as the field expands to include an increasing number of cultural groups, its initial focus on institutionalized racism and the achievement of students of color might wane. The discussions and debates within multicultural education reflect the vitality and growth of an emerging discipline.

An increasingly low-income and linguistically and culturally diverse student population requires a transformation of the deep structure of schooling in order to experience educational equity and cultural empowerment in the nation's schools. Multicultural education is a process of comprehensive school reform that challenges racism and prejudice by transforming the curriculum and instructional practices of schools, and by changing the relationships among teachers, students, and parents.

A major goal of multicultural education is to help students from diverse cultures learn how to transcend cultural borders and to engage in dialog and civic action in a diverse, democratic society. Multicultural education tries to actualize cultural democracy, and to include the dreams, hopes, and experiences of diverse groups in school knowledge and in a reconstructed and inclusive national identity. The future of democracy in the United States depends on the willingness and ability of citizens to function within and across cultures. The schools can play a major role in helping students to develop the knowledge and skills needed to cross cultural borders and to perpetuate a democratic and just society.

See also: AFRICAN-AMERICAN STUDIES; CURRICULUM, SCHOOL; ELEMENTARY EDUCATION, *subentries on* CURRENT TRENDS, HISTORY OF; RACE, ETHNICITY, AND CULTURE; SCHOOL REFORM; SECONDARY EDUCATION, *subentries on* CURRENT TRENDS, HISTORY OF; SOCIAL STUDIES EDUCATION; WOODSON, CARTER GODWIN.

BIBLIOGRAPHY

ALLPORT, GORDON W. 1954. *The Nature of Prejudice.* Reading, MA: Addison-Wesley.

BANKS, JAMES A. 1973. *Teaching Ethnic Studies: Concepts and Strategies.* Washington, DC: National Council for the Social Studies.

BANKS, JAMES A., ed. 1996. *Multicultural Education, Transformative Knowledge, and Action: Historical and Contemporary Perspectives.* New York: Teachers College Press.

BANKS, JAMES A. 2001a. *Cultural Diversity and Education: Foundations, Curriculum and Teaching,* 4th edition. Boston: Allyn and Bacon.

BANKS, JAMES A. 2001b. "Multicultural Education: Its Effects on Students' Racial and Gender Role Attitudes." In *Handbook of Research on Multicultural Education,* ed. James A. Banks and Cherry A. McGee Banks. San Francisco: Jossey-Bass.

BANKS, JAMES A., and BANKS, CHERRY A. MCGEE. 1995. "Equity Pedagogy: An Essential Component of Multicultural Education." *Theory into Practice* 34:152–158.

BANKS, JAMES A., and BANKS, CHERRY A. MCGEE, eds. 2001. *Handbook of Research on Multicultural Education.* San Francisco: Jossey-Bass.

BANKS, JAMES A.; CORTÉS, CARLOS E.; GAY, GENEVA; GARCIA, RICARDO L.; and OCHOA, ANNA S. 1991. *Curriculum Guidelines for Multicultural Education.* Washington, DC: National Council for the Social Studies.

BANKS, JAMES A., et al. 2001. *Diversity within Unity: Essential Principles for Teaching and Learning in a Multicultural Society.* Seattle: Center for Multicultural Education, University of Washington.

BOGATZ, GERRY A., and BALL, SAMUEL. 1971. *The Second Year of* Sesame Street: *A Continuing Evaluation.* Princeton, NJ: Educational Testing Service.

CODE, LORRAINE. 1991. *What Can She Know? Feminist Theory and the Construction of Knowledge.* Ithaca, NY: Cornell University Press.

COHEN, ELIZABETH G. 1994. *Designing Groupwork: Strategies for the Heterogeneous Classroom,* 2nd edition. New York: Teachers College Press.

COHEN, ELIZABETH G., and LOTAN, RACHEL A. 1995. "Producing Equal-Status Interaction in the Heterogeneous Classroom." *American Educational Research Journal* 32:99–120.

GIMMESTAD, BEVERLY J., and DE CHIARA, EDITH. 1982. "Dramatic Plays: A Vehicle for Prejudice Reduction in the Elementary School." *Journal of Educational Research* 76(1):45–49.

GAY, GENEVA. 2000. *Culturally Responsive Teaching: Theory, Research and Practice.* New York: Teachers College Press.

HARDING, SANDRA, ed. 1998. *Is Science Multicultural? Postcolonialisms, Feminisms, and Epistemologies.* Bloomington, IN: Indiana University Press.

IJAZ, M. AHMED, and IJAZ, I. HELENE. 1981. "A Cultural Program for Changing Racial Attitudes." *History and Social Science Teacher* 17(1):17–20.

LADSON-BILLINGS, GLORIA. 2001. *Crossing Over to Canaan: The Journey of New Teachers in Diverse Classrooms.* San Francisco: Jossey-Bass.

LEE, CAROL D. 1993. *Signifying as a Scaffold for Literary Interpretation.* Urbana, IL: National Council of Teachers of English.

LITCHER, JOHN H., and JOHNSON, DAVID. W. 1969. "Changes in Attitudes Toward Negroes of White Elementary School Students after Use of Multiethnic Readers." *Journal of Educational Psychology* 60:148–152.

McGREGOR, JOSSETTE. 1993. "Effectiveness of Role Playing and Antiracist Teaching in Reducing Student Prejudice." *Journal of Educational Research* 86 (4):215–226.

NATIONAL EDUCATION ASSOCIATION. 1997. *Status of the American Public School Teacher, 1996–1997.* Washington, DC: National Education Association.

PALLAS, AARON M.; NATRIELLO, GARY; and McDILL, EDWARD L. 1989. "The Changing Nature of the Disadvantaged Population: Current Dimensions and Future Trends." *Educational Researcher* 18(5):16–22.

ROCHE, AGNES M. 1996. "Carter G. Woodson and the Development of Transformative Scholarship." In *Multicultural Education, Transformative Knowledge and Action: Historical and Contemporary Perspectives,* ed. James A. Banks. New York: Teachers College Press.

SLAVIN, ROBERT E. 2001. "Cooperative Learning and Intergroup Relations." In *Handbook of Research on Multicultural Education,* ed. James A. Banks and Cherry A. McGee Banks. San Francisco: Jossey-Bass.

TERRY, DON. 2000. "U. S. Child Poverty Rate Fell as Economy Grew, But Is Above 1979 Level." *The New York Times,* August 11.

TRAGER, HELEN G., and YARROW, MARION R. 1952. *They Learn What They Live: Prejudice in Young Children.* New York: Harper.

U. S. CENSUS BUREAU. 1999. *Statistical Abstract of the United States: 1991,* 119th edition. Washington, DC: U.S. Government Printing Office.

WEINER, MICHAEL J., and WRIGHT, FRANCES E. 1973. "Effects of Undergoing Arbitrary Discrimination Upon Subsequent Attitudes toward a Minority Group." *Journal of Applied Social Psychology* 3:94–102.

YAWKEY, THOMAS D., and BLACKWELL, JACQUELINE. 1974. "Attitudes of 4-Year-Old Urban Black Children toward Themselves and Whites Based Upon Multi-Ethnic Social Studies Materials and Experiences." *The Journal of Educational Research* 67:373–377.

JAMES A. BANKS
JOHN AMBROSIO

MULTICULTURALISM IN HIGHER EDUCATION

There have always been debates about what knowledge should be included in the general education curriculum (often referred to as the *core curriculum*). However, since the mid-1960s the debate has focused largely on the inclusion of racial, ethnic, women, gay, and lesbian voices in the curriculum. At the beginning of the twenty-first century, the debate is not whether to do it, but how. Although many terms over the years have been used, such as *multiculturalism, multicultural education,* and *ethnic studies,* the term *diversity* will be used here. A more encompassing term, *diversity* is meant to represent all perspectives from groups that have traditionally been excluded from or insufficiently examined in the curriculum. The term also takes into account the external forces that influence how academic institutions meet their educational objectives. The legal struggle over affirmative action in admissions, for example, no longer rests on moral grounds of remedy for past discrimination, but on the compelling interest of the state in the educational value of having a diverse student body.

Demographics and Debates About Inclusion

Since the end of World War II, U. S. colleges and universities have become increasingly more diverse (by social class, race, gender, ethnicity, age, sexual orientation, and people with disabilities), even though some of these changes have often been fiercely resisted. Some demographic changes occurred not simply because of federal troops but also because of federal legislation. In the 1940s the G. I. Bill made college affordable for vast numbers of working-class men. The Civil Rights Act of 1964 opened the door of academia to African Americans and other people of color, while the Immigration Act of 1965 opened U.S. borders to new sections of the globe. Title IX radically altered how women fared on campuses, just as the Americans with Disabilities Act of 1990 removed barriers that previously barred many aspiring students. Other demographic shifts were fueled by policy changes or new programs, such as the establishment of community college systems, the creation of programs of continuing education for women, and the creation of the Equal Opportunities Commission. By the end of the twentieth century higher education had actually come close to fulfilling democracy's highest goal of an educated citizenry. In 2000 nearly 75 percent of high school graduates went on to some college experience within two years of graduating. The student profile in the late 1990s was 55 percent female and 28 percent students of color. Forty-three percent of students were over 25 years old, and nearly that same percentage were first generation college students.

Paralleling the shifting demographics of the students was the persistent call for inclusion of diverse perspectives in the curriculum. These calls have come not only from the groups that were previously excluded, but also from faculty, students, business leaders, and the general public. In a public poll of registered voters in 1998, the ordinary citizen was overwhelmingly in favor of diversifying students, faculty, and the courses taught. While 58 percent were concerned that the United States was splitting apart over differences, 71 percent believed that higher education could, and should, help people find a way to bring people together. Although Americans might differ in their rationales for broader inclusion, there is consensus overall about the intellectual, individual, economic, and societal benefits for doing so.

Calls for inclusion stem from the argument that a singular, Eurocentric perspective has had negative consequences for individual students and for the larger society. Proponents of diversity in higher education argue that excluding diverse perspectives in the curriculum has truncated students' learning, leaving them ill-prepared to function in an increasingly diverse democracy. The very purpose of higher education—to deepen students' understanding of what is known, how it has come to be known, and how to build on previous knowledge to create new knowledge—is thus undermined by eliminating the voices of those whose experiences differ from those traditionally represented. Such exclusions reveal an inconsistency between the rhetoric and the practice of democracy. Correcting this inconsistency eventually became the cornerstone of the civil rights, women's rights, and other movements that have pushed the higher education community to offer a more inclusive curriculum.

Conversely, opponents of diversity in the curriculum argue against including African American, Latina/Latino, Chicano, Asian American, women's, and gay and lesbian studies in the higher education curriculum, claiming that these issues are more appropriately discussed and debated in the political arena rather than in academia. They contend that institutions of higher education should be reserved for the pursuit of objective knowledge and truth through rigorous disciplinary study. Critics of diversity education claim that the focus on differences, which is often a characteristic of general-education

diversity requirements, weakens national unity and has only a limited (if any) role in institutions of higher learning. They contend that the curriculum of higher education should be the basis for inquiry, discovery, and dissemination of knowledge, open to students capable of contributing to its development, and devoid of social politics.

As the debate about inclusion grew louder, the research on, and practice of, diversity education has accelerated greatly over the years. Initially, diversity in the 1960s and 1970s was located primarily in newly established special departments and programs, usually organized around a single group, such as Asian-American studies, women's studies, or African-American studies. By the 1980s these specialized areas of knowledge eventually spawned hundreds of programs at colleges and universities in what came to be called *mainstreaming, integrating,* or *transforming* the curriculum. Such programs sought to incorporate new knowledge into existing courses, some of which were within a major course of study, others of which were in general education courses.

Eventually, the research on multicultural education began to lay out a compelling case that being attentive to diverse voices provides lenses through which richer conceptions of social, political, economic, and natural phenomenon could be revealed, underscoring that there are many ways of knowing. During the 1980s and 1990s in particular, colleges and universities moved from infusing diversity across the curriculum to also creating diversity requirements within their core curriculum. While a general education requirement alone is insufficient in and of itself to prepare students for the complexity of the diverse societies they will work and live in, it is a solid and significant start.

Before examining the emerging contours of twenty-first-century diversity requirements, it is important to recognize their context within general education as a whole. Some institutions, such as Wesleyan University in Connecticut, Bloomfield College in New Jersey, and Brookdale Community College in New Jersey, have invested significant institutional funds over many years in what they argue is a more pervasive strategy of infusion across the curriculum, rather than relying on a single required diversity course in general education. Nonetheless, because students take a prescribed number of general education courses, lodging diversity within core requirements is one visible indicator of an institution's commitment to diversity. While it is not the only measure, or even a sufficient measure, embedding diversity within general education makes a clear statement that knowledge about diversity is viewed as an essential component of a college education.

An Aerial View of National Diversity Requirements

The first formal adoption of a diversity requirement in the general education core occurred at Denison University in Ohio in 1979. By 1992, however, a survey conducted by researchers Richard Light and Jeanette Cureton reported that 34 percent of colleges and universities had multicultural general education requirements, 12 percent of which were on domestic diversity; 29 percent on global diversity; and 57 percent addressing both. Of those colleges queried, one-third offered course work in ethnic and women's studies, while a far greater number—54 percent—had introduced multiculturalism into their departmental course offerings. It is not surprising that there is more activity at departmental levels than at general education levels, since, in most cases, general education needs majority support from the faculty to secure approval. But departmental activity is unevenly dispersed and some departments and divisions have almost no multicultural courses or requirements.

Light and Cureton also found that four-year colleges are more active than two-year colleges in integrating multiculturalism into the curriculum, despite the greater diversity of the student body in community colleges. While demographics clearly drive the push for diversity requirements and courses, they are, it seems, not the only factor. Public institutions exceed private colleges in the number of multicultural indicators, just as research universities have more comprehensive multicultural efforts than either comprehensives or liberal arts colleges. Not surprisingly, geographical regions varied significantly in the amount of multicultural programming, with the Mid-Atlantic states and the West outpacing New England and the South.

In a 2000 national survey about diversity requirements, the Association of American Colleges and Universities (AAC&U) found striking progress among the percentage of colleges and universities polled—the number of institutions with diversity requirements had almost doubled from Light and Cureton's figures in 1992. Sixty-three percent of colleges and universities reported either having a diversity requirement in place or being in the process of developing one. Fifty-four percent of survey respondents had diversity requirements in place; another 8 percent were in the process of establishing them. Of institutions with requirements, 25 percent had been in place for more than ten years, 45 percent had put them in place during the previous five to ten years, and 30 percent had requirements in place for less than five years. All indications are, therefore, that the number of colleges with diversity requirements is likely to continue to expand.

Regional distinctions were also found in AAC&U's survey. For example, 78 percent of colleges responding from the West had diversity requirements, while 68 percent of those in the Middle States (Mid-Atlantic) region and 60 percent in the North Central region had such requirements. By contrast, only 45 percent of the institutions in the New England region had diversity requirements in 2000, followed by 36 percent of those in the South and 35 percent in the Northwest.

Incorporating Diversity into General Education Designs

But what do diversity requirements look like? A majority (58 percent) of institutions with such requirements demand that students take one course; while 42 percent require two or more courses. Not surprisingly, the most common model, surfacing at 68 percent of the AAC&U survey respondents, asks students to take one diversity course among many offerings. Typically these courses examine attitudes and cultures that are different from the dominant culture. At the University of Arizona, students can take a class that focuses on gender, race, class, or ethnicity, while the requirement at the University of Maryland focuses on all those plus non-Western culture as well.

Some institutions include several courses, but more restrictively define their purpose. At the University of Michigan, for instance, while there are many different courses to choose from, each course needs to pay attention to (1) race, racism, and ethnicity; (2) intolerance and resulting inequality; and (3) comparisons across race, religion, ethnicity, religion, social class, or gender. Similarly, Denison University in Ohio, whose requirement dates back to 1979, requires a course on women and/or minorities in twentieth century America that examines the effects of discrimination in the American context. Haverford College in Pennsylvania, whose original 1983 diversity requirement asked that students be introduced either to cultures they did not know or to systems of inequality and discrimination, revised its requirement after ten years to a social justice requirement focused on analyzing systems of inequality and discrimination.

The advantage of a more flexible diversity requirement is that it creates fewer turf battles between departments, is more easily approved by curriculum committees, and often needs less faculty development because the people who already have the expertise in a given area submit their existing courses as possible choices for the diversity requirement. These broad diversity requirements typically involve people across disciplines. When paired with faculty development opportunities, as it is at the University of Maryland, they can be a significant source for change in the curriculum overall, since newly acquired faculty expertise and perspectives will extend beyond the approved general-education diversity courses. The disadvantage of this approach is that without more tightly defined learning goals for the students, it is not always clear exactly what knowledge the institutions want students to acquire from taking such wide-ranging diversity courses. Students taking a course in twelfth-century Chinese art, for example, will learn very different things than those taking a course on the U.S. civil rights movement.

By contrast, only 17 percent of respondents in AAC&U's survey require all students to take a single diversity course that is part of a more tightly defined core curriculum. The great advantage of required cores is that every student is introduced to diversity issues, regardless of their major. Implementing a core curriculum, especially a newly designed one, typically calls for offering faculty development opportunities, which will, as a by-product, result in widespread influence on the content and pedagogy of many other courses outside the core.

Having a required core curriculum seems to work more easily and effectively at smaller institutions, for obvious staffing reason, but there are examples of large research universities implementing core curricula as well. The State University of New York at Buffalo, with approximately 16,000 undergraduate students, has such a core curriculum. After careful piloting and faculty development workshops, it instituted a well-thought-out required core course called "American Pluralism and the Search for Equality." While a variety of different courses meet the curriculum requirement, all such approved courses are united by their commitment to a com-

mon set of learning goals for students. Buffalo's 1992 American Pluralism Subcommittee included specifically defined learning goals for students, such as: (1) to develop within students a sense of informed, active citizenship by focusing on contemporary and historical issues of race, ethnicity, gender, social class, and religious sectarianism in American life; (2) to provide students with an intellectual awareness of the causes and effects of structured inequality and prejudicial exclusion in American society; (3) to provide students with increased self-awareness of what it means in our culture to be a person of their own gender, race, class, ethnicity, and religion as well as an understanding of how these categories affect those who are different from themselves; (4) to expand students' ability to think critically, and with an open mind, about controversial contemporary issues; and (5) to provide students with an intellectual awareness of diverse visions of the future as well as processes leading to a more equitable society.

A much smaller institution, St. Edward's University in Texas (approximately 3,300 undergraduates), adopted a fifty-seven-hour core that includes two first-year courses, "The American Experience" and "American Dilemmas." They have also adopted a vertical core that extends from freshman through senior year, thus allowing students opportunities to develop advanced analytical skills and revisit issues over time. By their senior year, students are asked to use insights acquired through their major to solve a pressing social problem as part of their senior culminating education requirement.

Yet another example of an interesting approach to a core diversity requirement is the regionally focused one adopted by the University of Memphis, where the general-education core requirement, "Cultural Confrontations," focuses on the relationships among the three major populations in the mid-South: European Americans, African Americans, and Native Americans. Parallel comparative courses that analyze power and justice can be found in the expanding number of general education courses focused on world cultures.

A newly developing approach to diversity that is located both in general-education diversity courses and in electives and majors focuses on what is called *service learning*, or, less frequently, *community-based learning*. Such credit-bearing courses teach students new intellectual knowledge about diversity, while also providing hands-on experiences that help them become more informed and skilled in creating more just societies. At Rutgers University in New Jersey, the Civic Education and Community Service Program combines community service with academic investigations about how to work alongside people with diverse backgrounds, while also teaching students more about what is needed to sustain an egalitarian, pluralist democracy. Hobart and William Smith Colleges in Connecticut created more than seventeen courses within two years' time that integrated service learning into academic courses that sought to expand students' capacities to be nation builders through a commitment to justice. Wagner College, located on Staten Island in New York, adopted a new curriculum in 1998 that integrates service learning as a thread woven through all four years as part of the general education requirement.

Whatever model is chosen for diversity requirements, courses across all these designs are more frequently organized through a comparative approach between groups, rather than by focusing on a single group alone. Conceptually, more courses also use an integrative analysis by helping students learn how to analyze multiple kinds of intersecting differences, either within a single group (studying gender or ethnic differences within Latinos/Latinas) or across several groups (studying class and religious differences across European Americans, African Americans, and Asian Americans). Diversity courses within general education also more typically explore moral and ethical questions, and are more likely to analyze systems of injustice, intolerance, inequality, and discrimination—as exemplified in Oregon State University's general education course, "Diversity, Power, and Discrimination."

Another emerging characteristic of diversity courses in general education is their interdisciplinary approach and the reliance on collaborative, student-centered pedagogies where intergroup dialogue and engagement are deliberately cultivated. In addition, there are also growing examples of innovative couplings between curricular and cocurricular activities, often but not exclusively incorporating living/learning residential dimensions to enrich classroom experiences. In an effort to escape the too prevalent option of choosing either a course on U.S. diversity or a course on world cultures, there is some evidence that more institutions are seeking ways to explore the interconnections between global and domestic diversity, sometimes by teaching U.S. diversity within a global context.

AAC&U's president, Carol Geary Schneider, argues that diversity requirements are, as she puts it, "filling the curricular 'civic' space once assigned to 'Western Civ.' That is, diversity requirements signal the academy's conviction that in the early twenty-first century citizens need to acquire significant knowledge both of cultures other than their own and of disparate cultures' struggles for recognition and equity" in order to be adequately prepared for the contentious, complex world they face (p. 2). But Schneider asserts more progress needs to be made in developing general education courses that examine diversity in the context of democratic values, histories, and aspirations. Students have too few opportunities to systematically debate the premises and meanings of democracy itself.

Conclusion

Despite the remarkable transformation and innovation in general education courses and models since 1980, the job is not done —and rightly so. In the best tradition of academic practices, most institutions would admit they don't always get it right the first time and need to submit their established general education designs to regular critique and assessment. While there has been increasing local and national attention paid to evaluating the impact of diversity courses, assessment needs to be more systematically embedded in the institutional life of the college and its faculty. Moreover, in the distinctively fluid, ever-changing environment of higher education, re-examining the effectiveness of the curriculum is a necessity, especially in light of what has become a common fact that students might attend two or three different institutions before acquiring their college degree.

Getting it right also matters because so much is at stake, both educationally and civically. Research examining the impact of curriculum transformation efforts reveals some significant findings. Several studies, for instance, confirm that serious engagement of diversity in the curriculum and the classroom has a positive impact on attitudes toward racial issues, on opportunities to interact in deeper ways with those who are different, on cognitive development, and on overall satisfaction with institutions. Longitudinal research on the effects of the focused use of intergroup dialogues confirm measurable progress in identity development, more comfort with conflict as a normal part of social life, more positive intergroup interactions, and long-term effects on participation in activities with members of other racial and ethnic groups among dialogue participants.

For all the notably proud progress of U.S. democracy, the United States is a stratified society that continues to be segregated racially in its residential patterns, whether within inner cities or in surrounding suburbia. Higher education is therefore precious mediating public space where, unlike most of American society, different groups live, study, and think side by side. As such, it offers the genuinely authentic daily experience of a multicultural, pluralist, democratic environment. If higher education can seize the rich educational and societal benefits inherent in such a mix, it promises to have far-reaching consequences on the quality of the nation's, and the world's, communal life.

Research has conclusively shown that a racially and ethnically diverse student body has far-ranging and significant benefits for all students. Students learn better in such an environment and are better prepared to become active participants in a pluralistic, democratic society once they leave school. Patterns of racial segregation can be broken by diversity experiences in institutions of higher education.

So it matters that general education courses incorporate diversity in ways that capitalize on the presence of diverse students and the potential for deep and lasting knowledge that affects actions during and after graduation. As Bobby Fong, the president of Butler University, said so eloquently at his inauguration, "The ideal of the academy is to be able to represent fairly the viewpoint of those with whom one most disagrees. But dialogue, however necessary, is not sufficient. The unending conversation is what we must, at all costs, preserve in the academy, but our students need to be equipped for living, in most cases, beyond the academy, in a world where moral decisions, in all their contingency and uncertainty, must be made."

Of course, general education courses cannot carry the intellectual and moral weight of accomplishing all this in one required course, or even in a sequenced series of courses. Each institution needs to take a holistic look at the entire curriculum, the interrelationship between general education and the major, the cumulative kinds of developmental experiences a student might have in progressing towards a degree, and the increasingly complex and demanding questions students are able to pose and answer

as they are challenged to use their new knowledge and civic, intercultural capacities to address real-world problems. If students graduate with the ability to think critically, act responsibly, and negotiate borders that might otherwise divide, then higher education will come closer to meeting its historic mission of not only advancing knowledge, but contributing to stable, more equitable democratic societies.

See also: AFRICAN-AMERICAN STUDIES; GAY AND LESBIAN STUDIES; GENERAL EDUCATION IN HIGHER EDUCATION; MULTICULTURAL EDUCATION; RACE, ETHNICITY, AND CULTURE; SERVICE LEARNING; WOMEN'S STUDIES.

BIBLIOGRAPHY

ASANTE, MOLEFI K., and RAVITCH, DIANE. 1991. "Multiculturalism: An Exchange." *American Scholar* 60:267–277.

ASSOCIATION OF AMERICAN COLLEGES AND UNIVERSITIES. 1995. *American Pluralism and the College Curriculum: Higher Education in a Diverse Democracy.* Washington, DC: Association of American Colleges and Universities.

ASSOCIATION OF AMERICAN COLLEGES AND UNIVERSITIES. 1995. *Integrity in the College Curriculum: A Report to the Academic Community.* Washington, DC: Association of American Colleges and Universities.

ASTIN, ALEXANDER W. 1993. *What Matters in College? Four Critical Years Revisited.* San Francisco: Jossey-Bass.

BANKS, JAMES A., and BANKS, CHERRY A. McGEE, eds. 1993. *Multicultural Education: Issues and Perspectives,* 2nd edition. Boston: Allyn and Bacon.

BENNETT, CHRISTINE. 2001. "Genres of Research in Multicultural Education." *Review of Educational Research* 71(2):171–217.

BLOOM, ALEXANDER. 1987. *The Closing of the American Mind.* New York: Simon & Schuster.

BOSSMAN, DAVID M. 1991. "Cross-cultural Values for a Pluralistic Core Curriculum." *Journal of Higher Education* 62: 661–681.

BOYER, ERNEST L. 1987. *College: The Undergraduate Experience in America.* New York: Harper and Row.

BUTLER, JOHNNELLA E., and WALTER, JOHN C., eds. 1991. *Transforming the Curriculum: Ethnic*

Studies and Women's Studies. Albany, NY: State University of New York.

CARNOCHAN, WALTER B. 1993. *The Battleground of the Curriculum: Liberal Education and American Experience.* Stanford, CA: Stanford University Press.

CORNWELL, GRANT H., and STODDARD, EVE W. 1994. "Things Fall Together: A Critique of Multicultural Curricular Reform." *Liberal Education* 80(4):40–51.

DUDERSTADT, JAMES J. 2000. *A University for the Twenty-First Century.* Ann Arbor: University of Michigan Press.

FITZGERALD, ANN K., and LAUTER, PAUL. 1995. "Multiculturalism and Core Curricula." In *Handbook of Research on Multicultural Education,* ed. James A. Banks. New York: Macmillan.

GAFF, JERRY G. 1992. "Beyond Politics: The Educational Issues Inherent in Multicultural Education." *Change* 24: 31–35.

GEYER, MICHAEL. 1993. "Multiculturalism and the Politics of General Education." *Critical Inquiry* 19:499–533.

GURIN, PATRICIA. 1999. "New Research on the Benefits of Diversity in College and Beyond: An Empirical Analysis." *Diversity Digest* 3(3):5,15.

HUMPHREYS, DEBRA. 1997. *General Education and American Commitments: A National Report on Diversity Courses and Requirements.* Washington, DC: Association of American Colleges and Universities.

HUMPHREYS, DEBRA. 2000. "National Survey Finds Diversity Requirements Common Around the Country." *Diversity Digest* 5(1):1–2.

HURTADO, SILVIA; MILEM, JEFFREY; CLAYTON-PEDERSEN, ALMA; and ALLEN, WALTER. 1999. *Enacting Diverse Learning Environments: Improving the Climate for Racial/Ethnic Diversity in Higher Education.* ASHE-ERIC Higher Education Report 26, Number 8. Washington, DC: George Washington University, Graduate School of Education and Human Development.

LEVINE, ARTHUR, and CURETON, JEANNETTE. 1992. "The Quiet Revolution: Eleven Facts About Multiculturalism and the Curriculum." *Change* 24:25–29.

LEVINE, LAWRENCE W. 1996. *The Opening of the American Mind: Canons, Culture, and History.* Boston: Beacon Press.

LIGHT, RICHARD, and CURETON, JEANNETTE. 1992. "The Quiet Revolution: Eleven Facts About Multiculturalism and the Curriculum." *Change* 24(1):24–29.

MARABLE, MANNING. 1997. "Diversity and Democracy in Higher Education." *Race and Reason* 3:3–9.

MONTALTO, NICHOLAS V. 1982. *A History of the Intercultural Educational Movement, 1924–1941.* New York: Garland.

MUSIL, CARYN M. 1999. "Education for Global Citizenship." *Liberal Education* 85(1): 22–27.

MUSIL, CARYN M.; GARCÍA, MILDRED; HUDGINS, CYNTHIA A.; NETTLES, MICHAEL T.; SEDLACEK, WILLIAM E.; and SMITH, DARYL G. 1999. *To Form a More Perfect Union: Campus Diversity Initiatives.* Washington, DC: Association of American Colleges and Universities.

"National Poll Reveals Strong Public Support for Diversity in Higher Education." 1998. *Diversity Digest* 3(1):1, 4–5.

NORDQUIST, JOAN. 1992. *The Multicultural Education Debate in the University: A Bibliography.* Santa Cruz, CA: Reference and Research Service.

SCHMITZ, BETTY. 1992. *Core Curriculum and Cultural Pluralism: A Guide for Campus Planners.* Washington, DC: Association of American Colleges and Universities.

SCHMITZ, BETTY. 1992. "Cultural Pluralism and Core Curricula." In *Promoting Diversity in College Classrooms: Innovative Responses for the Curriculum, Faculty, and Institutions,* ed. Maurianne Adams. San Francisco: Jossey-Bass.

SCHNEIDER, BARBARA, and STEVENSON, DAVID. 1999. *The Ambitious Generation.* New Haven, CT: Yale University Press.

SCHNEIDER, CAROL G. 2001. "Diversity Requirements: Part of a Renewed Civic Education Agenda?" *Diversity Digest* (5)2:2–3.

SCHNEIDER, CAROL G., and KNEFELKAMP, LEE. 1997. "Education for a World Lived in Common with Others." In *Education and Democracy: Re-Imagining Liberal Learning in America,* ed. Robert Orrill. New York: College Entrance Examination Board.

SMITH, DARYL G., and ASSOCIATES. 1997. *Diversity Works: The Emerging Picture of How Students Benefit.* Washington, DC: Association of American Colleges and Universities.

Spanier, Bonnie; Bloom, Alexander; and Boroviak, Darlene, eds. 1984. *Toward a Balanced Curriculum: A Sourcebook for Initiating Gender Integration Projects.* Cambridge: Schenkman.

Takaki, Ronald. 1991. "The Value of Multiculturalism." *Liberal Education* 77:8–10.

Taylor, Charles. 1992. *Multiculturalism and The Politics of Recognition.* Princeton, NJ: Princeton University Press.

Tirado, Isabel A. 1987. "Integrating Issues of Gender in the Survey of Western Civilization Since 1648." In *Initiating Curriculum Transformation in the Humanities: Integrating Women and Issues of Race and Gender.* Wayne, NJ: William Patterson College.

Zúñiga, Ximena, and Nagda, Biren (Ratnesh) A. 2001. "Design Considerations in Intergroup Dialogue." In *Intergroup Dialogue: Deliberative Democracy in School, College, Community, and Workplace,* ed. David Schoem and Sylvia Hurtado. Ann Arbor: University of Michigan Press.

Alma R. Clayton-Pedersen
Caryn McTighe Musil

MUSEUM AS AN EDUCATIONAL INSTITUTION, THE

In ancient Greece the museum was for pure study and contemplation. Culture came first, learning second. In American museums, the earliest examples of the term *education* in museum mission statements were directed toward promoting democracy. In this way education in American museums was tied to the very identity of the nation.

The Birth of Public Museums

In the late eighteenth century, America saw the development of the public museum. As industrialization progressed, more people moved into cities. The nation's policymakers were taking on more responsibility for social services and the welfare of the nation. Government-funded schooling in industrialized areas was developing. This was a time of great public interest in science, in which citizens were embracing the Founding Fathers' zeal for natural history while finding that technology and industry were affecting daily life. Amateur collectors formed membership societies for the preservation and study of specimens, which were displayed in what came to be called *cabinets of curiosities.* Leisure activities, such as public lectures on the arts and sciences, had intellectual value.

During the late 1700s and early 1800s education in American museums can be simplified as a time of conflict between scholarship and popularization. Arguably, many of the early American public museums were little more than sideshows of curiosities. The infamous American showman P. T. Barnum exploited public interest in natural history by exhibiting the supposed skeleton of a mermaid and entertaining crowds in institutions that were theatrical venues as much as museums. Two exceptions were the Peale museums in Baltimore, Maryland, and Philadelphia, Pennsylvania. They were created as institutions to help people better their lives. The Peale Museum in Philadelphia used its exhibition space for public health campaigns and demonstrations of the latest technological wonders. For example, its exhibition of piped gas lighting was an entertaining, but convincing, display of how gas lighting could transform Philadelphia. This was the beginning of the public museum where the display of objects was for the enlightenment and entertainment of the public.

Museums after the Civil War

Education in American museums developed further after the Civil War. In the late 1800s theories of learning proposed that new knowledge was revealed not just through books but also through objects. Consequently, museums, not universities, were places for the production of knowledge. At that time universities were seen as inactive as they were not institutions that created new knowledge. Instead, universities taught knowledge that was already known. The most prestigious universities of the mid- to late nineteenth century tended to be theological institutions that focused on the interpretation of texts, not object-based research.

Producing new knowledge required object-based research. Consider natural history museums, full of objects used in the daily research of scientists. These institutions were central to the pursuit of science. But education existed alongside research. In museums, as new information was discovered, it was made public through exhibitions. This was a striking contrast to universities, where any new knowledge produced was available only to the select audience there. Museums were seen as democratic institutions, more accessible to the public than universities.

The late 1800s were a boom time for American museums. Great institutions, such as the Metropolitan Museum of Art and the American Museum of Natural History, both in the New York City, and the Art Institute of Chicago opened during these years. Amateur-scientist societies were opening the doors to their cabinets of curiosities for the betterment of the public. American librarian John Cotton Dana was writing about the museum as an instrument for popular culture. He wanted museums to be founded out of the highest ideals for citizens. Yet this period marked a shift in public education institutions, and by the first quarter of the twentieth century, universities had become the primary institutions for public education.

A Shift in Education

One theory of how public education shifted from museums to universities in the early 1900s points to differences in assessment. As schooling became more common, a large system of assessment grew along with it. Museums did not embrace assessment in their educational activities. Assessment in schools provided the leverage necessary for additional public and government support. Another theory was that the educational activities of museums relied too much on the inherent ability of objects to speak for themselves. It was thought that anyone who studied the object carefully enough, even untrained observers, would understand the object's meaning. Public interest waned when faced with multitudes of objects and little interpretation. In addition, museums faced increasing competition from world fairs, which offered more entertainment than the usually serious museums.

By the 1930s there was already a need to argue that museums could provide a role in public education, even as an assistant to the education that took place in schools. A new generation of curators in museums was focused on collections, not education. Education in museums was no longer built on the production of new knowledge, and instead focused on entertaining and educating the public about information (that was not necessarily up to date). Museums began to turn increasingly to educating schoolchildren.

There was also an increasing diversity and professionalization of methods used to educate the public. Museums began to appoint instructors to their staff and early scientific studies of museum visitors' activities were carried out. By 1932, 15 percent of all museums offered educational programs. Lectures, tours, demonstrations, and labels became features of many museums. Public outreach was offered through tours for schoolchildren and through printed educational materials along with the loan of objects for classroom use. The presentation of objects in museums changed. Exhibits now included combinations of related objects, dioramas, period rooms, and more realistic taxidermy.

By the 1940s labels, brochures, and lectures were regular features of museums, but they tended to be strictly information based. Education programming now included teacher-training courses, junior museums for children, branch museums at local libraries, and programs for the unemployed. Museums loaned materials to schools, but also shops, hospitals, and community groups. Museum exhibitions and programs were even used to promote patriotism during World War II.

The National Education Infrastructure

The 1970s saw the development of new educational interpretation methods. Exhibitions of objects began to include film, audio, and even the first computers. There was also a growing awareness of a new type of exhibit, best described as a hands-on display, used to demonstrate scientific phenomena in the earliest science centers, including COSI in Columbus, Ohio, and the Exploratorium in San Francisco, California, which opened in 1964 and 1969 respectively. Perhaps most important, in 1973 the American Association of Museums created a standing professional committee on education. The education committee's purposes include promoting high professional standards for museum educators, advocating for the support of the educational purpose of museums, and promoting excellence in museum learning. This committee signaled a national recognition of the professionalization of education in museums.

In the 1980s education was placed squarely in the center of American museums and their role in the impending new century with the 1984 report of the American Association of Museums, *Museums for a New Century*. This report, and the later *Excellence and Equity*, published in 1992, spotlight education as the central focus of museums' public service. Notably, the reports describe education in broad, pluralistic terms, encouraging museums to provide educational experiences "by fostering the ability to live productively in a pluralistic society and to contribute to the resolution of the challenges we face as global citizens" (American Association of Museums 1992, p. 6). Museums were once again positioned to make a major contribution to public education.

In the 1990s research showed that museums not only provided rich education experiences for families but also provided direct support for schools. Museums played a role in the national infrastructure that supported public education. Some argued that museums played a unique role by offering benefits not found in schools: Museums were nonthreatening environments that appealed to a wide range of audiences; they offered an interdisciplinary approach; they had more flexibility than schools; and they had the capacity to bring students, teachers, and the public together in new ways. Museum education at the end of the twentieth century was much more than school group tours and classes for adults.

New Directions

As museums positioned themselves in the educational infrastructure at the beginning of the twenty-first century, there was increasing pressure to address public issues, including failing school systems, community building, and diversifying audiences. Museums responded to this pressure by expanding the range of their educational activities. Education came to encompass the development and interpretation of exhibitions, events, workshops, and even the study of visitors' experiences and educational outcomes. Museum staff has been involved at a national level in establishing standards for education. Educational training for teachers has been offered through pre-service classes and professional development. Education for children and adults has reached diversified audiences through new programs in new locations, including access programs for visitors with physical or mental impairments, and after-school clubs and activities in museums, churches, and public housing. Education in American museums, as Stephen E. Weil summarized it, has shifted from being about something to being for somebody.

See also: NATIONAL ART EDUCATION ASSOCIATION; NATIONAL ENDOWMENT FOR THE ARTS.

BIBLIOGRAPHY

ALEXANDER, EDWARD P. 1998. *The Museum in America: Innovation and Pioneers.* Nashville, TN: American Association for State and Local History.

AMERICAN ASSOCIATION OF MUSEUMS. 1984. *Museums for a New Century.* Washington, DC: American Association of Museums.

AMERICAN ASSOCIATION OF MUSEUMS. 1992. *Excellence and Equity: Education and the Public Dimension of Museums.* Washington, DC: American Association of Museums.

CONN, STEVEN. 1998. *Museums and American Intellectual Life, 1876–1926.* Chicago: University of Chicago Press.

FALK, JOHN H., and DIERKING, LYNN D. 2000. *Learning from Museums: Visitor Experiences and the Making of Meaning.* Walnut Creek, CA: Alta Mira.

HARRIS, NEIL. 1978. "Museums, Merchandising and Popular Taste: The Struggle for Influence." In *Material Culture and the Study of American Life,* ed. Ian Quimby. New York: Norton.

HEIN, GEORGE E. 1998. *Learning in the Museum.* New York: Routledge.

HIRSCH, JOANNE S., and SILVERMAN, LOIS H. 2000. *Transforming Practice: Selections for the Journal of Museum Education 1992–1999.* Washington, DC: Museum Education Roundtable.

HOOPER-GREENHILL, EILEAN, ed. 1994. *The Educational Role of the Museum.* London: Routledge.

ROBERTS, LISA C. 1997. *From Knowledge to Narrative: Educators and the Changing Museum.* Washington, DC: Smithsonian Institution Press.

WEIL, STEPHEN E. 1999. "From Being about Something to Being for Somebody: The Ongoing Transformation of the American Museum." *Daedalus: Journal of the American Academy of Arts and Sciences* 128:229–258.

KIRSTEN M. ELLENBOGEN

MUSIC EDUCATION

OVERVIEW
Richard Colwell

PREPARATION OF TEACHERS
Carlos Xavier Rodriguez

OVERVIEW

An observation of music classes in the public schools reveals that little changed in the last half of the twentieth century, including the education of music teachers. The value and role of music education in American schools has been affected, however, by the education reform movement and changes in the organization and delivery of instruction. One major change is that music often is not regarded as a stand-alone subject but is incorporated into an arts education.

Almost all K–6 schools offer some type of required instruction in music. At the middle school level, changes in the instructional format and the addition of electives in other arts courses have reduced the importance of music. The secondary school music program consists largely of performance ensembles, which comprise bands (wind ensembles), choirs, and string or full orchestras. These ensembles are elective although an increasing number of states (about half in 2001) mandate a unit of fine arts at the secondary level. To enable the nonperformer to meet this graduation requirement, courses are offered that may include advanced placement (AP) music theory (usually taken by students who are already enrolled in a music class), beginning guitar and keyboard classes, or an extension of the general music class similar to that offered in the elementary school. The prevalence of the new requirement for an arts course at the secondary level is somewhat misleading as some states define grades seven through twelve as secondary education. There is also a broad interpretation of what constitutes an arts course; some states include literature, foreign language, and photography, as well as music, visual arts, theatre, and dance, while others include the arts as a choice among required electives. The most identifiable change in the music curriculum, found primarily in general music, is a greater emphasis on composition, the instruction of which has been facilitated by computers and the use of multicultural music.

It is difficult to generalize the percentage of students participating in music at the secondary level. Percentage of participation varies greatly depending upon the size of the school, ranging from 5 percent in large schools to as much as half the student body in small or magnet schools. About 35 percent of the student body are enrolled in music for one semester, a percentage that would be about 20 percent at any one time. Well over 90 percent of the secondary schools offer band and nearly 85 percent offer choral music. String programs are found in approximately 20 percent of high schools, although this dearth is compensated by the all-city/region youth orchestras that provide stunning musical experiences, often rivaling the quality of the local symphony orchestra. String students commonly study music privately outside of school and often began instruction at an early age through a Suzuki-type program.

An important variable in secondary music is the establishment of numerous magnet arts high schools. Students enrolled in these programs do very well academically, as shown through past experience with arts magnet schools like the Interlochen Arts Academy and the North Carolina School for the Arts. James Catterall's research on students enrolled in music for four years reveals that they score appreciably better than average on SAT and ACT tests. This relationship between academic success and the arts is frequently used to promote the concept of "learning through the arts." In 2001 the U.S. Department of Education provided a $2.5 million grant to the Berkeley County School District in South Carolina to initiate an integrated arts/academic magnet school curriculum.

Elementary School Music

The required general music program in grades K–6 is less vibrant than it was at the midpoint of the twentieth century. The reduction in curriculum time occurred gradually during the 1970s and 1980s, making it difficult to pinpoint any single cause. Budget reductions are most often cited as the cause, perhaps due to the publicity given to budget caps passed by the legislatures in California and Massachusetts. Whether the caps were causal is a matter of debate but the reduction in curriculum time for music was more likely the result of changes in priorities and not fiscal change. During the 1970s and 1980s fewer discretionary funds were available to school districts due to steep increases in shared costs for special education. Second, greater emphasis was placed on test scores in language arts and mathematics. In addition, elementary classroom teachers were relieved of responsibility for teaching or helping to teach music, due to an extensive campaign by the Music Educators National Conference in behalf of certified music teachers. Fourth, colleges of education reduced the coursework in music required of classroom teachers, making music the area in which these teachers felt least competent to model and to teach. Also during this period instructional time was reduced from daily classes of 20–30 minutes to a weekly offering of the same length. However, expectations of student competency in music were not lowered and in fact new objectives were added. No public reaction to this change occurred, as school administrators and the public never had a clear idea of the important competencies in music that all students should possess upon completion of a K–6 curriculum. Thus, inadequate time became the norm. Instructional time in the secondary schools was not reduced; thus there was no change in the more visible components of the secondary school's music program.

Music appreciation as an objective in the elementary curriculum lost any cachet it once had (the AP course in music listening was dropped at the secondary level for lack of interest) despite a warning by the National School Board Association in 1988 that performance had replaced appreciation. Singing as an objective became a lower priority. Texts for general music for K–6, consisting of songs with related listening materials for all students, were replaced by specialized programs based on the method and materials of the founder. These programs, primarily Orff, Kodaly, and Dalcroze, became ascendant, along with teacher-constructed offerings consisting of popular and ethnic music, music games, videos, and activities tangentially related to music. When the specialist teacher came in contact with students only once per week and met as many as 500 students during that week, the idea of a sequential curriculum became infeasible, as did the possibility of assisting the student who fell behind. In all states except Louisiana specialists are the primary deliverers of instruction.

The reform movement promotion of basic or core subjects mobilized those interested in elementary music education to demand that music be included as a core subject, returning it to its century-long importance. Music was joined by visual arts, theatre, and dance to create a requirement in arts education. Arts Content Standards were quickly formulated in each of the four arts and in 1994 these standards were the first core addition to be accepted (after the long-standing mathematics standards) by the Secretary of Education. Performance and Opportunity to Learn Standards were also constructed and distributed to members of the four arts professions but these two standards have received scant attention, especially the Opportunity to Learn Standards that

are necessary for students to attain at least a proficient performance level in nine content areas. The Music Educators National Conference (now named MENC: The National Association for Music Education) has vigorously promoted the content standards since their adoption. (The suggestion has been made that if the standards in all of the subjects were adopted that it would add five years to the K–12 curriculum). Two of the content standards in each art form emphasized the importance of relating the four art forms to one another and relating the arts to other subjects in the curriculum. Although it is difficult to imagine how social studies or most other subjects could be taught without consideration of the arts, this content standard shifted the perception of responsibility so that the arts teacher is seen as an aide to the subject matter teacher when the reverse should be true, logically and educationally. The arts standards will not be taken seriously where the classroom teacher is given the responsibility but not the competency to teach in the arts area.

Middle School

With the recommendations of the Carnegie Foundation for the middle school, new curriculum emphasis was placed on student development of a positive outlook toward educational success that would contribute to improved self-confidence and self-esteem. To accomplish this, the middle school curriculum was to be taught by teacher teams in the more basic subjects that, in turn, were to be supplemented by a rich offering of exploratory courses. The arts became part of these elective exploratory courses, frequently competing with chess club and Tae Kwon-Do for available curricular time. (The arts are often a required exploratory for six to nine weeks at one or more of the grade levels of middle school, an arrangement that interferes with any sequential music curriculum during middle school and lacks any connection to elementary school music objectives or to the offerings in the secondary school.)

The involvement of the arts community in supporting the inclusion of the arts as a basic school subject has raised many substantive issues. First, could a national or community artist supplement or replace the certified teacher at a lower cost and provide more authentic instruction? The massive Annenberg grant to the public schools established partnerships between the schools and cultural organizations, a provision that brought performers and composers who had no teacher training into the schools much like the Ford Foundation's Young Composers Project did in the late 1950s and 1960s and programs of the National Endowment of the Arts, state arts councils, and Young Audiences do in the early twenty-first century. Second, arts organizations raise or find money to support their own curricular vision of a music program or music experience. These organizations provide musical instruments, music scores, and instruction, as well as field experiences such as attendance at concerts and operas. Third, arts organizations have found it easier to work with classroom teachers and their objectives rather than with the heavily scheduled music teacher. The Lincoln Center Institute has operated such a program for twenty-five years, bringing classroom teachers and professional musicians together to facilitate the classroom teacher's objective of an enriched classroom and to aid teachers in attaining goals in their extant curriculums. Fourth, other arts and nonarts organizations have taken a broad approach to education (as opposed to schooling) and initiated after-school programs in music to accomplish several purposes: to provide a balance to remedial programs in the more basic subjects that are offered after school; to provide a safe environment for that time period between the end of the school day and when parents are at home; and to free up the basic curriculum by avoiding the interruption for music class. Fifth, community music centers have a presence in many cities, offering not only private lessons but often ensemble experiences and short-term educational instructional units in the public schools (with their own staff); these offerings consist of content that fits a particular school's monthly or yearly focus. Sixth, all major and community orchestras have initiated educational programs that include youth concerts and preparation for attendance at these concerts. These multiple offers of assistance from the local community are difficult to reject; they cost the schools nothing, are designed for all students in K–6, and administratively count as part, or all, of the music program.

To describe the music education of Americans one must take into account the value of private music lessons (especially piano and guitar); the impact of radio, television, and compact discs and the listening experiences they provide; and the many informal performing experiences such as garage bands. Should a student's competency in music be the issue, many students could test out of classroom music. However, the opportunity to learn to play an instrument is provided in most schools around fourth grade—the decision of when to offer instrumental music instruction is based more upon the budget than the student's likelihood of success. Also, music educators in K–6 general music have adopted a role in supporting multicultural education. It is interesting to identify music from other cultures and to compare and contrast these types of music. Learning to perform on ethnic instruments is fun and listening exercises are more concrete as much ethnic music has a practical value in its relationship to social studies and other core courses. Western music, written for the concert hall, often does not contain many cultural or historical references; its meaning and importance are based on its formal and aesthetic qualities. Thus, it is no longer possible to definitively describe the K–6 music program in American schools, as the content is not only diverse but also affected greatly by the political currents of the educational reform movement.

Early Childhood Music

Early childhood education frequently includes rich music experiences whether in the private early childhood programs such as Waldorf and Montessori (which extend beyond early childhood) or in public school programs for disadvantaged children. Research, including the Perry Early Childhood Program (HighScope) that has impressive longitudinal data on a sample of students for some twenty years, indicates that music competencies achieved from birth to age five assist students in later school experience. Other research, whose findings are often mislabeled the "Mozart effect," indicates that music listening experiences with very young children play a role in how the brain is wired. This research is focused on temporal-spatial ability and how it relates to the abstract thinking required in mathematics and science. Keyboard experience also may provide a spatial-temporal advantage. These research results also support programs labeled "learning through music" where music is taught not for its musical benefits but for other reasons. The interest in justifying music instruction on the basis of what is learned about other subjects is a contemporary worry, although the powerful instrumental music programs in the secondary schools have long been valued for their role in accomplishing general, nonarts objectives. Students do learn character, responsibility, cooperative learning, how to budget their time, and much more as part of being a contributing member to an ensemble that has high standards. Students participate because their peers participate and they are attracted by the chance to do things well with their friends. The power of these side objectives does not necessitate the sacrifice of unique musical objectives; however, the perception of school administrators and board members is important for long-term goals.

Music continues to play an important role in special education programs, in music therapy, and with English as a Second Language students. The nonverbal nature of music allows students with special needs to participate in many music experiences and to obtain educational benefits as well as enjoyment.

Secondary Schools

The instrumental performance program (grades 9–12) is edging toward becoming a semi-independent part of the school day in that it is not fully supported by school funds. Participating students do receive academic credit but that credit is not always computed in a student's overall grade average and many colleges exclude such grades and credit in making admission decisions. *The Instrumentalist* magazine reported in 2001 that more than half of the budget required to support secondary instrumental music programs was raised by students, businesses, and parents through fund-raising or assessments. This percentage likely represents the more advanced band programs. The quality of band programs is steadily increasing with graduates often able to matriculate into college applied music curricula. A study completed by Educational Research Service indicates that slightly more than 20 percent of the funds required to support secondary music programs, including general music, music theory, choral performance, and other academic classes, is raised from outside sources. No longer automatically providing instruments for students, schools have gradually come to expect students to own or rent their own instruments and to pay for expenses associated with contests, festivals, and travel. There are also expenses involved with choral music but these are more limited, restricted to appropriate concert dress and travel funds. Secondary music is, therefore, not affordable for everyone unless support exists for special students.

In other aspects, music education in the secondary schools has not changed significantly. Secondary music teachers have not been affected by the educa-

tional reform movement (except for block scheduling and the addition of more required courses) and are generally unconcerned about the voluntary national standards as some do not relate to ensembles and others are too rudimentary to cause much trouble.

Philosophy

A single philosophy of music education for K–12 is inappropriate except when speaking of music in the broadest of terms. The need for more than one philosophy is not surprising with a subject as broad and diverse as music, one that provides so many beneficial outcomes. Two distinct philosophies exist in K–12 education, one based on the importance of music education for all students and one based upon the benefits of performance, including aesthetics and opportunities for excellence, for those with interest and talent. Teachers usually adhere to one philosophy or the other based on whether they have interests in elective music or in providing music to all students, regardless of ability. There are somewhat more than 45,000 public secondary school music teachers involved with performance; this represents slightly less than half the music teaching force. MENC reports an estimated 105,000 public school music teachers with an additional 15,000 teaching in private schools (2000a). The complexity of music (Western music has been increasing in complexity for centuries) means that not everyone can adequately perform the music that is important to them. Those who have the ability and time to develop high level performance skills can derive enormous satisfaction, enjoyment, and understanding from performing alone and with others.

External financial support is also important in supporting national arts (music) programs. The Getty Center has taken a special interest in visual arts education, supporting activities and publications to promote Discipline-Based Arts Education, a movement that has had some influence in music as well. Without Getty support, adoption of the voluntary national standards would have been delayed or lost, as would have been the arts assessment in 1997 of the National Association of Educational Progress and the development of the arts teacher component of the National Board of Professional Teaching Students.

See also: CURRICULUM, SCHOOL; ELEMENTARY EDUCATION, *subentry on* CURRENT TRENDS; MONTESsori, Maria; Secondary Education, *subentry on* Current Trends.

BIBLIOGRAPHY

Bickell, Henry M., and Paul, Regina H. 1988. *Time for Curriculum.* Alexandria, VA: National School Boards Association.

Brown, J. D. 1994. "Opportunities and Solutions for U.S. Instrumental Music Programs." *The Gemeinhardt Report* 4:11.

Carnegie Council on Adolescent Development. 1989. *Turning Points: Preparing American Youth for the 21st Century.* New York: Carnegie Council on Adolescent Development.

Carnegie Council on Adolescent Development. 1995. *Great Transitions: Preparing Adolescents for a New Century.* New York: Carnegie Council on Adolescent Development.

Catterall, James; Chapleau, Richard; and Iwanga, John. 1999. "Involvement in the Arts and Human Development." In *Champions of Change,* ed. Ed Fiske. Washington, DC: Arts Education Partnership.

Educational Research Service. 2000. *The National Survey of Music Education in Public Secondary Schools.* Arlington, VA: Educational Research Service.

Eisner, Elliot. 2001. "Music Education Six Months After the Turn of the Century." *Arts Education Policy Review* 102(3):20–24.

Instrumentalist. 2001. "2001 Survey of School Music Budgets." *Instrumentalist*(August):34–38.

Leonhard, Charles. 1991. *The Status of Arts Education in American Public Schools.* Urbana, IL: Council for Research in Music Education.

Music Educators National Conference. 1994a. *National Standards for Arts Education.* Reston, VA: Music Educators National Conference.

Music Educators National Conference. 1994b. *Opportunity to Learn Standards, PreK–12.* Reston, VA: Music Educators National Conference.

Music Educators National Conference. 1996. *Performance Standards for Music.* Reston, VA: Music Educators National Conference.

Music Educators National Conference. 2000a. "FYI: How Many Teachers Are There?" *Teaching Music* (October):69.

Music Educators National Conference. 2000b. "FYI: How Many Teachers Are There?" *Teaching Music* (December):66–67.

Strong, Richard W.; Silver, Harvey F.; and Perini, Matthew J. 2001. *Teaching What Matters Most: Standards and Strategies for Raising Student Achievement.* Alexandria, VA: Association for Supervision and Curriculum Development.

U.S. Department of Education, National Center for Educational Statistics. 1999. *Digest of Educational Statistics 1998.* Washington, DC: U.S. Department of Education.

Richard Colwell

PREPARATION OF TEACHERS

Prior to the 1960s the preparation of music teachers in the United States included study in music history, theory, and literature, performance experience in vocal and/or instrumental music, and initial teaching experience in a music classroom. The social and educational upheavals of the 1960s brought about significant changes in this curriculum to include new emphases on contemporary music, world music, contributions of related fields such as psychology and philosophy, and competency-based teacher preparation programs. By the 1970s, the aesthetic education movement, first introduced in widely read texts by Charles Leonhard and Robert W. House, dominated music education. Perhaps the most influential writing on this topic was Bennett Reimer's 1971 explication of the relationship between aesthetic principles and music education. His subsequent monograph (1972, revised in 1989) broadly influenced music teachers to legitimatize music instruction that was based on more deeply felt beliefs regarding the nature and importance of musical experience. During the 1990s music teacher education was influenced by the publication of national standards for music instruction formulated by the Music Educators National Conference (1994), which also sparked renewed interest in competency-based programs.

Dominant Themes in Music Teacher Education

During the last two decades of the twentieth century, much of the research concerning undergraduate music education programs focused on the student, the instructor, and the program content. Studies emphasizing student roles included the essential characteristics of the effective teacher; teaching styles; musical, intellectual, and personal development; teaching time management skills; formation of classroom and rehearsal strategies; behavior management skills; leadership skills; and attrition variables. Studies involving faculty included supervisory roles, use of modeling techniques, motivational skills, and professional responsibilities. Studies involving program content included the following:

- descriptive research by regions or type (instrumental/choral)
- use of innovations
- course sequencing
- feedback systems
- use of computers and technology
- use of simulation techniques
- evaluation
- observation
- the content and structure of methods courses
- multicultural components
- interdisciplinary studies
- field-based experiences and student teaching
- the importance of developing a philosophy of music education

Additional studies included historical accounts of music education programs, suggestions for improving evaluation systems, and reports of various educational task forces, which recommend guidelines for curriculum reform.

Problems in Music Teacher Education

Two competing perspectives have dominated writings and discussions in music teacher education. On the one hand, there is a search for new ways to teach more effectively what has long been regarded as standard curriculum content. On the other hand, there have been attempts to study the role of higher institutions in preparing educators, the systems through which a program's effectiveness is measured, and new emphases in educational psychology that require amendments to program philosophy and procedures. Some writers have expressed continuing concern for the conflict between the conservatory, liberal arts, and educational/professional imperatives present in the modern music education undergraduate program. Adequate coverage of these diverse components is typically not manageable within the context of a four-year program, so many institutions have added a fifth year of study.

Advocates of improved evaluation procedures in undergraduate music education programs cite the need for evaluation of learning as well as teaching. It has also been recommended that evaluation be presented as a distinct subject within the curriculum as well as used by faculty members to assess student learning. The term *assessment as instruction* is used to describe evaluative measures that are built into the learning process, and pre-service teachers in music performance and general music are encountering more course activities that include such measures.

The role of student teaching in the curriculum continues to be problematic. College faculty are hard-pressed to intensify their roles as supervisors and provide more time within the curriculum for field experiences. Provisions, however, have been identified by in-service teachers as the most important critical to an effective and relevant pre-service education.

Perhaps the most critical problem facing music teacher educators is the need for an increased effort to bridge the gap between educational theory and instructional practice. Few, if any, critics attribute this problem to insufficient study of either. Rather, it is traced to the segregation of these subjects in coursework and a lack of modeling by music education faculty in their own teaching. The success of such an effort requires increased focus and ingenuity on the part of faculty and increased emphasis on the development of problem-solving and independent thinking skills.

Future Issues

The results of research in musical preference need greater prominence in the undergraduate teaching program. There continues to be a cultural dividing line between "school music" and the world of music beyond the classroom, namely, popular music. The Housewright Declaration, a statement on the future of music education drafted by a subcommittee of the Music Educators National Conference (2000), espouses the increased presence of popular music in American music classrooms, and warns that music teacher training must proceed accordingly by becoming more flexible in its purview of teaching competencies. The implication for pre-service music educators is that they should begin preparing now by learning to teach composition and improvisation, broadening their music vocabularies to encompass pop genres and all types of progressive music, exploring alternative notational systems, designing interdisciplinary projects, and otherwise developing their creative reasoning skills.

There appears to be increasing emphasis on the development of interpersonal skills. As mentioned above, the personal characteristics of effective teachers are well known, but those most highly valued are the ability to detect and accommodate individual learning styles in the classroom, to demonstrate superior communication skills, and to balance efficiently the use of criticism and praise. Although it has not been established how undergraduate programs might best meet this challenge, college faculty will need to utilize measures that increase the individualization of degree programs through assessment of students' interpersonal strengths and weaknesses.

Technological advancements have given rise to more affordable, portable, powerful, and user-friendly systems whose educational worth is difficult to ignore. A required course in computer proficiency for music teaching is common across the nation. Many areas of music learning have been revolutionized by the computer—most profoundly, music composition. Although it is common for instructional curricula to be designed in accordance with available software, the inverse is decidedly optimal for teachers and teaching. Computers should serve to enhance a broad understanding of music and the related arts. The issue of humanism versus technology must be mediated by music education faculty, who can demonstrate proper computer applications to the teaching and learning of music.

A view of musicianship as a world phenomenon has been recommended since the Tanglewood Symposium of 1967. Its importance in a program appears to be largely a matter of faculty expertise and/or interest, as there are no federal, state, or task force mandates for a multicultural component. It should be noted here that the National Association of Schools of Music (NASM) has requirements in this area (and others) to qualify for accreditation, but such accreditation is voluntary. Multicultural music advocates cite the abundance of accessible information, the need for exposure to the many sources of influence in popular music, and the increasingly pluralistic profile of the average American classroom as reasons for a global perspective on music-making. Critics are primarily concerned with the more practical issues of additional time allotments in an already overflowing course load, the selection of certain musics over others for study, the extent of such studies, and issues of authenticity.

Many of the reforms prescribed for undergraduate music education programs continue to involve a rethinking of balances between the musical, professional and academic components. These translate into decisions regarding classwork versus field experience, musicianship versus teacher training, and whether to emphasize educational theory over instructional practice. A common theme that appears to underlie virtually all teacher education programs is the need for pre-service teachers to develop the cognitive skills necessary to analyze and evaluate effective teaching.

Finally, contemporary conceptions of intelligence have significantly extended the forms of understanding believed to be necessary for teaching. David Elliott posits four types of knowledge—formal, informal, impressionistic, and supervisory—each distinct in its origin and usage in the teaching process. Postmodern philosophy and thinking, regarded by academic professionals as a confounding yet indispensable guiding principle, reminds those entering the teaching profession they must address the difficult questions of what constitutes quality, integrity, and relevancy in instruction as they enter a new millennium of music teacher education.

See also: ART EDUCATION.

BIBLIOGRAPHY

ELLIOTT, DAVID. 1995. *Music Matters: A New Philosophy of Music Education.* New York: Oxford University Press.

LABUTA, JOSEPH A., and SMITH, DEBORAH A. 1997. *Music Education: Historical Contexts and Perspectives.* Upper Saddle River, NJ: Prentice-Hall.

LEONHARD, CHARLES, and HOUSE, ROBERT W. 1972. *Foundations and Principles of Music Education* (1959). New York: McGraw-Hill.

MADSEN, CLIFFORD K., ed. 2000. *Vision 2020: The Housewright Symposium on the Future of Music Education.* Reston, VA: Music Educators National Conference.

MARK, MICHAEL L. 1996. *Contemporary Music Education,* 3rd edition. New York: Schirmer.

REIMER, BENNETT. 1971. "Aesthetic Behaviors in Music." In *Toward an Aesthetic Education,* ed. Bennett Reimer. Washington, DC: Music Educators National Conference.

REIMER, BENNETT. 1989. *A Philosophy of Music Education,* 2nd edition. Englewood Cliffs, NJ: Prentice-Hall.

CARLOS XAVIER RODRIGUEZ

N

NATIONAL ACADEMY OF SCIENCES

The National Academy of Sciences (NAS) is one of three honorific societies which, with the National Research Council, are grouped together under the umbrella organization called the National Academies. The other organizations include the National Academy of Engineering (established in 1964) and the Institute of Medicine (1970). Together, the National Academies institutions marshal the talent, expertise, and public spiritedness of roughly 10,000 volunteers and 1,000 staff who work together in more than 500 committees and issue about one report every working day (230 in 2001).

National Academy of Sciences History

The National Academy of Sciences (NAS) was established in 1863 by an act of Congress that was signed into law by President Abraham Lincoln. This act of incorporation, or charter, created an academy of fifty specified members, with the authority to fill membership vacancies and to create its own laws and organization. Most important, in the words of its charter, the new organization would, "whenever called upon by any department of the government, investigate, examine, experiment, and report upon any subject of science or art, the actual expense of such investigations, examinations, experiments, and reports to be paid from appropriations which may be made for the purpose, but the academy shall receive no compensation whatever for any services to the government of the United States."

The academy had several historical and national antecedents. In Europe, honorific scientific organizations such as Great Britain's Royal Society and the French Academy of Sciences had been founded as far back as the 1660s. In America, the academy's forerunners included the American Philosophical Society, formed in 1743 by Benjamin Franklin; the American Academy of Arts and Sciences, established by the Massachusetts legislature in 1780; the Columbian Institution for the Promotion of Arts and Sciences, formed in 1816; and the American Association for the Advancement of Science, founded in 1848. But with the founding of the NAS a new type of organization was created, one that combined an American equivalent to the venerable academies of sciences of Europe with a mission of providing scientific and technological advice to the government. The high honor of election to the academy was thus accompanied by an expectation of public service.

By 1916 the demand for scientific and technical advice exceeded the capacity of the small academy as the United States would soon find itself embroiled in a war and as it faced both domestic and world issues that warranted careful attention to empirical evidence, scientific knowledge, and technological know-how. President Woodrow Wilson therefore called upon the NAS to establish the National Research Council (NRC). Through this body the institution could broaden the participation of scientists, engineers, and other experts who were not elected members of the Academy; perhaps most important, it could engage the expertise of scientists and engineers in industry as well as in academic institutions, again with the principal ethos of voluntary public service.

President Wilson recognized the value of the NRC's wartime service by asking the NAS to continue the NRC as part of its peacetime organization. Accordingly, it was made permanent by Wilson's

Executive Order No. 2859 of May 11, 1918, which cited the NRC's capacity for larger service. This larger service was reflected in the NRC's postwar organizational structure, which encompassed fields outside of the traditional physical and natural sciences. Although important work in psychology had been accomplished by the NRC during World War I, this work was placed under other divisions, such as Medical Sciences, or was classified as Special Projects. By contrast, the peacetime organization provided for a Division of Anthropology and Psychology, as well as a Division of Educational Relations. The role of the latter division was to maintain relationships with university and college research activities, "and to study the conditions attending the progress of research in these institutions."

Behavioral and Social Sciences

From its creation in 1863 the academy provided a place for the behavioral and social sciences in its section of Ethnology and Philology; later its reorganization provided for a standing committee of anthropology in 1899, later renamed Anthropology and Psychology. Members included William James and John Dewey.

Among the early forays of the NRC into the behavioral and social sciences was its involvement in the famous Army Alpha testing program, during World War I, which ultimately led to the application of intelligence tests to thousands of new recruits to the armed services. Other efforts included studies of human biological and sexual function; a study of the feasibility of developing an international auxiliary language (such as Esperanto) in 1919; and studies on human migration from 1922 to 1927. As part of the work of the Committee on Industrial Lighting (1926–1936), the famous Hawthorne experiments on productivity and motivation were initially designed and carried out, as described by Rexmond C. Cochrane in *The National Academy of Sciences: The First Hundred Years 1863–1963* (1978).

In the early twenty-first century the NRC's Division of Behavioral and Social Sciences and Education produces approximately forty reports per year, in the diverse fields of economics, population, child health and development, law and justice, statistics, cognitive sciences, human factors, testing, and education.

Education

Educational issues were embedded in the Alpha testing program and work studies of the 1920s and 1930s. Other early attention to education in the academy and NRC was focused on problems of education in science—mainly at the postsecondary, graduate, and postdoctoral level. Following the founding of the NRC, the academy's concern in this area had two principal aspects: advanced training in science through a wide variety of fellowship programs, and the maintenance and publication of comprehensive data on the production of Ph.D.'s in the United States.

More recently, however, attention to education has broadened from science education to a concern for the science *of* education. Amid the cacophony of data and proposed innovations for the nation's educational system, the general public as well as policy makers at all levels of government thirst for the disciplined, honest, and dispassionate rationality of science. The federal government's major elementary and secondary education bill, known as the No Child Left Behind Act of 2001, uses the phrase "scientifically based research" more than 100 times. Growing public concern with the quality of the entire American educational enterprise, in particular with the apparent weaknesses in the elementary and secondary systems—coupled with persistent faith in Lincoln's notion of decision-making informed by rational empirical inquiry—has vastly increased the demand for science-based evidence generally, as well as for the specific consensus-seeking processes of the NRC.

The NRC's current portfolio in education—more than 150 reports since 1993 alone—has been shaped by the confluence of several powerful forces: the advent of the standards-based education movement, which involves focused attention by the science, mathematics, and other academic communities on the content appropriate and necessary for K–12 schooling; significant findings from cognitive, behavioral, and organizational research on how people learn; and increased pressure to find solutions to real-world education problems that are grounded in scientific evidence. As part of a broad reorganization undertaken in 2000, the NRC consolidated most of its education activities in the Center for Education, a unit of the Division of Behavioral and Social Sciences and Education.

Although the gap between research and practice is still formidable, there is no question that the twin goals of improved education research quality and improved use of the results of that research are prominent in the education policy agenda of the early twenty-first century. This theme—making scientific research accessible by and useful to educators at all levels—pervades much of the academies' current portfolio.

Notable Studies

Notable education studies conducted by NRC committees and boards in the decade 1992–2001 include the following, organized by major topic area.

Standards-based reform. *National Science Education Standards,* published in 1996, offers a coherent vision of what it means to be scientifically literate and describes what all students must understand and be able to do as a result of their cumulative learning experiences. The document integrates content, teaching, assessment, program, and system standards that are key to improving science education.

Inquiry and the National Science Education Standards: A Guide for Teaching and Learning (2000) is a practical guide to teaching inquiry and teaching through inquiry, as recommended in the *National Science Education Standards* (the *Standards*) by explaining and illustrating how inquiry helps students to learn science content; mastering how to do science; understanding the nature of science; exploring the dimensions of teaching; and learning science as inquiry for K–12 students across a range of science topics. This volume also examines ways that educators can offer students the opportunities to develop not only an understanding of scientific concepts, but also the ability to solve science problems through experiential learning.

Science and mathematics education. *Classroom Assessment and the National Science Education Standards* (2001) focuses on a key kind of assessment: the evaluation that occurs regularly in the classroom by the teacher and his or her students as interacting participants. Focusing on the teacher as the primary player in assessment, the book offers assessment guidelines and explores how they can be adapted to the individual classroom. It features examples, definitions, illustrative vignettes, and practical suggestions to help teachers obtain the greatest benefit from this daily evaluation and tailoring process. The volume discusses how classroom assessment differs from conventional testing and grading—and how it fits into the larger, comprehensive assessment system.

Adding It Up: Helping Children Learn Mathematics (2001) examines mathematics education in the United States from pre-kindergarten through eighth grade, discusses the ways that children learn mathematics, and characterizes effective instruction. The report also recommends ways to improve teaching, learning, and teacher education in the subject.

Teacher professional development. As a framework for addressing this task, *Educating Teachers of Science, Mathematics, and Technology: New Practices for a New Millennium,* published in 2001, advocates partnerships among school districts, colleges, and universities, with contributions from scientists, mathematicians, teacher educators, and teachers. It then looks carefully at the status of the education reform movement and explores the motives for raising the bar for how well teachers teach and how well students learn. Also examined are important issues in teacher professionalism: what teachers should be taught about their subjects, the utility of in-service education, the challenge of program funding, and the merits of credentialing. Professional Development Schools are reviewed and vignettes presented that describe exemplary teacher development practices.

The 1997 *Science Teacher Preparation in an Era of Standards-Based Reform* is a report that offers a vision of what science teacher preparation will look like in a standards-based program, and then recommends ways in which the National Science Foundation can mobilize the postsecondary education community to achieve these goals.

Reading. Large numbers of American schoolchildren have difficulty learning to read well enough to meet the growing demands of a technological society. Failure to read adequately is especially acute among poor children, minorities, and those whose native language is not English. *Preventing Reading Difficulties in Young Children* is a 1998 report that examines effective methods used to teach young children to read. It reviews relevant research on preventing reading difficulties, highlighting ways to build a learning environment that is conducive to good instruction, to proper diagnosis of problems, and to effective interventions for children at risk. The report recommends key research findings that should be integrated into reading programs for children in preschool and early elementary school, and discusses the policy implications raised by these findings.

Starting Out Right: A Guide to Promoting Children's Reading Success (1999), a guidebook for parents, teachers, and child-care providers, builds on recommendations from the 1998 report, *Preventing Reading Difficulties in Young Children*. The guide offers the key elements all children need in order to become good readers; activities that parents and others can do with children so they are prepared for reading instruction by the time they reach school; concepts about language and literacy that should be included in beginning reading instruction; and ways to prevent reading difficulties in early childhood and the early grades.

Early childhood education. *Eager to Learn: Educating Our Preschoolers* is a book about the education of children age two to five, focusing on programs outside the home, such as preschool, Head Start, and child-care centers. This report from 2000 argues that promoting young children's growth calls for early childhood settings that support the development of the full range of capacities that will serve as a foundation for school learning.

Testing and assessment. *High Stakes: Testing for Tracking, Promotion, and Graduation* (1999) reviews the legal, educational, and psychometric foundations of testing, and recommends policies and practices to promote appropriate use of tests. This book sorts out the controversies that emerge when a test score can open or close gates on a student's educational pathway. The expert panel proposes how to judge the appropriateness of a test; explores how to make tests reliable, valid, and fair; puts forward strategies and practices to promote proper test use; and recommends how decision makers in education should—and should not—use test results. The book discusses common misuses of testing, their political and social context, what happens when test issues are taken to court, special student populations, social promotion, and more.

The movement to improve schools by setting high standards for all students poses new challenges for students with disabilities, whose education is rooted in individual goals and instruction. *Educating One and All: Students with Disabilities and Standards-Based Reform* (1997) is a congressionally requested report that examines how the seemingly contradictory goals of special education and standards-based reform can be reconciled.

Education research. The 2001 report *Scientific Inquiry in Education* examines the nature of scientific research and considers the implications for a federal education research agency.

Education in the United States does not rest on a strong research base. The 1999 report *Improving Student Learning: A Strategic Plan for Education Research and Its Utilization* proposes a long-term, highly focused program of research that involves the collaboration of researchers, educators, and policy experts. The plan is designed to increase the usefulness of research to educational practice.

International studies. Video technology can help education researchers examine teaching strategies in countries around the world and create a record of classroom practices for future studies. *The Power of Video Technology in International Comparative Research in Education* (2001) discusses how such technology can best be used.

U.S. students' mathematics and science achievement often lags behind that of their peers in other developed nations, but root causes of the disparity are not always clear. Based on a comprehensive analysis of results from the Third International Mathematics and Science Study (TIMSS), the 1999 report *Global Perspectives for Local Action: Using TIMSS to Improve U.S. Mathematics and Science Education* points out how the achievement gap between U.S. students and those in several other industrialized countries can be traced to differences in teaching methods, curriculum content, and school-support systems. The report also contains practical information that American schools can use to improve local programs and student learning. In addition, a supplementary professional development guide offers materials and strategies to help educators lead workshops and planning sessions aimed at enhancing mathematics and science education in the nation's classrooms.

The Third International Mathematics and Science Study (TIMSS) has provided a remarkable volume of intriguing data about the educational performance of students around the world. However, there is a great deal of important follow-up analysis still to be done. The report, *Next Steps for TIMSS: Directions for Secondary Analysis* (1999), based in part on a workshop, summarizes recommendations regarding research strategies that could yield the understanding of student learning that TIMSS was intended to make possible.

See also: INTERNATIONAL ASSESSMENTS, *subentry on* IEA THIRD INTERNATIONAL MATHEMATICS AND SCIENCE STUDY; MATHEMATICS LEARNING; SCIENCE EDUCATION; SCIENCE LEARNING.

BIBLIOGRAPHY

AMBROSE, STEPHEN E. 1996. *Undaunted Courage: Meriwether Lewis, Thomas Jefferson, and the Opening of the American West.* New York: Simon and Schuster.

ATKIN, J. MYRON; BLACK, PAUL; and COFFEY, JANET, eds. 2001. *Classroom Assessment and the National Science Education Standards: A Guide for Teaching and Learning.* Washington, DC: National Academy Press.

BEATTY, ALEXANDRA; PAINE, LYNN W.; and RAMIREZ, FRANCISCO O., eds. 1999. *Next Steps for TIMSS: Directions for Secondary Analysis.* Washington, DC: National Academy Press.

BEATTY, ALEXANDRA, et al., eds. 2001. *Understanding Dropouts: Statistics, Strategies, and High-Stakes Testing.* Washington, DC: National Academy Press.

BOWMAN, BARBARA T.; DONOVAN, SUZANNE; and BURNS, M. SUSAN, eds. 2000. *Eager to Learn: Educating our Preschoolers.* Washington, DC: National Academy Press.

COCHRANE, REXMOND C. 1978. *The National Academy of Sciences: The First Hundred Years 1863–1963.* Washington, DC: National Academy Press.

HEUBERT, JAY PHILIP, and HAUSER, ROBERT MASON, eds. 1999. *High Stakes: Testing for Tracking, Promotion, and Graduation.* Washington, DC: National Academy Press.

KILPATRICK, JEREMY; SWAFFORD, JANE; and FINDELL, BRADFORD, eds. 2001. *Adding It Up: Helping Children Learn Mathematics.* Washington, DC: National Academy Press.

MCDONNELL, LORRAINE M.; MCLAUGHLIN, MARGARET J.; and MORISON, PATRICIA, eds. 1997. *Educating One and All: Students with Disabilities and Standards-Based Reform.* Washington, DC: National Academy Press.

NATIONAL RESEARCH COUNCIL. 1996. *National Science Education Standards.* Washington, DC: National Academy Press.

NATIONAL RESEARCH COUNCIL. 1997. *Science Teacher Preparation in an Era of Standards-Based Reform.* Washington, DC: National Academy Press.

NATIONAL RESEARCH COUNCIL. 1999a. *Global Perspectives for Local Action: Using TIMSS to Improve U.S. Mathematics and Science Education.* Washington, DC: National Academy Press.

NATIONAL RESEARCH COUNCIL. 1999b. *Improving Student Learning: A Strategic Plan for Education Research and Its Utilization.* Washington, DC: National Academy Press.

NATIONAL RESEARCH COUNCIL. 2000. *Educating Teachers of Science, Mathematics, and Technology: New Practices for a New Millennium.* Washington, DC: National Academy Press.

OLSON, STEVE, and LOUCKS-HORSLEY, SUSAN. 2000. *Inquiry and the National Science Education Standards: A Guide for Teaching and Learning.* Washington, DC: National Academy Press.

SHAVELSON, RICHARD J., and TOWNE, LISA, eds. 2001. *Scientific Inquiry in Education.* Washington, DC: National Academy Press.

SNOW, CATHERINE M.; BURNS, M. SUSAN; and GRIFFIN, PEG. 1998. *Preventing Reading Difficulties in Young Children.* Washington, DC: National Academy Press.

SNOW, CATHERINE M.; BURNS, M. SUSAN; and GRIFFIN, PEG, eds. 1999. *Starting Out Right: A Guide to Promoting Children's Reading Success.* Washington, DC: National Academy Press.

ULEWICZ, MONICA, and BEATTY, ALEXANDRA, eds. 2001. *The Power of Video Technology in International Comparative Research in Education.* Washington, DC: National Academy Press.

WIGDOR, ALEXANDRA K. and GARNER, WENDELL R., eds. 1982. *Ability Testing: Uses, Consequences, and Controversies.* Washington, DC: National Academy Press.

BRUCE ALBERTS
MICHAEL FEUER

NATIONAL ARCHIVES AND RECORDS ADMINISTRATION

The National Archives and Records Administration (NARA) was established by an act of the U.S. Congress in 1934 for the purpose of housing, protecting, and displaying the documents and records of United States history. The functions of NARA include responsibility for record retention throughout the government. NARA also provides guidance to regional records centers and depositories.

Organization

NARA includes the offices of Administrative Services, Federal Register, Washington Records Services, Regional Records Services, Presidential Libraries, and National Historical Publications and Records Commission, as well as the offices of Contractor Services, Human Resources and Information Services, Information Security, and Inspector General. The administration is headed by the Archivist of the United States, who is supported by the Deputy Archivist and Chief of Staff, and a large permanent staff working at NARA facilities around the country.

NARA operates thirty-three facilities nationwide, including the main National Archive Building on Pennsylvania Avenue in Washington, D.C., the National Archives at College Park in Maryland, and the Washington National Records Center in Suitland, Maryland. Other NARA facilities include sixteen Regional Records Services Centers, ten presidential libraries, and the National Personnel Records Center in Saint Louis, Missouri.

NARA is responsible for managing all documents generated by the executive, legislative, and judicial branches of the federal government. NARA archivists estimate that less than three percent of documents from these sources have enough historical value to warrant retention. Determining which records should be preserved is one of the administration's major responsibilities. At the beginning of the twenty-first century, the National Archives possessed over 21 million cubic feet of textual materials. The vast NARA collection also included some 300,000 reels of film, 5 million maps and charts, about 200,000 sound and video recordings, 9 million aerial photographs, and 14 million still pictures and posters.

The central National Archives Building in Washington, D.C., was constructed in the mid-1930s. The building, which is open to the public, contains a theater, a central exhibit hall that houses the Formation of the Union exhibit, and a semicircular gallery for the States of the Union exhibit.

Office of Administrative Services. In addition to administrative functions, the Office of Administrative Services directs the educational programs of the National Archives. Among these are the publication of reports, bulletins, information papers, and guides to records. In 1969 the office began publication of *Prologue,* a scholarly journal that appears four times a year. The office also manages the various exhibits and produces and sells copies of documents and photographs contained in the archives. Documents of major historical importance, such as the three

great charters—the Declaration of Independence, the Constitution of the United States, and the Bill of Rights—are available in facsimile.

Office of the Federal Register. The Office of the Federal Register is responsible for publishing *The Federal Register,* a daily newspaper that contains presidential proclamations, executive orders, and administrative regulations, orders, and notices. Once published in *The Federal Register,* an order or regulation is official and binding until later amended or rescinded. *The Federal Register* also contains descriptions of the practices and procedures of federal agencies and departments.

The Office of the Federal Register codifies and publishes all regulatory documents in the *Code of Federal Regulations.* The organization and function of government agencies and departments are described in the *United States Government Organization Manual,* published annually. White House press releases and most of the public messages and statements of the president appear in the *Weekly Compilation of Presidential Documents* and semiannual volumes of *Public Papers of the Presidents.*

Office of Records Services. The Office of Records Services is responsible for preserving government records of permanent value and for providing access to them through published guides; microfilm, facsimile, and digital reproduction; research services; and use of the National Archives library and research rooms.

The office maintains a research staff that responds to thousands of inquiries every year. Among these inquires are many from individuals seeking genealogical, citizenship, or military records. The following collections of records provide extraordinary sources of information: census schedules, naturalization records, homestead applications, immigration passenger lists for ships arriving at various Atlantic and Gulf of Mexico ports, passport applications and related papers, seamen's protection certificates, and bounty-land warrant application files. The Office of Records Services also directs the records retention program of the federal government. It assists federal agencies and department in managing their records and evaluates their records maintenance and disposition programs.

Regional Records Services centers. The regional records services facilities were established to deal with the overwhelming volume of records originating in federal offices outside of Washington, D.C., which were far too numerous to be held within the National Archives Building. A nationwide survey of federal records in the late 1930s found collections of important papers originating in the lower federal courts, in customs offices, in offices of the Immigration and Naturalization Service, and in offices of Indian Affairs and the Bureau of Public Land Management. Many of these papers are on deposit at the regional records services sites.

Office of Presidential Libraries. The presidential library system was established in 1939 when Franklin D. Roosevelt donated his personal and presidential papers and part of his estate in Hyde Park, New York, to the federal government. Harry S. Truman did the same in 1950, and in 1955 Congress passed the Presidential Libraries Act, which gave presidents the opportunity to present their personal papers to the American public and to have them administered professionally as part of the archival resources of the United States. Libraries for the collections of presidents Herbert Hoover, Franklin D. Roosevelt, Harry S Truman, Dwight D. Eisenhower, John F. Kennedy, Lyndon B. Johnson, Jimmy Carter, George Bush, and Ronald Reagan were subsequently established. The William Jefferson Clinton Library was scheduled to open in 2006.

Presidential libraries function as repositories for preserving the papers, records, photographs, films, and other historical materials of U.S. presidents. Each library also includes a museum with exhibits about the life and times of the president. Most of the libraries offer tours, a series of public programs, and resources to aid researchers. The presidential libraries contain not only official materials, but also personal correspondence, diaries, and other records of the president's appointees and associates. These collections, along with related audiovisual materials, are identified by the name of the donor and are arranged, described, and preserved by archivists. The Presidential Libraries Act recognized the right of a donor to place restrictions on the use of his papers, for example, withholding for a period of years information relating to national security or personal family matters.

National Historical Publications and Records Commission. The National Historical Publications and Records Commission (NHPRC) was established by Congress in 1934; it is affiliated with the National Archives and Records Administration and chaired by the Archivist of the United States. The mission of the NHPRC is to encourage and fund programs to preserve, publish, and use archival materials relating to U.S. history. The NHPRC makes grants to state archives, local archives, colleges and universities, libraries, museums, historical societies, and other nonprofit organizations to help identify, preserve, and provide public access to important historical materials. Through grants, fellowships, publications, training programs, and special projects the commission offers assistance and funding to individuals and groups committed to preserving America's documentary resources.

National Archives Exhibits

The main exhibit hall of the National Archives Building houses the three great charters of American freedom—the Declaration of Independence, the Constitution of the United States, and the Bill of Rights. Until 1952, when the Constitution and the Bill of Rights were transferred to the National Archives, they were moved from place to place, chiefly in the charge of the State Department. Despite these moves, they are still in good condition. The Declaration of Independence was moved more often and treated with less care; consequently, its condition has been impaired. All three documents are now protected from further deterioration. The Formation of the Union exhibit consists of the three great charters and approximately 50 other important historical documents, all on permanent display. The States of the Union exhibit displays federal documents pertaining to the histories of the fifty states.

A fireproof, bombproof vault with a protective lid fifteen inches thick lies twenty feet below the floor of the exhibition hall. The three great charters can be lowered into the vault and the lid closed by an electrically powered mechanism. When the documents are not on display, they are housed in this vault, and in an emergency they can be lowered to safety there in less than a minute.

The exhibit hall and galleries of the National Archives Building in Washington, D.C., were closed for renovation in the early 2000s. While closed, some of the documents usually displayed there were sent to museums and libraries across the country as part of a traveling exhibit called *American Originals.*

Electronic Access Project

In the mid 1990s NARA launched the Electronic Access Project, which enables anyone with a computer and an Internet connection to access the holdings of the National Archives. NARA's Archival Information Locator (NAIL) is a searchable database containing information about thousands of archival holdings, as well as digital copies of approximately 125,000 of the archive's most popular and historically significant documents, photographs, and sound recordings. By 2001 NAIL offered access to only a small portion of NARA's vast holdings, but the project was ongoing and more records were being added to the live database daily.

NARA also produced an Online Exhibit Hall, which features digital copies of the documents displayed in the actual exhibit hall at Washington's National Archives Building. The Online Exhibit Hall also presents special educational exhibits featuring documents and still photographs from the NARA collection. Online exhibits have included *Powers of Persuasion: Posters From World War II; Portraits of Black Chicago; When Nixon Met Elvis;* and *Tokens and Treasure: Gifts Given to the Presidents.*

NARA's Digital Classroom features reproducible copies of primary documents from the holdings of the National Archives, as well as suggestions and activities for using these materials in the classroom. The NARA publication *Teaching With Documents* was designed to help teachers and students use primary documents effectively in their instruction and research.

BIBLIOGRAPHY

BREDHOFF, STACEY. 2001. *American Originals.* Washington, DC, and Seattle, WA: National Archives and Records Administration and Washington University Press.

BUSTARD, BRUCE. 1999. *Picturing the Century: One Hundred Years of Photography from the National Archives.* Washington, DC, and Seattle, WA: National Archives and Records Administration and Washington University Press.

NATIONAL ARCHIVES AND RECORDS ADMINISTRATION AND NATIONAL COUNCIL FOR THE SOCIAL STUDIES. 1990. *Teaching With Documents: Using Primary Sources from the National Archives.* Washington, DC: National Archives and Records Administration and National Council for the Social Studies.

INTERNET RESOURCE

NATIONAL ARCHIVES AND RECORDS ADMINISTRATION. 2002. <www.nara.gov>.

FRANK G. BURKE
Revised by
JUDITH J. CULLIGAN

NATIONAL ART EDUCATION ASSOCIATION

The National Art Education Association (NAEA) is a nonprofit professional association of art teachers and other people dedicated to the advancement of art in education and national life. The mission of the association is to promote the study of art at all levels of education; to encourage research and experimentation in art; to convince local, state, and federal government officials of the importance of art education; and to improve the status, working conditions, and skill levels of art teachers. The association seeks especially to improve the quality of art education in elementary and secondary schools and in college-level teacher education programs. The NAEA espouses the view that education through art is the means by which individuals realize their creative powers and that the promotion of aesthetic growth is the principal means by which quality art instruction is realized.

Program

The NAEA's goal of promoting the knowledge and skill level of art teachers is accomplished through the association's publications program and through its annual national convention, which feature hundreds workshops, panels, research presentations, addresses, and exhibits. The NAEA's regional groups conduct biennial conferences, where members can engage in direct discussion of problems and exchange ideas and research in the field of art education. In addition, the NAEA sponsors periodic national and international conferences on specific concerns in art education, such as curriculum and instructional development and the uses of new media and technologies.

The NAEA maintains contact with other education groups, such as American Association of School Administrators and the Association for Childhood Education International, in order to communicate the values and beliefs of art educators to those responsible for the administration and supervision of school art programs. The NAEA also engages in consultative activities and works closely with many organizations in the development of art publications for broad dissemination in the field.

In order to effect a favorable climate of opinion toward art in the community-at-large, the NAEA maintains liaison with organizations concerned with the broad promotion of the arts in society. In past years, the NAEA has contributed testimony on federal art legislation before committees of the U.S. Congress. The NAEA also engages in cooperative projects with state arts councils, state teachers associations, and other private organizations and governmental agencies with an interest in the arts.

The NAEA publishes two major periodicals: *Art Education* and *Studies in Art Education*. The bimonthly *Art Education* features articles exploring current views on theory and practice in art education, as well as curriculum and teaching strategies for studio arts, art criticism, or art history courses. Each issue includes four full-color art reproductions, with accompanying commentary and lesson suggestions, to be used in elementary and high school art classes. The quarterly *Studies in Art Education* covers issues and research in art education and is directed toward advanced researchers and scholars. *NAEA News,* published six times per year in alternating months with *Art Education,* details the activities of the association at both the national and regional level, and offers book reviews and information about grants and federal initiatives in art education and arts funding.

The NAEA also publishes monographs, books, and pamphlets on topics related to art curricula, instructional media, professional goals, and research. Many NAEA pamphlets are designed to communicate the value of art education to parents, school administrators, government officials, and others outside the field of art education. Other publications promulgate NAEA-devised guidelines for the safe use of art supplies and materials in the classroom and NAEA standards for art education programs. The association also publishes selected bibliographies and information on careers in art.

The NAEA gives out numerous national and regional awards during the year, most at its annual convention. Major annual NAEA awards include the Manual Barkan Memorial Award, the Lowenfeld

Award, the Marion Quin Dix Leadership Award, and the J. Eugene Grigsby Jr. Award. Each year the NAEA awards the Charles M. Robertson Memorial Scholarship to a high school student who has excelled in the arts. This four-year scholarship allows the student to attend the Pratt School of Art and Design in New York. Further grants available to NAEA members are awarded by the association's sister organization, the National Art Education Foundation.

In 1978 the NAEA established the National Art Honor Society to inspire and recognize outstanding art students in grades ten through twelve. The NAEA expanded this program in 1989 to include students in grades seven through nine in the hope of generating an early interest in art in younger students.

Organizational Structure

The NAEA is composed of six divisions representing particular areas of interest: elementary education, middle school education, secondary education, higher education, museum education, and supervision and administration. The national organization is also divided into four regional divisions: Eastern, Pacific, Southeastern, and Western.

The NAEA is governed by a board of directors that includes an executive committee lead by a president, a past president, and a president-elect. The board is advised by the officers of the four regional and six area divisions, and by three student chapter officers. The leadership of the regional divisions include a president, past president, president-elect, and one delegate from each state within the boundaries set for the region.

Membership and Financial Support

NAEA members come from each of the fifty states, the District of Columbia, most Canadian provinces, Guam, Puerto Rico, U.S. military bases around the world, and some foreign countries. All individuals who are directly or indirectly involved in art education are eligible for membership. The association maintains seven categories of membership: active, associate, student, institutional, life, patron, and honorary.

In 2001 NAEA had approximately 17,000 members representing every level of education from early preschool art programs to university degree programs, although most members teach in elementary and secondary schools. Not all NAEA members are art teachers, however; some work for publishers of art books and magazines, art supply manufacturers, museums, and other types of art-related organizations. Many members are students currently enrolled in art teacher education programs in U.S. universities. The NAEA is financed through membership dues, sales of publications, exhibit services, and grants from public, private, and corporate donors.

History and Development

Historic antecedents to the present NAEA are the art department of the National Education Association and four regional art associations—the Western Arts Association, the Pacific Arts Association, the Southeastern Arts Association, and the Eastern Arts Association. The first National Education Association department of art education was established in 1890 but was short-lived. In 1947 the four regional art associations merged under a single constitution to form the NAEA, which then became officially the Art Education Department of the National Education Association.

BIBLIOGRAPHY

MICHAEL, JOHN A., ed. 1998. *The National Art Education Association: Our History, Celebrating 50 Years 1947–1997.* Reston, VA: National Art Education Association.

INTERNET RESOURCE

NATIONAL ART EDUCATION ASSOCIATION. 2002. <www.naea-reston.org>.

CHARLES M. DORN
Revised by
JUDITH J. CULLIGAN

NATIONAL ASSESSMENT OF EDUCATIONAL PROGRESS

See: ASSESSMENT, *subentry on* NATIONAL ASSESSMENT OF EDUCATIONAL PROGRESS.

NATIONAL ASSOCIATION FOR THE EDUCATION OF YOUNG CHILDREN

The National Association for the Education of Young Children (NAEYC) is a nonprofit organization of early childhood professionals and others who are dedicated to improving the quality of early childhood education. More than 100,000 members strong, the association comprises a network of more than 400 affiliated local, state, and regional organizations, which share the belief that children's high-quality experiences at home and in child care, schools, and after-school programs lay the foundation for school readiness, academic success, and adult achievement.

Since its founding in 1926, NAEYC has promoted a vision of excellence in early childhood education that focuses on supporting the rights and needs of children. The association works with parents, teachers, business leaders, and policymakers to bring high-quality early education and care to all young children, from birth through age eight. NAEYC is best known for raising the quality of child care and other early learning programs. The association's voluntary national accreditation system helps improve early childhood education and recognizes high-quality programs so that parents and other decision makers can make informed choices. Its position statements, which are informed by research and practice, have addressed a wide range of topics: for example, developmentally appropriate teaching practices; the teaching of reading, writing, and mathematics in the early years; program licensing to ensure health and safety in child care settings; the role of early childhood professionals in preventing child abuse and neglect; and the support of diverse families.

NAEYC focuses on professional preparation, resources, and training for individuals who educate children birth through age eight. Working with higher education institutions to set standards for preparing teachers, NAEYC provides guidelines for appropriate teaching strategies, curriculum, and assessments for children in preschool through third grade. NAEYC promotes comprehensive training opportunities, high professional standards, and equitable compensation and working conditions so that qualified early childhood educators will stay and grow in the early childhood profession. The NAEYC annual conference is one of the largest educational meetings in the nation, bringing together 25,000 people each year for more than 1,000 seminars, workshops and other professional development opportunities.

NAEYC is a leading publisher and distributor of a wide range of books, videos, and other professional resources to help early childhood teachers and other professionals improve their knowledge and skills. NAEYC also publishes *Young Children,* an award-winning journal that combines the latest in early childhood research, theory and practice, with a readership of more than 250,000. The association also publishes the highly respected *Early Childhood Research Quarterly.*

To increase understanding and support for high-quality early childhood education. NAEYC works among policymakers and the public through its education, advocacy, and public awareness activities. NAEYC also sponsors the Week of the Young Child each spring to focus public attention on the rights and needs of young children.

A board of directors elected by the membership governs the association, and the executive director, responsible for the association's administration and management, sits on the board as an ex officio member. NAEYC is a private membership organization, supported primarily through fees for products and services. The association also accepts philanthropic support for projects that are aligned with its mission and goals and that further its strategic objectives.

In 1926 Patty Smith Hill and Lois Meek Stolz founded the NAEYC's precursor, National Association for Nursery Education, out of their concern about the proliferation of educational programs for preschool children staffed by individuals without adequate knowledge about child development and effective strategies for teaching young children. NANE was maintained primarily through the efforts of stalwart volunteers, who believed deeply in the association's mission. In the early 1960s a headquarters office was established in Washington, D.C., when the association was reorganized as the National Association for the Education of Young Children. The naming of a full-time executive director in the mid-1960s coincided with the creation of the federal Head Start program, designed to provide educational and social enrichment to preschool children living in poverty. Head Start not only focused public attention on the importance of early education, but also nurtured the early childhood profession by providing numerous opportunities for careers in teaching, program administration, and professional preparation and development.

NAEYC continued to grow in size and scope in the 1970s and 1980s, reaching a membership of 45,000 by 1985. That year, the Association created

the National Academy of Early Childhood Programs to accredit child-care centers, preschools, kindergartens, and before-school and after-school programs, again responding to the tremendous growth in the number of children attending preschool and child-care programs. Between 1985 and 2001, the association's membership climbed to more than 100,000, as more than 8,000 early childhood programs achieved accreditation and thousands more enrolled in the process.

By 2001, NAEYC completed major restructuring efforts to revitalize its membership and affiliate structure and to reinvent its accreditation process to meet the challenges of successful growth. In the early twenty-first century, NAEYC is poised for continued growth and success in promoting excellence in early childhood education for all young children and their families.

See also: EARLY CHILDHOOD EDUCATION.

BIBLIOGRAPHY

SMITH, MARILYN M., ed. 2001. *NAEYC at 75: Reflections of the Past; Challenges for the Future.* Washington, DC: National Association for the Education of Young Children.

INTERNET RESOURCE

NATIONAL ASSOCIATION FOR THE EDUCATION OF YOUNG CHILDREN. 2002. <www.naeyc.org>.

BARBARA WILLER

NATIONAL ASSOCIATION OF BIOLOGY TEACHERS

The National Association of Biology Teachers (NABT) is the only national association specifically organized to help educators at all levels improve the teaching of biology and life sciences. The purposes of the NABT are exclusively scientific, educational, literary, and charitable. Constitutionally, its objectives are to plan and administer projects for the advancement and utilization of knowledge in biology education; to make available to teachers information concerning the selection, organization, and presentation of biological materials in the classroom; to encourage research in biology education; and to promote understanding of the interrelationships between biology and society, ethics, and the other sciences.

Program

Since its formation in 1938 the NABT has concerned itself with an evolving series of issues facing educators of biology and life sciences. Early in its history the association recognized the need for improved conservation education in secondary schools. Later, the NABT promulgated strong positions on the ethical use of animals in the biology classroom. During the 1990s and early 2000s the NABT emphasized the importance of teaching evolutionary theory, the role of biology education in the prevention of HIV/AIDS, and the need to address the impact of global climate change, population growth, and genetic technology. The NABT encourages biology teachers to study such issues, and offers teachers resources for presenting these topics clearly and accurately in the classroom.

The association has also focused its attention on the plight of teachers who are concerned about the social implications of certain subjects pursued in their classrooms. Teachers react differently to controversial issues, depending on their own personalities and backgrounds, the mores of the local community, and the relative authoritarian nature of their school administrators. The NABT believes that biological concepts and discoveries have important implications for society, and the organization fights for the right of teachers to introduce students to these implications.

In 1962 the NABT initiated the nationwide Outstanding Biology Teacher Award program, which recognizes exceptional teachers working with seventh- through twelfth-grade students; one teacher is chosen from each of the fifty states, the District of Columbia, Puerto Rico, and Guam. This award represents the NABT's attempt to recognize and call attention to outstanding performance in the classroom. The Outstanding New Biology Teacher Achievement Award recognizes an educator who has been teaching for fewer than three years. The NABT also presents an annual Evolution Education Award to honor an educator who has made an outstanding effort to promote the accurate understanding of evolution in the community and the classroom. Other annual NABT awards include the Award for Excellence in Encouraging Equity, the Biotechnology Teaching Award, and the Distinguished Service Award.

The *American Biology Teacher,* published nine times per year, is the official journal of the NABT. It features ideas for biology projects, classroom demonstrations, and science experiments; editorials and book reviews; and articles discussing advances in the life sciences and the social and ethical issues of modern biology. NABT *News and Views,* published four times a year, is the newsletter of the association. It features articles of interest to active members and carries information about NABT programs and events, as well as teaching resources, professional opportunities, and activities of the organization's board, committees, and sections. The NABT also publishes numerous books about issues in biology education, and produces useful online resources for the teacher. The website *Biotechnology on a Shoestring* helps biology teachers in high schools and two-year colleges provide to high quality instruction on a limited budget. The NABT joined forced with the American Society for Microbiology to produce the *Microbial Literacy Collaborative,* a program to foster awareness of the world of microbiology through radio programs, books, and websites.

The NABT holds a national conventional each year and also sponsors one or more regional conferences. Thousands of educators attended the 2001 NABT convention, which featured 350 presentations and 140 exhibits. NABT also sponsors frequent seminars and workshops to improve and update biology teachers' knowledge of content and techniques.

Organizational Structure

The NABT is divided into six sections: elementary/middle school, two-year college, four-year college, multicultural affairs, the role and status of women in biology education, and retired members. Each section is responsible for developing programs in its area. The NABT is governed by a 25-member board of directors. An executive committee transacts business of the association between meetings of the board. A full-time headquarters staff manages the daily administration of the association and implements the policies set by the board of directors.

Membership and Financial Support

Membership in NABT is available to anyone expressing an interest in biological education. There are eight classes of membership: active, student, comprehensive, foreign, spouse, organizational, sustaining, and life. The dues differ with membership class. In 2001 the NABT's total membership exceeded 9,000. Dues and subscriptions accounted for most of the association's annual income. Private and institutional donations, advertising in the journal, and convention fees provided the rest.

INTERNET RESOURCE

NATIONAL ASSOCIATION OF BIOLOGY TEACHERS. 2002. <www.nabt.org>.

JERRY P. LIGHTNER
Revised by
JUDITH J. CULLIGAN

NATIONAL ASSOCIATION OF ELEMENTARY SCHOOL PRINCIPALS

The National Association of Elementary School Principals (NAESP) is a professional association dedicated to the professional development of principals serving grades kindergarten through eight. In addition, it seeks to provide a unified voice for its members in local, state, and national policy debates on issues affecting education and school administration. Finally, it seeks to make available resources and other forms of professional support to its members, with the aim of developing high standards of conduct and preparation within the profession.

Program

The association carries out its mission in three general spheres of activity. First among these is a series of newsletters. The official newsletter for the organization is the *Principal,* a magazine published bimonthly throughout the school year. Every issue is usually dedicated to a particular theme of interest to members of the profession. Recent issues have been devoted to such topics as the debate on establishing national curriculum standards, career development for veteran teachers, and children's health and safety in the schools. In addition to the magazine, the organization also publishes a number of newsletters devoted to special topics, including *Commentator,* which reports on policies and association news and events. Another newsletter, *Here's How,* offers practical solutions to common problems faced by elementary school administrators. Other special-

interest publications include *Streamlined Seminar* and *Research Roundup,* both of which present the results of recent research in school administration topics; *Middle Matters,* aimed specifically at principals serving in the nation's middle schools; and *Student News Today,* which focuses on working with student councils and other student organizations.

The national organization is also committed to working closely with local and regional associations, and the primary means of accomplishing this is through its field services program. Association members are available as speakers and consultants who can advise interested groups about school administration issues and about projects and programs that show promise in helping to strengthen schools. In addition, the NAESP provides a number of direct-to-members services, such as legal assistance for job-related concerns, both in the area of professional liability and for job-protection suits. It also offers access to a wide variety of educational resources at reduced cost.

The most important event on the NAESP annual calendar is the professional conference hosted by the association each year. In addition to seminars, panel discussions, and workshops, the annual conference provides members with an opportunity to raise their particular professional concerns with the governing board, to network with their peers, and to seek new employment opportunities. The association also sponsors smaller summer conferences in cooperation with other national educational organizations.

Organization

The NAESP is an autonomous organization with strong ties to the National Education Association (NEA). Its basic governing body is the delegate assembly, whose members are chosen by the individual state associations. This assembly meets annually during the convention and is responsible for establishing policy and responding to the concerns raised by the general membership. A smaller, fifteen-member board of directors is selected by the assembly and consists of three officers, nine regional representatives, a member representing ethnic minorities, a representative of middle school principals, and an executive director. The board appoints the various committees that help in carrying out NAESP business, including a nominating committee charged with selecting the next year's candidates for office and a publications committee, which works closely with the NAESP's full-time editorial staff. The executive director, supported by a professional staff, oversees the day-to-day operation of the association at the national headquarters.

Membership and Financial Support

The NAESP has several different categories of membership. At the heart of the organization are the active members who are all professionally engaged in the administration of elementary schools. Associate membership is available to faculty at universities and colleges who share the NAESP's interests but who are not themselves principals or vice principals. A growing membership category is the international associates, made up of principals, headmasters, and other elementary school administrators from outside the United States. The NAESP has in the late twentieth and early twenty-first century become increasingly interested in exploring strategies and policies that have worked well in school programs outside of the United States, with the hope that some may provide useful new insights in addressing local needs and problems. A final membership category comprises aspiring principals: teachers, students, and others who hope to become administrators in elementary and middle schools. Institutional and library memberships are also available.

The NAESP gains much of its operating revenues through its membership dues and through the sale of publications, resource kits, and other services. These funds are supplemented by support from a number of corporate and private donors, who contribute funds toward NAESP-sponsored awards programs. In addition, the association has forged a number of partnerships with corporations that offer services and resources, such as retirement plans or educational and administrative resources.

History

While taking a summer school course in school administration offered by the University of Chicago, a group of principals got together to discuss the possible usefulness of organizing a formal association that would directly address their special interests. At the end of the course, each of these principals returned to their home districts and began raising support for the plan, so that by the convocation of the 1921 annual convention of the NEA, there were fifty-one willing recruits. They drafted a mission statement, bylaws, and a constitution, thus forming the National Association of Elementary School Principals, and

were duly recognized by the NEA as an independent department of that organization.

The publication division of the NAESP was quickly launched, beginning with a bulletin that laid out the organization's goals and principles, followed by the publication of a yearbook, which contained articles on professional responsibility and leadership. The close association of the NAESP with the NEA continued over the next several decades.

By 1931 the NAESP had grown so much that it was granted permanent headquarters within the NEA offices in Washington, D.C. With this improvement in facilities, the publications division enjoyed a period of expansion as well, and the *National Elementary Principal* was launched. This publication, initially a newsletter, would eventually become the *Principal* magazine. The NAESP also began to move beyond its early focus on defining the administrator's role and status to include a consideration of related issues, such as community relations, controversies in educational standards and approaches, and other topics. Toward the end of the 1930s the organization began to offer additional services, notably a two-week summer workshop dedicated to enhancing professional skills.

In the 1950s the NAESP had grown substantially, and it was finally able to assert its independence from the NEA. Although it has always maintained a close professional cooperation with that organization, independence was important for it allowed the organization to devote all of its time exclusively to furthering the interests of its members. The organization continued to press for professional recognition, to advocate improvements in salary and working conditions, and to provide resources and support services to its members. In the 1980s and 1990s the NAESP focused on outreach to corporate, public, and private organizations to further the association's goals. The national organization remained housed within the NEA headquarters, however, until the 1990s, when it finally established its own independent offices.

See also: PRINCIPAL, SCHOOL.

INTERNET RESOURCE

NATIONAL ASSOCIATION OF ELEMENTARY SCHOOL PRINCIPALS. 2002. <www.naesp.org>.

WILLIAM L. PHARIS
Revised by
NANCY E. GRATTON

NATIONAL ASSOCIATION OF INDEPENDENT COLLEGES AND UNIVERSITIES

The National Association of Independent Colleges and Universities (NAICU) is a Washington, D.C.-based umbrella association comprising more than 900 private nonprofit colleges, universities, and associations. The association's purpose is to further the cause of its membership by representing the accomplishments and interests of independent higher education. To accomplish its aims, the NAICU staff represents private higher education to government officials, follows campus trends, conducts research, publishes newsletters and research results, issues papers, and coordinates a variety of nonprofit association activities at the national and state levels.

Activities and Membership

The association's major policy thrusts relate to student aid, taxation, and government regulation. Among the organization's projects has been leadership in the organization of the Student Aid Alliance, a grassroots effort aimed at substantially increasing funding for student aid programs in the federal budget. NAICU has led the effort during congressional election years to encourage member institutions to conduct on-campus nonpartisan voter registration drives through its National Campus Voter Registration project. NAICU is a participating member of the Big Six, an informal group of chief executive officers of the major higher education associations in Washington, who meet regularly to discuss common interests and develop collaborative approaches to lobby the federal government. The organization is represented in the deliberations of the six major Washington higher education associations' federal relations officers meetings, and it participates in the Secretariat, a body of forty associations representing postsecondary institutions that meets monthly to discuss events, activities, and mutual interests.

The NAICU's diverse membership includes liberal arts colleges, research universities, church-related institutions, historically black colleges and universities, women's colleges, performing and visual arts institutions, community colleges, and professional schools such as medicine and engineering.

The NAICU's activities include leadership of a secretariat whose membership is composed of the chief executive officers of national, regional, and other special purpose associations of independent colleges and universities, such as Associated Colleges of the South, Accrediting Association of Bible Colleges, and Association of Independent Colleges of Art and Design. In addition, NAICU collaborates with the Foundation for Independent Higher Education (FIHE) and the Council of Independent Colleges (CIC) to further the aims of independent higher education.

History

The National Association of Independent Colleges and Universities began as the Association of American Colleges (AAC) in 1916, an organization of denominational and independent colleges. AAC's founders were determined to counter charges that there was an oversupply of liberal arts colleges and to help withstand the threatening competition of state institutions.

AAC members had a long history of opposing government interference and, as late as 1963, were opposed to any federal aid to institutions of higher education. AAC suffered from a deep internal division. On the one hand AAC was the chief association advocate for the liberal arts, which meant that the organization included in its membership public institutions and large universities with liberal arts interests as well as small independent colleges, and the small independent colleges felt that they were not adequately represented. To remedy this the Federation of State Associations of Independent Colleges and Universities (FSAICU) was organized within AAC in the late 1960s as a coordinating agency for independent institutions. In a move to expand policy activity, FSAICU was reorganized in 1971 to become the National Council of Independent Colleges and Universities (NCICU), complete with a board independent of AAC and a full-time director of public affairs. The liberal arts versus independent college perspectives continued to divide AAC, and in 1975 an AAC study recommended that a completely separate organization be created to represent the interests of independent colleges and universities. In 1976 NCICU was disbanded and the National Association of Independent Colleges and Universities was formed, leaving the AAC free to pursue its continuing interest in liberal education. Later the AAC evolved to become the Association of American Colleges and Universities (AAC&U).

Because of its diverse membership, the problem of balance was particularly acute for NAICU. Thus, in the beginning, some NAICU members thought that there was an overrepresentation of presidents of large universities, such as Johns Hopkins and Stanford, on the board, when the membership was composed primarily of institutions with less than 2,500 students. However, NAICU worked at providing fair and equitable representation on its boards and became the peak organization for the large and diverse population of private colleges and universities in the United States, combining an active involvement in lobbying with the provision of a wide range of services to its membership, to government, and to the public.

BIBLIOGRAPHY

BLOLAND, HARLAND G. 1985. *Associations in Action: The Washington, D.C. Higher Education Community.* Washington, DC: Association for the Study of Higher Education.

HAWKINS, HUGH. 1992. *Banding Together: The Rise of National Associations in American Higher Education.* Baltimore: Johns Hopkins University Press.

INTERNET RESOURCE

NATIONAL ASSOCIATION OF INDEPENDENT COLLEGES AND UNIVERSITIES. 2002. <www.naicu.edu>.

HARLAND G. BLOLAND

NATIONAL ASSOCIATION OF INDEPENDENT SCHOOLS

The National Association of Independent Schools (NAIS) is an organization of independent elementary, middle, and secondary schools, as well as regional and local associations representing such schools. Sometimes called private schools, independent schools are nonprofit; supported by nonpublic funds such as tuition, charitable contributions, and endowments rather than tax or church funds; and governed by boards of trustees. Although independent schools must conform to state compulsory attendance laws, they have considerable freedom in setting standards, in developing curriculum, in admitting students, and in hiring teachers.

Program

The main responsibility of the NAIS is to represent member schools to the media, the general public, the U.S. Department of Education, and state and federal agencies and congressional committees that monitor and regulate education in the United States. The attitude of the state and federal governments toward independent schools and laws affecting them are of major concern to the association, which follows federal legislation closely and interprets relevant legislative action to its members.

The NAIS is also concerned with improving the quality of instruction in member schools. To this end, the association sponsors two annual conferences and periodic workshops and seminars, which provide a forum for teachers and administrators to share experiences and exchange ideas. The annual NAIS general conference draws some 4,000 administrators and teachers every year. The association's annual People of Color conference addresses issues of equity in schools and helps members learn how to build school communities that serve all students regardless of ethnicity, economic background, religious affiliation, physical disability, or sexual orientation. Many NAIS programs emphasize the importance of in-service training, refresher courses, and summer travel as part of the necessary, continuing development of teachers. The association also holds seminars on financial planning and advises member schools on fund-raising and business management.

NAIS committees, composed of faculty from member schools, have developed resources for mathematics, science, languages, social studies, art, and music curricula, as well as for the use of new media and computer technologies. The association's publications include the *Independent School Bulletin*, published three times per year, and various books, reports, and newsletters addressing topics of interest to the faculty and administration of independent schools. NAIS also releases publications aimed at independent school students and parents whose children attend independent schools.

One of the association's main concerns is the affordability of independent schools. To this end, the NAIS publishes numerous guides that describe financial aid opportunities and other ways by which parents can finance their child's education in an independent school. The NAIS also owns and operates the School and Student Service for Financial Aid, which processes financial aid applications for member schools.

Organizational Structure

The association's governing body is its twenty-six-member board of directors. Half of the board members are selected by national vote at the annual meeting, and half are appointed to represent geographic regions in the United States. Board members serve four-year terms. The board appoints the NAIS president, who oversees association business with the aid of a small staff. The president and board are also responsible for preparing and promulgating official public policy statements regarding legislation, regulations, and other issues.

Membership and Financial Support

More than 1,100 day schools and boarding schools held membership in NAIS in 2001, representing a total of 472,967 students and 48,385 teachers and school staff. Approximately 9 percent of member institutions were girls' schools; 8 percent were boys' schools. The remaining member schools were coeducational. Member schools ranged in size from several dozen students to several thousand and were located across the United States, Canada, Europe, and Asia in cities, small communities, and rural areas. All schools accepted for membership to NAIS must be nondiscriminatory in admission and employment, and they must demonstrate responsible management and sound fiscal practices.

There are three types of NAIS membership: active, affiliate, and new school. To qualify for active membership, a school must be located in the United States, be at least five years old, and have been recently accredited by a regional association of colleges and secondary schools or by a state department of education. Independent schools located outside the United States may qualify for affiliate membership if they have been in operation at least five years. Newly established schools may apply for new school membership with their status changing to affiliate or active after five years of operation and accreditation. Local, state, or regional associations of independent schools may also join the NAIS as nonvoting members.

Most of the association's income is from membership dues, sale of publications, and advertisements in the *Independent School Bulletin*. Some income is received from private donors and from foundation grants for special projects.

History

The NAIS was organized in 1962, the result of the merger of the Independent Schools Education Board and the National Council of Independent Schools. The Independent Schools Education Board was started in 1924 to establish uniform entrance requirements for boys' boarding schools; it gradually added service functions, including publication of the bulletin. The National Council of Independent Schools was formed in 1940 to provide liaison between the government and independent schools. Since the merger, the number of NAIS members has grown, and the association is recognized as the national spokesperson for independent schools.

BIBLIOGRAPHY

GRACE, CATHERINE O'NEILL. 2001. *Marketing Independent Schools in the Twenty-First Century.* Washington, DC: National Association of Independent Schools.

INTERNET RESOURCE

NATIONAL ASSOCIATION OF INDEPENDENT SCHOOLS. 2002. <www.nais.org>.

FRANCIS PARKMAN
Revised by
JUDITH J. CULLIGAN

NATIONAL ASSOCIATION OF SCHOOLS OF ART AND DESIGN

The National Association of Schools of Art (NASAD) is composed of schools, organizations, and individuals, representing the highest traditions and aims in the education of the artists and designers. NASAD is a voluntary, nonprofit agency with every major center of art education activity embodied in its membership. NASAD gives equal concern to each of the various visual arts. The association is recognized by the U.S. Department of Education and the Council for Higher Education Accreditation as the accrediting agency for college-level programs in art and design.

The aims and objectives of the association are to do the following:

1. Evaluate, through the processes of accreditation, schools of art and programs of studio art instruction—particularly those schools preparing students for careers in art—in terms of the quality of their instruction and the results achieved, as judged by experienced examiners.

2. Establish a national forum to stimulate the understanding and acceptance of the educational disciplines inherent in the creative arts in U.S. higher education.

3. Establish reasonable standards where quantitative measurements have validity, as in matters of budget, faculty qualifications, faculty–student ratios, and library and physical facilities.

4. Encourage varied and experimental approaches to the teaching of art and design, in the knowledge that creativity implies nonconformity and that values in art can be identified only in an appropriate context.

5. Assure students and parents that accredited art programs provide competent teachers, adequate facilities and equipment, and sound curricula and that these programs are capable of attaining their stated objectives.

6. Counsel and assist schools in developing instruction of the highest quality and to encourage self-evaluation and continuing improvement.

7. Invite and encourage the cooperation of professional art and design groups in the formulation of appropriate curricula and standards for the respective professions.

Program

The major responsibility of NASAD is the accreditation of U.S. higher educational programs in art and design. NASAD also sets guidelines and standards for graduate and undergraduate degrees in art and design, as well as certificate and credentialing programs for professional artists and designers. In addition, NASAD maintains a list of artists, designers, art teachers, and arts executives and professionals who are willing to serve as consultants. NASAD consultants help institutions with such issues as applications for new accreditation and re-accreditation, curriculum and institutional development, facility and equipment review, and state reviews. Many NASAD consultants are also available for speaking engagements on topics of concern to the art and design community.

NASAD also publishes books, reports, and pamphlets that outline accreditation requirements and procedures, describe research in art and design, record and evaluate statistics, and discuss issues and policies of concern to art students and art educators. The organization's major publications include the *NASAD Directory* and the *NASAD Handbook,* both published annually.

Representatives of member schools assemble annually for a conference on problems of mutual concern regarding the education of the artist and designer, and for an exchange of ideas concerning improvements in education processes. Prominent scholars and creative artists are regularly invited to participate in the program, and meetings are also open to individuals from nonmember institutions and allied fields.

NASAD participates in the Higher Education Arts Data Services (HEADS) Project along with the National Association of Schools of Music, the National Association of Schools of Theatre, and the National Association of Schools of Dance. Begun in 1982, the HEADS Project collects, compiles, evaluates, and publishes statistics from member and nonmember institutions with the goal of providing comprehensive management data on the arts in higher education. All NASAD member institutions must participation in the HEADS Project.

Organizational Structure

NASAD had 236 institutional members in 2001. The board of directors, elected by the membership, meets regularly during the year and is responsible for the proper conduct of association business. In addition to a commission on accreditation, standing committees of the board are maintained for membership, rules, program, research and development, public relations, nominations, and fellows and citations. Appointed representatives serve as liaison members with regional accrediting associations. There are no regional, state, or local units of the association.

Membership and Financial Support

The association offers both individual membership and accredited institution membership. Individual membership is available to artists, designers, and educators. Institutional membership is available to colleges, universities, and independent schools of art and design with NASAD accredited programs. These programs consist of professional schools and professionally oriented college and university art departments with programs leading to the bachelor of fine arts, bachelor of science in design, and similar professional degrees; liberal arts colleges with programs leading to the bachelor of arts degree with a major in art; and junior and community colleges and other schools offering programs of art instruction at the college level that do not lead to a bachelor's degree. Membership is also extended to appropriate professional organizations, societies, agencies, and institutions that are not functioning as schools.

To be eligible for membership, schools must be organized on a nonprofit basis, with appropriate physical facilities and resources, competent faculty and staff, and evidence of permanence and financial stability. Schools seeking fully accredited member status must be visited by an association evaluation team. All member schools and individuals are assessed annual membership dues, which constitute the main source of financial support for the association.

History and Development

In 1944 representatives of a number of art schools met at the Metropolitan Museum of Art in New York City to focus attention on schools that had or could develop education programs in the new field of industrial design. The meetings continued on a conference basis until 1948. Participants then decided to establish a firm organizational structure and to use the meetings as opportunities to visit schools as well as to exchange ideas and consider issues and problems facing art and design education. The organization thus formed was called the National Association of Schools of Design. In 1960, to more accurately reflect the broad interests of an expanding organization, the name was changed to National Association of Schools of Art, and later to the National Association of Schools of Art and Design.

INTERNET RESOURCE

NATIONAL ASSOCIATION OF SCHOOLS OF ART AND DESIGN. 2002. <www.arts-accredit.org/nasad/default.htm>.

FRANCIS A. RUZICKA
Revised by
JUDITH J. CULLIGAN

NATIONAL ASSOCIATION OF SECONDARY SCHOOL PRINCIPALS

The National Association of Secondary School Principals (NASSP) is a national voice for middle level and high school principals, assistant principals, and aspiring school leaders, providing its members the professional resources to serve as visionary leaders. The association was formed in 1916 by a group of seventy-eight high school principals from seven Midwestern states who met in Chicago, Illinois, to establish a professional organization. Headquartered in Reston, Virginia, the NASSP promotes the intellectual growth, academic achievement, character development, leadership development, and physical well-being of young people through its programs and student leadership services.

With nearly 37,000 members in the United States, Canada, and around the world, the NASSP is the largest organization serving middle level and high school administrators. Although most members are principals and assistant principals at public, private, and parochial secondary schools, the association's membership also includes aspiring principals, teachers, professors of secondary education, and retired educators.

A National Voice

Providing a national voice for principals across the United States is a key objective of the NASSP. As such, the association represents its members before the U.S. Congress and executive agencies of the federal government, monitors federal legislation directly affecting education, writes and delivers testimony before congressional committees, and assists members in advocating for state and federal policies to improve secondary education.

The NASSP supports federal policy initiatives that provide for secondary school programs under the Elementary and Secondary Education Act of 1965 (ESEA), that require mandatory funding for the federal government's share of the Individuals with Disabilities Act (IDEA), that provide efforts to lessen the impact of the principal shortage, and that guarantee that federal funding is available for the professional development of principals. Specifically, secondary school programs under the ESEA should include school safety initiatives, dropout prevention programs, enhanced curriculum, technology in schools, and developmental reading and writing programs in middle level and high schools.

Information and Resources

The NASSP provides a variety of publications, resources, and programs designed to assist school leaders in their school improvement process and to enhance student achievement. The NASSP *Bulletin,* a peer-refereed quarterly research journal, is aimed at secondary school administrators and is widely used in graduate-level principal preparation courses. Each issue of the *Bulletin* contains research and scholarly articles that develop a particular theme, such as instructional leadership, funding and equity, teacher recruitment and retention, standards and assessment, and alternative scheduling. Additional essays on other educational issues are also usually included. In September 2000, the NASSP launched the middle school and high school editions of *Principal Leadership* magazine. *Principal Leadership,* published monthly from September through May, offers practical, hands-on strategies for school leaders. Articles appearing in Principal Leadership are submitted by practitioners and offer personal insight into a host of educational issues.

Monographs, special reports, and in-depth studies supplement the regular NASSP publications. In 1996, in partnership with the Carnegie Foundation for the Advancement of Teaching, the NASSP released the groundbreaking report *Breaking Ranks: Changing an American Institution.* This report presents recommendations for restructuring high schools in ways that contribute to academic success. Unlike other reports, *Breaking Ranks* embodies a vision developed primarily by high school principals. It draws strength and authority from the fact that it arises from the inside.

Turning Points 2000, by Anthony W. Jackson and Gayle A. Davis, is a Carnegie Corporation project published by Teachers College Press and copublished and distributed by the NASSP and the National Middle School Association. Affirming and extending the original 1989 *Turning Points* model, which is considered the definitive work on reform at the middle school level, *Turning Points 2000* places greater emphasis on teaching and learning, and on the principal's role in ensuring that the focus of reform efforts is directed toward improving curriculum, assessment, and instruction. Together, *Turning Points 2000* and *Breaking Ranks* are the centerpieces for school improvement programs in the nation's middle level and high schools.

Programs

In 2001 the NASSP announced the formation of three national task forces—Middle School Principalship, High School Principalship, and Principal Preparation. Comprising principals, assistant principals, and professors, these task forces identify best practices in school leadership and in the preparation and development of school leaders; assist in disseminating these practices; advise the NASSP on the development and implementation of standards impacting principal preparation and practice; identify pertinent research topics; and contribute articles for NASSP publications.

To further support its legislative priorities, and in response to members' needs, the NASSP added two Resident Practitioners to the national staff in 2000—one with expertise in creating safe and orderly schools and one with expertise in special education. These practitioners are available to answer members' questions and conduct presentations to large groups of educational leaders.

Cities and states nationwide report principal vacancies and a lack of qualified candidates willing to fill the positions. *The Principal, Keystone of a High-Achieving School: Attracting and Keeping the Leaders We Need,* prepared in 2000 by the Educational Research Service for the NASSP and the National Association of Elementary School Principals, estimates that more than 40 percent of public school principals will retire by 2010. This report identifies the characteristics of effective principals, discusses factors contributing to the shortage, and suggests steps toward breaking down the barriers to attracting and retaining quality school leaders. With more than twenty years experience in assessment and development of instructional leaders, the NASSP, through its leadership development and assessment programs, assists school districts with the identification and development of potential school leaders. These highly personalized programs measure leadership potential by diagnosing individual strengths and development needs essential to effective leaders.

The association holds an annual convention that attracts more than 5,000 school leaders. The convention offers general sessions featuring speakers of national and international reputation; more than 200 concurrent sessions with distinct middle level and high school strands; exhibits featuring the latest in school technology, curriculum materials, and school supplies; school visits to explore exemplary programs; and informal networking opportunities.

Association programs and services, while most directly focused on the needs of secondary school leaders, also directly touch the lives of students. The NASSP sponsors the National Honor Society (NHS), National Junior Honor Society (NJHS), and National Association of Student Councils (NASC). In 2000 more than 18,000 local NHS/NJHS chapters recognized students for scholarship, character, service, and leadership. In addition, more than 18,000 schools affiliated with the NASC. *Leadership for Student Activities* magazine, published monthly from September through May, provides NHS, NJHS, and NASC advisers and their student leaders with timely articles on leadership topics and ideas for student-centered projects. Three standing committees, the Executive Board of the National Association of Student Councils, the NHS/NJHS Council, and the National Committee on Contests and Activities, ensure that the NASSP maintains its prominent position in the area of student leadership development.

The Trust to Reach Education Excellence (TREE) foundation was created to make grants available to educators and students who would ordinarily not have access to outstanding education opportunities. TREE makes grants to tax-exempt accredited school districts, individual public and private schools, and students. In addition, the TREE 5K, held at the annual convention, raises money for the foundation grants program.

Organizational Structure

The NASSP is a nonprofit 501(c)(3) organization. The association's twenty-four-member board of directors works with the executive director and staff to set the NASSP goals, priorities, and policies. The board includes two members from each of eight geographic regions; four members who speak for underrepresented groups; and two members elected at large (a middle level principal and an assistant principal). The association's president and president-elect also serve on the board of directors. A steering committee, composed of the president, president-elect, and a board member chosen by the board, oversees association operations between board meetings, which are held four times each year. The NASSP also works cooperatively with fifty-four affiliated state and regional principals' organizations throughout the United States. Individuals who hold membership in both national and state organizations enjoy a range of complementary services.

Membership

Several categories of membership are offered by the NASSP, each providing a wide range of benefits and services. Individual membership is open to persons engaged in the practice or supervision of middle level or high school administration. Individual membership is not transferable. Institutional membership is also open to persons engaged in the practice or supervision of middle level or high school administration. Institutional members receive all the benefits of individual membership. An institutional membership is in the name of an individual, but is owned by the school. Consequently, an institutional membership is transferable. Educator membership is open to graduate students enrolled in programs in educational administration, professors, parents, and teachers not engaged in administration. NASSP also offers a membership to retired school administrators.

INTERNET RESOURCE

NATIONAL ASSOCIATION OF SECONDARY SCHOOL PRINCIPALS. 2002. <www.nassp.org>.

TIMOTHY J. MCMANUS

NATIONAL ASSOCIATION OF STATE BOARDS OF EDUCATION

The National Association of State Boards of Education (NASBE) was established in Denver, Colorado, in 1959. Prior to the establishment of NASBE, individuals who served on state boards of education had limited opportunities to meet to discuss issues related to the development of state education policy. State board members, like many individuals involved in public education in the early fifties, were actually members of the National Education Association (NEA).

At its inception, the National Education Association was an umbrella organization for education professionals and policymakers, including members of state boards of education. The expansion of collective bargaining was incompatible with the concept of a single organization for education interests and resulted in the creation of targeted associations that represented the various components of public education. State and local boards of education initially banded together to form one organization. Several of the members of state boards of education, however, felt their unique interests and needs could not be met in the combined group because of the disproportionate number of local board members in the organization. Consequently, NASBE was created and continues to address the distinct needs of state school boards and their members.

In the early years of the organization, it was the usual custom for individuals to serve on state boards of education for several years. The services and activities of the organization focused on bringing members together and reflected a culture of long-term, extended ministration. During the late 1980s and into the 1990s, however, the average term of state board service diminished to four years, hence transforming the work of the association to one of assisting boards and members with the rapid pace of policy development. The primary focus of the association turned from one of simply a convener of state board members, to an organization that concentrated on the professional development of board members, training in policy development, and information dissemination.

The length of time individuals serve on state boards of education was not the only change that confronted the organization. With the standards-based reform movement, the nature and focus of policy development of state education changed dramatically. NASBE services in the early twenty-first century reflect the more complex work of state boards, the considerable diversity of views among the membership, and the external influence of legislatures and governors on the policymaking process. Recognizing the expansion of interest in state education policy development outside of the state boards of education, the association opened its doors to other educational leaders, still maintaining its core services to boards. Membership categories within the association have been developed for others who are interested in education policy development from a state perspective. Although the primary unit of membership is based on a state board of education, a person who does not currently sit on a state board of education may still join as an individual.

The association is a 501(c)3 nonprofit organization, which is governed by a board of directors that includes the offices of president, vice president, immediate past president, and eight area or regional directors. The officers are elected nationwide from four geographic regions, each of which has two representatives on the board of directors. A secretary-treasurer is elected from among the area directors, and there are ex-officio members representing the Council of Chief State School Officers, the National Council of State Education Attorneys, and the National Council of State Board of Education Executives. The board meets quarterly and holds an annual business meeting each October at the Annual Conference of the association. The organization has a Resolutions Committee that annually reviews the standing positions of the organization and each member state may cast a vote to change, affirm, or add resolutions to the association's governing document.

To guide its work between annual business meetings, the board of directors relies on a set of adopted beliefs that assert the following:

• Public education is essential.

• Public education must address the needs of all students.

• Public education is the most fundamental obligation of state government.

• Citizen governance is essential in making public education an enterprise that fulfills its purpose.

• Citizens who serve in position of governance over pubic education must do so without conflict of interest.

• Every state board member has national level roles and responsibilities.

• Differences among and between states should be recognized and considered when addressing education policy.

To promote those beliefs the association and its management relies on a mission statement that affirms the following:

ANASBE shall be the principal organization for policymakers involved in the field of education. It shall develop and provide information that anticipates critical issues formulated with active participation of state board members. NASBE shall promote policy frameworks that are clearly recognizable as scholarly, student-focused, nonpartisan and adaptable to state by state implementation.

NASBE is financed through a combination of state dues, associate memberships, publication sales, and grants and contracts for services and research projects. The range of issues addressed include, but are not limited to, the examination of policies that affect standards, assessments, accountability, certification, accreditation, special education, diversity, educational technology, and health education.

The organization provides a panoply of services to its members, including in-state technical assistance, annual and legislative conferences, an annual training institute for newly elected or appointed board members, chairs-leadership conference annual study groups, monthly policy and legislative updates, issue-specific publications, and a quarterly journal, the *State Education Standard.* The organization maintains a website, and is involved in numerous collaborative initiatives that augment its influence beyond the confines of state boards of Education. The association has been known for its scholarly approach to issues and consequently commands attention and influence beyond its basic membership.

The association is managed by an executive director, who is hired and evaluated by the board of directors, and who oversees a staff of nineteen professionals.

See also: STATES AND EDUCATION, *subentry on* STATE BOARDS OF EDUCATION.

INTERNET RESOURCE

NATIONAL ASSOCIATION OF STATE BOARDS OF EDUCATION. 2002. <www.nasbe.org>.

BRENDA LILIENTHAL WELBURN

NATIONAL ASSOCIATION OF STATE UNIVERSITIES AND LAND-GRANT COLLEGES

The National Association of State Universities and Land-Grant Colleges (NASULGC) is an organization of more than 200 public universities, land-grant colleges, and state university systems. Within this constituency, seventy-five are land-grant colleges, including seventeen historically black public colleges and universities, and twenty-eight are public higher education systems. Thirty tribal colleges are represented through the American Indian Higher Education Consortium (AIHEC).

Purpose and History of Association

The NASULGC has major interests in graduate education, research, and international education. The members' composition of mostly public institutions generates the association's policy interests in agriculture, economic development, and technology transfer. The NASULGC institutions annually grant one-third of the bachelor's and master's degrees and award 60 percent of the doctoral degrees in the United States. Seventy percent of U.S. engineering degrees are from NASULGC institutions.

Founded in 1887 as the Association of American Agricultural Colleges and Experiment Stations (AAACES), NASULGC is the oldest national association of institutions of higher education. The AAACES went through several name changes: the Association of Land-Grant Colleges (ALGC) in 1919; then the Association of Land-Grant Colleges and Universities (ALGCU) in 1926; before merging with National Association of State Universities (NASU), started in 1896, and the State Universities Association (SUA), founded in 1930, to form the National Association of State Universities and Land-Grant Colleges in 1963. The three organizations had overlapping memberships and similar interests but were competitive with each other for many years before a merger was effected.

The Association of Land-Grant Colleges and Universities (ALGCU) created a Washington, D.C., office in 1945, with Russell Thackrey as the full-time executive secretary, a position he held through the merger to 1969. After sharing headquarters on Massachusetts Avenue and One Dupont Circle with a number of other higher education associations since 1952, NASULGC moved to New York Avenue in

1998 to occupy a building it had purchased with three other higher education associations. The president of the association presides over a staff of forty.

The NASULGC shares with the American Association of State Colleges and Universities (AASCU) not only a public institution base but also mutual interests in promoting low tuition policies and equal educational opportunities for everyone who can benefit from a college education. Together, NASULGC and AASCU supported a bill favoring direct lending in the 1990s, and NASULGC was alone among the major Washington, D.C., associations in lobbying for national service legislation. A change in the association's bylaws in 1992 allowed most members of AASCU to become members of NASULGC. The two organizations had a history of working together over many decades. The land-grant association shares with the Association of American Universities (AAU) a longtime interest in graduate education and research, and the two organizations often cooperate in lobbying Congress on matters of mutual interest. The NASULGC is a member of the American Council on Education (ACE) and a member of the Big Six, an informal group of Washington, D.C.-based higher education associations whose members reflect the interests of most American higher education institutions.

The NASULGC has a special commitment, through its Office for the Advancement of Public Black Colleges, to promote historically black land-grant institutions and to aid urban universities in building their capacity to deal with urban interests and issues. In 1994 land-grant status was given to 30 tribal colleges, institutions now represented in NASULGC through their membership in the AIHEC.

Governance and Membership

The NASULGC's basic governing body is its Board of Directors, which consists of representatives from the organization's councils and commissions, six president/chancellor representatives, and three elected officers.

Although NASULGC is primarily a president's association, the organization's ten councils offer the opportunity for provosts, vice presidents, deans, presidents/chancellors, and presidents' spouses to interact with persons in similar roles in other institutions and to participate in the governance and other activities of the association. The six commissions of the organization deal with broad policy issues relat-

ed to the environment, social change, information technology, international affairs, technology transfer, and urban affairs.

Like other associations, NASULGC maintains an extensive information network to keep its members informed and involved in the activities and issues that concern public higher education at the national, state, and local levels. Its Office of Public Affairs deals with media relations, produces and distributes NASULGC publications, including *Newsline,* a newsletter published ten times per year, which keeps members informed on legislation, NASULGC programs, and other items of interest.

BIBLIOGRAPHY

COOK, CONSTANCE EWING. 1998. *Lobbying for Higher Education: How Colleges and Universities Influence Federal Policy.* Nashville, TN: Vanderbilt University Press.

NASULGC 2001: People and Programs. 2001. Washington, DC: NASULGC Office of Public Affairs.

INTERNET RESOURCE

NATIONAL ASSOCIATION OF STATE UNIVERSITIES AND LAND-GRANT COLLEGES. 2002. <www.nasulgc.org>.

HARLAND G. BLOLAND

NATIONAL BOARD FOR PROFESSIONAL TEACHING STANDARDS

The National Board for Professional Teaching Standards (NBPTS) was formed in 1987 as a response to *A Nation at Risk: The Imperative for Educational Reform* (1983), published by the National Commission on Excellence in Education, and its challenges to improve the quality of teaching and learning in U.S. schools. NBPTS has a three-part mission: (1) to establish high and rigorous standards for what accomplished teachers should know and be able to do; (2) to develop and operate a national voluntary system to assess and certify teachers who meet these standards; and (3) to advance related education reforms for the purpose of improving student learning in schools in the United States.

Validity

With standards and assessments in place to reach 95 percent of the nation's teachers, research has focused on the validity and the effects of National Board Certification processes. In 2000 Lloyd Bond, Tracy Smith, Wanda Baker, and John Hattie examined the consequential validity of the NBPTS standards and assessments. They sought to locate demonstrable differences between National Board Certified Teachers (NBCTs) and non–National Board Certified Teachers (non-NBCTs). These researchers created a sample of sixty-five teachers who completed all parts of the assessments and who received their scores on these assessments. These teachers were divided into two naturally formed groups, 31 NBCTs and 34 non-NBCTs.

For the next school year, these teachers were observed teaching in their classrooms and interviewed about their teaching. The researchers collected samples of the teachers' lessons, samples of their students' work, and of a variety of other writing assignments given to the students. The researchers interviewed three students in each teacher's classroom and conducted surveys of all children in each classroom. The researchers found that on the thirteen attributes of teaching effectiveness they had identified, NBCTs outscored non-NBCTs. The scores of the NBCTs were significantly higher, statistically, than the scores of the comparison group on eleven of the thirteen attributes. These findings offer firm foundation for the claim that NBPTS assessments actually measure highly accomplished teaching. It should be noted that all teachers scored rather high on all thirteen attributes, suggesting that just completing the entire assessment process enhances a teacher's skills as a practicing professional.

Candidate Support

Candidate support programs are offered by school districts, teachers organizations, and education schools to guide teachers through the National Board Certification process. In 2001 M. Cramer and J. Cramer conducted focus group interviews of 81 National Board candidates who participated in a support program. The researchers identified three major attributes of successful support programs. First, effective support programs require a knowledgeable and dedicated facilitator. Second, because of the unique demands placed on candidates, the support program must include a structured and sequenced curriculum. Third, creating a learning community with an ethos of egalitarianism in a high-stakes assessment environment seems to advance teacher growth and development.

In 1999 Iris Rotberg, Mary Futrell, and Anne Holmes surveyed candidates who had completed a local support program and found unequal access to information concerning National Board Certification. According to their report, the materials available from the National Board could be more explicit in their expectations. They also called for more venues for providing such information.

For a 2000 doctoral dissertation, D. B. Bohen compared the perceptions of candidates who participated in a cohort support program with those who did not. Both the cohort and noncohort candidates found the NBPTS certification process a powerful professional development experience that transformed their views on teaching. Both groups believed that completing the NBPTS processes in a structured and collegial environment enhanced their professional development. Bohen concludes that teachers seem to welcome the opportunity to study their teaching and the teaching of others in such group settings where deep inquiry and reflection are valued and encouraged.

Master's Degree Programs

Monographs by Peggy Blackwell and Mary Diez (1998) and Diez and Blackwell (1999) outline in clear and direct language the opportunities to use the NBPTS standards to re-design master's degree programs for teachers who want to remain in the classroom. The program designs they offer include these notions of inquiry, reflection, and using the classroom as a laboratory for learning.

In 1999 Karen Dawkins and John Penick surveyed 300 teachers in North Carolina to assess their beliefs and attitudes about a proposed master's degree program that was aligned with the NBPTS core propositions. The respondents expressed support for content and processes that directly target the capacity to improve teaching and daily interactions with children. The respondents did not dismiss the philosophical dimensions found in most graduate programs for teachers; however, they wanted them focused on professional development and improving teaching skills.

Candidate Performance

Data collected from the administration of NBPTS assessments indicate that the percentage of candidates achieving National Board Certification increases annually. In the 1999–2000 cycle, 52 percent of all first-time candidates achieved National Board Certification. However, within these data are differential achievement rates among racial and ethnic groups. In a series of studies, Bond and his colleagues inquired into the sources of adverse impacts on achievement rates in an effort to establish a set of conditions that would reduce their effects. These studies have included an external panel review of the standards and assessments, which found no bias inherent in either, and a study of the interaction of assessors and candidates, focusing on the factor race plays in these interactions. This study also yielded no evidence of systematic bias. In studying minority candidates who did not achieve National Board Certification but who retook exercises and who achieved National Board Certification on the next attempt, Bond and colleagues found that these candidates felt underprepared for the amount of reflective thinking required in the assessments, suggesting the need for better teacher preparation.

In 1998 Laura Onafowora studied six African-American candidates who did not initially gain National Board Certification and found that these candidates might not write well extemporaneously. She found the entries of these African-American candidates tended to focus on philosophical themes, such as instilling "survival imperatives" in their students, rather than on their teaching.

Assessing Accomplished Teaching

Results of studies on the reliable and valid measurement of accomplished teaching, as reported in separate 1998 articles by Bond and Richard Jaeger, offer insights into the process of scoring multidimensional representations of teaching. They highlight the need for new calculations of validity and needed research on measuring performance. In 1997 Drew Gitomer reviewed five major challenges faced in the design, development, and implementation of the NBPTS assessment process. These challenges were: (1) defining scoring; (2) handling a broad range of disciplines and contexts; (3) resolving bias issues; (4) interpreting unfamiliar representations of content; and (5) identifying the cut-score.

Changing the Profession and Advancing Reform

In a commissioned study of National Board Certified Teachers, Yankelovich and associates surveyed all NBCTs concerning the effects National Board Certification has had on their ability to change the profession. NBCTs reported, in significant numbers, that they are undertaking new roles and responsibilities in their schools and communities since gaining National Board Certification, including mentoring other teachers, coaching National Board Certification candidates, and serving as clinical faculty in teacher education programs.

The National Board is pursuing its mission to set the benchmark for accomplished teaching. It has overcome political, professional, and psychometric obstacles, and it has spawned a national inquiry into teacher quality. However, it is still a long way from having the kind of research evidence that solidifies its base. By creating the broad categories used to review the current literature, it is hoped further research will occur.

See also: SUPERVISION OF INSTRUCTION; TEACHER EVALUATION.

BIBLIOGRAPHY

BLACKWELL, PEGGY J., and DIEZ, MARY. 1998. *Toward a New Vision of Master's Education for Teachers.* Washington, DC: National Council for Accreditation of Teacher Education.

BOHEN, D. B. 2000. "How Teacher Candidates View and Value the Certification Process of the National Board for Professional Teaching Standards." Ph.D. diss., George Mason University.

BOND, LLOYD. 1995. "Unintended Consequences of Performance Assessment: Issues of Bias and Fairness." *Educational Measurement: Issues and Practice* 14(4):21–24.

BOND, LLOYD. 1998. "Culturally Responsive Pedagogy and the Assessment of Accomplished Teaching." *Journal of Negro Education* 67(3):242–254.

BOND, LLOYD. 1998. "Disparate Impact and Teacher Certification." *Journal of Personnel Evaluation in Education* 33(3):410–427.

BOND, LLOYD; SMITH, TRACY W.; BAKER, WANDA K.; and HATTIE, JOHN A. 2000. *Accomplished Teaching: A Validation of National Board Certification.* Arlington, VA: National Board for Professional Teaching Standards.

BUDAY, MARY CATHERINE, and KELLY, JAMES A. 1996. "National Board Certification and the Teaching Profession's Commitment to Quality Assurance." *Phi Delta Kappan* 77(2):215–219.

CARNEGIE FORUM ON EDUCATION AND THE ECONOMY. 1986. *A Nation Prepared: Teachers for the 21st Century.* Washington, DC: Carnegie Forum.

CRAMER, M., and CRAMER, J. 2001. *Candidates' Perceptions of Effective National Board for Professional Teaching Standards Support Programs..* Conway: Arkansas State University.

DAWKINS, KAREN, and PENICK, JOHN. 1999. *Teacher Preferences for an Advanced Masters Degree Based on NBPTS and NCATE Standards.* Chapel Hill: University of North Carolina, College of Education.

DIEZ, MARY, and BLACKWELL, PEGGY J. 1999. *Achieving the New Vision of Master's Education for Teachers.* Washington, DC: National Council for Accreditation of Teacher Education.

GITOMER, DREW. 1997. "Challenges for Scoring Performance Assessments in the NBPTS System." Paper presented at the annual meeting of the American Educational Research Association.

JAEGER, RICHARD M. 1998. "Evaluating the Psychometric Qualities of the National Board for Professional Teaching Standards." *Journal of Personnel Evaluation in Education* 12(2):189–210.

NATIONAL COMMISSION ON EXCELLENCE IN EDUCATION. 1983. *A Nation at Risk: The Imperative for Educational Reform.* Washington, DC: U.S. Government Printing Office.

ONAFOWORA, LAURA. 1998. "Measurement Consequences Reconsidered: African American Performance and Communication Styles in the Assessment for National Teacher Certification." Ph.D. diss.

ROTBERG, IRIS C.; FUTRELL, MARY HATWOOD; and HOLMES, ANNE E. 2000. "Increasing Access to National Board Certification." *Phi Delta Kappan* 81(5):379–382.

ELIZABETH B. CASTOR
GARY R. GALLUZZO

NATIONAL BUSINESS EDUCATION ASSOCIATION

The National Business Education Association (NBEA) is a private organization devoted to the use of education to advance ethical standards, professional conduct, diversity, and fairness in the field of business. It is the largest professional organization of its kind in the United States, and its influence is enhanced by the close ties it maintains to other business-related organizations both within the United States and in the international community. Its primary constituency comprises business educators and the administrators of programs of business instruction.

Program

The NBEA takes as its primary goal the improvement of business education and enhancing the status of the profession. Among the activities it conducts to achieve these ends are a publications program, through which the NBEA disseminates information on the latest innovations in teaching techniques; a strong leadership program designed to improve professionalism within the field of business education; and a lobbying arm, the Legislative Advocacy Committee, which works with lawmakers at the local, state, and federal level to improve the quality of business education. It also sponsors two student organizations, the Future Business Leaders of America (for high school students) and the college honor society Phi Beta Lamda, in the conviction that early education is key to developing business skills and a commitment to civic leadership.

The NBEA has an active publications division, which offers materials on topics of interest to business educators. Its official journal is the *Business Education Forum,* and it also publishes a newsletter, *Keying In.* In addition it publishes the *Business Education Standards,* which establishes standards of competency that should be attained by children from kindergarten to age fourteen in eleven areas of business-related education. Among the areas addressed are accounting principles, business law, marketing, computation, economics, and management. The NBEA also publishes an annual *Yearbook,* each issue of which is devoted to a single topic of importance to business educators. It maintains a website with links to a wide range of business organizations in the United States and abroad.

Organization

The NBEA has four divisions, each representing a distinct area of professional interest: International; Research; Teacher Education; and Teaching, Supervision, and Administration. The organization is broken into five regional associations: Eastern, Southern, North-Central, Mountain-Plains, and Western. Overseeing the organization's activities is an executive board, which consists of the presidents of each of the divisions and associations as well as elected representatives of the five regional associations. Conferences and workshops are sponsored at the divisional and regional levels.

The NBEA also has a representative assembly, composed of business and business education leaders from each state and from affiliated business organizations. This assembly provides recommendations on policy, planning, and future activities of the national organization. Through this structure, the NBEA is able to carry out its mission to serve as an information conduit, conveying information among affiliated business organizations for the betterment of all members.

Membership and Support

The NBEA welcomes all individuals who share its interest in improving business education and advancing the goals of fairness, diversity, and professionalism in the field. Interested parties may choose from five different categories of membership: professional, student, associate, lifetime, and honorary. Only professional and lifetime members are eligible to vote on NBEA issues, serve on the assembly, or be elected to the executive committee. Funding for the NBEA comes from membership dues, the sale of NBEA literature, and fees charged for workshops and seminars.

History

The NBEA got its start in 1878 when a group of educators from several private schools got together to form the Business Education Association (BEA). The group was chiefly concerned with the dissemination of information of interest to business teachers and published a series of monographs. In 1892 the BEA became a formal division of the National Education Association (NEA) and was renamed the Department of Business Education.

Groups of other independent organizations devoted to principles of sound business education were founded over the next several years, including the National Commercial Teachers Association (1895), the Eastern Commercial Teachers Association (1897), the Southern Commercial Teachers Association (1922), and the National Association of Commercial Teacher-Training Institutions. These and other like-minded groups joined together to form the National Council for Business Education (NCBE) in 1933, with the goal of establishing national standards in the field of business education.

In 1946 the NCBE merged with the NEA's Department of Business Education to form the United Business Education Association, and headquarters were established at the NEA Center in Washington, D.C. Regional divisions were formed over the next several years, leading to the organizational structure that now characterizes the NBEA. The organization took its present name in 1962.

See also: BUSINESS EDUCATION.

INTERNET RESOURCE

NATIONAL BUSINESS EDUCATION ASSOCIATION. 2002. <www.nbea.org>.

O. J. BYRNSIDE JR.
Revised by
NANCY E. GRATTON

NATIONAL CATHOLIC EDUCATIONAL ASSOCIATION

The National Catholic Educational Association (NCEA) is the largest professional organization for Catholic educators in the United States. The association's principal objectives are to promote the welfare of Catholic education; to provide Catholic educational institutions with national and regional representation; to enable Catholic educators to work together for professional growth; to foster cooperation between Catholic schools and other professional agencies in the field of education; to facilitate the interchange of ideas; to conduct educational research; and to increase public understanding and proclaim the uniqueness of Catholic education.

Program

The services provided by the NCEA include a broad spectrum of activities designed to aid Catholic educators. The association sponsors meetings, issues publications, and conducts informational programs. The annual convention and exposition, which attracts over 15,000 participants, is the most important annual forum for the exchange of ideas and information among Catholic educators. The NCEA sponsors an annual meeting for diocesan school superintendents, regional meetings related to the special needs of particular areas of the United States, and frequent professional workshops dealing with new educational and administrative methods for teachers and administrators.

The NCEA publishes books, monographs, journals, and directories. NCEA newsletters include *News for Catholic School Parent Leaders, National Catholic Educators Accent,* and *Pastor Education Digest.* The association's official journal is the quarterly *Momentum,* which includes articles and columns discussing educational theory and methodology, catechetical programs, and important educational issues. The association also makes available to members the services of consultants in guidance and counseling, religious education, accreditation, international education, and other areas of interest.

Other NCEA programs focus on leadership development and training for teachers and administrators at all levels of Catholic education. A retreat program called *Shepherding the Shepherd* is designed to foster the spirituality of teachers and administrators and help them integrate it into their educational efforts. *Sharing the Faith* is a faith development program that provides in-service training for Catholic educators and teaches them ways to balance personal reflection with community building. The *Frontiers of Justice* program, cosponsored by Catholic Relief Services, sends Catholic educators to developing countries to help local Catholic groups develop school systems.

Each year the NCEA, in association with the United States Catholic Conference, sponsors Catholic Schools Week to promote the value of Catholic education, to call attention to the role Catholic Schools play in their communities, and to raise money for school programs and scholarships. Since 1990 the Wednesday of Catholic Schools Week has been celebrated as National Appreciation Day for Catholic Schools.

The association also makes several annual awards, including the Elizabeth Ann Seton Awards to honor people who have made exceptional contributions to Catholic education, and the Leonard F. DeFiore Parental Choice Advocate Award to honor a person who has shown leadership in promoting educational choice.

Organizational Structure

The NCEA is made up of five departments: the religious education department, the seminary department, the secondary school department, the elementary school department, and the department of chief administrators of Catholic schools. The NCEA also includes a Commission for the National Association of Boards of Education and is an affiliate member of the Association of Catholic Colleges and Universities. Each NCEA department elects its own officers and designates two representatives who sit as voting members on the association's general executive board. The association also includes several sections dealing with special concerns, such as the special projects and public policy section; the leadership development section; and the communications, public relations, and production section. The executive board, headed by a president, oversees the work of the association.

Membership and Financial Support

Membership in the association is voluntary and open to anyone desiring to further its objectives. Most membership is on an institutional basis. In 2001 the NCEA had more than 200,000 members. The NCEA's chief financial support comes from institutional membership dues, which vary with the size and type of institution, and corporate and private donors. Individuals may join as sustaining members, adult education commission members, or regular members.

History and Development

The NCEA's founding convention was held in St. Louis, Missouri, in July 1904 when several Catholic education groups joined forces to form the Catholic Education Association. In 1927 the word *national* was added to the name. The growth of the NCEA in size and services parallels the growth of Catholic education in the United States. When the association was started, Catholic schools in the United States enrolled about 850,000 students; in 2001 there were Catholic schools in all fifty states and a nationwide enrollment of more than 7.5 million.

BIBLIOGRAPHY

BENSON, PETER L. and GUERRA, MICHAEL J. 1985. *Sharing the Faith: The Beliefs and Values of Catholic High School Teachers.* Washington, DC: National Catholic Educational Association.

Convery, John J.; McLellan, Jeffrey; and Youniss, James, eds. 2000. *The Catholic Character of Catholic Schools.* Notre Dame, IN: University of Notre Dame Press.

INTERNET RESOURCE

National Catholic Educational Association. 2002. <www.ncea.org>.

Russell Shaw
Revised by
Judith J. Culligan

NATIONAL CENTER FOR EDUCATION STATISTICS

The National Center for Education Statistics (NCES) is a federal agency responsible for collecting, analyzing, and disseminating statistical information related to the U.S. educational system. The principle goals of the NCES are to collect data concerning the condition and progress of American education and to make that data available to federal and state public policy makers, professional educators, the public, and the media. The NCES also reviews and reports on education in other countries.

Programs

The various programs of the NCES supply information and statistical data on such education-related matters as, for example, student enrollment, graduation rates, teacher staffing levels and teacher shortages, student skill and knowledge levels, and state and local educational expenditures. To obtain this information, the NCES conducts numerous surveys on the American educational system. Among the most important are the Schools and Staffing Survey, which monitors teacher supply and demand, as well as the composition of the educational work force in public and private schools across the country. Another survey, the National Assessment of Education Progress, evaluates the knowledge and skills of American fourth, eighth, and twelfth graders in reading, writing, science, mathematics, history, geography, and other subject areas. This survey also evaluates high school transcripts and provides state-by-state comparisons of its findings. The NCES National Study of Postsecondary Faculty reports on faculty and staff characteristics at the nation's colleges and universities. The National Adult Literacy Survey measures the reading and writing skills of the American adult population. In addition, the NCES conducts various longitudinal studies that follow different classes of students over a long period of time to asses such factors as academic growth, changes in attitude and motivation, and the ability to transition from one educational level to the next and from school into the labor market.

Federal, state, and local officials use data supplied by NCES to help them plan educational programs. The media use NCES data to inform the public about significant conditions and trends in American schools, such as school dropout and college enrollment rates, the relationship of educational achievement to class size, and the relative success of private and public schools. Members of the general public may examine NCES statistics to become more informed voters and to make knowledgeable decisions about their own and their children's education. Ultimately, wide access to the information collected and reported by the NCES can promote and accelerate the reform and improvement of education in the United States.

The NCES administers numerous programs to collect, process, and report educational data. The NCES Annual Reports Program conducts research on current and emerging topics in education and disseminates annual reports in support of other NCES programs. The Data on Vocational Education (DOVE) Program, established in 1998, collects and collates data from students and faculty involved in vocational education in secondary and postsecondary schools. DOVE also collects information about adults pursuing continuing education and work-related training. The NCES Education Financial Statistics Center conducts research related to the financing of public and private elementary, secondary, and post-secondary education. The Statistical Standards Program provides technical support and develops standards and procedures to ensure the quality and accuracy of NCES statistical surveys, analyses, and reports. The NCES established the National Forum on Education Statistics to improve methods for collecting, processing, and reporting elementary and secondary education statistics. The Forum also provides technical assistance to state and local data collection systems. Since 1994, a branch of the NCES called the Advisory Council on Education Statistics has deliberated problems facing the NCES and recommended solutions to the NCES Commissioner.

The NCES provides access to its statistical information through the online NCES Electronic Catalog, the National Education Data Resource Center, the National Library of Education, the Resource Sharing and Cooperation Division, and various web posting, CD-ROM releases, and nearly one hundred annual print publications. The major print publications of the NCES include the annual *Digest of Education Statistics,* a compilation of wide-ranging statistical data covering American educational institutions from preschool through graduate school. The *Digest* also compares American schools with schools in other countries. The *Projections of Education Statistics,* a periodic report first published in 1964, provides ten to fourteen year projections on enrollment, graduation rates, teacher levels, and expenditures in America elementary schools, high schools, colleges, and universities. Other periodical publications include the NCES *Education Statistics Quarterly,* which provides a comprehensive overview of work accomplished throughout the NCES over a three-month period.

The NCES also maintains a series of databases on a wide variety of topics addressing elementary, secondary, and postsecondary education at the local, state, and national level. These include *Common Core of Data,* which is the primary database for statistical information about public and private elementary and secondary schools. Another NCES database, the *School District Database,* provides demographic information derived from the most recent census about school districts around the country. The *K–12 Practitioners' Circle* is a website that provides links, resources, and other information for teachers and support staff, administrators, policymakers, librarians, and parents. The online *NCES Students' Classroom* offers children and parents information about schools and libraries, a kid's magazine called *Crunch,* and general educational data, as well as games and quizzes on history, mathematics, science, geography, and the arts.

Organizational Structure

The NCES is a division of the U.S. Department of Education's Office of Educational Research and Improvement. The NCES is headed by a commissioner and deputy commissioner, who set policy and oversee the operation of the center. There are four main divisions comprising the NCES: the Early Childhood and International and Crosscutting Studies Division, the Elementary/Secondary and Libraries Studies Division, the Postsecondary Studies Division, and the Assessment Division.

See also: INTERNATIONAL EDUCATION STATISTICS; U.S. DEPARTMENT OF EDUCATION.

BIBLIOGRAPHY

GEDDES, CLAIRE. 1999. *Learning about Education through Statistics.* Washington, DC: National Center for Education Statistics.

SNYDER, THOMAS D., ed. 1993. *120 Years of American Education: A Statistical Portrait.* Washington DC: National Center for Education Statistics.

INTERNET RESOURCES

NATIONAL CENTER FOR EDUCATION STATISTICS. 2002. <http://nces.ed.gov>.

NATIONAL CENTER FOR EDUCATION STATISTICS. 2002. "Common Core of Data: Information on Public Schools and School Districts in the United States." <http://nces.ed.gov/ccd>.

NATIONAL CENTER FOR EDUCATION STATISTICS. 2002. "K–12 Practitioner's Circle." <http://nces.ed.gov/practitioners>.

NATIONAL CENTER FOR EDUCATION STATISTICS. 2002. "NCES Student's Classroom." 2002. <http://nces.ed.gov/nceskids>.

JUDITH J. CULLIGAN

NATIONAL COMMITTEE FOR CHILDREN AND YOUTH

The National Committee for Children and Youth (NCCY) is a private association that was established in 1960 as a part of President Eisenhower's White House Conference on Children and Youth. It was thus part of a larger initiative intended to improve the federal, state, and local services provided to the nation's children.

The committee's original mandate was fivefold. It was to implement the findings of the White House conference, to achieve greater coordination among the various programs and associations that sought to serve the needs of children and youth, to improve and speed the flow of useful information among interested organizations and agencies, to provide guidance in the planning of activities aimed toward improving children's services, and to identify new problems and issues as they arose in the provision of services to children.

Program

Eisenhower's White House conference established the Council of National Organizations for Children and Youth, a national coordinating council serving some 400 individual youth and children's service providers, and state-based Committees for Children and Youth. The NCCY, as a committee within the national council, functions as an information clearinghouse and consultation service for these member organizations, acting as a liaison between federal agencies and local, regional, and state-based child-service providers. In addition, it plays an important role in reaching out to the community at large and educating the public about child-service goals and issues.

The NCCY fulfills its mission through its publications division. It produces a quarterly newsletter, distributed to service providers and individuals, which recounts the accomplishments and ongoing projects of the various service agencies at all levels of government. It also sponsors conferences that bring together professionals in the field of child services. It has also produced reports, books, and research articles, which are used to train educators, social workers, and other professional child-service providers.

Programs

A central concern of the NCCY since its inception has been to improve literacy among the nation's youth. One important project, aimed at young people in their teens, has been the establishment of remedial reading programs, which seek to improve reading skills in children who have been passed along through the school system without acquiring the ability to read at a basic level of competency. This type of project is typical of the work of the NCCY, involving as it does a collaboration between a number of independent agencies and individuals, such as the U.S. Department of Labor's Manpower Administration, local schools, and social workers. However, the NCCY does not maintain long-term control over such projects. As an initiative proves itself to be successful, the NCCY finds an appropriate agency to take over the service, thus freeing itself to explore new programs and initiatives.

Organizational Structure

The NCCY is a division within the Council of National Organizations for Children and Youth, and as such it serves the larger agenda of its parent agency. It also works closely with the National Council of State Committees for Children and Youth, each of which elects five of its members to three-year terms of service on the NCCY. The bylaws of the committee provide that at least two members must be under the age of twenty-five, to make certain that the concerns of the committee's target population are understood and adequately addressed.

History

The NCCY was born out of President Eisenhower's 1960 educational initiative, the 1960 Golden Anniversary White House Conference on Children and Youth. The original conference was part of a long tradition in which, at the start of each decade since 1909, the sitting president would call together a wide range of professionals, from educators to physicians, who served the needs of the nation's children and youth. The 1960 conference attracted more than 7,000 participants, drawn from every state and territory in the United States. During the course of the conference, it was determined that a permanent committee should be established to provide continuity, collaboration, and focus for the widely disparate individuals, organizations, and government agencies that shared an interest in child services.

At the 1970 White House Conference, it was decided that each state should establish its own Committee on Children and Youth, and the NCCY's role changed from direct involvement in developing projects to a more advisory and facilitative function. It assumed the responsibility of providing national leadership and serving as an informational clearinghouse through which the local initiatives could be communicated to interested parties, agencies, and committees elsewhere in the country.

ISABELLA J. JONES
Revised by
NANCY E. GRATTON

NATIONAL COMMUNICATION ASSOCIATION

The National Communication Association (NCA) is the oldest and largest nonprofit, scholarly society dedicated to the field of communication, with a special emphasis on public speaking and other forms of speech communication. Its mission is to promote excellence in the research, teaching, and application of the "artistic, humanistic, and scientific principles of communication." It has a membership of more than 7,100, representing all fifty states and twenty foreign countries.

Program

The NCA serves as an informational center and network for individuals working in the broadly defined field of communication. Its primary goal is to organize and disseminate information of relevance to its membership, and it accomplishes this goal through a variety of venues. Each year an annual convention is held, attracting some 4,000 attendees who participate in workshops, seminars, and panel discussions. Also offered are films and presentations on advances in the field of speech communication, employment placement services, and other special-interest activities. The annual convention is also the occasion for the NCA's various business and planning committees to meet. In addition to the annual convention, the NCA sponsors smaller conferences throughout the year.

In addition to meetings, the NCA disseminates information through a wide range of publications. The first NCA journal, founded in 1915 as the *Quarterly Journal of Public Speaking,* is now published as the *Quarterly Journal of Speech.* Since the inaugural issue of this journal, the NCA has added six others, each with a special focus (education, criticism, text, performance, and so on). The NCA also produces two annuals and an online index, as well as numerous books, monographs, brochures, and pamphlets. The monthly newsletter, *Spectra,* has an electronic counterpart available on the organization's website.

To encourage excellence in the field of communication, the NCA also sponsors numerous awards, conferred annually at the NCA convention. These awards, many of which carry significant cash grants, recognize achievement in a variety of communication applications, from teaching to "best dissertation." In addition, the organization sponsors exchange programs, which bring international debate and public speaking teams together for competitions. The official NCA collegiate honor societies are Lambda Pi Eta (for four-year institutions) and Sigma Pi Eta (for community colleges), in addition to which the organization encourages the formation of student clubs on university campuses throughout the country.

The NCA is also actively involved in outreach programs with public and private agencies. Through these programs, the NCA promotes its positions on such issues as communication education, freedom of speech, and presidential debates. The NCA also prepares position papers on legislation relevant to its areas of interest and makes these available to lawmakers at the federal and state level when appropriate.

Organization and Funding

The NCA is governed by a sixty-member legislative council, which meets annually at the NCA convention, and a ten-member administrative committee, which meets periodically throughout the year. Policy positions are determined by the legislative council, then disseminated throughout the organization in the form of resolutions. When deemed necessary, the legislative council may call for the formation of special committees to do research on special-interest topics, with the purpose of publishing the results of the research. Past examples of such projects include a brochure on careers in the field of speech communication and a book on the rhetoric of the antislavery movement. More recently, the NCA has published brochures on finding grant support for individual research and a volume on Mexican-American rhetoric and the activism of Cesar Chavez.

The NCA is an independent, not-for-profit organization, relying primarily on membership dues, conference and convention fees, and revenues from the sale of its publications to support the majority of its programs. Individual members and special projects receive support from private sponsors as well as from federal granting agencies. Although many of the NCA annual awards are supported by organization funds, it also solicits endowed awards, and as of 2002 there are ten such awards granted through the organization. In addition to individual memberships, the NCA recruits memberships from institutions and libraries. Undergraduate students receive a reduced membership rate.

History

The National Communication Association was founded on November 28, 1914, in Chicago, Illinois. The impetus for its founding arose from a dispute within the ranks of the National Council of Teachers of English, in which seventeen members broke away from the parent organization to form the National Association of Academic Teachers of Public Speaking. Within a year, the new organization had inaugurated its first publication, *The Quarterly Journal of Public Speaking*. Interest in the new organization was lively, and by 1916 it boasted 160 members.

Within ten years, membership grew to 910, and the organization underwent its first name change, to the National Association of Teachers of Speech (NATS). New services were added to the organizational profile, including job-placement service. In 1934 the organization began publication of *Speech Monographs* (now titled *Communication Monographs*), and membership had topped 2,000. In 1945 the group changed its name, once again, to the Speech Association of America (SAA), under which, five years later, the organization was officially incorporated. In 1953 the association launched its third quarterly publication, *Speech Teacher* (now *Communication Educator*). In 1963 the SAA established its headquarters in New York City and for the first time created full-time administrative positions to facilitate the running of the organization. In 1970 the organization adopted a new constitution and bylaws and once again chose a new name: the Speech Communication Association (SCA).

With professional offices and a national headquarters, the SCA grew rapidly over the next two decades, and its services expanded markedly. New publications were founded to address changes in the field, including *Journal of Applied Communication* (founded 1973), *Critical Studies in Media Communications* (1984), and *Text and Performance Quarterly* (1989). The conference and awards programs were expanded as well. In 1997 the organization underwent yet another name change to become the National Communication Association, and in 2001 the association launched its most recent publication, *Review of Communication*. In the 1990s the NCA outgrew its Manhattan-based headquarters and relocated to Washington, D.C.

See also: SPEECH AND THEATER EDUCATION.

INTERNET RESOURCE

NATIONAL COMMUNICATION ASSOCIATION. 2002. <www.natcom.org>.

WILLIAM WORK
Revised by
NANCY E. GRATTON

NATIONAL CONFERENCE OF STATE LEGISLATURES

The National Conference of State Legislatures (NCSL) was founded in 1975 with the conviction that legislative service is one of democracy's worthiest pursuits. Representing the citizens of a district and the people of a state is the very essence of free government.

NCSL is recognized as the preeminent bipartisan organization dedicated to serving the lawmakers and staffs of the nation's fifty states, its commonwealths, and its territories. It is known nationally for its leadership. All the nation's legislators and legislative staff are members of NCSL. A sixty-member executive committee, elected yearly and composed of legislators and staff, governs NCSL under the leadership of seven officers.

With a focus on service, NCSL is a source for research, publications, consulting assistance, meetings, and seminars. It is the only organization that provides an open, bipartisan, national forum for lawmakers to communicate with one another and share ideas. NCSL is an effective and respected voice for the states in Washington, D.C., representing their interests before the U.S. Congress, the presidential administration, and federal agencies.

The issues legislatures confront are increasingly complex. Each year NCSL answers more than 16,000 questions from legislators and staff. The researchers at NCSL provide lawmakers and their staffs with expert information on a variety of issues, including welfare reform, education, criminal justice, energy, environment, transportation, health care, children and families, the legislative institution, economic development, state finances, uninsured children, automobile insurance, workers' compensation, nuclear waste, clean air and water, gaming, education funding, immigrants, managed care, ethics, and many others.

Each year, NCSL produces some 160 books, newsletters, briefs, and other publications, including

State Legislatures magazine, on topics of interest to the states. Its Internet site provides thousands of documents from states as well as those published by NCSL. The site includes numerous databases, features listservs through which lawmakers and staff can communicate, and provides users the ability to perform comprehensive research using multistate searches of legislation, statutes, audits, and other legislative documents.

NCSL assists lawmakers in crafting legislation and in seeking expert witnesses to testify before committees. NCSL also conducts special workshops on specific issues and training programs for legislators and staff. NCSL specialists work with legislative leaders on direct consultation projects on legislative organization and management, rules and procedures, committee operations, personnel policies, strategic planning, and related institutional issues. Nearly half of the sixty-member NCSL executive committee is composed of state legislators.

Legislators and legislative staff have numerous opportunities to attend NCSL meetings on a variety of issues and topics throughout the year. The annual meeting provides more than 160 informative sessions and presents nationally renowned speakers on important concerns. Like legislatures, NCSL is structured to allow free and open debate in committees. The Assembly on Federal Issues is comprised of lawmakers who are interested in federal issues and how they relate to the states. The assembly helps guide NCSL's lobbying efforts in Washington, D.C., through the work of nine committees, and its members are appointed by the presiding leaders in the states. The leader-to-leader meeting, held in Washington, D.C., each year, is the premier gathering for state legislative leaders to discuss pressing federal issues with congressional leaders, cabinet officers, key members of the administration, and often the president. Both legislators and staff can be appointed to the Assembly on State Issues. Through its eight standing committees, members address a set of topics from cultural and economic development and fiscal matters to science and technology.

Legislatures cannot run effectively without professional, high-quality staff. NCSL offers a wealth of learning and professional development opportunities for staff. Among them are an annual seminar to help staff sharpen their skills in research, program evaluation, fiscal analysis, bill drafting, and legislative procedures. Specialized meetings cover presentation skills, media relations, legal research, and skills development in other areas.

NCSL has ten professional staff organizations for researchers, fiscal officers, leadership staff, legal services staff, legislative clerks, secretaries, computer staff, research librarians, program evaluators, and security personnel. With the Hubert H. Humphrey Institute of Public Affairs at the University of Minnesota, NCSL also cosponsors the Legislative Staff Management Institute, an intensive, two-week executive management seminar for senior legislative staff.

NCSL's Leaders' Center assists legislative leaders in meeting the challenges of managing the institution, crafting the best possible public policy, creating consensus out of dissension, communicating with Congress and key administration officials, and protecting and promoting the legislative institution. The Leaders' Center offers specialized services including publications, timely policy information, and ideas for innovative management, and sponsors the annual Leadership Institute for emerging leaders. NCSL offers leaders opportunities to enhance skills, communicate with colleagues in other states, and meet with members of Congress and the administration.

NCSL created the foundation for state legislatures in 1982 to support the innovative research, seminars, and publications for NCSL and the work of two major programs: the Acclaimed Trust for Representative Democracy and the Center for Ethics in Government. The foundation is committed to the important work of strengthening America's legislatures, counteracting cynicism and distrust of the legislative process, and helping lawmakers confront and solve the critical issues of the time.

NCSL's Center for Ethics in Government was created to address a most critical, fundamental and far-reaching problem facing the United States: the loss of public trust and confidence in representative democracy. The center is founded on the principles of belief in representative democracy and the legislative process and that all who work in the public sector have a particular responsibility to operate with high ethical standards. By facilitating ethics sessions for legislators, staff, and state government affairs professionals and through its research arm, the center is a leading force in promoting responsible behavior in legislatures and educating the public on the importance of the legislative process.

NCSL is an extension of the legislature. Its mission is to improve the quality and effectiveness of state legislatures, to serve as the forum for exchanging information and ideas among legislatures, and to ensure that legislatures have a strong, cohesive voice in the federal system.

INTERNET RESOURCE

NATIONAL CONFERENCE OF STATE LEGISLATURES. 2002. <www.ncsl.org>.

GINGER SAMPSON

NATIONAL COUNCIL FOR ACCREDITATION OF TEACHER EDUCATION

The National Council for Accreditation of Teacher Education (NCATE) is the accrediting body for colleges and universities that prepare teachers and other professional specialists for work in elementary and secondary schools. The NCATE accreditation process aims to ensure that accredited institutions produce competent, caring, and qualified teachers and other professional school personnel who can help all students learn.

NCATE is a nonprofit, 501 (c)(3), nongovernmental coalition of more than thirty national associations representing the education profession at large. The associations appoint representatives to NCATE's policy boards. The boards develop NCATE standards, policies, and procedures. Membership on policy boards includes representatives from organizations of (1) teacher educators, (2) teachers, (3) state and local policymakers, and (4) professional specialists. See Table 1 for a list of NCATE member organizations.

Mission

Accountability and improvement are central to NCATE's mission. The NCATE accreditation process determines whether schools, colleges, and departments of education meet demanding standards for the preparation of teachers and other school specialists. Through this process, NCATE seeks to provide assurance to the public that graduates of accredited institutions have acquired the knowledge, skills, and dispositions necessary to help all students learn.

Providing leadership for reform in teacher preparation is also central to NCATE's mission. Through

standards that focus on systematic assessment and performance-based learning, NCATE encourages accredited institutions to engage in continuous improvement based on accurate and consistent data. In this way, NCATE ensures that accredited institutions remain current, relevant, and productive, and that graduates of these institutions are able to have a positive impact on P–12 students.

Number of Accredited Institutions

As of 2002, more than six hundred institutions were a part of the NCATE system; 539 of these institutions are accredited, and another 80 to 108 are candidates for accreditation. NCATE institutions produce approximately two-thirds of new teacher graduates in the United States each year.

Process

Those institutions interested in attaining national professional accreditation complete an intent-to-seek accreditation form. A mutually convenient date for an on-site visit is set, usually two years in advance of the visit. The institution prepares a self-study, which explains how it believes it meets the NCATE standards. The self-study is sent to examining team members two months prior to the visit. Team members review the self-study and other documents, if available on the institution's website, before the visit. A five- or six-person team visits the institution, arriving on Saturday and leaving the following Wednesday. The weekend is spent examining documents of the institution (student evaluations, copies of curricula, student work, minutes of faculty meetings, etc.). Monday and Tuesday are devoted to interviewing faculty, students, staff, and teachers/principals at clinical sites. The team works in the evening to determine how well the institution is addressing the NCATE expectations. Wednesday at mid-day, an exit interview is held with the head of the education unit, explaining the team's recommendations.

The team finalizes its report in thirty days and returns it to NCATE's office. NCATE sends the report to the institution. The institution may wish to issue a rejoinder if it believes the team missed important information. All of the documents are sent to NCATE's Unit Accreditation Board, which makes a final accreditation decision.

History

NCATE was founded in 1954. Five groups were instrumental in the creation of NCATE: the American

Association of Colleges for Teacher Education, the National Association of State Directors of Teacher Education and Certification, the National Education Association, the Council of Chief State School Officers, and the National School Boards Association. When NCATE was founded as an independent accrediting body, it replaced the American Association of Colleges for Teacher Education as the agency responsible for accreditation in teacher education.

Influence

The NCATE of the new millennium is implementing a performance-based system of accreditation developed during the 1990s. This system is enhancing both accountability and improvement in educator preparation, as it requires compelling evidence of effective candidate performance for institutions to become accredited. Institutions must show that candidates know the subjects they plan to teach and that they can teach effectively so that students learn.

NCATE standards are increasingly the norm in teacher preparation, and NCATE serves as a resource to the states. Twenty-eight states have adopted or adapted NCATE standards as the state standards for teacher preparation, and seventeen states expect NCATE accreditation of all public colleges with teacher preparation units. In addition, NCATE works in partnership with forty-six states to conduct joint reviews of colleges of education, designed to streamline the quality assurance process and to mesh state and professional standards.

NCATE is part of a continuum of teacher preparation and development that begins with pre-service preparation, and continues with stages of teacher licensure and advanced professional development. Standards in each phase of teacher development are aligned for the first time, providing new coherence to teacher preparation and development.

See also: ACCREDITATION IN THE UNITED STATES, *subentry on* HIGHER EDUCATION; HIGHER EDUCATION, *subentry on* SYSTEM.

BIBLIOGRAPHY

NATIONAL COUNCIL FOR ACCREDITATION OF TEACHER EDUCATION. 2001. *Professional Standards for the Accreditation of Schools, Colleges, and Departments of Education.* Washington, DC: National Council for Accreditation of Teacher Education.

INTERNET RESOURCE

NATIONAL COUNCIL FOR ACCREDITATION OF TEACHER EDUCATION. 2002. <www.ncate.org>.

ARTHUR E. WISE

TABLE 1

List of constituent member organizations of NCATE

Teacher educator organizations
American Association of Colleges for Teacher Education (AACTE)
Association of Teacher Educators (ATE)

Teacher organizations
American Federation of Teachers (AFT)
National Education Association (NEA)

Policymaker organizations
Council of Chief State School Officers (CCSSO)
National Association of State Boards of Education (NASBE)
National School Boards Association (NSBA)

Subject-specific organizations
American Council on the Teaching of Foreign Languages (ACTFL)
American Alliance for Health, Physical Education, Recreation, and Dance (AAHPERD)*
International Reading Association (IRA)*
International Technology Education Association (ITEA)*
National Council for the Social Studies (NCSS)*
National Council of Teachers of English (NCTE)*
National Council of Teachers of Mathematics (NCTM)*
National Science Teachers Association (NSTA)*
Teachers of English To Speakers of Other Languages (TESOL)

Child-centered organizations
Association for Childhood Education International (ACEI)*
Council for Exceptional Children (CEC)*
National Association for the Education of Young Children (NAEYC)*
National Middle School Association (NMSA)*

Technology organizations
Association for Education Communications and Technology (AECT)*
International Society for Technology in Education (ISTE)*

Specialist organizations
American Educational Research Association (AERA)
American Library Association (ALA)*
Council for Social Foundations of Education (CSFE)
National Association of School Psychologists (NASP)*

Administrative organizations
American Association of School Administrators (AASA)**
Association for Supervision and Curriculum Development (ASCD)**
National Association of Black School Educators (NABSE)
National Association of Elementary School Principals (NAESP)**
National Association of Secondary School Principals (NASSP)**

Other
National Board for Professional Teaching Standards (NBPTS)
Public representatives
Student representatives

*These organizations have submitted program standards that have been approved by NCATE for use in program review.
**The Educational Leadership Constituent Council (ELCC), composed of four members associations—AASA, ASCD, NAESP, and NASSP—reviews educational leadership programs.

SOURCE: Courtesy of author.

NATIONAL COUNCIL FOR THE SOCIAL STUDIES

The National Council for the Social Studies (NCSS) is a private, nonprofit organization that, in the words of its mission statement, aims to "provide leadership, service, and support for social studies educators." It is inspired by the belief that all citizens in a participatory democracy must develop the content knowledge, intellectual skills, and civic values that a solid education in the social studies can impart.

Program

The central mission of the NCSS is to improve the integrated teaching of the social studies at all levels of education, from elementary school to college and graduate school. To further this end it produced its core publication, a study entitled *Expectations of Excellence: Curriculum Standards for Social Studies,* first published in 1994. In this report, the NCSS lays out a ten-theme, integrated approach to the teaching of history, geography, economics, political science, sociology, psychology, anthropology, and law-related subjects. However, the NCSS is also active in supporting research, encouraging experimentation, fostering dialog among educators and between educators and policymakers, and making available research data that may assist in all these endeavors.

Chief among the NCSS's services is the dissemination of information, which will help educators to improve their ability to communicate with their students. The NCSS flagship publication *Social Education* seeks to do this by publishing articles on curriculum development, teaching methods, the use of audio and visual aids, classroom projects, and relevant research results. The journal is published monthly throughout the academic year. The NCSS also publishes *Social Studies and the Young Learner,* a journal devoted to exploring the special educational needs of elementary school students, and *The Social Studies Professional,* the council's newsletter. Both of these are published bimonthly during the academic year.

In addition, the NCSS issues a number of bulletins on specific topics or specific subfields within the larger discipline of social studies. Bulletins appear twice each year in book form. Tightly defined "how-to" tips and techniques are featured in a series of six-to eight-page leaflets. At irregular intervals the NCSS also publishes books and monographs on topics of interest to its membership.

As the NCSS has long dedicated its energies toward developing standards in the teaching of social studies, it would seem that the trend favoring "standards-based education" would be highly compatible with NCSS philosophy. However, the organization has always taken a holistic approach, which brings together the various disciplines found in the social sciences, behavioral sciences, and humanities. This approach does not always fit comfortably within a curriculum that is strongly driven by objective testing. Thus publications in the early twenty-first century and other NCSS initiatives have begun to explore ways in which educators can remain faithful to NCSS standards while still helping their students pass the externally imposed regimen of objective testing found in many school districts across the nation.

Organizational Structure

The officers and board of directors are elected to office through the votes of the general membership. The board of directors is responsible for setting council policy, approving projects, and other such high-level decision-making. The board is assisted in its duties by the advice of delegates representing local, regional, and state councils. The board meets officially twice each year; when decisions must be made during the interim between board meetings, an executive council consisting of the president, vice president, president-elect, and two board-appointed members will convene to address the issues. The day-to-day affairs of the council are handled by an executive secretary who is assisted by a professional staff.

Membership

The NCSS has more than 20,000 members drawn from all fifty states and the District of Columbia, as well as affiliates in sixty-nine countries around the world. Its members include teachers at all educational levels, from first grade to graduate school, as well as nonteaching professionals, such as principals, curriculum designers, and educational specialists in local, state, and national governments. In addition, students who are completing a course of study geared to a career in education are eligible to join.

Direct membership is not the only way to become involved in the NCSS. The council has long been an active promoter of independent councils and offers such groups the opportunity to become affiliates if they share the general aims and philosophy of the national council.

History

The NCSS was founded in 1921, shortly after the close of World War I. This was a time when the public school system was undergoing rapid expansion and access to college was being extended well beyond the traditional elite few. Educators in all disciplines were finding that received standards and philosophies of teaching were inadequate to cope with a burgeoning student body, which represented a widely divergent set of skills and prior training.

In response to these pressures, colleges and public school districts across the country were all attempting to come up with workable solutions. Given the extremely independent nature of the public school organization, which was always locally controlled, the result of these efforts was an uncoordinated patchwork of programs, plans, and approaches, and the education received by students could vary wildly in quality and in content. To address this problem, a group of college professors and public school professionals met in Atlantic City, New Jersey. When this group drew up a constitution, elected officers, and agreed to continue to meet, the NCSS was born.

The NCSS set itself the task of finding a way to coordinate the efforts of educators and educational professionals across the country. It soon found some degree of success simply by making all the various groups aware of what their colleagues were doing elsewhere in the country. Thus, even at the outset, communication through publications was recognized to be a highly effective strategy for the NCSS in achieving its goals. Its journal, then titled *The Historical Outlook,* became influential throughout the national educational system. It was renamed *Social Education* in 1937, two years after the NCSS held its first annual conference independent of the National Education Association, on which it was initially dependent.

Over the years the NCSS has grown dramatically in size and influence, not just within the educational community but also with local, state, and federal policymakers. For all its growth and influence, however, it remains committed to the goals that inspired its founding: to serve and support the nation's teachers of the social studies, in the interest of educating new generations of informed, responsible citizens.

See also: SOCIAL STUDIES EDUCATION.

INTERNET RESOURCE

NATIONAL COUNCIL FOR THE SOCIAL STUDIES. 2002. <www.ncss.org>.

MERRILL F. HARTSHORN
Revised by
NANCY E. GRATTON

NATIONAL COUNCIL OF TEACHERS OF ENGLISH

The National Council of Teachers of English (NCTE) is, according to their literature, "a professional organization of educators in English studies, literacy, and language arts." This private, nonprofit organization is dedicated to promoting English language education at all levels, from kindergarten through graduate studies.

Program

The NCTE hosts four annual conferences, at which members have the opportunity to attend panel discussions, seminars, and workshops to improve their professional skills. In addition, it maintains a presence at the conferences and conventions of affiliated organizations, such as the Modern Language Association of America (MLA), the International Reading Association (IRA), and the Speech Association of America (SAA).

In addition to the national conferences, the NCTE produces several publications aimed at disseminating information it considers important to its general membership. The official newsletter is *The Council Chronicle,* in which are published articles on the issues, trends, and concerns facing teachers of English. Another publication of general interest is the *English Language Quarterly.* Other periodicals serve specific subgroups in the larger membership: *College English, Primary Voices K–6,* and *Teaching English in the Two-Year College,* for example, have clearly defined constituencies. All told, the NCTE supports the publication of twelve journals.

Each year the NCTE also produces twenty to twenty-five books, most of which are specifically intended as teacher's guides or texts. Among recent titles are *Teaching Poetry in High School, Lesson Plans for Substitute Teachers,* and *Evaluating Writing.* This continues a long tradition; the first full-length publication produced by the NCTE was *Current English Usage,* produced in 1935 and long a staple in high school classrooms.

The NCTE also sponsors a number of annual awards. Two are granted to individual students in every state and are meant to recognize outstanding achievement in writing. Candidates are nominated by their high-school English teacher and must submit three writing samples. A third award, also granted on a state-by-state basis, honors the best student publication of the year. Finally, there is the David H. Russell Award for Distinguished Research in the Teaching of English, awarded in recognition of scholarly achievement by a member of the NCTE.

Because professional development is an important aspect of the NCTE mission, the council is committed to supporting its membership in advancing their skills as well as their knowledge of the changing nature of American education, particularly as it affects the teaching of English. For this reason it maintains the NCTE Research Foundation, which makes available grants to support scholarly research.

A final aspect of the NCTE mandate is advocacy. The council is actively involved in providing guidance to policymakers at the local, state, and national level on all issues relevant to the teaching of English. For instance, the NCTE has been very active in the fight against censorship of reading materials in schools, and has been equally involved in advising policymakers on ways to expand and improve literacy among the nation's children.

Organization

As of 2002 the NCTE had 77,000 active members in the United States and Canada. The council recognizes the wide range of interests and specializations represented within its membership, which is therefore broken out into three separate divisions: elementary (K–6 grades), secondary (middle school and high school), and collegiate. In addition, there are several special-interest departments called *conferences.* These are the Conference on College Composition and Communication (CCCC), the Conference on English Education (CEE), the Conference for English Leadership (CEL), the Two-Year College English Association (TYCA), and the Whole Language Umbrella conference (WLU). Each division is run by a section committee and an independent governing board.

The publications arm of the NCTE is separately administered. In addition to the books and periodicals produced by the organization, there are bulletins, public information updates, and special reports issued to members as well as to the broader public.

The national council is overseen by a board of directors, made up of representatives from all the divisions as well as from affiliated, nonmember groups such as the MLA. A slate of nominees is developed by a nominating committee, then voted on by the current board. The board meets annually to discuss NCTE business. A smaller executive committee is responsible for the day-to-day activities of the council and includes a president, vice president, executive secretary, treasurer, and representatives from each of the council divisions, as well as the immediate past president. This group meets with greater frequency, three times a year on average, and reports its activities to the board of directors.

Affiliate organizations, from local English associations to national organizations with a strong interest in the promotion of English language use and literacy, are an independent but highly valued constituency within the NCTE. Their participation in national conferences is actively encouraged. In addition, such groups are frequently enlisted in the pursuit of NCTE-sponsored special projects, such as literacy campaigns, curriculum development, and teacher education.

Membership and Financial Support

The NCTE prides itself on keeping its membership open to all teachers of English and others in related professions. The council supports its programs by membership dues, paid annually, and through the sale of its books and other published materials. In addition, it receives government support in the form of grants.

History

The NCTE was founded in 1911 by a group of educators in Chicago, Illinois, known as the English Round Table of the National Education Association. This group wanted to create a professional response to changing needs and values regarding education, particularly English language education. The impetus for this early effort was a concern that school curriculums were becoming too narrow and were incapable of addressing the needs of an increasingly diverse student population. A special committee was formed to address these issues.

These concerned educators at first set themselves a limited task: to explore the problems arising from a rigid, narrowly defined approach to English language instruction. Soon, however, it became apparent that more was needed, and that only a national professional organization would have the ability to affect policy decisions. By 1919 the original investigatory committee had grown large enough to become such an organization. Because of its open-door policy regarding membership, the NCTE from the first maintained a divisional structure, with separate groups representing elementary, secondary, and postsecondary educators.

Over the next several decades the organization continued to grow. By 1948 it was clear that the simple divisions based on grade level were inadequate, and the CCCC was formed to address the special needs of communication and composition teachers at the college level. This reliance on committee organization proved to be extremely useful, for it permitted interested groups to concentrate their focus on particular issues or trends. Membership grew dramatically in the second half of the twentieth century, and over the years new committees were formed, leading to the five-conference structure in place at the beginning of the twenty-first century.

See also: LANGUAGE ARTS, TEACHING OF; SPEECH AND THEATER EDUCATION; WRITING, TEACHING OF.

INTERNET RESOURCE

NATIONAL COUNCIL OF TEACHERS OF ENGLISH. 2002. <www.ncte.org>.

DORA V. SMITH
JAMES R. SQUIRE
Revised by
NANCY E. GRATTON

NATIONAL COUNCIL OF TEACHERS OF MATHEMATICS

Since its inception in 1920, the National Council of Teachers of Mathematics (NCTM) has been dedicated to improving the teaching and learning of mathematics. NCTM has positioned itself as a leader in efforts to ensure an excellent mathematics education for every student and to provide sustained professional development opportunities for every mathematics teacher to grow professionally. The mission of the National Council of Teachers of Mathematics is to provide the vision and leadership necessary to ensure a mathematics education of the highest quality for all students.

With more than 100,000 members and more than 250 affiliates in the United States and Canada, NCTM is the world's largest organization dedicated to improving mathematics education in grades pre-kindergarten through twelve. NCTM offers vision, leadership, and avenues of communication for mathematics educators at the elementary school, middle school, high school, and college and university levels.

In representing the interests of its members in the debate of public issues, NCTM's government relations activities are dedicated to ongoing dialogue and constructive discussion with all stakeholders about what is best for students.

Principles and Standards

In April 2000 NCTM released its *Principles and Standards for School Mathematics,* which are guidelines for excellence in pre-K–12 mathematics education and a call for all students to engage in more challenging mathematics. The *Principles and Standards* provide a vision for mathematics education in the future, one with higher standards for both teachers and students.

Principles and Standards for School Mathematics has four major components. First, the principles reflect basic perspectives on which educators should base decisions that affect school mathematics. These principles establish a foundation for school mathematics programs by considering the broad issues of equity, curriculum, teaching, learning, assessment, and technology.

The NCTM standards describe an ambitious and comprehensive set of goals for mathematics instruction. The first five standards present goals in the mathematical content areas of number and operations, algebra, geometry, measurement, and data analysis and probability. The second five describe goals for the processes of problem solving, reasoning and proof, connections, communication, and representation. Together, these standards describe the basic skills and understanding that students will need to function effectively in the twenty-first century.

Resources

NCTM develops and publishes a wide array of resources for teachers. A series of thirty *Navigations* volumes is being published to assist teachers in bringing the *Principles and Standards for School Mathematics* into the classroom. The content of *Principles and Standards* is extended online at NCTM's website through *E-Standards* and *Illuminations*. The *Illuminations* website was developed to further illustrate the NCTM standards and provide teachers with lesson plans and learning activities for students to put the standards into practice. It provides standards-based Internet content for K–12 teachers and classrooms.

Professional Development

NCTM provides a range of professional development opportunities through annual, regional, and leadership conferences, and through the publication of professional journals and other publications. The association coordinates several regional conferences and one annual meeting each year, with a combined attendance of more than 30,000. Its Academy for Professional Development, founded in 2000, provides two- and five-day training institutes for mathematics teachers.

Reflections is another element of NCTM's professional development for teachers. The *Reflections* website offers online video examples of mathematics instruction to help teachers apply in-depth analysis and discussion to improve their own skills. Included are online discussions with lesson-study critiques, video of students' work during class and on their assignments, and a professional analysis with teachers' discussions.

NCTM publishes four professional journals: *Teaching Children Mathematics; Mathematics Teaching in the Middle School;* the *Mathematics Teacher;* and the *Journal for Research in Mathematics Education.* Other publications include the monthly member newsletter, the *NCTM News Bulletin,* and more than 200 educational books, videos, and other materials. Each year in April, the council sponsors the World's Largest Math Event and publishes a colorful activity booklet with related activities that teachers can use across the grades.

The National Council of Teachers of Mathematics also works closely with the National Council for Accreditation of Teacher Education (NCATE), which delegates to NCTM the review of its institutions' mathematics teacher preparation programs. NCATE accredits 519 institutions, which produce two-thirds of the nation's new teacher graduates each year. Through its review of these schools' mathematics programs, NCTM helps to ensure that future teachers will be prepared for the classroom.

In 1976 NCTM founded the Mathematics Education Trust (MET) to provide funds directly to teachers to enhance the teaching and learning of mathematics. MET offers twelve grant and scholarship award programs for teachers. In addition to grants to individual teachers, MET honors mathematics educators with its annual Lifetime Achievement Award for Distinguished Service to Mathematics Education.

Governance and Membership

The National Council of Teachers of Mathematics is a nonprofit organization governed by a fifteen-member board of directors consisting of the president, past president or president-elect, and twelve elected members who serve three-year terms. The executive director is an ex officio member of the board. The president serves a four-year term on the board, consisting of one year as president-elect, two years as president, and one year as past president.

As a professional association, NCTM derives its strength from its members. Membership is composed primarily of K–12 classroom teachers, university educators specializing in mathematics education, and educational institutions (such as college libraries and schools). Members participate in the work of approximately seventy national committees and task forces and contribute to all aspects of the council's work. Through its executive, conference services, finance and administration, human resources, information technology, member services and marketing, and publications divisions, the council's 110 employees manage an annual budget of $16 million.

See also: MATHEMATICS EDUCATION, TEACHER PREPARATION.

INTERNET RESOURCE

NATIONAL COUNCIL OF TEACHERS OF MATHEMATICS. 2002. <www.nctm.org>.

KEN KREHBIEL

NATIONAL EDUCATION ASSOCIATION

The National Education Association (NEA) is America's oldest and largest professional employee organization committed to the cause of public education (as well as to the well-being of its members). Founded in 1857 in Philadelphia, and now headquartered in Washington, D.C., in 2001 the NEA membership includes more than 2.6 million elementary and secondary school teachers, college faculty, education support professionals, school administrators, retired educators, and students preparing to become teachers. The NEA has affiliates in every state as well as in over 13,000 local communities across the United States.

Membership

Anyone who works for a public school district, a college or university, or any other public institution devoted primarily to education is eligible to join the NEA. The organization also has special membership categories for retired educators and college students studying to become teachers. More specific membership information can vary among state and local affiliates. Members pay dues to be part of the NEA, and in return are provided with a wide range of services from the organization. The NEA has long been active in trying to improve the economic status of teachers and education professionals by assisting in the negotiating of employment contracts with local school boards.

Issues the NEA includes in negotiations are salary schedules, grievance procedures, instruction methods, transfer policies, discipline, preparation periods, class size, extracurricular activities, sick leave, and school safety. The NEA assists local affiliates in negotiations through consultation by field representatives and through the production of resource materials. In defining the role of its members, the NEA developed the *Code of Ethics for the Educational Profession.* In 1975 NEA members adopted the code, which "indicates the aspiration of all educators and provides standards by which to judge conduct."

Governance

The NEA is a democratic organization, and the structure and policy of the NEA are outlined in the organization's constitution and bylaws. NEA members nationwide set association policy and change the bylaws and the constitution of the organization—most notably through the annual Representative Assembly (RA), which is held every July. The Representative Assembly is the primary legislative and policymaking body of the NEA. It derives its powers from, and is responsible to, the membership. NEA members at the state and local level elect the more than nine thousand RA delegates, who in turn elect NEA's top officers, debate issues, and set NEA policy at the Representative Assembly.

Between Representative Assemblies, NEA's top decision-making bodies throughout the year are the board of directors and the executive committee. The board of directors consists of at least one director from each association affiliated with the NEA, as well as an additional director for each twenty thousand active NEA members in each state, six directors for the retired members of the NEA, and three directors for the student members. The board meets four times a year, plus one meeting in conjunction with the Representative Assembly.

The executive committee consists of nine members: the three executive officers of president, vice president, and secretary treasurer, and six members elected at-large by delegates to the Representative Assembly. The executive committee meets approximately seven times a year.

Staff and Administration

NEA is a volunteer-based organization supported by a network of staff at the local, state, and national level. At the local and state level, NEA affiliates are active in a wide array of activities, ranging from conducting professional workshops on discipline and other issues that affect faculty and school support staff to bargaining contracts for school district employees. At the national level, more than five hundred employees work for the NEA at its headquarters in Washington, D.C. The NEA staffing structure is designed to help realize the NEA's strategic priorities.

Policies

During the 1998–2000 budget years, it was decided by the membership that the association's priority work would concentrate on three areas of concern: student achievement, teacher quality, and school system capacity to support student success. The organization's staff departments were assembled with these three core priorities in mind.

Student achievement. Increasing student achievement is NEA's first strategic priority. Making sure that all students have the skills and knowledge to function successfully in school so that they may also succeed as adults is critical to the Association's strategic focus on rebuilding public confidence in public education. This department is dedicated to helping local affiliates address issues such as high-stakes testing and implementing standards-based education. It also helps affiliates advocate for and influence instructional policy and practice at the local level and implement the NEA's annual Read Across America child literacy event, which is held every March 1 in honor of the birthday of Dr. Seuss (Theodor Geisel).

Teacher quality. The single most important factor in enhancing student achievement is teacher quality. The NEA stands by the belief that without a qualified teacher in every classroom, student learning is limited and access to quality education is compromised. NEA's Teacher Quality Department is designed to help all teachers achieve high standards for practice. Through this department, the NEA promotes rigorous standards for access to, and graduation from, teacher preparation programs; advocates that all teacher education institutions meet the high standards set by the National Council for Accreditation of Teacher Education (NCATE); and insists on comprehensive teacher induction programs, which include mentoring support systems for new teachers that enhance professional practice and teacher retention. The department also seeks to ensure that all personnel hired to teach are fully licensed; promotes the strategic recruitment and retention of licensed teachers in shortage areas; advocates standards-driven professional development and teacher evaluation systems that work to enhance performance; and advances strategies to increase the number of teachers, particularly minority teachers, who become National Board Certified.

School system capacity. The NEA is working to enhance school system capacity to assure that America's schools have the staff, structures, and resources needed to improve student achievement. Toward this end, work in this department establishes systems that support quality teaching and high levels of learning. The NEA is also seeking to increase financial support for public education, stimulate the recruiting and maintaining of quality school staffs, improve the physical learning environment, ensure safe and orderly schools, promote equity and excellence among school districts, and help educators, parents, and other interested citizens develop more

effective school management and decision-making processes.

Activities

At the state level, NEA activities are wide-ranging. NEA state affiliates, for instance, regularly lobby legislators for the resources schools need, campaign for higher professional standards for the teaching profession, and file legal actions to protect academic freedom.

At the national level, NEA's work ranges from coordinating innovative projects to restructuring how learning takes place and fighting congressional attempts to privatize public education. At the international level, NEA is linking educators around the world in an ongoing dialogue dedicated to making schools as effective as they can be. On an individual level, NEA members organize themselves into voluntary groups called *caucuses*.

NEA affiliates around the country celebrate three major events: Read Across America Day; American Education Week (the week before Thanksgiving); and National Teacher Day (the Tuesday that falls in the first full week of May, which is Teacher Appreciation Week).

Lobbying and elections. One of the most prominent education lobbying group in the nation, the NEA is influential in politics—ranging from school board elections to the presidential election. With 2.6 million members in America's schools, one in one hundred Americans is an NEA member. This makes NEA a loud voice in America's public-education policy debate.

NEA's lobbying efforts are based on the initiatives passed by the Representative Assembly, and usually involve school funding issues, student testing requirements, and federal funding for needy schools. The NEA has a political action committee (PAC) named the Fund for Children and Public Education, which is used to contribute funds to candidates running for office who uphold the principles of the NEA and its affiliates. Members donate to the PAC, but it is not funded through dues assessments like many other labor union PACs.

Communications. The NEA is often called upon to serve as a voice for teachers and public education in national media outlets. Usually the organization's president serves in this role, though oftentimes NEA staff are also asked to be spokespeople for the association. Additionally, the NEA produces and disseminates several publications. The most widely read is the *NEA Today* monthly magazine, which is sent to all NEA members. There are also publications put out by the NEA for its different constituencies, including retired members, student members, and members in higher education institutions.

Research. As a way of serving its members, the NEA has a research department that looks into issues concerning teachers and public education. The most widely used research document produced by the NEA is the yearly *Rankings and Estimates,* which ranks state school statistics such as teacher salaries, per-pupil expenditures, and student enrollment. Every five years, the NEA research department produces *Status of the American Public School Teacher,* which is an intensive look at the attitudes of members about their workloads and toward the profession and compensation.

History

The NEA was founded in 1857 as the National Teachers Association, "to elevate the character and advance the interests of the profession of teaching, and to promote the cause of popular education in the United States." In 1870 the NTA united with the National Association of School Superintendents and the American Normal School Association to form the National Educational Association. The organization was incorporated in 1886 in the District of Columbia as the National Education Association, and in 1906 it was chartered by an act of Congress. The charter was officially adopted at the association's annual meeting of 1907, with the name officially set down as the National Education Association of the United States. The original statement of purpose of the National Teachers Association remains unchanged in the present NEA charter.

In 1917 the association moved to Washington, D.C., where it acquired a permanent headquarters in 1920. In the same year the association, grown too large for the efficient transaction of business by the total membership, reorganized on a representative basis, with delegates drawn from NEA-affiliated state and local education associations. With this new arrangement the NEA increased efforts to organize professional associations of teachers at the state and local school district level. The emerging goal for the association became a united teaching profession with every teacher participating at three levels of association work—local, state, and national. Throughout the 1920s and 1930s, the association also expanded through the development or addition of departments devoted to subject matter and positional specialties.

The 1960s saw the merger of separate associations of white and African-American educators, a situation that had arisen as a result of dual school systems in the South. Although NEA membership had always been open to all qualified educators regardless of race, an independent national organization of African-American educators, the American Teachers Association, was in existence until 1966, when its 32,000 members merged with the NEA. Merger of state associations followed, and by 1969 had been completed in almost all states.

In the late 1990s the NEA was talking merger again. At that time, the NEA was close to merging with another sister union, the American Federation of Teachers (AFT), which is affiliated with the AFL-CIO labor union. In 1998, the Representative Assembly voted down a proposal to unite the two organizations. However, a partnership agreement was approved at the 2001 Representative Assembly. The partnership agreement allows the two organizations to work together and prevents the two unions from "raiding" each other's members.

See also: TEACHER UNIONS.

BIBLIOGRAPHY

NATIONAL EDUCATION ASSOCIATION. 2000. *NEA Handbook 2000–2001.* Washington, DC: NEA.

INTERNET RESOURCE

NATIONAL EDUCATION ASSOCIATION. 2002. <www.nea.org>.

DENISE CARDINAL

NATIONAL ENDOWMENT FOR THE ARTS

The National Endowment for the Arts (NEA) is an independent federal agency that supports and funds the arts in the United States. The endowment was established by the Arts and Humanities Act of 1965, which defines the arts to include music, dance, drama, folk art, graphic art, creative writing, architecture, painting, sculpture, photography, crafts, industrial design, costume and fashion design, motion pictures, television, radio, and sound recordings. The NEA is the country's largest single source of funding for nonprofit arts.

The endowment was established on the principle that the arts are as vital to the spirit, stability, and success of a democratic country as science and technology. Accordingly, the government and citizens of the United States must preserve the country's artistic heritage and cultivate new artistic expression. Through the NEA, the federal government fosters the preservation and development of the arts by financing new and classic artistic works and their presentation, making the arts accessible to people in all parts of the country, promoting art education at all levels, preserving the country's artistic heritage, and recognizing and honoring the country's national leaders in the arts.

Program

The NEA supports the arts through leadership initiatives; through partnerships with other federal agencies and with local, state, and regional arts organizations; and, primarily, through the making of grants to nonprofit arts organizations and, in some cases, to individual artists. It is not the intention of the federal government to fully subsidize the arts in the United States; rather the NEA aims at alleviating the financial stress prevalent in the arts by providing "seed" money to stimulate the private sector to provide support for the cultural growth of the country.

The NEA funds the work of individual artists through Literature Fellowships, American Jazz Masters Fellowships, and National Heritage Fellowships. Literature Fellowships of $20,000 are awarded to writers of poetry, fiction, and drama; fellowships of $10,000 to $20,000 are awarded for translation projects. Since the establishment of the Literature Fellowship in 1967, many National Book Awards, National Book Critics Circle Awards, and Pulitzer Prizes in poetry and fiction have been awarded for works funded in part by the NEA. American Jazz Masters Fellowships of $20,000 are awarded to distinguished jazz musicians. National Heritage Fellowships of $10,000 are annually awarded to up to thirteen master folk and traditional artists who hope to teach their skills and techniques to another generation of artists. All recipients of NEA fellowships must be citizens or permanent residents of the United States.

Grants that are awarded to nonprofit organizations support a variety of projects, such as developing new works, bringing the arts to new audiences, developing new and stronger arts organizations, and preserving America's cultural heritage. The NEA's heritage and preservation grants support such projects as the restoration of historic buildings and artworks, the preservation of historic sound recordings, the documentation of dance projects, and the publication of anthologies of American literature. In 2000 the NEA formed a partnership with Heritage Preservation to sponsor Save Outdoor Sculpture!, a program to repair and maintain damaged outdoor sculptures in the United States. Another NEA program, Save America's Treasures, offers grants in cooperation with the Department of the Interior and the National Park Service for the preservation and conservation of historically or culturally significant buildings, sites, artifacts, collections, and monuments.

The NEA's grants for arts education aim to strengthen the role of the arts in America's public educational system and encourage lifelong learning in the arts. The NEA recognizes that stimulation of young audiences is essential to its goal of developing a broad base of public appreciation and support for the arts. In partnership with state arts agencies and regional arts organizations, the NEA has provided millions of dollars to support K–12 arts education projects in communities across the country. In a program conducted in cooperation with local school boards and the U.S. Department of Education, professional theater companies have received financial assistance to give free performances for student audiences. Similarly, the endowment provided support for a program aimed at sending poets into secondary schools to read and discuss their works. Other grants in support of art education have funded master classes, artist-in-residence programs, and training for elementary and high school art teachers.

To further achieve the expansion of audiences the NEA has initiated programs that bring the performing and visual arts to small towns, rural areas, and other regions of the United States where the arts would otherwise be unavailable. In 1996 the NEA helped finance the New England Foundation for the Arts, which sends contemporary dance companies on tours that include cities where few dance companies reside. The endowment has also provided funds for an experimental rural arts program to explore methods of increasing public receptivity to cultural programs. In many states, grants have been made to develop new audiences for opera by providing funds for additional performances for neighborhood and community organizations, labor groups, and students.

The endowment has provided new opportunities for arts programming on television through grants to public television stations for the production of arts programs and their free distribution to other public television stations throughout the country. The NEA helped fund the popular series *Live from Lincoln Center, American Masters,* and *Great Performances,* which are broadcast around the country and seen by millions of people each year. These grants have served as an incentive to the further development of educational programming on the arts and have helped many smaller stations get access to local cultural resources.

The American Film Institute was established with funding from the NEA in order to focus national attention on motion pictures as a contemporary art. One of the institute's central responsibilities is that of promoting and guiding the burgeoning interest in this art in secondary schools and higher education. The institute is providing assistance to the entire academic community.

Organizational Structure

The endowment's advisory body is the National Council on the Arts, which includes fourteen private citizens appointed by the president of the United States for six-year terms and six members of Congress who are appointed by congressional leaders and serve in a nonvoting capacity for two-year terms. The private members of the council are persons who have distinguished themselves through their training, experience, and interest in the arts. Past council members have included singer Marian Anderson, composer Leonard Bernstein, dancer and choreographer Agnes de Mille, artist Richard Diebenkorn, composer Duke Ellington, author Harper Lee, actor Gregory Peck, actor Sidney Poitier, author John Steinbeck, and violinist Isaac Stern. The council, which meets three times each year, advises the chairman on NEA policies, programs, and procedures and makes recommendations on applications for financial assistance.

History and Development

The National Council on the Arts was created by the National Arts and Cultural Development Act of 1964 (Pub. L. 88-579). The National Endowment for the Arts began its work in 1965, when President Lyndon B. Johnson signed legislation (Pub. L. 89-209) creating the National Foundation on the Arts and the Humanities, consisting of both the NEA and its sister agency the National Endowment for the Humanities. The 1965 act transferred the functions of the council from the executive office of the president of the United States to the NEA.

The NEA came under attack during the 1980s and 1990s as some citizens and public officials questioned the value, quality, and appropriateness of certain NEA-supported projects. President Ronald Reagan established a Presidential Task Force on the Arts and Humanities in 1981 to develop "ideas to stimulate increased private giving for cultural activities." The task force, however, recommended that the NEA continue public funding of humanities and art projects. Between 1965 and 2000 the NEA awarded more than 115,000 grants to artists and art organizations in all fifty states, Puerto Rico, and Guam. In the 2001 fiscal year the endowment's budget was approximately $105 million.

BIBLIOGRAPHY

DOWLEY, JENNIFER, and PRINCENTHAL, NANCY. 2001. *A Creative Legacy: A History of the National Endowment for the Arts Visual Artists Fellowship Program.* New York: Abrams.

NATIONAL ENDOWMENT FOR THE ARTS. 2000. *A Legacy of Leadership: Investing in America's Living Cultural Heritage since 1965.* Washington, DC: National Endowment for the Arts.

NATIONAL ENDOWMENT FOR THE ARTS. 2000. *The National Endowment for the Arts 1965–2000: A Brief Chronology of Federal Support for the Arts,* revised edition. Washington, DC: National Endowment for the Arts.

ZEIGLER, JOSEPH WESLEY. 1994. *Arts in Crisis: The National Endowment for the Arts Versus America.* Pennington, NJ: A Cappella Books.

INTERNET RESOURCE

NATIONAL ENDOWMENT FOR THE ARTS. 2002. <http://arts.endow.gov>.

KAREN SZUREK
Revised by
JUDITH J. CULLIGAN

NATIONAL ENDOWMENT FOR THE HUMANITIES

On September 29, 1965 U.S. President Lyndon B. Johnson signed legislation enacted by the eighty-ninth Congress creating the National Foundation on the Arts and the Humanities, an independent federal agency consisting of two separate but cooperating organizations, the National Endowment for the Arts (NEA) and the National Endowment for the Humanities (NEH). Through this legislation tangible expression was given to the concept that support of the arts and the humanities is in the national interest. The formation of the NEH lent credence to the belief that the humanities stimulate reflection on the values that Americans hold as a nation and as individuals, and that they offer, through their common historical orientation, interpretations of the process by which cultures and societies have reached their present complex form.

The National Endowment for the Humanities is a public body whose purpose is to bring the substance of the humanities to bear on the mainstream of American thinking and life. It attempts to do so by increasing knowledge, improving the competence of scholars and teachers, and improving public understanding of the humanities through education. The humanities include a broad list of fields, including literature, history, languages and linguistics, archaeology, comparative religion, philosophy, jurisprudence, journalism, and art history and criticism.

Program

The NEH accomplishes its mission primarily by making grants and fellowships dedicated to supporting research, education, preservation, and public programs in the humanities. Most NEH grants are awarded to cultural institutions such as museums, historical societies, libraries, universities, and public television and radio stations. Many grants and fellowships are also made to individuals to support such activities as the writing of a book or the production of a film. The NEH does not fund creative or performing arts; the National Endowment for the Arts supports these activities.

Any citizen of the United States or a permanent resident who has lived in the United States for more than three years can apply for an NEH grant, although most grants are given to institutions. NEH grants are awarded on a competitive basis. Each application is assessed by panels of experts outside the endowment. The National Council on the Humanities meets three times a year to review the applications and outside assessments. The council makes recommendations to the NEH chairperson, who makes the final decisions.

The NEH runs numerous grant programs. Some grants are awarded annually or on a running basis, some are awarded only once. Some grants are only available to institutions; others only to individuals. Representative NEH grant programs include the Preservation Assistance Grant of up to $5,000 to help libraries, museums, and historical societies increase their capacity to preserve their humanities collections; Schools for a New Millennium grants of up to $100,000 for educational institutions wishing to improve elementary, middle, and high school teaching of humanities; Institutional Grants of up to $25,000 for historically black, Hispanic-serving, and tribal colleges and universities that wish to improve the teaching of humanities; and the Lewis and Clark Bicentennial Initiative Grant for a project relating to the history and accomplishments of this expedition.

The NEH has funded hundreds of important educational and preservation projects, as well as books, films, and exhibitions since its founding. In 1969 an NEH grant to the University of Virginia supported a project to produce the first comprehensive edition of *The Papers of George Washington*. In 1971 the NEH began funding the compilation of the groundbreaking *Dictionary of American Regional English*. In 1976 the NEH funded the preparation and publication of *The States and the Nation*, a multivolume series of state histories published in honor of the American bicentennial. In 1980 the NEH awarded a grant to the Ancient Biblical Manuscript Center in Claremont, California, to make archival photographs of the Dead Sea scrolls. In 1988 *Voices and Visions*, a thirteen-part television series on American poetry, aired on public television stations with NEH support.

Throughout its history the NEH has helped historians, literary critics, and other scholars research, write, and publish books. Many NEH supported books have gone on to win Pulitzer Prizes and other major awards. The NEH helped fund the Pulitzer Prize–winning *Gotham: A History of New York City to 1898* (1998) by Edwin G. Burrows and Mike Wallace. The NEH also helped fund David M. Kennedy's Pulitzer Prize–winning *Freedom from Fear: The American People in Depression and War, 1929–45*

(1999). In addition, the NEH funds the production, distribution, and broadcast of numerous documentary films. Filmmaker Ken Burns's documentaries *The Brooklyn Bridge* (1982), *The Life and Times of Huey Long* (1986), *The Civil War* (1990), and *Baseball* (1994) were all made and broadcast with NEH support. The NEH also supported the Academy Award nominated *Scottsboro: An American Tragedy* (2001), a documentary film written and directed by Barak Goodman.

NEH-funded projects that were underway in the early 2000s included the United States Newspaper Program, a major effort to locate, catalog, and preserve newspapers published in the United States since the eighteenth century; and the Papers Projects, which funded a number of projects to collect and publish the papers of American presidents and other historical and literary figures. The NEH was also actively funding numerous online humanities projects, including the Mystic Seaport's *Exploring Amistad* website; the Academy of American Poets' *Online Poetry Classroom,* and Indiana University's *Prehistoric Puzzles* website. Descriptions of NEH-funded projects, and other NEH news and information, are published in the bimonthly magazine *Humanities.*

Since 1997, the NEH has presented annual National Humanities Medals to individuals or groups who have helped deepen people's understanding of the humanities. Notable past winners of the National Humanities Medal have included Quincy Jones, Garrison Keillor, Jim Lehrer, August Wilson, Henry Louis Gates Jr., Garry Wills, Maxine Hong Kingston, and Doris Kearns Goodwin. Since 1972 the NEH has also selected an outstanding individual to give the prestigious Jefferson Lecture in the Humanities, delivered every spring in Washington, D.C. The Jefferson Lecture, which includes a $10,000 honorarium, is awarded to an important American scholar who has demonstrated the ability to communicate about the humanities in a accessible and appealing way. Notable Jefferson lecturers have included poet Robert Penn Warren (1974), novelist Saul Bellow (1977), novelist Toni Morrison (1996), and playwright Arthur Miller (2001).

Organizational Structure

The NEH is composed of four divisions and three offices. Divisions include the Preservation and Access Division, the Public Programs Division, the Research Division, and the Education Division. Offices include the Challenge Grants Office, the Office of Federal-State Partnership, and the Enterprise Office. The Office of Federal-State Partnership links NEH with fifty-six regional humanities councils located across the United States and in Puerto Rico, American Samoa, Guam, the U.S. Virgin Islands, and the Northern Mariana Islands. Each regional council funds humanities programs in its area. The responsibility of the Enterprise Office is to raise funds for Endowment projects and initiatives, to forge relationships with other federal and state agencies and with private organizations, and to implement special programs.

The NEH is directed by a chairperson who is appointed by the president of the United States for a four-year term. The chairperson is advised by the National Council on the Humanities, a group of twenty-six private citizens who are appointed by the president and approved by the United States Senate. The NEH chairperson and council coordinate and advise the endowments for the arts and the humanities.

Financial Support

In order to utilize as much private money as possible in its activities, the endowment is authorized by Congress to receive gifts from private sources for unrestricted purposes. These funds are then matched equally with funds conditionally appropriated by Congress for this purpose. This provision was amended in 1968 to also permit the matching of restricted gifts for purposes recommended by the council and approved by the chairperson.

History and Development

Before the creation of the National Foundation on the Arts and the Humanities, the effort to secure federal support for the arts had gone on for about a century, and minor support for the arts did exist in many departments of the government. The most conspicuous success prior to 1965 was the establishment in 1964 of an arts council—without funds. In contrast, government support for the sciences grew rapidly after World War II, first through research support, particularly from the military, and then through the establishment and funding of the National Science Foundation. The results created an imbalance in the universities and colleges—despite the evident benefits for education in general. Federal funds were relatively abundant for the sciences, but they were entirely lacking for the humanities and the arts. In an attempt to rectify this situation, several members of Congress introduced legislation calling for increased support of the humanities, but none was successful.

In 1963 the American Council of Learned Societies, the Council of Graduate Schools in the United States, and the United Chapters of Phi Beta Kappa Society sponsored the Commission on the Humanities to study the needs of the humanities. The members of this group included university professors and presidents, business and professional men, and school administrators. It accepted in principle the inseparability of the humanities and the arts, but concentrated on the humanities in their educational context. This commission's report, issues in the spring of 1964, received wide distribution and had considerable effect.

In Congress, Senator Claiborne Pell of Rhode Island and Representative Frank Thompson Jr., of New Jersey, who had led the effort to secure meaningful support for the arts, took the opportunity offered by this increased attention to the humanities and introduced new bills to include the arts and the humanities in a single organization. The joining of congressional and public support for both the humanities and the arts resulted in the passage of the bill and the establishment of the foundation.

The NEH, along with the National Endowment for the Arts, came under attack beginning in the 1980s as some citizens and public officials questioned the quality and appropriateness of projects funded by the endowments. President Ronald Reagan established a Presidential Task Force on the Arts and the Humanities in 1981 to develop "ideas to stimulate increased private giving for cultural activities." The Task Force, however, recommended that the NEH and NEA continue public funding of humanities and art projects. From 1965 through 1998 the NEH awarded more than $3 billion in fellowships and grants.

BIBLIOGRAPHY

NATIONAL ENDOWMENT FOR THE HUMANITIES. 2001. *Rediscovering America: Thirty-five Years of the National Endowment for the Humanities.* Washington, DC: National Endowment for the Humanities.

INTERNET RESOURCE

NATIONAL ENDOWMENT FOR THE HUMANITIES. 2002. <www.neh.fed.us>.

BARNABY C. KEENEY
Revised by
JUDITH J. CULLIGAN

NATIONAL GOVERNORS ASSOCIATION

The National Governors Association (NGA) is powerful, bipartisan public policy and lobbying organization made up of the chief executives of America's fifty states, American Samoa, Guam, Virgin Islands, Northern Mariana Islands, and Puerto Rico. The NGA serves as the collective voice of the nation's state governments and provides a forum by which governors and their staffs can examine policy, share problems, and development solutions to issues of concern to the states. The NGA also represents state interests before the federal government, and provides advice and technical assistance to governors and their staffs.

Organizational Structure

The NGA is headed by a nine-member bipartisan executive committee, from which body the members annually elect a chairperson and vice chairperson from different parties. Former governors Bill Clinton, John Ashcroft, and Tommy Thompson have all served as NGA chairs. The NGA maintains three standing committees: economic development and commerce, human resources, and natural resources. In addition, the association forms task forces and special committees made up of at least two governors to address high-priority issues of immediate importance.

One of the association's principle bodies is the NGA Center for Best Practices. The center helps governors and their public policy staffs study problems and challenges facing their states and develop innovative approaches and solutions. The center examines practices in various states, then disseminates information on which states have the "best practices" in dealing with education, health care, the environment, social services, trade, workforce development, crime, and terrorism, so that other states can shape and reform their own policies using these practices as models.

Education Initiatives

The NGA takes great interest in education policy and practice because the U.S. Constitution grants to state governments the primary responsibility for public education. Governors recognize their leadership role in education policymaking, and during the 2001–2002 session the NGA included task forces on both postsecondary and K–12 education.

The Center for Best Practices includes the Education Policy Studies Division, which is staffed by policy analysts with expertise in education. During the late twentieth and early twenty-first centuries, the Education Policy Studies Division focused its work on early childhood education, school health, extra learning opportunities for elementary and high school children, standards-based education reform and performance-based accountability, teacher quality and teacher preparation, and the use of technology in education.

In 1999 the NGA and Center for Best Practices launched an initiative in cooperation with seven states (Georgia, Illinois, Maryland, New Hampshire, Ohio, Washington, and Wisconsin) to build public and political support for improving access to affordable health care and education for infants and toddlers by offering, among other things, incentives such as tax credits and family leave. In October 2001 the center launched the Interdisciplinary Network on School-Health Partnerships, a two-year initiative involving Mississippi, Missouri, Utah, Vermont, and Wyoming. This initiative was designed to increase the role of the governors in school health issues, examine the relationship between health care and student performance, develop strategies for states that need to improve student health programs, and help states build partnerships that promote the health of school children.

During the late 1990s and early 2000s the center's policy analysts were also examining state practices to expand extra learning opportunities (ELOs) for children ages five to eighteen. ELOs include activities such as organized sports, dance, tutoring, and community service, which take place outside of the regular school day and supplement a child's classroom education.

In 2001 the NGA, in cooperation with the National Conference of State Legislatures, launched a two-year project to improve teacher preparation and ensure quality teaching at all levels of education. The Colleges and Classrooms: State Strategies for Redesigning Teacher Preparation Policies project involved five states: California, Georgia, Idaho, Ohio, and Vermont. The project brought together officials and legislators in these states with members of the higher education community and Center for Best Practices staff to address key issues related to teacher preparation. The goal of the project was to help states design legislation and regulations that would improve teacher preparation, leading to better teaching and learning in the state's schools.

Meeting and Funding

The members of the NGA meet twice each year for three-day sessions. In the winter the governors meet in Washington, D.C.; the summer meeting is hosted by one of the states. The work of the NGA and the Center for Best Practices is funded by dues from individual states, federal grants and contracts, private foundation grants, and dues from Corporate Fellows who pay $12,000 per year.

INTERNET RESOURCE

NATIONAL GOVERNORS ASSOCIATION. 2002. <www.nga.org>.

JUDITH J. CULLIGAN

NATIONAL HONOR SOCIETY

The National Honor Society of Secondary Schools (NHS) was established in 1921 by the National Association of Secondary School Principals (NASSP) to recognize and encourage scholastically outstanding high school students. Its founders wanted to form a society modeled after Phi Beta Kappa, the undergraduate collegiate honor society. The National Junior Honor Society of Secondary Schools (NJHS) was established in 1929 to honor younger, middle-level students for similar reasons.

The founding committee viewed education as a total experience and the new honor society as more than just an honor roll—they emphasized the promotion of scholarship, along with leadership, service, and character, in the original constitution. As stated in the 1997 revised constitution, the purposes of the National Honor Society are to create an enthusiasm for scholarship, to stimulate a desire to render service, to promote leadership, and to develop character in the students of secondary schools.

The constitution of NJHS is similar to that of the high school honor society, except for the addition of citizenship as a fifth criterion for membership.

Formation and Growth

The National Honor Society is one of the most widely recognized cocurricular student activities in American high schools. The student activity program of the secondary school, essentially a development of the twentieth century, has been accepted as a vital and integral part of education. This status of student activities was re-emphasized by NASSP in its 1996 report, *Breaking Ranks: Changing an American Institution*: "The high school will promote cocurricular activities as integral to an education, providing opportunities for all students that support and extend academic learning. The concept of 'extracurricular' serves no useful purpose. . . . We propose to scrap this outmoded term and instead call these activities 'cocurricular,' emphasizing that they are integral to the educational program" (p. 18).

However, during the first part of the twentieth century, leading educators expressed considerable concern over the great amount of attention given to social and athletic achievements, and over the lack of emphasis placed on scholarship. In response to this concern, a number of educators organized local and regional societies to recognize academic excellence. Among the first was Phi Beta Sigma, founded in 1903 at South Side Academy in Chicago, Illinois. In 1906 the Cum Laude Society was organized at Tome School in Port Deposit, Maryland. By 1919 other honor societies had been established in New York City, Los Angeles, western Massachusetts, and Fargo, North Dakota. The organization of the National Honor Society in 1921 was a logical outgrowth of this developing interest.

Efforts to form a national organization were initiated at the 1919 annual convention of the National Association of Secondary School Principals in Chicago. The first chapter of the new society was chartered in 1921 at the Fifth Avenue High School in Pittsburgh, Pennsylvania, the school at which Edward Rynearson, considered the father and founder of NHS, was principal. The first official charter for the NJHS was awarded in 1929 to Webster Groves High School in Missouri.

Immediate acceptance led to continuous growth in the number of chapters and the size of the membership. Fourteen chapters were chartered during 1922; by 1930 there were 962 chapters of NHS and 128 chapters of NJHS. In 2001, the national office recognized 13,553 chapters of NHS and 5,316 chapters of NJHS. It is estimated that active membership in the two societies exceeds 1 million students per year. Chapters exist in all fifty states, the District of Columbia, all U.S. territories and possessions, and in American schools in more than forty foreign countries. Throughout the history of NHS and NJHS, membership has reflected a gender breakdown of two females to one male.

In 1921 an official emblem for the society was created in the form of a keystone and flaming torch. Widely recognized, the keystone bears at its base the letters *C*, *S*, *L*, and *S*, which stand for the four fundamental virtues of character, scholarship, leadership, and service. The torch symbolized the search for truth and is also the emblem of the National Junior Honor Society. The colors of NHS are blue and gold; navy blue and white are the colors for NJHS. The official flower for NHS is the yellow rose; for NJHS, the white rose.

Chapter Formation and Membership

Any public or approved or accredited private secondary school in the United States may apply for a chapter by submitting an application and agreeing to operate under the society's constitutional guidelines. Each chapter remains on the active list with the national office as long as it submits the annual affiliation payment. No individual fees are required of students, although local chapters can establish chapter dues, not to exceed ten dollars per member per year.

One or more faculty members (the chapter advisers) are appointed by the principal to administer each chapter. To assist in the selection, discipline, and dismissal of members, the principal also appoints a five-member faculty council. Specific guidelines are provided in the national handbook for the faculty councils to assist them in their duties. According to the society's constitution, the principal reserves authority over all actions of the chapter.

To be eligible for active membership in a chapter, students must have a cumulative grade point average of 3.0 (on a 4.0 scale), 85, B, or a cumulative average that is an equivalent standard of excellence. Local chapters may raise this average to meet local standards of excellence as long as such standards are applied fairly and consistently. National guidelines indicate that students may be considered as candidates in their sophomore, junior, or senior year; however, chapters are given the flexibility to limit candidacy to one or more of these years. Candidates must be enrolled at the school for a minimum of one semester, although exceptions can be made for transfer students.

Once this scholastic eligibility has been determined, candidates are then considered for membership on the basis of their leadership, service, and character. To ascertain how each candidate compares to the chapter standards in these three areas, the selection process recommended in the *National Honor Society Handbook* (1997) indicates that all candidates submit an information sheet detailing their relevant experiences. The local chapter may add additional qualifications or steps in the selection process. Once sufficient information has been gathered and reviewed, the faculty council votes on each candidate. Candidates become members at an induction ceremony. For the National Junior Honor Society, the selection process is the same, although membership is limited to second-semester sixth, seventh, eighth, and ninth grades, and includes citizenship as the fifth criterion needed for selection.

All local chapters are required to publish the local selection process, including the standards for the membership criteria, for all students, parents, and faculty. The national office provides information concerning these procedures on its website and offers the national handbooks for sale to the public.

Chapter Activities

The most important ceremony in the life of any chapter of the National Honor Society is the induction ceremony at which new members of the chapter are publicly recognized. Traditionally this ceremony has included a candle-lighting component, during which the flame from the central candle (the lamp of knowledge) is used to light four candles, one for each of the four core values of the society.

At the induction ceremony, new members are often given symbols of their new membership that can include a membership pin, card, or certificate, and are asked to sign the official roll of members. A suggested format for this ceremony is provided to all chapters, but the national office mandates no single format or script, preferring to encourage chapters to compose a ceremony that has local meaning and significance.

For other activities, the rules and regulations of NHS permit considerable latitude for local chapter initiative. Though no schedule of meetings is mandated by the national guidelines, all chapter meetings must be open and under the direction of one or more professional staff members of the school.

All chapters are required to undertake an annual service project. With the growth of a new volunteer service ethic among students and educators in America during the 1990s, NHS and NJHS members have been leading contributors, in service hours, to the improvement of their schools and communities. According to the society's annual reports for 1999–2000, the average chapter commits more than twenty-five hours per member of service to the school and community through an average of more than four projects per year. The total of service contributions by NHS and NJHS members exceeds 500,000 hours per year. This high degree of involvement indicates that chapters are living up to the society's motto, *Noblesse Oblige*, or, loosely translated, "to whom much is given, much is expected."

Typical service projects include tutoring programs for underclassmen, reading development for elementary students, fundraising for local or national charities, blood drives, serving meals at local food banks and soup kitchens, and servicing the needs of the elderly in the community. Regardless of the nature of the activity, all service projects and other activities of the chapter, including fundraising activities, meet the following criteria: they fulfill a need within the school or community; they have the support and sanction of the administration and the faculty; they are appropriate and educationally defensible; and they are well planned, organized, and executed.

In order to undertake these responsibilities efficiently, most chapters elect officers to lead the chapter and assist the adviser during the year. An important responsibility for chapter officers is ensuring that all chapter members maintain their membership obligations and live up to the standards of the chapter by being positive role models on campus and in the community.

National Control and Services

The board of directors of NASSP is also the governing board of the National Honor Society. General operational control is vested in the NHS/NJHS National Council, composed of ten principals and advisers. The executive director of NASSP is an ex officio member of the national council, and the NASSP director of student activities serves ex officio as secretary to the council. National activities of NHS are coordinated by the national office staff, located at the headquarters of NASSP in Reston, Virginia.

In 2001, twenty-two organizations existed at the state level supporting NHS and NJHS activities. These organizations are all affiliated with the national office, but operate independently. Whereas on the national level, chapters are required to maintain an active affiliation with the national office, participation in state activities is voluntary.

Conferences

In 1993 the first national conference of the NHS was held in the city that hosted the first chapter of NHS, Pittsburgh, Pennsylvania. The annual meeting is open to student members and advisers of NHS and NJHS, providing motivation and leadership training for students and professional development services for advisers.

In addition, in 2000, the national office expanded its regional student council leadership conferences (the National Association of Student Councils is also sponsored by NASSP) to include NHS and NJHS members and advisers. State conferences for NHS are held annually in those states maintaining a state association.

Scholarship Programs

NHS scholarships are awarded each year to outstanding graduating senior members of local chapters. NASSP organized this program in 1945, and since then more than $10 million has been dispensed. Two hundred scholarships of $1,000 each were distributed to the membership in 2001. In addition to the NHS Scholarship, the national office administers the following scholarship and award programs: the Principal's Leadership Award, sponsored by Herff Jones, Inc.; the Prudential Spirit of Community Awards; and the Wendy's High School Heisman Awards.

In the early twenty-first century, because it is the oldest, largest, and most prestigious school-based student recognition program in the country, the National Honor Society is considered the highest honor that can be bestowed upon students in secondary schools.

See also: HONOR SOCIETIES.

BIBLIOGRAPHY

HOOTON, COLBURN E. 1964 "The National Honor Society: Its Establishment and Growth, 1921 to 1963." *Student Life Highlights* 37:1–5.

NATIONAL ASSOCIATION OF SECONDARY SCHOOL PRINCIPALS. 1995. *Breaking Ranks: Changing an American Institution.* Reston, VA: National Association of Secondary School Principals.

NATIONAL HONOR SOCIETY OF SECONDARY SCHOOLS. 1997. *National Honor Society Handbook.* Reston, VA: National Association of Secondary School Principals.

NATIONAL JUNIOR HONOR SOCIETY OF SECONDARY SCHOOLS. 1998. *National Junior Honor Society Handbook.* Reston, VA: National Association of Secondary School Principals.

INTERNET RESOURCE

NATIONAL HONOR SOCIETY. 2002. <http://dsa.principals.org/nhs>.

DAVID P. CORDTS

NATIONAL MERIT SCHOLARSHIPS

Established in 1955, the National Merit Scholarship Corporation (NMSC) is an independent, not-for-profit organization that conducts the National Merit Scholarship Program. NMSC was initially funded by a $20 million Ford Foundation grant and a $500,000 grant from the Carnegie Corporation of New York. The National Merit Scholarship Program's purpose is to recognize academic achievement and grant undergraduate college scholarships to able high school students, based on their performance on the Preliminary SAT/National Merit Scholarship Qualifying Test (PSAT/NMSQT). Students take the PSAT/NMSQT for guidance purposes, to practice for the SAT, and to enter the competition for National Merit Scholarships. Though some sophomore students take the exam, typically only students in their third year of high school are eligible for the National Merit Scholarship competition. Additional eligibility requirements for the competition include full-time enrollment as a high school student with plans to enter college no later than the fall following completion of high school and one of the following: U.S. citizenship, permanent U.S. resident status, or current involvement in the U.S. citizenship-qualification process.

Recognition and Awards Program

NMSC recognizes students who earn high scores on the PSAT/NMSQT through press releases to the news media and by sharing their information with colleges and universities to assist with recruiting academically able students. Students who meet rigorous scholarship criteria are also recognized by receiving monetary scholarships. The National Merit Scholarship program offers several different types and levels of recognition and scholarships, including commended students, semifinalists, finalists, and Merit scholars. In addition, students compete for corporate- and university-sponsored Special Scholarships and the National Achievement Scholarship program.

Because there is a lengthy screening process throughout the scholarship competition (approximately eighteen months), high school juniors who took the PSAT/NMSQT in October 2000 would not receive scholarships until spring 2002, the student's senior year. Of the 2.9 million students who took the test in 2000 (an estimated 45% of the projected 2002 high school graduates), 1.2 million were eligible to enter the competition for scholarships. From this smaller group, approximately 50,000 of the highest-scoring students qualified for merit-program recognition. Of the 50,000 highest scorers, approximately 34,000 students received letters of commendation to recognize their academic potential. Though they were no longer eligible for the Merit Scholarship, some students in this group were eligible for Special or National Achievement Scholarships.

The remaining 16,000 students were notified that they qualified as semifinalists, which allowed them to remain eligible to be Merit scholars. The National Merit Scholarship Corporation then sent scholarship applications to the semifinalists to compete for finalist standing. About 90 percent of semifinalists who met academic and all other requirements then progressed to finalist standing. As finalists, students were then eligible for approximately 7,900 Merit Scholarships, which include the following three types of awards: National Merit Scholarships (one-time $2,500 awards), corporate-sponsored Merit Scholarships, and college-sponsored Merit Scholarships. Corporate- and college-sponsored scholarship awards vary in amount and duration, depending on the sponsors.

In addition to granting 7,900 National Merit Scholarships, the National Merit Scholarship Program awards approximately 1,700 Special Scholarships to high-scoring applicants who did not qualify to be Merit scholars but met specific criteria designated by scholarship sponsors, such as businesses or corporations. For example, a company might fund a fixed number of scholarships for its employees' children who achieved a high score on the PSAT/NMSQT. The NMSC reviews the eligible students' applications and selects the recipients.

The third type of scholarship program coordinated by NMSC is the National Achievement Scholarship program. Established in the early 1960s as the National Achievement Scholarship Program for Outstanding Negro Students, the Achievement Scholarship competition seeks to honor outstanding African-American students and improve their opportunities for higher education. Thus far, awards worth about $70 million have been offered to student participants. Though it is run simultaneously with the National Merit Scholarship program, and the two programs appear parallel in design, the National Achievement Scholarship is operated and funded independently. The participation requirements for the Achievement Scholarship are the same as those for the National Merit Scholarship awards, with one addition: African-American students must request entry into the Achievement Scholarship program when they fill out the PSAT/NMSQT answer sheet.

Approximately 110,000 students enter the National Achievement Scholarship program each year, and about 1,500 of the top-scoring students (represented regionally) are designated as semifinalists. Semifinalists complete an Achievement Scholarship application, and more than 1,200 then advance to finalist standing. From this group, Achievement Scholarship recipients are selected.

NMSC, professional organizations, corporations, and college sponsors fund more than 700 Achievement Scholarships each year. The three types of Achievement Scholarship awards are: National Achievement Scholarship ($2,500), corporate-sponsored Achievement Scholarships, and college-sponsored Achievement Scholarships. Students can compete in the competitions for both the National Merit Scholarships and the National Achievement Scholarships in the same year, but they can only receive one monetary reward.

The Test

Cosponsored by NMSC and the College Board, the PSAT/NMSQT comprises five sections: two verbal, two mathematical, and one writing-skills section. The verbal sections include sentence completions, analogies, and critical-reading questions. The mathematical sections include multiple choice questions, quantitative comparisons, and student-produced responses. Finally, the writing portion includes identifying sentence errors, improving sentences, and improving paragraph items.

The PSAT/NMSQT is administered in October, and the score reports are usually sent to high school principals by Thanksgiving. The range of scores for each section of the PSAT/NMSQT is 20 to 80. The scores for the PSAT/NMSQT can be compared to an estimated SAT score by multiplying the PSAT/NMSQT score by 10. For example, if a student's combined score for the verbal section was 48, the corresponding SAT score would be 480. Based on the PSAT/NMSQT results, the individual's test report provides estimates for SAT scores.

In 1999 the average PSAT/NMSQT results for juniors were 48.3 (verbal), 49.2 (mathematics), and 49.2 (writing skills), for a Selection Index of about 147 (the sum of the verbal, mathematics, and writing scores). The Selection Index ranges from 60 to 240, and those students with the highest Selection Index scores are eligible for recognition and scholarships coordinated by the National Merit Scholarship Corporation.

See also: ADVANCED PLACEMENT COURSES/EXAMS; COLLEGE ADMISSIONS; COLLEGE ADMISSIONS TESTS; COLLEGE FINANCIAL AID; COLLEGE SEARCH AND SELECTION.

BIBLIOGRAPHY

NATIONAL MERIT SCHOLARSHIP CORPORATION. 2000. *2000 PSAT/NMSQT Student Bulletin.* Evanston, IL: National Merit Scholarship Corporation.

INTERNET RESOURCES

COLLEGE BOARD. 2001. "What's on the PSAT/NMSQT?" <www.collegeboard.org>.

NATIONAL MERIT SCHOLARSHIP CORPORATION. 2001. <www.nationalmerit.org>.

AMY HIRSCHY

NATIONAL PTA

National PTA is the oldest and largest volunteer child advocacy organization in the United States. Founded in 1897, National PTA is a not-for-profit organization of parents, educators, students, and other citizens who are active in their schools and communities. Membership in National PTA is open to anyone who is concerned with the education, health, and welfare of children and youth.

National PTA's 6.5 million members work in 26,000 local chapters in all 50 states, the District of Columbia, the U.S. Virgin Islands, and in Department of Defense schools in Europe and the Pacific. The association's bylaws govern its affairs; a twenty-eight-member board of directors, including National PTA officers, other PTA leaders, and members at-large, oversees National PTA's business. Professional staff at the association's headquarters in Chicago, Illinois, and its office in Washington, D.C., carries out National PTA's day-to-day operations and lobbying efforts.

History

From its founding in 1897 in Washington, D.C., as the National Congress of Mothers by Alice McLellan Birney and Phoebe Apperson Hearst, National PTA has spoken out in support of children and their families. Among its earliest efforts, the Congress called for the establishment of a public health bureau to stem the tide of child mortality caused by childhood illnesses such as measles, whooping cough, and diphtheria; encouraged juvenile justice reforms; and began serving hot lunches to children in schools across the country in 1912. These efforts were rewarded at the state and federal levels with the establishment of the U.S. Public Health Service in 1913, emerging state laws establishing juvenile courts and probation systems in the first decade of the twentieth century, and the passage of the National School Lunch Act in 1946.

Throughout the remainder of the twentieth century, National PTA continued to champion children's rights. In the 1950s, the PTA promoted participation in the field testing of the Salk polio vaccine, initiated a nationwide campaign to prevent youth smoking in cooperation with the U.S. Department of Health, Education, and Welfare in the 1960s, sponsored a project to combat violence on television in the mid-1970s, launched an HIV/AIDS education project in cooperation with the Centers for Disease Control and Prevention in Atlanta in the 1980s, and made sure the parent voice was represented in major education reforms put forth by the U.S. government in the 1990s. As the PTA moved into the twenty-first century, it focused its efforts in three broad areas as identified by its 1999 strategic plan. These areas include promoting parent involvement, advocating for safe and nurturing environments for children and youth, and continuing support of public education.

Parent Involvement

At the root of all PTA work is its commitment to parent involvement in education; one of the association's founding objectives was to bring the home and school into closer relationship. National PTA worked with Congress to initiate the Parent Act, which sought to strengthen the parent participation policies in the Elementary and Secondary Education Act (ESEA). In January 2002 the ESEA was signed into law as the No Child Left Behind Act, authorizing more than 40 programs that provide federal funds to nearly every school district in the nation. This law includes many of the parent involvement provisions of the Parent Act and, for the first time, defines the term *parent involvement* based on National PTA's standards for parent/family involvement programs. These standards, developed and published in 1997 and based on research from Johns Hopkins University that affirmed that parent and family involvement increases student success, guide the development of quality parent involvement programs in schools and to help evaluate their effectiveness.

In 2000 National PTA published a comprehensive work, *Building Successful Partnerships: A Guide for Developing Parent and Family Involvement Programs,* which incorporates the six standards and field-tested strategies for building effective parent involvement programs. The PTA created a nationwide training program based on the book, as well as a complementary parent education program *How to Help Your Child Succeed,* which focuses on ten practical strategies for helping children succeed in school and in life.

National PTA has long supported arts education as an essential element in the education of children and has encouraged parents to nurture their children's artistic expressions. As a result, for more than thirty-two years National PTA has sponsored a nationwide arts recognition initiative, Reflections Pro-

gram, which encourages young artists in grades pre-K–12 to express themselves through literature, musical composition, photography, or the visual arts. In 2000 almost 700,000 young people participated in the program through their local PTA chapters.

Safe and Nurturing Environments

In response to the issue of intolerance purported to be at the heart of such violence as the September 11, 2001, tragedy and the rash of U.S. school shootings in 1998 and 1999, the PTA published the *Respecting Differences Resource Guide* in 2001. The guide is intended for use by PTAs and schools to promote diversity and inclusiveness in their communities in the hopes of eliminating episodes of intolerance, discrimination, and violence. It reflects the PTA's longstanding commitment to the individual worth of all people as articulated by founder Alice Birney, "The National Congress of Mothers, irrespective of creed, color, or condition, stands for all parenthood, childhood, homehood."

An early example of this commitment was seen in the PTA's support of parent teacher associations in African-American schools in the segregated south during the first quarter of the twentieth century. This support evolved into the creation of the National Congress of Colored Parents and Teachers (NCCPT) in 1926, headed by Selena Sloan Butler.

The PTA responded to the television industry's increasing promotion of violence, sex, and stereotyping in programming by launching its *Take Charge of Your TV* project in 1995. Developed in cooperation with the National Cable and Telecommunications Association and Cable in the Classroom—cable TV's educational arm—the project is a workshop that teaches parents to become more discriminating viewers of television so that they, in turn, can educate their children.

In collaboration with the International Truck and Engine Corporation (a manufacturer of school bus chassis), the PTA created a school bus safety program, *Be Cool. Follow the Rules* in 1993. The program uses a host of resources that convey multiple messages promoting school bus safety to multiple audiences including parents, schoolchildren, school administrators, and school bus drivers.

Support of Public Education

Throughout its history, National PTA has advocated for a strong public education system. Its efforts have focused on adequate federal funding of public schools, education equity, ongoing teacher training, and support of comprehensive education reforms among other issues. The PTA consistently has fought against voucher and tax credit programs that would divert federal money away from public schools. Currently, National PTA supports federal education policies that expand parent involvement, promote equity, and help states and schools build the capacity they need to provide high quality educational services for all children.

Child Advocacy

As identified in National PTA's strategic plan, a primary objective of the PTA is to train all 6.5 million members to be effective advocates for children and youth by the year 2020. Part of that objective will be accomplished through National PTA's programming and training efforts, and through its advocacy and legislative work in Washington, D.C. With a network of 6.5 million advocates, the PTA will be an even more powerful voice to express its concerns regarding children in classrooms, in communities, in state legislatures, and on Capitol Hill.

Other Resources

Through its many resources, National PTA keeps members and the public apprised of the issues affecting children and youth, and provides the means to help parents, teachers, and others work effectively for children. Some of these resources include *Our Children,* National PTA's magazine for members and others concerned about the health, education, and welfare of children; *Building Successful Partnerships: A Guide for Developing Parent and Family Involvement Programs;* and the *National Standards for Parent/Family Involvement Programs.*

National PTA's online presence, www.pta.org, includes parent involvement information and tips, resources regarding children's health and safety, and updates on legislation affecting families. There is also a password-protected members' area filled with materials exclusively for PTAs, including several electronic newsletters providing timely information on a range of child- and member-related topics.

Each June, National PTA holds a convention, enabling PTA members and nonmembers from across the country to attend workshops and other education sessions on a range of subjects focusing on National PTA's three-fold mission of child advocacy, parent education, and parent involvement. National

PTA also hosts a biannual legislative conference in Washington, D.C., where participants hone their advocacy skills and legislative knowledge.

Raising Awareness of the PTA

To better identify itself as the national association, in the summer of 2001 National PTA launched a nationwide media campaign to raise public awareness of its identity as the oldest and largest volunteer child advocacy association in the United States.

See also: FAMILY, SCHOOL, AND COMMUNITY CONNECTIONS; PARENTAL INVOLVEMENT.

INTERNET RESOURCES

NATIONAL PTA. 2002. <www.pta.org>.

PAMELA J. GROTZ

NATIONAL SCHOOL BOARDS ASSOCIATION

The National School Boards Association (NSBA) is the nationwide organization representing public school governance. NSBA's mission is to foster excellence and equity in public elementary and secondary education through school board leadership. NSBA achieves its mission by representing the school board perspective before federal government agencies and national organizations that affect education and by providing vital information and services to state associations of school boards and local school boards throughout the nation.

Founded in 1940, NSBA is a not-for-profit federation of state associations of school boards across the United States and its territories. NSBA represents the nation's 95,000 school board members who govern nearly 15,000 local school districts serving the nation's more than 47 million public school students. Nearly all school board members are elected; the rest are appointed by elected officials.

A 150-member delegate assembly of local school board members determines NSBA policy. The board of directors, which comprises twenty-five members, translates this policy into action. The NSBA executive director and staff administer programs and services.

NSBA advocates local school boards as the ultimate expression of grassroots democracy. The organization supports the capacity of each school board—working with the people of its community—to envision the future of education, to establish a structure and environment that allows all students to reach their maximum potential, to provide accountability for the people of its community on performance in the schools, and to serve as a community advocate for children and youth and their public schools.

History and Development

The advantages of forming an association of school boards were recognized as early as 1895. Pennsylvania became the first state to organize a state association in 1895; New York followed in 1896. Although some states organized associations in the years immediately following, it was not until 1913 that numerous other associations emerged. After 1913 the school board association movement showed steady growth. In the 1950s fifteen associations were organized, making this decade the time of greatest development.

The idea of establishing a national organization of school boards took shape during the 1938 convention of the National Education Association. The first name given to this group was the National Association of Public School Boards. However, the NSBA was formally organized in St. Louis, Missouri, on February 28, 1940, as the National Council of State School Boards Association. The name was later changed to the National School Boards Association.

Program

NSBA's major services include:

- The National Affiliate Program, which enables school boards to work with their state association and NSBA to identify and influence federal and national trends and issues affecting public school governance.
- The Council of Urban Boards of Education (CUBE), which serves the governance needs of urban school boards. CUBE publishes *Urban Advocate,* a quarterly newsletter that addresses the programmatic, fiscal, and governance challenges of urban public schools on behalf of its members and the 7.5 million students they serve.
- The Federal Relations Network, which helps school board members from each congressional district actively participate in NSBA's federal and national advocacy efforts.

- ITTE: Education Technology Programs and Technology Leadership Network, which helps advance public education through best uses of technology in the classroom and school district operation. Formerly known as the Institute for the Transfer of Technology to Education (ITTE) the organization publishes *Technology Leadership News* nine times per year. NSBA's technology publication *Electronic School* is produced in cooperation with ITTE.
- The Council of School Attorneys (COSA), which focuses on school law issues and services to school board attorneys. COSA publishes *Inquiry and Analysis (I&A).* Published ten times per year, *I&A* keeps members up-to-date on the latest developments in the field of school law.
- The National Education Policy Network, which provides the latest policy information nationwide and a framework for public school governance through written policies.
- *School Board News (SBN),* NSBA's member newspaper, which began publication in 1981. *SBN* covers trends in public education and has won many awards for its content.
- *American School Board Journal (ASBJ),* which is an award-winning, editorially independent education magazine housed at NSBA's offices. *ASBJ* began publication in 1891 and in the early twenty-first century had a circulation of more than 35,000 paid subscribers.
- NSBA's Annual Conference and Exposition, which is the nation's largest policy and training conference for local education officials on national and federal issues affecting the public schools in the United States.
- NSBA's Technology + Learning (T+L) Conference, which brings together school district leaders, technology specialists, and the leading vendors in education technology.

Organizational Structure

The NSBA is a federation of state school boards associations, which includes the school boards of the fifty states, the District of Columbia, and the U.S. Virgin Islands.

Local school boards are eligible for membership in their own state school boards association and are not district members of the NSBA. However, the NSBA maintains contact with local school boards and their members through the National Affiliate program.

The National Affiliate program is a partnership that includes NSBA, its federation of state school boards associations, and local school districts across the country, which is dedicated to ensuring education excellence and improved student achievement through effective school board leadership. Official association publications supplement state association publications in helping to supply school board members with vital educational information. The National Affiliate program began in 1980 and now boasts more than 2,500 member districts.

The major policymaking body of the association is the delegate assembly, which meets during the annual conference. Two voting delegates, who are chosen at the state level, represent each member association. The delegate assembly determines official NSBA policies and resolutions. Policy decisions require a two-thirds vote and resolutions a majority vote.

Goals

NSBA and its federation members are dedicated to educating every child to his or her fullest potential and are committed to leadership for student achievement. This commitment has coalesced into a strategic vision for the NSBA as a powerful, united, energetic federation; as an influential force for achieving equity and excellence in public education; and as a catalyst for aligning the power of the community on behalf of education.

Underlying this shared vision are certain fundamental convictions:

- belief that effective local school boards can enable all children to reach their potential
- conviction that local governance of public education is a cornerstone of democracy
- belief in the power of local school boards to convene the community around education issues
- conviction that together, local school boards can influence education policy and governance at the state and national levels
- commitment to the principle that through collaboration comes impact
- belief that the strength of local school board leadership arises from the board's capacity to represent the diversity of students and communities

Central to NSBA's vision is the "Key Work of School Boards" initiative. The "Key Work of School Boards" is NSBA's framework for raising student achievement through community engagement. It is designed to give school boards the concrete action tools to be even more effective in the role of school board member and community leader and is based on the premise that excellence in the classroom begins with excellence in the boardroom.

The "Key Work" initiative is framed around eight key areas: vision, standards, assessment, accountability, alignment, climate, collaborative relationships, and continuous improvement. It means engaging the community, identifying priorities, and setting standards for student performance. It requires establishing assessment and accountability measures, demanding student data to drive decision-making, and aligning district resources to support priorities. All of this involves setting the right climate for learning, forming collaborative relationships, and always continually improving performance.

Through these goals and its longstanding commitment to excellence and equity in public education through school board leadership, the NSBA is a powerful force in education policy.

See also: SCHOOL BOARD RELATIONS; SCHOOL BOARDS.

INTERNET RESOURCE

NATIONAL SCHOOL BOARDS ASSOCIATION. 2002. <www.nsba.org>.

ANNE L. BRYANT

NATIONAL SCHOOL PUBLIC RELATIONS ASSOCIATION

The National School Public Relations Association (NSPRA) defines itself in its mission statement as "a professional organization dedicated to building support for education through responsible public relations that leads to success for all students." Founded in 1935, NSPRA is the professional association for school communications specialists, superintendents, and others who are responsible for improving communication within school districts and between districts and the citizens they serve.

The association's Articles of Incorporation state that its primary purposes are to serve the citizenry of the nation by promoting a better understanding of the objectives, accomplishments, and needs of public education. It seeks to accomplish those purposes by: (1) developing materials that will assist educational leaders in building both an increased public understanding of the role of education and increased awareness, knowledge, and understanding of current management practices and educational development; (2) placing before the public facts and viewpoints that will lead to a better understanding, appreciation, and support of public education; and (3) encouraging the use of sound public relations procedures by all those at work in education.

Programs and Activities

NSPRA had approximately 1,800 members in 2001, comprising both individual and organizational memberships. Members are eligible for discounted prices on association publications and seminars. In addition, the association has approximately thirty-five state chapters throughout the United States, which enable national members and chapter members to create local networks and programs for professional development.

A four-day NSPRA annual seminar is held each July, attracting more than 600 participants to different locations each year. NSPRA offers other professional development opportunities, including two print newsletters, several electronic newsletters, and workshops. In 2000 the association initiated hour-long conference calls featuring experts in various areas of communication who make brief presentations and discuss participants' questions. One of the association's print newsletters, *Network,* is designed primarily for school public relations practitioners and superintendents, while the other, *PRincipal Communicator,* is designed for elementary and middle school principals.

NSPRA initiated an accreditation program for school public relations professionals in 1976. More than 150 members achieved accredited status before the program was combined with that of the Universal Accreditation Board's Accredited in Public Relations (APR) program. The association continues to urge its members to become accredited. In 2001 NSPRA was also developing standards of good practices that educational organizations could strive for in improving their communication efforts.

The association has been a publisher of documents to help improve educational public relations since its founding. *School Public Relations: Building Confidence in Education,* published in 1999, gives education leaders a comprehensive overview of what school public relations is and what it can do for schools and communities. Other association publications include *Dream Big: Creating and Growing Your School Foundation, Principals in the Public: Engaging Community Support, The Complete Crisis Communication Management Manual for Schools, Win at the Polls,* and many others. In addition to its own publications, the association's catalog lists public relations and communications products created by other organizations.

In 1985 the association created the Flag of Learning and Liberty and coordinated an introductory campaign that saw the flag raised over all fifty state capitols on the Fourth of July that year. The flag is a visible reminder that education is critical to continuing a healthy, democratic society.

Another important service that NSPRA provides to local and intermediate school districts is a communication audit. For a modest fee, the district collects samples of its communication efforts and sends them to NSPRA for inspection by experienced public relations professionals. One or two of these professionals then conduct fifteen to twenty focus group sessions in a site visit to the district. Based on the review of district communication efforts and comments from the focus groups, the association provides an audit report with recommendations that will help improve the district's communication efforts.

Organizational Structure

NSPRA is an incorporated, not-for-profit organization. It has a twelve-member board of directors, consisting of a president, president-elect, and ten vice presidents, eight of whom are elected by association members. Of these elected vice presidents, who serve three-year terms, seven represent geographic regions of the United States and Canada, while one represents ethnic and racial minorities. Two vice presidents, representing specific constituencies, are appointed by the board to two-year terms. The first two of these vice presidents' constituencies were urban school districts and superintendents of schools.

The board, which meets three times annually, hires an executive director to carry on the business and program of the association. It develops and approves association policies, conveys ideas and interests from the membership, and approves an annual association budget. In addition to the executive director, the association has a staff of eight.

History

Initially, NSPRA was part of the National Education Association's (NEA's) Division of Press and Radio, created to help teachers and schools improve their communication efforts. It became an NEA department in 1950 and retained that status until the early 1970s, when it became independent.

INTERNET RESOURCE

NATIONAL SCHOOL PUBLIC RELATIONS ASSOCIATION. 2002. <www.nspra.org>.

RICHARD D. BAGIN
KENNETH K. MUIR

NATIONAL SCIENCE FOUNDATION

The National Science Foundation (NSF) is an independent agency of the federal government, created by the National Science Foundation Act of 1950, as amended (Pub. L. 81-597). The agency is responsible for promoting the progress of science and advancing the nation's health, prosperity, welfare, and security by supporting research and education in all fields of science and engineering. It is also responsible for monitoring the status of the U.S. science and engineering enterprise and for collecting and analyzing data that support the formulation of national policy.

By statute, NSF consists of the National Science Board and the director. These twenty-five eminent scientists, engineers, and administrators are appointed by the president and confirmed by the U.S. Senate. The board is responsible for establishing NSF's policies and is mandated to advise the president and the U.S. Congress on policy matters related to science and engineering research and education. The director, who is a member of the board ex officio, is responsible for directing the programs of the agency.

Unique among federal agencies, NSF is devoted to strengthening the overall health of the science and engineering enterprise. Other federal agencies support research and education related to their specific missions, such as energy or defense. NSF's mission is to support scientific inquiry in all fields, encourage emerging areas of research, and help ensure an adequate supply of scientists, engineers, and science and engineering educators. In any year, more than 200,000 people receive support through NSF programs and activities nationwide, and millions more benefit from NSF investments in education and other areas.

With a budget of $4.7 billion for fiscal year 2002, NSF accounts for 4 percent of the total annual federal expenditure on research and development and 23 percent of federal support for all basic research performed at academic institutions. NSF provides more than a third of all federal funding in the physical sciences and about 50 percent in environmental sciences and engineering. In some fields, NSF provides the preponderant support: approximately two-thirds in mathematics and computer science research and nearly 100 percent in anthropology.

Scope of Programs

NSF investments act as a catalyst to expand new knowledge. NSF supports cutting-edge research and education in the core disciplines, ranging from mathematics, the physical and life sciences, and engineering to the social, behavioral, and economic sciences. Its investments support three goals: to provide the nation with the necessary

- people—developing a diverse, internationally competitive, and globally engaged work force of scientists, engineers, and well-prepared citizens;
- ideas—enabling discovery across the frontiers of science and engineering, connected to learning, innovation, and service to society; and
- tools—providing broadly accessible research and education tools.

NSF is organized into directorates and offices, which support research and education in the various fields and administer grants to lead researchers and institutions. The directorates include biological sciences; computer and information science and engineering; education and human resources; engineering; geosciences; mathematical and physical sciences; and social, behavioral, and economic sciences.

In addition to support for core fields, NSF funds interdisciplinary research teams and centers, such as its science and technology centers, which encourage the integration of research and education. NSF also provides grants to small businesses through its Small Business Innovation Research Program to encourage them to focus on important science, engineering, and education problems and opportunities with potential for commercial and public benefit.

Partnerships among academic institutions, industry, and government entities are integral to the way NSF implements its mission. Partnerships foster the use of new knowledge to stimulate innovation that will create new wealth and benefit the public. Some major programs are the Engineering Research Centers, Partnerships for Advanced Computational Infrastructure, and the U.S. Global Change Research Program.

Since its beginning, NSF has recognized that the conduct of science is intrinsically global, and the agency has encouraged international cooperation. NSF supports cooperative international activities, such as research collaborations, data sharing, and international partnerships in large-scale research facilities.

Although NSF itself operates no laboratories or research facilities, it provides funding for large, multiuser, state-of-the-art facilities, such as the Laser Interferometer Gravity Wave Observatory, the National Superconducting Cyclotron Laboratory, the International Gemini Observatory, and the Terascale Computing Facility. NSF also is the designated federal manager of the U.S. Antarctic Program.

Within NSF's broad portfolio, a few opportunities emerge that are so revolutionary that they promise to reshape science and engineering and ultimately change the way people think and live. Typically, these opportunities cross disciplinary boundaries, encompass the full range of NSF programs, and require coordination with other federal agencies. NSF investments that evolved into high-performance computing exemplify this type of emerging opportunity.

Priority areas that NSF has selected for increased attention during the early years of the twenty-first century are:

- information technology research: support for the people who will create new knowledge, and an upgrade of computational infrastructures;
- nanoscale science and engineering: research and technology at the confluence of the smallest human-made devices and the largest molecules of living systems;
- biocomplexity in the environment: the dynamic web of often-surprising interrelationships that arise when components of the global ecosystem interact; and
- learning for the twenty-first century: building and sustaining a competent, diverse work force and integrating research and education to produce that work force.

Involvement with the External Scientific Community

Researchers and educators in all fifty states and the U.S. territories receive NSF support through competitively awarded grants and cooperative agreements. More than 2,000 colleges, universities, academic consortia, pre-kindergarten through grade twelve (pre-K–12) school systems, small businesses, nonprofit institutions, informal science organizations, and other research institutions receive such support.

Funding decisions are made through the process of competitive merit review, in which expert evaluation by external peer reviewers contributes to recommendations by NSF program managers. Each year, NSF receives approximately 30,000 proposals, solicits reviews from approximately 50,000 scientists and engineers, and funds approximately 10,000 proposals. Reviewers evaluate proposals according to two criteria:

- the intellectual merit of the proposed activity: the importance of the proposed activity to advancing knowledge and understanding within its own field or across different fields; the extent to which the proposed activity explores creative, original concepts; and
- the broader impacts of the proposed activity: how well the activity promotes teaching, training, and learning; how well it broadens the participation of underrepresented groups; and the extent of benefits to U.S. society.

In addition to the use of external reviewers, NSF recruits outstanding scientists, engineers, and mathematicians to serve on advisory committees or to join the NSF staff for short periods through the Intergovernmental Personnel Act and the Visiting Scientists, Engineers and Educators programs. Through these mechanisms, NSF involves thousands of working scientists in evaluating emerging opportunities for new knowledge and ensures its access to cutting-edge ideas in all fields of science and engineering.

Support for Education

NSF's support for research is highly integrated with its investment in science and engineering education. Thousands of students at the undergraduate, graduate, and postdoctoral levels contribute to research activities at their education institutions and benefit from involvement with them. In addition, each year NSF provides graduate research fellowships to approximately 900 outstanding graduate students in science, mathematics, and engineering. To provide teaching experience for graduate students and strengthen pre-K–12 education, NSF provides graduate teaching fellowships to graduate students who assist teachers with the content of their mathematics and science classes. NSF's Integrative Graduate Education and Research Traineeships help prepare doctoral candidates for a broad spectrum of career opportunities in education. Through its Experimental Program to Stimulate Competitive Research, NSF provides funding to educational institutions to increase the research and development competitiveness of twenty-one states and the Commonwealth of Puerto Rico.

Although the integration of research and education is most obvious at the graduate and postdoctoral levels, NSF also funds pre-K–12 science and mathematics education in state, urban, and rural school systems and invests in comprehensive reform of undergraduate science, technology, engineering, and mathematics (STEM) education. NSF supports the development of high-quality instructional materials, teacher enhancement, and the use of learning technologies in the classroom. Its funding encourages educational systems to prepare all students—not just STEM majors—for the demands of a highly technological society.

NSF's systemic initiatives in education have catalyzed change in the teaching of mathematics and science by cultivating partnerships between local school systems and other organizations involved in education. Each partnership addresses curriculum, professional development, assessment, policies, resources, stakeholder support, evaluation, and improved student performance as the ultimate goal of any reform effort. As of 2001 NSF had encouraged experiments in comprehensive reform in twenty-six states, fifty-eight urban school districts, and twenty-eight rural initiatives in regions usually composed of more than one state. In the 1999/2000 school year, NSF systemic initiatives affected 227,000 teachers in 11,900 schools with approximately 4.6 million students.

In fiscal year 2002 NSF began implementing the Math and Science Partnerships program, which provides funds for states and local school districts to join with institutions of higher education in strengthening mathematics and science education. The goals are to improve mathematics and science standards, provide teachers with mathematics and science training, and create innovative ways to reach underserved schools and students.

See also: SCIENCE EDUCATION; SCIENCE LEARNING.

BIBLIOGRAPHY

NATIONAL SCIENCE BOARD. 2000. *National Science Board: A History in Highlights, 1950–2000.* Arlington, VA: National Science Foundation.

NATIONAL SCIENCE FOUNDATION. 2000. *America's Investment in the Future.* Arlington, VA: National Science Foundation.

NATIONAL SCIENCE FOUNDATION. 2000. *Guide to Programs FY 2001.* Arlington, VA: National Science Foundation.

NATIONAL SCIENCE FOUNDATION. 2000. *NSF GPRA Strategic Plan, FY 2001–2006.* Arlington, VA: National Science Foundation.

NATIONAL SCIENCE FOUNDATION. 2000. *Resource Guide 2000: National Science Foundation Celebrating 50 Years.* Arlington, VA: National Science Foundation.

National Science Foundation Act of 1950. Public Law 81-597. *U.S. Code.* Vol. 42, secs. 1861 et seq.

U.S. OFFICE OF SCIENTIFIC RESEARCH AND DEVELOPMENT. 1945. *Science, The Endless Frontier: A Report to the President by Vannevar Bush, Director of the Office of Scientific Research and Development.* Washington, DC: U.S. Office of Scientific Research and Development.

INTERNET RESOURCE

NATIONAL SCIENCE FOUNDATION. 2002. <www.nsf.gov>.

MARTA CEHELSKY

NATIONAL SCIENCE TEACHERS ASSOCIATION

The National Science Teachers Association (NSTA) promotes excellence and innovation in science teaching and learning for all. Its guiding principles are to model excellence; to embrace and model diversity through equity, respect, and opportunity for all; to provide and expand professional development to support standards-based science education; to serve as a voice for excellence and innovation in science teaching and learning, curriculum and instruction, and assessment; to promote interest in and support for science education collaboratively and proactively throughout society; and to exemplify a dynamic professional organization that values and practices self-renewal. NSTA was founded in 1944 and is headquartered in Arlington, Virginia. Its 2001 membership of more than 53,000 included science teachers, science supervisors, administrators, scientists, business and industry representatives, and others involved in science education.

The association publishes professional journals, a newspaper, and many publications for teachers, and it conducts world-class conventions that attract more than 30,000 attendees annually. NSTA offers many services for science educators, including the NSTA Institute, which provides online and site-based professional development programs; teacher recognition and grant programs; and competitions for students. NSTA also maintains a website that provides grade-specific resources for teachers, the latest news and information affecting science education, and opportunities for educators to connect with one another. NSTA participates in cooperative working arrangements with numerous educational organizations, government agencies, and private industries on a variety of projects.

History

NSTA originated in Pittsburgh, Pennsylvania, on July 4, 1944. It was created by a merger of the American Council of Science Teachers and the American Science Teachers Association, both of which ceased to exist after the merger. At the time, the organizations had approximately 2,000 members combined. Years later, NSTA became an affiliate organization of the National Education Association (NEA) and was housed with NEA and its affiliates in downtown Washington, DC. Eventually becoming an independent organization, NSTA purchased and moved into

its own headquarters on Connecticut Avenue in 1974. In 1994 NSTA moved its headquarters to Arlington, Virginia.

Legal Status and Governance

The National Science Teachers Association is a 501(c)(3) organization, incorporated under the laws of the District of Columbia by Articles of Incorporation filed on July 1, 1960. The association filed a Statement of Election to Accept Title 29, Chapter 10 of the District of Columbia Code, and a Certificate of Acceptance was issued on January 30, 1974. NSTA is governed by bylaws, which are amended from time to time.

The organization is governed by a board of directors with two advisory bodies: the NSTA Council and NSTA Congress. The board of directors consists of elected officers, including a president (chair), president-elect, and retiring president, as well as ten division directors. The council serves as the advisory body to the board of directors and consists of eighteen elected district directors and presidents from each of NSTA's seven affiliates. The council receives reports from NSTA committees and the congress and makes recommendations to the board. The congress is composed of a large body of science education leaders who gather to discuss and bring forth recommendations of interest to NSTA. Members include delegates from each NSTA state chapter and each NSTA-associated group.

Membership

NSTA offers both individual teacher memberships and institutional memberships for schools and libraries. Special discount memberships are also given to students and retired educators. Members receive their choice of one of four award-winning journals, a newspaper, discounts on more than 300 books and publications, and reduced prices at NSTA regional and national conventions.

Publications

NSTA publishes four award-winning, peer-reviewed journals geared to the specific needs of science educators at every level. They include *Science and Children* for elementary teachers, *Science Scope* for those at the middle and junior high level, *The Science Teacher* for high school science educators, and the *Journal of College Science Teaching* for educators at the college level. Considered a popular benefit of NSTA membership, these journals help teachers learn about the latest teaching strategies and identify new activities to use in the classroom.

NSTA's news publication, *NSTA Reports!*, has been a timely source of news and information about science education. The newspaper is published six times a year as a free member service. It includes national news on science education and education in general; information on teaching materials; announcements of programs for teachers; and advance notice about all NSTA programs, conventions, and publications.

NSTA is also a major publisher of quality science materials for teachers. In 2000 the association revamped its publishing division, calling it *NSTA Press* to reflect its efforts to deepen its involvement in the science publishing arena. NSTA Press produces a wide variety of books, websites, CD-ROMs, and posters on popular science topics, including astronomy, biology, chemistry, earth science, environmental science, and physical science. Resources also focus on the diverse curriculum needs of teachers, such as teaching in alignment with the National Science Education Standards, mentoring, and assessment, as well as on creative teaching strategies, such as organizing science fairs and addressing questions about evolution.

Influence and Significance

With more than 53,000 members worldwide, NSTA is a major voice of science teachers and strong supporter of quality science education. It is the largest member organization in the world committed to quality science teaching and learning for all and is a key player in setting the nation's science education agenda. In the mid-1990s, the organization was instrumental in the development of the National Science Education Standards, which guide the science education community in improving science teaching and learning. The association is an ardent advocate for long-term, sustained professional development for all teachers of science.

NSTA has a presence on Capitol Hill. The organization works closely with key members of the U.S. Congress and their staff, and is asked to present testimony to Congress and provide input to legislators on key issues. NSTA reaches more than 40,000 educators with its electronic *Legislative Update*, which reports the latest news of legislative and regulatory activities affecting science education. Through the *Legislative Update*, the association encourages its members to contact members of Congress to voice their support for legislation bolstering quality science education. As a result of these efforts, NSTA has helped to maintain a high level of federal funding for science teaching and learning.

The association keeps its members and the general public informed on national issues and trends in science education. NSTA conducts and disseminates national surveys on science teaching. Many of these surveys, along with other NSTA opinions, have been featured in major news media outlets. In addition, NSTA has position statements on issues, such as teacher preparation, evolution, and laboratory safety that help guide policies and practices in education institutions around the country.

NSTA also has an impact on science education through its resources and programs. One successful program is *Building a Presence for Science*. Sponsored by the Exxon Education Foundation, this national education program seeks to strengthen the quality of science teaching and learning by creating a network of science advocates in public and private schools nationwide. It promotes standards-based science teaching instruction and hands-on, inquiry-based learning. A key component of the program is its dynamic national electronic network that enables information sharing among teachers and serves as a viable two-way communications conduit that is used by state and federal agencies and other organizations to share information with science teachers. As of 2001 the program had been implemented in twenty-four states and the District of Columbia.

INTERNET RESOURCE

NATIONAL SCIENCE TEACHERS ASSOCIATION. 2002. <www.nsta.org>.

HAROLD PRATT

NATION AT RISK, A
See: EDUCATION REFORM; SCHOOL REFORM.

NEGLIGENCE AND SCHOOL PERSONNEL
See: LIABILITY OF SCHOOL DISTRICTS AND SCHOOL PERSONNEL FOR NEGLIGENCE.

NEIGHBORHOODS

The *neighborhood* has long been an icon of school quality, local responsiveness, and home/parent centeredness in U.S. education. The mythology of the neighborhood has been heavily reinforced by the deep popularity of the long-running children's television show *Mr. Rogers' Neighborhood*. A romantic image of the neighborhood has also often been at the heart of opposition to busing, school closings, redefined attendance areas, or reallocations of personnel. Nostalgia connects the neighborhood school to the *old-time schoolhouse*—a facility remembered as being at the very center of the community, with its potluck suppers, spelling bees, family softball games, and Fourth of July picnics.

Reality, of course, has been a different story. Desegregation policies, population growth, magnet schooling, diversity goals, *pairings* of schools, and an increasing array of other choice options have reduced significantly the percentage of schools that have an identifiable neighborhood flavor. Nevertheless, at the start of the twenty-first century the significance of the neighborhood is returning to discussions of and inquiry into matters of school improvement.

Among the forces spurring this rediscovery of the neighborhood are: (1) a new appreciation of out-of-school (alongside in-school) learning and development; (2) a return in many communities to neighborhood assignment patterns under renegotiated desegregation agreements; (3) a renewed interest in cultural elements, and matters of cultural diversity, in varied patterns of development among children; and (4) a realization that school-centered learning (typically academic) and neighborhood-based learning (heavily social and emotional) can be, but are not necessarily, effectively linked.

A New Linkages Lexicon

The renewed fascination with the neighborhood has been accompanied by a re-explored lexicon of linkages terminology and neighborhoods-centered theorizing. The most commonly employed term is *social capital,* which captures the notion that the strengths of families and their surrounding neighborhoods can provide a social foundation of norms, networks, and relationships upon which the schools can build. In pushing the concept of social capital, James Coleman has suggested that, in neighborhoods lacking or weak in social capital, it should be the job of the local

school to reach out to families with sets of capital-creating activities.

Other terms gaining an increased frequency of use are: *social cohesion, agency,* and a *sense-of-place.* Social cohesion proceeds beyond matters of capital toward an interest in the connective tissues of neighborhoods, as well as between neighborhoods and schools. Connective "webs," collaborative endeavors, and ecological systems are key elements—as are such administrative acts as networking and a building of civic capacity.

Social cohesiveness exists when members of a school community adhere to the understood cultural norms of that community, and when members display tolerance in interactions across social groups. Stephen Heyneman suggests schools perform five essential functions in fostering social cohesion: (1) teach the "rules of the game" (i.e., principles underpinning good citizenship and consequences for not adhering to these principles) through curriculum content; (2) support school and classroom cultures; (3) decrease the distance between individuals of different origins, thus building social capital; (4) provide an equality of opportunity for all students, thus creating the public perception that the available opportunities for education are distributed fairly; and (5) adjudicate disagreements across social groups.

The concept of *agency* reflects a closer attention to the centeredness of a school within its neighborhood, reflecting a deep cultural embeddedness between school and community, as well as the agency work of the school in both preserving and passing on the values of the community. In like manner, the idea of a *sense-of-place* includes notions of social and cultural embeddedness, but adds a territorial, or *boundary,* dimension to the discussion—just what is a central part of each neighborhood, and what is not?

A New Set of Neighborhood Models

To the extent that the neighborhood was "modeled" in past years, the central image was that of an entity of importance in the immediate environment around the school, but not *of* the school. Important were studies of neighborhood and community structures (e.g., community type, socioeconomic status); distributions of power and specialized interests; the array of concerns and issues in the community; and varying sources of support in the surrounding community (e.g., financial, public opinion). The neighborhood, with its structures, issues, and supports, was regarded as an important context around the work of the school, but it was still external and "outside."

More recent modeling (as with the above lexicon) has emphasized a more interactive set of neighborhood theories. Among these are: (a) an activism, or *alliances*, approach, (b) community-development modeling, (c) *regime* theorizing, and (d) a family-preferences, or *choice*, model. Alliance schools have been under experimentation for some time in the state of Texas. The central concept in the alliance approach has been an in-reach from neighborhood-to-school, rather than the other way around. A mobilization of the resources and strengths of the neighborhood and its institutions (including religious organizations) has been employed in the program to reach into the schools and assist the schools to reach back out to the community.

An initiation of alliances, but starting with the school, is also central to community-development modeling. Neighborhood revitalization has become a front-burner endeavor in many communities across the United States. Lizbeth Schorr, among others, would place the neighborhood school at the heart of the development effort. Indeed, Schorr advises that an improvement of learning opportunities in low-income neighborhoods requires nothing less than a key place for the school "at the table where community reform is being organized" (p. 291). In like fashion, William Boyd, Robert Crowson, and Aaron Gresson have suggested an extended role for the local school as an *enterprise school*, in which it joins an array of other community institutions in the regeneration of the neighborhood environment.

A third model takes the political science term *regime* as its central idea. From a regime perspective, the essential strengths, and indeed the power, of a neighborhood are to be found in a deeply structural embodiment of the neighborhood's own culture and overall ecology (e.g., its essential lifeways, social institutions, local history, values, norms, expectations, and market forces). While activism and redevelopment are at the heart of the earlier two models, regime theorizing looks more closely at the neighborhood and its various institutions (including the schools) as participants in a *sustaining habitat*—a notion not unlike the centeredness celebrated in agency theorizing or the collective memories built into a sense-of-place. A key role for persons exercising leadership, from this perspective, may be action

as a cultural broker who bridges between the lifeways of a community and the institutions that serve it.

Finally, a neighborhood model that is extremely problematic but must be addressed is the *effects* model, which is based heavily upon the steadily increasing opportunities for choice found in modern-day schooling. An argument in favor of choice of schooling (e.g., through magnets, charters, transfer options, or vouchers) is that families are no longer locked in to underperforming neighborhood schools in poverty-stricken settings. A counterargument is that it is usually the families in a neighborhood with the most social capital and greatest intellectual resources and expectations who will avail themselves of choice—leaving the rest of a neighborhood even less empowered and enabled than before. A caveat is that at least these families stay in the neighborhood physically, if not educationally.

Interestingly, there have been comparative analyses of the effects upon neighborhoods when there are large disparities in the availability of community and social service resources (e.g., playgrounds, libraries). There have not yet been comparable studies of the neighborhood effects of differences in the availability of human capital resources at a family-to-family level.

Neighborhoods and the Development of Children

There are still some neighborhoods to be found that can elicit memories of an old-fashioned bonding, familiarity, stoop-sitting, watching-one-another's-children, stopping-to-chat-awhile community. More common in the early twenty-first century, however, are neighborhoods where the streets are considered danger zones rather than playgrounds, where social interaction is minimal, and where there seems to be little sense of communal responsibility for children. Under these altered and less-cohesive conditions of life, it becomes difficult to conceptualize, and more difficult to study, a set of neighborhood effects upon the development of children and their success in school.

Nevertheless, the recognition is that if a new lexicon of linkages and new models of alliances, regimes, and the like are to bear fruit, then attention must be paid to what have been called "connection impacts." There is evidence, for example, that there are connections of significance to be found in the recent and rapid expansion of out-of-school connections, or when-school-is-out programming that provides activities for children outside of regular school hours. After-school options (e.g., tutoring, recreation, art and music education) are on the rise nationally—with public libraries, Boys and Girls Clubs, YMCAs and YWCAs, youth groups, faith-based organizations, and some private businesses leading the charge. While there is some disagreement regarding the effectiveness of many after-school programs, interest and experimentation has continued to build.

Halpern has observed that it is a lack of old-fashioned connectiveness in neighborhoods that is reflected in the expansion of after-school activities, including a belief that such public spaces as streets and playgrounds are no longer safe, and that it is "stressful and unproductive for children to be left on their own after school" (p. 81). A growing literature on out-of-school connections has identified as key developmental effects progress in identity-building for youngsters, in emotional support and guidance, in helping to bridge and broker cultural challenges for immigrant youth, in overcoming loneliness, and in providing protection against negative neighborhood influences.

A second major category of connections pays attention to the in-school effects of the neighborhood. A 1999 review by Wynn, Meyer, and Richards-Schuster, for example, has explored the steadily growing case-study literature on the in-school developmental effects of partnerships, service relationships, parental involvement, and community volunteerism. Among the specific benefits can be a sense of *the village,* meaning a broadened arena of support and caring; improved relationships between home and school; enhanced access to such learning-related services as counseling or medical care; increased school attendance; and improved student perceptions of the community's interest in school. In one of the few empirical studies of neighborhood influences, Lee Shumow, Deborah Vandell, and Jill Posner discovered that a broad exposure to positive adult role models throughout a neighborhood can contribute to better academic performance for children in school.

Summary

Public schools have often been *in* but not *of* their neighborhoods. The late twentieth century saw a rediscovery of the importance of neighborhood—both as a potentially vital complement to the work of the school and as an important educator in its own right. Linkages between the many components of neighborhoods and between neighborhoods and their schools are receiving new emphasis, including establishing a linkages terminology ranging from concepts of social capital to social cohesion, agency, and sense-of-place. Models of neighborhood involvement are also surfacing anew, including community activism and special alliances, the effects of community revitalization, the idea of *regime,* and a better understanding of the effects of individual family preferences. Although the notion of neighborhood effects upon the development of children is still an emerging arena for research interest, there are indications that neighborhood connections (both out-of-school and in-school) represent a productive line of inquiry.

See also: FAMILY, SCHOOL, AND COMMUNITY CONNECTIONS; PARENTING, *subentry on* HIGH-RISK NEIGHBORHOODS; SOCIAL CAPITAL AND EDUCATION; VIOLENCE, CHILDREN'S EXPOSURE TO, *subentry on* COMMUNITY VIOLENCE.

BIBLIOGRAPHY

BEHRMAN, RICHARD E., ed. 1999. "When School Is Out." *The Future of Children* 9(2).

BOYD, WILLIAM L.; CROWSON, ROBERT L.; and GRESSON, AARON. 1999. "Neighborhood Initiatives, Community Agencies, and the Public Schools: A Changing Scene for the Development and Learning of Children." In *Development and Learning of Children and Youth in Urban America,* ed. Margaret C. Wang and Maynard C. Reynolds. Philadelphia: Temple University Center for Research in Human Development and Education.

BURLINGAME, MARTIN. 1988. "The Politics of Education and Educational Policy: The Local Level." In *Handbook of Research on Educational Administration,* ed. Norman J. Boyan. New York: Longman.

CHRISPEELS, JANET H., and RIVERO, ELVIA. 2001. "Engaging Latino Families for Student Success: How Parent Education Can Reshape Parents' Sense of Place in the Education of Their Children." *Peabody Journal of Education* 76(2):119–169.

COLEMAN, JAMES S. 1987. "Families and Schools." *Educational Researcher* 16(6):527–532.

COLEMAN, JAMES S. 1988. "Social Capital in the Creation of Human Capital." *American Journal of Sociology* 94:S95–S120.

CROWSON, ROBERT L. 2002. "Empowerment Models." In *Interprofessional Collaboration and Comprehensive School Services,* ed. Mary M. Brabeck and M. E. Walsh (102nd Yearbook of the National Society for The Study of Education). Chicago: University of Chicago Press.

DORSCH, NINA G. 1998. *Community, Collaboration, and Collegiality in School Reform: An Odyssey Toward Connections.* Albany: State University of New York Press.

DRISCOLL, MARY ERINA. 2001. "The Sense of Place and the Neighborhood School: Implications for Building Social Capital and for Community Development." In *Community Development and School Reform,* ed. Robert L. Crowson. Oxford: Elsevier Science.

DRISCOLL, MARY ERINA, and KERCHNER, CHARLES T. 1999. "The Implications of Social Capital for Schools, Communities, and Cities: Educational Administration As If a Sense of Place Mattered." In *Handbook of Research on Educational Administration,* 2nd edition, ed. Joseph Murphy and Karen S. Louis. San Francisco: Jossey-Bass.

ELKIN, STEPHEN L. 1987. *City and Regime in the American Republic.* Chicago: University of Chicago Press.

GOLDRING, ELLEN B., and HAUSMAN, CHARLES S. 2001. "Civic Capacity and School Principals: The Missing Links for Community Development." In *Community Development and School Reform,* ed. Robert L. Crowson. Oxford: Elsevier Science.

HALPERN, ROBERT. 1999. "After-School Programs for Low-Income Children: Promise and Challenges." *The Future of Children* 9(2):64–81.

LITTELL, JULIA, and WYNN, JOAN. 1989. *The Availability and Use of Community Resources for Young Adolescents in an Inner-City and a Suburban Community.* Chicago: Chapin Hall Center for Children, University of Chicago.

MAWHINNEY, HANNE B. 2001. "Schools in the Bowling League of the New American Economy: Theorising on Social/Economic Integration in School-to-Work Opportunity Systems." In *Community Development and School Reform,* ed. Robert L. Crowson. Oxford: Elsevier Science.

RAMSAY, MEREDITH. 1996. *Community, Culture, and Economic Development: The Social Roots of Local Action.* Albany: State University of New York Press.

SAVAGE, CARTER JULIAN. 2001. "'Because We Did More With Less,' The Agency of African American Teachers in Franklin, Tennessee: 1890–1967." *Peabody Journal of Education* 76(2).

SCHORR, LISBETH B. 1997. *Common Purposes: Strengthening Families and Neighborhoods to Rebuild America.* New York: Anchor Books.

SHIRLEY, DENNIS. 1997. *Community Organizing for Urban School Reform.* Austin: University of Texas Press.

SHIRLEY, DENNIS. 2001. "Linking Community Organizing and School Reform." In *Community Development and School Reform* ed. Robert L. Crowson. Oxford: Elsevier Science.

SHUMOW, LEE; VANDELL, DEBORAH LOVE; and POSNER, JILL. 1999. "Risk and Resilience in the Urban Neighborhood: Predictors of Academic Performance Among Low-Income Elementary School Children." *Merrill-Palmer Quarterly* 45:309–334.

SMREKAR, CLAIRE, and GOLDRING, ELLEN. 1999. *School Choice in Urban America: Magnet Schools and the Pursuit of Equity.* New York: Teachers College Press.

STONE, CLARENCE N. 1989. *Regime Politics: Governing Atlanta, 1946–1988.* Lawrence: University Press of Kansas

WYNN, JOAN; MEYER, STEPHEN; and RICHARDS-SCHUSTER, KATHERINE. 1999. *Furthering Education: The Relationship of Schools and Other Organizations.* Working Paper, Chapin Hall Center for Children, University of Chicago.

ANDREW J. FINCH
ROBERT L. CROWSON

NEILL, A. S. (1883–1973)

Alexander Sutherland Neill flouted educational convention with utopian faith in individuals' ability to direct their own learning. His romantic Progressive beliefs concerning students' rights and freedoms, his refusal to conform to popular moral and intellectual standards, and his emphasis on social and character development led him to found his own school, Summerhill, in 1921. Neill's radically humanistic, Freudian-based work later joined with Jean-Jacques Rousseau's natural philosophy to greatly influence the free/alternative schools movement of the 1960s and 1970s.

Early Life and Career

A. S. Neill was born in Forfar, Scotland. Working as a pupil teacher in his father's school, Neill's experiences as a young educator were colored by traditional educational expectations: strict discipline, teacher-centered learning practices, and excessive control. At the age of twenty-five, Neill enrolled in Edinburgh University, where he studied English and later became a journalist. In 1915, while working as headmaster, or *dominie*, at a small school in Scotland he wrote the first book in his *Dominie* series, *A Dominie's Log*. This five-book series, which also included *A Dominie Dismissed* (1917), *A Dominie in Doubt* (1921), *A Dominie Abroad* (1923), and *A Dominie's Five* (1924) represented Neill's informal diary interspersed with stories and observations of people, places, and adventures. Most importantly, Neill used the series to explore his thoughts concerning freedom and children—chronicling dramatic transformation in his own ideology from his early teaching experiences.

Although Neill's vocabulary in *A Dominie's Log* connected to traditional psychoanalysis, it was not until he visited "Little Commonwealth," educator Homer Lane's community for delinquent adolescents, that he became familiar with the work of Austrian psychoanalyst Sigmund Freud. There, Lane introduced Neill to Freud's New Psychology, to the notion that children possessed innate goodness, and to the pedagogical practice of student self-government. Neill's emerging understanding of education seemed to be heavily influenced by other psychologists of his time as well, including Wilhem Stekel and Wilhem Reich.

Dissatisfied with traditional schooling—with its lack of freedom, democracy, and self-determination—Neill began searching for a place to establish his own school and to experiment with his developing ideas. In 1921 Neill became involved as co-director of the Dalcroze School in Hellerau, a suburb of Dresden, Germany. Part of an international school called Neue Schule, the Dalcroze supported the study of Eurythmics. Yet despite the school's bohemian atmosphere, Neill soon began to feel that the staff was more interested in education than children, and that the conflict between freedom and rigor was untenable. Additionally, the political climate after World War I caused financial difficulties for many of his students' families and contributed to feelings of anti-Semitism. When parents began removing their children from the school Neill decided it was time to leave Germany.

Once again, Neill was off in search of a site for his experimental educational venture. Neill, together with Lillian Neustatter (who later became Neill's first wife), opened a school in a scenic Austrian mountaintop town called Sonntagsberg. However, conflicts with townspeople over the teaching of religion combined with financial difficulties caused Neill to dismantle the school and renew his search for a suitable location.

Significance to Education

By 1923 Neill had returned to England, to the town of Lyme Regis in the south, to a house called Summerhill. There, he re-established his experimental school and enrolled a variety of so-called problem children in Summerhill. In 1926 Neill departed from his *Dominie* series and wrote *The Problem Child*. In this book, Neill clarified his ideology of freedom as a protest of his experiences both as a child and as a pupil teacher. As a result of this publication, Summerhill garnered greater attention and more students.

The school moved in 1927 to Leiston in the county of Suffolk, which would continue to be its location into the twenty-first century. Despite the move, Neill's ideals and aims remained firm: allowing children freedom to grow emotionally; offering children power over their own lives; giving children the time to develop naturally; and creating a happier childhood by removing fear of and coercion by adults. Summerhill offered numerous activities to help students work toward the above aims. In particular, students took part in private lessons or therapy sessions with Neill. Moreover, students participated in *Schulgemeinde*, or weekly community meetings designed to help them define limits and establish community rules. Following the lead of Homer Lane, Neill viewed these meetings as a way for children to transfer their emotions onto the community. Because freedom and self-determination were of utmost priority, the learning of lessons became a necessary concession at Summerhill. As such, Neill was less concerned with hiring teachers with strong pedagogical skills than he was with hiring teachers who cared about children and who followed the aims and vision of Summerhill.

Neill's first wife, Lillian, died in April 1944. Soon after her death, Neill married Ena Wood, and together they oversaw Summerhill until Neill's death in 1973. Upon his second wife's retirement in 1985, Zoe Readhead, the daughter of A. S. Neill and Ena Neill, took over as headmistress of Summerhill.

Critics argue that A. S. Neill interpreted education in an overly romantic and apolitical fashion, suggesting that offering a stimulating environment with minimum direction was not a proper way to run a school. Also under review are Neill's beliefs about his Freudian-based pedagogy as well as those concerning the innate goodness of children. Despite his critics, Neill's book *Summerhill* (1962) gained him a worldwide audience.

See also: ALTERNATIVE SCHOOLING; EDUCATIONAL REFORM; PROGRESSIVE EDUCATION; ROUSSEAU, JEAN-JACQUES.

BIBLIOGRAPHY

CROALL, JONATHAN. 1983. *Neill of Summerhill.* New York: Pantheon.

HEMMINGS, RAY 1972. *Fifty Years of Freedom: A Study of the Development of the Ideas of Alexander Sutherland Neill.* London: Allen and Unwin.

LAMB, ALBERT. 1992. *Summerhill School: A New View of Childhood.* New York: St Martins.

NEILL, ALEXANDER SUTHERLAND. 1928. *The Problem Child* (1926). London: McBride.

NEILL, ALEXANDER SUTHERLAND. 1937. *That Dreadful School.* Middlesex, Eng.: Jenkins.

NEILL, ALEXANDER SUTHERLAND. 1968. *Summerhill* (1962). Middlesex, Eng.: Penguin.

NEILL, ALEXANDER SUTHERLAND. 1972. *Neill, Neill Orange Peel.* New York: Hart.

NEILL, ALEXANDER SUTHERLAND. 1975. *A Dominie's Log* (1916). New York: Hart.

DEBRA M. FREEDMAN
J. DAN MARSHALL

NEW AMERICAN SCHOOLS

New American Schools (NAS) is a business-led nonprofit organization whose mission is to significantly increase student achievement through comprehensive school improvement. Comprehensive school improvement is an effort to support high student achievement at the school, district, and state levels through the coherent alignment of five essential components: (1) leadership, management, and governance; (2) resource allocation; (3) professional development; (4) evaluation and accountability; and (5) educator, family, and community engagement.

History

In 1991 NAS began investing in specific approaches, later known as "designs," to help turn around low-performing schools. The idea behind this concept was to launch comprehensive approaches to improve student performance by applying the best research available on what works in classrooms in as many schools as possible throughout the country. Through a national competition, NAS selected the best research-based ideas in the country. With private and public partners, NAS then invested more than $130 million in these efforts and others. By the beginning of the twenty-first century, these designs had been implemented in almost 4,000 schools and collectively were in every state in the United States.

In 1997 in response to NAS's initial successes and the long-term potential for comprehensive school improvement, the U.S. Congress passed the Comprehensive School Reform Demonstration (CSRD) program. Since its passage, almost $900 million has been appropriated to help schools and districts start comprehensive school improvement efforts. As a result, hundreds of organizations have begun to offer systems-based school reform services and products. In its 2001 reauthorization of the Elementary and Secondary School Education Act, Congress identified comprehensive school reform as a key strategy in turning around low-performing schools. Congress also authorized new funding streams and provided greater flexibility of education dollars for comprehensive school reform efforts.

In 1999 NAS convened a highly respected panel of educational and business leaders to develop a set of national guidelines of quality to assist consumers. NAS provides the resulting guidelines to educators, parents, and others in an effort to help stakeholders make decisions about an array of educational programs.

In 2001 NAS built on the work of the panel by helping to form the Education Quality Institute. The aim of this independent organization is to help consumers of education products and services select programs that meet locally defined needs and adhere to quality guidelines, are research based, and have been proven to work. Importantly, that same year, NAS shaped a decade's worth of classroom experience, extensive research, and independent evaluations into a coherent set of consulting and operational services, products, and tools, offered through two new divisions within New American Schools—the Education Performance Network and the Center for Evidence-Based Education Development Network—and through the organization's funding arm, the Education Entrepreneurs Fund, which launched a School Funding Services unit.

Education Entrepreneurs Fund

The Education Entrepreneurs Fund operates as a financial intermediary for social investment in education. It seeks grants from corporations, foundations, and government; leverages these funds with social capital loans and program-related investment; and uses the funds to make loans to and investments in education organizations. The fund invests in organizations that contribute to raising student achievement and that have the potential to achieve sustained quality at scale. The fund also provides technical consultation to education entrepreneurs. Additionally, the fund assists educators in identifying and accessing the billions of federal, state, and private dollars available for education improvement programs through its School Funding Services unit launched in 2002.

Education Performance Network (EPN)

The mission of the Education Performances Network is to align education policies and practices to foster strong organizational performance and high student achievement. EPN assists clients in the following areas: accountability and evaluation, charter and contract schools, special education, and community engagement.

Center for Evidence-Based Education

The Center for Evidence-Based Education conducts applied research on the use of school improvement strategies in schools and at the state and district levels. It also supports the development of successful leaders for quality reform and promotes the use of evidence-based approaches to school improvement nationally.

Legal Status and Governance

New American Schools is a nonprofit 501 (c)(3) organization. It is guided by a fourteen-member board of directors.

Membership

New American Schools does not have members but is affiliated with independently operating design teams. Schools and school districts contract with design teams to provide comprehensive school improvement services on a fee basis. In 2002 nine design teams were affiliated with New American Schools: Accelerated Schools Project, ATLAS Communities, Co-nect Schools, Different Ways of Knowing, Expeditionary Learning Outward Bound, the Bernstein Center for Learning, Modern Red Schoolhouse, Turning Points, and Urban Learning Centers.

Publications

New American Schools offers several publications to assist in the implementation of comprehensive school improvement. NAS offers a "how-to" series that provides current research about comprehensive school improvement. This series includes the following papers: *Design-Based Assistance as Cornerstone of a School Improvement Strategy; How to Create and Manage a Decentralized Education System; How to Rethink School Budgets to Support School Transformation; Strategies for Improving Professional Development: A Guide for School Districts; How to Make the Link between Standards, Assessment, and Real Student Achievement; How to Create Incentives for Design-Based Schools; How to Build Local Support for Comprehensive School Reform; How to Evaluate Comprehensive School Reform Models;* and *Revising School Schedules to Create Common Planning Time and Literacy Blocks.* NAS also offers several publications helpful in design selection, including *Guidelines for Ensuring the Quality of National Design-Based Assistance Providers; Design Teams Portfolio;* and *Working toward Excellence: Examining the Effectiveness of New American Schools Designs.*

Influence

By the most meaningful objective criteria, "comprehensive school reform" has become the dominant school reform effort in the nation's public school classrooms. By the early twenty-first century, public schools were investing some $1 billion every year in the staff working with comprehensive school reform designs. Almost 6 percent—more than 5,400—of the nation's 92,000 public schools have used the federal CSRD program to finance design implementation. Thousands more schools have paid for work with comprehensive school reform models from other funding sources, including Title I. Comprehensive school reform is even part of the charter school movement. From 1999 to 2001 the design teams alone entered into partnerships with sixty-five charter schools. Comprehensive school improvement is considered one of the best hopes for the U.S. public school system to make significant progress on a national scale in the near term.

INTERNET RESOURCE

NEW AMERICAN SCHOOLS. 2002. <www.naschools. org>.

LOUISE KENNELLY

NEWLON, JESSE (1882–1941)

Superintendent of Denver, Colorado, schools, director of the Lincoln Experimental School of Teachers College, Columbia University, and president of the National Education Association, Jesse Homer Newlon was one of the most well known progressive educational administrators of the early twentieth century.

Born in Salem, Indiana, Newlon graduated from Indiana University in 1907. He earned a master's degree in 1914 from Columbia University, and began a series of educational appointments as teacher, principal, and superintendent of schools in Indiana, Illinois, and Nebraska. In 1920, he accepted the position for which he is best known—superintendent of schools in Denver, Colorado. In this role, Newlon had the opportunity to further develop his ideas of progressive education and administration. Whereas many academics explored the implications of progressive educational thought at a conceptual level, Newlon, more than any other educator of his generation, proved that an educational administrator could adhere to progressive ideals and, at the same time, involve himself in the community while overseeing the operation of a large school complex.

During the early 1920s in the United States, the ideals of progressive education, espoused by John Dewey and others, were inspiring curriculum reform efforts in a number of public schools. In 1922

Newlon persuaded the Denver school board to support such a project with the argument that he could make the curriculum of the Denver schools more efficient. What set Newlon's plan apart from any other curriculum reform effort of the time was his inclusion of teachers into the curriculum revision process. He believed that teachers, not school boards, should be involved in curriculum development, and he appointed teacher committees to revise curricula and courses of study. Teachers, not administrators, chaired these committees, and Newlon scheduled time during the school week for teachers to work on these revision processes with administrative and supervisory personnel. Newlon thus orchestrated official acknowledgment of the significance of teachers' collaborative participation in curriculum development.

The Denver Plan attracted considerable attention from teachers and administrators as well as community members across the country. Teachers especially applauded Newlon's insistence that the Denver school board provide support and structure for the teachers' labor outside the classroom. For example, Newlon proposed that teachers who served as members or chairs of curriculum revision committees be provided relief from regular classroom work, with a few days to a few months release time. He also insisted on the formation of a clerical staff to support all committee work, thus freeing teachers from those clerical responsibilities.

Throughout the duration of the Denver Curriculum Project, committees worked to reconstruct courses of study in subject areas at each of the three instructional levels: elementary, junior high, and high school. Newlon also secured funds to print the courses of study completed by the committees. By 1923, a professional library was completed and was staffed by a full-time librarian. According to Newlon and his committees of teachers, administrators, and supervisory staff, curriculum revision needed to be a continuous process and therefore needed also to draw on the latest educational research and theories.

Further, Newlon posited that development and enactment of the curriculum were simultaneous: curriculum was shaped not only by committees outside the classroom but also by the interactions of teachers and students who used—and therefore reshaped according to their particular situations and needs—those courses of study.

At the same time, Newlon concluded that teachers' and students' participation in curriculum development and revision did not obviate the need for curriculum specialists. During his tenure as Denver superintendent, Newlon appointed the first district-wide curriculum administrator in the nation. Some argue that because that district-wide curriculum administrator was educated in a department of educational administration (at Teachers College, Columbia University), the ensuing first generation of curriculum specialists established the bureaucratic and administrative character of the curriculum development paradigm. That administrative character finally was challenged in the 1970s by a group of curriculum theorists intent on the reconceptualization of the field.

Nonetheless, Newlon's conceptions of curriculum development and school administration attracted national attention, not only through his support of teachers and students as curriculum creators, but also through his establishment of an equal salary schedule, development of an exceptional school library system, and organization of a permanent curriculum department. These accomplishments all took place during his overseeing of the construction of fifteen schools in the Denver area.

By 1933 the Denver Plan and the materials generated by teachers, administrators, supervisors, and students were widely known, circulated, and used nationally. As a result, the Denver high schools were selected to be participants in the Progressive Education Association's Eight-Year Study (1934–1942). Although Newlon had resigned as Denver superintendent of schools in 1927 to become professor of education at Teachers College, Columbia University, most viewed his foundational work as the major reason the Denver schools were selected as one of the six most experimental and successful schools in the study.

From 1927 to 1941 Newlon served as professor of education at Teachers College, Columbia University, and from 1927 to 1934 as director of the Lincoln Experimental School at Columbia. The Lincoln School, under his directorship, also participated in the Eight-Year Study. During his tenure at Teachers College, Newlon served as director of the Division of Instruction (1934–1938), and of the Division of Foundations of Education (1938–1941). He participated in the Teachers College discussion group "The Social Frontier," the Committee for Academic Freedom of the American Civil Liberties Union, and the American Historical Association's Commission on Social Studies.

Newlon visited the Soviet Union in 1937, and as a result of that visit, became increasingly fearful of rising totalitarianism abroad. Upon his return, he devoted himself further to spreading the ideals of Progressive education by speaking frequently about the values of democracy and the school's role in the preservation of freedom. Some note that Newlon became so distraught over the loyalty oaths and authoritarian conditions he witnessed in the schools that his health seemed to be adversely and permanently affected. He died on September 1, 1941.

See also: EDUCATION REFORM; EIGHT-YEAR STUDY; PROGRESSIVE EDUCATION.

BIBLIOGRAPHY

JOHNSTON, CHARLES H.; NEWLON, JESSE H.; and PICKELL, FRANK G. 1922. *Junior-Senior High School Administration.* New York: Scribners.

NEWLON, JESSE H. 1923. *Twentieth Annual Report of School District Number One in the City and County of Denver and State of Colorado.* Denver, CO: Denver School Press.

NEWLON, JESSE H. 1934. *Educational Administration as Social Policy.* New York: Scribners.

NEWLON, JESSE H. 1939. *Education for Democracy in Our Times.* New York: McGraw-Hill.

JANET L. MILLER

NGOS AND FOUNDATIONS

See: NONGOVERNMENTAL ORGANIZATIONS AND FOUNDATIONS.

NO CHILD LEFT BEHIND ACT OF 2001

On January 8, 2002, President George W. Bush signed into law the No Child Left Behind Act. This act was a congressional reauthorization of the Elementary and Secondary Education Act of 1965 (ESEA) and is also known technically as Public Law 107-87.

In April 1965, almost thirty-seven years prior to the enactment of Public Law 107-87, the 89th Congress and President Lyndon Baines Johnson had overseen enactment of the original ESEA (Pub. L.

89-10). This federal government statue proved enormously important for American education. It also proved enormously difficult to implement and manage. The nature and complexity of the No Child Left Behind Act suggests that it too will be both equally important and equally challenging to those charged with overseeing its operation.

The Original ESEA

The significance of the original ESEA resided in its emphasis on the schooling of students from low-income households. The ESEA, through a remarkably creative financing formula, distributed federal funds to states, and thence to counties and school districts, proportionate to the number of enrolled students from low-income households. By the turn of the twenty-first century, this act was responsible for distributing more than $13 billion each school year to public and, through a few minimal provisions, private and religious K–12 schools. The act also supplied substantial financial subsidies for the operation of state education departments.

Prior to 1965, not only did the federal government have only the most minimal presence in education, education also had only a minimal presence in the lives of low-income students. These were children who had legal access to public schooling. But public schooling had few mechanisms, other than the dedication of certain teachers and principals, for educating them. Low-income students were permitted to stay in school, often being promoted from one grade to the next. Prior to the ESEA, however, there were few expectations that schools would expend on their behalf the added resources that might be necessary to compensate for the poverty-impacted nature of their neighborhoods and households. The ESEA was, if nothing else, a powerful symbolic message that even poor children were to be schooled.

Administration of the ESEA proved challenging. School districts frequently did not realize that the added federal funding was intended for low-income children. They accepted the money as "general financial aid," suitable for whatever purpose they chose to spend it. Congressional amendments in 1968 made the statute's purposes more clear. Nevertheless, these new regulations were so strict that it became equally clear that the federally funded poverty programs, however much needed, were intruding deeply into the operation of schools. The narrowly focused instructional programs they financed were at best wasteful and possibly counterproductive to the education of children.

By the mid-1990s, Congress undertook another midcourse correction and began to permit schools to deploy the ESEA funds with greater local discretion. Still, by 1998, a General Accounting Office report suggested that only fifteen states were adequately implementing the ESEA. This was more than three decades after its enactment.

The New Act

The No Child Left Behind Act promises to be as important as the original ESEA not only because of the added federal funding it authorizes for education but also because of the pathbreaking measures required of states accepting the money.

The new ESEA is also symbolic of a major shift in American education. Until the latter part of the twentieth century, it was generally sufficient simply to offer schooling and to ensure that all children had equal access to it. By the turn of the twenty-first century, however, global economic changes had so altered that societal landscape that Americans were expecting far more of their education systems. Now, simple access was no longer sufficient. Learning was coming to be expected—and not simply learning for the slender elite that for more than a century had graduated from privileged public and private schools and attended the nation's highest-ranking universities. Now learning was expected of all children, and performance was expected of all schools. The No Child Left Behind Act is filled with accountability provisions to ensure that states and participating schools understand the new expectations.

The No Child Left Behind Act is symbolic of the transition in American education from a period where the main concern was that the inputs of schooling be present to a period where it is the outcomes of schooling that matter. To accomplish this new purpose—to render schools effective—the reauthorized ESEA provides added funding to school districts, through states. In addition, it requires that states have learning standards and testing programs capable of assessing each child's performance in achieving those standards. The accountability mechanisms in the statute provide for negative sanctions to schools and districts that persistently fail to elevate student achievement.

However important practically, financially, or symbolically, the No Child Left Behind Act will doubtless prove difficult to implement. The statutory language offers only the most rudimentary solutions to a number of issues and questions, such as the comparability of testing forms across states, or whether improvement in student achievement is sufficient or must a school attain absolute standards of achievement to be approved.

In that the original ESEA was not fully understood nor faultlessly managed even three decades after its enactment, it is unlikely that the 2002-enacted version, which if anything is even more complicated, will achieve success at a faster pace.

INTERNET RESOURCE

U.S. Department of Education. 2002. *No Child Left Behind.* <www.nochildleftbehind.gov>.

James W. Guthrie

NONGOVERNMENTAL ORGANIZATIONS AND FOUNDATIONS

Nongovernmental organizations (NGOs) are entities, usually international nonprofits, which work in an independent fashion yet complement the work of governments for the benefit of constituencies in civil society. The nature of NGOs runs the gamut from lobbying and advocacy to operations and project-oriented organizations. Their mandates often but not always include working to complement the efforts of state and local governments. Since becoming players in the international economic development world in the early 1980s, NGOs have proliferated in both developed and developing countries.

Foundations are institutions through which private wealth is contributed and distributed for public purposes. They are institutions financed by charitable contributions or endowments and can either be for-profit or nonprofit entities depending on the manner in which their money is invested and managed. Foundations generally grant funds to certain causes in keeping with their mandate and mission. In the case of education, foundations often supplement the public provision of financing for education, many times specifically channeling funds to needy or underserved populations. The board of a given foundation establishes the grant-making poli-

cies from which the programming agenda is then derived. Foundations provide grant money to a variety of types of organizations, including nonprofits and NGOs, as well as to universities and schools. The programming agenda is periodically revised to keep abreast of changes in society. For example, following the 2000 U.S. presidential election controversy, the Carnegie Foundation changed its programming agenda to include strengthening U.S. democracy as one of its four main programmatic areas.

Although the work of foundations may be regarded collectively, several people have written scholarly pieces on the work of specific foundations (Robert F. Arnove on the Carnegie, Ford, and Rockefeller foundations; Jeffrey Puryear on the impact of the Ford Foundation's programs in Chile; and James S. Coleman and David Court on the Rockefeller Foundation's impact in Africa). The debate about foundations includes the position that foundations promote the causes that the elite and powerful determine worthwhile (Arnove) versus the argument that they facilitate institution building (Puryear, Coleman, and Court). Although these two positions may seem diametrically opposed, they both start with the premise that social change and development—as a result of the planning, research, expertise, and leadership of people interested in particular social causes—becomes more viable with funding from private charitable contributions. It is frequently NGOs that are conduits or tangential beneficiaries of the programming decisions or internal policies of these very foundations. Without trying to resolve the debate, it is imperative to recognize the role in international development that both foundations and NGOs play, together with the multilateral development banks, bilateral aid agencies, and governments. The descriptions that follow provide details on the individual organizations, their mandates, objectives, programming agendas, and target populations.

Nongovernmental Organizations

CARE. The Cooperative for Assistance and Relief Everywhere (CARE) is a nonprofit, nonsectarian federation of agencies and NGOs devoted to channeling relief and self-help materials to needy people in foreign countries. Originally organized in the United States in 1945 to help war-ravaged Europe, CARE soon expanded its program to include developing nations in Asia, Africa, and Latin America. Famous for its "CARE packages" of food and other necessities, CARE in now also involved in population, health care, land management, and small economic activity. It is an international organization with ten member countries and headquarters in Brussels, Belgium.

CARE's goal is to build self-sufficiency by helping families meet three basic needs: income, education, and health and population services. Its work in education includes promoting literacy, numeracy, and school attendance, particularly among girls who are often denied schooling. Programs improve education for all children, with an emphasis on keeping girls in school. Groups are created so parents and teachers can discuss traditional educational barriers, such as housework or baby-sitting, which keep girls from attending school. CARE also provides economic incentives to help parents cover the cost of keeping their daughters in school.

CARE first began its education program in 1994 with pilot projects in Peru, Guatemala, India, and Togo. Within four years of its inception, it expanded this number to twenty-nine projects in eighteen countries.

Education International. Located in Brussels, Belgium, Education International (EI) has become an important organization for many NGOs, such as teachers unions, in their advocacy work at the national and international level. As an international association of teacher unions, with local teacher associations or unions as members, EI's mission is based on a growing conviction that basic education is a key factor in the eradication of poverty and a cornerstone of freedom, democracy, and sustainable human development. Education also plays a role in eliminating the worst forms of child labor.

Through the Global Campaign for Education (GCE), this NGO brings together organizations working in 180 countries and seeks to hold governments accountable for the fact that 125 million children are denied an education. Education International, Action Aid, Oxfam International, and Global March Against Child Labor jointly launched this program. In terms of teacher evaluation, EI advocates a type of evaluation that is perceived by teachers as being affirmative and supportive as well as balanced and fair and that can contribute to promoting quality in education.

Education Trust. Located in Washington, D.C., the Education Trust is an independent, nonpartisan, nonprofit organization. Established in 1990 by the American Association for Higher Education as a special project to encourage colleges and universities to support K–12 reform efforts, in the early twenty-first century it strives to promote high academic achievement for students at all levels from kindergarten through college (K–16). The organization functions on the premise that in order to achieve significant change in K–12 it must simultaneously change the way that postsecondary education does business. Similarly, the Education Trust maintains that postsecondary education needs as much improvement as the K–12 level.

The Education Trust works for the high academic achievement of all students. It abides by the tenet that all children taught at high levels will learn at high levels. The students and institutions most often left behind in plans to improve education are its focus, in particular those institutions serving low-income Hispanic, African-American, and Native American youth. Education Trust strives to close the achievement gaps that separate poor and minority students from their more advantaged peers. Efforts to improve elementary and secondary education must be undertaken in conjunction with postsecondary education. The organization places emphasis on high standards, rigorous curriculum, good teaching, and accountability for results. Participating in education debates at the national and state policy level, the Education Trust works alongside policymakers, parents, education professionals, and community and business leaders in communities across the United States to transform schools and colleges into institutions that genuinely serve all students.

Oxfam International. Oxfam International is an international confederation of eleven autonomous NGOs committed to working together to fight poverty and injustice around the world. Each shares the commitment to end waste and the injustice of poverty, in long-term development work and during times of urgent humanitarian need. The common mandate for all of the Oxfams is to address the structural causes of poverty and related injustices and create lasting solutions to hunger, poverty, and social injustice through long-term partnerships with poor communities around the world. The organization has an advocacy office in Washington, D.C., which lobbies the World Bank, the International Monetary Fund, and the United Nations on issues agreed upon by the eleven member organizations. As a privately funded organization, it strives to speak "with conviction and integrity to challenge the structural barriers that foster conflict and human suffering and limit people from gaining the skills, resources, and power to become self-sufficient."

Oxfam invests privately raised funds and technical expertise in local organizations around the world that hold promise in their efforts to help poor people move out of poverty. These projects are characterized by partnerships with local organizations, a unique and highly successful approach that ensures lasting change. Through the local partnerships, Oxfam listens to the local needs and works jointly toward solutions that enable communities to prosper and organize for economic stability and democratic opportunity. Oxfam is committed to these long-term relationships in search of lasting solutions to hunger, poverty, and social inequities. As part of this commitment, Oxfam is dedicated to educating the public worldwide on the realities of poverty and the universal obligation to establish a future that is equitable, environmentally sustainable, and respectful of the rights of all peoples.

In education, Oxfam plays an active role in ensuring that aid resources are channeled to education, which plays a vital role in poverty reduction, economic growth, and democracy. The organization plays an advocacy role, regularly issuing policy and position papers that react to the policies of G8 countries, large donor organizations, and international summits.

Save the Children. Save the Children is an international nonprofit child-assistance organization (or NGO) based in Westport, Connecticut, which works in forty-six countries worldwide, including the United States. Its mission is to make lasting, positive change in the lives of children in need. Save the Children is a member of the International Save the Children Alliance, a worldwide network of twenty-six independent Save the Children organizations working in more than 100 countries to ensure the well-being of children everywhere.

Nearly seventy years of experience working alongside families and communities in the United States, Latin America, the Caribbean, the Middle East, Eurasia, Africa, and Asia has convinced Save the Children that poverty "need not be a life sentence." To help children get the best possible start in life, Save the Children promotes locally appropriate programs in education, health care, environmentally sound agriculture, and economic productivity.

In a world where the majority of illiterate adults are women, improving access to education for girls is urgent. At the outset of the twenty-first century, nearly two-thirds of the 125 million children not attending primary school are girls. The cycle of illiteracy traps millions of girls and women throughout the developing world. But with education, this cycle can be broken. Studies show that an educated mother is more likely to provide her children with adequate nutrition, seek needed health care, and send her girls, as well as boys, to school. Save the Children focuses on education as a critical means of improving the quality of life for both mothers and their families.

In an effort to address the lack of access to quality education experienced by more than one billion people, Save the Children's programs support communities in the development of quality education programs. Working with communities, the organization explores initial concepts to bring Strong Beginnings programs to the area. The programs include research and project development in each community, which leads to the implementation of active intergenerational-learning programs for all ages, early childhood development, primary education, and youth and adult nonformal education.

Save the Children's education programs have produced many dramatic results in the lives of women and girls around the world. In Afghanistan, where prior to 2002 girls were kept in seclusion and not allowed to attend formal school, the program has established home-based classrooms to provide basic education that would otherwise be denied. More than 20,000 girls in remote villages of Mali, where schools were once rare, are learning to read and count. And women participating in literacy programs in Guatemala are learning to manage their lives and take on leadership roles in their communities.

World Vision. Based in the United Kingdom, World Vision is an international Christian relief and development NGO, which works to promote the well-being of all people, especially children. World Vision strives to enable families and communities to transform their conditions and gain self-reliance in a sustainable manner. It achieves this by working with the poor in their communities; it helps them gain access to clean water, better agricultural production, improved health care, and primary education.

World Vision's advocacy initiatives draw on the expertise and experience of staff throughout the world who work in countries and communities that are afflicted by poverty. World Vision works to raise their concerns in the United Kingdom, with ministers and members of Parliament, through meetings, briefing papers, a discussion paper series, and special reports. World Vision has policy staff working on the areas of child rights, conflict, peace building, and also global economic issues. Each of these advocacy themes has the potential to bring real benefits to ordinary communities in developing countries.

Although World Vision is a Christian organization, the organization has child-focused projects that are offered freely, regardless of belief, ethnic background, or gender. The organization's literature claims that "faith fuels our work and supplies our staff with wisdom and ability, our donors with the resources they share, and enables our recipients to work toward the fulfillment of their dreams."

Foundations

The Broad Foundation. Located in Los Angeles, California, and established in 1999, the Broad Foundation supports innovative efforts to strengthen local, state, regional, and national initiatives to improve governance, management, and labor relations in large urban school systems. The foundation is dedicated to building K–12 educational leadership capacity, strengthening union-management relations, and supporting aggressive, systemwide strategies to increase student achievement. It aims to infuse a new kind of school system leadership in order to strengthen the state of public education.

The Broad Foundation's investments are targeted toward the following five program areas: (1) support for entrepreneurial and nontraditional leaders; (2) leadership training; (3) recruitment and selection strategies; (4) visibility for high performers; and (5) venture philanthropy.

The area of support for entrepreneurial and nontraditional leaders provides funding to current innovators, such as superintendents, school boards, union presidents, and other leaders in the K–12 public education system, through rewards for high performance, grants for specific district and union projects, and funding for ongoing networking and assistance. A leadership training area provides grants for the support and development of training for aspiring and current innovators. The area of recruitment and selection strategies provides assistance to districts and to business and community organizations interested in securing the next generation of

entrepreneurial educational leaders and managerial talent. Visibility for high performers is an area that permits the foundation to engage in public visibility campaigns that showcase the results of systemwide improvements in urban districts. The foundation also supports research and dissemination projects that actively communicate the results of high-potential endeavors. Finally, the venture philanthropy area funds entrepreneurial ideas from inside and outside the current system that offer high-leverage opportunities to improve K–12 education.

Carnegie Corporation of New York. Founded in 1911 by Andrew Carnegie for the "advancement and diffusion of knowledge and understanding among people of the United States," the Carnegie Corporation is a general-purpose, grant-making foundation. Charter amendments made subsequent to its founding permit the corporation to channel close to 7.5 percent of its income for the same purpose in countries that are currently or have been members of the British Commonwealth. Most such grants are in British Commonwealth Africa. As a grant-making foundation, the corporation seeks to carry out Carnegie's vision of philanthropy, which he said should aim "to do real and permanent good in this world."

The focus of the corporation's work has evolved over time, adapting its program areas to changing circumstances as Andrew Carnegie wished. Although current program directions have been designed to correspond with the corporation's historic mission and legacy and to maintain the continuity of its work, they are also intended to serve as catalysts for change. A current challenge facing the Carnegie Corporation is how to support the development of a global community in an age when both isolationism and nationalism seem to be fostering a fractured view of the world. This raises the question of how to use the current glut of information to foster a sense of community, rather than letting it disintegrate community.

After a review of the foundation's management structure and grant programs under the leadership of Vartan Gregorian, the corporation refined its programmatic focus, which in the early twenty-first century includes education, international peace and security, international development, and strengthening U.S. democracy. In addition, a new program, Carnegie Corporation Scholars Program, strives to support fundamental research by young scholars with outstanding promise and also by established experts who stand to contribute significantly to the corporation's mission.

In education, the Carnegie Corporation dedicates a large majority of its funds to education reform ranging from early childhood education to higher education. The education program focuses on three key areas: early childhood education, urban school reform, and higher education. Within these areas, the corporation's goals are to promote the creation of high-quality early learning opportunities on a large scale; accelerate urban school reform; strengthen the education of teachers; and stimulate an examination and strengthening of liberal arts education. In education, the corporation has traditionally had a significant impact on public policy for children, teachers, and other stakeholders in the educational process. Through its focus on education, Carnegie has successfully convened special bodies of experts and opinion leaders to study related issues and publish several key reports.

Carnegie Foundation for the Advancement of Teaching. The Carnegie Foundation for the Advancement of Teaching is a national and international center for research and policy studies about teaching and is an ancillary philanthropy of the Carnegie Foundation. With a focus on the scholarship of teaching, the foundation seeks to generate discussion and promulgate sustainable, long-term changes in educational research, policy, and practice. Foundation programs are designed to foster deep, significant, lasting learning for all students and to improve the ability of education to develop students' understanding, skills, and integrity.

The Ford Foundation. Established in 1936 by Henry Ford, the founder of Ford Motor Company, and his son Edsel, the Ford Foundation is one of the most important and prominent foundations in the field of education. From 1936 to 1950 the foundation made grants mostly to organizations in its home state of Michigan. In 1951 the foundation moved to New York City and began its focus on national and international giving.

The Ford Foundation is a private philanthropic institution, which seeks to improve the well-being of people around the world by funding "experimental, demonstration, and developmental efforts that give promise of producing significant advances in various fields."

The foundation is governed by a board of trustees and administered by a professional staff. The board of trustees includes CEOs, senior officials in higher education, and people involved in Native American interests. The trustees determine general policies and budgets. The staff evaluates grant applications, identifies institutions to administer programs, and makes recommendations for grants.

The foundation has identified certain program areas in which it is interested in funding projects. It generally does not make grants for normal operating costs of an organization, construction of buildings, or for strictly religious activities.

The foundation has identified six broad categories of programs in which it is interested: urban poverty, rural poverty and resources, human rights and social justice, governance and public policy, education and culture, and international affairs.

The type of work the foundation funds is equally diverse. The foundation funds projects, which involve direct assistance to the needy, and grants to organizations, which seek to influence public policy. Over the years the foundation has provided grants to establish new organizations, found new academic departments at universities, fund demonstration projects, and assist other philanthropies. The foundation has organized coalitions with other philanthropies, government, and nonprofit organizations to work on projects. It also administers its own projects.

In some cases the foundation has funded programs on an ongoing basis, which over time become established institutions, such as community development corporations (CDCs). Since the late 1960s it has made grants of nearly $200 million to CDCs in depressed urban areas, which initiate economic development projects; raise additional funds; offer job training, day care, and credit; and advocate for improved government services.

The Ford Foundation has sixteen offices overseas. Approximately 35 percent of the annual budget is allocated for overseas projects. Programs include agricultural development in Latin America, Africa, and Asia; a training program for judges in China; international studies in Chile; and philanthropy in Egypt.

The Bill and Melinda Gates Foundation. The William H. Gates Foundation (founded in 1994 with a focus on health issues in developing countries) and the Gates Learning Foundation (founded in 1997 but renamed the Gates Library Foundation) merged in August 1999 to become the Bill and Melinda

Gates Foundation, which encompasses those two foundations and the Gates Center for Technology Access. The Gates Foundation ranks as one of the wealthiest private foundations in the world. Established by the Microsoft cofounder and chief executive officer, the Seattle, Washington-based foundation is led by Bill Gates's father, William Gates Sr., and supports initiatives in education, technology, global health, and community giving in the Pacific Northwest.

Although many benefit from the linking of the globe in a digital web of communications and information flow, the foundation strives to pay attention to those who have not shared in the promise of the digital age. The Bill and Melinda Gates Foundation is dedicated to sharing the promise of new technologies with all citizens. The foundation is focusing its efforts in three critical areas: (1) U.S. education; (2) libraries; and (3) public access to information.

In its work on education, the foundation perceives the education system as an immensely important strategic front for forging a future in which all children can participate in the opportunities of the digital age. In March 2000 the foundation announced a $350 million, three-year investment in a series of education grants designed to help all students achieve at high levels by improving teaching and learning and enhancing access to technology.

In 1999 Bill and Melinda Gates made a defining gift of $1 billion to establish the Gates Millennium Scholars program, which will provide scholarships for academically talented minority students (African-Americans, Asian-Americans, Hispanics, and Native Americans) who would otherwise not have the financial resources to attend college. Additional scholarships are available for minority scholars pursuing graduate degrees in science, mathematics, engineering, education, or library science.

The Charles Stewart Mott Foundation. Based in Flint, Michigan, the Charles Stewart Mott Foundation was the brainchild of the sailor, automotive engineer, industrial pioneer, banker, educational innovator, and community leader by the same name. In addition to these attributes, Mott was also a philanthropist.

The grant-making activities of the foundation focus on four main areas: civil society; the environment; development in Flint, Michigan; and pathways out of poverty. In addition, the Exploratory and Special Projects program permits the founda-

tion to explore new opportunities. About 20 percent of the foundations grants are international in scope.

Of particular interest to educators are the program for civil society and the efforts to decrease poverty. The mission of the civil society program is to "strengthen citizen and nonprofit-sector engagement in support of free and pluralistic democratic societies," with primary geographic focus on the United States, central and eastern Europe, Russia, South Africa, and at the global level. In the United States the efforts focus on strengthening the fabric of civil society in the face of public apathy and cynicism, extremist forces, and an economically and racially divided society.

Within the program area of Pathways Out of Poverty, efforts include improving community education, expanding economic opportunity, building organized communities, and special initiatives. The mission for the programmatic area of improving community education is to "ensure that community education serves as a pathway out of poverty for children in low-income communities by building a continuum of quality learning opportunities that stretches from the preschool years through preparation for higher education and the work force." This includes promoting school readiness, success in school, and learning that spans beyond the classroom.

Lilly Endowment. Founded in 1937 by pharmaceutical manufacturer Josiah K. Lilly, this foundation, based in Indianapolis, Indiana, grants funds for religious, educational, and charitable purposes. Of special interest to the foundation are programs designed to foster the growth and development of Christian character.

Its endeavors in education include aid to Protestant theological seminaries, other colleges, and elementary and secondary education. Most of the foundation's work in education focuses on raising the educational-attainment level of citizens of the state of Indiana. The endowment also provides grants to private, historically black colleges and universities (HBCUs) throughout the United States. In addition, the endowment focuses on positive development of youth by providing support to direct-service organizations, building the capacity of intermediary organizations, and providing professional development for staff members in such organizations.

The Pew Charitable Trusts. Based in Philadelphia, Pennsylvania, the Pew Charitable Trusts support nonprofit activities in the areas of culture, education, the environment, health and human services, public policy, and religion. The trusts consist of seven individual charitable funds established between 1948 and 1979 by two sons and two daughters of Sun Oil Company founder Joseph N. Pew and his wife, Mary Anderson Pew. Though the trusts are separate legal entities, their grant-making activities are managed collectively and guided by a single set of program priorities. The trusts make strategic investments that encourage and support citizen participation in addressing critical issues and effecting social change.

The work of this foundation in education seeks to raise the performance of students at all levels of education, especially the capabilities of students to learn for understanding and to acquire the types of literacy necessary for productive employment and effective citizenship in an increasingly complex society. The foundation's broad efforts in education include an interest in publicly funded preschool education programs, standards based reform in K–12 education, other K–12 reform efforts, and support to higher education. In higher education, the foundation is interested in issues of access to higher education, the quality of higher education, and the means for keeping the United States competitive in the emerging global and technology-intensive economy.

Rockefeller Foundation. Based in New York City, the Rockefeller Foundation is a knowledge-based, global foundation with a commitment to enrich and sustain the lives and livelihoods of poor and excluded people throughout the world. The foundation seeks to identify, and address at their source, the causes of human suffering and need. The foundation's approach to current global challenges focuses on poor people's daily existence, and how the process of globalization can be turned to their advantage. Program funding is focused on grant-making areas that reflect the interconnections between people's health, food, work, creative expression, and the impact of globalization on the poor. The Rockefeller Foundation's central goal is to "give full expression to the creative impulses of individuals and communities in order to enhance the well-being of societies and better equip them to interact in a globalized world."

Within the unit that encompasses education, knowledge, and religion, the foundation seeks to enhance educational opportunity, especially for low-income and chronically disadvantaged groups, and to address the challenges of pluralism and diversity using interdisciplinary and collaborative approaches. Through education reform, the foundation seeks to enhance the capacity of schools and higher education institutions to broaden access and increase levels of student achievement, particularly for historically unserved populations. In higher education and scholarship, the foundation seeks to build fields of knowledge that deepen scholarship and public understanding of pluralism and identity. The foundation emphasizes the importance of social science training as a means to educate a new generation of leaders and scholars who can be more effective in their civic roles.

Smith Richardson Foundation. H. Smith Richardson, son of the founder of Vicks Family Remedies, and his wife, Grace Jones Richardson, created the Smith Richardson Foundation in 1935. Located in Westport, Connecticut, the Smith Richardson Foundation seeks to "help ensure the vitality of our social, economic, and governmental institutions," and "assist with the development of effective policies to compete internationally and advance U.S. interests and values abroad." This mission is embodied in its international and domestic grant programs.

The foundation has two grant programs: the International Security and Foreign Policy Program, which supports research and policy projects on issues central to the strategic interests of the United States; and the Domestic Public Policy Program, which supports research, writing, and analysis on public policy issues and strives to help inform policymakers and the public on domestic issues. Education policy and school reform are two of the foundation's most important areas of grant making. Such grants support research at universities, think tanks, and research organizations on important education policy issues, such as charter schools, school choice, teacher training and pay, class size, and educational standards. This grant making is focused on policy debates in the United States. Although the grant-making efforts do not include a particular focus on certain levels of education, research on higher education is not supported.

Soros Foundation. American stock trader and philanthropist George Soros has used his wealth to create a network of foundations, most of which are intended to aid former Communist countries in creating an "open society." Other Soros foundations fund health initiatives and aid immigrants in the United States.

In the parlance of the Soros foundations network, the term *national foundation* refers to an autonomous nonprofit organization founded by George Soros in a particular country to promote the development of open society in that country. National foundations are located primarily in the countries of central and eastern Europe and the former Soviet Union, although there are some in other parts of the world. A local board of directors comprising distinguished citizens from different ethnic, geographic, political, and professional backgrounds determines the specific priorities and activities of each foundation. Given the diversity of social, political, and economic conditions in the countries of the network, programs vary greatly in nature and urgency from one foundation to another. Yet all of the foundations' activities share an overarching common mission: to support the development of an open society. The local nature of the decision-making process at the foundations is one of the distinctive features of George Soros's approach to philanthropy.

In promoting an open society, education plays a role in the work of most of the foundations; however, the focus varies from country to country. For example, the Soros Foundation provided education to 300,000 Burmese refugees in Thailand, India, and Bangladesh, serving otherwise underserved populations. In Armenia the Internet and National Education programs, redesigned in 1999, increased school outreach and community involvement in education. A network of schools and organizations provided the training and support required to develop the idea of community schools. The aim is not only to strengthen community participation but also to improve the quality of the education system by introducing modern methodology and criteria for curriculum development.

In other countries such as Latvia, the Soros Foundation emphasizes the importance of raising critically thinking, tolerant, and creative young people. In such countries the foundations provide continued support to primary and secondary education while simultaneously devoting efforts to the strengthening of higher education, especially in terms of the study of law and pedagogy.

Stuart Foundation. Based in San Francisco, California, the Stuart Foundation's overarching purpose is to help the children and youth of California and Washington states become responsible citizens. The foundation's approach is to help strengthen the public systems and community supports that contribute to children's development. Three grant program areas exist: (1) strengthening the public school system; (2) strengthening the child welfare system; and (3) strengthening communities to support families.

The Stuart Foundation employs a systemic approach to change. The following themes characterize the foundation's approach to strengthening public systems and communities in all three grant-making programs: (1) making public policies more effective by supporting efforts to improve statewide or local policies so that public systems and communities can support the development of children and youth more effectively; (2) policy analysis and policy development by supporting projects that examine the effectiveness of policies for children and youth; that improve the quality of information available to policymakers, stakeholders, and the public; and that provide a nonpartisan forum for discussion and dialogue to build understanding and consensus for improvements; (3) standards or accountability through support to the development of standards and systems for measuring results that promote greater accountability and program improvements, and that can gain the support of policymakers, practitioners, communities, and business leaders; and (4) making connections and building understanding to solve social problems by uniting people and organizations with different perspectives (e.g., educators, parents, policymakers, business people, and service providers) to build a shared understanding and reach agreement on what needs to be done.

The foundation seeks to foster stronger connections among policymakers, practitioners, and researchers to foster information exchange, fresh thinking, and creative solutions. It promotes collaboration across agencies and disciplines in which closely related programs integrate their work to achieve greater benefits for children and youth. It strives to build public understanding of key issues in education, child welfare, and community well-being, and to secure a more supportive environment for effective policies and practices. It seeks to improve practice through the development and dissemination of more effective practices, through the promotion and dissemination of successful innovations, and through effective methods to promote widespread improvements in practice.

Spencer Foundation. Located in Chicago, Illinois, the Spencer Foundation was established by Lyle M. Spencer, founder of the educational publishing firm Science Research Associates. The foundation investigates "ways in which education, broadly conceived, can be improved around the world." A basic research foundation with both international and domestic interests, the foundation supports high quality investigation of education through its research programs by promoting scholarship through various grant programs for research, postdoctoral fellowships, predissertation research, conferences, and training. Such grants are open to people from an array of backgrounds—researchers, practitioners, and young professionals.

The foundation's programs are organized within three divisions: Research, Fellowships, and Training. In addition, a handful of programs are also operated out of the office of the vice president. Programs in the research division support work that shows promise of contributing new knowledge, understanding, and improvement of educational thought and practice. Programs in the fellowship division support educational researchers at different stages of their professional careers, providing resources to both beginning and senior researchers to pursue concentrated intellectual activity. Programs in the training division are aimed at improving the work and performance of agencies and institutions, mainly universities and graduate schools of education at universities, which hold a mission of training and apprenticing educational researchers. Funding programs within the vice president's office are experimental or developmental, spanning and augmenting the other divisions' programmatic objectives. The majority of the programs administered within the training division and the office of the vice president are invitational.

See also: INTERNATIONAL DEVELOPMENT AGENCIES AND EDUCATION.

BIBLIOGRAPHY

ARNOVE, ROBERT F. 1977. "The Ford Foundation and 'Competence Building' Overseas: Assumptions, Approaches, and Outcomes." *Studies in Comparative International Development* 12(fall):100–126.

ARNOVE, ROBERT F., ed. 1980. *Philanthropy and Cultural Imperialism: The Foundations at Home and Abroad.* Boston: G. K. Hall.

ARNOVE, ROBERT F. 1981. "Foundations and the Transfer of Knowledge: Implications for India." *Social Action, New Delhi, India* (April).

ARNOVE, ROBERT F. 1982. "The Ford Foundation and the Transfer of Knowledge: Convergence and Divergence in the World System." *Compare* 13:724.

CLOTFELTER, CHARLES T., and EHRLICK, THOMAS, eds. 1999. *Philanthropy and the Nonprofit Sector in a Changing America.* Bloomington: Indiana University Press.

COLEMAN, JAMES S., and DAVID COURT. 1993. *University Development in the Third World: The Rockefeller Foundation Experience.* New York: Pergamon.

PURYEAR, JEFFREY. 1994. *Thinking Politics: Intellectuals and Democracy in Chile, 1973–1988.* Baltimore: Johns Hopkins University Press.

INTERNET RESOURCES

BILL AND MELINDA GATES FOUNDATION. 2002. <www.gatesfoundation.org>.

BROAD FOUNDATION. 2002. <www.broadfoundation.org>.

CARE. 2002. <www.care.org/>.

CARNEGIE FOUNDATION FOR THE ADVANCEMENT OF TEACHING. 2002. <www.carnegiefoundation.org>.

EDUCATION INTERNATIONAL. 2002. <www.ei-ie.org>.

EDUCATION TRUST. 2002. <www.edtrust.org>.

OXFAM INTERNATIONAL. 2002. <www.oxfam.org>.

PEW CHARITABLE TRUSTS. 2002. <www.pewtrusts.com>.

ROCKEFELLER FOUNDATION. 2002. <www.rockfound.org>.

SAVE THE CHILDREN. 2002. "Education." <www.savethechildren.org/education.shtml>.

SMITH RICHARDSON FOUNDATION. 2002. <www.srf.org/>.

SOROS FOUNDATION. 2002. <www.soros.org/>.

SPENCER FOUNDATION. 2002. <www.spencer.org/>.

STUART FOUNDATION. 2002. <www.stuartfoundation.org/funding.html>.

WORLD VISION. 2002. <www.wvi.org/>.

KATHERINE TAYLOR HAYNES

NONGRADED SCHOOLS

This entry will seek to identify and clarify the opposite of graded schools, for which the term *nongraded schools* is used. Although there are secondary schools that also seek to develop nongraded structures, the primary beneficiaries of the arrangement are children at the elementary school level.

Brief Definition

Briefly, nongradedness is defined in terms of respect for, and optimism about, individual differences. It calls for the provision of a pleasurable, challenging, and rewarding learning atmosphere where there are maximum opportunities for productive interaction between the learners. Within a nongraded setting the curriculum is both integrated and flexible. Similarly the timetable for the academic progress of each unique child is flexible. The learning of facts, although important, is recognized as subordinate to the mastery of concepts and methods of inquiry. The assessment of students is holistic and individualized, and evaluation is continuous, comprehensive, and diagnostic. The entire program within the nongraded setting, especially if there is a team of teachers involved, is more under the control of the teacher(s) than is the case in grade-structured situations. Research and experience generally support the conclusion that pupils in nongraded settings work harder, albeit more comfortably, and achieve more and better results than graded students do. There is also rather strong research evidence that children in nongraded settings enjoy better physical and emotional health.

Development of Graded Education

Graded education was introduced and developed during the years 1848 to 1870, beginning with the Quincy Grammar School in Boston. The Quincy school came into being largely to provide a manageable school organization at a time when schooling in expanding cities became a much larger enterprise than had existed in the familiar one-room school serving pupils of multiple ages. It also grew out of assumptions that undergirded and made possible efforts toward universal education. Because little was known or believed in those years about stages of human development and the unevenness of readiness within age groups, the assumption was made that students may logically be grouped together by age, or actually within a twelve-month span, and

taught a specific and common body of skills and subject matter.

Well into the twentieth century, the patterns of fairly rigid gradedness, with attendant nonpromotion/promotion practices, launched at the Quincy school became, in effect, universal. All the same, at that point in social history the system was in fact a significant and creative advance, appropriate to the assumptions and perceptions involved. The teachers were usually quite uneducated and insufficiently trained, and therefore there evolved the system of requiring them to master only a one-year segment of the educational program. In this way, a form of primitive specialization occurred. There was also a pattern of very strict supervision by the employers.

Search for Other Models

Before long, the disadvantages of the graded system's rigidity had become apparent, and by the end of the nineteenth century there were various efforts to create different schooling models and achieve greater flexibility. These efforts continued well into the twentieth century, handicapped to some extent by the publishing industry's success in producing age-graded textbook series that made it easier for teachers to manage their work. In the same period, so-called normal schools and later, colleges, produced teachers whose preparation assumed that each would work alone in a self-contained classroom and, except for those in smaller multigraded schools, with materials deemed suitable for one age-group of children.

Along with the search for more appropriate, flexible, and child-oriented arrangements to replace the entrenched gradedness, several influential and helpful developments occurred. Progressive education was very likely the most dramatic example. Also influential were some well-known examples of nongradedness in Europe, which in the 1920s caused many venturesome American teachers, especially from cities in Wisconsin and New York, to visit pilot programs that were located in Jena, Germany, and in several cities in Holland. Some of these programs continue to flourish in the early twenty-first century.

Over the years the label "nongraded" proved to be slightly confusing and insufficiently informative, and scholars and administrators found that labels such as "continuous progress" were more descriptive. Beginning with milestone research and related articles by Walter Rehwoldt and Warren W. Hamilton in 1956 and 1957, the discussion of nongradedness increasingly involved reference to interage or intergrade grouping, for which the term *multiage* was soon frequently substituted. Also in the 1950s, the nation's first experience with formally organized team teaching, and with a related notion, the use of teacher aides/helpers, redefined the organizational framework within which, it was increasingly argued with the support of research evidence, a demonstrably preferable setting could be provided not only for the pupils but also for the collaborating adults who worked with them.

Some elementary schools chose to organize classes in a pattern similar to departmentalization, with each teacher responsible for one content area, such as math or social studies; but it was not until 1957 when there was a sudden burst of interest, nurtured by seventeen universities being funded by Ford Foundation grants to support teacher-teaming and related arrangements, that the virtues of self-containment came to be seriously questioned. Some of the funded model projects, which soon sparked nationwide interest, called for aggregating multiage pupil groups (e.g., children six to seven and eight years of age) to be taught by teams of four to eight collaborating teachers. This development led to a kind of architectural revolution, because standard-size classrooms could no longer accommodate various-sized pupil aggregations. It is of interest to note that, as of the beginning of the twenty-first century, it seems probable that a great many elementary schools continue to provide at least some space flexibility to accommodate teaming arrangements.

Research Findings

The 1993 book *Nongradedness: Helping It to Happen* presents what is probably the most comprehensive analysis/summary of research about nongradedness. It provides a conservative yet positive story about the "substantial and generally favorable body of research on nongradedness." Not surprisingly, several of the studies show that benefits increase over time: that is, the longer that pupils are in such programs, the greater the improvement in achievement scores. Another conclusion of interest is that boys, African Americans, underachievers, and lower-socioeconomic pupils perform better and feel more positive toward themselves and their schools in a nongraded environment. Mental health and school attitudes also benefit.

In summary, then, both logical analysis and examination of the sparse but convincing research now available support the organizational arrangement that calls for (1) multiage pupil grouping to permit numerous learning opportunities, (2) teacher teaming to enable both specialization of functions and continuous professional partnerships and exchanges, (3) flexible architecture to permit a great variety of instructional groupings, and (4) the absence of grade-related nomenclature and the psychological pressure it presents. It is to be noted and appreciated that the classroom procedures and the flexible structure of a multiple-year curriculum enhance the atmosphere and, as research indicates, stimulate both good learning and what can accurately be described as the mental health of all participants.

See also: CURRICULUM, SCHOOL; ELEMENTARY EDUCATION, *subentry on* HISTORY OF; SCHOOL REFORM; SOCIAL ORGANIZATION OF SCHOOLS.

BIBLIOGRAPHY

ANDERSON, ROBERT H. 2000. "Rediscovering Lost Chords." *Phi Delta Kappan* 81:402–404.

ANDERSON, ROBERT H., and PAVAN, BARBARA NELSON. 1993. *Nongradedness: Helping It to Happen.* Lancaster, PA: Technomic.

GOODLAD, JOHN I., and ANDERSON, ROBERT H. 1987. *The Nongraded Elementary School,* revised edition. New York: Teachers College Press.

HEATHERS, GLEN. 1967. "Influencing Change at the Elementary Level." In *Perspectives on Educational Change,* ed. Richard I. Miller. New York: Appleton.

MCLOUGHLIN, WILLIAM F. 1967. *The Nongraded School: A Critical Assessment.* Albany, NY: University of the State of New York, State Education Department.

REHWOLDT, WALTER, and HAMILTON, WARREN W. 1956. "An Analysis of Some of the Effects of Interage and Intergrade Grouping in an Elementary School." Ph.D. diss., University of Southern California.

REHWOLDT, WALTER, and HAMILTON, WARREN W. 1957. "By Their Differences They Learn." *National Elementary Principal* 37(December):27–29.

ROBERT H. ANDERSON

NONTRADITIONAL STUDENTS IN HIGHER EDUCATION

The term *traditional students* describes the characteristics of most students attending colleges and universities before 1970. These included: age between the late teens and early twenties; immediate entry to higher education following high school; full-time attendance and completion of a four year degree in four to five years; residence at the college or in its vicinity; and primary financial dependence on family sources. Traditional students also generally were neither married nor responsible for other family members.

In North America, beginning about 1970, higher education institutions began to see an influx of significantly different students, to whom the term *nontraditional students* was applied. The most prominent differences were that these students were older and had interrupted formal education either before or after finishing secondary school. Postsecondary schools in other developed countries, for instance Organisation for Economic Co-operation and Development (OECD) members, also experienced increases in older students. In the early twenty-first century, some believe nontraditional students have become the new majority, and traditional students the exception.

Direct comparisons of nontraditional students across countries are difficult because of varying frameworks of data collection. Examples can be seen from the United States, United Kingdom, and selected OECD countries such as Canada, Germany, and Japan. Initially, the simple age criterion of twenty-five years of age or older was used to define nontraditional students. According to the National Center for Education Statistics (NCES), by the mid-1990s the proportion of these students in institutions of higher education had grown to more than 40 percent. A later mid-1990s NCES study of beginning undergraduates broadened the factors to seven characteristics, including later than usual initial enrollment, financial independence, full-time employment, part-time attendance, responsibility for dependents other than a spouse, being a single parent, and high school equivalency by means other than a diploma. It also classified nontraditionals as minimally (one factor), moderately (two or three factors), or highly (four or more factors) nontraditional. The study described nearly three-quarters of beginning undergraduates as at least minimally non-

traditonal. A Canadian-American association concerned with nontraditionals even proposed a new classification, *New Trads,* to include younger students attending part-time but lacking extensive adult life experience.

Elsewhere, other factors applied. A 1997 United Kingdom study described nontraditional students as having later age on entry, but also included ethnic, disability, and socioeconomic level factors. Germany explicitly counted senior students and part-timers, but its university system is difficult for part-time students to access. Ireland and Japan increased access for nontraditional students only in the 1990s, so their rates of increase are smaller than other countries. Clearly, nontraditional students are somewhat older and have alternative qualifications for admission than do traditional students, and, depending on country, perhaps other adult-like or situational factors.

Types of Nontraditional Students in the United States

In 1997, using only the age criterion of twenty-five or older, nontraditional enrollments numbered 6,149,000, or nearly 43 percent of all students in higher education. Such a broad group probably includes some representation of all aspects of the total population, but in important considerations, such as gender, ethnicity, socioeconomic status, and regionalism, nontraditional learners do not mirror American society precisely. Some salient characteristics of the group have implications for how providers plan, design, and conduct programs for nontraditional learners, and the supporting services they should provide.

Even including younger people with adult characteristics of autonomy and financial independence, nontraditional learners generally are older than traditional students at the same level. This accounts for why so much of the discussion of nontraditional learners takes place in the context of adult learning, although counselors should be sensitive to the varying circumstances of younger students. Adults are likely to have maturity and experience that can benefit their study, but they may also have formed fixed convictions that restrict their openness. Nontraditional learners often lead complex lives with many responsibilities that compete with their educational goals. They tend to be employed full-time or for extensive part-time periods. Similarly, many are married with demanding family responsibilities and community involvements. Demands on their time often limit them to part-time enrollment and longer times to complete degree and certificate sequences.

Adult women have entered at a higher rate than men, and are helping to outnumber the greater proportion of male enrollment that prevailed before 1970. Women are more likely than men to be responsible for younger or older dependents and a larger portion of them attend part-time.

Other situational factors affect participation. Nontraditional learners are more likely to reside in urban or suburban areas, rather than rural areas. This may be related to the proximity of educational institutions and could be relieved by the growth of distance learning systems. Proportionally, more nontraditional students come from the western or Rocky Mountain states than the rest of the United States, and fewer come from the New England and the mid-Atlantic states. In addition, the ethnicity of nontraditional students does not parallel that of the national population. Asian and non-Hispanic white students enroll at a higher rate than their proportion of the general population, while African Americans and Hispanics participate at a lower rate. In their thirties, however, the proportion of African Americans enrolled in higher education is higher than that of the general population, which suggests that gap may be closing for them. The same is not true of Hispanics, whose numbers may be affected by the immigration of less educated persons. Immigrants make up an increasing number of nontraditional participants in higher education, with needs ranging from English as a second language to revalidation of high-level professional qualifications for certification or licensure in the United States.

Surveys over several decades confirm that the primary motivation for nontraditional enrollment has been career improvement. For younger participants, obtaining credentials necessary to enter desired employment has been critical. People between thirty-five and fifty years of age often seek to improve their career prospects with expanded qualifications. This marks an important shift in motivation toward growing one's capabilities to keep up with changing knowledge demands or to assume greater responsibility. People in their later years, on the other hand, are more likely to pursue personal enrichment goals, and even to seek degree credentials for their own sake. A great many nontraditional learners come to higher education with credit earned in earlier enrollments and are eligible for assessment of informal learning for credit. Nontraditional learners are likely to take longer to complete their degrees than traditional students and to have higher attrition in their first year. Those who continue to the second year have persistence rates closer to traditional students.

Support for Nontraditional Learners

The greater maturity of most nontraditional learners, and the complexity of their daily lives, means that they have different expectations for their learning experiences and different needs for services responsive to their circumstances. Many institutions have made adjustments to assist nontraditional learners, and that practical experience can be an invaluable resource to others who wish to follow their example.

Innovations have involved three major shifts in perspective. These changes have their roots in an emphasis on fulfilling human potential and realizing individual autonomy. Leading exponents have been Malcolm Knowles, Jerold Apps, and Stephen Brookfield.

First, there has been an effort to remove barriers, both situational and dispositional, to nontraditional learner participation. The most daunting of these has been a rigidity in attendance requirements that are incompatible with the other responsibilities of these students. New time and place options have brought much greater choice and flexibility. The growth of asynchronous distance-learning offerings through electronic technology could eliminate this barrier entirely. More flexible access to other important services has become more common as well. Clearer information on institutions and the specific programs needed for career or other learning goals is available. Access and guidance to financial aid has improved. Programs for nontraditional learners provide reentry or orientation workshops to reacquaint applicants with college level study or to reduce anxiety about reentry after an interruption. Some of these are linked to resources to refresh college study skills.

The second major change has been to reorient the learning transaction to focus on learners. Instructors assume roles as facilitators or mentors to work with learners to design individualized curricula. Often working in groups, they establish a climate of mutual respect, trust, and feedback. These groups take account of the contribution that previous experience can offer, but try to foster a spirit of critical reflection and openness to new ideas and information. According to Brookfield, "the aim of facilitation is the nurturing of self-directed, empowered adults" (p. 11).

Finally, nontraditional institutions increasingly provide continuing academic and personal support to sometimes-vulnerable nontraditional learners. On the academic side, there is greater recognition of the value of ongoing counseling and developmental monitoring, in addition to close attention at entry. The support can include preparation for leaving the program, such as career counseling and exit seminars to deal with the anxiety of a new transition.

Learners also may need a variety of nonacademic services throughout the program. These include food or refreshment services and lounge spaces at late afternoon or evening times, convenient parking and campus security, child care for young children, and perhaps personal counseling to assist with stress or unanticipated emergencies.

The recognition of, and the adaptation to, nontraditional learners since the 1970s has been impressive. Any institution that pretends to serve society must take responsibility for nontraditional learners in the knowledge age. The National Association of State Universities and Land-Grant Colleges (NASULGC) recognized this in their 1999 report *Returning to Our Roots: A Learning Society*. Yet there is much more many higher education institutions can do to serve nontraditional learners with full commitment.

See also: COMMUTER STUDENTS; ENROLLMENT MANAGEMENT IN HIGHER EDUCATION; LIFE EXPERIENCE FOR COLLEGE CREDIT.

BIBLIOGRAPHY

APPS, JEROLD W. 1981. *The Adult Learner on Campus: A Guide for Instructors and Administrators.* Chicago: Follett.

BROOKFIELD, STEPHEN D. 1986. *Understanding and Facilitating Adult Learning.* San Francisco: Jossey-Bass.

KELLOGG COMMISSION ON THE FUTURE OF STATE AND LAND-GRANT UNIVERSITIES. 1999. *Returning to Our Roots: A Learning Society.* Washington, DC: National Association of State Universities and Land-Grant Colleges.

KNOWLES, MALCOLM S. 1980. *The Modern Practice of Adult Education: From Pedagogy to Andragogy,* revised edition. Chicago: Follett.

KNOWLES, MALCOLM S., et al. 1985. *Andragogy in Action: Applying Modern Principles of Adult Learning.* San Francisco: Jossey-Bass.

MAEHL, WILLIAM H. 2000. *Lifelong Learning at its Best: Innovative Practices in Adult Credit Programs.* San Francisco: Jossey-Bass.

NATIONAL CENTER FOR EDUCATION STATISTICS. 1997. *Nontraditonal Undergraduates: Trends in Enrollment from 1986 to 1992 and Persistence and Attainment among 1989–90 Beginning Postsecondary Students.* Statistical Analysis Report NCES 97-578. Washington, DC: U.S. Department of Education.

NATIONAL CENTER FOR EDUCATION STATISTICS. 2000. *Digest of Education Statistics, 1999.* NCES Report 2000-031. Washington, DC: U.S. Department of Education.

SCHLOSSBERG, NANCY K.; LYNCH, ANN Q.; and CHICKERING, ARTHUR W. 1989. *Improving Higher Education Environments for Adults: Responsive Programs and Services from Entry to Departure.* San Francisco: Jossey-Bass.

SCHUETZE, HANS G., and SLOWEY, MARIA, eds. 2000. *Higher Education and Lifelong Learners: International Perspectives on Change.* London: Routledge/Falmer.

INTERNET RESOURCES

DEGABRIELE, GABE. 2001. "Keynote Speech, ANTSHE Conference, June 3–6, 2001." <www.antshe.org/keynote.htm>.

HIGHER EDUCATION FUNDING COUNCIL FOR ENGLAND. 1997. "The Participation of Nontraditional Students in Higher Education." <www.hefce.ac.uk/Pubs/HEFCE/1997/M8_97.htm>.

POSTSECONDARY EDUCATION OPPORTUNITY. 2001. "College Enrollment by Age, 1950 to 2000." <www.postsecondary.org>.

WILLIAM H. MAEHL

NORTH AFRICA

See: MIDDLE EAST AND NORTH AFRICA.

NTL INSTITUTE FOR APPLIED BEHAVIORAL SCIENCE

The NTL Institute for Applied Behavioral Science originated in the 1940s as an experiment in group relations called the National Training Laboratory. Directed toward the adult learner, NTL, which is a not-for-profit membership corporation, designs and delivers programs to reeducate adults to help them become better leaders at the group and systems level and to become sensitive to interpersonal dynamics.

NTL's original mission was to train and develop *change agents,* as they came to be called. NTL's T-Group methodology, along with other innovations—such as experiential learning ("learning by doing"), sensitivity training, and the feedback method—have influenced social institutions, industry, and organizations of every variety worldwide. The NTL Institute also developed methods and programs to link teacher training and classroom teaching.

Four scholars are directly associated with NTL's beginnings. Kurt Lewin, considered by many as the father of NTL, began a project in 1946 in which forty-one community leaders examined interracial and intergroup conflict in their home settings—and learned skills to deal with those conflicts. This workshop led to the discovery of the T-Group and eventually to the founding of NTL; however, Lewin died before the first workshop was held in Bethel, Maine, in 1947. Other founders were educational psychologist Leland P. Bradford, who was director of the Division of Adult Service of the NEA before cofounding NTL; Kenneth Benne, who had an interest in teaching techniques as a faculty member in the College of Education at the University of Iowa; and Ronald Lippitt, who is recognized for his early work in group leadership and analyzing group processes and who became a research assistant to Kurt Lewin at Iowa.

Lewin's research and work played a key role in NTL's *reeducation of the adult learner,* a process where people alter, replace, or transcend their usual patterns of thinking. It is a process more complex than learning anew. Lewin's field theory, "human behavior is the function of both the person and the environment, expressed in symbolic terms, $B=f(P, E)$" led to development of actual field research on human behavior and was incorporated into all NTL training.

NTL developed and perfected the Work Conference model during the 1940s and 1950s. This model continues to influence conference and meeting design. NTL helped transform the field of applied behavioral science and made seminal contributions to the field of organizational development, including *The Journal of Applied Behavioral Science,* which was founded in 1965 to advance the field of applied behavioral science and to foster NTL's core values.

From NTL's most widely recognized innovation, the T-Group method—the basic method of laboratory learning about self, groups, and interpersonal relations—emerged the concept of sensitivity training, which psychologist Carl Rogers, who revolutionized the course of therapy, regarded as "perhaps the most significant social invention of the century . . . it is one of the most rapidly growing social phenomena in the United States. It has permeated industry and education and is reaching families and professionals in the helping fields and many others." Sensitivity training is a technique that uses intense small-group discussion and interaction to increase individual awareness of self and others.

Besides NTL's wide array of training and education programs in personal and professional development, NTL offers certificate programs in advanced technology for senior organization-development practitioners; change management and diversity leadership; experience-based learning and training; and organization development. In addition, through partnerships with American University and Cleveland State University, NTL provides a graduate program that culminates in a master's degree in organization development or diversity management. NTL works internationally as well, offering programs and training in Asia and other areas.

NTL straddles many contradictions. It began as an organization of academics who wanted to extend their praxis beyond the academy and who were intrigued with the possibility of bridging the divide between social science and social action. Thus, NTL occupied a unique place between the behavioral and social sciences. Through NTL, researchers, scholars, educators, and activists are brought together to solve social problems, to create programs of human change, and to integrate action, education, and research.

NTL has grown since its inception and, like other educational entities, is reexamining its market to discover the provocative possibilities of human interaction across time and space; to answer the questions raised by the dynamics of human interaction in an electronic environment; to continue to meet the challenge of unraveling the possibility of work-life balance; to manage rapid change, rather than react to it; and to continue a focus on managing and valuing diversity and various societal problems, while at the same time strengthening the design and delivery of its training to meet a changing environment.

See also: CONTINUING PROFESSIONAL EDUCATION.

BIBLIOGRAPHY

BRADFORD, LELAND P. 1974. *National Training Laboratories: Its History: 1947–1970.* Bethel, ME: Leland Bradford.

HIRSCH, JERROLD I. 1987. *The History of the National Training Laboratories 1947–1986.* New York: Peter Lang.

IRENE V. JACKSON-BROWN
DIANE M. PORTER

NURSING EDUCATION

To place nursing education into perspective, it is helpful to reflect on the health care environment and the role of the nurse in that environment. The health care landscape in the United States has been changing at an unprecedented rate. Nursing education also has undergone changes to keep pace and to prepare leaders who are highly educated and technically sharp decision-makers and clinicians. What is most noteworthy, however, is not that change has occurred but rather that the rate of change since 1980 has been greater than during similar periods. Factors driving the transformations include new medical and technological advances, new health care delivery systems, and expanded roles for nurses.

Nurses are the largest single group of health care professionals but they do not practice in isolation. Rather they are an integral part of health care teams, institutions, and systems. As health care continues to move outside the hospital, the demand for nurses who can function across systems and direct a continuum of care is rising. The changing health care environment has not only changed the role of the nurse, it has also affected the supply–demand ratio. Hospitalized patients have multiple health problems, are more acutely ill, and are discharged sooner. This has

increased the demand for nurses in acute care institutions at the same time that more nurses are needed in home and community settings. Given trends that emphasize health promotion and disease prevention, the need for acute and chronic care is skyrocketing.

The Federal Division of Nursing predicts that by 2010, the growing demand for nurses with bachelor of science in nursing (B.S.N.) and master of science in nursing (M.S.N.) degrees will outstrip the supply and that by 2020, the demand for B.S.N. and M.S.N. graduates will grow nearly twice as fast as the expected increase in the workforce. The predicted need for nurses is sobering, yet it is important to acknowledge that the impending crisis is not solely numbers based. The question is not only how many nurses will be available, but more importantly, will their educational preparation be appropriate to meet future health care needs. Based on the Federal Nursing Division's data, the answer is to increase the number of bachelor's, master's, and doctorate-level nurses.

Bachelor of Science in Nursing Degree

In 1996 the American Association of Colleges of Nursing affirmed nursing's place in American higher education by stating that the minimum educational requirement for professional nursing is the bachelor of science in nursing (B.S.N.) degree. B.S.N. programs are offered by four-year colleges and universities. Most generic B.S.N. programs are four academic years, although some students who have other responsibilities may choose to extend their programs. The term *generic* refers to a program designed for students studying nursing for the first time. By comparison, some B.S.N. programs have degree completion tracks for registered nurses (RNs) and licensed practical nurses (LPNs) who have completed basic nursing programs in hospitals or community colleges. Some programs also offer tracks for individuals with bachelor's degrees in other majors. B.S.N. programs must be approved by the state board of nursing.

A B.S.N. degree enables graduates to not only launch a successful career in nursing, but also to appreciate a more meaningful life. Therefore, the curriculum includes courses in nursing as well as the arts and sciences. Because the B.S.N. graduate is prepared as a generalist, nursing courses include both theory and clinical experiences and in most specialty areas, such as adult, community, maternal-child, pediatric, psychiatric, and critical care nursing. In some B.S.N. programs, students enroll in nursing courses at the freshman or sophomore level with courses in the major along with arts and sciences integrated throughout the program. In other programs, nursing courses are concentrated at the junior and senior levels. The number of credit hours required for a B.S.N. degree usually ranges from 120 to 130. Upon completing the degree, graduates are eligible to take the National Council Licensing Examination (NCLEX) to become licensed as a registered nurse. By law, nurses must be licensed to practice in the state where they work.

A strong background in science, mathematics, and verbal skills is needed to succeed in nursing. The admission process varies among institutions but typical criteria include: official transcripts with a minimum grade point average (GPA) of 2.0; SAT or ACT Assessment score, and TOEFL (Test of English as a Foreign Language) for foreign students; essay; and letters of recommendation. Some B.S.N. programs admit students directly into the major. Others admit students initially to the institution and require students to apply for admission to the major after completing prerequisite courses including the sciences.

Master of Science in Nursing Degree

Whereas bachelor's degree graduates are generalists, master's degree graduates are specialists. The master of science in nursing (M.S.N.) degree program prepares graduates to be advanced practice nurses (APNs) with in-depth theory and practice in a clinical specialty. Some M.S.N. programs combine both clinical and functional roles (e.g. education, administration, case management). However, the American Association of Colleges of Nursing (1996) concluded that the clinical role should be the primary focus for all master's programs.

Most master's students select one of four tracks or primary roles: clinical nurse specialist (CNS), nurse practitioner (NP), certified registered nurse anesthetist (CRNA), or certified nurse midwife (CNM). The CNS is an APN with expertise in theory and research-based clinical nursing practice. In addition to clinical practice, major roles of the CNS include teaching, research, consulting, and management, all within an area of specialization, such as acute care, adult health, community health, critical care, gerontology, maternal-child, mental health, neonatology, oncology, pediatrics, or women's health. The NP is an APN who is a primary care provider to individuals and families in multiple settings.

Originally developed to function as a physician extender, the NP role has evolved to incorporate a more holistic nursing approach to illness prevention and health promotion. NPs assess, diagnose, treat, prescribe, monitor, and refer patients as appropriate. The CRNA works closely with a physician and administers anesthesia in hospitals and outpatient settings. The CNM manages routine obstetrical cases. APNs have a collaborative agreement with a physician.

Although M.S.N. programs offer a wide choice of clinical specialties, most curricula include core courses such as statistics, research, professional role, concepts and theories, health policy, ethics, and economics. Other required courses include advanced study in physiology and pathology, pharmacology, and health assessment. The number of clinical hours is program specific but ranges between 500 and 750 are common. M.S.N. programs may require a thesis or other culminating project, and a comprehensive examination. The number of credit hours required for the M.S.N. degree typically ranges from 36 to 48. Although the master of science in nursing (M.S.N.) is the degree awarded most frequently, some institutions award a master of nursing (M.N.), a master of science (M.S.), or a master of arts (M.A.) degree. The difference is more a function of institutional organization, not the graduate nursing curriculum.

The admission process is institution specific but typical admission criteria include the following: official transcript verifying a B.S.N. degree from an accredited program with a minimum GPA of 3.0; undergraduate courses or demonstrated competency in health assessment, statistics, and informatics; practice in nursing; Graduate Record Exam (GRE), Miller Analogy Test (MAT), or TOEFL for foreign students; letters of recommendation; résumé; and an essay. The above discussion assumes that a M.S.N. applicant has a B.S.N. degree, but it is possible for nurses with no bachelor's degree or a non-nursing bachelor's degree, and for individuals with no background in nursing to be admitted into some graduate nursing degree programs.

After completing a master's degree or postmaster's certificate, CNSs and NPs may take national certifying examinations such as those offered by the American Nurses Credentialing Center (ANCC) providing their programs included the requisite content and hours in a clinical specialty. This credentialing system further demonstrates nursing's ever-increasing standards and commitment to excellence.

Doctoral Degrees in Nursing

The quality of nursing education has increased further as evidenced by the fact that doctoral degree programs in nursing, and even postdoctoral programs, have become an integral part of American higher education. Prior to 1960 there were no doctoral programs in nursing. During the 1960s nursing was added as a minor to other Ph.D. degree programs. It was not until 1970 that Ph.D. programs in nursing emerged, but the number of programs has increased significantly. At the beginning of the twenty-first century, there are more than seventy-five doctoral programs in nursing leading to a Doctor of Philosophy (Ph.D.) or a Doctor of Science in Nursing (D.N.S., D.S.N., or D.N.Sc.) degree.

Both the Ph.D. and D.N.S. degree programs focus on research and "prepare students to pursue intellectual inquiry and conduct independent research for the purpose of extending knowledge" (American Association of Colleges of Nursing, 2001b, p. 2). Stated differently, doctoral programs in nursing enhance the scientific foundation for nursing theory and practice. A research-focused doctoral degree prepares graduates for a variety of positions within higher education, health care, government, and the private sector, such as educator, researcher, administrator, and advanced practice. Career options for nurses prepared at the doctoral level are virtually limitless.

Directed toward preparing graduates for a wide range of scholarly pursuits, most doctoral programs require courses in history, philosophy, and theory of nursing; informatics; research; and in related issues from health care ethics to economics. However, curricula do vary depending upon philosophy, faculty expertise, and other resources. Other requirements include a dissertation, oral defense, and comprehensive examination. The number of credit hours required for the doctoral degree is institution specific.

Criteria for admission to a doctoral program are similar to those for a master's program. Typical criteria include an official transcript verifying a M.S.N. degree with a minimum GPA of 3.0; a strong foundation in statistics; GRE score; practice in nursing; curriculum vitae; letters of recommendation; essay; and interview by a faculty committee.

Higher education is a lifelong investment. Undergraduate and graduate students should investigate several programs to determine which one correlates best with their academic and clinical interests and career goals. Students also should carefully assess multiple institution and program characteristics, especially accreditation status. Colleges and universities are accredited by nationally recognized, regional accrediting associations. Undergraduate and graduate nursing programs may apply for specialty accreditation by the Commission on Collegiate Nursing Education (CCNE) or the National League for Nursing Accrediting Commission (NLNAC). Although accreditation is voluntary, it demonstrates an institution's and program's commitment to continuous improvement and quality education.

See also: MEDICAL EDUCATION.

BIBLIOGRAPHY

AMERICAN ASSOCIATION OF COLLEGES OF NURSING. 1993. *Position Statement on Nursing Education's Agenda for the Twenty-First Century.* Washington, DC: American Association of Colleges of Nursing.

AMERICAN ASSOCIATION OF COLLEGES OF NURSING. 1996. *The Essentials of Master's Education for Advanced Practice Nursing.* Washington, DC: American Association of Colleges of Nursing.

AMERICAN ASSOCIATION OF COLLEGES OF NURSING. 1996. *Position Statement on the Baccalaureate Degree in Nursing as Minimal Preparation for Professional Practice.* Washington, DC: American Association of Colleges of Nursing.

AMERICAN ASSOCIATION OF COLLEGES OF NURSING. 1997. *Position Statement on Vision of Baccalaureate and Graduate Nursing Education: The Next Decade.* Washington, DC: American Association of Colleges of Nursing.

AMERICAN ASSOCIATION OF COLLEGES OF NURSING. 1998. *The Essentials of Baccalaureate Education for Professional Nursing Practice.* Washington, DC: American Association of Colleges of Nursing.

AMERICAN ASSOCIATION OF COLLEGES OF NURSING. 2001a. *Envisioning Doctoral Education for the Future.* Washington, DC: American Association of Colleges of Nursing.

AMERICAN ASSOCIATION OF COLLEGES OF NURSING. 2001b. *Position Statement on Indicators of Quality in Research-Focused Doctoral Programs in Nursing.* Washington, DC: American Association of Colleges of Nursing.

ANDERSON, NORMA E. 1981. "The Historical Development of American Nursing Education." *Journal of Nursing Education* 20:18–36.

BEDNASH, GERALDINE, ed. 2001. *Ask a Nurse—From Home Remedies to Hospital Care.* New York: Simon and Schuster Source.

CHASKA, NORMA L., ed. 2001. *The Nursing Profession Tomorrow and Beyond.* Thousand Oaks: Sage.

HAMRIC, ANN B.; SPROSS, JUDITH A.; and HANSON, CHARLENE M., eds. 2000. *Advanced Nursing Practice.* Philadelphia: Saunders.

CAROLE F. CASHION

NUTRITION AND CHILDREN'S PHYSICAL HEALTH

Proper nutrition is crucial for the appropriate growth and development of children. Undernourished children are at risk for illness, cognitive delay, and poor social skills. Overnourished children are at risk for obesity, diabetes, heart disease, and a shortened life span.

Proper nutrition implies adequate caloric intake for optimal growth and development. At birth, a child's metabolic rate per unit weight is at its peak. This period is coincidental with the highest rate of brain growth and development. Therefore, it is imperative that newborns be adequately nourished. Human breast milk is the ideal food for newborns, and remains the gold standard by which all formulas are measured. Breast-fed infants are healthier, have better cognitive development, and are provided with a more secure mother–infant bond. Research has shown that breast-fed infants are less prone to infection and food allergies, and have IQ scores three to five points higher than their non-breast-fed counterparts. The American Academy of Pediatrics recommends breast-feeding for the first twelve months of life. Solid foods should be introduced around age six months, and supplemented with breast milk. It is recognized, however, that most of the immunologic and cognitive benefits of breast-feeding decrease after the first six months. Thus, the first six months of life provide the greatest return on breast-feeding.

In the newborn period, babies require approximately 100 kilocalories per kilogram of body mass each day. This requirement decreases approximately 10 kilocalories per kilogram every three years, until reaching adult needs of approximately 40 kilocalories per kilogram of lean body mass. It is important to ensure that in addition to adequate energy intake each child has a well-balanced diet to provide appropriate vitamins and minerals as well. The U.S. Department of Agriculture has provided a "food pyramid" as a guide to healthy eating for adults and older children. It suggests that a daily regimen consist of six to eleven servings of bread, rice, cereal, or pasta; two to four servings of fruit; three to five servings of vegetables; two to three servings of dairy products; two to three servings of meat, beans, eggs, or nuts. Sweets and fats are to be consumed sparingly.

Research in the decade 1989–1998 has shown that undernutrition, even in a mild form, can have detrimental effects during childhood, and the younger the child, the more at risk he or she is for undernutrition. It is clear that the greater degree of malnutrition, the worse the outcomes. Inadequate nutrition ranges from the starvation states seen during famines, to the more familiar mild undernutrition common among children of poor socioeconomic standing. The body, when in a starvation state, preserves vital functions first. Thus, energy is shunted to basic metabolic tasks, leaving little energy for cognitive development and social activity. Two distinct types of starvation are recognized: marasmus, or general caloric insufficiency, and kwashiorkor, or protein deficiency. Marasmus results from inadequate caloric intake. Physically, children with marasmus have a wasted appearance throughout the body. Generally, in the face of inadequate calories, weight is first lost, then vertical growth becomes stunted, and the last growth parameter affected is the head circumference. Although correction of this condition with adequate calories can be achieved, cognitive abilities and height may remain stunted. Kwashiorkor results from inadequate protein intake. The appearance of kwashiorkor is a skinny child with a protuberant belly. This appearance is due to the fatty infiltrate of the liver and water retention of the surrounding tissues. The treatment of this condition is to provide adequate protein. As with marasmus, the damage done while in this state is often not reversible.

Mild to moderate undernutrition is a threat to a child's achieving his or her potential cognitive abilities. Undernourished children are typically easily distracted and fatigued. A 1998 study demonstrated that children who skip breakfast perform worse on tasks of memory and concentration than when they eat breakfast. Other studies have suggested that children with inadequate amounts of protein in the diet had lower achievement scores than their counterparts with adequate protein intake.

Iron deficiency is the most common nutritional deficiency in the United States. Anemia, or decreased red blood cell mass, results from a lack of adequate iron in the body. This lack of iron causes an irreversible decrease in IQ. One of the most common reasons for anemia in toddlers is a crowding out of iron-rich foods by excessive milk intake. In older children, iron deficiency likely results from dietary inadequacies as well as from menstruation in females. Lower socioeconomic classes are at particular risk for iron deficiency.

During the 1990s overnutrition became a concern in industrialized nations. In the United States obesity is the most common preventable health problem affecting both children and adults. Fourteen percent of children and adolescents in the United States were obese in 1999. This represents an increase of 50 percent from the previous decade. Obesity is usually a result of chronic mild overeating, as opposed to repeated binge eating. Consuming five hundred kilocalories more than needed each day will result in a weight gain of approximately one pound per week. Obesity has not only negative psychological effects on the individual, but also negative health effects. People who are obese have shorter life spans, higher than average blood pressure, higher cholesterol levels, increased incidence of diabetes, and more difficulties with the hip and knee joints. Obesity is most effectively treated when interventions are at an early age. Only 25 percent of children who are obese at age six years will go on to be obese adults.

However, 75 percent of obese teenagers will go on to be obese adults. Treatment includes increased exercise, decreased food intake, and family counseling about good food choices. As of the year 2002 there are no safe and effective drug therapies for obese children. Despite millions of dollars spent every year in the weight loss industry, it still appears that the best way to combat obesity is to prevent it.

See also: HEALTH AND EDUCATION; HEALTH SERVICES, *subentry on* SCHOOL; SCHOOL FOOD PROGRAMS.

BIBLIOGRAPHY

AMERICAN ACADEMY OF PEDIATRICS. 1997. "Breastfeeding and the Use of Human Milk." *Pediatrics* 100:1035–1039.

BEHRMAN, RICHARD E. 1996. *Nelson Textbook of Pediatrics,* 15th edition. Philadelphia: Saunders.

STRAUSS, RICHARD S. 2001. "Epidemic Increase in Childhood Overweight, 1986–1998." *Journal of the American Medical Association* 286:2845–2848.

INTERNET RESOURCES

EDUCATIONAL RESOURCES INFORMATION CENTER. "Children's Nutrition and Learning." 1994. <http://ericps.crc.uiuc.edu/eece/pubs/digests/1994/nhec194.html>.

TUFTS CENTER ON HUNGER, POVERTY, AND NUTRITION POLICY. 1998. "New Findings about Child Nutrition and Cognitive Development." <http://nutrition.tufts.edu/publications/hunger>.

PAUL D. HAIN

O

OPEN CLASSROOM SCHOOLS

Open education is a philosophy which values the natural development and experience of the child as the primary determinants for the appropriate curriculum and methods. During the 1960s the world witnessed a remarkable amount of social change and the emergence of new philosophies in various aspects of society. Groups seeking reform challenged many institutional practices. Criticism from these groups often reflected their lack of trust in decision-making structures. Educators were prompted to examine issues of control within their traditional philosophy, notions of curricula, and protocols of teaching and learning. Educators began a search for an institutional model of child-centered pedagogy.

In the mid-1960s Americans visited the English infant schools, which promoted self-determination. These elementary schools advocated "informal" or "open" education and the "integrated day." The "integrated day" refers to an interdisciplinary approach in which content from various subjects is woven and presented in a hands-on, problem-solving context. Educators from several continents adapted and applied these concepts in new open space or open plan facilities.

The open classroom school generally had an architectural configuration of large pods containing six to twelve classrooms, each with an outside access and no interior walls. Children were not assigned individual desks; they sat in cooperative small groups at tables. Teachers usually defined their workspace by their arrangements of bookshelves and cabinets. The lack of hallways meant more space was available for instructional use. The outside accesses and lack of walls allowed for greater accessibility. These design changes also resulted in a more efficient use of energy at a time when energy was becoming more costly.

The changes in the internal structure of the pod accommodated changes in the philosophical approach taken by educators. Without traditional rooms, teachers could redefine the nature of their role. The teacher shifted from the dispenser of knowledge to the facilitator of learning. Teachers were no longer isolated from each other. They were better able to confer and plan. Learning became an activity that was child centered rather than teacher-oriented. Standard grade-level skill checklists were set aside and the differences in individual needs provided the rationale for the curricula. Students' progress was not based on rankings, which define success in a competitive context; instead, evaluation of progress was reported in terms of the individual's achievement in relation to growth from previous levels and the individual's initiative and responsibility as demonstrated in academic and related arts areas.

As the role of the teacher changed, methods of instructional delivery were necessarily challenged. Traditional instruction involved discrete subject areas with generalized class expectations for performance. The open space philosophy altered the format of instruction. Classes were replaced with interest centers, which offered topical activities. Center choices promoted the discovery method, a precedent to constructivism. Learners were prompted to explore and develop their own connections in order to promote concept development and the scientific method. Students moved among the centers largely by choice and often without specific schedules.

Class composition was reminiscent of the one-room schoolhouse. Teachers arranged flexible multi-age grouping within the interest centers. Mindful of individual needs, teachers were challenged to maintain fluid group membership. In this manner, they could naturally develop a disposition towards diversity and citizenship. In some open classroom schools, homerooms or "family groups" were not configured by grade level. A class may have contained five students at each level, kindergarten through fourth grade. Each year, five would enter, and five would graduate. The stability of relationships over a number of years allowed a different social dynamic. The homeroom was designed to reflect the cooperative nature of learning. Over time the teacher could develop a richer knowledge of each student and serve as a long-term counselor and mentor.

The construction of open classroom schools declined by the mid-1970s. Concerns about noise and distraction encouraged educators to return to a traditional approach. Although the open classroom movement lost popularity, certain aspects of its philosophy and methods were reshaped and used. Many open-space facilities have been remodeled with the addition of inside walls, or become magnet programs, which have located technology labs and computer stations conveniently in the open spaces. Schools with open space classrooms varied to the degree in which the philosophies were operationalized. This variability limits the degree to which one evaluates the concept's effectiveness. Research has indicated that the open classroom approach may not have significantly improved learning, but it certainly did not impede achievement. Additional research suggested that children in open classroom programs did score higher than traditional classroom students in self-concept, attitudes towards school, and creativity.

See also: ELEMENTARY EDUCATION, *subentry on* HISTORY OF; INFANT SCHOOLS IN ENGLAND; INSTRUCTIONAL DESIGN; NEILL, A. S.; OPEN EDUCATION; PROGRESSIVE EDUCATION.

BIBLIOGRAPHY

BARTH, ROLAND. 1972. *Open Education and the American School.* New York: Agathon.

ROTHENBERG, PHILLIP. 1989. "The Open Classroom Reconsidered." *The Elementary School Journal* 90:69–86.

SILBERMAN, CHARLES E., ed. 1973. *The Open Classroom Reader.* New York: Vintage.

STEVEN R. BAUM

OPEN EDUCATION

Open education refers to a philosophy, a set of practices, and a reform movement in early childhood and elementary education that flourished in the late 1960s and early 1970s in the United States. It received support from similar work that had been developing for many years in England, where it was simply termed *modern* education. Its development in both countries relied upon the long tradition of Progressive education.

Known for its spirited, child-centered classrooms, open education was viewed by proponents as a humane, liberating alternative to the more formal classrooms of its day. To detractors, its informalities represented an abdication by teachers of their duty to instruct, an indulgence that failed to hold students or teachers accountable. Where adherents saw independent, individualized learning, critics saw chaos. At the height of its popularity, the ideas of open education influenced at most 20 percent of infant (ages 5–7) or junior (ages 8–11) schools in England and perhaps half that number of comparable schools in the United States.

The Classroom

The open classroom, at its best, is a busy laboratory, richly provisioned with materials for learning. Alone or in small groups, children move from one work area to another, using balance beams, colored beads, blocks, and other hands-on material in the mathematics corner; working on art projects in paint, clay, or construction scraps; reading quietly or aloud to others from books or from their own illustrated reports. The room itself is arranged into several separate learning centers, a functional organization that invites choice of participation in a variety of activities. The school day is flexibly scheduled, allowing students to determine for themselves when an activity merits more time and when it is completed. Class meetings often start and end each day, providing time to give announcements and news, negotiate assignments, and share projects. The teacher rarely calls the entire class together for group instruction. Classes are composed of mixed ages, a vertical group setting in which children encounter points of view and abilities other than their own. This "family grouping" also encourages cooperative learning and social responsibility, with older students helping younger ones. Within the classroom, the teacher circulates among students, extending their learning by commenting and responding to their work, asking leading questions, and suggesting further directions for them to explore. The curriculum is necessarily flexible, responsive, and organic.

Philosophical Underpinnings

Open education believes in the following tenets:

- Children's fundamental desire and capacity to conduct their own inquiries and to learn in their own way from direct experience
- The right of children to take significant responsibility for their own education
- A "whole child" approach that includes the emotional and social aspects of learning
- A reciprocal relationship between school and community
- School as an environment for personal choice and fulfillment, not as mere training ground for pre-selected social roles
- The curriculum as better learned through direct experience than from textbook formulation
- Teachers functioning as observers, guides, and providers of resources, materials, and experiences suited to the needs and interests of students

A general optimism prevails, both about children's capacity to respond positively to freedom and independence, and about school as a miniature democracy preparing a self-motivated, responsible citizenry.

These ideas are grounded in the Progressive philosophy of American educator John Dewey (1859–1952), and in the developmental psychology of Swiss clinician and theoretician Jean Piaget (1896–1980). Dewey believed that learning results from the real-life experiences of a growing mind; it is the "process of learning to think through the solution of real problems" (Dworkin, p. 20) by means of active inquiry and experience, not by memorization and recitation. The school is a microcosm of society, not to be separated from the child's familiar context of family, community, social norms, daily life—all areas that children need to confront and comprehend. Education is a process of living in the here and now, not a preparation for future life. If each child is brought into "membership within a little community, saturating him with the spirit of service, and providing him with the instruments of effective self-direction, we shall have the deepest and best guarantee of a larger society which is worthy, lovely, and harmonious," Dewey wrote (Dworkin, p. 49). Throughout, he emphasized the value and importance of childhood and the influence of social environment upon individual development. All this reflects a long-standing American faith in the civilizing power of education via the common school.

As a "genetic psychologist," Piaget studied the quality, sequence, and development of mental concepts in children. Through exploration and interaction with things around them, children build structures that explain the world and how it works. New experience and deeper understanding force modification of earlier formulations, as the child's inner framework is reshaped and restructured to accommodate new realities. This process commences in very concrete ways when the child is small; later, at ages seven or eight, the mind begins to develop more structured thought, and in early adolescence moves on to abstract conceptualization. Every child goes through this process: the sequence is invariable, though the speed, style, and quality of growth vary. According to Piaget, children are the architects of their own individual intellectual growth, and this concept provides the link to Dewey and Progressive education: children are born with the natural ability to do their own learning, a capability that in part defines the evolutionary heritage of the human race.

English Beginnings

In England, the formative period of open education was protracted. Before 1900, some teachers had begun to work in less formal ways, often in isolated, one-room village schools, and with little official or administrative support. By 1931 the Consultative Committee on the Primary School proclaimed in the Hadow Report, "The curriculum is to be thought of in terms of activity and experience rather than of knowledge to be acquired and facts to be stored" (p. 1). World War II was also an influential factor, as children and their teachers were taken out of the cities into the countryside where they were left to improvise. But it was with the release of *Children and Their Primary Schools* (the Plowden Report) in 1967 that these "modern methods" received their most authoritative support. "At the heart of the educational process lies the child," began the Central Advisory for Education, "Children need to be themselves . . . . The child is the agent in his own learning" (paragraphs 2.6 and 2.7). Educators such as Sir Alec Clegg in the West Riding of Yorkshire, Edith Moorhouse and John Coe in Oxfordshire, and Stewart Mason in Leicestershire asserted strong personal leadership. In-service teacher centers, Her Majesty's Inspectorate, and key teacher training colleges, especially the Froebel Institute with its demonstration school and influential publications, and Goldsmiths' College at the University of London, provided institutional support.

The American Experience

By the mid-1960s many Americans were considering basic educational change. Motivated by the launching of *Sputnik* by the Soviet Union in 1957 and cold war competition, business leaders called for the revitalization of mathematics and science curricula. Meanwhile, rebellious youths challenged many social institutions for their fairness and "relevance." Schools were portrayed as racist, sexist, and oppressive. Teachers hoped to rekindle their sense of creativity and love of teaching by turning to less formal methods and materials. Parents responded both to the high quality of student work and to their children's obvious enthusiasm for school.

On learning that informal, child-centered classrooms were already established in Britain, Americans flocked to see for themselves. Some, like Joseph Featherstone, wrote about their experiences; others, such as Lillian Weber and Edward Yeomans, set about to educate or reeducate teachers. Soon open education took its place alongside schools without walls, schools within schools, storefront academies, community schools, and other alternative practices. Some new converts understood the underlying philosophy and recognized the enormous demands open education placed on the classroom teacher; others copied carelessly.

Questions, Controversies, and Criticisms

Criticism of open education was of two sorts. Some disagreed with its basic aims, finding the goals of self-actualization, independence, and social responsibility to be seriously misguided. This was a philosophical, ideological opposition that was part of a longstanding debate about the aims of education. Others questioned its effectiveness, especially in public schools. They challenged its appropriateness

for all students; they queried whether its open structure produced discipline problems; they worried that school transfer would be complicated by the absence of a structured curriculum; they wondered whether students would really learn the "basics." They also perceived inefficiency, unclear objectives, and what seemed a lack of accountability.

In England, such questions had begun in the late 1960s; and, by 1971, a collection of "Black Papers" was published by a group of Oxford and Cambridge intellectuals. They were especially critical of Progressive assumptions about children's learning and about the absence of any agreed-upon common body of knowledge that all educated people should possess. Evaluation was the focus of intense debate. To adherents, proof of success was to be found in the children's enjoyment of school and the high quality of their work. To critics, however, neither this raw data, nor the potential of portfolio assessment, nor positive testimonials from school administrators sufficed: they required objective, quantifiable evidence.

In fact, for many reasons, open education defied empirical evaluation, as it favored:

- Collaborative learning, where it is difficult to determine individual achievement
- Student participation in planning and in setting goals
- An evolving curriculum rather than the set scope-and-sequence chart of a more traditional school
- Standardized testing to be used only as a diagnostic tool
- Process over product, long-term goals over short, and affective as well as academic ends.

Because open education included a variety of similar but not identical classrooms, no standard measure of "openness" was ever established. For researchers, it proved impossible to establish clear experimental and control groups, a basic necessity for conventional studies.

Thus on the one hand, there was considerable misunderstanding of open education; on the other, there were some very real methodological problems in evaluating its effectiveness. Both left the movement vulnerable to attack. In the end, several factors account for the failure of open education to thrive:

- Miscalculation of the demands of teaching in this manner

• Failure to understand the centrality of teacher support services in the effort to reform schools

• Institutional inertia.

The movement failed to develop sufficient political strength to override its critics' concerns, and the times simply changed, as the mid-1970s saw a general shift toward more conservative social policies, and, in education, a call for increased structure and formal accountability. Nonetheless, the influence of open education remains in American schools, the lasting legacy of a promising effort at Progressive educational reform.

See also: ALTERNATIVE SCHOOLING; DEWEY, JOHN; ELEMENTARY EDUCATION, *subentry on* HISTORY OF; INDIVIDUALIZED INSTRUCTION; PHILOSOPHY OF EDUCATION; PIAGET, JEAN; PROGRESSIVE EDUCATION; SCHOOL REFORM.

BIBLIOGRAPHY

BARTH, ROLAND S. 1972. *Open Education and the American School.* New York: Agathon.

CENTRAL ADVISORY FOR EDUCATION. 1967. *Children and Their Primary Schools,* Vol. 1. London: Her Majesty's Stationery Office.

CONSULTATIVE COMMITTEE ON THE PRIMARY SCHOOL. 1931. *The Primary School.* London: Her Majesty's Stationery Office.

COX, C. B., and DYSON, A. E., eds. 1971. *Black Papers.* London: Davis-Poynter.

DWORKIN, MARTIN. 1959. *Dewey on Education: Selections.* New York: Teachers College Press.

FEATHERSTONE, JOSEPH. 1967. "The Primary School Revolution in Britain." *The New Republic* August 10, September 2, and September 9.

HAWKINS, DAVID. 1974. *The Informed Vision.* New York: Agathon.

NYQUIST, EWALD B., and HAWES, GENE R., eds. 1972. *Open Education: A Sourcebook for Parents and Teachers.* New York: Bantam.

RATHBONE, CHARLES H., ed. 1971. *Open Education: The Informal Classroom.* New York: Citation.

RATHBONE, CHARLES H. 1972. "Examining the Open Education Classroom." *School Review* 80:521–549.

SILBERMAN, CHARLES E., ed. 1973. *The Open Classroom Reader.* New York: Random House.

SMITH, LYDIA A. H. 1976. *Activity and Experience: Sources of Informal Education in England.* New York: Agathon.

SMITH, LYDIA A. H. 1997. "'Open Education' Revisited: Promise and Problems in American Educational Reform." *Teachers College Record* 99:371–415.

SPODEK, BERNARD, and WALBERG, HERBERT J., eds. 1975. *Studies in Open Education.* New York: Agathon.

WEBER, LILLIAN. 1971. *The English Infant School and Informal Education.* Englewood Cliffs, NJ: Prentice-Hall.

YEOMANS, EDWARD. 1967. *Education for Initiative and Responsibility.* Boston: National Association of Independent Schools.

CHARLES H. RATHBONE

LYDIA A. H. SMITH

OUTCOME BASED EDUCATION

Few educational concepts have sparked as much interest, enthusiasm, misunderstanding, and controversy during the 1990s as Outcome Based Education (OBE). In one form or another, and sometimes against their political wills, educators the world over are increasingly focusing their efforts on what are variously being called outcomes, results, performances, competencies, or standards.

Whether proposed by national governments, as in Scotland, South Africa, or the United Kingdom; by state or provincial policy bodies, as in Australia, Canada, and the United States; or by local jurisdictions and institutions, as is happening on virtually every continent, how these changes are being applied to traditional forms of education vary as much as the terms themselves.

The Dilemma of Defining Outcome Based Education

One can begin to bring some clarity to this melange of meanings and models, however, by looking systematically at the term *outcome based education* itself. At face value, the concept is quite simple and straightforward: Start by developing a clear picture of what learners should ultimately be able to do successfully at the end of a significant educational experience (i.e., the outcome). Then base (i.e., develop) the curriculum, instruction, assessment, and reporting (i.e., education) directly on that clear picture. This is a simple matter of clearly defining what one wants learners to be able to do (the end) before the beginning, teaching them how to accomplish that end, and then assessing and documenting the end they were to achieve in the first place. Notice the fundamental cause-and-effect logic of this model: Education (the means) is based on the outcome (the end), not the other way around.

When are learners successful in such a system? When or whenever they can demonstrate the intended learning outcome. How many chances are they given to succeed? Usually there is more than one and sometimes there are several chances.

Real world examples. If these basic ends/means elements of OBE sound simple and straightforward, they are, and there are many examples from the "real world" to illustrate them. They include skill and technical training of all kinds (that sometimes reaches back hundreds of years to the craft guilds of the Middle Ages in Europe); ski schools; Boy Scouts' merit and honor badges; pilot and transportation licenses of all kinds; first-aid training; almost all military and athletic training; and virtually all licensure programs in the practical arts.

What is the essence of each of these examples? In some cases successful performance is a matter of life and death, but in all cases two factors stand out: (1) A clear criterion of success or standard of performance (the intended end) guides both instructors and learners; and (2) there is variability in the time and number of opportunities (critical means) that learners might take to achieve the standard. Having learners successfully demonstrate the outcome is what counts the most in these models. In OBE language, successful learning or performance (the end) is the constant, and the time required to attain it is flexible.

The education system reversal. But in virtually all formal educational systems across the globe, just the opposite configuration of these two defining conditions prevails. There, time is the constant, and learning or performance is the variable. Consequently, defining exactly what is and is not OBE on the education scene is extremely problematic in formal education because the two factors that most fundamentally define OBE are not only not present, they are actually reversed.

As William Spady described it in both 1994 and 1998, the world's education systems are time based: that is, they are defined by, organized around, focused on, and managed according to the calendar and clock, not outcomes. Virtually everything that happens within them is forced to exist within fixed, predefined blocks of time, no matter how much actually needs to be accomplished by either instructors or learners. When an official time block ends, so does the learner's opportunity to pursue the outcomes and improve performance on them.

From this perspective, introducing outcomes into a time-based system is like trying to force soft, large, round pegs into rigid, small, square holes. To date, the holes have emerged the overwhelming winners. Across the globe time has remained the given and the constant, even though outcomes have increasingly been emphasized as the reason the time blocks exist.

The other set of rigid square means—holes into which outcomes are being forced—is the curriculum, and it too has prevailed as a dominant force in this implementation dynamic. Although some countries and states have adopted frameworks of outcomes that reach across or go beyond existing curriculum areas—frameworks that contain complex kinds of performance abilities, which link to eventual career and life performances—the overwhelming approach to OBE across the globe has been one of developing outcome frameworks for the major subject areas in the existing curriculum. The latter are variously called program outcomes, specific outcomes, learning area outcomes, curricular outcomes, and standards. In this approach, the curriculum's content structures are the givens, and outcomes are derived from them, resulting in a "tail-wags-dog" approach. As a result the system's means are used to determine its ends, even though the term outcome-based implies just the opposite.

Better to call it "CBO"? Given the fundamental discrepancy between what the term OBE implies and how it has been so overwhelmingly applied, it is wise to distinguish between its conceptual meaning and its implementation realities. Those interested in upholding the inherent meaning of the OBE concept and its reform ideals view the broad sweep of imitation implementation practices in a skeptical light, often referring to them as "CBO" rather than OBE. Among other things, CBO stands for curriculum-based outcomes, calendar-based organizations, content-bound objectives, convention-bound orientations, and convenience-based operations.

Objective Based Education as a Reform Ideal

Those who generated the OBE movement in the United States during the 1970s through the 1990s were deeply influenced by the research and concepts of two key individuals: John Carroll (1963) and Benjamin Bloom (1968). Carroll's revolutionary ideas about *aptitude* as rate of learning rather than fixed ability opened the door to an expanded view of learner potential, which Bloom promoted and tested over the next twenty years. The resulting reform initiative was both a philosophy of expanded learning success for all learners and a classroom instructional strategy called *mastery learning*.

Based on the documented successes of a variety of mastery learning initiatives in the 1970s, a coalition of researchers, practitioners, and reformers founded an organization called the Network for Outcome Based Schools (NOBS) in 1980. The NOBS and its members generated major interest in both mastery learning and the expanded notion of OBE throughout North America during the 1980s and early 1990s, hosting many national and regional conferences featuring practitioners who had achieved major improvements in student learning through the systematic application of the network's key operating premises and principles. Several of the most notable of these local successes are documented in Spady's 1994 book.

Objective based education's four power principles. The spirit and intent of the NOBS operational philosophy was to convince educators that they could dramatically improve student learning success and their professional effectiveness by consistently, creatively, and simultaneously applying four key operating principles in their schools and classrooms. These power principles are:

1. clarity of focus on culminating outcomes of significance,
2. expanding opportunity and support for success,
3. high expectations for all to succeed,
4. designing down from ultimate outcomes.

Over time the network's members became convinced that if any form of OBE was to exist, it needed to consistently embody these four principles because without them educators would lose the leverage these principles gave them in expanding what NOBS called the *conditions of success*—the basic ground rules around which learning and learning opportunities are fundamentally structured.

Do all learners have a clear picture of what they are ultimately expected to demonstrate before a learning experience begins? Is every learner given more than one routine chance or block of time in which to reach or exceed the expected standard? Are positive and challenging expectations for learning success applied equally to all learners, with no bell curves or success quotas applied? Has the curriculum been systematically designed back from the end point that learners are expected to reach, so that there is a clear path for getting there? If the answer to any of these four questions is no, then constraining conditions of success are deemed to exist and, as such, the model in question falls short of the substance, integrity, and spirit of the four power principles. For more than a decade, models of OBE were held to this exacting standard.

Outcomes as Competence

By the mid-1980s the leaders of the rapidly growing OBE movement had come to understand that outcomes were culminating demonstrations of learning, which required learners to do things of significance with what they knew and understood. As such outcomes required both complex mental processing and the ability to carry out visible and accessible processes—processes that were specified by the verbs used in defining the outcome (e.g., describe, explain, design, negotiate, organize, produce, disseminate), this demonstration component brought skill, competence, and performance to center stage in outcome-based models and sent implementation efforts down three quite distinctive paths, depending on the designer's conception of a learning demonstration.

The disciplinary path. The disciplinary path focused on student mastery of quite specific skills, often the skills and tasks imbedded in daily lessons and multiweek units of instruction. Usually these were skills inherent in the curriculum content itself. This approach was quite consistent with the original mastery learning model, was subject-focused and disciplinary in nature, and invited minimal change in curriculum structures and instructional delivery patterns. The application of the power principles took on a distinctive "micro" focus, usually within self-contained classrooms.

Because of its focus on specific content and skills, the disciplinary path eventually led to the development of standards in the subject areas and to the standardized testing efforts being employed by education systems worldwide in the late 1990s and early 2000s. Its proponents, however, see in the latter efforts virtually no attempt to systematically address OBE's four power principles and would in no way regard these initiatives as real OBE.

The interdisciplinary path. A second path took a much more interdisciplinary and change-oriented tack, prompted by its proponents' conviction that learning performance could and should take more complex forms than content-focused skills. In the main these were educators who saw what many called higher-order skills as having no exclusive disciplinary home—abilities such as communication, critical thinking, planning, and problem solving. Nor did these abilities fall into age-specific categories. These higher-order competencies, they argued, were fundamentally developmental, increasing in complexity as learners matured, and needed to be taught that way. Consequently they needed to be addressed and fostered in all subject areas and grade levels for all learners.

By connecting the concepts of higher-order, interdisciplinary abilities with outcomes, these reformers intended to take both OBE and educational change to a new level. That level involved an elevated, more complex notion of learning and competence; a developmental approach to curriculum design and instruction; an authentic approach to assessment and reporting; a dramatic expansion of what was meant by instructional time and opportunity; a frontal challenge to traditional tracking, streaming, and promotion systems; and an intensive connection and collaboration among all players within the education system in addressing student learning and success. It forced both thinking and practice out of the traditional square holes, and it gave the four power principles a whole new meaning and expanded scope of application.

Much of this approach is embodied in the cross-disciplinary outcomes of the national system in South Africa, several of the states or provinces in Australia and Canada, as well as numerous local districts in North America. Because of its developmental, interdisciplinary nature, however, it is fundamentally inconsistent with national and state policy emphases on content standards and time-based standardized testing.

The future-focused path. The third path represents an even more dramatic break from the small, square holes of time-based, curriculum-bound traditional educational practice. The future-focused path emerged in the late 1980s as some leaders of the OBE movement took the notion of culminating demonstrations of learning to its logical limit, recognizing that real outcomes matter and occur after students have finished their formal educational experiences. In other words, authentic outcomes are only known after all of the instructional preparation is complete, and for graduates that means they will be played out in the future they face, not simply in the schooling they have had.

This transformational departure from the norm further elevated the notion of competence beyond education itself to the life and role performances in which individuals engage in their career, family, and community lives. Life, not school, is the real measure of an education's significance and impact, argued these future-focused proponents, and the design of outcomes and learning systems must begin precisely there: with the challenges and conditions that the constantly evolving future inevitably offers.

This future-focused approach to OBE both invited and challenged educators to look far beyond the curriculum and system structures in which they were currently immersed, to examine the kinds of performance abilities required of successful adults in this world, and to design and model their efforts on this dynamic and expansive template. Only then could they ensure that the education their students were getting was actually aligned with the realities and challenges they faced in a world of continuous discovery and constant change. In so doing, they would add a third critical dimension to the OBE learning model: content, competence, and context—the actual settings and conditions in which performance abilities are ultimately tested.

Without question this third role-performance conception of competence represents a radical departure from the standards-based models of reform that have taken such a powerful hold of education in the 2000s. It further expands the meaning, applications, and implications of OBE's four power principles, and it openly challenges the very paradigm on which the education systems of the past century are based.

The Future of OBE

The enormous inertia that surrounds and pervades traditional education systems leaves the widespread implementation of authentic Outcome Based Education very much in doubt. Because they are under enormous public pressure to show results, public systems will continue to advocate outcomes, but almost inevitably in a CBO format. Externally imposed accountability reforms will keep things constrained in small, rigid means holes, with educators compelled to find ways to engage and empower a very diverse population of learners within those inflexible constraints.

Consequently, in the early twenty-first century, trends suggest that true OBE may only survive in alternative settings—schools that are given the flexibility to meet the needs of nontraditional learners in ways that transcend the constraints and inflexibilities of traditional education as we have known it. Outcome Based Education is fundamentally about system change, but the forces of system inertia are prevailing in the accountability-driven world of the 2000s.

See also: CURRICULUM, SCHOOL; LEARNING; SCHOOL REFORM.

BIBLIOGRAPHY

BLOCK, JAMES H. 1971. *Mastery Learning: Theory and Practice.* New York: Holt, Rinehart, and Winston.

BLOCK, JAMES H., ed. 1974. *Schools, Society, and Mastery Learning.* New York: Holt, Rinehart, and Winston.

BLOOM, BENJAMIN S. 1968. "Learning for Mastery." *UCLA Evaluation Comment* 1(2):1–12.

BLOOM, BENJAMIN S. 1976. *Human Characteristics and School Learning.* New York: McGraw-Hill.

CARROLL, JOHN B. 1963. "A Model of School Learning." *Teachers College Record* 64:723–733.

SPADY, WILLIAM G. 1994. *Outcome Based Education: Critical Issues and Answers.* Arlington, VA: American Association of School Administrators.

SPADY, WILLIAM G. 1998. *Paradigm Lost: Reclaiming America's Educational Future.* Arlington, VA: American Association of School Administrators.

SPADY, WILLIAM G. 2001. *Beyond Counterfeit Reforms: Forging an Authentic Future for All Learners.* Lanham, MD: Scarecrow Press.

SPADY, WILLIAM G., and KIT J. MARSHALL. 1991. "Beyond Traditional Outcome-Based Education." *Educational Leadership* 49(2):67–72.

WILLIAM G. SPADY

OUTDOOR AND ENVIRONMENTAL EDUCATION

Outdoor education and environmental education are separate but closely related areas of study within the field of education. They share some common content and processes, although they are distinctive in other important ways. Various interpretations have appeared in the literature, but their original purposes have changed very little since their inceptions. This article will define the terms and show their relation to each other and to other related educational movements, describe their objectives and purposes, outline their commonly used instructional methods, briefly trace their historical development in the United States and abroad, discuss their status in American school curricula, and suggest several key issues, controversies, and trends.

Defining Terms

The term *outdoor education* emerged in the early 1940s to describe the instructional use of natural and built areas to meet student learning objectives in a variety of subject-matter disciplines through direct experiences. This type of contextual learning involving the local surroundings has also been referred to as taking field trips, excursions, journeys, or doing field studies. During the late nineteenth century in the United States, some educators realized that taking students out of the classroom to teach appropriate concepts, skills, attitudes, and values could improve education. Some of the early outdoor educators used camp settings during the regular school year to meet academic objectives and to improve students' social development and leisure skills. Because outdoor education activities were usually tied closely to the school curriculum, the field has adapted to early-twenty-first century reforms affecting the broader educational field.

The term *environmental education* arose in the late 1960s in the United States as a result of a national social phenomenon called the environmental movement. The classic definition, developed by William B. Stapp and his graduate students, appeared originally in the 1969 issue of the *Journal of Environmental Education*: "Environmental education is aimed at producing a citizenry that is knowledgeable concerning the biophysical environment and its associated problems, aware of how to help solve these problems, and motivated to work toward their solution" (Hungerford et al., p. 34).

Although public concern for improving and preserving quality environments existed earlier when national parks were set aside, and windblown soil created the dust bowl of the 1930s, resource use or conservation education increased in the 1970s. Some historians point to Rachel Carson's book *Silent Spring,* published in 1962, as one event that helped to spawn the first Earth Day in April 1970. Spurred by federal legislation during the next several decades, environmental education expanded in public and private schools across the nation. Some critics accused educators of simply changing the names of their outdoor science, nature study, or outdoor education programs to environmental education but continuing the same programs as in the past. This practice of changing the names of these closely related fields in order to modernize the program content, methodology, or focus continues today.

Some of the practices in outdoor and environmental education programs do overlap. Although both fields are interdisciplinary, one difference is that outdoor education can be applied to any discipline that can be effectively taught and learned outside. For example, outdoor education could mean teaching the concept of an acre by measuring a playing field (mathematics); or visiting a park to write poetry or draw pictures inspired by the setting (language arts and art); or recording the information found in a cemetery to learn about past events (history); or testing the pH to determine if a nearby stream is acid or alkaline (science); or climbing a hill to calculate student heart rates (physical education). It could also mean visiting zoos, parks, museums, fire stations, factories, water treatment plants, or any other built environment to create more effective learning opportunities. Environmental education can take place outside as well as inside classrooms and take local as well as global perspectives, but the focus is usually on studying an issue such as water, air, and soil pollution; solid waste and toxic disposal; urban sprawl and population; deforestation; endangered plants and animals; or drought and flooding, especially at upper grade levels. The line separating the two fields is blurred when teachers take students outside to study nature awareness and culture's impact on ecosystems. It makes little sense to argue over which label to apply to these kinds of outdoor lessons when their purposes blend.

Objectives and Purposes

The definitions of these fields reveal several similarities and differences. Simply stated, outdoor educa-

tion programs are designed to help make the learning of certain knowledge more effective through firsthand experiences outside the school. According to Lloyd B. Sharp (1895–1963), outdoor education pioneer, a key principle is "that which ought and can best be taught inside the schoolrooms should there be taught, and that which can best be learned through experience dealing directly with native materials and life situations outside the school should there be learned" (Knapp 1996, p. 77). Most environmental education programs are designed to prepare students to investigate environmental problems. The question of whether or not students should try to resolve these problems is controversial. Gregory A. Smith (2001) and others critique this debate in detail. Although both fields advocate the use of broad subject-matter content, environmental education is generally taught within the social studies and/or sciences at the upper grades. At elementary levels activities usually span more of the academic curriculum and also incorporate social and recreational objectives leading to teamwork, cooperative and service learning, citizenship skills, and lifelong outdoor pastimes. Nature awareness activities can be justified at all levels as integral aspects of both fields. One indication that these are distinct fields of study can be found in the organizational structure of the U.S. Department of Education's Educational Resources Information Center (ERIC) system. Across the country there are sixteen information clearinghouses covering the field of education. Outdoor education informational services are offered through the Clearinghouse for Rural Education and Small Schools (CRESS), and environmental education informational services are offered through the Clearinghouse for Science, Mathematics, and Environmental Education (CSMEE). Each clearinghouse is responsible for collecting and disseminating a wide variety of educational resources in their assigned areas, although some overlap does occur. The CRESS center also has assumed the responsibility for collecting information from adventure or experiential education, another similar but distinctive field.

Instructional Methods

Although both outdoor education and environmental education are offered mainly through schools, nature centers, and outdoor residential facilities, the instructional methodologies are selected from the general field of education. Environmental and outdoor educators primarily advocate experiential (hands-on) learning strategies. Although both fields draw from conventional instructional technologies, such as textbooks, periodicals, computers, videos, and overhead transparencies, these educators stress the importance of contextual, direct, and unmediated experiences used in problem-based learning situations. They want their students to use a variety of senses in exploring the content to maximize active learning.

History and Status in the United States and Abroad

Both fields are considered as innovative, educational reforms designed to accomplish specific objectives that are not being met effectively by traditional practices. Although the idea of using direct experiences existed for hundreds of years in Europe (e.g., the Czech theologian and educator Johann Comenius [1592–1670], the French philosopher and author Jean-Jacques Rousseau [1712–1778], and the Swiss educational reformer Johann Pestalozzi [1746–1827]), little was written in the professional literature. Beginning in the early 1900s the American nature study and camping movements gained momentum. Their purposes were to expand the students' cognitive and affective connections with basic processes, such as obtaining food, shelter, recreation, spiritual inspiration, and other life needs. These nature contacts countered the negative effects of increased urbanization and more complex technologies. Attempts were made to make learning conditions more active and less passive, more closely linked with community activities and less abstract, and more focused on practical knowledge for immediate social use rather than only for the future. These and other goals were incorporated into the Progressive education movement, which was introduced in some U.S. schools during the first half of the twentieth century. The American philosopher, psychologist, and educator John Dewey's Laboratory School, operating in Chicago from 1896 to 1904, exemplified this Progressive philosophy. As Progressivism began to wane in the public schools in the 1940s and 1950s, outdoor education gained in importance. American outdoor education reformers looked to Germany, Britain, Australia, South Africa, British Honduras, and Scandinavia for program models. Because many outdoor educators saw the value of immersion-type programs, camp settings were used in the beginning. Lloyd B. Sharp, who earned his doctorate at Columbia University in 1930, was instrumental in establishing leadership programs for many future outdoor educators in 1940. As residential outdoor education programs grew throughout the nation (mainly in Texas, Indiana, Illinois, California, Washington, Michigan, Ohio, Georgia, New York, and New Jersey), the field flourished. During the late 1940s and early 1950s selected colleges and universities established camping and outdoor education courses to prepare teachers. Another key leadership development occurred in Michigan when the W. K. Kellogg Foundation pioneered community school camps in 1940 and supported further experimentation over the next few decades. Julian Smith (1901–1975), a Michigan administrator, was also influential as a pioneer outdoor educator. Additional support for outdoor education was given through state departments of conservation and education, as well as national educational agencies, professional teacher organizations, and other nongovernmental groups.

By the late 1960s conservation education was also contributing to the outdoor experiences and knowledge of many American and Canadian youth through federal, state, and provincial conservation agencies, although it maintained its largely rural focus. In the U.S. the funding of the Elementary and Secondary Education Act in 1965 led to many innovative outdoor-related programs. The stage was now set for the emergence of environmental education. The U.S. Department of Health Education and Welfare established an office of environmental education in 1968. In 1971 the National Association for Environmental Education (later the North American Association for Environmental Education) was formed to serve as one of the leading professional organizations. From then on, environmental education received federal, state, and local support to promote education about the many complex interrelations between culture and ecosystems. Because of the politics of environmental decision making, the field has faced numerous controversies. Some debates have centered on questions such as: What is the correct definition and purpose of environmental education? Should the curriculum include environmental values and ethics as well as ecological and economic concepts and skills? What is the role of student action projects in remedying environmental problems? What is the proper role for teachers in conducting lessons about the environment? At what ages should students be introduced to environmental problems? What types of educational experiences should urban, suburban, and rural youth receive?

What kinds of technologies can slow ecological destruction?

Issues and Trends

Some of the issues facing outdoor and environmental educators have already been suggested. Because of the politics inherent in many educational and environmental decisions, the field of outdoor and environmental education has never been static. Educators continually devise better ways to define and refine their philosophies and practices. One way to accomplish this has been to change the names of the fields and redesign their theories and practices. Some early-twenty-first century terms include earth education, bioregional education, Expeditionary Learning Outward Bound, use of the environment as an integrating context for learning, ecological education, nature awareness, locally focused teaching, and place-based education. The more than sixty labels for educational movements related to the outdoors and the environment demonstrate the importance and vitality of the fields. One promising development has been the identification of an eighth category of human multiple intelligences by Harvard professor Howard Gardner—the *naturalist intelligence.* This way of demonstrating expertise in recognizing and classifying the flora, fauna, and other physical and cultural artifacts is important because it provides another justification for integrating outdoor and environmental education into curriculum and instruction.

Summary

Outdoor education has served as a significant educational reform since the early 1940s by promoting the use of outdoor learning settings. When environmental education emerged in the 1970s, it focused more directly on knowledge leading to quality local and global environments. Their forerunners—camping, nature study, conservation, and adventure education—paved the way for early school and community leaders to develop experiential programs aimed at living well on earth though understanding how it works.

See also: ALTERNATIVE SCHOOLING; CURRICULUM, SCHOOL; EXPERIENTIAL EDUCATION; PROGRESSIVE EDUCATION; SCHOOL REFORM.

BIBLIOGRAPHY

CAMPBELL, MEG; LIEBOWITZ, MARTIN; MEDNICK, AMY; and RUGEN, LEAH. 1998. *Guide for Planning a Learning Expedition.* Dubuque, IA: Kendall/Hunt.

CARSON, RACHEL. 1962. *Silent Spring.* Boston: Houghton Mifflin.

CORNELL, JOSEPH. 1998. *Sharing Nature with Children,* revised and expanded. Nevada City, CA: Dawn.

DISINGER, JOHN F. 1998. "Tensions in Environmental Education: Yesterday, Today, and Tomorrow." In *Essential Readings in Environmental Education,* eds. Harold R. Hungerford, William J. Bluhm, Trudi L. Volk, and John M. Ramsey. Champaign, IL: Stipes.

GARDNER, HOWARD. 1999. *Intelligence Reframed: Multiple Intelligences for the 21st Century.* New York: Basic Books.

HAMMERMAN, DONALD R.; HAMMERMAN, WILLIAM M.; and HAMMERMAN, ELIZABETH, L. 2001. *Teaching in the Outdoors,* 5th edition. Danville, IL: Interstate.

HUNGERFORD, HAROLD; BLUHM, WILLIAM J.; VOLK, TRUDI L.; and RAMSEY, JOHN M., eds. 1998. *Essential Readings in Environmental Education.* Champaign, IL: Stipes.

KNAPP, CLIFFORD E. 1996. *Just Beyond the Classroom: Community Adventures for Interdisciplinary Learning.* Charleston, WV: ERIC Clearinghouse on Rural Education and Small Schools.

KNAPP, CLIFFORD E. 2000. "Learning from an Outdoor Education Hero: Personal Reflections about L. B. Sharp." *Taproot* 12:7–11.

LESLIE, CLARE WALKER; TALLMADGE, JOHN; and WESSELS, TOM. 1999. *Into the Field: A Guide to Locally Focused Teaching.* Barrington, MA: Orion Society.

LIEBERMAN, GERALD A., and HOODY, LINDA L. 1998. *Closing the Achievement Gap: Using the Environment as an Integrating Context for Learning.* Poway, CA: Science Wizards.

SMITH, GREGORY A. 2001. "Defusing Environmental Education: An Evaluation of the Critique of the Environmental Education Movement." *Clearing: Environmental Education Resources for Teachers* 108(winter):22–28.

SMITH, GREGORY A., and WILLIAMS, DILAFRUZ R. 1999. *Ecological Education in Action: On Weaving Education, Culture, and the Environment.* Albany, NY: State University of New York Press.

STAPP, WILLIAM B. 1998. "The Concept of Environmental Education." In *Essential Readings in Environmental Education*, eds. Harold R. Hungerford, William J. Bluhm, Trudi L. Volk, and John M. Ramsey. Champaign, IL: Stipes.

TANNER, LAUREL N. 1997. *Dewey's Laboratory School: Lessons for Today.* New York: Teachers College Press.

TRAINA, FRANK, and DARLEY-HILL, SUSAN, eds. 1995. *Perspectives in Bioregional Education.* Rock Springs, GA: North American Association for Environmental Education.

VAN MATRE, STEVE. 1990. *Earth Education: A New Beginning.* Warrenville, IL: Institute for Earth Education.

WOODHOUSE, JANICE, L., and KNAPP, CLIFFORD E. 2000. "Place-Based Curriculum and Instruction: Outdoor and Environmental Education Approaches." *ERIC Digest*, EDO-RC-00-6. Charleston, WV: AEL.

CLIFFORD E. KNAPP

OUT-OF-SCHOOL INFLUENCES AND ACADEMIC SUCCESS

From birth to age eighteen, children spend just a fraction of their lives in school. Thus it is not surprising that many factors outside the school environment can significantly influence students' prospects for academic success in school. These factors are in play both during the years before children begin formal schooling and while they are actually enrolled in elementary and secondary school.

A diverse array of issues, including (but not limited to) parents' beliefs and expectations about education; the availability and quality of child care; family economic status; the persistence, or absence, of violence in a child's life; access to social services; physical and mental health issues; opportunities for constructive, healthy activities outside of school; and the nature and strength of school-community connections, can make a difference in a child's opportunities to do well in school.

Background

Much of the work concerning out-of-school influences on students' prospects for academic success stems from James Coleman's 1966 study of racial and ethnic segregation, student and family characteristics, and student achievement. In *Equality of Educational Opportunity* (1966), prepared for the United States Department of Education, Coleman found that family factors such as household composition, socioeconomic status, and parents' level of education were stronger predictors of students' educational attainment than were direct school-related factors.

The Coleman study gave rise to decades of research and writing, particularly in the 1970s and 1980s, on so-called family effects on students' academic achievement. These studies generally concluded that the factors Coleman identified do exert enormous influence on students' achievement, though they are not necessarily deterministic of it. Students who come from backgrounds that would seem to doom them to school failure often find a way to beat the odds and achieve at high academic levels. And some students who hail from seemingly ideal life situations never thrive academically.

During the 1990s, as the United States education system was focused intensely on raising academic achievement across the board under the banner "All Students Can Learn," many educators, researchers, and policymakers began to adopt the *no excuses* philosophy. Regardless of a child's life circumstances, they asserted, an effective education environment can overcome other challenges and enable all children to achieve at high levels.

As is the case with most complicated issues, both points of view have considerable merit. All (or nearly all) students can learn. But the circumstances of a child's life, the social indicators that paint a cumulative picture of a child's total environment, are important signposts pinpointing conditions that either make learning possible or present challenges that must be overcome to pave the way for learning.

Parental Influence

A commonly used phrase, but one that has the ring of substantial truth, is that parents are their children's first teachers. The home environment shapes a child's initial views of learning. Parents' beliefs, expectations, and attitudes about education and their children's achievement have a profound early impact on students' conceptions of the place of education in their lives. What parents think about the importance (or unimportance) of doing well in school is often mirrored in student results. A study by the Metropolitan Life Insurance Company found that nearly all students (97%) who earned mostly A's and B's on their report cards reported that their parents encouraged them to do well in school. Among students who earned mostly C's, nearly half (49%) said they received little parental encouragement.

Some families clearly have more resources to devote to their children and can more easily find time to spend nurturing and encouraging them. When both parents work (an increasingly common phenomenon) or when a child is being raised by a single parent, finding time to read to the child, to encourage the completion of homework, or to participate in school functions—all known to have a salutary effect on student success in school—become more difficult. The problem is often compounded for parents who speak limited or no English.

However, regardless of family composition or circumstance, the research is clear. Children whose families provide supervision and support, and who have aspirations for their children, tend to multiply those children's chances of being successful students.

Family Economic Status

Many children grow up in homes with an abundance of fiscal and material resources. But not all do. As of 1998, 13 million children in the United States (19% of children age eighteen or younger) lived below the federally established poverty line. Children eighteen and under make up just 26 percent of the total U.S. population, but they represent 40 percent of the population living in poverty. Stated more starkly, the United States, the richest nation in the world, ranks highest in childhood poverty among all the industrialized nations of the world.

Poverty takes a toll on students' school performance. Poor children are twice as likely as their more affluent counterparts to repeat a grade; to be suspended, expelled, or drop out of high school; and to be placed in special education classes.

Family composition and economic circumstance are often intertwined. More than half of the poor families in the United States are headed by an unmarried mother who must balance employment issues (these women are often trapped in low-wage jobs) with child care and parenting responsibilities. In sum, children from more economically affluent home circumstances have a leg up in many areas of life, including education.

Preparing for School

Children begin learning from the time they are born. Where children spend their time before they enter kindergarten has an effect on both their readiness for school and their chances for good long-term achievement results.

Six in ten children in the United States, or nearly 12 million children younger than age five, spend part of their waking hours being cared for by someone other than their parents. There are a variety of care circumstances. Sometimes young children are looked after by a relative, such as a grandmother or an aunt. Some young children spend part of their day in the care of a licensed provider who may watch over several children at the same time. Some preschoolers attend organized preschool or early childhood education programs.

Studies show that early childhood care and education make a difference. The quality of care young children receive establishes the foundation for their future academic success. Young children who are exposed to high-quality care settings, geared to their social, emotional, and intellectual development, exhibit better language and mathematics skills, better cognitive and social skills, and better relationships with classmates than do children in low-quality care.

The nature of quality of early care has been shown to have lasting impacts. Children in high-quality care environments are less likely than children in low-quality care circumstances to repeat a grade, require special education services, drop out of school, or find themselves in future trouble with the law.

For many families, the child-care issue revolves around two central concerns: cost and access. Even if quality care is available, many families cannot afford to pay for it. And for many families, quality care is simply not available.

Physical and Mental Health

Overall, children's health improved substantially during the last decades of the twentieth century. Infant mortality rates went down, and many childhood diseases once thought incurable attained high cure rates or became preventable altogether.

Health—both physical and mental well-being—has obvious links to students' prospects for doing well in school. Children who are physically ill fail to attend school regularly, and when they do attend they are often unable to focus on their schoolwork.

Children with untreated mental health problems experience a range of school-related difficulties, from acting-out behavior in the classroom to an inability to make friends and develop collegial attachments.

Research shows that attention to children's health is important even before a child is born. Low-birthweight babies, often born to mothers who smoke, drink, or eat unhealthy diets during pregnancy, are at greater risk of becoming children with a host of developmental difficulties.

Despite the compelling importance of robust physical and mental health to students' prospects for academic success, large numbers of American children have inadequate access to appropriate health care services. Not surprisingly, access to quality services is often a function of family income. The less financially stable the child's family, the less likely the child is to have regular medical care.

Children covered by health insurance are more likely to have better access to health care than are children not covered by such insurance. As of 1999, 10 million children in the United States (14% of the child population) were uninsured.

Other significant risk factors, particularly for adolescents, are drugs and alcohol. Drinking, smoking cigarettes, and using harder drugs, from marijuana to cocaine, can cause substantial long-term physical and mental health problems. In the short-term, use of many of these substances can cause reduced school attendance and general inattention to school studies.

The Impact of Violence

Violence in children's lives can come in many forms. Sometimes it is violence children witness, such as violence between their parents or caregivers, or violence in the communities in which they live. Sometimes children themselves are the victims of violence, whether it be abuse by a parent or relative, or physical (or verbal) attacks in their neighborhoods. These kinds of violence have long-term impacts on children, affecting their expectations about life and their views of the world.

Violence outside of school can shape students' attitudes about school. A child surrounded by a violent environment who does not expect to live to adulthood may see little purpose in completing an education. Violence in the home increases the likelihood that a student will spend at least part of childhood and/or adolescence in the child protective services system, perhaps in foster care. For children who live with violence, the situation is quite often just one of a constellation of challenging circumstances. Violence is often a partner to poverty and an unstable home life.

One of the most prevalent contemporary milieus for youth violence is gangs. Gang activity exists in all fifty states. Membership in gangs—often seen by adolescents as a kind of badge of honor or admission to a privileged club—increases the likelihood of involvement in criminal activities. Effective anti-gang programs have been shown to include intervention by police and officers of the juvenile justice system, family and youth education programs, and providing alternative outlets for youths' time and energy.

An important research finding is that gang activity, or at least attraction to it, begins early. As early as the third or fourth grade, students (particularly boys) can be lured into believing that becoming a member of a gang is an important social goal. Thus, programs to prevent students from joining gangs need to begin in elementary school.

Out-of-School Activities: Recreation and Employment

How students spend their time when they are not in school can have a significant impact on their opportunity to succeed in school.

Youth organizations. Research suggests that participation in various kinds of youth organizations contributes to better behavior in school, improved social skills, more self-confidence, and higher academic expectations. Organizations such as the YMCA and YWCA, Boys and Girls Clubs, 4-H, and Boy Scouts and Girl Scouts often provide academic support as a complement to activities designed to foster social and emotional development. Athletic programs, such as Little League and those organized by local recreation and parks departments, offer healthy outlets for children's and adolescents' energy, while also building skills such as personal responsibility and teamwork.

Mentoring relationships can ensure that a caring adult is part of a child's life, and they have been shown to offer important benefits. Research has shown that programs such as the Big Brothers and Big Sisters of America contribute to lower rates of drug and alcohol use, reduced violence, and better school attendance, performance, and attitudes.

Youth employment. As many as 76 percent of youth in the United States are working, or have worked, in paid employment by age sixteen. Researchers differ regarding the impact of work on adolescents' academic achievement. Some studies conclude that work provides students with useful skills and attributes, among them instilling a sense of responsibility and heightening students' sense of self-efficacy, and that these have a positive spillover effect in school. However, other research concludes that work is just a distraction for most students, in that it competes with school for students' time and attention.

Of course, students work for different reasons. Some students are significant breadwinners for their families. Their earnings represent an important part of the families' income. Some students work specifically to save money for college. Most studies, however, show that the vast majority of students who work do so to earn spending money for things they want to buy.

Research has shown that the amount of time a student works is a factor in determining employment's impact on educational performance. For students working twenty or fewer hours per week, few problems seem to arise. But for students working more than twenty hours per week, work can present education-related problems where the job takes precedence over school.

Connecting Schools, Families, and Neighborhoods

For most students, school creates an important community setting—a safe place where time is structured (which children and teens do crave, even if they do not always appreciate it) and friends are present. Families and neighborhoods complete a student's community, and consciously connecting schools, families, and neighborhoods offers significant advantages for students, particularly those at academic risk.

Students who are struggling in school are often plagued by a host of problems outside of school. Offering students the best opportunity to succeed in school may require helping not just the student, but also treating the student's entire family.

Among the systems devised for this purpose are school-linked and school-based programs of social services. The goal of these programs is to directly connect family support services—such as health care, income support, English language acquisition,

and job training—with schools as a way of increasing families' access to these services. Located either on school grounds (school-based) or nearby in the surrounding neighborhood (school-linked), these efforts foster partnerships between schools and social services agencies, ideally giving each a chance to do what it does best.

Despite the promise of such programs, they have not been problem-free. Difficulties arise around allocation of resources, turf (who is in charge of what?), and misunderstandings about the roles and responsibilities of various involved professionals. Research has shown that for school-based or school-linked programs to produce the desired results, social services need not just to be linked to schools, but must be integrated into schools' activities and functions, creating new pressures for schools regarding what they are expected to do and under what circumstances. Whatever kind of program is employed, what is important is for services to reach students and their families so that education can be a student's primary responsibility.

Conclusion

Schools do not exist in a vacuum. A host of factors contribute to students' prospects for academic success. Some students come to school with all they need: stable and supportive families, adequate financial resources, and good health. For students who do not enjoy these advantages, making provision to help them meet outside-of-school challenges can provide just the boost they need to succeed in school.

See also: COLEMAN, JAMES S.; FAMILY COMPOSITION AND CIRCUMSTANCE; FAMILY, SCHOOL, AND COMMUNITY CONNECTIONS; HEALTH AND EDUCATION; PARENTING; VIOLENCE, CHILDREN'S EXPOSURE TO.

BIBLIOGRAPHY

BROOKS-GUNN, JEANNE; DUNCAN, GREG G.; KLEBANOV, PAMELA K.; and SEALAND, NAOMI. 1993. "Do Neighborhoods Influence Child and Adolescent Development?" *American Journal of Sociology* 99:353–395.

COLEMAN, JAMES S., et al. 1966. *Equality of Educational Opportunity.* Washington, DC: U.S. Office of Education.

McLANAHAN, SARA, and SANDEFUR, GARY. 1994. *Growing Up with a Single Parent.* Cambridge, MA: Harvard University Press.

MᴄLᴀᴜɢʜʟɪɴ, Mɪʟʙʀᴇʏ W., et al. 1994. *Urban Sanctuaries.* San Francisco: Jossey-Bass.

Mᴇᴛʀᴏᴘᴏʟɪᴛᴀɴ Iɴsᴜʀᴀɴᴄᴇ Cᴏᴍᴘᴀɴʏ. 1998. *The Metropolitan Life American Teacher Survey of 1998.* New York: Metropolitan Insurance Company.

Mɪʜᴀʟɪᴄ, Sʜᴀʀᴏɴ W., and Eʟʟɪᴏᴛᴛ, Dᴇʟʙᴇʀᴛ S. 1997. "Short and Long-term Consequences of Adolescent Work." *Youth and Society* 28(4):464–498.

Qᴜᴀʟɪᴛʏ Cᴏᴜɴᴛs. 2002. "Building Blocks for Success: State Efforts in Early Childhood Education." Bethesda, MD: Education Week.

Tɪᴇʀɴᴇʏ, Jᴏsᴇᴘʜ P.; Gʀᴏssᴍᴀɴ, J. Bᴀʟᴅᴡɪɴ; and Rᴇsᴄʜ, Nᴀɴᴄʏ L. 1995. *Making a Difference: An Impact Study of Big Brothers/Big Sisters.* Philadelphia: Public/Private Ventures.

Uɴɪᴛᴇᴅ Sᴛᴀᴛᴇs Hᴏᴜsᴇ ᴏғ Rᴇᴘʀᴇsᴇɴᴛᴀᴛɪᴠᴇs, Cᴏᴍᴍɪᴛᴛᴇᴇ ᴏɴ Wᴀʏs ᴀɴᴅ Mᴇᴀɴs. 2000. *The 2000 Green Book.* Washington, DC: U.S. Government Accounting Office.

Wᴇʜʟᴀɢᴇ, Gᴀʀʏ; Sᴍɪᴛʜ, Gʀᴇɢᴏʀʏ; and Lɪᴘᴍᴀɴ, Pᴀᴜʟɪɴᴇ. 1992. "Restructuring Urban Schools: The New Futures Experience." *American Educational Research Journal* 29(1):51–93.

INTERNET RESOURCE

Sᴄʜᴡᴀʀᴛᴢ, Wᴇɴᴅʏ. 1996. "An Overview of Strategies to Reduce School Violence." ERIC Identifier ED410321. New York: Eric Clearinghouse on Urban Education. <www.ed.gov/databases/ERIC_Digests/ed410321.html>.

Jᴜʟɪᴀ E. Kᴏᴘᴘɪᴄʜ

P

PACIFIC REGION

See: EAST ASIA AND THE PACIFIC.

PAIDEIA PROGRAM

In 1982 a group of scholars and educators headed by philosopher Mortimer Adler published *The Paideia Proposal,* and it is difficult to name a leading educational reform program since that has not been directly or indirectly influenced by Paideia principles. *Paideia* is the Greek word for the nurturing of children, and the Paideia Group was dedicated to providing a powerful public education for all. In the years immediately following the proposal, Adler and the original Paideia Group published two more books—*Paideia Problems and Possibilities* (1983) and *The Paideia Program* (1984)—intended in part to answer practical questions about program implementation. The National Paideia Center was established at the University of North Carolina in 1988, and in 1992 began working in close, classroom-based partnership with schools. By the year 2000 the center was working with well over a hundred schools in over a dozen states, and the list was growing continually. Paideia has grown steadily since the early 1990s for several reasons.

The first reason is that the original Paideia principles have appealed to many as a powerful condensation of the best thinking about public education. Adler focused on the profound connection between school reform and the United States as a functional democracy. The Paideia philosophy stated a litany of principles that in 1982 seemed radical but by 1995 had became accepted wisdom. Such principles as "all children can learn" and "therefore they deserve the same quality, not just quantity, of education," anticipated many of the later American reform movements, and documented Paideia's origin in a philosophy of human development.

The second reason why interest in Paideia has continued to grow rapidly is that the program marries a fundamentally conservative idea, the beneficial rigors of a classical education, and a fundamentally liberal one, inclusive teaching and learning practices. These seemingly contradictory ideas—intellectual rigor and equal access to a quality education—are the bedrock upon which successful Paideia schools have been built.

Perhaps the most important reason for Paideia's steady growth is that the program includes all subjects and embraces important curriculum from diverse cultures. Increasingly, the National Paideia Center has provided schools with curricular information on how to use Paideia instructional techniques in mathematics, science, music, literature, writing, and physical education—all the subjects in a strong core curriculum. In addition, the center has broadened the use of the term *classical* to include the study of texts by African Americans, Hispanics, Asians, and representatives of other cultures.

Implementing the Paideia Program

The recent work of the National Paideia Center is based on a mix of teaching strategies called the "three columns" of teaching. They are made up of the didactic instruction of curricular information, intellectual coaching of the skills necessary to manipulate and apply information, and seminar discussion of the ideas and values inherent to that information. Paideia does not require a specific curriculum, but rather provides a system for fostering student engagement with the standard curriculum of a state or district. In contrast to the heavy use of teacher-centered, didactic instruction characterizing traditional American schools, the Paideia program focuses on limiting didactic instruction to less that 15 percent of classroom time and devoting the remaining 85 to 90 percent to increased student learning activity.

Typically, in the first year of partnership with the center, a school focuses on implementing the Paideia seminar schoolwide. The Paideia seminar is a formal discussion of a text in which the leader of the seminar (the teacher) simply asks open-ended questions, leaving it up to the students to generate a dialogue about the ideas and values inherent to the text. (The text may be a map or historical document, a chart or skeleton, a math problem or a poem, a photograph or painting.) In this way, students are brought into active engagement with the conceptual framework behind the curriculum.

In the second year of implementation, Paideia schools focus on implementing the Paideia-coached project, revising traditional units of study in each classroom to make them much more product–oriented, resulting both in more authentic assessment and active student learning. "Product–oriented" means that most or all student work is produced for an authentic audience (parents or other community members) and will be assessed by that audience. Typically, this phase of Paideia implementation takes several years as teachers move from teaching a few units each year as coached projects to developing an entire curriculum based on the production of real work for authentic audiences. In the third year of partnership with the center, most Paideia schools implement more student-centered assessment practices in the classroom, and the entire school community develops a cyclical plan for continuous improvement.

Detailed program evaluations, notably one comprehensive study by the Center for Research and Evaluation at the University of North Carolina at Greensboro, have shown that Paideia schools consistently produce a greater increase in standardized test scores for all students than do non-Paideia schools. In addition, Paideia schools consistently show an improved school climate, including a more inviting environment for minority students.

The eventual goal of the Paideia program is schools that offer every student access to a rigorous education. To accomplish this goal, the Paideia program prescribes schools that are themselves communities of thought, where adults and students alike focus on the skills and attitudes of lifelong learning and continuous improvement.

See also: ALTERNATIVE SCHOOLING; CURRICULUM, SCHOOL; ELEMENTARY EDUCATION, *subentry on* CURRENT TRENDS; SCHOOL REFORM; SECONDARY EDUCATION, *subentry on* CURRENT TRENDS.

BIBLIOGRAPHY

ALDER, MORTIMER J. 1982. *The Paideia Proposal.* New York: Macmillan.

ADLER, MORTIMER J. 1983. *Paideia Problems and Possibilities.* New York: Macmillan.

ADLER, MORTIMER J. 1984. *The Paideia Program.* New York: Macmillan.

ROBERTS, TERRY, and BILLINGS, LAURA. 1999. *The Paideia Classroom: Teaching for Understanding.* Larchmont, NY: Eye of Education.

ROBERTS, TERRY, and the STAFF OF THE NATIONAL PAIDEIA CENTER. 1998. *The Power of Paideia Schools: Defining Lives Through Learning.* Alexandria, VA: Association for Supervision and Curriculum Development.

TERRY ROBERTS

PALMER, ALICE FREEMAN
(1855–1902)

The first female college president and the first president of Wellesley College, Alice Freeman Palmer was the founding dean of women at the University of Chicago.

Born on a farm in mid-state New York, Palmer grew up with the rural expectation that women would work hard to help support their families. At age fifteen she surprised her parents by announcing that she intended to go to college. She was already engaged to the only college graduate she had ever met, a teacher at the local academy where she was a star student, and when he discouraged her plans she broke the engagement. A college education, she insisted to all opponents, would best prepare her to serve others and to earn money by teaching. Palmer matriculated at the University of Michigan in 1872, two years after the university was first forced to admit women. During and after college she took a variety of teaching positions, and a year after graduation she became her family's primary support when her father went bankrupt.

In 1879 Palmer accepted a position as professor of history at Wellesley College, which had opened four years earlier with an all-female faculty. Wellesley's founder, Henry Durant, was greatly impressed by Palmer's intellectual abilities, charismatic leadership, and persistent yet charming personality. She became his protégé, and when he died in 1882 the trustees appointed her president even though, at age twenty-seven, she was the youngest member of the faculty.

Palmer soon gained a national reputation as a promoter of women's higher education. She strengthened Wellesley's faculty, student body, and financial status, established a network of secondary schools to prepare girls for college work, and insisted that Wellesley pursue high intellectual standards. College education, she argued at every opportunity, prepares women for civic leadership as well as self-knowledge and self-respect. She expected many of her students to support themselves, as she had. The rest she expected to lead libraries and museums, serve on school boards and town governments, and pursue other forms of civic service.

In 1887 Palmer shocked her colleagues by marrying George Herbert Palmer, a professor of philosophy at Harvard University, and resigning from Wellesley's presidency. She spent the next year recovering from her active tuberculosis, and then renewed her career as a public speaker. For the next four years she toured the country to preach the importance of women's higher education to university audiences, women's clubs, religious societies, and anyone else who would pay her. A powerful and passionate speaker, she presented herself as a model of an educated woman: intellectual yet emotional, dedicated to serving others yet happy in her personal life, willing to work hard for causes she believed in, yet retaining the feminine graces of beauty, wit, and attentiveness to others. Many people still believed that education de-sexed women, and Palmer intended to prove them wrong.

Palmer also joined the Massachusetts State Board of Education, eventually becoming its most senior member, and gained a reputation as a formidable lobbyist on Beacon Hill. She served as a trustee for several educational institutions, including Wellesley College, was active in several education-oriented voluntary associations, including the forerunner of the American Association of University Women, and was one of five people chosen to represent Massachusetts at the 1893 World's Fair. With her husband, George Palmer, she tried to persuade Harvard to admit women on equal terms with men. After she led a campaign to create a $250,000 endowment for female students, Harvard reneged on its agreement to admit women if the money were raised.

In 1892, when the University of Chicago was preparing to open, Palmer was the most prominent woman in the field of higher education. Chicago was then a rough western city, and the university's president, William Rainey Harper, feared that parents would refuse to send their daughters to a new university in a city best known for its stockyards. If Palmer were dean of women, Harper believed, her reputation would help give the young university the stamp of approval it desperately needed. He hoped to hire both Palmers—George as well as Alice—but when George decided to remain at Harvard, Harper continued to court Alice persistently. Finally she agreed to his suggestion that she commute from Cambridge to Chicago and be in residence only twelve weeks a year.

Palmer was one of the few Chicago founders with solid administrative experience, so she quickly became involved in every aspect of the new university. Harper repeatedly claimed that he would not have survived the university's first year without her. Palmer gave special attention, however, to making the university an appealing intellectual and social environment for women. She succeeded. When Chicago opened, women were 24 percent of its student body. The next year they were 33 percent, and the percentage climbed each year until 1898, when 43 percent of the students were women. Many male students, faculty, administrators, trustees, and donors—including Harper—were alarmed by this trend, which they interpreted as the "feminization" of the university, and university policies quickly shifted to attract men and discourage women. Palmer, not surprisingly, was marginalized and her policy suggestions ignored. After three years she decided to resign.

Palmer never again held a paid, professional position. Instead, she gave all of her time to the Massachusetts Board of Education, the numerous institutions of which she was trustee, and other cultural and political activities. She always, even during her Wellesley years, preferred coeducation to single-sex education. Men and women, she believed, belonged beside each other, working and learning together as peers. After her experiences at Harvard and Chicago, however, she lost her early optimism that men needed only a few years of adjustment and then would be happy to treat women as equals. For the rest of her life, she nurtured institutions—schools, colleges, and scholarships for advanced graduate work—that would enable other women to pursue education and professional work.

See also: HIGHER EDUCATION IN THE UNITED STATES, *subentry on* HISTORICAL DEVELOPMENT.

BIBLIOGRAPHY

BORDIN, RUTH. 1993. *Alice Freeman Palmer: The Evolution of a New Woman.* Ann Arbor: University of Michigan Press.

KENSCHAFT, LORI. 1999. "Marriage, Gender, and Higher Education: The Personal and Public Partnership of Alice Freeman Palmer and George Herbert Palmer, 1886–1902." Ph.D. diss., Boston University.

LINENTHAL, ARTHUR J. 1995. *Two Academic Lives: George Herbert Palmer and Alice Freeman Palmer.* Boston: privately printed.

PALMER, ALICE FREEMAN. 1897. *Why Go To College.* Boston: Crowell.

PALMER, ALICE FREEMAN, and PALMER, GEORGE HERBERT. 1908. *The Teacher: Essays and Addresses on Education.* Boston: Houghton Mifflin.

LORI KENSCHAFT

PARENTAL INVOLVEMENT IN EDUCATION

Although widespread support for parental involvement is reflected in current educational policies and practices, what this means is not always clear. Parental involvement includes a wide range of behaviors but generally refers to parents' and family members' use and investment of resources in their children's schooling. These investments can take place in or outside of school, with the intention of improving children's learning. Parental involvement at home can include activities such as discussions about school, helping with homework, and reading with children. Involvement at school may include parents volunteering in the classroom, attending workshops, or attending school plays and sporting events.

Research on Parental Involvement

Research on the effects of parental involvement has shown a consistent, positive relationship between parents' engagement in their children's education and student outcomes. Studies have also shown that parental involvement is associated with student outcomes such as lower dropout and truancy rates. Whether or not parental involvement can improve student outcomes is no longer in question.

Researchers have begun to focus on how parental involvement affects students, why parents do and do not get involved in their children's education, and what role schools and teachers can play in creating parental involvement. Three frameworks for exploring the precursors to and effects of parental involvement have been the foundation of a majority of the research on parental involvement. Each approach highlights a different aspect of the dynamics that exist in school-home-community relationships.

Wendy S. Grolnick and her colleagues, in articles published in 1994 and 1997, conceptualized three dimensions of parental involvement based on how parent–child interactions affect students' schooling and motivation. Behavioral involvement refers to parents' public actions representing their interest in their child's education, such as attending an open house or volunteering at the school. Personal involvement includes parent–child interactions that communicate positive attitudes about school and the importance of education to the child. Cognitive/intellectual involvement refers to behaviors that promote children's skill development and knowledge, such as reading books and going to museums. Parental involvement, according to this theory, affects student achievement because these interactions affect students' motivation, their sense of competence, and the belief that they have control over their success in school.

Kathleen V. Hoover-Dempsey and Howard M. Sandler, in articles published in 1995 and 1997, defined parental involvement broadly to include home-based activities (e.g., helping with homework, discussing school events or courses) and school-based activities (e.g., volunteering at school, coming to school events). They argued that parental involvement is a function of a parent's beliefs about parental roles and responsibilities, a parent's sense that she can help her children succeed in school, and the opportunities for involvement provided by the school or teacher. In this theory, when parents get involved, children's schooling is affected through their acquisition of knowledge, skills, and an increased sense of confidence that they can succeed in school.

Joyce L. Epstein, in a 1995 article and a 2001 book titled *School, Family, and Community Partnerships*, argued that school, family, and community are important "spheres of influence" on children's development and that a child's educational development is enhanced when these three environments work collaboratively toward shared goals. Epstein encouraged schools to create greater "overlap" between the school, home, and community through the implementation of activities across six types of involvement: parenting, communication, volunteering, learning at home, decision-making, and collaboration with the community. By implementing activities across all six types of involvement, educators can help improve student achievement and experiences in school.

Effects on Parental Involvement

Research has shown that student and family characteristics affect levels of parental involvement. Working-class families and families in which mothers work full-time tend to be less involved in their children's education. Also, parents of elementary school students tend to be more involved in their children's education than parents of older students. Other factors, however, have been shown to be more important predictors of parental involvement than family income or structure.

Schools play a significant role in getting parents and family members involved in students' education. In their study published in the 1993 book *Families and Schools in a Pluralistic Society*, Susan L. Dauber and Joyce L. Epstein found that school and teacher practices were the strongest predictors of parental involvement. Specific practices that have been shown to predict parental involvement include: assigning homework designed to increase student-parent interactions, holding workshops for families, and communicating to parents about their children's education.

Parental beliefs and perceptions have also been shown to be a strong predictor of parental involvement. Parents' educational aspirations and level of comfort with the school and staff have been shown to predict levels of involvement. In addition, parents' beliefs about their responsibilities as a parent, their ability to affect their children's education, and their perceptions of their children's interests in school subjects have been shown to predict their involvement at home and at school.

Obstacles to Parental Involvement

Important obstacles that constrain parents' ability to become actively involved in their children's education include teachers' attitudes and family resources. These obstacles, however, can be overcome by schools and through teacher training. Each is discussed below.

Teacher attitudes may be one obstacle to parental involvement. For example, teacher beliefs about the impact of their efforts to involve parents in students' learning predict their efforts to encourage family involvement. In a study published in 1991, Epstein and Dauber found that, compared to middle school teachers, elementary school teachers more strongly believed that parental involvement is important for students and provide more opportunities and help for parents to be involved in their children's education. Low levels of parental involvement at some schools may be the result of the staff's perceptions of parents or the degree to which they feel parental involvement is important for their students.

Although all families want their children to succeed in school, not all families have the same resources or opportunities to be involved in their children's education. Families in which all caregivers work full-time, where there are multiple children, or where English is not spoken or read well face significant barriers to participation in their children's education. It is important for schools to understand the demands that exist on the families of their students and to work to overcome them. In her 1995 article Epstein argued that schools need to overcome these challenges by providing opportunities for school-to-home and home-to-school communications with families; providing communications to families in a language and at a reading level all families can understand; ensuring adequate representation of the entire community of parents on school advisory committees; and distributing information provided at workshops to the families who could not attend.

Schools that work to meet these challenges and try to make involvement easier and more convenient for all families will gain support from parents and improve student achievement.

One approach to overcoming these obstacles to parental involvement is to increase the degree to which teacher training covers the topic of parental involvement. Teacher-training programs spend very little time helping students understand the impact of parents in student learning and how teachers can help parents become involved in their children's education. Without this training, teachers may not understand the importance of parental involvement or how to facilitate it. As a result, working with parents can become one of the greatest challenges faced by new teachers.

Controversies

In spite of the evidence to suggest parental involvement can help improve student achievement and educational attainment, many are skeptical of parent-involvement programs. Michelle Fine, in a 1993 article, and Annette Lareau, in her 1989 book *Home Advantage,* raise concerns about the widespread implementation of parent-involvement policy and practices. Their concern about the effect of parent involvement programs stems from their observations that many schools and teachers use a "one-size-fits-all" approach. The result is that schools reinforce white, upper- and middle-class values and disadvantage students from other backgrounds.

Research has shown differences in parental involvement, parental beliefs, and the home-school relationship across socioeconomic, ethnic, and racial groups. The existence of different beliefs between parents and teachers can lead to misperceptions and the development of negative home-school relationships. Whether and how parent-involvement programs can be sensitive and equitable to families from all backgrounds remains an issue of discussion.

Current Issues

An area of research on parental involvement emerging in the late 1990s and early twenty-first century is the systematic examination of the role of community. Mavis G. Sanders, in an article published in 2001, reported that schools have a wide range of community resources available but use only a small percentage of these in their efforts to educate students. Also, Sophia Catsambis and Andrew Beveridge, in a 2001 article, showed that neighborhood conditions can dilute the effect of parental involvement and argued that this has an indirect affect on student achievement. The full role of community, and its impact on schools and families, is still unclear.

Understanding parental involvement as a developmental phenomenon is also emerging as an important issue. Research is needed to understand the most appropriate forms of involvement given students' age and maturation. Although parental involvement is an important influence on students throughout their schooling, effective elementary school parent-involvement activities may not be appropriate with high school students. Related to this issue, schools need to understand how parent-involvement activities can help students and families successfully transition from one level of schooling to another. Understanding the influences and effects of parental involvement and different forms of involvement as students move through school remains an understudied process.

The importance of having parents and family members support students' efforts in school is well known and well documented. Research shows a positive connection between parental involvement and student achievement. Furthermore, when schools and teachers work to involve parents, studies show that they can increase student achievement. Concern that schools may not be reaching out to all families and that they may not be aware of how families from different cultures perceive schools and school staff have raised questions about the effects of parental involvement for some students. Nevertheless, it appears that when schools reach out, understand the needs of all families, and create parental involvement, children are more likely to experience success in school.

See also: FAMILY, SCHOOL, AND COMMUNITY CONNECTIONS.

BIBLIOGRAPHY

CATSAMBIS, SOPHIA, and BEVERIDGE, ANDREW. 2001. "Does Neighborhood Matter? Family, Neighborhood, and School Influences on Eighth-Grade Mathematics Achievement." *Sociological Focus* 34:435–457.

CHAVKIN, NANCY F., ed. 1993. *Families and Schools in a Pluralistic Society.* Albany: State University of New York Press.

DAUBER, SUSAN L., and EPSTEIN, JOYCE L. 1993. "Parents' Attitudes and Practices of Involvement in Inner-City Elementary and Middle Schools." In *Families and Schools in a Pluralistic Society,* ed. Nancy F. Chavkin. Albany: State University of New York Press.

EPSTEIN, JOYCE L. 1995. "School/Family/Community Partnerships: Caring for the Children We Share." *Phi Delta Kappan* 76:701–712.

EPSTEIN, JOYCE L. 2001. *School, Family, and Community Partnerships: Preparing Educators and Improving Schools.* Boulder, CO: Westview.

EPSTEIN, JOYCE L., and DAUBER, SUSAN L. 1991. "School Programs and Teacher Practices of Parent Involvement in Inner-City Elementary and Middle Schools." *Elementary School Journal* 91:289–305.

FINE, MICHELLE. 1993. "[Ap]parent Involvement: Reflections on Parents, Power, and Urban Public Schools." *Teachers College Record* 94:682–710.

GROLNICK, WENDY S.; BENJET, CORINA; KUROWSKI, CAROLYN O.; and APOSTOLERIS, NICHOLAS H. 1997. "Predictors of Parent Involvement in Children's Schooling." *Journal of Educational Psychology* 89:538–548.

GROLNICK, WENDY S., and SLOWIACZEK, MARIA L. 1994. "Parents' Involvement in Children's Schooling: A Multidimensional Conceptualization and Motivational Model." *Child Development* 65:237–252.

HOOVER-DEMPSEY, KATHLEEN V., and SANDLER, HOWARD M. 1995. "Parent Involvement in Children's Education: Why Does It Make a Difference?" *Teachers College Record* 97:310–331.

HOOVER-DEMPSEY, KATHLEEN V., and SANDLER, HOWARD M. 1997. "Why Do Parents Become Involved in Their Children's Education?" *Review of Educational Research* 67:3–42.

LAREAU, ANNETTE. 1989. *Home Advantage.* London: Falmer Press.

SANDERS, MAVIS G. 2001. "The Role of 'Community' in Comprehensive School, Family, and Community Partnerships." *Elementary School Journal* 102:19–34.

STEVEN B. SHELDON

PARENTING

OVERVIEW

The study of parenting and its impact on children and adolescents has long been a central concern to scholars interested in child development and education. Although some contemporary commentators have suggested that social scientists have overestimated the influence of parents on their children's development and have underemphasized the importance of genetic factors and forces outside the family, most experts continue to believe that children's emotional, cognitive, and behavioral development is profoundly affected by the ways in which their parents have raised them.

This confidence in parental influence notwithstanding, it is important to note that much research on parenting and child development, which tends to be correlational in nature, leaves open the question of causal direction. The observation that children with certain characteristics are more likely than not to come from parents who engage in certain ways of parenting can be accounted for with a variety of explanations, of which parental influence is just one. Consider, for example, the commonly observed correlation between parental harshness and childhood aggression. Although it is reasonable to suggest that this observation reflects the fact that parental hostility creates aggressive children, it is also reasonable to suppose that parents are influenced by their children (i.e., that aggressive children elicit harsh parenting), that other environmental or genetic factors influence both parents and children in certain directions (e.g., that poverty makes parents harsh and children aggressive, or that harsh parents and aggressive children share a genetic predisposition for violence).

Researchers interested in disentangling these different accounts have generally followed one of three approaches. First, through the use of longitudinal designs, researchers have studied the links between parenting and child adjustment over time, examining whether certain types of parenting precede, rather than simply accompany or follow from, the emergence of certain child characteristics. Second, in studies of animals, researchers have been able to randomly assign infants and juveniles to rearing environments in which adults vary in their parenting practices, and by doing so, scientists have been able to examine the impact of variations in parenting on adjustment through experimentation. Finally, a number of investigators have studied the impact of parent-focused interventions on child adjustment. In these studies, parents' behavior is changed through some sort of psychoeducational treatment, and any resultant change in child adjustment is examined in relation to the parenting intervention. All three designs (longitudinal, experimental, and interventional) have buttressed the findings from correlational work.

Parenting, of course, encompasses many different phenomena. Nancy Darling and Laurence Steinberg (1993) have suggested that researchers distinguish between parenting style and parenting practices. They define *parenting style* as a constellation of attitudes toward the child communicated to the child by the parent, that taken together create an emotional climate in which the parent's behaviors are expressed. These behaviors include both the specific, goal-directed behaviors through which parents perform their parental duties (what Darling and Steinberg refer to as *parenting practices*) as well as non-goal-directed parental behaviors, such as gestures, changes in tone of voice, or the spontaneous expression of emotion. The focus of the current entry is on parenting style. Information on specific parenting practices, especially those related to parenting practices designed to influence educational achievement, may be found in other entries.

Dimensional Approaches to Research on Parenting

Whether through correlational, longitudinal, or experimental designs, research on parenting style and its impact has traditionally followed one of two approaches. In the *dimensional* approach, researchers isolate critical dimensions of parenting along which parents differ and examine the relations between variability on one or more of these dimensions and variability in one or more child outcomes. The most frequently studied dimensions of parenting have been warmth (sometimes referred to as acceptance or responsiveness), firmness (sometimes referred to as demandingness or behavioral control), and restrictiveness (sometimes referred to as intrusiveness or psychological control). Four broad sets of child adjustment indicators have been examined in relation to each of these dimensions of parenting: psychosocial development (including social competence, self-conceptions, and self-reliance); school achievement (including school performance, school engagement, and academic motivation); internalized distress (including depression, anxiety, and psychosomatic problems); and problem behavior (including delinquency, aggression, and drug and alcohol use).

Generally speaking, research shows that children and adolescents fare better when their parents are warm, firm, and nonrestrictive. Although variability in parental warmth has been associated with variability in all four areas of child adjustment listed in the preceding paragraph, it appears that variations in parents' firmness and restrictiveness contribute relatively more to some aspects of children's development than to others. In general, variations in firmness are linked most strongly to variations in problem behavior (with children whose parents are low in firmness exhibiting more problem behavior than their more vigilantly reared peers), whereas variations in restrictiveness are linked most strongly to variations in internalized distress (with children whose parents are high in restrictiveness scoring higher on measures of depression, anxiety, and the like). Thus the distinction between behavioral and psychological control is important not only because each is related to different outcomes but also because optimal child development is associated with high levels of one type of control (behavioral) but low levels of the other (psychological).

Configurational Approaches to Research on Parenting

The dimensional approach attempts to separate various aspects of parenting from one another, to isolate their independent relations to child outcomes. In contrast, the *configurational* approach to parenting attempts to identify particular types or styles of parenting that are defined by certain constellations of parenting characteristics (e.g., a group of parents who are high on warmth, low on behavioral control, and low on psychological control; a group who are high on warmth, high on behavioral control, and low on psychological control, etc.). This has been done by using configurations that are defined a priori on the basis of theory as well as by identifying naturally occurring clusters of parents whose parenting has been assessed on several of the key dimensions identified earlier. The advantage of the a priori approach is that all possible constellations of parents are identified, even those that are relatively rare. The advantage of identifying naturally occurring clusters of parents is that the end result is a categorization system that accurately reflects the type of parenting found within the particular ecological niche studied. This can be an important consideration for researchers who are interested in cultural groups whose parenting may not be easily classified using preexisting configurational models. Some critics, for example, contend that the most commonly used configurational models of parenting have greater applicability within white, middle-class, American samples than within samples of parents from other backgrounds.

The most widely used configurational model of parenting is one that derives from the work of Diana Baumrind (1971), whose theory of parenting style has been enormously influential. Although Baumrind's initial conceptualization of parenting styles was not explicitly based on the dimensions of parental warmth, behavioral control, and psychological control, more contemporary models of parenting, such as those of Darling and Steinberg, have attempted to bridge Baumrind's configurational approach with research on these three dimensions of parenting. Within this parenting-style framework, parents are classified as authoritative (high in warmth, high in firmness, and low in restrictiveness), authoritarian (low in warmth, high in firmness, and high in restrictiveness), or indulgent (high in warmth, low in firmness, and low in restrictiveness). Contemporary variations of this framework have also included a fourth group, indifferent parents, who are characteristically low in warmth, low in firmness, and low in restrictiveness. Although it is theoretically possible to derive additional configurations of parents based on other combinations of warmth, firmness, and restrictiveness, most empirical research suggests that, at least in contemporary Western cultures, the authoritative, authoritarian, permissive, and indifferent styles account for the vast majority of parents.

Authoritative parents. These four general styles of parenting can be distinguished in many respects beyond their scores on measures of parental warmth, firmness, or restrictiveness. For example, in addition to being both warm and firm, authoritative parents set standards for the child's conduct but form expectations that are consistent with the child's developing needs and capabilities. They place a high value on the development of autonomy and self-direction but assume the ultimate responsibility for their child's behavior. Authoritative parents deal with their child in a rational, issue-oriented manner, frequently engaging in discussion and explanation with their children over matters of discipline.

Authoritarian parents. In contrast, authoritarian parents place a high value on obedience and conformity, favoring more punitive, absolute, and forceful disciplinary measures. Verbal give-and-take is not common in authoritarian households, because the underlying belief of authoritarian parents is that the child should accept without question the rules and standards established by the parents. They tend not to encourage independent behavior and, instead, place a good deal of importance on restricting the child's autonomy.

Indulgent parents. Indulgent parents behave in an accepting, benign, and somewhat more passive way in matters of discipline. They place relatively few demands on the child's behavior, giving the child a high degree of freedom to act as he or she wishes. Indulgent parents are more likely to believe that control is an infringement on the child's freedom that may interfere with the child's healthy development. Instead of actively shaping their child's behavior, indulgent parents are more likely to view themselves as resources that the child may or may not use.

Indifferent parents. Finally, indifferent parents try to do whatever is necessary to minimize the time and energy that they must devote to interacting with their child. In extreme cases, indifferent parents may be neglectful. They know little about their child's activities and whereabouts, show little interest in their child's experiences at school or with friends, rarely converse with their child, and rarely consider their child's opinion when making decisions. Rather than raising their child according to a set of beliefs about what is good for the child's development (as do the other three parent types), indifferent parents are "parent centered"—they structure their home life primarily around their own needs and interests.

In light of research findings linking positive child adjustment to the presence of parental warmth and firmness, and to a lack of parental restrictiveness, it is not surprising to find that child adjustment varies as a function of parenting style, with children from authoritative households exhibiting relatively healthier adjustment than their peers and children from neglectful homes exhibiting poorer functioning on virtually all measured indicators. More specifically, children and adolescents from authoritative homes score better than their peers on measures of psychosocial development, school achievement, internalized distress, and problem behavior, whereas those from neglectful homes score worse across all four sets of outcomes. Youngsters raised in authoritarian or permissive homes score somewhere between the two extremes, with authoritarian parenting associated with special problems in self-reliance, social competence, and internalized distress, and permissive parenting associated with somewhat lower school achievement and elevated rates of problem behavior.

Although occasional exceptions to these general patterns have been noted from time to time, the evidence linking authoritative parenting and healthy child and adolescent development is remarkably strong, and it has been found in studies of a wide range of ethnicities, cultures, regions, social classes, and family structures. At the other extreme, parenting that is indifferent, neglectful, or abusive has been shown consistently to have harmful effects on the adolescent's mental health and development, leading to depression and a variety of behavior problems, including, in cases of physical abuse, aggression toward others.

The Power of Authoritative Parenting

Why is authoritative parenting so consistently associated with healthy child and adolescent development? First, authoritative parents provide an appropriate balance between restrictiveness and autonomy, giving the child opportunities to develop self-reliance but providing the sorts of standards, limits, and guidelines that developing individuals need. Authoritative parents, for instance, are more likely to give children more independence gradually as they get older, which helps children develop self-reliance and self-assurance. Because of this, authoritative parenting promotes the development of and enhances their ability to withstand a variety of potentially negative influences, including life stress and exposure to antisocial peers.

Second, because authoritative parents are more likely to engage their children in verbal give-and-take, they are likely to promote the sort of intellec-

tual development that provides an important foundation for the development of psychosocial competence. Family discussions in which decisions, rules, and expectations are explained help the child to understand social systems and social relationships. This understanding plays an important part in the development of reasoning abilities, role taking, moral judgment, and empathy.

Finally, because authoritative parenting is based on a warm parent-child relationship, adolescents are more likely to identify with, admire, and form strong attachments to their parents, which leaves them more open to their parents' influence. Adolescents who have had warm and close relationships with their parents are more likely, for example, to have similar attitudes and values. Adolescents who are raised by indifferent parents, in contrast, often end up having friends their parents disapprove of, including those involved in antisocial activity.

Cultural Differences in Parenting

A number of researchers have asked whether parents from different ethnic groups vary in their child rearing and whether the relation between parenting and child and adolescent outcomes is the same across different ethnic groups. These, of course, are two different questions: The first concerns average differences between groups in their approaches to parenting (e.g., whether ethnic minority parents are firmer than white parents), whereas the second concerns the correlation between parenting practices and child adjustment in different groups (e.g., whether the effect of firmness is the same in ethnic minority families as it is in white families).

In general, researchers find that authoritative parenting is less prevalent among African-American, Asian-American, or Hispanic families than among European-American families, no doubt reflecting the fact that parenting practices are often linked to cultural values and beliefs. Nevertheless, even though authoritative parenting is less common in ethnic minority families, its *effects* on adolescent adjustment are beneficial in all ethnic groups. In other words, ethnic minority youngsters for the most part benefit just as much from parenting that is responsive and demanding as do their nonminority peers.

Research has also indicated that authoritarian parenting is more prevalent among ethnic minority than among white families, even after taking ethnic differences in socioeconomic status into account. As opposed to research on authoritative parenting, however, which suggests comparable effects across ethnic groups, research on authoritarian parenting indicates that the adverse effects of this style of parenting may be greater among white youngsters than among their ethnic minority counterparts. Several explanations have been offered for this finding.

First, some writers have suggested that because ethnic minority families are more likely to live in dangerous communities, authoritarian parenting, with its emphasis on control, may not be as harmful and may even carry some benefits. Second, as several researchers (Ruth Chao, 1994; Nancy Gonzales, Ana Mari Cauce, and Craig Mason, 1996) have pointed out, the distinction between "authoritative" versus "authoritarian" parenting may not always make sense when applied to parents from other cultures. For example, nonwhite parents frequently combine a very high degree of restrictiveness (like white authoritarian parents) with warmth (like white authoritative parents). If they focus too much on parents' strictness when observing family relationships, European-American researchers may mislabel other ethnic groups' approaches to child rearing (which appear very controlling, but which are neither aloof nor hostile) as authoritarian.

In the last years of the twentieth century, new models of parenting began to emerge, which attempted to move beyond the traditional, often stale, debates between those who believe that parents are relatively impotent in the face of genetic and non-familial influence on child development and those who believe that parents' influence is limitless. These new models emphasize the importance of studying parenting as a bidirectional process, in which parents both influence and are influenced by their child, and as an embedded process, in which a range of forces in the proximal and distal environment influence the parent-child relationship. New research on parenting examines such questions as whether and in what ways the child's temperament moderates the impact of certain types of parenting on child adjustment; whether and how the impact of parenting varies across neighborhood and community contexts; and whether and through what processes the influence of parents on their children is itself affected by the other settings in which the child spends time, such as the peer group, day-care center, or classroom.

See also: ADOLESCENT PEER CULTURE, *subentry on* PARENTS' ROLE; PARENTAL INVOLVEMENT IN EDU-CATION; PARENTING, *subentries on* HIGH-RISK NEIGHBORHOODS, INFLUENCE OF PARENTS' LEVEL OF EDUCATION, INFLUENCE ON CHILD'S EDUCATIONAL ASPIRATIONS AND ATTAINMENT.

BIBLIOGRAPHY

BAUMRIND, DIANA. 1971. "Current Patterns of Parental Authority." *Developmental Psychology Monograph* 4(1), part 2.

CHAO, RUTH. 1994. "Beyond Parental Control and Authoritarian Parenting Style: Understanding Chinese Parenting through the Cultural Notion of Training." *Child Development* 65:1111–1119.

COLLINS, W. ANDREW, et al. 2000. "Contemporary Research on Parenting: The Case for Nature and Nurture." *American Psychologist* 55:218–232.

DARLING, NANCY, and STEINBERG, LAURENCE. 1993. "Parenting Style as Context: An Integrative Model." *Psychological Bulletin* 113:487–496.

GONZALES, NANCY; CAUSE, ANA MARI; and MASON, CRAIG. 1996. "Interobserver Agreement in the Assessment of Parental Behavior and Parent-Adolescent Conflict: African American Mothers, Daughters, and Independent Observers." *Child Development* 67:1483–1498.

HARRIS, JUDITH R. 1998. *The Nurture Assumption: Why Children Turn Out the Way They Do.* New York: Free Press.

STEINBERG, LAURENCE. 2001. "We Know Some Things: Adolescent-Parent Relationships in Retrospect and Prospect." *Journal of Research on Adolescence* 11:1–20.

STEINBERG, LAURENCE, et al. 1994. "Over-Time Changes in Adjustment and Competence Among Adolescents from Authoritative, Authoritarian, Indulgent, and Neglectful Families." *Child Development* 65:754–770.

LAURENCE STEINBERG

HIGH-RISK NEIGHBORHOODS

Avenues of inquiry regarding successful parenting in high-risk neighborhoods, particularly as it relates to students' ability to succeed in school, include the following: How do researchers define "high-risk," and how does the concept differ from "disadvantaged"? What is known about the socio-demographic conditions associated with individuals and neighborhoods characterized by "risk"?

To answer these questions, three intersecting lenses of analysis are examined: (1) individual: parenting and resilience; (2) community: social capital and capacity; and (3) interinstitutional: ecology of schooling. The discussion focuses upon the elements associated with educational management functions among families in high-risk neighborhoods.

Definition of "At-Risk"

The concept of a high-risk neighborhood is derived from the set of social and economic conditions that place individuals "at-risk" of failure, or of encountering significant problems related to employment, education, self-sufficiency, or a healthy lifestyle. At-risk conditions include both environmental or community characteristics, such as crime and limited employment opportunities, and individual qualities, such as poverty and low educational attainment. The problems or failures encountered by those labeled at-risk are oriented toward the future but linked to current conditions.

The understanding that interactions between particular environmental and individual characteristics may lead to a heightened risk of negative outcomes is rooted in the health and medical literature, and is widely examined in studies of social stratification, educational inequality, and social policy. Common arguments, such as those of sociologists Karl Alexander and Doris Entwisle, among others, suggest that individuals "disadvantaged" by low socioeconomic status are more susceptible to adverse environmental or community conditions, such as unsafe housing and poor quality schooling. Decades of social science research provide compelling evidence that the extent and concentration of neighborhood poverty and the presence (or absence) of affluent neighbors are associated with an array of outcomes, including rates of teenage pregnancy and school dropout. But policymakers and social scientists also underscore the finding that in socially depleted neighborhoods, residents are often constrained in their efforts to transmit positive values and productive norms because of a lack of community structure and effective social controls.

High-Risk Neighborhoods

Historically, neighborhoods have functioned as the social, political, and cultural webbing for families and children. This context links families and individuals to a set of norms, routines, and traditions. The social scripts embedded in the geography and culture of the neighborhood, if well known and well defined, become institutionalized practices for children and adults. Social actions flow from perceptions of safety and opportunity, expectations regarding appropriate parenting styles and child behavior, norms regarding home maintenance and respect for property. The neighborhood environment defines the formation of particular social networks among families and the levels of trust, familiarity, and face-to-face engagement among members.

Clusters of interlocking and corrosive conditions are persistent in high-risk neighborhoods, and are evidenced by the dense and dilapidated housing, a real and constant threat of violent crime, inadequate and inaccessible health care, a lack of employment opportunities that pay a living wage, and unreliable and limited public transportation. These concrete indicators of poverty and social isolation give rise to an insidious and entrenched culture of fear, disconnection, and distrust in high-risk neighborhoods. Families may be paralyzed by fear of gangs and guns. Omnipresent drug traffic and a constant threat of victimization minimize opportunities for interdependence and delimit social interaction among neighbors within the community. High transience rates in these neighborhoods lead to blocks of unstable and abandoned housing.

How does this social fabric influence children's well-being, particularly their success in schooling, when the population is so heavily marked by concentrated poverty, unemployment, low levels of education, and large numbers of struggling, single parents? How is a parent's pattern of involvement in home- and school-based learning activities affected by these neighborhood-level conditions—beyond individual characteristics (income, education, family structure)? These community-level conditions frame the challenging conditions for parents engaged in managing their children's educational experiences at home and at the school site. Researchers agree that these out-of-school environments constitute vital components that are deeply connected but external to students' experiences in formal school settings.

Resiliency and Community Capacity

Although it is clear that certain family conditions are associated with higher rates of poverty—low parent education, young parental age, and single parent status—it is less well understood how parenting practices in circumstances of poverty may overcome or mediate these "high-risk" conditions to produce successful educational outcomes for children. Emerging research findings point to the important role of resiliency in guiding the actions of individuals. Resiliency research refers to a long tradition of studies aimed at understanding how individuals or groups overcome high-risk conditions, such as poverty, or succeed despite severely adverse family situations, such as an alcoholic or abusive parent.

Certain elements present in the individual or community, known as "protective factors" function to assist people in high-risk environments to overcome the adverse conditions. Internal protective factors include social competence (ability to form positive and productive relationships with others); problem solving (the ability to identify problems and apply appropriate resources to solving them); autonomy (an ability to act independently and with control over their environment); and sense of purpose (the disposition to set goals, persist in achieving them, and maintain a focus). These internal elements function in partnership with external protective factors to produce resiliency and positive outcomes. Thus, schools and neighborhoods that offer resiliency to individuals include the following properties: a sense of caring and heightened familiarity for individual members or students; high expectations coupled with appropriate resources to reach these goals; opportunities for meaningful participation and demands for personal responsibility.

The research literature on community capacity extends and elaborates upon the important influence that neighborhood conditions exert in shaping social action in positive ways that lead to productive outcomes among members. Robert Chaskin has identified four central elements that are often weak or tenuous in high-risk neighborhoods.

1. A sense of community or degree of connectedness among neighbors—their sense of being similarly situated socially, economically, and geographically

2. Level of commitment among neighbors who view themselves as stakeholders and assume responsibility for collective outcomes

3. A mechanism for problem identification, planning and priority-setting, and problem solving

4. Access to financial, political, and human resources

Community capacity focuses upon the significance of social interaction across individuals, organizations, and networks of organizations. A central asset required for community capacity is human capital—the skills, knowledge, and dispositions among individual members of a community that are profitable for both individuals and the neighborhood in optimizing the processes outlined in the community-building literature. As James Coleman and Thomas Hoffer note, residents in high-risk neighborhoods who fit the traditional definition of "disadvantaged," that is, are marked by low levels of education and low income, have little human capital and face challenging obstacles in their efforts to build community capacity.

Social capital bridges human capital theory, which underscores the economic value of individuals for collective purposes, and social organization theory. The capacity of neighborhoods to provide constructive assets for parents engaged in managing their children's educational success can be examined through the concepts embedded in social capital.

Social Capital

The concept of social capital emphasizes the role of organizational (e.g., school) relationships in establishing social ties between members who share similar attitudes, norms, and values instrumental in promoting a strong sense of obligation, shared expectations, and trust. These critical elements of social capital help promote trust, facilitate open and fluid communication, and produce purposeful and meaningful activities that benefit students and adults alike. Social capital is sustained when there is "a sense of community" or a set of organizational and institutional affiliations (e.g., civic, religious, professional) that bind families in stable, predictable, and enduring social ties.

The economic and social environments in high-risk neighborhoods may militate against the development and sustainability of social capital. These neighborhoods often reflect their social and economic context: scarce economic resources, unstable social networks, limited social trust, and a perceived lack of consensus on parenting. There are few after-school programs, church-related youth groups, or recreation/civic programs for children, youth, and families. Research studies of parenting practices in high-risk neighborhoods—community contexts bereft of social capital assets—describe parenting as a highly private, protected, and isolated set of activities. Under manifestly dangerous conditions, parents in high-risk neighborhoods manage risk and opportunity by adopting stringent child monitoring and youth control, or "lock-down" strategies. These individual patterns of confinement and insularity in childrearing and parenting reflect the larger, collective neighborhood dynamics. As more and more parents adopt these defensive tactics, increasing numbers of neighbors are disconnected and social networks of support dissolve.

Thus, the capacity of parents in high-risk neighborhoods to manage and promote educational success and healthy outcomes for their children is powerfully influenced by the nature of, and the ability to activate, social capital assets and community capacity-building in the neighborhood. Successful parents, that is, parents whose children are thriving socially and academically despite the distracting and disabling conditions in their neighborhood environments, demonstrate resiliency and an ability to activate internal protective factors. These parents manage to capture "scarce opportunities" in ways that suggest "super motivation" and "unusual diligence," according to Frank Furstenberg and his colleagues, who have studied urban neighborhoods and youth development for decades in Baltimore.

What role do schools play in promoting enduring social ties between families and educators in high-risk neighborhoods? Against this backdrop of distracting and disabling social contexts, how does a school community bind families in networks of support that enhance parents' abilities to promote positive educational outcomes for their children?

School Community

Research suggests that the type and strength of community in schools differentially affects the critical social connections that bond families and schools in the joint enterprise of education. This concept of community refers to two types: functional and value. Functional communities are characterized by structural consistency between generations in which social norms and sanctions arise out of the social structure itself, and both reinforce and perpetuate that structure. Functional communities exhibit a high degree of uniformity and cohesion within geographical, social, economic, and ideological boundaries. Value communities describe a collection of people who share similar values about education and childrearing but who are not a functional community; they are strangers from various neighborhoods, backgrounds, and occupations united around an educational organization—their children's school. Re-

search findings indicate that Catholic schools often reflect the elements of functional communities; magnet schools sometimes suggest the elements of a value community.

The families of students in high-risk neighborhoods, however, may possess few if any of the constitutive elements of either a functional or value community. Although public neighborhood schools a century ago served residential areas that were functional communities, social, economic, and technological changes have transformed many of these communities from enclaves of shared values and daily face-to-face talk, to somewhat disparate sets of interests and weak affiliations.

Parent Involvement

Substantial research evidence indicates the positive effects of both home- and school-based parent involvement programs for all parents, teachers, and students. Findings, such as those of Carole Ames in 1993, indicate that parent involvement enhances parents' attitudes about themselves, school, school personnel, and the role each plays in the development of the child. This increased understanding promotes greater cooperation, commitment, and trust between parents and teachers. Finally, evidence, such as that of James Comer in 1980 suggests that students' achievement and cognitive development increases when effective parent involvement practices are in place.

Most significant in the generally positive and optimistic reports on parent involvement may be the evidence that patterns of parental participation are related to differences in socioeconomic status: Higher income and more educated parents participate at higher rates than lower class parents, both in terms of school-based activities and home learning exercises. Studies have identified educative enrichment activities that are crucial for children's cognitive development and school success (reading to children, taking children to the library, attending school-based events) that middle-class parents engage in more frequently than lower class parents. Beyond the benefit of home-based activities (reading, math games, inquisitive conversation) on children's learning, there are strong indications of the connection between teachers' expectations for student performance and the actions and attitudes of parents. Decisions regarding retention/promotion and ability grouping may well hinge on teachers' perceptions of parental interest and commitment.

Research by Deborah Vandell and colleagues in 1999 suggests that parents' patterns of participation (as reported by teachers) may be an important factor in mediating the negative impact of neighborhood risk on academic performance of elementary school students. The types of involvement reported by teachers to benefit children in high-risk neighborhoods include visiting the school for discussions with teachers, supervising homework, and providing children with enrichment activities at home. Vandell and colleagues point to resilience factors evidenced among parents to explain these families' active and purposeful participation in a range of home and school-based activities that benefit their children's academic performance.

School-Linked Social Services

The critical interaction between social structure and school organization in high-risk neighborhoods is amplified by the school-linked social services movement launched more than 100 years ago and rekindled with new programmatic priorities in the late 1980s. The school-linked social services movement has triggered a shift from a model of education based upon separate spheres between home and school to an ecological perspective of family life that considers the human context of need and locates the school as the nexus for expanded social and economic services.

Rebuilding community-based groups and youth development organizations, such as neighborhood centers, recreation programs, youth groups, and after-school art and educational enrichment programs, is critical to improved family functioning in high-risk neighborhoods. The research on family functioning, poverty, and neighborhoods is clear: A multipronged community-capacity building effort is necessary to enhance the ability of parents who are embedded in a context of economic survival and social isolation. Only then can parents overcome the daunting array of formidable obstacles to manage successfully their children's educational experiences in the neighborhood and inside the classroom.

See also: ADOLESCENT PEER CULTURE, *subentry on* PARENTS' ROLE; FAMILY, SCHOOL, AND COMMUNITY CONNECTIONS; PARENTAL INVOLVEMENT IN EDUCATION; PARENTING, *subentry on* INFLUENCE ON CHILD'S EDUCATIONAL ASPIRATIONS AND ATTAINMENT.

BIBLIOGRAPHY

ALEXANDER, KARL L., and ENTWISLE, DORIS R. 1996. "Schools and Children at Risk." In *Family-School Links,* ed. Alan Booth and Judith Dunn. Mahwah, NJ: Erlbaum.

AMES, CAROLE; KHOJU, MADHAB; and WATKINS, TOM. 1993. *Parents and Schools: The Impact of School-to-Home Communications on Parents' Beliefs and Perceptions.* Baltimore, MD: Center on Families, Communities, Schools and Children's Learning, Johns Hopkins University.

BAKER, DAVID P., and STEVENSON, DAVID L. 1986. "Mothers' Strategies for Children's School Achievement." *Sociology of Education* 59:156–166.

BECHER, RHODA M. 1986. "Parent Involvement: A Review of Research and Principles of Successful Practice." In *Current Topics in Early Childhood Education,* ed. Lillian G. Katz. Norwood, NJ: Ablex.

BOOTH, ALAN, and DUNN, JUDITH. 1996. "Preface." In *Family-School Links,* ed. Alan Booth and Judith Dunn. Mahwah, NJ: Erlbaum.

BRYK, ANTHONY S.; LEE, VALERIE E.; and HOLLAND, PETER B. 1993. *Catholic Schools and the Common Good.* Cambridge, MA: Harvard University Press.

CATHEY, D. 2001. "Building Resiliency: Exploring the Link between After School Programs and Youth Resiliency." Ph.D. diss., Vanderbilt University.

CHASKIN, ROBERT J. 1999. *Defining Community Capacity: A Framework and Implications from a Comprehensive Community Initiative.* Chicago: The Chapin Hall Center for Children at the University of Chicago.

CLARK, REGINALD M. 1983. *Family Life and School Achievement: Why Poor Black Children Succeed or Fail.* Chicago: University of Chicago Press.

COLEMAN, JAMES. 1987. "Families and Schools." *Educational Researcher* 16:32–38.

COLEMAN, JAMES, and HOFFER, THOMAS. 1987. *Public and Private High Schools: The Impact of Communities.* New York: Basic Books.

COMER, JAMES P. 1980. *School Power.* New York: University Press.

DORNBUSCH, SANFORD M., and RITTER, PHILIP L. 1988. "Parents of High School Students: A Neglected Resource." *Educational Horizons* 66:75–77.

DRISCOLL, MARY E., and KERCHNER, CHARLES T. 1999. "The Implications of Social Capital for Schools, Communities and Cities: Educational Administration as if a Sense of Place Mattered." In *Handbook of Research on Educational Administration,* ed. Joseph Murphy and Karen S. Louis. San Francisco: Jossey-Bass.

EPSTEIN, JOYCE L. 1987. "Toward a Theory of Family-School Connections: Teacher Practices and Parent Involvement." In *Social Intervention: Potential and Constraints,* ed. Klaus Hurrelmann, Franz Kaufmann, and Friedrich Losel. New York: DeGruyter.

EPSTEIN, JOYCE L., and DAUBER, SUSAN L. 1991. "School Programs and Teacher Practices of Parent Involvement in Inner-City Elementary and Middle Schools." *Elementary School Journal* 91:289–303.

FURSTENBERG, FRANK F. 1993. "How Families Manage Risk and Opportunities in Dangerous Neighborhoods." In *Sociology and the Public Agenda,* ed. William J. Wilson. Newbury Park, CA: Sage.

GOODSON, BARBARA D., and HESS, ROBERT P. 1975. *Parents as Teachers of Young Children.* Washington, DC: Bureau of Educational Personnel Development, Department of Health, Education, and Welfare, Office of Education.

HENDERSON, ANNE. 1981. *Parent Participation–Student Achievement: The Evidence Grows.* Columbia, MD: National Committee for Citizens in Education.

KOZOL, JONATHAN. 1995. *Amazing Grace.* New York: Crown.

LAREAU, ANNETTE. 1989. *Home Advantage.* New York: Falmer.

NATRIELLO, GARY; MCDILL, EDWARD L.; and PALLAS, AARON M. 1990. *Schooling Disadvantaged Children.* New York: Teachers College Press.

PUTNAM, ROBERT. 1995. "Bowling Alone." *Journal of Democracy* 6(1):65–78.

RICH, DOROTHY. 1987. *Schools and Families: Issues and Actions.* Washington, DC: National Endowment of the Arts Press.

SCHORR, LISBETH B. 1997. *Common Purpose.* New York: Doubleday.

SCOTT-JONES, DIANE. 1987. "Mother-as-Teacher in the Families of High- and Low-Achieving Low-Income Black First-Graders." *Journal of Negro Education* 56:21–34.

SMREKAR, CLAIRE. 1996. *The Impact of School Choice and Community.* Albany, NY: State University of New York Press.

SMREKAR, CLAIRE, and MAWHINNEY, HANNE B. 1999. "Integrated Services: Challenges in Linking Schools, Families, and Communities." In *Handbook of Research on Educational Administration,* ed. Joseph Murphy and Karen S. Louis. San Francisco: Jossey-Bass.

STEVENSON, DAVID L., and BAKER, DAVID P. 1987. "The Family-School Relation and the Child's School Performance." *Child Development* 58:1348–1357.

VANDELL, DEBORAH; SHUMOW, LEE; and POSNER, JILL. 1999. "Risk and Resilience in the Urban Neighborhood." *Merrill-Palmer Quarterly* 45:2.

WANG, MARGARET C., and GORDON, EDMUND W., eds. 1994. *Educational Resilience in Inner-City America.* Hillsdale, NJ: Erlbaum.

WANG, MARGARET C.; HAERTEL, GENEVA D.; and WALBERG, HERBERT J. 1996. "Educational Resilience in Inner-City America." In *Strategies for Improving Education in Urban Communities,* ed. Edmund W. Gordon and Maynard C. Reynolds. Philadelphia: Temple University Center for Research in Human Development and Education.

WERNER, EMMY E., and SMITH, RUTH S. 1982. *Vulnerable but Invincible: A Longitudinal Study of Resilient Children and Youth.* New York: McGraw-Hill.

WERNER, EMMY E., and SMITH, RUTH S. 1992. *Overcoming the Odds: High Risk Children from Birth to Adulthood.* Ithaca, NY: Cornell University Press.

WILSON, WILLIAM J. 1987. *The Truly Disadvantaged.* Chicago: University of Chicago Press.

ZILL, NICHOLAS, and NORD, CHRISTINE W. 1994. *Running in Place.* Washington, DC: Child Trends.

CLAIRE SMREKAR

INFLUENCE OF PARENTS' LEVEL OF EDUCATION

Traditionally, family status variables such as parents' level of education have been regarded as predictors of children's academic achievement. Increasingly, research has suggested that, rather than having a direct association with children's academic achievement, parents' level of education is part of a larger constellation of psychological and sociological variables influencing children's school outcomes.

Attendant on higher levels of education may be access to resources, such as income, time, energy, and community contacts, that allow for greater parental involvement in a child's education. Thus, the influence of parents' level of education on student outcomes might best be represented as a relationship mediated by interactions among status and process variables.

The literature also suggests that level of education influences parents' knowledge, beliefs, values, and goals about childrearing, so that a variety of parental behaviors are indirectly related to children's school performance. For example, higher levels of education may enhance parents' facility at becoming involved in their children's education, and also enable parents to acquire and model social skills and problem-solving strategies conducive to children's school success. Thus, students whose parents have higher levels of education may have an enhanced regard for learning, more positive ability beliefs, a stronger work orientation, and they may use more effective learning strategies than children of parents with lower levels of education.

While many theorists and researchers argue that student attributes conducive to achievement are deeply rooted in processes of socialization, such as learning through observation of parental modeling, others contend that through their personal qualities, children actively shape the parenting they receive: Parents socialize their children, but children also influence their parents. Supporting both theoretical perspectives is research indicating that the combination of learning behavior and intelligence exceeds the contributions of any single source in predicting children's scholastic achievement.

Parents with higher levels of education are also more likely to believe strongly in their abilities to help their children learn. A recent study exploring the relationships between level of parent education, parent self-efficacy, children's academic abilities, and participation in a Head Start program found that level of parent education and program participation was significantly related to parental self-efficacy. In turn, parental self-efficacy beliefs significantly predicted children's academic abilities.

However, examinations across varied cultural and ethnic groups within the United States suggest that level of education does not appear to determine the value parents place on education, their interest in their children's schooling or their aspirations for their children's academic success. For example, in a 1997 study comparing the relative value of varied predictors of parental involvement, Thomas Watkins found that parents' efficacy for involvement and educational goals for their children were stronger predictors of school success than parental level of education and ethnicity. Additionally, this study found that teacher communications to parents predicted parental involvement, suggesting that, regardless of education level, parents need encouragement from educators to become involved in their children's education.

In sum, it appears that process variables, or factors susceptible to the influence of parents, their children, and school personnel (e.g., educational expectations, level of involvement, child attributes conducive to achievement, and teacher invitations for parental involvement) are more predictive of children's school success than status variables such as parental level of education. This is an important conclusion, for while educators and researchers cannot influence the status of students' families, they may improve students' educational outcomes by influencing selected mediating process variables.

See also: PARENTING, *subentries on* HIGH-RISK NEIGHBORHOODS, INFLUENCE ON CHILD'S EDUCATIONAL ASPIRATIONS AND ATTAINMENT, OVERVIEW.

BIBLIOGRAPHY

BAUMRIND, DIANA. 1989. "Rearing Competent Children." In *Child Development Today and Tomorrow,* ed. William Damon. San Francisco: Jossey-Bass.

CLARK, REGINALD. 1983. *Family Life and School Achievement: Why Poor Black Children Succeed of Fail.* Chicago: University of Chicago Press.

HESS, ROBERT D., and HOLLOWAY, SUSAN D. 1984. "Family and School as Educational Institutions." In *Review of Child Development Research,* Vol. 7: *The Family,* ed. Ross D. Parke. Chicago: University of Chicago Press.

HOOVER-DEMPSEY, KATHLEEN V., and SANDLER, HOWARD M. 1997. "Why Do Parents Become Involved in Their Children's Education?" *Review of Educational Research* 67(1):3–42.

LAREAU, ANNETTE. 1989. *Home Advantage: Social Class and Parental Intervention in Elementary Education.* New York: Falmer Press.

McGILLICUDDY-DeLISI, ANN V. 1992. "Parents' Beliefs and Children's Personal-Social Development." In *Parental Belief Systems: The Psychological Consequences for Children,* ed. Irving E. Sigel, Ann V. McGillicuddy-De Lisi, and Jacqueline J. Goodnow. Hilllsdale, NJ: Erlbaum.

SCARR, SANDRA, and McCARTNEY, KATHLEEN. 1983. "How People Make Their Own Environments: A Theory of Genotype-Environment Effects." *Child Development* 54:424–435.

SCHAEFER, BARBARA A., and McDERMOTT, PAUL A. 1999. "Learning Behavior and Intelligence as Explanations for Children's Scholastic Achievement." *Journal of School Psychology* 37(3):299–313.

SCHUNK, DALE H., and ZIMMERMAN, BARRY J. 1997. "Social Origins of Self-Regulatory Competence." *Educational Psychologist* 32(4):195–208.

SEEFELDT, CAROL; DENTON, KRISTIN; GALPER, ALICE; and YOUNOSZAI, TINA. 1999. "The Relation between Head Start Parents' Participation in a Transition Demonstration, Education, Efficacy and Their Children's Academic Abilities." *Early Childhood Research Quarterly* 14(1):99–109.

STEINBERG, LAURENCE; ELMEN, JULIE; and MOUNTS, NINA. 1989. "Authoritative Parenting, Psychosocial Maturity and Academic Success among Adolescents." *Child Development* 60:1424–1436.

WATKINS, THOMAS J. 1997. "Teacher Communications, Child Achievement and Parent Traits in Parent Involvement Models." *Journal of Educational Research* 91(1):3–14.

JOAN M. T. WALKER
CLAIRE SMREKAR

INFLUENCE ON CHILD'S EDUCATIONAL ASPIRATIONS AND ATTAINMENT

A considerable body of research conducted within the United States and across countries has overwhelmingly demonstrated the profound influence of parents' beliefs and behaviors on children's educational aspirations and academic achievement. What remains unclear is how parental belief systems are transmitted to and manifested in children, and how belief systems function among families of varied socioeconomic and ethnic backgrounds.

Effects of Socialization

Many theorists and researchers regard the development of student beliefs and behaviors conducive to achievement (e.g., belief in one's ability, effective learning strategy use, motivation for academic tasks, strong work orientation) as the product of socialization processes. In a 1996 study, Manuel Martinez-Pons tested a theoretical model indicating that parental belief and behavior systems induce their children's educational aspirations—through parental modeling of attitudes and strategies, encouragement and facilitation of academically related goals and activities, and reinforcement or rewarding of student achievement.

Examples of specific parental behaviors that may influence children's educational aspirations can be found in recent reviews of parental involvement in homework. This literature suggests that parents use a wide array of cognitive and social strategies to facilitate their children's learning. These strategies range from simple efforts such as creating a physical space for completing homework and providing general oversight and encouragement of the homework process to interacting with the child's school or teacher about homework and engaging in homework tasks with the child. Parents also appear to use more sophisticated strategies that are designed to create a "fit" between a particular task and the child's abilities (e.g., breaking tasks into discrete, manageable parts), support children's understanding of specific homework tasks (e.g., helping the child organize personal thinking about the assignment), and support their understanding of strategies conducive to achievement (e.g., developing problem-solving skills).

Parenting Styles

In addition to their involvement in specific aspects of their children's education, styles of parenting also affect children's attitudes toward academic achievement. For example, adolescents who described their parents as "warm, democratic, and firm" (i.e., a parenting style characterized as *authoritative parenting*) were more likely than their peers to develop positive attitudes toward and beliefs about their achievement. These results, however, were true for a predominantly white middle-class to upper-middle-class population. Investigation of links between parenting practices and academic achievement among varied ethnic groups have suggested that the relationship between parenting style and achievement is more complex.

Students' educational aspirations appear to be influenced not only by parents, but also by peers. For example, Laurence Steinberg, Sanford Dornbusch, and B. Bradford Brown (1992) found that high-achieving white students benefited from the combination of authoritative parenting and peer support for achievement, while lower-achieving Hispanic students suffered from a combination of *authoritarian* parenting (characterized by high demands and low warmth) and low peer support. For African-American students, the benefits of authoritative parenting appeared to be offset by low peer support for achievement, while the negative consequences on Asian-American students of authoritarian parenting were tempered by peer support.

Theories of Influence

The combined influence of parents and peers supports theorists who argue that parents' educational aspirations for their children, and children's own aspirations, stem from socially constructed roles. *Role theory* suggests that beliefs are derived from expectations held by groups for the behavior of its individual members (e.g., a family's expectations for a child's academic achievement). Roles are also sets of behaviors characteristic of specific kinds of group members (e.g., minority elementary-school students). As such, role construction involves three interactive processes: (1) structural demands (i.e., What do others expect of me?), (2) personal role conceptions (i.e., What do I expect of myself?), and (3) role behavior (i.e., What do I/should I do?). Put simply, *role* can be characterized by two components: beliefs individuals hold and actions that individuals take.

Because it accounts for interactions among varied psychological and sociological factors experienced by members of different races, social classes, and ethnicities, role theory is a valuable tool for explaining the conflicting evidence surrounding parents' influence on children's educational aspirations. Further, some researchers speculate that understanding how parental roles are constructed may enhance educators' abilities to effectively involve parents in their children's education, and thus enhance student outcomes.

Another useful theoretical tool for disentangling differential patterns of parental belief and behavior systems is John U. Ogbu's *cultural ecological theory.* From this perspective, within minority groups, students' choice of strategies for succeeding in school are believed to stem from their desire to take the path of least resistance to the dominant social group, and to improve their status within their own peer group. Further, Ogbu characterizes minority groups' status as voluntary (i.e., immigrant families) and involuntary (i.e., native-born families), and he contends that voluntary minorities have more social pressure to do well in school than involuntary minorities. His argument is supported by a collection of ethnographies and other qualitative studies describing the combined influence of self, peer, and parental expectations and valuing of education among immigrant students and their native-born peers.

Specifically, these studies have noted that while many immigrant students invest personal time and energy in studying and seeking extra help, what appears to drive these self-regulatory efforts is a constellation of self, peer, and parental values that place great importance on the role of education. Moreover, when voluntary and involuntary minority families are compared, the children of immigrant families appear to have higher educational aspirations and academic achievement than their native-born peers.

Compounding the difficulty in understanding how parental aspirations influence children's ability beliefs and learning behaviors is the fact that children receive and require differing levels of support and guidance from parents and peers according to their cognitive, social, and emotional development. In general, educational psychologists view the development of beliefs and behaviors conducive to achievement as a movement from largely socially regulated experiences in the early grades to more self-regulated learning experiences in middle and high school. Thus, the quality and quantity of parental influence on students' positive aspirations for achievement differ as children move from elementary to high school.

See also: PARENTAL INVOLVEMENT IN EDUCATION; PARENTING, *subentries on* HIGH-RISK NEIGHBORHOODS, INFLUENCE OF PARENTS' LEVEL OF EDUCATION, OVERVIEW.

BIBLIOGRAPHY

BIDDLE, BRUCE J. 1979. *Role Theory: Expectations, Identities, and Behavior.* New York: Academic Press.

FULIGNI, ANDREW J. 1997. "The Academic Achievement of Adolescents from Immigrant Families: The Roles of Family Background, Attitudes and Behavior."*Child Development* 68(2):351–363.

HALLE, TAMARA G.; KURTZ-COSTES, BETH; and MAHONEY, JOSEPH L. 1997. "Family Influences on School Achievement in Low-Income, African-American Children." *Journal of Educational Psychology* 89(3):527–537.

HOOVER-DEMPSEY, KATHLEEN V., and SANDLER, HOWARD M. 1997. "Why Do Parents Become Involved in Their Children's Education?" *Review of Educational Research* 67(1):3–42.

MARTINEZ-PONS, MANUAL. 1996. "Test of a Model of Parental Inducement of Academic Self-Regulation." *The Journal of Experimental Education* 64(3):213–227.

OGBU, JOHN U. 1978. *Minority Education and Caste: The American System in Cross-Cultural Perspective.* New York: Academic Press.

SCHUNK, DALE H., and ZIMMERMAN, BARRY J. 1997. "Social Origins of Self-Regulatory Competence." *Educational Psychologist* 32(4):195–208.

SINGH, KUSUM; BICKLEY, PATRICIA G.; TRIVETTE, PAUL; and KEITH, TIMOTHY Z. 1995. "The Effects of Four Components of Parental Involvement on Eighth-Grade Student Achievement: Structural Analysis of NELS-88 Data." *School Psychology Review* 24(2):299–317.

STEINBERG, LAURENCE; DORNBUSCH, SANFORD M.; and BROWN, B. BRADFORD. 1992. "Ethnic Differences in Adolescent Achievement: An Ecological Perspective." *American Psychologist* 47(6):723–729.

STEINBERG, LAURENCE; ELMEN, JULIE; and MOUNTS, NINA. 1989. "Authoritative Parenting, Psychosocial Maturity and Academic Success among Adolescents." *Child Development* 60:1424–1436.

SUAREZ-OROZCO, MARCELO M. 1989. *Central American Refugees and U.S. High Schools: A Psychosocial Study of Motivation and Achievement.* Stanford, CA: Stanford University Press.

JOAN M. T. WALKER
CLAIRE SMREKAR

PEACE EDUCATION

Peace education encompasses the key concepts of education and peace. While it is possible to define education as a process of systematic institutionalized transmission of knowledge and skills, as well as of basic values and norms that are accepted in a certain society, the concept of peace is less clearly defined. Many writers make an important distinction between positive and negative peace. Negative peace is defined as the absence of large-scale physical violence—the absence of the condition of war. Positive peace involves the development of a society in which, except for the absence of direct violence, there is no structural violence or social injustice. Accordingly, peace education could be defined as an interdisciplinary area of education whose goal is institutionalized and noninstitutionalized teaching about peace and for peace. Peace education aims to help students acquire skills for nonviolent conflict resolution and to reinforce these skills for active and responsible action in the society for the promotion of the values of peace. Therefore, unlike the concept of conflict resolution, which can be considered to be retroactive—trying to solve a conflict after it has already occurred—peace education has a more proactive approach. Its aim is to prevent a conflict in advance or rather to educate individuals and a society for a peaceful existence on the basis of nonviolence, tolerance, equality, respect for differences, and social justice.

The Development of Peace Education and Its Basic Principles

The understanding of the concept of peace has changed throughout history, and so has its role and importance in the educational system from the very beginnings of the institutionalized socialization of children. When discussing the evolution of peace education, however, there have been a few important points in history that defined its aims and actions. The end of World War I (1914–1918) brought powerful support for the need for international cooperation and understanding and helped instill a desire to include these ideas in educational systems. The League of Nations and a number of nongovernmental organizations worked together on these ideas, especially through the International Institute of Intellectual Cooperation, an organization that was the predecessor of the United Nations Educational, Scientific and Cultural Organization (UNESCO).

World War II (1939–1945) ended with millions of victims and the frightening use of atomic weapons against Japan, at Hiroshima and Nagasaki. In 1946 UNESCO was founded as an umbrella institution of the United Nations, and it was charged with planning, developing, and implementing general changes in education according to the international politics of peace and security. The statute of this organization reinforced the principle of the role of education in the development of peace, and a framework was created for including and applying the principles of peace in the general world education systems. The cold war division of the world after World War II and the strategy of the balance of fear between the so-called West and East blocs redirected the peace efforts. The peace movement began concentrating on stopping the threat of nuclear war, halting the arms race, and encouraging disarmament. Somewhat parallel to this, the issues of environmental protection and development found their place in peace education programs. The contemporary sociopolitical environment (particularly the events in eastern Europe since the early 1990s, the fear of terrorism, and the increasing gap between developed and undeveloped countries) has created new challenges for the understanding of peace and for the development of the underlying principles of responsibility and security.

A 1996 book by Robin Burns and Robert Aspeslagh showed that the field and the themes that are included in peace education are diverse. The diversity is evident in theoretical approaches, underlying philosophies, basic methodology, and goals. Within the field of peace education, therefore, one can find a variety of issues, ranging from violence in schools to international security and cooperation, from the conflict between the developed world and the undeveloped world to peace as the ideal for the future, from the question of human rights to the teaching of sustainable development and environmental protection. A critic could say that the field is too wide and that peace education is full of people with good intentions but without a unique theoretical framework, firm methodology, and an evaluation of the outcomes of the practical efforts and programs of peace education. Some within the field would generally agree with this criticism. Nevertheless, the importance of accepting the specific situations in which programs for peace are being implemented and held should be emphasized. Owing to these specifics, difficulties emerge when one tries to define the unique approach, methodology, and evaluation of the efficiency of applied programs. The complex systems of society, the circumstances, and the context make the peace education field very active and diverse.

Peace Education Discrepancies: Individual, Group Conflict

In the active process of achieving positive peace, peace education is faced with a few basic discrepancies: discrepancy between the individual and the group, discrepancy between groups within one society or from different societies, and the discrepancy of conflict as an imbalance of different interests that need to be resolved without violence.

Discrepancies between individual and group. The modern liberal theory puts the individual's equality, values, and rights in the center of a successfully functioning society. This basic thesis is the beginning of the philosophy and practical protection of human rights. From the individual psychological point of view one thinks in terms of educating a complete person. In the educational system this does not mean transmitting only the facts, but it includes the complete social, emotional, and moral development of an individual; the development of a positive self-concept and positive self-esteem; and the acquisition of knowledge and skills to accept responsibility for one's own benefit as well as for the benefit of society. The development of a positive self-concept is the foundation for the development of sympathy for others and building trust, as well as the foundation for developing awareness of interconnectedness with others. In that sense a *social individual* is a starting point and a final target of peace education efforts.

Discrepancies between groups. People are by nature social beings, fulfilling their needs within society. Many social psychologists believe that there is a basic tendency in people to evaluate groups they belong to as more valuable than groups they do not belong to. This ingroup bias is the foundation of stereotypes, negative feelings toward outgroups, prejudices, and, finally, discrimination. In the psychological sense, the feeling of an individual that his or her group is discriminated against, or that he or she as an individual is discriminated against just for belonging to a particular group, leads to a sense of deep injustice and a desire to rectify the situation. Injustice and discrimination do not shape only the psychological world of an individual but also shape the collective world of the group that is discriminated against—shaping the group memory that is transmitted from generation to generation and that greatly influences the collective identity. Belonging to a minority group that is discriminated against could have a series of negative consequences on the psychological and social functioning of its members, for example, leading to lower academic achievement or negatively influencing the self-concept and self-esteem. Therefore, peace education is dealing with key elements of individual and group identity formed by historical and cultural heritage, balancing the values of both of these, and trying to teach people how to enjoy their own rights without endangering the rights of others, and especially how to advocate for the rights of others when such rights are threatened. This motivating element of defense and advocating for the rights of others is the foundation of shared responsibility for the process of building peace.

Conflict and its role in peace education. Conflict is a part of life, and its nature is neither good nor bad. On the interpersonal and intergroup level, conflict describes an imbalance or an existence of difference between the needs and interests of two sides. It becomes negative only when the answer to a conflict is aggression. It is possible, however, to resolve the difference positively, by recognizing the problem and recognizing one's own needs and interests and also acknowledging the needs of the opposing sides. In this way, constructive nonviolent conflict resolutions are possible. An important aspect of conflict is that it includes potential for change, and it is in this context that peace education addresses the issues of conflict and conflict resolution by teaching students how to take creative approaches to the conflict and how to find different possibilities for the conflict resolution. Thus students gain knowledge and skills that encourage personal growth and development, contribute to self-esteem and respect of others, and develop competence for a nonviolent approach to future conflict situations.

Peace Education in Schools

From the very beginnings of the development of systematic peace education, there has been discussion about whether it should be added as a separate program in the schools, or if the principles of peace education should be applied through the regular school subjects. The variety of approaches and attitudes on what peace education actually is leads to the introduction of a series of titles, such as multicultural training, education for democracy and human rights, and education for development. Many in the field, however, believe that the implementation of *principles* of peace education into the institutionalized educational system is a better approach, especially within the subjects encompassing the cultural heritage of the dominant society and the ethnic groups belonging to it. Consistent with this view, Aspeslagh in 1996 wrote about the need to internationalize national curriculum. For example, including within the curriculum the contributions of minority groups to literature, history, art, the general cultural heritage, and the development of the particular nation-state may significantly contribute to intercultural closeness and understanding.

The Principles and Theoretical Foundations of Peace Education Programs

Since the psychologist Gordon Allport formulated his well-known contact hypothesis in 1954, this theoretical framework became the most applicable principle for programs whose main goal is to change the relationships between groups in conflict. According to Allport's theory, for the intergroup contact to be successful and accomplish positive changes in attitudes and behavior, it must fulfill four basic conditions: the contact groups must be of equal status, the contact must be personal and manifold, the groups must depend on each other working for a superordinate goal, and there must be institutional support for the equality norm. The numerous research projects that tried to verify the predictions of the contact hypothesis provided contradictory results, raising serious doubts about the major cognitive, affective, and behavioral shifts that occur as a result of organized meetings between representatives of conflicting groups. Almost every new study added new conditions that must be fulfilled in order for the contact to be successful.

Even if there is a positive change in the attitude toward members of the outgroup in direct contact, there is a question of the generalization of the newly formed attitude to the other members of the outgroup. The key problem of peace education is not the interpersonal conflict but the collective conflict between groups, races, nations, or states. Therefore, the issue of transferring the positive attitudes toward members of other groups—attitudes achieved in safe environments such as classrooms, schools, workshops, and the like—to all members of the outgroup and all other outgroups remains the pivotal issue of peace education. Children learn about peace and the need for peace in safe protected environments and then return to a wider society where there is still injustice, asymmetry of power, a hierarchical structure, discrimination, and xenophobia. Therefore, each program for peace education must not only strengthen the capacity of an individual for critical thinking but also strengthen the individual's ability to resist the majority, if the majority is one that discriminates. As stated by Ervin Staub in 1999, for change to happen and spread there is a need for a *minimum mass of people* who share attitudes, a culture in which they can express those attitudes, and a society that accepts the attitudes.

Based on the contact hypothesis, a very successful technique was developed for improving the relations among groups, highly applicable as a general teaching and learning method. It is the *cooperative learning technique* in which a smaller group of students study in face-to-face interaction, cooperating to complete a common task. This technique was very successful both in lower and higher grades of elementary school, not only as a teaching method but also for creating a positive atmosphere in the classroom, reinforcing students relationships, and creating intergroup friendships.

On the other hand, based on the idea that adopting knowledge and developing skills is the basis for gaining positive attitudes and behavior, *intercultural training programs* were also developed. These basically involve a group of techniques that accept the primary notion that differences between cultures are what lead to misunderstandings and conflicts between groups. Such programs assume that information about the values, customs, and practices of the members of a different culture contributes to better understanding of others, thereby reducing prejudices, negative stereotypes, and tensions between people who belong to different cultures. Research has shown that ignorance about others plays a significant role in the development and perpetuation of prejudices. Educating students about both cultural similarities and differences is a significant factor in reducing prejudice.

Conclusion

Peace education is a diverse field that includes the theoretical, research, and practical activities of experts from many disciplines assembled in a number of professional and research associations. The best known among these is the International Peace Research Association, which was founded in 1964.

The programs of peace education exist within the academic discipline of peace studies on many universities, especially in the United States. The dissemination of research results and theoretical approaches is ensured by the existence of a number of periodicals, for example *Peace and Conflict: Journal of Peace Psychology; Journal of Peace Research;* and *Peace and Change.*. The measure of the success of these efforts will be seen in the ending of conflicts between countries and nations, in a more just distribution of goods, and in reducing the differences in economic development and life standards between the countries of the underdeveloped and developed worlds. For the culture of peace to become established, it is necessary to accept the principles of uniqueness in diversity and to establish the social norms of respect, dignity, and the rights of every individual.

See also: INDIVIDUAL DIFFERENCES.

BIBLIOGRAPHY

ALLPORT, GORDON. 1979. *The Nature of Prejudice,* unabridged 25th edition. Reading, MA: Perseus Books.

ASPESLAGH, ROBERT. 1996. "Educating for a Peace Culture." In *Three Decades of Peace Education around the World: An Anthology,* ed. Robin J. Burns and Robert Aspeslagh. New York: Garland.

BURNS, ROBIN J., and ASPESLAGH, ROBERT, eds. 1996. *Three Decades of Peace Education around the World: An Anthology.* New York: Garland.

DEUTSCH, MORTON. 1998. "Constructive Conflict Resolution: Principles, Training, and Research." In *The Handbook of Interethnic Coexistence,* ed. Eugene Weiner. New York: Continuum.

DUGAN, MÁIRE A., and CAREY, DENNIS. 1996. "Toward a Definition of Peace Studies." In *Three Decades of Peace Education around the World: An Anthology,* ed. Robin J. Burns and Robert Aspeslagh. New York: Garland.

FOLGER, JOSEPH P., and BARUCH BUSH, ROBERT A. 1994. "Ideology, Orientation to Conflict, and Mediation Discourse." In *New Directions in Mediation: Communication Research and Perspectives,* ed. Joseph P. Folger and Tricia S. Jones. Thousand Oaks, CA: Sage.

SALOMON, GAVRIEL, and NEVO, BARUCH. 2002. *Peace Education: The Concept, Principles, and Practices around the World.* New York: Erlbaum.

SHONHOLTZ, RAYMOND. 1998. "Conflict Resolution Moves East: How the Emerging Democracies of Central and Eastern Europe Are Facing Interethnic Conflict." In *The Handbook of Interethnic Coexistence,* ed. Eugene Weiner. New York: Continuum.

SIDANIUS, JIM, and PRATTO, FELICIA. 1999. *Social Dominance: An Intergroup Theory of Social Hierarchy and Oppression.* Cambridge, Eng.: Cambridge University Press.

SLAVIN, ROBERT E. 1990. *Cooperative Learning: Theory, Research, and Practice.* Needham, MA: Allyn and Bacon.

STAUB, ERVIN. 1989. *The Roots of Evil: The Origins of Genocide and Other Group Violence.* Cambridge, Eng.: Cambridge University Press.

STEPHAN, WALTER G., and WHITE STEPHAN, COOKIE. 1984. "The Role of Ignorance in Intergroup Relations." In *Groups in Contact: The Psychology of Desegregation,* ed. Norman Miller and Marilyn B. Brewer. Orlando, FL: Academic Press.

TAJFEL, HENRI, and TURNER, JOHN C. 1986. "The Social Identity Theory of Intergroup Behavior." In *Psychology of Intergroup Relations,* ed. Stephen Worchel and William G. Austin. Chicago: Nelson-Hall.

DINKA CORKALO

PEER GROUPS

See: ADOLESCENT PEER CULTURE; PEER RELATIONS AND LEARNING.

PEER RELATIONS AND LEARNING

Influences on student learning in an academic environment can be numerous and contradictory. Determining the accuracy and relevance of information from teachers, friends, and classroom materials can be overwhelming. Which classroom features an individual student attends to depends, in part, on what that student values and prioritizes.

The interactions among peers in the classroom are a normal and essential part of the learning process that influence the lifelong learning habits of students. The potential effects of peer relationships are reciprocal: Some students are more receptive than others. On one extreme, for example, is the student who values and seeks peer input on every decision; on the other is the social isolate who avoids interaction in and out of the classroom. This entry examines selected variables that can influence learners, including developmental differences, motivational and learning considerations, and the function of the classroom contexts.

Peer Relationships

In a 1953 book, Henry Stack Sullivan outlined a developmental theory describing the changes in interpersonal needs as an individual matures. He observed that elementary school students tend to work with larger peer groups, which are usually the whole class with whom the young student spends their academic days. Classroom peer groups give way to same-sex "chums" in early adolescence. These same-sex chums fit the best friend/confidant role. Late-elementary and middle school students usually confine their social activities to include these one or two friends. High school and early adulthood individuals seek out and spend time with love interests who satisfy emotional and physical intimacy needs.

With entrance into education, the influence of the family plateaus, if not decreases, as the importance of peers increases. Adolescence marks the peak of peer influence. The demands and opinions of friends can overwhelm the needs of family and, at times, can overwhelm the individuals themselves. As the individual matures biologically and cognitively, the culture of education also changes, moving the student through a system marked by a single class in early elementary school to a system of hour-long classes in middle and high school. Student peer preferences also change during these years. Friendships of two to three students give way to larger group networks.

It comes as no surprise, then, that the relative consistency of peers allows them to take precedence over academics and educators in later education. In addition to school structure, factors such as biology, home life, and increased personal responsibilities have also been explanations for students' decreased academic motivation and increased receptivity to peer influence. Whatever the causes, the subculture of the peer group can be very telling in determining students' motivation to succeed in academics.

In short, the relative influence of peers or peer groups typically increases with the age and development of the student. So, too, do the multiple functions of peers increase. A younger student may be able to find the motivation and desire to learn apart from classmates and friends, looking instead to values from home and teacher. Older students are more apt to seek out those who have similar interests and values.

Motivation, Learning, and Relationships

Age of the student is one consideration in weighing the importance and application of motivation to learn. Human relationships have varying degrees of importance in motivational and learning theories. Most approaches tend to agree, however, that students who surround themselves with peers and influences who value learning and the educational process will also value their own learning and strive to enhance their education.

Abraham H. Maslow viewed the need for love and belongingness as a step toward achievement in his hierarchy of motivation model, which he described in 1954. In this view, the deprivation of more basic needs hinders progress along the path to achievement. In Maslow's model, people must have love and belongingness issues satisfied in order to address needs of achievement. For example, a student with deprived relationship concerns will be less able to participate in classroom learning opportunities. The ability to learn is built on a foundation of comfortable relationships with others, including peers and family, and classroom learning is all about learning with and in the presence of others.

"Expectancy by value" theories define motivation as the product of the amount of success on a task that an individual expects to earn times the amount of value the individual places on the task. Thus, a task that the individual values and expects to be successful at will be motivating compared to a task with lower expected success or value. Whereas past experience can predict the expectancy aspect of this model (e.g., the student has done well on prior essay exams), the value placed on the task is more mediated by outside factors, such as peers and family (e.g., the student's opinions are respected). Related motivational theories include the incentive or rewarding aspects of motivation, which may also stem from relationships with others.

Behaviorism provides one way to explain the association between motivation to learn and peer interactions. In basic behaviorist theories, relationships between people affect learning only as much as people reinforce each other (or not) in the academic arena. For example, if the peer group encourages education and learning, then the individual student within that group will value learning, because the individual is reinforced, or rewarded, for behavior that indicates that learning is valued. Students in peer groups that do not value education lack the stimulation and reinforcement needed to encourage personal learning. These peer groups presumably stimulate and reinforce other values.

Albert Bandura's social learning theory speaks precisely to the human interactions involved in learning. Observational, or "vicarious" learning is based upon learning by watching then "modeling" or acting similarly to others. If the student views and works with people who appreciate learning by engaging in learning activities, then the student too will engage in learning and might work harder at learning. Peers with positive attitudes and behaviors toward education will allow and teach each other to set goals that include opportunities to learn and achieve. If peer models do not convey positive attitudes toward learning, then the students observing these models will not prioritize learning in their own lives. They will learn to prioritize other goals.

In 1978 Lev Vygotsky also presented ideas on the facilitation of learning through experiences mediated by other people. In his explanations, the learner cannot reach full potential without the aid of others. The processes of guiding the learner to higher stages of cognitive functioning rely on interactive human relationships. Mentors—for example, teachers or more capable peers—can raise the student's competence through the zone of proximal development (ZPD). ZPD is defined as the gap between what a student can do alone and what the student can achieve with assistance. In this view assistance is transitional, a "scaffold" that is removed when it is no longer needed and the student has internalized another's support.

In sum, varied theories agree that the values and attitudes of the peer group are essential elements in motivation and learning. Students who surround themselves with academically focused, goal-oriented peers will be more likely to appreciate, internalize, and exhibit these features themselves.

Classroom Dynamics

With consideration of these social determinants, how then can the educational process be structured to boost the learning of individuals? For younger students, providing a whole-class environment that enriches learning opportunities with teachers who model positive learning values will set the new learner on a path toward academic achievement. Encouraging elementary students to interact with peers, adults, and family members who have strong learning desires can support the students' development as learners. Although peer influences may not yet be as powerful as they will become in student achievement motivation, the effects of young students' interactions cannot be disregarded.

As the learner matures, the importance of how peers view the learner's actions and decisions may well supercede the opinions of others, possibly even the views of the learners themselves. The academic environment needs to be structured in a fashion that allows for student interaction but sets boundaries that afford pro-social behavior. Students who are concentrating on unresolved issues in their social life, whether these issues result from social isolation or from social or home crisis, will be less able to profit from classroom opportunities. Recognition of the strategic effort required to maintain classroom social and academic order can help both the learner and the teacher decide how to approach problems addressed in either domain.

Within the classroom, time and organization can be established to focus students on their learning. Pairing and grouping students by their devotion to academics, for example, may benefit all involved. Those who value learning can share their enthusiasm and act as mentors for those who have other priorities. Students who motivate themselves in nonacademic directions can view and appreciate the choices of peer learners.

These dynamics must include consideration of the types of classroom curricula. The well-known and intended analytic curriculum taught to preservice educators and recorded in the lesson plans and assignments may easily disregard the underlying informal curriculum of social and human interaction. As Mary McCaslin and Tom L. Good noted in 1996, "Learning is socially situated" (p. 642); the achievement of the student is a small part of who the student is and what she does. The responsibilities of education include helping students recognize their own place as social contributors and maximizing the resources available to them through interpersonal relationships. For example, cooperative learning and help-seeking behaviors are essential resources for students in the classroom that facilitate both student achievement and social competence. Some students and educators view help-seeking as a sign of dependence or weakness, but research supports the contention that help-seeking is a sign of social competence that increases students' chances of academic success. Negative attitudes toward help-seeking may discourage low-achieving students from approaching peers and teachers and may further isolate them. This is especially detrimental to older students.

Students are not isolated in the pursuit of knowledge. They are social beings who need to interact and establish social contacts. Social learning is as much a part of any classroom curriculum as the printed guidelines. At a minimum, the influence of peers and a student's relationships with them can be understood as a function of student age, motivation, learning, and classroom opportunities.

See also: ADOLESCENT PEER CULTURE; COOPERATIVE AND COLLABORATIVE LEARNING.

BIBLIOGRAPHY

BANDURA, ALBERT. 1996. "Multifacted Impact of Self-Efficacy Beliefs on Academic Functioning." *Child Development* 67:1,206–1,222.

ECCLES, JACQUELYNNE. 1983. "Expectancies, Values, and Academic Behaviors." In *The Development of Achievement Motivation,* ed. Janet T. Spence. Greenwich, CT: JAI Press.

ECCLES, JACQUELYNNE; MIDGLEY, CAROL; WIGFIELD, ALLAN; BUCHANAN, CHRISTY M.; REUMAN, DAVID; FLANAGAN, CONSTANCE; and MAC IVER, DOUGLAS. 1993. "Development during Adolescence: The Impact of Stage-Environment Fit on Young Adolescents' Experience in Schools and Families." *American Psychologist* 48:90–101.

GOOD, TOM L.; SLAVINGS, RICKY L.; HAREL, KATHLEEN H.; and EMERSON, HUGH. 1987. "Student Passivity: A Study of Question Asking in K–12 Classrooms." *Sociology of Education* 60:181–199.

MASLOW, ABRAHAM H. 1954. *Motivation and Personality.* New York: Harper and Row.

MCCASLIN, MARY, and GOOD, TOM. L. 1996. "The Informal Curriculum." In *The Handbook of Ed-*

ucational Psychology, ed. David C. Berliner and Robert C. Calfee. New York: American Psychological Association/Macmillan.

NEWMAN, RICHARD S., and SCHWAGER, MAHNA T. 1992. "Student Perceptions and Academic Help Seeking." In *Student Perceptions in the Classroom,* ed. Dale Schunk and Judith Meece. Hillsdale, NJ: Erlbaum.

SULLIVAN, HENRY S. 1953. *The Interpersonal Theory of Psychiatry.* New York: Norton.

VYGOTSKY, LEV. 1978. *Mind in Society: The Development of Higher Psychological Processes.* Cambridge, MA: Harvard University Press.

HEIDI LEGG BURROSS
MARY MCCASLIN

PEOPLE WITH DISABILITIES, FEDERAL PROGRAMS TO ASSIST

Programs to assist people with disabilities initiated by the federal government in the early decades of the twentieth century were designed strictly with vocational rehabilitation in mind, that is, with an emphasis on assisting men injured in military service or work-related injuries to sufficiently overcome disabling conditions to return to the work force. Other programs were developed to provide income assistance to workers who were temporarily or permanently disabled and unable to earn an income. The last decades of the twentieth century increased the magnitude of federal programs to protect the rights of people with disabilities in such areas as employment, education, public transportation, and building accessibility. (The term *disability* instead of *handicap* and the phrase *individual with a disability* instead of *individual with handicaps* reflects legislative language and accepted terminology in the late twentieth and early twenty-first centuries. As with racial and ethnic epithets, the choice of terms to apply to a person with a disability is overlaid with stereotypes, patronizing attitudes, and other emotional connotations. Many individuals with disabilities, and organizations representing such individuals, object to the use of such phrases as *handicapped person* or *the handicapped.* Congress has recognized this shift in terminology in all legislative actions since about 1990.)

Federal Vocational Rehabilitation Programs

The earliest federal programs created to develop some level of aid for people with disabilities date to the period following World War I. The Smith-Sears Veterans' Rehabilitation Act of 1918 initiated a program to vocationally rehabilitate veterans who were disabled during the war. The Smith-Fess Act of 1920 (the Civilian Vocational Rehabilitation Act) established the first broad-based federal program to provide vocational assistance to people whose disabilities were not the result of war. This program provided federal funds at a 50 percent matching rate to state rehabilitation agencies for counseling, vocational training, and job placement services for people with physical disabilities.

After the 1920s federal rehabilitation systems initially conceived to serve injured veterans expanded in magnitude. The Social Security Act of 1935 gave permanent status to these federal programs for the first time. Subsequent legislative changes expanded the nature of vocational rehabilitation programs, including the provision of medical services and prosthetic devices; creation of programs to serve people with mental disabilities, migratory workers, and disadvantaged youth; and provision of assistance to families of people with disabilities. The focus of vocational rehabilitation programs remains true to its original foundation of attaining and maintaining employment, although the definition of employment has expanded to support efforts of people with disabilities to gain access to their communities, live independently, and direct the course of their own lives.

Federal Income Support for People with Disabilities

As the United States became more industrialized and sophisticated in its understanding of the role of the federal and state governments in increasing the American standard of living, services for people with disabilities also developed beyond their original mission to include programs that provided support through direct income subsistence to individuals born with disabilities. The Social Security Act of 1935 provided funds to states to assist indigent dependent children, elderly adults, and people who are blind. In the early 1930s, people who were blind, and shortly thereafter, those who were deaf, were the first disability advocates to organize and work collectively to advance their own positions at the federal level. For this reason, the first disability-related institutions in many states, including disability-specific schools, were those that served people who were blind or deaf. While the act also initiated unemployment and old age insurance programs, it did not create a permanent program of disability insurance, although the idea was considered at the time.

As with other disability programs, amendments to the original legislation served to expand the program, in this case by removing the age limitation for eligibility and changing the definition of disability in the Social Security Act. In 1972 Congress created another federal income support program, Supplemental Security Income, that authorized uniform national benefits for people with disabilities, regardless of geographic location. Thus, the next stages in federal involvement led to the beginning of financial assistance and the right of children with disabilities to public education.

Federal Involvement in Access to Education for Children with Disabilities

Federal government involvement in educating children with disabilities generally parallels the development of federal support for elementary and secondary education as a whole. Until the 1960s elementary and secondary education was viewed almost entirely as a state and local function and federal intervention was almost nonexistent. The Elementary and Secondary Education Act (ESEA) of 1965 (Pub. L. 80-10) was amended in 1966 to specifically provide federal support for the education of children with disabilities through the creation of Title VI. Title VI authorized funds to assist states in the initiation, expansion, and improvement of programs for the education of children with disabilities. Over the next five years, interest groups representing children with disabilities amassed major political support sufficient to expand federal involvement.

The legal underpinnings of the right to education for children with disabilities stems from the civil rights movement and the landmark *Brown v. Board of Education* (1954) and the Civil Rights Acts of 1964 and 1968. By the early 1970s the foundation was established for federal legislation ensuring the special education of disabled children. Active litigation and legislative efforts enacted from 1964 to 1974 produced strong legal and political support for expanded federal oversight of the education of children with disabilities, most significantly through *Pennsylvania Association for Retarded Children (PARC) v. Commonwealth of Pennsylvania* and *Mills v. Board of Edu-*

cation of the District of Columbia. The Rehabilitation Act of 1973 provided the initial protections to children with disabilities in public schools. This act requires nondiscrimination on the basis of disability in all federally conducted and assisted programs. State and local educational agencies (i.e., public school districts) that receive federal funding are required to provide programmatic access for children and others with disabilities. The Rehabilitation Act did not mandate special education services, but set the foundation of civil rights protections for people with disabilities.

The late 1960s and early 1970s saw a dramatic increase in federal involvement for children with disabilities. In 1966 the Bureau of Education of the Handicapped was created within the Office of Education and in 1975 the Education for All Handicapped Children Act (EAHCA; Pub. L. 94-142) was enacted for the education of children with disabilities needing special education and related services. Since 1975 EAHCA, now renamed the Individuals with Disabilities Education Act (IDEA), has evolved and remains the most significant legislation for special education.

IDEA mandates "a free appropriate public education" for all children with disabilities that require special education services. All fifty states, the District of Columbia, and freely associated states accept federal funding under IDEA and are thus compelled to implement all of IDEA's requirements. IDEA specifies that children with disabilities be educated in the "least restrictive environment" with their nondisabled peers to the maximum extent appropriate. IDEA serves all eligible children with disabilities from birth through age twenty-one, and moves beyond the traditional school-age population aged five to seventeen or eighteen. IDEA extends federally mandated education to all children with disabilities from birth through age three through early intervention services and to young adults with disabilities aged eighteen to twenty-one who have not graduated with a regular high school diploma.

IDEA, together with the Rehabilitation Act of 1973 and the Americans with Disabilities Act of 1990 (ADA; Pub. L. 101-336), represent the world's most comprehensive civil rights initiatives, providing inclusion in regular educational environments for children with disabilities in public and private elementary and secondary education and for adults with disabilities in public and private colleges and universities in the United States. An exception applies to religiously affiliated or controlled schools, which may be exempt from coverage depending on the specific circumstances.

ADA extends the right to public and private education for all individuals with disabilities in previous areas not covered by federal law, such as activities open to parents or other individuals with disabilities, graduation ceremonies, parent-teacher organization meetings, plays, and adult education classes regardless of the source of funding.

See also: College Students with Disabilities; Federal Educational Activities; Special Education.

BIBLIOGRAPHY

Americans with Disabilities Act of 1990. U.S. Public Law 101-336. *U.S. Code.* Vol. 42, secs. 12101–12213 (Supp. II 1990).

Civil Rights Act of 1964. U.S. Public Law 88-352. *U.S. Code.* Vol. 42, secs. 2000 et seq.

Civil Rights Act of 1968. U.S. Public Law 90-284. *U.S. Code.* Vols. 18, 25, 42.

Education for All Handicapped Children Act of 1975. U.S. Public Law 94-142. *U.S. Code.* Vol. 20, secs. 1232, 1401, 1405–1420, 1453.

Elementary and Secondary Education Act of 1965. U.S. Public Law 80-10. *U.S. Code.* Vol. 20, secs. 2701 et seq.

Individuals with Disabilities Education Act Amendments of 1997. U.S. Public Law 105-17. *U.S. Code.* Vol. 20, secs. 1400 et seq.

Section 503 of the Rehabilitation Act of 1973, amended. 1988–1989. U.S. Public Law 93-112. *U.S. Code.* Vol. 29, secs. 791–794.

Turnbull, H. Rutherford, and Turnbull, Ann P. 2000. *Free Appropriate Public Education: The Law and Children with Disabilities.* Denver, CO: Love Publishing.

Yell, Mitchell L. 1998. *The Law and Special Education.* Upper Saddle River, NJ: Merrill/ Prentice-Hall.

INTERNET RESOURCE

Office of Special Education and Rehabilitative Services. 2001. <www.ed.gov/offices/ osers>.

Troy R. Justesen

PERSONAL AND PSYCHOLOGICAL COUNSELING AT COLLEGES AND UNIVERSITIES

College and university students must adapt to environments plagued by rapid change, ambiguity, uncertainty, and depleted support systems. Students must also cope with a myriad of personal and psychological problems that range from basic adjustment and developmental, academic and learning, and career concerns to clinical-level mental illness. Within higher education, there exists general consensus that the ubiquitous role of personal and psychological counseling is to contribute to student development, adjustment, and learning while preventing dangerous and self-defeating behavior, thus enabling the individual to thrive in the college community. The mechanisms that colleges and universities utilize to achieve this goal vary dramatically from one institution to another, depending heavily on the institution's philosophy or mission, available resources, and campus need.

American colleges and universities confront the daunting task of serving the needs of a highly diverse campus. Within this environment, personal and psychological counseling incorporates an expanded interpretation of its role and responsibility. A comprehensive view of counseling within higher education reveals a set of role domains that include psychotherapy, career, academic and learning, and educational and psychological outreach. Not all institutions of higher education share this systemic perspective. Some schools define counseling within the strict confines of academics, devoid of a mental health dimension, offering only educational, career, and developmental services. Others adopt a more inclusive perspective of counseling in higher education—one that incorporates all domains. This holistic view of counseling enables services to reach and assist a vast majority of the campus community while contributing to an environment of support and encouragement.

Psychotherapy

Students arrive on campus with personal and psychological problems centered on dysfunctional family situations; anxiety around social, academic, and career concerns; and mental health issues. For many students, transition and adjustment to college is marked by debilitating stress and anxiety. Deleterious effects result from personal and psychological problems stemming from these experiences and often manifest during the college experience, requiring psychotherapeutic attention. At an alarming rate, students are also experiencing serious mental disorders diagnosed prior to or following their admittance to college. Mood, anxiety, eating, substance, or other disorders complicate adjustment and the ability to meet personal, familial, and collegiate expectations.

The traditional-aged student typically presents developmental, career, and adjustment issues and crises. Identity development, sexuality, intimacy, relationships, substance use, grief and loss, family dysfunction, and values clarification denote challenges this group encounters. Generally, the adult returning student tackles different dilemmas, which focus on stress and time management, career and life transition and changes, family and relationship issues, and financial stress. Minority and other groups on campus require continual attention and support pertaining to such issues as racism, discrimination, marginalization, and academic and social integration.

Personal and psychological problems interfere with innumerable aspects of a student's life, causing significant impairment and distress. Attending to these mental heath concerns, psychotherapy represents a viable mechanism in providing support and guidance across cognitive, affective, and spiritual dimensions within a confidential and safe environment. Utilizing individual, group, couples, and children and family counseling opportunities, therapists attend to the whole individual. Assessment, referral, and treatment extend the mental health counselor's ability to meet students' disparate needs. Collaborations with community mental health providers, support groups, and Twelve Step programs allow students to access services the college or university does not furnish.

Academics and Learning

The general role of counseling, within the realm of academic and learning, is to improve academic proficiency. Programming and support services place considerable attention on strengthening basic reading and writing skills, while addressing issues of time management, test taking, comprehension and retention, and study strategies. With the advent of novel research aimed at enhancing campus programming and student services, diagnostic criterion and tools, supportive programs, and medication, students diagnosed with varying degrees of learning disabilities and attention-deficit disorders are better equipped to successfully matriculate and prosper in higher education. Encouraging student interactions with academic advisers, faculty, and campus learning centers significantly strengthens a student's chances of being successful and contributes to a student sense of academic and social connection.

Career Counseling

Counseling on a college and university campus inevitably involves issues encompassing career and vocational exploration. Within this domain, counseling assists individuals in selecting an area of study, choosing a career, or clarifying attributes that facilitate or detract from their present work. Exploration of personal values, goals, and characteristics, combined with assessments of career interests, enhance the student's successful transition through higher education. Facilitating student–faculty interactions represents another essential facet of career counseling. Such significant relationships are positively associated with changes in students' occupational values.

Educational and Psychological Outreach

Educational and psychological outreach is critical if college counselors desire to serve as initiators and catalysts for change on the campus and in surrounding communities. Education and prevention comprise the foundation of outreach initiatives. Via thematic presentations, decimation of educational materials, special events, and educational programs counselors effectively address topics such as stress and time management, eating disorders, substance abuse, depression, study skills, career issues, and cross-cultural adjustment.

College counseling services typically acknowledge the scope of problems for which students seek assistance, yet disagree as to the resource feasibility and the level of responsibility schools have in meeting all these counseling provisions. Balancing the needs of traditional-aged students, returning adult students, minority students, and other groups represents a challenging and resource-exhaustive process.

The prevalence of developmental and adjustment problems as well as various forms and degrees of mental illness on college and university campuses cannot be ignored. Within the context of higher education, the role counseling assumes depends largely on the specific needs of the individual and the broad requirements of the campus community. Abetting student adjustment, development, and learning, counseling provides the means for clients to explore problems related to normal developmental issues such as careers, academics and learning, relationships, and identity. For a large number of students, problems of mental illness require more intensive therapy in order to maneuver life's daily tasks and successfully meet personal, parental, and school expectations. In recognizing the comprehensive role of personal and psychological counseling in higher education, colleges and universities substantially counteract student's perception of academic, social, and personal isolation by addressing all facets of the human being.

See also: ACADEMIC ADVISING IN HIGHER EDUCATION; ADJUSTMENT TO COLLEGE; CAREER COUNSELING IN HIGHER EDUCATION; COLLEGE STUDENT RETENTION; DRUG AND ALCOHOL ABUSE, *subentry on* COLLEGE; PERSONAL AND PSYCHOLOGICAL PROBLEMS OF COLLEGE STUDENTS; STUDENT SERVICES.

BIBLIOGRAPHY

AMERICAN PSYCHIATRIC ASSOCIATION (APA). 1994. *Diagnostic and Statistical Manual of Mental Disorders,* 4th edition. Washington, DC: American Psychiatric Association.

ARCHER, JAMES, JR., and COOPER, STEWART. 1998. *Counseling and Mental Health Services on Campus: Handbook of Contemporary Practices and Challenges.* San Francisco: Jossey-Bass.

MULL, CHARLOTTE; SITLINGTON, PATRICIA L.; and ALPER, SANDRA. 2001. "Postsecondary Education for Students with Learning Disabilities: A Synthesis of the Literature." *Council for Exceptional Children* 68(1):97–118.

PASCARELLA, ERNEST T., and TERENZINI, PATRICK T. 1991. *How College Affects Students.* San Francisco: Jossey-Bass.

WALLACE, BEVERLY A.; WINSLER, ADAM; and NESMITH, PAT. 1999. "Factors Associated with Success for College Students with ADHD: Are Standard Accommodations Helping?" Paper presented at the American Education Research Association Annual Conference, Montreal, Canada.

LEIGH Z. GILCHRIST

PERSONAL AND PSYCHOLOGICAL PROBLEMS OF COLLEGE STUDENTS

An increasing amount of attention is being directed to the transition to higher education as experienced by traditional-age and adult students. It is a movement that incorporates a great deal of stress and challenge. Although some students are able to experience this transition as a challenge to personal growth, other students are overwhelmed by the changes and experience emotional maladjustment and depression.

Issues of adjustment and general development require persistent attention by campus professionals due to the immediate relevance to college success. Complex psychological histories often underpin these problems, further complicating treatment. These difficulties are often present as inefficiencies in coping with familial separation, time and stress management, basic study techniques, goal setting, relationship formation, handling emotions, and self-esteem crystallization. Personal, academic, social, and professional success depend on the student's ability to manage these aspects of their lives.

Family Dynamics

Families in the United States are experiencing significant stress and functional discourse marked by unparalleled changes in family structures. The home environment for many young people represents a place of instability and emotional upheaval where security, caring, and nurturing are depleted or nonexistent. Separation, divorce, death, or abandonment removes one or both parents from the family. The lack of attention and affection that may accompany such change adversely impacts children. Subsequent emotional and financial difficulties of a single parent household further strain the family dynamic.

Substance abuse; domestic violence; emotional, physical, and sexual abuse; and mental illness plague some families. At an alarming rate, young people enter higher education with dysfunctional family backgrounds that evoke stress and trepidation in students. For children of alcoholics, for example, the college social climate that is impressed by alcohol use produces significant anxiety as the student grapples with the personal and familial implications of watching and participating in drinking practices. It is imperative that schools recognize the existence and impact of family discourse and childhood trauma on students, and provide them with the support necessary to enable them to cope with their situations and succeed within the collegiate environment.

Depression

With a lifetime prevalence rate of 17 percent in the general population, a significant number of men and women suffer from a clinical episode of depression at some time in their lives, according to Chris Segrin and Jeanne Flora in 2000. An estimated 7 million women and 3.5 million men can be diagnosed with major depression in the United States; similar numbers are diagnosed as experiencing dysthymia, or minor depressive symptoms. College students are twice as likely to have clinical depression compared to people of similar ages and backgrounds in the workforce, according to Wayne A. Dixon and Jon K. Reid in 2000.

Depression manifests in varying degree from general symptomology to a clinical disorder. Symptoms occur in four general domains of human functioning: emotional, cognitive, physical, and behavioral, with mood disturbance being the predominant feature. Typical symptoms of depression include a change in appetite or weight, sleep, and psychomotor activity; decreased energy; feelings of worthlessness or guilt; difficulty thinking, concentrating, or making decisions; or recurrent thoughts of death or suicidal ideation. Anhedonia, or a loss of interest in activities that were once considered pleasurable, accompany social withdrawal. Depression is a risk factor for a number of other negative health outcomes including diminished immune function and poor illness recovery.

Depression constitutes a problem of enormous personal and social significance, and its impact on American college students is indisputable. Depression interferes with intra- and interpersonal processes, academic and social integration, and retention. Some depressed individuals may evince a hostile, uncooperative, and self-criticizing interpersonal style eliciting negative responses from others. Poor social skills and social acuity are thought to make people vulnerable to the onset of depressive symptomology and other psychosocial problems pursuant to the experience of negative stressful life events.

Eating Disorders

Typically developing between the ages of twelve and twenty-five, eating disorders are a life-threatening reality for 5 to 10 percent of American women and girls past puberty. An estimated 64 percent of college women exhibit some degree of eating disorder behavior, a situation that pushes the body image issue to the forefront of concern in higher education. Although most people diagnosed with anorexia or bulimia nervosa are women, men also suffer from these disorders.

Problematic eating behavior is best conceptualized on a continuum that illustrates the range of eating behavior from normal to weight-preoccupied to chronic dieter to subthreshold bulimia/anorexia and full bulimia/anorexia. Compulsive dieting and overeating behaviors fail to meet the clinical criteria for a label of disorder. These practices, however, often intensify and reach eating disorder status.

Eating disorders stem from a complex interaction of biological, psychological, sociological, spiritual, and cultural factors. American culture's emphasis on thinness and physical beauty, the prevalence of dieting, myths about food and nutrition, and perfectionistic expectations contribute to this growing problem. Eating disorders often start when an individual experiences a major problem and feels helpless and out of control. It is not uncommon for a student suffering from an eating disorder to report a personal or family history of eating or mood disorders. They typically possess a character profile of achievement-oriented personality, low self-esteem, and drive for perfectionism. Obsession, loneliness, anxiety, depression, guilt, fear of sexual maturation, and feelings of inadequacy are psychological correlates often associated with problematic eating behaviors.

Substance Use

Alcohol, tobacco, and other drug use on college and university campuses poses tremendous concern for parents, students, higher education professionals, governmental officials, and the general community. No school is immune to substance use and resulting adverse consequences. Alcohol, tobacco, and marijuana are the most commonly used drugs on college campuses, but this use encompasses drugs of varying forms including amphetamine, caffeine, cocaine, hallucinogen, inhalants, opioid, phencyclidine, sedative, hypnotic, anxiolytic, steroids, and polysubstances. An essential feature of substance abuse is a maladaptive pattern of substance use leading to recurrent and clinically significant impairment or adverse consequences. Substance use and abuse are characterized by noted inefficiencies in life functioning, impaired relationships, high-risk behavior, and recurrent legal troubles. Substance dependency emerges from repeated use of the substance despite significant problems related to its use.

Substance abuse appears to be etiologically linked to "complex interactions of genetic predisposition, psychological vulnerability, and sociocultural influences" (Archer and Cooper, p. 77). Extensive family history of addiction, poor self-esteem, negative emotional orientation, and few coping skills actively play a role in substance dependency. Skewed perceptions of social norms, peer values and behaviors, and pre-college substance use influence a student's use patterns. Many students who abuse substances are unready to recognize how their life is being adversely affected by their use, and believe substance use to be a part of normal development and experimentation.

The negative effects of student substance use are not campus centered, and impact both the campus and wider communities. Substance use is associated with increased absenteeism from class and poor academic performance. The majority of injuries, accidents, vandalism, sexual assaults and rape, fighting, and other crime on- and off-college campus are linked to alcohol and other drug use. Unplanned and uninhibited sexual behavior may lead to pregnancy, exposure to sexually transmitted diseases, and HIV/AIDS. Driving under the influence, tragic accidents, alcohol poisoning, overdosing, and even death from accidents, high-risk behaviors, and suicide carry tremendous, life-threatening implications for all involved. Tobacco use is associated with severe health risks and illness, physical inefficiency, and even death. Fires caused by careless smoking practices place all students at risk.

Students who abstain, use legally, or use in moderation often suffer secondhand effects from the behaviors of students who use substances in excess. Nonbinging and abstaining students may become the targets of insults and arguments, physical assaults, unwanted sexual advances, vandalism, and humiliation. Sleep depravation and study interruption results when these students find themselves caring for intoxicated students.

Other Psychological Disorders

Summer M. Berman and colleagues estimated in 2000 that 37 percent of Americans between the ages of fifteen and twenty-four, many of whom are college students, have a diagnosable mental illness. The fact that the age of onset for many major illnesses is the years from eighteen to twenty-four, the range in which most traditional-age students fall, further complicates the matter. Higher education must realize that a large percentage of college students are, or will be, affected by mental illness. These disorders range from mild and short-lived to chronic and severe, including such illnesses as depression, anxiety, schizophrenia, and bipolar disorder, and appear at varying rates on campuses.

The early-twenty-first-century student brings a set of experiences and personal and psychological problems that may predispose them to mental illness. It is not unusual for a college counseling and mental health center to diagnose students with anxiety, mood, eating, impulse-control, personality, substance-related or other mental disorders. Students may enter college with challenges originating from learning, attention-deficit, and disruptive behavior disorders that are first diagnosed in infancy, childhood, or adolescence. Dual diagnosis further complicates students' social and academic integration and success.

If detected, most mental illnesses are treatable or manageable, allowing the individual to proceed effectively through life's daily routines. Unfortunately, many cases are not diagnosed or treated, and the consequences for the college student are life altering. Many students diagnosed with mental illness withdraw from college before earning a bachelor's degree; however, with proper attention and support they may have been successful in the collegiate environment.

Campus Services

The services that institutions provide to address students' personal and psychological problems depend heavily on the school's philosophy, available resources, and campus need. Colleges and universities of all types should develop and implement confidential services that span multiple policy arenas in order to sufficiently address these problems. Creating partnerships with various facets of the institution, such as the college counseling and mental health center, student health services, women's center, learning center, spiritual and religious organizations, and other associations, expands the scope of programs offered and students affected.

Comprehensive initiatives that incorporate the domains of psychotherapy, treatment, prevention, outreach, academics and learning, and career, enable institutions of higher education to sufficiently ensure that services are meeting the diverse personal and psychological needs of students. Individual, group, couples, and children and family counseling opportunities address issues related to family, relationship, and personal dynamics. Psychological, neuropsychological, alcohol and drug, and career assessments provide information necessary to better serve the student. Colleges and universities also disperse self-help and educational materials as well as employ standardized programs and interactive computer systems. Schools may outsource counseling services or develop a referral system to direct students to services offered in the community. Connections with twelve step and support groups within the community further assist students. Outreach within and outside the campus enables schools to educate society about the issues surrounding personal and psychological problems and programs.

See also: ADJUSTMENT TO COLLEGE; DRUG AND ALCOHOL ABUSE, *subentry on* COLLEGE; HEALTH SERVICES, *subentry on* COLLEGES AND UNIVERSITIES; PERSONAL AND PSYCHOLOGICAL COUNSELING AT COLLEGES AND UNIVERSITIES.

BIBLIOGRAPHY

AMERICAN PSYCHIATRIC ASSOCIATION. 1994. *Diagnostic and Statistical Manual of Mental Disorders,* 4th edition. Washington, DC: American Psychiatric Association.

ARCHER, JAMES, JR., and COOPER, STEWART. 1998. *Counseling and Mental Health Services on Campus: Handbook of Contemporary Practices and Challenges.* San Francisco: Jossey-Bass.

AUBE, JENNIFER, and WHIFFEN, VALERIE E. 1996. "Depressive Styles and Social Acuity: Further Evidence for Distinct Interpersonal Correlates of Dependency and Self-Criticism." *Communication Research* 23(4):407–424.

BACHMAN, JERALD G.; WADSWORTH, KATHERINE N.; O'MALLEY, PATRICK M.; JOHNSTON, LLOYD D.; and SCHULENBERG, JOHN E. 1997. *Smoking, Drinking, and Drug Use in Young Adulthood: The Impacts of New Freedoms and New Responsibilities.* Mahwah, NJ: Erlbaum.

BERMAN, SUMMER M.; STRAUSS, SHARI; and VERHAGE, NATASHA. 2000. "Treating Mental Illness in Students: A New Strategy." *The Chronicle of Higher Education* 46(June 16):B9.

BRAY, NATHANIEL J.; BRAXTON, JOHN M.; and SULLIVAN, ANNA. 1999. "The Influences of Stress-Related Coping Strategies of College Student Departure Decisions." *Journal of College Student Development* 40(6):645–657.

DIXON, WAYNE A. and REID, JON K. 2000. "Positive Life Events as a Moderator of Stress-Related Depressive Symptoms." *Journal of Counseling and Development* 78:343–347.

LEVINE, ARTHUR, and CURETON, JEANETTE S. 1998. *When Hope and Fear Collide: A Portrait of Today's College Student.* San Francisco: Jossey-Bass.

SCARANO, GINA M., and KALODNER-MARTIN, CYNTHIA R. 1994. "A Description of the Continuum of Eating Disorders: Implications for Intervention and Research." *Journal of Counseling and Development* 72:356–361.

SEGRIN, CHRIS, and FLORA, JEANNE. 2000. "Poor Social Skills Are a Vulnerability Factor in the Development of Psychosocial Problems." *Human Communication Research* 26(3):489–514.

LEIGH Z. GILCHRIST

PESTALOZZI, JOHANN (1746–1827)

In the history of education, the significant contributions of Johann Heinrich Pestalozzi are (1) his educational philosophy and instructional method that encouraged harmonious intellectual, moral, and physical development; (2) his methodology of empirical sensory learning, especially through object lessons; and (3) his use of activities, excursions, and nature studies that anticipated Progressive education.

Career and Development of Educational Theory

The development of Pestalozzi's educational theory is closely tied to his career as an educator. Born in Zurich, Switzerland, Pestalozzi was the son of Johann Baptiste Pestalozzi, a middle-class Protestant physician, and Susanna Hotz Pestalozzi. Pestalozzi's grandfather, Andreas Pestalozzi, a minister in the rural village of Hongg, inspired his evolving philanthropic mission to uplift the disadvantaged Swiss peasantry.

Pestalozzi, who had an overly protected and isolated childhood, considered himself to be socially inept and physically uncoordinated as an adult. His formal education was in institutions in Zurich. He first attended a local primary school and then took the preparatory course in Latin and Greek at the Schola Abbatissana and the Schola Carolina. His higher education was at the Collegium Humanitatis and the Collegium Carolinum, where he specialized in languages and philosophy.

With other university students, Pestalozzi was influenced by Jean Jacques Bodmer, an historian and literary critic, whose reformist ideology urged regenerating Swiss life by renewing the rustic values of the Swiss mountaineers. Pestalozzi joined the Helvetic Society, an association committed to Bodmer's ideals, and wrote for *The Monitor,* a journal critical of Zurich's officials. Pestalozzi was jailed briefly for his activities, which the authorities deemed subversive.

In 1767 Pestalozzi studied scientific agriculture with Johann Rudolf Tschiffeli, a physiocrat and experimental farmer near Kirchberg. Pestalozzi married Anna Schulthess, daughter of an upper-middle-class Zurich family in 1769. His only child, named Jean Jacques after Rousseau, was born in 1770. After using Rousseau's work *Émile* as a guide to educating his son, Pestalozzi revised Rousseau's method in *How Father Pestalozzi Instructed His Three and a Half Year Old Son* (1774). Though still committed to Rousseauean natural education, Pestalozzi began to base instruction on a more empirically based psychology.

In 1774 Pestalozzi established his first institute, a self-supporting agricultural and handicraft school at Neuhof. At its height, the school enrolled fifty pupils, many of whom were indigent or orphaned. Here, Pestalozzi devised *simultaneous instruction,* a group method to teach reading, writing, and arithmetic. However, financial indebtedness forced the school's closing in 1779.

Pestalozzi published *Leonard and Gertrude,* a popular didactic novel in 1781, which was followed by a less successful sequel, *Christopher and Elizabeth* in 1782. Between 1782 and 1784 he wrote educational essays for *Ein Schweizer Blatt,* the Swiss newspaper. His *On Legislation and Infanticide,* (1783), condemned killing or abandoning unwanted children. He wrote two children's books: *Illustrations for My ABC Book* (1787) and *Fables for My ABC Book*

(1795). Pestalozzi's *Researches into the Course of Nature in the Development of the Human Race* (1797) was a pioneering work in educational sociology.

Pestalozzi re-entered active educational service in 1799 when the Napoleonic-backed Helvetian Republic appointed him director of the orphanage at Stans. Here, he developed his concept of a residential school in which children were educated within an emotionally secure setting. Operating for less than a year, the orphanage closed when French and Austrian armies battled in its vicinity.

Pestalozzi then conducted a residential and teacher training school at Burgdorf from 1800 to 1804. He trained such educators as Joseph Neef, who would introduce Pestalozzianism to the United States, and Friedrich Froebel, the kindergarten's founder.

Pestalozzi's most systematic work, *How Gertrude Teaches Her Children* (1801) was a critique of conventional schooling and a prescription for educational reform. Rejecting corporal punishment, rote memorization, and bookishness, Pestalozzi envisioned schools that were homelike institutions where teachers actively engaged students in learning by sensory experiences. Such schools were to educate individuals who were well rounded intellectually, morally, and physically. Through engagement in activities, students were to learn useful vocations that complemented their other studies.

Pestalozzi's method rested on two major premises: (1) children need an emotionally secure environment as the setting for successful learning; and (2) instruction should follow the generalized process of human conceptualization that begins with sensation. Emphasizing sensory learning, the special method used the *Anschauung* principle, a process that involved forming clear concepts from sense impressions. Pestalozzi designed object lessons in which children, guided by teachers, examined the form (shape), number (quantity and weight) of objects, and named them after direct experience with them. Object teaching was the most popular and widely adopted element of Pestalozzianism.

Pestalozzi developed two related phases of instruction: the general and special methods. The general method in which teachers were to create an emotionally secure school environment was a necessary condition for implementing the special method. Emphasizing sensory learning, the special method, using the *Anschauung* principle, involved forming clear concepts from sense impressions. Pestalozzi designed an elaborate series of graded object lessons, by which children examined minerals, plants, and animals and human-made artifacts found in their environment. Following a sequence, instruction moved from the simple to the complex, the easy to the difficult, and the concrete to the abstract.

Pestalozzi's object lessons and emphasis on sense experience encouraged the entry of natural science and geography, two hitherto neglected areas, into the elementary school curriculum. On guided field trips, children explored the surrounding countryside, observing the local natural environment, topography, and economy. A further consequence of Pestalozzi's work was the movement to redirect instruction from the traditional recitation in which each child recited a previously assigned lesson to simultaneous group-centered instruction.

In 1804 Pestalozzi relocated his institute to Yverdon, where he worked until 1825. He died on February 17, 1827 and was buried at Neuhof, site of his first school.

Diffusion of Educational Ideas

Pestalozzianism was carried throughout Europe and America by individuals he had trained as teachers and by visitors who were impressed with his method. After Gottlieb Fichte promoted Pestalozzianism in his *Addresses to the German Nation* in 1808, Prussia incorporated selected elements of Pestalozzi's method in its educational reform of 1809 and dispatched teachers to study with him. In the United Kingdom, the Home and Colonial School Society in 1836 established a Pestalozzian teacher training school.

William Maclure, a philanthropist and natural scientist, began Pestalozzianism's introduction to the United States in 1806, when he subsidized Neef's school near Philadelphia. Neef's *A Sketch of a Plan and Method of Education* (1808) and *The Method of Instructing Children Rationally in the Arts of Writing and Reading* (1813) promoted Pestalozzian education in the United States. Under Maclure's auspices, Neef, Marie Duclos Fretageot, and William D'Arusmont conducted Pestalozzian schools at Robert Owen's communitarian experiment at New Harmony, Indiana, from 1824 to 1828.

Other American proponents of Pestalozzianism were Henry Barnard and Edward A. Sheldon. Barnard (1811–1900), a common school leader and U.S. Commissioner of Education, endorsed Pestalozzian education in *Pestalozzi and Pestalozzianism* (1859). Sheldon (1823–1897) incorporated the Pestalozzian object lesson in the teacher education program at the Oswego normal school in New York. In 1865 a report of the National Teachers' Association endorsed object teaching.

Certain Pestalozzian elements could be found among American progressive educators of the late nineteenth and early twentieth centuries who, like Pestalozzi, opposed traditional schools' formalism and verbalism and emphasized children's interests and needs. Such educational emphases as the *child-centered school, child permissiveness,* and *hands-on process learning* had their origins with Pestalozzi.

Pestalozzi's paramount contribution to education was his general philosophy of *natural education* that stressed the dignity of children and the importance of actively engaging children in using their senses to explore the environment.

Specifically, his legacy to later educators was his emphasis on children's holistic physical, mental and psychological development; his emphasis on empirical learning; his reforms of elementary and teacher education; and his anticipation of child-centered progressivism.

See also: INSTRUCTIONAL STRATEGIES; PROGRESSIVE EDUCATION; SHELDON, EDWARD.

BIBLIOGRAPHY

BARLOW, THOMAS A. 1997. *Pestalozzi and American Education.* Boulder: Este Es Press, University of Colorado Libraries.

GUTEK, GERALD L. 1999. *Pestalozzi and Education.* Prospect Heights, IL: Waveland.

MONROE, WILL S. 1907. *History of the Pestalozzian Movement in the United States.* Syracuse, NY: Bardeen.

PESTALOZZI, JOHANN HEINRICH. 1891. *Leonard and Gertrude,* tr. Eva Channing. Boston: Heath.

PESTALOZZI, JOHANN HEINRICH. 1946. *Complete Works and Letters; Critical Education,* ed. Emanuel Dejung. Zurich: Orell Fussli Verlag.

SILBER, KATE. 1973. *Pestalozzi: The Man and His Work.* New York: Schocken Books.

GERALD L. GUTEK

PHILOSOPHY OF EDUCATION

HISTORICAL OVERVIEW
William K. Frankena
CURRENT TRENDS
Nicholas C. Burbules
Nathan Raybeck

HISTORICAL OVERVIEW

The word *education* is used sometimes to signify the activity, process, or enterprise of educating or being educated and sometimes to signify the discipline or field of study taught in schools of education that concerns itself with this activity, process, or enterprise. As an activity or process, education may be formal or informal, private or public, individual or social, but it always consists in cultivating dispositions (abilities, skills, knowledges, beliefs, attitudes, values, and character traits) by certain methods. As a discipline, education studies or reflects on the activity or enterprise by asking questions about its aims, methods, effects, forms, history, costs, value, and relations to society.

Definition

The philosophy of education may be either the philosophy of the process of education or the philosophy of the discipline of education. That is, it may be part of the discipline in the sense of being concerned with the aims, forms, methods, or results of the process of educating or being educated; or it may be metadisciplinary in the sense of being concerned with the concepts, aims, and methods of the discipline. However, even in the latter case it may be thought of as part of the discipline, just as metaphilosophy is thought of as a part of philosophy, although the philosophy of science is not regarded as a part of science. Historically, philosophies of education have usually taken the first form, but under the influence of analytical philosophy, they have sometimes taken the second.

In the first form, philosophy of education was traditionally developed by philosophers—for example, Aristotle, Augustine, and John Locke—as part of their philosophical systems, in the context of their ethical theories. However, in the twentieth century philosophy of education tended to be developed in schools of education in the context of what is called *foundations of education,* thus linking it with other parts of the discipline of education—educational history, psychology, and sociology—rather than with other parts of philosophy. It was also developed by writers such as Paul Goodman and Robert M. Hutchins who were neither professional philosophers nor members of schools of education.

Types

As there are many kinds of philosophy, many philosophies, and many ways of philosophizing, so there are many kinds of educational philosophy and ways of doing it. In a sense there is no such thing as *the* philosophy of education; there are only philosophies of education that can be classified in many different ways.

Philosophy of education as such does not describe, compare, or explain any enterprises to systems of education, past or present; except insofar as it is concerned with the tracing of its own history, it leaves such inquiries to the history and sociology of education. Analytical philosophy of education is *meta* to the discipline of education—to all the inquiries and thinking about education—in the sense that it does not seek to propound substantive propositions, either factual or normative, about education. It conceives of its task as that of analysis: the definition or elucidation of educational concepts like teaching, indoctrination, ability, and trait, including the concept of education itself; the clarification and criticism of educational slogans like "Teach children, not subjects"; the exploration of models used in thinking about education (e.g., growth); and the analysis and evaluation of arguments and methods used in reaching conclusions about education, whether by teachers, administrators, philosophers, scientists, or laymen.

To accomplish this task, analytical philosophy uses the tools of logic and linguistics as well as techniques of analysis that vary from philosopher to philosopher. Its results may be valued for their own sake, but they may also be helpful to those who seek more substantive empirical of normative conclusions about education and who try to be careful about how they reach them. This entry is itself an exercise in analytical philosophy of education.

Normative philosophies or theories of education may make use of the results of such analytical work and of factual inquiries about human beings and the psychology of learning, but in any case they propound views about what education should be, what dispositions it should cultivate, why it ought to cultivate them, how and in whom it should do so, and what forms it should take. Some such normative theory of education is implied in every instance of educational endeavor, for whatever education is purposely engaged in, it explicitly or implicitly assumed that certain dispositions are desirable and that certain methods are to be used in acquiring or fostering them, and any view on such matters is a normative theory of philosophy of education. But not all such theories may be regarded as properly philosophical. They may, in fact, be of several sorts. Some simply seek to foster the dispositions regarded as desirable by a society using methods laid down by its culture. Here both the ends and the means of education are defined by the cultural tradition. Others also look to the prevailing culture for the dispositions to be fostered but appeal as well to experience, possibly even to science, for the methods to be used. In a more pluralistic society, an educational theory of a sort may arise as a compromise between conflicting views about the aids, if not the methods, of education, especially in the case of public schools. Then, individuals or groups within the society may have conflicting full-fledged philosophies of education, but the public philosophy of education is a working accommodation between them. More comprehensive theories of education rest their views about the aims and methods of education neither on the prevailing culture nor on compromise but on basic factual premises about humans and their world and on basic normative premises about what is good or right for individuals to seek or do. Proponents of such theories may reach their premises either by reason (including science) and philosophy or by faith and divine authority. Both types of theories are called philosophies of education, but only those based on reason and philosophy are properly philosophical in character; the others might better be called theologies of education. Even those that are purely philosophical may vary in complexity and sophistication.

In such a full-fledged philosophical normative theory of education, besides analysis of the sorts described, there will normally be propositions of the following kinds:

1. Basic normative premises about what is good or right;

2. Basic factual premises about humanity and the world;

3. Conclusions, based on these two kinds of premises, about the dispositions education should foster;

4. Further factual premises about such things as the psychology of learning and methods of teaching; and

5. Further conclusions about such things as the methods that education should use.

For example, Aristotle argued that the Good equals happiness equals excellent activity; that for a individual there are two kinds of excellent activity, one intellectual (e.g., doing geometry) and one moral (e.g., doing just actions); that therefore everyone who is capable of these types of excellent activity should acquire a knowledge of geometry and a disposition to be just; that a knowledge of geometry can be acquired by instruction and a disposition to be just by practice, by doing just actions; and that the young should be given instruction in geometry and practice in doing just actions. In general, the more properly philosophical part of such a full normative theory of education will be the proposition it asserts in (1), (2), and (3); for the propositions in (4) and hence (5) it will, given those in (3), most appropriately appeal to experience and science. Different philosophers will hold different views about the propositions they use in (1) and (2) and the ways in which these propositions may be established.

Although some normative premises are required in (1) as a basis for any line of reasoning leading to conclusions in (3) or (5) about what education should foster or how it should do this, the premises appearing in (2) may be of various sorts—empirical, scientific, historical, metaphysical, theological, or epistemological. No one kind of premise is always necessary in (2) in every educational context. Different philosophers of education will, in any case, have different views about what sorts of premises it is permissible to appeal to in (2). All must agree, however, that normative premises of the kind indicated in (1) must be appealed to. Thus, what is central and crucial in any normative philosophy of education is not epistemology, metaphysics, or theology, as is sometimes thought, but ethics, value theory, and social philosophy.

Role

Let us assume, as we have been doing, that philosophy may be analytical, speculative, or narrative and remember that it is normally going on in a society in which there already is an educational system. Then, in the first place, philosophy may turn its attention to education, thus generating philosophy of education proper and becoming part of the discipline of education.

Second, general philosophy may be one of the subjects in the curriculum of higher education and philosophy of education may be, and presumably should be, part of the curriculum of teacher education, if teachers are to think clearly and carefully about what they are doing.

Third, in a society in which there is a single system of education governed by a single prevailing theory of education, a philosopher may do any of four things with respect to education: he may analyze the concepts and reasoning used in connection with education in order to make people's thinking about it as clear, explicit, and logical as possible; he may seek to support the prevailing system by providing more philosophical arguments for the dispositions aimed at and the methods used; he may criticize the system and seek to reform it in the light of some more philosophical theory of education he has arrived at; or he may simply teach logic and philosophy to future educators and parents in the hope that they will apply them to educational matters.

Fourth, in a pluralistic society like the United States, in which the existing educational enterprise or a large segment of it is based on a working compromise between conflicting views, a philosopher may again do several sorts of things. He may do any of the things just mentioned. In the United States in the first half of the twentieth century professional philosophers tended to do only the last, but at the end of the twentieth century they began to try to do more. Indeed, there will be more occasions for all of these activities in a pluralistic society, for debate about education will always be going on or threatening to be resumed. A philosopher may even take the lead in formulating and improving a compromise theory of education. He might then be a mere eclectic, but he need not be, since he might defend his compromise plan on the basis of a whole social philosophy. In particular, he might propound a whole public philosophy for public school education, making clear which dispositions it can and should seek to promote, how it should promote them, and which ones should be left for the home, the church, and other private means of education to cultivate. In any case, he might advocate appealing to scientific inquiry and experiment whenever possible. A philosopher may also work out a fully developed educational philosophy of his own and start an experimental school in which to put it into practice, as John Dewey did;

like Dewey, too, he may even try to persuade his entire society to adopt it. Then he would argue for the desirability of fostering certain dispositions by certain methods, partly on the basis of experience and science and partly on the basis of premises taken from other parts of his philosophy—from his ethics and value theory, from his political and social philosophy, or from his epistemology, metaphysics, or philosophy of mind.

It seems plausible to maintain that in a pluralistic society philosophers should do all of these things, some one and some another. In such a society a philosopher may at least seek to help educators concerned about moral, scientific, historical, aesthetic, or religious education by presenting them, respectively, with a philosophy of morality, science, history, art, or religion from which they may draw conclusions about their aims and methods. He may also philosophize about the discipline of education, asking whether it is a discipline, what its subject matter is, and what its methods, including the methods of the philosophy of education, should be. Insofar as the discipline of education is a science (and one question here would be whether it *is* a science) this would be a job for the philosopher of science in addition to one just mentioned. Logicians, linguistic philosophers, and philosophers of science may also be able to contribute to the technology of education, as it has come to be called, for example, to the theory of testing or of language instruction.

Finally, in a society that has been broken down by some kind of revolution or has newly emerged from colonialism, a philosopher may even supply a new full-fledged normative philosophy for its educational system, as Karl Marx did for Russia and China. In fact, as in the case of Marx, he may provide the ideology that guided the revolution in the first place. Plato tried to do this for Syracuse, and the philosophes did it for France in the eighteenth century. Something like this may be done wherever the schools "dare to build a new society," as many ask schools to do.

Dewey once said that since education is the process of forming fundamental dispositions toward nature and our fellow human beings, philosophy may even be defined as the most general theory of education. Here Dewey was thinking that philosophy is the most general normative theory of education, and what he said is true if it means that philosophy, understood in its widest sense as including theology and poetry as well as philosophy proper, is what tells us what to believe and how to feel about humanity and the universe. It is, however, not necessarily true if it refers to philosophy in the narrower sense or means that all philosophy is philosophy of education in the sense of having the guidance of education as its end. This is not the whole end of classical philosophy or even of philosophy as reconstructed by Dewey; the former aimed at the truth rather than at the guidance of practice, and the latter has other practical ends besides that of guiding the educational enterprise. Certainly, analytical philosophy has other ends. However, although Dewey did not have analytical philosophy in mind, there is nevertheless a sense in which analytical philosophy can also be said to be the most general theory of education. Although it does not seek to tell us what dispositions we should form, it does analyze and criticize the concepts, arguments, and methods employed in any study of or reflection upon education. Again it does not follow that this is all analytical philosophy is concerned with doing. Even if the other things it does—for example, the philosophy of mind or of science—are useful to educators and normative theorists of education, as, it is hoped, is the case, they are not all developed with this use in mind.

See also: ARISTOTLE; AUGUSTINE, ST.; BAGLEY, WILLIAM C.; BODE, BOYD H.; BRAMELD, THEODORE; CHILDS, JOHN L.; COMENIUS, JOHANN; COUNTS, GEORGE S.; DEWEY, JOHN; FREIRE, PAULO; HERBERT, JOHANN; JAMES, WILLIAM; KILPATRICK, WILLIAM H.; MONTESSORI, MARIA; NEILL, A. S.; PESTALOZZI, JOHANN; PLATO; ROUSSEAU, JEAN-JACQUES; WHITEHEAD, ALFRED NORTH.

BIBLIOGRAPHY

ANDERSON, R. N., et al. 1968. *Foundation Disciplines and the Study of Education.* Toronto: Macmillan.

ARCHAMBAULT, REGINALD D., ed. 1965. *Philosophical Analysis and Education.* New York: Humanities Press.

FRANKENA, WILLIAM K., ed. 1965. *Philosophy of Education.* New York: Macmillan.

JARRET, JAMES L., ed. 1969. *Philosophy for the Study of Education.* Boston: Houghton Mifflin.

LUCAS, CHRISTOPHER J. 1969. *What Is Philosophy of Education?* New York: Macmillan.

MORRIS, VAN CLEVE. 1969. *Modern Movements in Educational Philosophy.* Boston: Houghton Mifflin.

O'CONNOR, DANIEL JOHN. 1957. *Introduction to the Philosophy of Education.* London: Routledge.

PARK, JOE. 1968. *Selected Readings in the Philosophy of Education,* 3rd edition. New York: Macmillan.

SCHEFFLER, ISRAEL, ed. 1966. *Philosophy and Education,* 2nd edition. Boston: Allyn and Bacon.

WILLIAM K. FRANKENA

CURRENT TRENDS

Philosophy of education is a field characterized not only by broad theoretical eclecticism but also by a perennial dispute, which started in the mid-twentieth century, over what the scope and purposes of the discipline even ought to be. In the "Philosophy of Education" article that was included in the previous edition of this encyclopedia, William Frankena wrote, "In a sense there is no such thing as *the* philosophy of education" (p. 101). During certain periods of the history of the philosophy of education, there have been dominant perspectives, to be sure: At one time, the field was defined around canonical works on education by great philosophers (Plato of ancient Greece, the eighteenth-century Swiss-born Frenchman Jean-Jacques Rousseau, and others); at other times, the field was dominated, in the United States at least, by the figure of John Dewey (1859–1952) and educational Progressivism; at other times, the field was characterized by an austere analytical approach that explicitly rejected much of what had come before in the field as not even being proper "philosophy" at all. But even during these periods of dominance there were sharp internal disputes within the field (such as feminist criticisms of the "Great Man" approach to philosophy of education and vigorous critiques of the analytical method). Such disputes can be read off the history of the professional societies, journals, and graduate programs that institutionalize the field, and they can be documented through a succession of previous encyclopedia articles, which by definition attempt to define and delimit their subject matter.

These sorts of struggles over the maintenance of the disciplinary boundary, and the attempt to define and enforce certain methods as paramount, are hardly unique to philosophy of education. But such concerns have so preoccupied its practitioners that at times these very questions seem to become the substance of the discipline, nearly to the exclusion of thinking about actual educational problems. And so it is not very surprising to find, for example, a book such as *Philosophers on Education.* Consisting of a series of essays written by professional philosophers entirely outside the discipline of philosophy of education, the collection cites almost none of the work published within the discipline; because the philosophers have no doubts about the status of the discipline of philosophy of education, they have few qualms about speaking authoritatively about what philosophy has to say to educators. On the other hand, a fruitful topic for reflection is whether a more self-critical approach to philosophy of education, even if at times it seems to be pulling up its own roots for examination, might prove more productive for thinking about education, because this very tendency toward self-criticism keeps fundamental questions alive and open to reexamination.

Any encyclopedia article must take a stance in relation to such disputes. However much one attempts to be comprehensive and dispassionate in describing the scope and purpose of a field, it is impossible to write anything about it without imagining some argument, somewhere, that would put such claims to challenge. This is especially true of "categorical" approaches, that is, those built around a list of types of philosophy of education, or of discrete schools of thought, or of specific disciplinary methods. During the period of particular diversity and interdisciplinarity in the field that has continued into the twenty-first century, such characterizations seem especially artificial—but even worse than this, potentially imperial and exclusionary. And so the challenge is to find a way of characterizing the field that is true to its eclecticism but that also looks back reflexively at the effects of such characterizations, including itself, in the dynamics of disciplinary boundary maintenance and methodological rule-setting that are continually under dispute.

One way to begin such an examination is by thinking about the *impulses* that draw one into this activity at all: What is philosophy of education for? Perhaps these impulses can be more easily generalized about the field than any particular set of categories, schools of thought, or disciplinary methods. Moreover, these impulses cut across and interrelate approaches that might otherwise look quite different. And they coexist as impulses within broad philosophical movements, and even within the thought of individual philosophers themselves, sometimes conflicting in a way that might help explain the tendency toward reflexive self-examination

and uncertainty that so exercises philosophy of education as a field.

The Prescriptive Impulse

The first impulse is prescriptive. In many respects this is the oldest and most pervasive inclination: to offer a philosophically defended conception of what the aims and activities of teaching ought to be. In some instances, as in Plato's *Republic,* these prescriptions derive from an overall utopian vision; in other instances, such as seventeenth-century English philosopher John Locke's *Some Thoughts Concerning Education* or Rousseau's *Émile,* they derive from a fairly detailed reconception of what the day-to-day activities of teaching should look like; in still other instances, such prescriptions are derived from other social or moral principles, as in various Kantian views of education (even though eighteenth-century German philosopher Immanuel Kant himself had very little to say on the subject). These prescriptive inclinations are in many respects what people expect from philosophy of education: a wiser perspective, a more encompassing social vision, a sense of inspiration and higher purpose. It is what people usually mean when they talk about having a "philosophy of education."

A broad range of perspectives in the field share this prescriptive impulse: many of these perspectives can be comprised in what was once called the "isms" approach (perennialism, idealism, realism, Thomism, and so on)—the idea that a set of philosophical premises could generate a comprehensive and consistent educational program. For many years, working out the details of these "philosophies of education" was considered the main substance of the field, and the debates among the "isms" were typically at the very basic level debates among fundamentally different philosophical premises. An implication of this approach was that disagreements tended to be broadly "paradigmatic" in the sense that they were based on all-or-none commitments; one could not, of course, talk about a synthesis of realist and idealist worldviews.

One wag has suggested that the "isms" have more recently been replaced by the "ists"—less purely philosophical and more social/political theories that now typify many scholars working in philosophy of education (Marxists, feminists, multiculturalists, postmodernists, and so on). These will be characterized as critically oriented philosophies below, but at this stage it is important to see that these perspectives can be equally driven by the prescriptive impulse: many writers (for example, neo-Marxist advocates of Paulo Freire's "critical pedagogy") offer quite explicit accounts of how education ought to proceed, what it is for, and whose interests it ought to serve.

The Analytical Impulse

The second impulse that drives much of philosophy of education is analytical. In a broad sense this includes not only philosophical approaches specifically termed "analytical philosophy" (such as conceptual analysis or ordinary language analysis), but also a broader orientation that approaches the philosophical task as spelling out a set of rational conditions that educational aims and practices ought to satisfy, while leaving it up to other public deliberative processes to work out what they might be in specific. In this enlarged sense, the analytical impulse can be seen not only in analytical philosophy per se but also in studies that focus on the logical and epistemological criteria of critical thinking; in the diagnosis of informal fallacies in reasoning; in certain kinds of liberal theory that spell out broad principles of rights and justice but that remain silent on the specific ends that education ought to serve; and even in some versions of German philosopher Jürgen Habermas's theory, which proposes a structure of communicative deliberation in which conversations must satisfy what he calls a set of general "validity" claims, but which does not specify or constrain in advance what that process of deliberation might yield.

The analytical impulse is often seen as expressing a certain philosophical modesty: that philosophers do not prescribe to others what their educational choices ought to be, but simply try to clarify the rational procedures by which those choices should be arrived at. Here metaphors such as referees who try to adjudicate an ongoing activity but remain nonpartisan within it, or groundskeepers who pull up weeds and prepare the soil but do not decide what to plant, tend to predominate in how this version of philosophy of education is presented and justified to others. The idea that philosophy provides a set of *tools*, and that "doing philosophy of education" (as opposed to "having a philosophy of education") offers a more workmanlike self-conception of the philosopher, stands in sharp contrast with the idea of philosophy as a system-building endeavor.

Of course, it must be said that this impulse is not entirely free of the prescriptive inclination, either. For one thing, there is a prescriptiveness about the very tools, criteria, principles, and analytical distinctions that get imported into how problems are framed. These are implicitly (and often explicitly) presented as educational ideals themselves: promoting critical thinking or fostering the conditions for Habermasian communication in the classroom, for example. However rationally defended these might be, they will undoubtedly appear to some as imposed from "on high." Moreover, at a deeper level, the analytic/prescriptive distinction is less than clear-cut: a theory of logic, or a theory of communication, however purely "procedural" it aspires to be, always expresses conceptions of human nature, of society, of knowledge, of language, that contains social and cultural elements that might appear "natural" or "neutral" to the advocates of those procedures, but that will be regarded as foreign and particularistic by others ("why must I justify my educational choices by *your* criteria?"). This is not meant as a criticism of the analytical orientation, but it just shows how these impulses can and do coexist, even within accounts that regard themselves as primarily one or the other.

The Critical Impulse

Similarly, the third impulse, a critical orientation, can coexist with either or both of the others. The critical impulse, like the analytical one, shares the characteristic of trying to clear the ground of misconceptions and ideologies, where these misrepresent the needs and interests of disadvantaged groups; like the prescriptive impulse, the critical impulse is driven by a positive conception of a better, more just and equitable, society. Where the critical impulse differs from the others is in its conception of the contribution philosophy can play in serving these ends. From this orientation, philosophy is not just a set of tools or an abstract, programmatic theory; it is itself a substantive personal and political commitment, and it grows out of deeper inclinations to protect and serve the interests of specific groups. Hence the key philosophical ideas stressed in critically oriented philosophies of education (reflection, counterhegemony, a critique of power, an emphasis upon difference, and so on) derive their force from their capacity to challenge a presumably oppressive dominant society and enable put-upon individuals and groups to recognize and question their circumstances and to be moved to change them.

As there are prescriptive and analytical elements in critically oriented philosophies of education, so there can be critical elements in the others. Philosophers of education more driven by a prescriptive or analytical impulse can and do share many of the same social and political commitments as critically oriented philosophers of education; and some of them may see their work as ultimately serving many of the same goals of criticizing hegemonic ideologies and promoting human emancipation. This is why these three impulses or orientations must not be seen as simple categories to which particular philosophies (or philosophers) can be assigned. Stressing their character as impulses highlights the motivational qualities that underlie, and frequently drive, the adoption of particular philosophical views. While philosophers tend to stress the force of argument in driving their adoption of such views, and while they do certainly change their minds because of argument and evidence, at some deeper level they are less prone to changing the very impulses that drive and give vigor to their philosophical investigations. By stressing the ways in which all three impulses can coexist within different philosophical schools of thought, and even within the inclinations of a given philosopher, this account highlights the complex and sometimes even contradictory character of the philosophical spirit. When philosophers of education teach or speak about their views, although they certainly put forth arguments, quotations of and references to literature, and so forth, at a deeper level they are appealing to a shared impulse in their audience, one that is more difficult to argue for directly, and without which the arguments themselves are unlikely to take hold.

Implications of the Impulses for Philosophy of Education

Given the existence of these three impulses, how can they help in providing an overview of the field of philosophy of education that does not fall into arguments about disciplinary boundary maintenance? First, these very broad orientations are in many respects easier to generalize within the field than would be any specific set of disciplinary criteria; many different kinds of philosophy of education can manifest these sorts of inclinations. Indeed, it makes for strange bedfellows when people consider that despite their vigorous paradigmatic differences they are actually motivated by very similar underlying philosophical commitments. Perhaps this recognition might create a stronger incentive for them to engage one another respectfully across those differences.

Second, it is beneficial for philosophers to consider that the validity they attribute to certain kinds of arguments may not be driven simply by the objective force of those arguments, but also by a particular appeal those kinds of arguments have *for them*. This sort of reflectiveness might be fruitful for various reasons, but a significant benefit could be in raising a person's appreciation for why others may not be moved by the arguments that seem so patently obvious to that person; and why the force of argument alone may not be sufficient to generate philosophical agreement or reconcile disagreement. Given the pervasively eclectic and interdisciplinary nature of the field of philosophy of education, such a spirit of tolerance and inclusiveness, while not needing to be unbounded entirely, would be a valuable corrective to the historical tendency to establish *the* methods or *the* philosophical school that will separate proper philosophy of education from the imposters.

Advocates of more prescriptive approaches typically buttress their case for dominance by reference to canonical Great Works (Plato, ancient Greek philosopher Aristotle, Locke, Rousseau, Dewey). This sort of system-building across epistemological, ethical, and social/political issues is what the great philosophers *do,* and it is revealing that for them philosophy of education was rarely seen as a distinct area of inquiry but merely the working out in practice of implications for teaching and learning that were derived from their larger positions about truth, value, justice, and so on.

Advocates of more analytical approaches, as noted, tend to put more reliance upon the tools of philosophical investigation, and less on particular authors or sources. In the twentieth century, versions of these approaches tended to dominate philosophy of education, especially in the English-speaking world, as they have many departments of philosophy itself. Indeed, when one surveys accounts of the field of philosophy of education from the 1990s forward, they nearly all chart the history as one of the rise to dominance of an analytical approach and then a succession of critiques and attacks upon it.

Advocates of more critical approaches suffer from a particular difficulty—carrying out their philosophical work in a way that is consistent with their broader commitments. Naturally, any philosophical approach aspires to consistency of some sort; but to the extent that critically oriented philosophers are concerned with challenging power structures, hegemonic belief systems, and universalisms that obscure, not to say squelch, the particular beliefs, values, and experiences of those whom they seem to empower, such philosophers must also endeavor to avoid these potentially oppressive tendencies in their own writing and teaching. This tension is perhaps felt most acutely by contemporary postmodern philosophers of education, but it can be seen in much of the work of neo-Marxists, critical theorists, feminists, and Foucauldians as well: how to argue for and promote an emancipatory approach to education that does not itself fall into the habits of exclusionary language, authoritative (if not authoritarian) postures, and universalizing generalizations that are excoriated when detected in the work of others.

Summary

This entry has tried to provide an overview of how the field of philosophy of education has seen itself, and it has recounted major elements in the narratives by which the history of the field has been traced by others. At the same time it has tried to reveal problems with the ways in which these different accounts have been driven in part by various agendas to define a scope and boundary for the field, and often to privilege one or another approach to philosophy of education, even when they have endeavored to be comprehensive and fair to all views. This entry has taken a different approach, first, by resisting the temptation to provide a single definition or characterization of the field; and, second, by stressing not schools of thought or methodological divisions as the categories for thinking about the field, but rather the underlying inclinations, or impulses, that animate philosophical inquiry. As noted, for a field that tends to resist and argue over every attempt to define it, such caution is probably prudent, but it has an added benefit as well. When philosophers think about the impulses that motivate their areas of inquiry and ways of thinking about them, they relate their philosophical work not solely to an abstract order of truth but to themselves; and it is a short step from that recognition to extending that way of thinking to others as well. The generosity of outlook that results might be the one thing that all philosophers of education can share.

See also: RESEARCH METHODS.

BIBLIOGRAPHY

BARROW, ROBIN. 1994. "Philosophy of Education: Analytic Tradition." In *The International Encyclopedia of Education,* 2nd edition, ed. Torsten Husén and T. Neville Postlethwaite. Oxford: Pergamon Press.

BLAKE, NIGEL; SMEYERS, PAUL; SMITH, RICHARD; and STANDISH, PAUL, eds. 2002. *Blackwell Guide to Philosophy of Education.* Boston: Blackwell.

BURBULES, NICHOLAS C. 2000. "Philosophy of Education." In *Routledge International Companion to Education,* ed. Bob Moon, Miriam Ben-Peretz, and Sally Brown. New York: Routledge.

CHAMBLISS, J. J. 1996. "History of Philosophy of Education." In *Philosophy of Education: An Encyclopedia,* ed. J. J. Chambliss. New York: Garland.

EDEL, ABRAHAM. 1972. "Analytic Philosophy of Education at the Cross-Roads." *Educational Theory* 22:131–152.

ERICSON, DAVID. 1992. "Philosophical Issues in Education." In *Encyclopedia of Educational Research,* ed. Marvin Alkin. New York: Macmillan.

FRANKENA, WILLIAM K. 1971. "Philosophy of Education: Overview." In *The Encyclopedia of Education,* ed. Lee C. Deighton. New York: Macmillan.

GIARELLI, JAMES M., and CHAMBLISS, J. J. 1991. "The Foundations of Professionalism: Fifty Years of the Philosophy of Education Society in Retrospect." *Educational Theory* 41:265–274.

KAMINSKY, JAMES S. 1993. *A New History of Educational Philosophy.* Westport, CT: Greenwood.

KAMINSKY, JAMES S. 1996. "Professional Organizations in Philosophy of Education." In *Philosophy of Education: An Encyclopedia,* ed. J. J. Chambliss. New York: Garland.

LEACH, MARY S. 1991. "Mothers of In(ter)vention: Women's Writing in Philosophy of Education." *Educational Theory* 41:287–300.

LUCAS, CHRISTOPHER J. 1969. *What Is Philosophy of Education?* New York: Macmillan.

MALONEY, KAREN E. 1985. "Philosophy of Education: Definitions of the Field, 1942–1982." *Educational Studies* 16:235–258.

MARTIN, JANE ROLAND. 1985. *Reclaiming a Conversation: The Ideal of the Educated Woman.* New Haven, CT: Yale University Press.

NELSON, THOMAS W. 1996. "Literature in Philosophy of Education." In *Philosophy of Education: An Encyclopedia*, ed. J. J. Chambliss. New York: Garland.

NODDINGS, NEL. 1995. *Philosophy of Education.* Boulder, CO: Westview.

PHILLIPS, D. C. 1994. "Philosophy of Education: Historical Overview." In *The International Encyclopedia of Education*, 2nd edition, ed. Torsten Husén and T. Neville Postlethwaite. Oxford: Pergamon Press.

RORTY, AMELIE OKSENBERG, ed. 1998. *Philosophers on Education: New Historical Perspectives.* New York: Routledge.

SMEYERS, PAUL. 1994. "Philosophy of Education: Western European Perspectives." In *The International Encyclopedia of Education*, 2nd edition, ed. Torsten Husén and T. Neville Postlethwaite. Oxford: Pergamon Press.

NICHOLAS C. BURBULES
NATHAN RAYBECK

PHYSICAL DISABILITIES, EDUCATION OF INDIVIDUALS WITH

In special education, physical disabilities are physical limitations or health problems that interfere with school attendance or learning to such an extent that special services, training, equipment, materials, or facilities are required. In the early twenty-first century, approximately 500,000 school children in the United States were classified as having physical disabilities or other health impairments for special education purposes. Since 1975, federal law (under the Education for All Handicapped Children Act, and since 1990, the Individuals with Disabilities Education Act [IDEA]) has mandated special education and related services for all students with physical disabilities that interfere with their education. Major classifications include neurological conditions, musculoskeletal conditions, and other health impairments.

Types and Causes of Physical Disabilities

Neurological conditions involve damage to the central nervous system (brain or spinal cord). In 1990 traumatic brain injury became a separate category of disability under IDEA. Other major neurological conditions include cerebral palsy, seizure disorder (or epilepsy), and spina bifida, a congenital condition in which the spinal cord protrudes through the backbone resulting in partial or total paralysis below the site of the nerve damage. Disabilities associated with neurological conditions vary from very mild to severe and may involve physical, cognitive, speech-language, or sensory abilities, or a combination thereof.

Musculoskeletal conditions include muscular dystrophy, juvenile rheumatoid arthritis, limb deficiencies or amputations, and a wide variety of other deformities or degeneration of muscles or bones affecting the ability to move, walk, stand, sit, or use the hands or feet normally. Other health impairments include a wide variety of infectious diseases and chronic problems such as diabetes, asthma, cystic fibrosis, immunodeficiency (including HIV and AIDS), hemophilia, fetal alcohol syndrome, and the malfunction or failure of vital organs.

Causes include infectious disease, congenital conditions or malformations, and developmental problems or chronic health problems that are poorly understood. A wide variety of disabilities, especially those associated with traumatic brain injury, result from vehicular accidents, gunshot wounds, burns, falls, and poisoning. Substance abuse and physical abuse by caretakers, infectious diseases, and substance abuse by the child or by the mother during pregnancy cause some disabilities. Advances in medicine and related treatments are reducing or eliminating physical disabilities resulting from some diseases, injuries, and chronic conditions. Advances in medicine, however, also increase the number of children surviving congenital anomalies, accidents, and diseases with severe disabilities.

The Basics and History of Special Education

Special education includes helping students have as normal an experience as possible in school. Much depends on access to the typical curriculum and use of adaptive devices when necessary. Emphasis is on overcoming attitudinal barriers among persons without disabilities to participation of students with physical disabilities in school and the community. Special educators must understand the operation of prostheses (artificial body parts), orthotics (braces and other corrective devices), and adaptive devices (wheelchairs, communication boards, and other gadgets enabling people to accomplish tasks).

Special education in public schools dates from the early twentieth century. Programs have emphasized major health problems of the era. In the first half of the twentieth century the focus was on crippling conditions and the effects of infectious diseases, particularly tuberculosis and polio. After antibiotic drugs and vaccines dramatically reduced or eliminated many infectious diseases in the mid-twentieth century, the focus changed to cerebral palsy, spina bifida, and other congenital conditions or chronic health problems. In the late twentieth century, increasing attention was given to traumatic brain injury, spinal cord injuries, and AIDS.

Trends and Controversies

Trends in the field are determined largely by changes in epidemiology and advances in medicine. The number of students needing special education and the focus of programs may change because of a resurgence of an infectious disease (e.g., tuberculosis), an advance in immunology (e.g., an effective vaccine for AIDS), or medical advances such as gene therapy, transplants, artificial organs, or extremely effective new treatments that reduce or eliminate a chronic health problem (as may occur for such conditions as diabetes, cystic fibrosis, and asthma). Advances in medicine and related services, such as physical therapy, technological applications, and adaptive devices that allow more normal functioning, may reduce or eliminate the need for special education or make education in a typical classroom feasible.

Issues and controversies include the extent to which placement in typical school environments is appropriate. Many students with even severe physical disabilities can attend regular schools and classes, given improved accessibility of school buildings, the use of technologies of treatment and adaptive devices, and improved attitudes of acceptance of disabilities in the school. Some students need highly specialized medical care and are thought to need education in the hospital where they are being treated or in a special class or school. A controversial issue is whether to include in regular schools and classes students who are near death or who have extreme physical and cognitive disabilities that leave them unresponsive to typical instruction.

See also: Adapted Physical Education; Council for Exceptional Children; Motor Learning;

Severe and Multiple Disabilities, Education of Individuals with; Special Education, *subentries on* Current Trends, History of.

BIBLIOGRAPHY

Hallahan, Daniel P., and Kauffman, James M. 2000. *Exceptional Learners: Introduction to Special Education,* 8th edition. Needham Heights, MA: Allyn and Bacon.

Kauffman, James M. 1981. "Historical Trends and Contemporary Issues in Special Education in the United States." In *Handbook of Special Education,* ed. James M. Kauffman and Daniel P. Hallahan. Englewood Cliffs, NJ: Prentice-Hall.

Smita Shukla-Mehta
James M. Kauffman

PHYSICAL EDUCATION

OVERVIEW
B. Ann Boyce
PREPARATION OF TEACHERS
Murray Mitchell

OVERVIEW

"Physical education is the study, practice, and appreciation of the art and science of human movement" (Harrison, Blakemore, and Buck, p. 15). While movement is both innate and essential to an individual's growth and development, it is the role of physical education to provide instructional activities that not only promote skill development and proficiency, but also enhance an individual's overall health. Physical education not only fulfills a unique role in education, but is also an integral part of the schooling process.

Historical Perspectives

From the late 1700s to the mid-1800s, three nations—Germany, Sweden, and England—influenced the early development of physical education in the United States. German immigrants introduced the Turner Societies, which advocated a system of gymnastics training that utilized heavy apparatus (e.g., side horse, parallel and horizontal bars) in the pursuit of fitness. In contrast, the Swedish system of exercise promoted health through the performance of a series of prescribed movement patterns with light apparatus (e.g., wands, climbing ropes). The English brought sports and games to America with a system that stressed moral development through participation in physical activities. The influence of these three nations laid the foundation for sport and physical education in America.

The 1800s were an important time for the inclusion of physical education in schools across America. The Round Hill School, a private school established in 1823 in Northampton, Massachusetts, was the first to include physical education as an integral part of the curriculum. In 1824 Catherine Beecher, founder of the Hartford Female Seminary, included calisthenics in her school's curriculum and "was the first American to design a program of exercise for American children" (Lumpkin, p. 202). She also advocated the inclusion of daily physical education in public schools. However, physical education was not offered in the public schools until 1855, when Cincinnati, Ohio, became the first city school system to offer this type of program to children.

In 1866 California became the first state to pass a law requiring twice-per-day exercise periods in public schools. Beecher's influence started the American system of exercise, and, along with her contemporaries Dio Lewis, Edward Hitchcock, and Dudley Allen Sargent, she was an early leader in physical education. In the profession's early years, between 1855 and 1900, there were several debates, referred to as the *Battle of the Systems,* regarding which system (American, Swedish, German, or English) could best provide a national physical education program for America.

During the 1890s traditional education was challenged by John Dewey and his colleagues, whose educational reforms led to the expansion of the "three R's" to include physical education. It was also during this time that several *normal schools* (training schools for physical education teachers) were established. All of these schools offered a strong background in the sciences that included courses in anatomy and physiology, with many of the early professors holding medical degrees.

In 1893 Thomas Wood stated that "the great thought of physical education is not the education of the physical nature, but the relation of physical training to complete education, and then the effort to make the physical contribute its full share to the life of the individual" (National Education Associa-

tion, p. 621). During the early twentieth century, several educational psychologists, including Dewey, Stanley G. Hall, and Edward Thorndike, supported the important role of children's play in a child's ability to learn. In line with the work of Wood in physical education, and the theoretical work of prominent educational psychologists, *The New Physical Education* was published in 1927 by Wood and Rosalind Cassidy, who advocated *education through the physical.*

This position supported the thesis that physical education contributed to the physical well-being of children, as well as to their social, emotional, and intellectual development. However, Charles McCloy argued against this expanded role of physical education, arguing that *education of the physical,* which emphasized the development of skills and the maintenance of the body, was the primary objective of physical education. The testing of motor skills was a part of McCloy's contribution to physical education, and his philosophy of testing paralleled the scientific movement in education.

The evolution of physical education, along with other educational professions, reflected contemporary changes in society. Throughout the early twentieth century, into the 1950s, there was a steady growth of physical education in the public schools. During the early 1920s many states passed legislation requiring physical education. However, shifts in curricular emphasis were evident when wars occurred and when the results of national reports were published. For example, as a result of the bombing of Pearl Harbor and the United States' entrance into World War II, the emphasis in physical education shifted from games and sport to physical conditioning. Similar curricular shifts were noted in 1953 when the Kraus-Weber study found that American children were far less fit than their European counterparts. As a result of this report, the President's Council on Physical Fitness was established to help combat the falling fitness levels of America's youth.

During the 1950s and the 1960s, physical education at the elementary level experienced tremendous growth. Today, many physical education programs emphasize overall fitness, referred to as *wellness,* as well as skill development. However, since the 1970s the number of schools offering daily physical education has drastically decreased—1995 statistics from the Centers for Disease Control and Prevention (CDC) show a drop from 43 percent in 1991 to 25 percent in 1995.

Rationale

In the 1990s three national reports—*The Surgeon General's Report on Physical Activity and Health* (1996), *Healthy People 2000* (1990), and the CDC's *Guidelines for School and Community Programs* (1997)—have focused on the deplorable physical condition of Americans. These reports cited physical inactivity as a national health risk, based on statistics such as: (1) 13 percent of young people are classified as overweight; (2) only half of all youths are physically active on a regular basis (and this percentage decreases with age); and (3) inactivity and poor diet cause at least 300,000 deaths per year.

These reports advocated the need for daily physical activity, citing the following health benefits from moderate participation: improved strength and endurance, healthier bones and muscles, weight control, reduced anxiety and increased self-esteem, and, often, improved blood pressure and cholesterol levels. Physical education is the major vehicle for improving the health and fitness of the nations' youth. *Healthy People 2000* recommended the increase of daily physical education to a level of at least 50 percent of students in public schools by the year 2000.

In addition to the health benefits, cognitive performance can also be enhanced through physical education. There is a growing body of research that supports the important relationship between physical activity and brain development and cognitive performance. C. Edwin Bencraft (1999) found that "sensory and motor experiences play a prominent role in reinforcing. . . synaptic connections and neural pathways" (p. 45). Eric Jensen's 1998 research revealed that the cerebellum is not solely dedicated to motor activity, but includes both cognitive and sensory operations. Further, Jensen points out the strong relationship of the cerebellum to memory, perception, language, and decision-making, citing physical activity as a way to enhance cognition. In a summary of research findings, Bencraft suggests providing the following applications that could increase cognitive performance: (1) challenging motor tasks before the age of ten can increase cognitive ability due to a heavier, more dendrite-rich brain; (2) aerobic exercise improves cognitive functioning by increasing the number of capillaries serving the brain through the delivery of more oxygen and glucose and removal of carbon dioxide; (3) cross-lateral movements increase the communication ability between the brain's hemispheres; and (4) physical activity reduces the production of stress chemicals that inhibit cognitive processing.

From the mounting evidence favoring physical activity, it appears that physical education in schools plays a dual role in serving both mind and body. The challenge to physical educators will be to implement programs that address the health crisis while building the child's mind through physical activity.

Curriculum

According to the American Alliance for Health, Physical Education, Recreation and Dance (AAHPERD), a quality physical education program for grades K–12 includes instructional periods totaling at least 150 minutes per week at the elementary level and 225 minutes at the secondary level, qualified physical education specialists, and adequate equipment and facilities. In general, the curriculum should consist of: (a) instruction in a variety of developmentally appropriate motor skills that challenge students to develop physically, cognitively, socially, and emotionally; (b) fitness activities that educate and help students understand and improve or maintain optimal fitness levels; (c) instruction in concepts that lead to a better understanding of motor skills and fitness development; (d) opportunities to engage in experiences that enhance cooperation and develop multicultural awareness; and (e) experiences that foster the desire for lifelong participation in physical activity.

More specifically, the elementary curriculum should include many enjoyable activities that lead to the acquisition and refinement of fundamental motor patterns (e.g., running, skipping, jumping, catching, throwing, striking, balancing) that can be applied in game, sport, dance, and gymnastics contexts. The *movement-based curriculum* proposed and adapted by George Graham, Shirley Ann Holt/Hale, and Melissa Parker in 1998 introduces skill themes (fundamental motor patterns) and movement concepts that describe how a movement is performed (e.g., speed, direction, relationship). This curriculum pattern teaches children to move while challenging them to explore, modify, and refine motor patterns, and it can be used as a vehicle for teaching physical education. The *activity based* approach is the most common curriculum pattern used in both middle schools and high schools. This curricular pattern uses activity units in sport, fitness, and dance (e.g., volleyball, aerobic dance, swimming) to teach physical education.

Middle school curriculums should include a wide variety of team and individual sports utilizing motor skills introduced and refined at the elementary level. High school curriculums should focus on lifetime sports skills (e.g., golf, tennis, aerobic dance), with a secondary emphasis on team sports. During the high school years, students should become highly proficient in one (or more) sport and/or fitness activity of their own choosing. However, regardless of the level of schooling, fitness forms the base of the curriculum and it is an integral part of the program.

Trends, Issues, and Controversies

School accountability, a major trend of the 1990s, has driven the need for national assessment (testing) and standards. This trend has become an issue and has created debate throughout education, including physical education. Proponents on both sides have valid points to make. Those who oppose national testing point out the need for people to enjoy physical activity. They believe that testing does not foster the desire for lifelong participation. In contrast, proponents of testing think it would parallel work completed in other disciplines, such as math and science, while helping students gauge their progress towards a national standard for fitness and/or skill competence.

The National Association for Sport and Physical Education has provided guidelines in the form of grade-level benchmarks, as well as an operational definition of the *physically educated person.* Such a person is skillful in a variety of physical activities, physically fit, participates regularly in physical activity, knows the benefits of physical activity, values physical activity and its contributions to a healthy lifestyle, respects diversity, and acts in a socially responsible manner. The question remains, however, of how much direction and specificity in the form of standards and assessment are needed.

In many school programs and business settings, the term *wellness* has replaced *fitness* and *health.* In general, this term refers to optimal health and well-being, but it has been broadened to include the dimensions of emotional, mental, spiritual, social, and environmental well-being.

There are many issues that are of interest to all educators, issues that pose a challenge to all of those who seek to teach children. These include discipline problems, student drug abuse, violence, insufficient resources, lack of parental support for education, large classes, teacher burnout, and perhaps most importantly, a concern for the health and well-being of all children.

By far the greatest issue facing physical education in K–12 institutions is the reduction of time in the curriculum allotted to this important subject. The need for daily physical education is obviously important for the well-being of students, but it presents a dilemma for those who must balance academics, accountability, and what is best for the child's overall education. Given the support for the physical and psychological contributions of exercise, along with the health risks associated with inactivity, it is clear that daily physical education plays a crucial and unique role in each child's cognitive, psychological, and physical development.

See also: ELEMENTARY EDUCATION, *subentries on* CURRENT TRENDS, HISTORY OF; HEALTH EDUCATION, SCHOOL; SECONDARY EDUCATION, *subentries on* CURRENT TRENDS, HISTORY OF; SPORTS, SCHOOL.

BIBLIOGRAPHY

AMERICAN ALLIANCE FOR HEALTH, PHYSICAL EDUCATION, RECREATION AND DANCE. 1999. *Speak II: Sport and Physical Education Advocacy Kit II.* Reston, VA: American Alliance for Health, Physical Education, Recreation and Dance.

BENCRAFT, C. EDWIN. 1999. "Relationship between Physical Activity, Brain Development and Cognitive Performance." *Brain Research and Physical Activity: Maryland Physical Education Study Group Report. SPEAK Kit,* Vol. 2. Reston, VA: American Alliance for Health, Physical Education, Recreation and Dance.

CENTERS FOR DISEASE CONTROL AND PREVENTION. 1995. *Youth Risk Behavior Survey.* Atlanta, GA: Centers for Disease Control and Prevention.

CENTERS FOR DISEASE CONTROL AND PREVENTION. 1997. *Guidelines for School and Community Programs: Lifelong Physical Activity.* Washington, DC: U.S. Department of Health and Human Services.

FAHEY, THOMAS D.; INSEL, PAUL M.; and ROTH, WALTON T. 1994. *Fit and Well.* Mountain View, CA: Mayfield.

GRAHAM, GEORGE; HOLT/HALE, SHIRLEY ANN; and PARKER, MELISSA. 1998. *Children Moving: A Reflective Approach to Teaching Physical Education,* 4th edition. Mountain View, CA: Mayfield.

HARRISON, JOYCE M.; BLAKEMORE, CONNIE L.; and BUCK, MARILYN M. 2001. *Instructional Strategies for Secondary School Physical Education,* 5th edition. Boston, MA: McGraw-Hill.

JENSEN, ERIC. 1998. *Teaching with the Brain in Mind.* Alexandria, VA: Association for Supervision and Curriculum Development.

LUMPKIN, ANGELA. 1994. *Physical Education and Sport: A Contemporary Introduction,* 3rd edition. St. Louis: Mosby.

NATIONAL ASSOCIATION FOR SPORT AND PHYSICAL EDUCATION. 1992. *The Physically Educated Person.* Reston, VA: National Association for Sport and Physical Education.

NATIONAL ASSOCIATION FOR SPORT AND PHYSICAL EDUCATION. 1995. *Moving into the Future: National Standard for Physical Education.* St Louis, MO: Mosby.

NATIONAL EDUCATION ASSOCIATION. 1893. *NEA Proceedings* 32:621.

SWANSON, RICHARD A., and SPEARS, BETTY MARY. 1995. *History of Sport and Physical Education in the United States,* 4th edition. Madison, WI: WCB Brown and Benchmark.

U.S. DEPARTMENT OF HEALTH AND HUMAN SERVICES. 1990. *Healthy People 2000: National Health Promotion Disease Prevention Objectives.* DHHS Publication Number PSH 91-50212. Washington, DC: U.S. Government Printing Office.

U.S. DEPARTMENT OF HEALTH AND HUMAN SERVICES. 1996. *Physical Activity and Health: A Report of the Surgeon General.* Atlanta, GA: Centers for Disease Control and Prevention.

B. ANN BOYCE

PREPARATION OF TEACHERS

In the United States, teacher preparation in physical education originally had close links to medicine. A program of study would commonly include anatomy, physiology, health, first aid, history and philosophy, educational psychology, and various physical skills—from gymnastics through dance, games, and sport. Major shifts across time have largely involved the length of programs of study on each of these topics.

A Brief History

The early roots of physical education teacher preparation in the United States can be traced to the northeastern part of the country during the latter part of the 1800s. In 1952 Charles Bucher described a ten-week course at the Normal Institute of Physical Education in Boston (founded by Dio Lewis) as graduating the nation's first class of physical education teachers in 1861. A one-year course of study was developed in 1866 in New York City under the name of the North American Turnerbund. The Sargent School in Cambridge, Massachusetts, under the direction of Dr. Dudley Allen Sargent, began preparing teachers in 1881, and in 1886 the Brooklyn Normal School for Physical Education was opened.

In 1886 the International Young Men's Christian Association College at Springfield Massachusetts began operations. This institution, which evolved into the Springfield College, began with the mission to prepare physical education teachers for the Young Men's Christian Association (YMCA). Later, degrees at the bachelor's, master's and doctoral levels for study in physical education were awarded by this institution. In general, the preparation of physical education teachers in the late 1800s and early 1900s ranged from as little as two months to as much as five years.

Prior to World War I, preparation to teach physical education was primarily completed in normal schools. The poor condition of many of the men in the country who were called to serve in the war heightened interest in physical education. As a result of such concerns, there was some form of compulsory public school physical education in thirty-eight states by 1930.

At the beginning of the twenty-first century, the requirements for physical education teachers vary somewhat by state, since education is governed at that level rather than by national standards. The National Association for Sport and Physical Education (NASPE) has published guidelines for beginning teachers in an attempt to provide some professional leadership. These guidelines are not binding on either institutions preparing teachers or on state governments, where the responsibility of licensing teachers rests. In a collaborative effort with one of the major accrediting agencies for teacher preparation programs, the National Council for Accreditation of Teacher Education (NCATE), NASPE has created guidelines for programs seeking accreditation in the preparation of physical educators for initial certification.

Current Structure

Physical education teacher education (PETE) programs in the United States are designed around at least three models and five conceptual orientations. One model is delivered at the undergraduate level and two at the graduate level. At the undergraduate level, programs are usually delivered in a four-year program with course work in three major areas: general education (e.g., the broad concepts in many fields that the general public associates with an educated citizen), professional education (e.g., concepts specifically linked with what is known about teaching and learning), and content knowledge (e.g., the information unique to the field, often represented in a variety of subdisciplinary areas such as exercise physiology, biomechanics, and motor learning). The actual number of credits and sequence of these courses varies and is often dependent upon the philosophical orientation of the program and resources available to the faculty.

One type of graduate PETE program has evolved from various reform efforts, including the Holmes Group initiative. In this approach, students study for a four-year degree in the content area supporting the type of licensure they seek. In physical education, an undergraduate degree could be in sport studies, exercise physiology, biomechanics, or some other related subdisciplinary field. At the master's level, students then study the pedagogical content to learn how to deliver the content knowledge to students. This approach is a response to perceived needs of teachers to be better prepared in the content knowledge of their field.

A second type of graduate PETE program is sometimes characterized as a response to teacher shortages. In this approach, candidates have typically acquired an undergraduate degree in some field other than physical education. Graduate programs for this approach must include a combination of content knowledge and professional education. Students changing careers are often attracted to this model.

In 1990 Sharon Feiman-Nemser described five conceptual orientations to teacher education, regardless of the model; three years later Judith Rink provided adaptations to these models using examples appropriate to PETE programs. Both authors suggest that the conceptual orientation guides the delivery of content. In contrast to Feiman-Nemser, however, Rink suggests that it is possible for parts of each orientation to exist in any program.

The *academic* orientation holds that the subject matter knowledge is central. The focus of these programs is on games, sports, dance, and fitness knowledge. In the *practical* orientation, experience and conventional wisdom are the focal points. Field experiences are key parts of these programs, where students are given ample practice time with practice-proven methods of teaching. The *technological* orientation has also been characterized as systematic, science-based instruction where there is an emphasis on mastering teacher effectiveness skills. Instruction is based on research-based teaching for student skill development. The *personal* orientation is a more humanistic approach where the teacher and learner are considered as people first; teaching, learning, and content are secondary concerns. Individualization, nurturing personal meaning, and growth are hallmarks of this approach to teacher education. In the *critical/social* orientation, the relationship between schools and the structure of society becomes central. Attention is drawn to the moral obligations of teachers to include all members of society, regardless of age, gender, race, religion, skill level, or socioeconomic level.

Michael Metzler and Bonnie Tjeerdsma (2000) suggest that teacher educators have a responsibility to assess the effectiveness of what they do, with whatever model or conceptual orientation is selected. They suggest that few teacher educators have spent much effort doing this type of assessment. In an effort to be of assistance, Metzler and Tjeerdsma provide a variety of tools for assessing and improving program delivery.

Daryl Siedentop and Larry Locke provided an alternative perspective on assessing PETE programs in 1997. They describe the minimum conditions necessary for the effective operation of a PETE program, and also suggest that the responsibility of PETE programs goes beyond educating new recruits and includes a duty to "create and sustain good school programs" (p. 27). These authors go on to lament that few PETE faculty have assumed any responsibility for the quality of programs in schools, instead adopting an "us" (e.g., faculty in higher education) versus "them" (e.g., teachers in the K–12 schools) mentality. The outcome of this adversarial relationship has been a declining level of competent program delivery, with national health-related consequences. In 1990 John Goodlad identified a similar concern when he suggested that the reform or renewal of schools, teachers, and teacher preparation programs has to occur simultaneously.

In-Service and Staff Development

Most states require some sort of ongoing accumulation of continuing education credits for teachers to retain their licensure. Most school districts create opportunities for continuing education related to topics relevant to the purposes of schools and needs of students in their community. Unfortunately, these opportunities are often too generic to address the specific needs of physical educators, and are often perceived to be ineffective.

Beyond state and school district requirements, there is a key challenge for licensure programs: convincing graduates that their preparation to become true professionals has not ended, but has just begun. Without an internal commitment to ongoing professional growth, few in-service or staff development efforts are effective at eliciting change. Indeed, although specific examples of successful change efforts can be cited, Linda Bain (1990) describes practice in physical education as "generally resistant to change" (p. 771).

Michael Eraut (1987) describes four approaches to in-service education that can be used to categorize some of the work in physical education. The *defect* approach involves behavioral training to build skills that teachers lack. In physical education, targets of this approach have included different verbal behaviors (e.g., feedback, prompts, questions, use of student names, etc.), teacher movement, task selection, and others. The *growth* approach is about helping teachers seek greater fulfillment, rather than helping them simply become competent. In physical education, this approach is difficult to distinguish from the *problem-solving* approach, where efforts are made to help teachers diagnose problems in their own instructional setting. Program research from places like Teachers College at Columbia University and the University of Massachusetts would be examples of this kind of in-service program. Lastly, the *change* paradigm involves efforts to make changes in programs that are responsive to greater societal needs. Attention to gender equity, mainstreaming, and nondiscrimination would be examples of this work in physical education.

Trends and Controversies

The most critical concern facing physical educators in the United States is the viability of physical education programs as a required subject in schools. As opportunities for advanced placement courses; electives in art, music, and foreign languages; and other varied courses have occurred, time in the required curriculum for physical education has declined. There are consequences to this on at least two levels. First, the health of the nation is at risk when the most equitable delivery system for ensuring active lifestyles is curtailed. Second, there is a declining need for teacher education programs when there are fewer teaching positions available for program graduates.

Related to the time available for physical education programs in schools is an ongoing debate over the most appropriate content for programs. In some states (e.g., West Virginia and Florida) there is a major emphasis on student performance on fitness tests as an indication of physical education program effectiveness. In other states (e.g., Missouri) there is more of an emphasis on the demonstration of written competence in health-related fitness knowledge. In at least one other approach (South Carolina), there is an attempt to hold teachers accountable for fitness levels and fitness knowledge, as well as out-of-class behaviors and movement competence. There are obvious implications for teacher preparation programs in each of these states with respect to what will be expected of program graduates. It is also worth noting that none of these approaches is an exact match with NASPE guidelines.

Part of the debate over appropriate content for teacher preparation can be traced back to a classic 1964 work by Franklin Henry, where physical education was first conceptualized as an academic discipline in the United States. For the first time, the study of human movement spawned viable areas of study, leading to degrees and careers other than teaching. Today, locating departments of physical education in colleges and universities is a challenge, partly because such departments can go by so many different names: 114 have been counted by P. Stanley Brassie and Jack Razor, including Biomechanics, Kinesiological Studies, Kinesiology, Sport Science, and Sport Studies, to cite just a few. Approximately half of these departments are in colleges of education, while others are in colleges of liberal arts, applied sciences, health, or elsewhere. This identity crisis has lead to marginal status for physical educators at all levels.

A common trend in teacher preparation programs is for early and frequent field-based experiences for students. The challenge is to find (or create) placements where desirable practices are being modeled. An additional challenge is to determine the amount and type of training required to prepare school-based supervisors.

The last major controversy that warrants mention in teacher preparation involves determining the most appropriate level for initial licensure. In some institutions (e.g., the Ohio State University), initial licensure in physical education is only available at the graduate level. In other schools (e.g., University of South Carolina), initial licensure is available at both the undergraduate and graduate level. In most of the rest of the country, initial licensure is predominantly delivered at the undergraduate level. There is no definitive evidence on which (if any) of these approaches is the most appropriate way to prepare physical education teachers.

See also: CURRICULUM, HIGHER EDUCATION, *subentry on* TRADITIONAL AND CONTEMPORARY PERSPECTIVES; CURRICULUM, SCHOOL; HEALTH EDUCATION, SCHOOL; SPORTS, SCHOOL.

BIBLIOGRAPHY

BAIN, LINDA. 1990. "Physical Education Teacher Education." In *Handbook of Research on Teacher Education,* ed. W. Robert Houston. New York: Macmillan.

BRASSIE, P. STANLEY, and RAZOR, JACK. 1989. "HPER Unit Names in Higher Education: A View toward the Future." *Journal of Physical Education, Recreation and Dance* 60(7):33–40.

BUCHER, CHARLES AUGUSTUS. 1952. *Foundations of Physical Education.* St. Louis, MO: C.V. Mosby.

COLEMAN, MARGARET, and MITCHELL, MURRAY. 2000. "Assessing Observation Focus and Conference Targets of Cooperating Teachers." *Journal of Teaching in Physical Education* 20:40–54.

ERAUT, MICHAEL. 1987. "Inservice Teacher Education." In *The International Encyclopedia of Teaching and Teacher Education,* ed. Michael J. Dunkin. Elmsford, NY: Pergamon Press.

FEIMAN-NEMSER, SHARON. 1990. *Conceptual Orientations in Teacher Education.* East Lansing, MI: Michigan State University, National Center for Research on Teacher Education.

GOODLAD, JOHN. 1990. *Teachers for Our Nation's Schools.* San Francisco: Jossey-Bass.

HENRY, FRANKLIN. 1964. "Physical Education As an Academic Discipline." *Journal of Health, Physical Education and Recreation* 37(9):32–33.

HOLMES GROUP. 1986. *Tomorrow's Teachers.* East Lansing, MI: Holmes Group.

HOUSNER, LYNN. 1996. "Innovation and Change in Physical Education." In *Student Learning in Physical Education: Applying Research to Enhance Instruction,* ed. Stephen Silverman and Catherine Ennis. Champaign, IL: Human Kinetics.

MECHIKOFF, ROBERT, and ESTES, STEVEN. 1993. *A History and Philosophy of Sport and Physical Education.* Madison, WI: Brown and Benchmark.

METZLER, MICHAEL, and TJEERDSMA, BONNIE. 2000. *Assessment of Physical Education Teacher Education Programs.* Reston, VA: National Association for Sport and Physical Education.

NATIONAL ASSOCIATION FOR SPORT AND PHYSICAL EDUCATION. 1992. *Developmentally Appropriate Physical Education Practices for Children.* Washington, DC: American Alliance for Health, Physical Education, Recreation and Dance.

NATIONAL ASSOCIATION FOR SPORT AND PHYSICAL EDUCATION. 1995. *Moving into the Future: National Standards for Physical Education.* St. Louis: C.V. Mosby.

NATIONAL ASSOCIATION FOR SPORT AND PHYSICAL EDUCATION. 1995. *National Standards for Beginning Physical Education Teachers.* Reston, VA: National Association for Sport and Physical Education.

NATIONAL ASSOCIATION FOR SPORT AND PHYSICAL EDUCATION. 1997. *Shape of the Nation.* Reston, VA: National Association for Sport and Physical Education.

NATIONAL ASSOCIATION FOR SPORT AND PHYSICAL EDUCATION. 1998. *National Association for Sport and Physical Education / National Council for Accreditation of Teacher Education Guidelines for Teacher Preparation in Physical Education.* Reston, VA: National Association for Sport and Physical Education.

RINK, JUDITH E. 1993. "Teacher Education: A Focus on Action." *Quest* 45:308–320.

SIEDENTOP, DARYL, and LOCKE, LARRY. 1997. "Making a Difference for Physical Education: What

Professors and Practitioners Must Build Together." *Journal of Physical Education, Recreation and Dance* 68(4):25–33.

MURRAY MITCHELL

PHYSICAL EDUCATION: ADAPTED

See: ADAPTED PHYSICAL EDUCATION.

PIAGET, JEAN (1896–1980)

Director of the Institute of Educational Science in Geneva and professor of experimental psychology at the University of Geneva, Jean Piaget was the most influential developmental psychologist of the twentieth century. Many of Piaget's concepts and research methods have become so much a part of the conventional wisdom and practice that psychologists are often unaware of their origin. The stages of development that Piaget observed and conceptualized are given extended treatment in every introductory psychology and developmental psychology textbook. In addition, much of contemporary research on infancy grows directly out of Piaget's innovative studies of his own three infants. Moreover, a great deal of present day research and theory regarding adolescence starts from Piaget's demonstration of the appearance of new, higher level, mental abilities during this age period. In these and in many other ways, Piaget's research and theory continue to be a powerful stimulus in many different fields and areas of investigation.

Piaget's work, however, has had an impact on other disciplines as well. The contemporary emphasis upon constructivism in education, for example, stems directly from Piaget's theory of intellectual development. According to Piaget the child does not copy reality, but rather constructs it. Reality is developmentally relative; it is always a joint product of the child's developing mental abilities and his or her experiences with the world. Piaget's research and theory has also had considerable impact upon psychiatry. His description of the intellectual stages of development has provided a very important complement to the psychosexual stages of development outlined by the Austrian psychologist Sigmund Freud. In these, and in many other ways, the power of Piaget's work continues to be felt in many diverse fields.

Jean Piaget was born in Neuchâtel, Switzerland. His father was a classics professor at the University of Neuchâtel while his mother was a deeply devout Christian. In his autobiography, Piaget suggests that the ongoing conflict between his father's scientific beliefs and his mother's spiritual convictions contributed to his theory of mental development. He came to regard the development of intelligence as motivated by the progressive resolution of conflicting ideas. Be that as it may, Piaget showed his genius early. At the age of fourteen he published his first scientific paper, his observations of an albino sparrow. He also became, thanks to the mentorship of the curator of the Neuchâtel natural history museum, a student of mollusks. He began experimenting with crustaceans and publishing his findings in the biological journals. These articles were so well received that he was offered the curatorship of a natural history museum in another Swiss canton. Piaget, however, had to refuse because he had not yet graduated from high school.

Once at the university, Piaget took courses in both philosophy and biology and struggled to find some way to reconcile his philosophical interests with his commitment to science. He hit upon a unique solution in an unexpected place. After receiving his doctorate, Piaget explored a number of different professions including psychiatry. He eventually took a position in Paris, translating some of the intelligence tests created by the English psychologist, Sir Cyril Burt, into French. As part of this endeavor, it was necessary for Piaget to test a number of children in order to ensure that his translations had not made the items easier or more difficult than they were for English children of comparable age. While administering these tests, Piaget became fascinated with the children's wrong answers. To Piaget, these wrong answers did not seem random. Rather they appeared to be generated by a systematic way of seeing things that was not wrong, but simply reflected a different world view than that held by adults.

Piaget was fascinated by his unexpected discovery that children's perception of reality was not learned from adults, as had heretofore been assumed, but was constructed. Children's conception of the world, Piaget reasoned, was different than that of adults because their thought processes were different. Piaget assumed that he would pursue this problem, the development of children's thinking, for a few years and then move on to other things. Instead, this pursuit of the ways in which children construct reality, became the foundation of a lifelong professional career. Piaget came to realize that the study of the development of children's adaptive thought and action, of their intelligence, was a way of pursuing both his philosophical and his scientific interests.

One field of philosophy is epistemology, the study of how people come to know the world. Most philosophers approach this topic by means of introspection and logical analysis. Piaget, however, believed that he could put epistemological questions to the test by studying the development of thought and action in children. Accordingly Piaget created his own new discipline with its own methods and problems. The field was genetic epistemology, the study of child development as a means of answering epistemological questions. Piaget's career exploration of genetic epistemology can be roughly divided into four different stages.

Stage 1: The Sociological Model of Development

During this first stage, roughly corresponding to the 1920s, Piaget investigated children's heretofore unexplored conceptions of the world, the hidden side of children's minds. To further this exploration Piaget made use of a combination of psychological and clinical methods that he described as the *semiclinical interview*. He began with a standardized question, but followed up with nonstandard questions that were prompted by the child's answer. In order to get what Piaget called children's "spontaneous convictions" he often asked questions that the children neither expected nor anticipated. In his study of children's conception of the world, for example, he asked children whether a stone was alive and where dreams came from. He made a comparative study of children's answers and found that for these and for similar questions there was a gradual progression from intuitive to scientific and socially acceptable responses.

During this early period, Piaget published *The Language and Thought of the Child, The Child's Conception of the World, The Child's Conception of Physical Causality,* and *The Moral Judgment of the Child.* Each of these books was highly original and they made Piaget world famous before he was thirty. In these books he elaborated his first theory of development, which postulated the mental development was fueled by a social dynamic. He proposed that children moved from a position of egocentrism (a fail-

ure to take the other person's point of view into account) to sociocentrism (the recognition that others see the world differently than they do). Children moved from the egocentric to the sociocentric position thanks to social interaction and the challenge to younger children's ideas by the ideas of those children who were more advanced. Piaget made it clear, however, that the young children's egocentric ideas were not wrong, but merely different from those of the older children. Egocentric ideas are developmentally appropriate for young children, if not for older ones.

Stage 2: The Biological Model of Intellectual Development

In 1928 Piaget married one of his graduate students and started a family in the 1930s. Having his own infant children set the stage for the second phase of Piaget's work, the exploration of the development of intelligence in infants. During this period, Piaget studied his own three offspring. The semiclinical interview was clearly not of much use with infants who could not talk. Piaget, therefore, invented a number of ingenious experiments to test the infant's knowledge about the world. For example, he placed a cloth over a toy that the infant was playing with to see whether or not the baby would try to remove the cloth to recover the toy. If the baby removed the cloth this would be evidence that he or she had some mental representation of the toy. If the baby did not remove the cloth, but merely cried in frustration, this would be evidence that the infant had not yet attained representational thought.

During this second period of his work, Piaget elaborated a biological model of intellectual development, which he combined with the sociological model of the earlier period. He now described intelligence as having two closely interrelated facets. One of these, carried over from the earlier period, was the content of children's thinking. The other, new to this period, was the process of intellectual activity. Piaget now introduced a truly powerful idea, namely, that the process of thinking could be regarded as an extension of the biological process of adaptation.

He argued, for example, that the child who sucked on anything and everything in his or her reach was engaging in an act of assimilation, comparable to the assimilation of food by the digestive system. Just as the digestive system transforms a variety of foodstuffs into the nutriments needed by the body, so the infant transforms every object into an object to be sucked. At much higher level, whenever one classifies an object, say a dog, he or she in effect assimilates this exemplar to their more general dog concept. In so doing the particular dog is transformed into the universal, conceptual dog. At all stages of development, therefore, whenever one transforms the world to meet individual needs or conceptions, one is, in effect, assimilating it.

Piaget also observed that his infant children not only transformed some stimuli to conform to their own mental structures but also modified some of their mental structures to meet the demands of the environment. He called this facet of adaptation *accommodation*. At the biological level the body accommodates when, for example, its blood vessels constrict in response to cold and expand in response to heat. Piaget observed similar accommodations at the behavioral and conceptual levels. The young infant engages primarily in reflex actions, such as sucking the thumb or grasping. But shortly thereafter the infant will grasp some object and proceed to put that in his or her mouth. In this instance the child has modified his or her reflex response to accommodate an external object into the reflex action. That is to say, the infant's instinctual thumbsucking reflex has been adapted to objects in the environment. Piaget regarded this behavioral adaptation as a model for what happens at higher intellectual levels as well. Whenever one learns new facts, values, or skills, he or she is, in effect, modifying mental structures to meet the demands of the external world.

In Piaget's view, assimilation and accommodation are the invariant processes of intellectual processing and are present throughout life. Furthermore, because the two are often in conflict they provide the power for intellectual development. The child's first tendency is to assimilate, but when this is not possible, he or she must accommodate. It is the constant tension between assimilation and accommodation and the need for some form of equilibrium between them that triggers intellectual growth. For example, in the "hiding the toy experiment" described above, the six-month-old infant simply cried while the one-year-old infant lifted the cloth to reveal the hidden object. This initial upset, and failure of assimilation, thus led to the infant's construction of a mental image of the object. This new construction allows the child to solve the problem and remove the cloth from the toy. At each level of development, the failure of assimilation leads to a new accommodations that result in a new equilib-rium that prepares for yet another level of disequi-librium.

Piaget published the results of these infant studies in three books, *The Origins of Intelligence in the Child, The Construction of Reality in the Child,* and *Play Dreams and Imitation.* These books continue to stimulate a wide range of investigations into the developing abilities of infants.

Stage 3: The Elaboration of the Logical Model of Intellectual Development

During the third period of his work, from the 1940s through the 1960s, Piaget explored the development of many different physical and mathematical concepts in children and adolescents. To explore the physical and mathematical conceptions of children and adolescents, Piaget returned to the semiclinical interview, but in modified form. He decided that the way to test children's level of conceptual development was to challenge their understanding of conservation, that is, their understanding that an object's physical or mathematical properties do not change despite a change in its appearance. Piaget based this methodology on the fact that scientific progress occurs when judgments of reason win out over judgments based upon appearance. The discovery of the roundness of the earth is a good example. The ancients believed that the world was flat. It was only from later observations and reasoning about the disappearance of ships on the horizon and the shadow of the earth on the moon that the perception of flatness could be overcome.

To test children's understanding of conservation, Piaget presented children with a wide array of tasks in which the child had to make a judgment on the basis of either perception or reason. Only when the child made his or her judgment on the basis of reason was the child said to have attained conservation. For example, in his studies of children's conception of number, Piaget confronted children with two rows of six pennies, one spread apart so that it was longer than the other. Young children judge the longer row to have more pennies, while older children judge both rows to have the same amount. Older children have attained the conservation of number while younger children have not.

With this conservation methodology, Piaget and his longtime colleague, Barbel Inhelder, explored how children constructed their concepts of number, space, time, geometry, speed, and much more. In this third phase of his work, Piaget introduced a logical model to explain children's attainment of conservation in different domains and at different age levels. It is this logical model of intellectual development for which he is perhaps best known. Piaget argued that intelligence develops in a series of stages that are related to age and that are progressive in the sense that each is a necessary prerequisite of the next. There is no skipping of stages. In addition, he contended that each stage was characterized by a set of mental operations that are logical in nature but vary in complexity. At each stage of development the child constructs a view of reality in keeping with the operations at that age period. At the next stage, however, with the attainment of new mental abilities the child has to reconstruct the concepts formed at the earlier level in keeping with his or her new mental abilities. In effect, therefore, Piaget conceived of intellectual development as an upward expanding spiral wherein the child must constantly reconstruct the ideas formed at an earlier level with new, higher order concepts acquired at the next level.

The first stage, infancy or the first two years of life, Piaget described as the *sensori-motor period.* In the first two years of life, the baby constructs elementary concepts of space, time, and causality but these are at the visual, auditory, tactual, and motoric level, and do not go beyond the here and now. At the next stage of development, the *pre-operational level,* children acquire the symbolic function and are able to represent their experience. Children now begin to use words and symbols to convey their experience and to go beyond the immediate. Concepts of space, time, and causality, for example, begin to be understood with terms like *now* and *later,* as well as *day* and *night.* Once the child's thought moves from the sensori-motor to the symbolic level, it has much more breadth and depth.

By the age of six or seven children attain a new set of mental abilities that Piaget termed *concrete operations,* which resemble the operations of arithmetic and which lift school-age children to a whole new plane of thinking. Concrete operations enable young children to reason in a syllogistic way. That may be the reason the ancients called these years the age of reason. Concrete operations enable children to deal with verbal rules and that is why formal education is usually begun at about this time. Following rules is in effect reasoning syllogistically. Consider the classic model of the syllogism.

All men are mortal.

Socrates is a man.

Therefore Socrates is mortal.

This is the same form of reasoning the child must employ if he or she is to follow the rule that says "when two vowels go walking, the first one does the talking."

When two vowels go walking the first one does the talking.

In the word *ate* there are two vowels and the first is an *a.*

In this word, a does the talking.

Concrete operations enable young children to construct their conceptions of space, time, number, and causality on a higher quantitative plane. It is during the elementary years that children are able to learn clock and calendar time, map and geographical space, and experimental causality.

At about the age of eleven or twelve young people develop yet a higher level of mental operations that Piaget labeled *formal.* These operations are formal in the sense that they are no longer tied to the here and now and are abstract in the sense that they can be in conflict with reality. For example, if you ask a younger child to imagine a world in which snow was black and to guess what color, in that world, Mickey Mouse's ears would be, the child would have trouble saying they were white. Adolescents who have attained formal operations have no trouble with this problem. Formal operations enable young people to understand celestial space, historical time, and multivariable causality. They can construct ideals, think in terms of possibilities, and deal with multiple variables at the same time. Formal operations move young people to a new plane of thought, which is on a level with adult thinking.

Stage 4: The Study of Figurative Thought

During the last stage of Piaget's work, which lasted until his death in 1980, Piaget explored what he called the *figurative facets of intelligence.* By figurative Piaget meant those aspects of intelligence such as perception and memory that were not entirely logical. Logical concepts are completely reversible in the sense that one can always get back to the starting point. The logical addition of concepts, such as "boys plus girls equals children," can be undone by logical subtraction, such as "children minus boys equals girls" or "children minus girls equals boys." But perceptual concepts cannot be manipulated in this way. The figure and ground of a picture, for example, cannot be separated because contours cannot be separated from the forms they outline. Memory too is figurative in that it is never completely reversible. Piaget and Inhelder published books on perception, memory and other figurative processes such as learning during this last period of his work.

Conclusion

Jean Piaget is clearly the giant of developmental psychology. His experimental paradigms have been replicated in almost every country in the world and with quite extraordinary comparability of results. Piaget's observations, then, are among the hardiest, if not the hardiest, data in all of psychology. No other research paradigm has received such extensive cross-cultural confirmation. In the early twenty-first century there has been a tendency of investigators to dismiss Piaget's work as passé. This would be a mistake. While it is important to challenge Piaget and to build upon the foundation he has provided, it would be wrong to discount his work without having a comparable database on which to found such a rejection. Indeed, the opposite is more likely the case, namely, that the value of much of Piaget's work both for developmental psychology education and for other disciplines is yet to be fully realized.

See also: LEARNING THEORY, *subentry on* CONSTRUCTIVIST APPROACH.

BIBLIOGRAPHY

BEARD, RUTH M. 1983. *An Outline of Piaget's Developmental Psychology.* Boston: Routledge and Kegan Paul.

EVANS, RICHARD I. 1973. *Jean Piaget: The Man and His Ideas.* New York: E. P. Dutton.

KAMII, CONSTANCE. 1993. *Physical Knowledge in Preschool Education: Implications of Piaget's Theory.* New York: Teacher's College Press.

PIAGET, JEAN. 1926. *The Language and Thought of the Child.* London: Routledge and Kegan Paul.

PIAGET, JEAN. 1929. *The Child's Conception of the World.* New York: Harcourt, Brace.

PIAGET, JEAN. 1948. *The Moral Judgment of the Child,* trans. M. Gabain. Glencoe, IL: Free Press.

PIAGET, JEAN. 1950. *The Psychology of Intelligence.* London: Routledge and Kegan Paul.

PIAGET, JEAN. 1951. *Play Dreams and Imitation in Childhood.* New York: Norton.

PIAGET, JEAN. 1952. *The Origins of Intelligence in the Child.* New York: International Universities Press.

PIAGET, JEAN. 1970. *Science of Education and the Psychology of the Child.* New York: Orion.

PIAGET, JEAN, and INHELDER, BARBEL. 1958. *The Growth of Logical Thinking from Childhood to Adolescence.* New York: Basic Books.

PIAGET, JEAN, and INHELDER, B. 1971. *Mental Imagery in the Child.* London: Routledge and Kegan Paul.

DAVID ELKIND

PLATO (427?–347 B.C.E.)

Plato (427?–347 B.C.E.) was a prominent Athenian philosopher who posed fundamental questions about education, human nature, and justice.

A student of the famous philosopher Socrates, Plato left Athens upon his mentor's death in 399 B.C.E. After traveling to other parts of Greece, Italy, and Sicily, Plato returned to Athens in 387 B.C.E. and founded a school of mathematics and philosophy called the Academy, which became the most prominent intellectual institution in all of ancient Greece. Plato authored a number of dialogues that often depicted Socrates engaging in the educational mode of dialectic. Like his mentor, Plato suspected that most people did not know what they claimed to know, and hence wondered why rigorous qualifications for rulers did not exist. Challenging the Sophists' claims that knowledge and truth were relative to the perspective of each individual, Plato developed an epistemology and metaphysics that suggested an absolute truth that could only be gleaned through rigorous self-examination and the development of reason—skills crucial for enlightened political leaders.

The Ideal State

Plato's educational ideas derived in part from his conception of justice, both for individuals and for the ideal state. He viewed individuals as mutually dependent for their survival and well-being, and he proposed that justice in the ideal state was congruent with justice in the individual's soul.

Plato's ideal state was a republic with three categories of citizens: artisans, auxiliaries, and philosopher-kings, each of whom possessed distinct natures and capacities. Those proclivities, moreover, reflected a particular combination of elements within one's tripartite soul, composed of appetite, spirit, and reason. Artisans, for example, were dominated by their appetites or desires, and therefore destined to produce material goods. Auxiliaries, a class of guardians, were ruled by spirit in their souls and possessed the courage necessary to protect the state from invasion. Philosopher-kings, the leaders of the ideal state, had souls in which reason reigned over spirit and appetite, and as a result possessed the foresight and knowledge to rule wisely. In Plato's view, these rulers were not merely elite intellectuals, but moral leaders. In the just state, each class of citizen had a distinct duty to remain faithful to its determined nature and engage solely in its destined occupation. The proper management of one's soul would yield immediate happiness and well-being, and specific educational methods would cultivate this brand of spiritual and civic harmony.

The Dialectical Method

Plato's educational priorities also reflected his distinct pedagogy. Challenging the Sophists—who prized rhetoric, believed in ethical and epistemological relativism, and claimed to teach "excellence"—Plato argued that training in "excellence" was meaningless without content and that knowledge was absolute, certain, and good. As a result, teachers assumed a high moral responsibility. Plato doubted whether a standard method of teaching existed for all subjects, and he argued that morally neutral education would corrupt most citizens. He preferred the dialectical method over the Sophists' rhetorical pedagogy. For Plato, the role of the teacher was not to fill an empty reservoir with specific skills, but to encourage the student to redirect his or her soul and to rearrange the priorities within it to allow reason to rule over the irrational elements of spirit and appetite.

In the *Meno,* Plato examined a paradox that challenged the dialectical method of education: if one knows nothing, then how will one come to recognize knowledge when he encounters it? In response, Plato's Socrates proposed a different idea. Through a geometry lesson with a slave boy, he attempted to demonstrate that all possessed some minimal knowledge that served as a window into one's eternal and omniscient soul. Through dialectic, the teacher could refute the student's false opin-

ions until the student pursued a true opinion that survived the rigors of critical examination. Unacquainted with the storehouse of knowledge in one's soul, a person needed to learn how to access or "recollect" it. Plato distanced himself further from the Sophists by distinguishing knowledge (eternal and certain) from opinion (unreliable and ephemeral).

Plato developed this idea more fully in the *Republic,* declaring knowledge superior to opinion in both an epistemological and ontological sense. Opinion reflected a misapprehension of reality, while knowledge belonged to an essential or "intelligible" realm. In particular, Plato proposed a linear hierarchy of knowledge starting with the "visible" realms of imagination and then belief, and moving to the "intelligible" realms of reason, and ultimately, knowledge. In his celebrated cave metaphor, Plato's Socrates depicted chained prisoners, who presumed shadows of representations cast by artificial light to be real. The first step of education, then, was to turn one's soul away from this artificial world of shadows and toward the representations of objects and ideas themselves—leading one to the realm of belief. The objects of belief, however, were still empirical, and thus, ephemeral, relative, and unreliable. Beyond the cave lay the intelligible realm of reason and knowledge. Plato asserted that ideas did not possess any physical qualities, and to ascend beyond the world of tangible objects and ideas, one needed to develop the power of abstract thinking through the use of postulates to draw conclusions about the universal essence or "form" of an object or idea. Mathematics constituted a particularly useful tool for the development of reason, as it relied heavily on logic and abstract thought. The ultimate stage of awareness for Plato was knowledge of the "form of the good"—a transcendence of all postulates and assumptions through abstract reasoning that yielded a certain and comprehensive understanding of all things.

Educational Programs

Plato also made clear that not all citizens of the ideal state possessed the same capacity to realize the "form of the good." As a result, he proposed distinct educational programs for future artisans, auxiliaries, and philosopher-kings. Plato favored mathematics as a precise and abstract model for the development of thought in the future rulers of the just state. Knowledge, however, could only be attained through the use of dialectic to shed all assumptions and to glean the first principle of all, the "form of the good." After many years of mathematical and dialectical study, followed by fifteen years of public service, the best of this group would have come to understand the "form of the good" and have become philosopher-kings. Cognizant of the interrelationship of all things and confident of the reasons behind them, the intellectually and morally elite would be equipped to rule the just state in an enlightened manner.

The Cultivation of Morals

In addition, Plato advocated the removal of all infants from their natural families to receive a proper aesthetic education—literary, musical, and physical—for the development of character in the soul and the cultivation of morals necessary for sustaining the just state. Suspecting that most writers and musicians did not know the subjects they depicted—that they cast mere shadows of representations of real objects, ideas, and people—Plato feared that artistic works could endanger the health of the just state. Consequently, he wanted to hold artists and potential leaders accountable for the consequences of their creations and policies. This is why Plato advocated the censorship of all forms of art that did not accurately depict the good in behavior. Art, as a powerful medium that threatened the harmony of the soul, was best suited for philosophers who had developed the capacity to know and could resist its dangerous and irrational allures. Exposure to the right kinds of stories and music, although not sufficient to make a citizen beautiful and good, would contribute to the proper development of the elements within one's soul. For Plato, aesthetics and morality were inextricable; the value of a work of art hinged on its propensity to lead to moral development and behavior.

A Less-Ideal State

In the *Laws,* Plato considered the possibility that not only the majority, but all citizens could be incapable of reaching the "form of the good." He thus envisioned a second-best state with rulers ignorant of the "form of the good" but capable of thought. Such a society had absolute and unyielding rulers who eradicated any idea or thing that questioned their authority. Acting as if they possessed wisdom, such leaders established laws that reflected their opinions and their imperfect conception of the good.

Modern Scholarship

Contemporary advocates of popular democracy have criticized Plato's republican scheme as elitist and tyrannical in prizing order over individual liberty. Indeed, Plato believed that individuals could not stand alone, and as most would never reach internal harmony or virtue, the majority needed to be told how to conduct its life by those who possessed that knowledge. Incapable of understanding the reasons behind the laws, most citizens needed merely to obey them.

Some scholars have also questioned Plato's treatment of women in his just state. For instance, Jane Roland Martin has argued that although he did not differentiate education or societal roles on the basis of sex, Plato was not committed to gender equality. Despite his abolition of the family, gender distinctions would have likely persisted, as Plato did not seek to ensure the equal portrayal of men and women in literature. According to this view, Plato's female guardians-in-training warranted a distinct education from men to help mitigate the cultural, symbolic, and epistemological assumptions of female subordination. Identical education, then, did not necessarily constitute equal education, a point that holds significant implications for contemporary assumptions about the effects of coeducation.

These criticisms illustrate the longevity of Plato's educational, metaphysical, and ethical ideas. In addition, other scholars have eschewed the tendency to evaluate the modern implications of Plato's specific educational doctrines, and instead have highlighted his assumption that education could address fundamental social problems. They view Plato's method of inquiry—critical self-examination through the dialectical interplay of teacher and student—as his primary contribution to educational thought. Indeed, perhaps education itself embodied the highest virtue of Plato's just state.

See also: PHILOSOPHY OF EDUCATION.

BIBLIOGRAPHY

BARROW, ROBIN. 1976. *Plato and Education.* London: Routledge and Kegan Paul.

BLANKENSHIP, J. DAVID. 1996. "Education and the Arts in Plato's *Republic.*" *Journal of Education* 178:67–98.

MARTIN, JANE ROLAND. 1985. *Reclaiming a Conversation: The Ideal of the Educated Woman.* New Haven, CT: Yale University Press.

PARRY, RICHARD D. 1996. "Morality and Happiness: Book IV of Plato's *Republic*." *Journal of Education* 178:31–47.

PLATO. 1976. *Meno,* trans. G. M. A. Grube. Indianapolis, IN: Hackett.

PLATO. 1976. *Protagoras,* trans. C. C. W. Taylor. Oxford: Clarendon Press.

PLATO. 1980. *The Laws of Plato,* trans. Thomas L. Pangle. New York: Basic Books.

PLATO. 1992. *Republic,* trans. G. M. A. Grube and rev. C. D. C. Reeve. Indianapolis, IN: Hackett.

SCOLNICOV, SAMUEL. 1988. *Plato's Metaphysics of Education.* London and New York: Routledge.

SEVAN G. TERZIAN

POLICY

See: EDUCATIONAL POLICY.

POPULATION AND EDUCATION

The relationship between education and population has attracted the attention of both scholars and policymakers, especially since the mid-1970s. The rate of population growth and the number of people living on earth have both increased spectacularly since the beginning of the nineteenth century. During the twentieth century, the human population increased at an average annual rate that was about fifty times as fast as the rate over the previous 10,000 years. Between 1800 and 2000, the number of people alive increased nearly seven-fold. Following World War II, the rate of population growth exploded—during the 1970s it was about four times as great as it had been a century earlier. By 2000, the living population exceeded the entire population born between the beginning of settled agriculture and the year 1900—a period of 10,000 years.

The implications of this explosive growth for both the physical environment and human well-being alarmed many observers and prompted an intense public policy debate. Many scholars and policymakers noted that high levels of educational achievement were associated with more moderate rates of population growth, suggesting that important opportunities for alleviating population pressures might be found in ensuring greater access to education, particularly for females. The ensuing public policy debate has prompted an examination of how education affects the birth rate.

The explosive growth of the human population in the nineteenth and twentieth centuries was the result of a historically unprecedented decline in the rate of mortality, rather than an increase in the birth rate. The proportion of children dying before reaching the age of five fell from nearly one in three in most of the world to less than one in one hundred in the most advanced societies over this period, and to one in ten in low-income countries. In the wealthiest countries, birth rates adjusted quickly to restore a balance between births and deaths and establish a rate of population growth of less than 1 percent a year. In economically advanced societies, the average number of children born to each woman over her reproductive life has fallen from about seven to less than two. However, in the poorest countries, a sharp drop in death rates has not been accompanied by a corresponding fall in birth rates. As a result, the rate of population growth—the difference between the average birth rate and the average mortality rate—has increased dramatically in most of the world. The growth of population has been greatest in countries that are both poorest and least able to invest in social and educational services. The combined effects of these forces seem to imply that the gulf between rich and poor is likely to widen over the foreseeable future if aggressive policy measures are not introduced.

These facts suggest that the key to ensuring a sustainable rate of population growth lies in reducing the fertility rate. However, in a highly influential 1979 review of the research literature on the relationship between education and fertility, the economist Susan Hill Cochrane concluded that too little was known about the mechanisms through which education affects population growth to allow policymakers to rely on improvements in educational opportunities to slow the rate of population growth. Since 1976 a large number of scholars have focused on the impact of education—especially the education of the girl child—on fertility, mortality, and population growth. The central purpose of these studies has been to determine whether the nearly universal association of low fertility and high levels of educational attainment are causally linked or merely the result of their association with other forces that directly affect fertility. For example, the inverse relationship between female literacy and fertility might have nothing to do with education as such, but might instead simply reveal that societies that seriously attempt to educate females also care about the welfare of women and therefore seek to control fertility in order to protect their health.

Social and Economic Factors

The research literature has sought to identify the causal pathways that link education and fertility. The scholars working in this area have been drawn primarily from the disciplines of economics, sociology, and demography, and they have brought with them the conceptual and methodological traditions of their respective disciplines. Economists have suggested that the issues be organized around the familiar (for economists) ideas of supply and demand. They have argued that the number of children actually born to a couple is determined by the capacity to bear children, the factors that determine desired family size, and the couple's ability to achieve its aims. The capacity for meeting fertility goals is determined by such factors as age at marriage, the health of the woman, her fertility, and customs and taboos that affect sexual relations. Women who marry early or enter into sexual unions at a younger age have a greater potential for childbearing than those who marry late. Nutritional status and disease history affect a woman's ability to conceive or to carry a pregnancy to full term. Cultural prohibitions against sexual relations for a prescribed period following childbirth or during breast-feeding reduce the period during which a woman may become pregnant. Failure to ovulate during breast-feeding also reduces the period during which a woman might become pregnant.

The demand for children (the number of children that a couple desires) is also the outcome of complex calculations. Economists have predictably focused on the net contributions of children to the income and material welfare of the family. In very-low-income communities, children typically become contributors to the economic welfare of the family at a very young age. Small children care for younger siblings, thereby releasing their mothers to work either in the fields or in shops. Often, very small children also assist in the herding of small animals and in the care of kitchen gardens. In addition, children provide parents with economic security in their old age. As average incomes and aspirations rise, parents typically seek to have fewer children and to provide these children with more and better education.

Labor market demands and the cultural values of higher-income communities stress education as a requisite of social success. Therefore, as incomes rise, families tend to have fewer children but to invest much more in the nurturing and education of each child. The demand for children is also affected by the costs of providing daughters with dowries and wedding celebrations.

The ability of a couple to achieve its desired family size depends in part on access to contraception. The decision to control fertility is affected by a very complex set of customs and interpersonal forces. Cultural norms that value large families make the limitation of fertility a very difficult choice for many couples living in traditional societies. The social status of the couple and its autonomy relative to mothers-in-law and other members of the extended family, clan, or community influence the choices that are made. The research literature has focused on the impact that formal education has on the decision-making autonomy of women concerning contraception and fertility choices. The literature posits that women who are better educated are not only more knowledgeable about the available options for limiting fertility, but also better equipped to negotiate these subjects with husbands and extended families. The impact of educational status on the openness of communication between husband and wife has received particular attention.

A second approach to the organization of discussions of the determinants of fertility has relied on a framework based on macrosociological theories. Researchers have argued that the average educational attainment of members of a community, and the values and aspirations that emerge as a result, affect desired family size and access to contraception. These researchers have suggested that more-educated communities value smaller, higher-quality families. They have further argued that communities that have adopted modern values are more supportive of decisions to limit fertility.

Conclusions

Empirical research into the relationship between education and fertility has drawn varied conclusions. At the most aggregate level—comparisons of countries—the conclusion is fairly consistent: countries in which women are better educated typically have smaller families and lower rates of population growth. However, when efforts are made to examine the relationship between education and fertility at the level of the household, the findings become more ambiguous. The World Fertility Survey and the Demographic and Health Surveys (large-scale international surveys of the characteristics and behavior of individual households) have revealed that cultural norms play a significant role in mediating the impact of education on fertility. The inverse relationship between female education and fertility cannot be found in nearly half of the fifty countries that the two surveys have covered. The failures have been most notable in the Middle East, where Islamic cultural values appear to collide with efforts to limit fertility, and in sub-Saharan Africa, where education levels are often very low. A common generalization arising from research based on these surveys is that the education of females does not affect fertility until an average of four or five years of schooling is provided to most girls.

Quantitative research into the relationship between education and fertility has focused primarily on the relationship between girls' schooling and achieved family size. Efforts to examine simultaneously the impact of boys' education on fertility suggest that perhaps a third of the effect of education on family size operates through boys' education.

The extensive research literature on female education and fertility has been undertaken primarily in order to document the likely effect of additional investments in the education of girls on the rate of population growth. The literature has grown enormously since the mid-1970s. The complexity of the forces that determine desired and actual family size has grown more apparent as a result of this research. However, until a more powerful way of organizing and interpreting the facts can be developed, it will remain impossible to predict with reasonable accuracy the impact of improvements in girls' education on fertility, family size, or population growth. Nonetheless, the contributions that education makes to the economic productivity and the quality of life for both individual women and their families argue persuasively for investing in the education of girls.

See also: GENDER ISSUES, INTERNATIONAL; HEALTH AND EDUCATION.

BIBLIOGRAPHY

BLEDSOE, CAROLINE H.; CASTERLINE, JOHN B.; JOHNSON-KUHN, JENNIFER A.; and HAAGA, JOHN G. 1999. *Critical Perspectives on Schooling and Fertility in the Developing World.* Washington, DC: National Academy Press.

COCHRANE, SUSAN H. 1979. *Fertility and Education: What Do We Really Know?* Baltimore: Johns Hopkins University Press.

JEJEEBHOY, SHIREEN J. 1995. *Women's Education, Autonomy and Reproductive Behavior.* Oxford: Clarendon Press.

POPULATION REFERENCE BUREAU. 2001. *2001 World Population Data Sheet.* Washington, DC: Population Reference Bureau.

FREDRICK L. GOLLADAY

POSTDOCTORAL EDUCATION

As graduate students complete their doctoral training, they have several options for employment. A natural step for a new Ph.D. is to enter the professoriate by accepting a faculty position at a college or university. Others choose to accept nonacademic positions in either private or public businesses. A third option is to enter a postdoctoral position (postdoc), with opportunities for continued research as neither a graduate student nor a permanent university employee.

The National Research Council notes that the "postdoc is difficult to quantify and describe because it as both 'further study' and 'employment'" (p. 2). A senior faculty member supervises (or mentors) the postdoc for a period of one to several years as the postdoc continues to research and expand her knowledge base. The postdoc receives a stipend or salary for the position and in most cases will also receive some benefits such as medical insurance. However, the postdoc is not a permanent position. There is also no standard job description for postdocs as each university, department, and supervisor may have different expectations of postdoctorate education. In the right situation, a postdoc can provide extra time for the new Ph.D. to hone research skills and increase publication productivity. In other cases, it is the best path to choose because of a poor job market and increased competition for faculty positions.

For years, postdoctorate positions have been standard in high-consensus disciplines such as chemistry and other science-based fields. Only at the end of the twentieth century did disciplines within the humanities begin to offer postdoctoral positions to recent graduates in their fields, in order to give these graduates the opportunity to begin a strong research program prior to the start of tenure-track responsibilities.

There are several considerations one must take into account before pursuing and accepting a postdoctoral position. The first is what will ultimately happen to the new Ph.D. by delaying entry into the workforce. Will the position make the new Ph.D. a stronger candidate for future positions, or is she decreasing her chances of finding the best-ranking position by not pursuing a "real" job? Second, it is also important to consider the scope of the postdoctoral position. Will the postdoctorate education allow a Ph.D. to have responsibilities for all areas of a typical faculty position or will he be limited to one or two specific jobs? Either of these scenarios could hinder or assist a new faculty member as he pursues a chosen career path. Finally, those in the hard sciences may have the option to continue a project after the end of the postdoctoral job. This could make the candidate more marketable for prime faculty positions, but the postdoc supervisor may be reluctant to allow this.

Although postdocs have traditionally been temporary appointments under seasoned researchers at universities, a growing trend is for industry to offer postdoctoral opportunities to scholars in fields such as chemistry, biology, and physics. Industry jobs can provide a steady supply of funds and research equipment that may lead to more collaboration with other researchers because of reduced competition for research funds. However, these positions often afford the new Ph.D. less autonomy as companies often have specific research goals set for their researchers. Proprietary research may limit what the postdoc is allowed to publish as well.

The number of recent graduates actively searching for postdoctorate positions is contingent on several factors; the most prominent is the condition of the job market. In the hard sciences, for example, the number of research jobs available each year may be limited due to several factors, including industrial restructuring and reductions in the growth of federal research and development spending. At the same time, the number of Ph.D.s continue to rise in both the hard sciences and the humanities. Thus a greater number of new Ph.D.s are forced to compete for openings, leading many to pursue a postdoc as an alternative.

See also: DOCTORAL DEGREE, THE; FACULTY, ROLES AND RESPONSIBLITIES; FEDERAL FUNDING FOR ACADEMIC RESEARCH; GRADUATE SCHOOL TRAINING.

BIBLIOGRAPHY

NATIONAL ACADEMY OF SCIENCES–NATIONAL RESEARCH COUNCIL. 1995. "Ph.D.s and Postdoctoral Appointments. Issues Brief." Washington, DC: Office of Scientific and Engineering Personnel.

RADETSKY, PETER. 1994. "The Modern Postdoc: Prepping for the Job Market." *Science* 265:1909–1910.

PATRICIA A. HELLAND

POVERTY AND EDUCATION

OVERVIEW
Christy Brady-Smith
Rebecca C. Fauth
Jeanne Brooks-Gunn
CHILDREN AND ADOLESCENTS
Rebecca C. Fauth
Christy Brady-Smith
Jeanne Brooks-Gunn

OVERVIEW

In 1998, more than 13 million children (19 percent of all children) under age eighteen lived in families with incomes below the official poverty threshold. Although children age eighteen and under represent 26 percent of the United States population, they comprise nearly 40 percent of the poverty population. Despite a steady decrease from 1993 (23%) to 1999 (17%) in the rate of children in poverty, the United States still ranks highest in childhood poverty among all industrialized nations.

In the United States, income poverty is defined by the poverty threshold, developed in 1959 and based on expected food expenditures (thrifty food basket) for families of varying sizes. Each year the threshold is adjusted for the Consumer Price Index cost of living. In 1999, the poverty threshold for a single mother raising two children was $13,423. Researchers have criticized the poverty threshold on numerous counts. First, government transfers such as food stamps and housing subsidies as well as tax benefits (e.g., the Earned Income Tax Credit) and tax payments are not included when assessing the poverty threshold. Second, regional and urban differences in the cost of living are not considered when computing the poverty threshold. Despite the criticisms levied against the way poverty is assessed in the United States, the current review highlights research that has used this definition of poverty, while acknowledging its weaknesses.

This article reviews the literature linking family poverty to children's cognitive and educational outcomes such as achievement tests, grade completion, and high school graduation. Timing of poverty has been shown to make a difference vis-à-vis child outcomes; thus, the discussion focuses on three stages of childhood: early childhood (age two to four), middle childhood (age five to twelve), and adolescence (age thirteen to eighteen). For each stage, we examine the effect of income poverty on children's cognitive ability and school achievement. Depth and duration of poverty are also considered, as these features have been linked to numerous domains of child development.

Consequences of Income Poverty on Children's Educational Outcomes

Simple comparisons between children in poor families and children in non-poor families using national datasets indicate that poor children are more likely to do worse on indices of school achievement than non-poor children are. Poor children are twice as likely as non-poor children to have repeated a grade, to have been expelled or suspended from school, or to have dropped out of high school. They are also 1.4 times as likely to be identified as having a learning disability in elementary or high school than their non-poor counterparts.

As with many studies examining the effect of poverty on children, correlational research is deficient in many ways. Simple comparisons between poor and non-poor children do not account for other family or child characteristics—such as single-parent households, maternal education, or child health problems—that may contribute to child development apart from the effect of poverty itself. Selection bias is another potential problem. Some researchers, such as Susan Mayer (1997), argue that poverty status often depends upon decisions made by family members, such as whether to apply for government services or seek employment, resulting in upwardly biased estimates of the relationship between income and child outcomes. Few feasible

strategies are available that are capable of completely eliminating the problem of selection bias, though some are more successful than others are.

Recently released national data sources address many of the inherent problems in research on family income and child development. These studies include longitudinal indicators of socioeconomic variables (e.g., occupational status and prestige, years of schooling, and family and neighborhood income), measures of family income, and numerous child development assessments. Utilization of the data from these longitudinal studies has made possible the distinction between family income and its correlates on child development and outcomes. Moreover, longitudinal designs allow for an assessment of how the timing (early vs. late) and duration (transient vs. persistent) of poverty may differentially affect children's outcomes. When possible, this discussion presents finding from studies that used standardized tests of school readiness, achievement, and cognitive ability, and controlled for key family and child characteristics, in its review of the impact of poverty on children's educational outcomes.

Early childhood. During the 1990s, the nation was inundated with reports on the importance of the early years on children's brain development and later cognitive achievement. While some of the reports may have overstated the issue and understated the importance of a child's later years on development, evidence suggests that the early years may be a critical period of development in which family poverty has particularly strong effects on young children. As seen in Table 1, poverty occurring early in a child's life (age two to four) is associated with large effects on indices of child school readiness and cognitive outcomes.

Judith Smith and colleagues (1997), using data from two national datasets, showed that family poverty was significantly associated with lower scores on several measures of child cognitive and school readiness outcomes for children age three to four years, even after controlling for the effect of mother's education, family structure, and child race, birth weight, and gender. Moreover, according to Pamela Klebanov (1998), the effect of poverty was seen among children as young as two years of age.

Judith Smith, Jeanne Brooke-Gunn, and Pamela Klebanov (1997) found that children living in families with incomes less than half the poverty threshold (deep poverty) scored nine to ten points lower on

TABLE 1

Effects of family income on measures of children's ability and achievement by developmental period

Developmental Period	Size of Effect		
	None	Small or Moderate	Large
Early childhood (age 2–4)			BSID PPVT-R Stanford-Binet
Middle childhood (age 5–12)		Completed schooling Behind in grade for age	PPVT-R PIAT-Math PIAT-Reading

Adolescence (age 13–18)	Self-reported grades
	Completed schooling
	Odds of completing
	  high school
	Odds of attending
	  college
		Completed schooling
		Odds of completing
		  high school
		Odds of attending
		  college
		AFQT score	

Note: Analyses control for mother's education, family structure, and other demographic characteristics.
  Large effects: all income coefficients from income-based models were significant at $p \leq .05$ and effect size was $\geq$ one-third of a standard deviation.
  Small to moderate effects: most income coefficients were significant at $p \leq .05$ and effect size was consistently < one-third of a standard deviation.
  None: few or no income coefficients were significant at $p \leq .05$.
  BSID: Bayley Scales of Infant Development; PPVT-R: Peabody Picture Vocabulary Test-Revised; PIAT: Peabody Individual Achievement Test; AFQT: Armed Forces Qualification Test.

SOURCE: Adapted from Duncan, Greg J., and Brooks-Gunn, Jeanne. 1997. "Income Effects across the Life Span: Integration and Interpretation." In *Consequences of Growing Up Poor,* ed. Greg J. Duncan and Jeanne Brooks-Gunn. New York: Russell Sage Foundation Press.

cognitive ability than children in near-poor families (150 percent to 200 percent of the poverty threshold) at age three to four. Persistently poor children, those who spend all of their childhood years in poverty, experience more negative cognitive and educational outcomes than their peers who encountered only short-term or transient poverty. Children who lived in persistent poverty scored six to nine points lower on measures of cognitive ability and school readiness than children who were never in poverty. Although transient poverty was associated with worse child outcomes, the effect was not significant—children who had experienced short-term poverty scored only two to three points lower, on average, than children who were never in poverty.

Middle childhood. Measures of child educational outcomes in elementary school typically include school achievement test scores, grade failure, and learning and attention problems. Among school-age children, the effect of family poverty on child achievement parallels the findings for young children. Family poverty was significantly associated with lower reading and mathematics achievement scores for children at age five to eight. Other researchers, such as Thomas Hanson, Sara McLanahan, and Elizabeth Thomson, have found modest

associations between family income-to-needs ratio (income divided by poverty threshold for family) and school performance and grade point average.

Children living in deep poverty scored ten to twelve points lower than near-poor children on measures of achievement and cognitive ability at age five to six. This effect was also found for older children—those in deep poverty scored seven to nine points lower on the achievement measures at age seven to eight. The differential effects of persistent and transient poverty were also seen in middle childhood. Five- to eight-year-old children who lived in persistent poverty scored six to ten points lower on measures of cognitive ability and school readiness than children who were never poor. Children who had experienced transient poverty scored three to six points lower, on average, than children who were never in poverty. A study in Canada by Linda Pagani and colleagues also found that persistent poverty was significantly related to academic failure. Children who had experienced poverty throughout their lives were twice as likely as never-poor children to be placed in a non-age-appropriate classroom.

Adolescence. Academic measures of adolescent educational outcomes include high school dropout and graduation rates, school engagement, GPA, and achievement test scores. Overall, the effect of poverty in adolescence on educational outcomes is relatively small. Findings suggest that a 10 percent increase in family income is associated with a .2 percent to 2 percent increase in the number of school years completed. Income poverty in the early years, however, is more strongly associated with high school completion than poverty during later childhood and adolescence, and most pronounced among those in deep poverty.

Pathways through Which Poverty Affects Children's Educational Outcomes

Poverty's effect seems to be the strongest when it occurs early in the child's life, when it is persistent, and when children live well below the poverty threshold. Poverty may influence child development through at least five pathways: (1) child health and nutrition, (2) parent mental health and affective interactions, (3) provision of a stimulating home environment, (4) school and child care quality, and (5) neighborhood conditions. Emerging evidence suggests that the influence of family poverty on children's cognitive outcomes may be entirely mediated by these pathways. The latter four pathways are briefly reviewed below.

Parental mental health and affective interactions. Parents who are poor or who have a history of welfare receipt are more likely to have worse emotional and physical health than those who are not poor. Researchers such as Rand Conger and colleagues, using the family stress model, have linked parental depressive symptoms to more conflict with adolescent children, which in turn results in less optimal emotional, social, and cognitive outcomes. Poor parental mental health also is associated with less stimulating home environments and more discordant parent-child interactions.

Provision of a stimulating home environment. Family income directly influences the material resources available to children in their homes. Higher income children benefit from higher levels of cognitively stimulating materials available in their homes compared to low-income children. The provision of a stimulating home environment, in turn, accounts for much of the effect of income on the cognitive development of preschool and elementary school children and may be the most important pathway through which poverty operates.

School and child care quality. Children from poor families are also exposed to lower quality school and child care settings compared to their non-poor counterparts. Findings from two national child care studies, as described by Deborah Phillips et al. (1994), indicate that up to 60 percent of subsidized and low-income child care centers failed to conform to legal child to staff ratios in toddler classrooms and most (70%) received low ratings on scales of appropriate caregiving and the provision of appropriate activities. Lower quality child care is associated with lower math and language ability, negative peer interactions, and more behavior problems.

Neighborhood conditions. The neighborhoods in which poor families reside are another pathway through which income poverty may negatively affect children's educational outcomes. Financial strain limits the housing and neighborhood choices available to low-income families, constraining these families to live in neighborhoods characterized by high levels of crime and unemployment, low levels of resources, and a lack of collective efficacy among the residents. Neighborhood residence, in turn, is associated with child and adolescent school outcomes above and beyond the effect of family poverty.

Conclusion

The challenge currently facing researchers is how to accurately estimate the effect of income poverty net of other factors, such as measured and unmeasured family and individual characteristics. There are several statistical options available that may provide upper and lower bounds of effects. Regressions, such as those reviewed above, that control for a host of demographic and parental characteristics are one option that provide an upper bound of effects. Including more specific controls, such as maternal verbal ability or IQ scores (which most of the findings in this article did not do), would provide a more accurate estimated effect of poverty on child outcomes. Another option is to control for assets or permanent income. Sibling analyses, which control for many unmeasured family characteristics, also provide a more accurate effect of poverty. Experimental studies, in which participants were randomly assigned to receive income supplements or the usual welfare program, provide some of the most powerful evidence thus far that income influences child achievement. Parents randomly assigned to programs that increased earnings had elementary school-aged children who scored consistently higher in the area of school achievement, compared to those in the control program.

Although the complex pathways through which family poverty affects child educational outcomes have yet to be fully understood, it is clear that childhood poverty compromises the educational prospects of children and adolescents. Many poor children begin life at a disadvantage, due to family income, low maternal education, single parents, young parents, or a combination of these factors. The level of disadvantage may become exacerbated through the lack of cognitively stimulating or safe home environments, conflicted parent-child interactions, poor school and child care environments, and poor neighborhood conditions. As knowledge of the pathways through which income poverty affects child cognitive and educational outcomes expands, this nation will come closer to understanding how best to address the problem of childhood poverty.

See also: FAMILY SUPPORT SERVICES; NEIGHBORHOODS; NUTRITION AND CHILDREN'S PHYSICAL HEALTH; PARENTING; WELFARE REFORM.

BIBLIOGRAPHY

ADLER, NANCY E., et al. 1993. "Socioeconomic Inequalities in Health: No Easy Solution." *Journal of the American Medical Association* 69:3140–3145.

BAYDAR, NAZLI; BROOKS-GUNN, JEANNE; and FURSTENBERG, FRANK F. 1993. "Early Warning Signs of Functional Illiteracy: Predictors in Childhood and Adolescence." *Child Development* 64(3):815–829.

BETSON, DAVID M., and MICHAEL, ROBERT T. 1997. "Why So Many Children Are Poor." *The Future of Children* 7(2):25–39.

BLAU, DAVID M. 1999. "The Effect of Income on Child Development." *Review of Economics and Statistics* 81(2):261–276.

BRADLEY, ROBERT H. 1995. "Home Environment and Parenting." In *Handbook of Parenting*, Vol. 2: *Biology and Ecology of Parenting,* ed. Marc H. Bornstein. Mahwah, NJ: Erlbaum.

BROOKS-GUNN, JEANNE; BRITTO, PIA R.; and BRADY, CHRISTY. 1999. "Struggling to Make Ends Meet: Poverty and Child Development." In *Parenting and Child Development in "Nontraditional" Families,* ed. Michael E. Lamb. Mahwah, NJ: Erlbaum.

BROOKS-GUNN, JEANNE, and DUNCAN, GREG J. 1997. "The Effects of Poverty on Children." *Future of Children* 7:55–71.

BROOKS-GUNN, JEANNE; DUNCAN, GREG J.; and ABER, J. LAWRENCE, eds. 1997. *Neighborhood Poverty,* Vol. 1: *Context and Consequences for Children.* New York: Russell Sage.

BROOKS-GUNN, JEANNE, et al. 1993. "Do Neighborhoods Influence Child and Adolescent Development?" *American Journal of Sociology* 99:353–395.

BROOKS-GUNN, JEANNE, et al. 2001. "Effects of Combining Public Assistance and Employment on Mothers and their Young Children." *Women and Health* 32:179–210.

BROOKS-GUNN, JEANNE; KLEBANOV, PAMELA K.; and FONG-RUEY LIAW. 1995. "The Learning, Physical, and Emotional Environment of the Home in the Context of Poverty: The Infant Health and Development Program." *Children and Youth Services Review* 17(1–2):251–276.

BRUER, JOHN T. 1999. *The Myth of the First Three Years.* New York: The Free Press.

CHUGANI, HARRY T. 1998. "A Critical Period of Brain Development: Studies of Cerebral Glucose Utilization with PET." *Preventive Medicine* 27:184–188.

COMMITTEE ON WAYS AND MEANS. 2000. *The 2000 Green Book.* Washington, DC: U.S. Government Accounting Office.

CONGER, RAND D.; CONGER, KATHERINE J.; and ELDER, GLEN H. 1997. "Family Economic Hardship and Adolescent Adjustment: Mediating and Moderating Processes." In *Consequences of Growing Up Poor,* ed. Greg J. Duncan and Jeanne Brooks-Gunn. New York: Russell Sage.

CONGER, RAND D., et al. 1994. "Economic Stress, Coercive Family Process, and Development Problems of Adolescents." *Child Development* 65:541–561.

DALAKER, JOSEPH, and PROCTER, BERNADETTE D. 2000. *Poverty in the United States: 1999.* Washington, DC: U.S. Government Printing Office.

DUNCAN, GREG J., and BROOKS-GUNN, JEANNE. 1997. "Income Effects across the Life Span: Integration and Interpretation." In *Consequences of Growing Up Poor,* ed. Greg J. Duncan and Jeanne Brooks-Gunn. New York: Russell Sage.

DUNCAN, GREG J.; BROOKS-GUNN, JEANNE; and KLEBANOV, PAMELA K. 1994. "Economic Deprivation and Early-Childhood Development." *Child Development* 65:296–318.

DUNCAN, GREG J., et al. 1998. "How Much Does Childhood Poverty Affect the Life Chances of Children?" *American Sociological Review* 63:406–423.

GUO, GUANG, and HARRIS, KATHLEEN MULLAN. 2000. "The Mechanisms Mediating the Effects of Poverty on Children's Intellectual Development." *Demography* 37:431–447.

HANSON, THOMAS L.; MCLANAHAN, SARA; and THOMSON, ELIZABETH. 1997. "Economic Resources, Parental Practices, and Children's Well-Being." In *Consequences of Growing Up Poor,* edited by Greg J. Duncan and Jeanne Brooks-Gunn. New York: Russell Sage.

HAVEMAN, ROBERT H., and WOLFE, BARBARA S. 1994. *Succeeding Generations: On the Effects of Investments in Children.* New York: Russell Sage.

HELBURN, SUZANNE W., ed. 1995. *Cost, Quality, and Child Outcomes in Child Care Centers: Technical Report.* Denver: Department of Economics, Center for Research in Economic and Social Policy, University of Colorado.

KLEBANOV, PAMELA K., et al. 1998. "The Contribution of Neighborhood and Family Income to Developmental Test Scores over the First Three Years of Life." *Child Development* 69:1420–1436.

KORENMAN, SANDERS; MILLER, JANE E.; and SJAASTAD, JOHN E. 1995. "Long-Term Poverty and Child Development in the United States: Results from the NLSY." *Children and Youth Services Review* 17:127–155.

LEVENTHAL, TAMA, and BROOKS-GUNN, JEANNE. 2000. "The Neighborhoods They Live In: Effects of Neighborhood Residence on Child and Adolescent Outcomes." *Psychological Bulletin* 126(2):309–337.

LIAW, FONG-RUEY, and BROOKS-GUNN, JEANNE. 1993. "Patterns of Low Birth Weight Children's Cognitive Development and their Determinants." *Developmental Psychology* 29:1024–1035.

LINVER, MIRIAM R.; BROOKS-GUNN, JEANNE; and KOHEN, DAPHNA E. 2000. *Do Maternal Parenting and Emotional Distress Mediate Associations between Income and Young Children's Development?* New York: Columbia University.

MAYER, SUSAN E. 1997. *What Money Can't Buy: Family Income and Children's Life Chances.* Cambridge, MA: Harvard University Press.

MCLOYD, VONNIE C., et al. 1994. "Unemployment and Work Interruption among African American Single Mothers: Effects on Parenting and Adolescent Socioemotional Functioning." *Child Development* 65(2):562–589.

MOORE, KRISTIN A., et al. 1995. *How Well Are They Faring? AFDC Families with Preschool-Aged Children at the Outset of the JOBS Program.* Washington, DC: U.S. Department of Health and Human Services, Office of the Assistant Secretary for Planning and Evaluation and U.S. Department of Education.

MORRIS, PAMELA A. 2002. "The Effects of Welfare Reform Policies on Children." *Social Policy Report.* 16(1):4–8

NICHD EARLY CHILD CARE RESEARCH NETWORK. 1997. "Child Care in the First Year of Life." *Merrill-Palmer Quarterly* 43 (3):340–360.

NICHD EARLY CHILD CARE RESEARCH NETWORK. 2000. "The Relation of Child Care to Cognitive and Language Development." *Child Development* 71(4):960–980.

PAGANI, LINDA; BOULERICE, BERNARD; and TREMBLAY, RICHARD E. 1997. "The Influence of Poverty on Children's Classroom Placement and Behavior Problems." In *Consequences of Growing Up Poor,* ed. Greg J. Duncan and Jeanne Brooks-Gunn. New York: Russell Sage.

PHILLIPS, DEBORAH A., et al. 1994. "Child Care for Children in Poverty: Opportunity or Inequity?" *Child Development* 65(2):472–492.

SAMPSON, ROBERT J.; RAUDENBUSH, STEPHEN W.; and EARLS, FELTON. 1997. "Neighborhoods and Violent Crime: A Multilevel Study of Collective Efficacy." *Science* 277:918–924.

SHATZ, CARLA J. 1992. "The Developing Brain." *Scientific American* 267(3):60–67.

SHORE, RIMA. 1997. *Rethinking the Brain: Early Insights into Brain Development.* New York: Families and Work Institute.

SMITH, JUDITH R.; BROOKS-GUNN, JEANNE; and KLEBANOV, PAMELA K. 1997. "The Consequences of Living in Poverty for Young Children's Cognitive and Verbal Ability and Early School Achievement." In *Consequences of Growing Up Poor,* ed. Greg J. Duncan and Jeanne Brooks-Gunn. New York: Russell Sage.

SMITH, JUDITH R., et al. 2000. "Welfare and Work: Complementary Strategies for Low-Income

Women?" *Journal of Marriage and the Family* 62:808–821.

TEACHMAN, JAY D.; PAASCH, KATHLEEN; and CARVER, KAREN. 1996. "Social Capital and Dropping Out of School Early." *Journal of Marriage and the Family* 58(3):773–783.

VLEMINCKX, KOEN, and SMEEDING, TIMOTHY M., eds. 2001. *Child Well-Being, Child Poverty and Child Policy in Modern Nations.* Bristol, Eng. The Policy Press.

WILSON, WILLIAM JULIUS. 1987. *The Truly Disadvantaged: The Inner City, the Underclass, and Public Policy.* Chicago: University of Chicago Press.

CHRISTY BRADY-SMITH
REBECCA C. FAUTH
JEANNE BROOKS-GUNN

CHILDREN AND ADOLESCENTS

Although the percentage of children ages 18 and under living in poverty in the United States dropped from 18.9 percent in 1998 to 16.9 percent in 1999, children in the United States are more likely to be poor than any other age group. Moreover, U.S. child poverty rates are well above those in other industrialized nations, such as Spain, Canada, and Australia. Put simply, 12.1 million children in the United States are living in families with earnings at or below the conservative income poverty line ($17,601 or less for a family of four, according to the U.S. Census Bureau's 2001 guidelines), indicating they are likely to be lacking the finances to fund basic needs such as food, shelter, and clothing.

The rise in both divorce rates and out-of-wedlock births in the last quarter of the twentieth century is partially responsible for the staggering number of poor children in the United States. One-third of U.S. births in the early 1990s were to unmarried mothers. Single-parent families are more likely to be poor due to both their dependence on a single wage earner for income and the probability that the household heads are younger and less educated than their dual-parent counterparts. Given this information, it is not surprising that 53 percent of poor families are headed solely by a female adult.

Changes in employment patterns, declines in the manufacturing sector, relocation of jobs into the suburbs, and wage polarization may also explain the high national poverty rates. The Personal Responsibility and Work Opportunity Reconciliation Act (PRWORA) of 1996 also has the potential to affect U.S. poverty rates. With PRWORA's prescribed time limits, work requirements, sanctions, and categorical restrictions for cash assistance, many families may find themselves unable to receive needed benefits. Moreover, the current welfare legislation does not offer a safety net for parents facing difficulties transitioning into full-time work.

Effects of Income on Child Outcomes

Findings are modest but significant regarding the direct role of poverty in influencing children's cognitive and school-related outcomes throughout early, middle, and late childhood. Children reared in conditions of poverty face more adverse developmental outcomes than their non-poor counterparts. Much of the research prior to the mid-1990s on the impact of poverty status on children suffered from shortcomings such as flawed measures or unrepresentative samples. Additionally, the differences between income and socioeconomic status (SES) were often blurred, elevating the risk of using inappropriate indicators of SES such as occupational prestige or level of maternal education (fairly stable variables) as proxies for income (which is often quite volatile). Large, longitudinal studies such as the National Longitudinal Survey of Youth (NLSY), the Infant Health and Development Program (IHDP), and the Panel Study of Income Dynamics (PSID) have remedied many of these methodological problems and include adequate child development assessment instruments, measures of family income, and socioeconomic status indicators. A common current practice of researchers is to calculate an income-to-needs ratio, which takes into account family size relative to the current poverty line; a ratio of one or below denotes living in poverty. Utilization of this poverty measure compared with a two-pronged (poor versus not poor) approach allows for a more thorough analysis of how different depths of poverty affect children's outcomes.

Physical health. Beginning prior to birth, poor children experience more health problems than their non-poor counterparts, even after adjusting for potentially confounding factors. Controlling for mothers' age, education, marital status, and smoking status, women with incomes below the federally established poverty line were found to be 80 percent more likely to bear an infant at low birth weight

(2500 grams or less) than women whose incomes remained above the poverty line. Children born at a low birth weight are at risk for negative outcomes well into their childhoods. Compared to full-term children, neurologically intact very-low-birth-weight children (1500 grams or less) present more impairments in arithmetic, motor and spatial skills, language, and memory, and perform worse on measures of achievement. Children with birth weights of less than 1000 grams are at the highest risk. One study revealed that 34 percent of low-birth-weight children were either repeating grades or placed in special education classrooms in school; only 14 percent of normal-birth-weight children experienced the same outcomes. Other research also reports elevated levels of grade repetition as a result of low birth weight. One study of siblings found that low birth weight reduces children's chances of graduating high school by nearly 75 percent when compared with their full-term siblings regardless of family income. Sibling studies control for unmeasured family characteristics and for selection bias—the fact that families with low-birth-weight children may be different in important ways from those who do not have low-birth-weight children—and therefore may provide more nuanced results and greater effects. The detrimental effects of low birth weight remain intact, though diminished, through the adolescent years and possibly into adulthood.

Although the rates of child malnutrition are lower in the United States compared with other countries, poverty is associated with nutrition-related disorders. Often linked with nutritional deficits, poor children in America experience higher rates of growth stunting (low height-for-age) and wasting (low weight-for-height) than their non-poor counterparts (13% and 5% respectively). These height and weight differences between poor and non-poor children are greater when long-term rather than single-year measures of income are used. Stunting and wasting are associated with lower cognitive test scores; short-term memory is especially diminished. Chronic malnutrition, often the cause of stunting, is associated with low cognitive test scores even after controlling for poverty status and its correlates. Children who are born both at low birth weight and short for their age have lower test scores that children who fit in only one of these categories.

Exposure to lead poisoning presents yet another heightened risk for poor children. The prevalence of elevated blood lead levels (20 to 44 μ per deciliter) was four times greater for children from low-income families (16.3%) compared with their peers from high-income backgrounds (4.0%). Rates were especially high (28.4%) for low-income black children. The deleterious effects of lead exposure on children vary depending on the severity of exposure, and also on the developmental stage of the child. At young ages, elevated blood lead levels are associated with stunted growth, decreases in IQ, and various physical impairments. A study conducted by Walter J. Rogan and his colleagues explored the effect of chelation therapy to reduce blood lead levels in poor children ages twelve to thirty-three months. The study found that although the treatment did lower children's blood lead levels, IQ scores were lower and parent-reported behavior problems were higher for treated children than for controls who only received a placebo at a thirty-six-month follow-up. Chelation therapy proved unable to successfully prevent deleterious outcomes for lead-exposed children; therefore, prevention of lead exposure for poor children needs to be a priority.

Health problems and nutritional deficits are important ways through which poverty affects children's cognitive and school-related outcomes. Poor children face an increased probability of being born at a low birth weight and experiencing both nutritional deficits and elevated blood lead levels. Past research suggests that the prevalence of these conditions in addition to other health problems can account for as much as 20 percent of the difference in IQ scores between poor children and their non-poor peers during preschool. Efforts to improve the health and well-being of poor children, including improved access to affordable health care and the provision of nutritional supplements and food stamps, are necessary to promote school-related success and competence.

Mental health. Children's mental health can be assessed via dimensional scales that screen children for various types of less severe subclinical symptoms (e.g., behavior problems) or with scales that more formally determine whether or not a child's behavior falls within a clinical diagnostic category according to the *Diagnostic and Statistical Manual of Mental Disorders—Fourth Edition* (DSM-IV). Most large national studies contain measures that assess dimensionality/level, such as the Child Behavior Checklist. Parental reports of behavior problems are the most common indicator of children's mental health and are generally classified along two dimensions: *externalizing* or undercontrolled behaviors including aggression, fighting, and acting out, and *internalizing* or overcontrolled behaviors such as depression, anxiety, and withdrawal. The reliance on maternal reports of behavior problems is a shortcoming in many of the large national studies. While these studies do control for maternal mental health and other characteristics that may influence how parents rate their children's behavior, higher instances of teacher-rated behavior problems are needed to corroborate mothers' responses.

Studies have established a negative link between income and behavior problems, although modest in size compared to the effects of income on both physical and cognitive outcomes. After controlling for a host of family-level variables including maternal education and single parenthood, the effects of income or poverty on children's emotional and behavioral outcomes are often muted or dissipate altogether. Some researchers, however, have found significant effects of poverty on children's mental health.

Using data from both the IHDP and the NLSY, researchers found that kindergarten-aged children growing up in persistently poor homes had substantially higher internalizing behavior problem scores than their peers who were never poor. Lower self-esteem, which is related to internalizing problems, most notably depression, may also result from persistent poverty, although mothers who are actively involved in their children's lives may lessen this effect. The timing of poverty in children's lives may also be relevant. Children who suffered from persistent poverty early in their lives maintained heightened levels of depression through the age nine in one study. Children who experienced economic hardship were also less popular among their peers than those who did not face economic adversity, possibly due to their higher levels of behavior problems.

Research is mixed as to whether current poverty status or persistent poverty contributes to children's externalizing behavior problems, including antisocial behavior. Data from the Charlottesville Longitudinal Study, examining elementary-school-aged children, found that children who endured even one year of family economic hardship possessed higher levels of externalizing behaviors than children who did not experience poverty; boys were more adversely affected than girls. Other research, using an income-to-needs ratio as an index of family poverty, reported a link between poverty and delinquency for

young boys studied longitudinally between the ages of 6 and 16 years. Boys experiencing transitory poverty were at greater risk of engaging in extreme delinquent acts than boys who were never poor. Less severe manifestations of externalizing behavior were not influenced by family poverty in this particular study. Thus, families' poverty status may have its greatest impact on externalizing behaviors in their most severe form.

Due to the confounding of race/ethnicity and class and the fact that poverty rates among blacks and Hispanics living in the United States are two to three times higher than that of non-Hispanic whites, it is important for researchers to consider children's racial/ethnic backgrounds when examining links between poverty and child outcomes. One line of research suggests that the effects of persistent poverty on children's behavior problems, both internalizing and externalizing scales, may be stronger for white than for African-American children, possibly explaining some of the discrepancies regarding the relationship between poverty and externalizing problems. Other research found the opposite pattern emerging with internalizing scores. For black children, internalizing behaviors increased with the number of years spent in poverty, whereas the inverse was found for persistently poor white children.

Thus far, the direct impacts of income on children's mental health have been considered. Risk indices, which take into account other factors correlated with family poverty status (i.e., low maternal education, single parenthood, and parental substance abuse and mental health), provide an alternate way of examining the effects of poverty on children. Not surprisingly, the more risk factors children experience, the greater the number of behavioral problems they show at six and seven years of age. Moreover, behavioral maladaptation is more likely to occur for children experiencing numerous risk factors simultaneously rather than one individually. Parental attributes or behaviors such as substance abuse, antisocial behavior, negative life events, and psychiatric episodes tend to be the most devastating risks for children. Thus, it may not be poverty per se that has a negative impact on poor children, but other risks experienced more frequently by poor children than by their nonpoor counterparts.

Parenting behavior and parent mental health. The Family Stress Model has been used by researchers to examine the indirect links between poverty and child development. According to this model, stress generated by economic hardship and income loss results in parenting that is less consistent, less supportive, less involved, and more coercive and harsh. These lower quality parent-child interactions lead to higher rates of behavioral and school-related problems among poor children. Maternal mental health, most notably depression, is also negatively affected by poverty. The higher incidences of maternal depression and distress in poor families most likely drives the use of these less effective parenting styles. Many studies have documented the link between maternal depression and children's internalizing and externalizing behavior problems, indicating that the emotional detachment and disengagement resulting from depression is quite harmful to children. Other indirect influences include the home environment, child care and schools, neighborhoods, health care, and exposure to violence.

Implications of mental health on children's educational outcomes. Poor children's academic performance may be hindered due to the higher rates of behavior problems within this group. A large body of research has established a link between behavior problems and outcomes in the academic or cognitive domain early and late in children's school careers. Difficulty in paying attention, a form of externalizing behavior, is highly associated with underachievement for younger, elementary-school-aged children. Aggression toward peers in fifth grade has been found to predict school dropout. Compared with peers who were never poor, persistently poor children were found to be most at risk for fighting with peers in the sixth grade, even after teacher-rated behavior problems in kindergarten are taken into account. These same children were two times more likely than their never–poor peers to be in a non–age appropriate classroom and to be at risk for experiencing academic failure.

Other studies indicate that both externalizing and internalizing symptoms (including hyperactivity, intrapersonal adjustment, lethargy, and withdrawn behaviors) in kindergarten or first grade may be associated with poor reading and math achievement the following academic year. Early behavior problems have been found to have relatively long-term effects on reading skills, IQ, and class placement during later school years, possibly even into high school. Teacher-reported ratings of internalizing and externalizing symptoms in second and fifth grades predicted grade point averages and achievement test scores during children's freshman and senior years of high school.

Past research has shown that teachers at high socioeconomic level who teach poor children tend to regard their pupils in a more negative light, in terms of behavioral characteristics (maturity/immaturity), academic expectations and performance, even in the early school years. These teachers were also more likely to view the school and classroom contexts less positively than teachers of children at higher socioeconomic levels, possibly creating a self-fulfilling prophecy in which these children begin to act, behaviorally and academically, in line with their teachers' thoughts at very early ages. Some have argued that in order to mitigate the powerful effects of poverty and its correlates on children's school outcomes, teachers must allow students greater autonomy and decision-making, have positive expectations for all of their students, possess good management, disciplinary control, and exemplary organizational skills, and provide a variety of challenging, yet meaningful tasks.

Policy Implications

It is always important to contemplate how government social policy concerning income transfers, employment, child care and schooling, social services, housing, and health care can potentially help or hinder our nation's poor families. Preliminary results from ongoing research examining the effects of mothers transitioning off welfare and obtaining employment suggest that job earnings often are not lifting families out of poverty. Without a significant increase in earnings, it is likely that these working families may not see any marked improvements in children's well-being. Moreover, if these families continue to live in high-poverty neighborhoods with elevated crime rates and inferior public schools, are unable to afford high-quality child care for their children, and do not receive family health benefits, the situation seems dire still. Policy efforts may need to go beyond cash transfers and concentrate instead on the provision of high-quality services such as medical care (e.g., Medicaid), the provision of nutritional information and supplements (e.g., food stamps; Women, Infants, and Children; and the National School Lunch Program), early childhood education (e.g., Head Start and Early Head Start), and housing (e.g., Section 8 vouchers). It is not clear whether programs that target some of the indirect effects of poverty, such as in-home interventions, are effective in improving adults' parenting skills and their ability to facilitate literacy and learning within the home, which are crucial for children's school success. Continued investment in creating new and unique policies and programs that are aimed at either preventing economic deprivation altogether or help to assuage its negative effects are needed.

Conclusion

The effect of poverty on children's physical and mental health begins early and often continues to leave its mark well into the adolescent years. While many researchers have examined the connections between growing up poor, children's health, and their cognitive and school-related outcomes, few independent research efforts have made similar connections between the pernicious effects of low income on youngsters' mental health and the subsequent impact of poor mental health and behavior problems on children's academic performance. The association between income poverty and mental health is not as strong as its effects on physical and cognitive and/or academic outcomes. In fact, when effects are found, they are often mediated by parenting and parental mental health. Children are negatively affected by poverty throughout their lives in many domains, especially when the poverty occurs at a young age and in severe form. Policy efforts to assist poor families in order to bolster children's chances of succeeding in school need to start early and target the entire family and their environs.

See also: FAMILY SUPPORT SERVICES; NEIGHBORHOODS; NUTRITION AND CHILDREN'S PHYSICAL HEALTH; MENTAL HEALTH SERVICES AND CHILDREN; PARENTING.

BIBLIOGRAPHY

ACKERMAN, BRUCE P.; IZARD, CARROLL E.; SCHOFF, KRISTEN; YOUNGSTROM, ERIC A; and KOGOS, JEN. 1999. "Contextual Risk, Caregiver Emotionality, and the Problem Behaviors of Six- and Seven-Year-Old Children from Economically Disadvantaged Families." *Child Development* 70:1415–1427.

BOLGER, KERRY E.; PATTERSON, CHARLOTTE J.; THOMPSON, WILLIAM W.; and KUPERSMIDT, JANIS B. 1995. "Psychosocial Adjustment Among Children Experiencing Persistent and Intermittent Family" *Child Development* 66:1107–1129.

BROOKS-GUNN, JEANNE; BERLIN, LISA J.; and FULIGNI, ALLISON SIDLE. 2000. "Early Childhood Intervention Programs: What About the Family?" In *Handbook of Early Childhood Intervention,* ed. Samuel J. Meisels and Jack P. Shonkoff. New York: Cambridge University Press.

BROOKS-GUNN, JEANNE, and DUNCAN, GREG J. 1997. "The Effects of Poverty on Children." *Future of Children* 7:55–71.

CONGER, RAND D.; GE, XIAOJIA; ELDER, GLEN H.; LORENZ, FREDERICK O.; and SIMONS, RONALD L. 1994. "Economic Stress, Coercive Family Process, and Development Problems of Adolescents." *Child Development* 65:541–561.

DUNCAN, GREG J., and BROOKS-GUNN, JEANNE, eds. 1997. *Consequences of Growing Up Poor.* New York: Russell Sage Foundation Press.

DUNCAN, GREG J., and BROOKS-GUNN, JEANNE. 2000. "Family Poverty, Welfare Reform, and Child Development." *Child Development* 71(1):188–196.

DUNCAN, GREG J.; BROOKS-GUNN, JEANNE; and KLEBANOV, PAMELA K., eds. 1994. "Economic Deprivation and Early-Childhood Development." *Child Development* 65:296–318.

HACK, MAUREEN; KLEIN, NANCY K.; and TAYLOR, H. GERRY. 1995. "Long-Term Developmental Outcomes of Low Birth Weight Infants." *The Future of Children* 5:176–196.

HINSHAW, STEPHEN P. 1992. "Externalizing Behavior Problems and Academic Underachievement in Childhood and Adolescence: Causal Relationships and Underlying Mechanisms." *Psychological Bulletin* 111:127–155.

HUSTON, ALETHA C. 1994. "Children in Poverty: Developmental and Policy Issues." In *Children in Poverty: Child Development and Public Policy,* ed. Aletha C. Huston. New York: Cambridge University Press.

KLEBANOV, PAMELA K.; BROOKS-GUNN, JEANNE; and McCORMICK, MARIE C. 1994. "Classroom Behavior of Very Low Birth Weight Elementary School Children." *Pediatrics* 94:700–708.

KORENMAN, SANDERS; MILLER, JANE E.; and SJAASTAD, JOHN E. 1995. "Long-Term Poverty and Child Development in the United States: Results from the NLSY." *Children and Youth Services Review* 17:127–155.

KUPERSMIDT, JANIS B., and COIE, JOHN D. 1990. "Preadolescent Peer Status, Aggression, and School Adjustment as Predictors of Externalizing Problems in Adolescence." *Child Development* 61:1350–1362.

MCCORMICK, MARIE C.; BROOKS-GUNN, JEANNE; WORKMAN-DANIELS, KATHRYN; TURNER, J.; and PECKHAM, GEORGE. 1992. "The Health and Developmental Status of Very Low Birth Weight Children at School Age." *Journal of the American Medical Association* 267:2204–2208.

MCLEOD, JANE D., and SHANAHAN, MICHAEL J. 1993. "Poverty, Parenting, and Children's Mental Health." *American Sociological Review* 58:351–366.

PAGANI, LINDA; BOULERICE, BERNARD; VITARO, FRANK; and TREMBLAY, RICHARD E. 1999. "Effects of Poverty on Academic Failure and Delinquency in Boys: A Change and Process Model Approach." *Journal of Child Psychology & Psychiatry* 40:1209–1219.

RIST, RAY C. 2000. "Student Social Class and Teacher Expectations." *Harvard Educational Review* 70:266–301.

ROGAN, WALTER J.; DIETRICH, KIM N.; WARE, JAMES H.; DOCKERY DOUGLAS W.; SALGANIK, MIKHAIL; RADCLIFFE, JERILYNN; JONES, ROBERT L.; RAGAN, N. BETH; CHISOLM, J. JULIAN; and RHOADS, GEORGE G. 2001. "The Effect of Chelation Therapy with Succimer on Neuropsychological Development in Children Exposed to Lead." *The New England Journal of Medicine* 344:1421–1426.

SCHWARTZ, JOEL. 1994. "Low Level Lead Exposure and Children's IQ: A Meta-Analysis and Search for Threshold." *Environmental Research* 65:42–55.

SMITH, JUDITH R.; BROOKS-GUNN, JEANNE; KOHEN, DAPHNA; and MCCARTON, CECILIA. 2001. "Transitions On and Off Welfare: Implications for Parenting and Children's Cognitive Development." *Child Development* 72:1512–1533.

YOSHIKAWA, HIROKAZU. 1995. "Long-Term Effects of Early Childhood Programs on Social Outcomes and Delinquency." *The Future of Children* 5:51–75.

REBECCA C. FAUTH
CHRISTY BRADY-SMITH
JEANNE BROOKS-GUNN

PREGNANCY

See: RISK BEHAVIORS, *subentries on* SEXUAL ACTIVITY AMONG TEENS; TEEN PREGNANCY.

PRESCHOOL EDUCATION

See: EARLY CHILDHOOD EDUCATION.

PRESIDENCY, COLLEGE AND UNIVERSITY

The chief executive officer of an institution of higher education in the United States is commonly known as *president*. There are some campuses, however, which use the titles of chancellor, dean, or chief executive officer in lieu of president. The diversity of higher education institutions in the United States has resulted in chief executive officers at U.S. colleges and universities with a wide variety of background characteristics and job responsibilities.

Characteristics

Historically, college presidents have been overwhelmingly white, Protestant, and male. By the late 1990s more than 19 percent of college presidents were women and 11 percent were members of other minority groups. The average age for presidents was 57.6 years, with 30 percent never having served as a full-time faculty member. More than 80 percent hold an earned doctorate, with the single largest field of study being education. Most college and university presidents are members of their institution's governing board, although not all have voting rights. The average length of service for a president is seven years.

Career Path

The path to the college presidency was historically pursued by ordained ministers. This held true especially for those institutions created to educate future religious leaders. As institutions began to educate beyond theology and law, presidents with educational backgrounds in the arts and sciences became predominant. These academic presidents still constitute the single largest type of all college presidents, particularly at four-year institutions. In the latter half of the twentieth century great changes occurred in higher education, shifting the role of the U.S. college president. Two-year public community college systems were created in most states as a means to provide greater access to higher education, and a number of four-year institutions were founded to accommodate the rising number of students going on to college. This exponential growth required the addition of many presidential positions. Many of those named to the presidency of the two-year colleges came from the ranks of professional educators, in particular from the staff of local school systems. Selection of presidents at four-year institutions shifted from academic ranks to mostly those from administrative positions at a college or university.

Increasingly, more chief executive officers are arriving at the presidency from areas other than the traditional vice president of academic affairs position. These nontraditional presidents are typically individuals who have worked in other areas of college or university administration, such as finance, institutional advancement, or student affairs. Some institutions have even gone to the business community for individuals to fill the presidency. This shift stems from the need of higher education institutions to run more like a business and to use skills of management and finance that are not as prevalent in academe.

Even with these changes in a president's educational and experiential background, it is still uncommon for college presidents to shift between different types of institutions. Individuals who have worked at two-year colleges typically remain at two-year institutions. The same is true for doctorate-granting, comprehensive, baccalaureate, and specialized institutions. For all institutional types, presidents are usually hired from another institution rather than from within the same institution. Due to the extensive nature of the position, the search process to select a college or university president often involves a number of individuals with a vested interest and often takes an entire year.

Roles and Responsibilities

The college president is typically responsible to a governing board for the successful operation of the institution. Some presidents lead an institution affiliated with a church denomination or a state system, and may therefore report to the chief executive officer of that particular organization. The president's relationship with the institution's board of trustees is critical. One of the board's primary duties is to hire and fire the president, and thus it is important

for the president to be attentive to the needs and desires of the board.

Many presidents gain the full trust and support of their boards, which allows them to establish and carry out a vision for the institution. The construction of a vision for an institution by the president is critical because it tells the story of where an institution has been and provides direction for where the institution is headed. "This vision, if believed in by the faculty, administrators, staff and students, has the potential to transform an institution. The degree to which the president is respected and admired by the faculty will be the extent to which he or she is able to inspire trust and confidence, the extent to which he or she is believable, and can deliver" (Fisher, p. 101). Although the president is the voice for the vision, the president does not usually create this vision alone. The college or university president must identify, and be attentive to, the strengths and weaknesses of the institution. Understanding the capacity of those who work for the college or university and how the institution fits within the larger higher education sector allows the president to determine what the institution can achieve. The president must craft this vision, with members of the college community taking ownership in its development. Once the vision is crafted, the president must share it at every opportunity.

A significant aspect of the college president's role is symbolic in nature. Whether it is leading the opening convocation, dedicating a new facility, or presiding over commencement ceremonies, the president represents the institution. Within the college community, the president can use the influence derived from the symbolic nature of his or her position to move the institution in a given direction. Out in the greater community the president's role is often more prominent. Individuals not directly involved with the college typically believe a college or university president has authority and control over more than he or she really does. As a result, presidents may find themselves under greater pressure from external constituents than internal constituents. The resulting role for many presidents becomes one of mediator, facilitator, and consensus maker for issues both internal and external to the institution.

Internally, a college president is responsible for the effective operation of the institution. Most presidents have an advisory cabinet composed of vice presidents and potentially one or two other key individuals who help the president ensure that the goals and vision are being implemented in a positive fashion. The president's broad areas of responsibility include academic affairs, which encompasses development of the curriculum and new educational programs; oversight and maintenance of facilities; fund-raising and communicating the image of the institution through institutional advancement; enrollment management, which tracks graduation, admission rates, and financial aid to ensure stable student enrollment; the finances of the institution; and finally, the management of out-of-classroom issues in student affairs, such as judicial hearings, residence life, and health services. Although there are countless variations in the organizational structure and scope of responsibilities, these areas, in most instances, are overseen by a vice president. For example, many institutions combine facilities and finance into one functional area. The organizational structure of the president's cabinet reflects institutional as well as presidential values and goals.

Although the president has vice presidents and their staffs to carry out each functional role, the president will be involved at varying levels at different times, depending on the issue at hand. A president may serve as the final arbiter for a student judicial hearing, determine whether a faculty member receives tenure, or assist in the detailed development of a new facility for the campus. However, it is a rare campus where the president has developed authority in a top-down fashion. The president relies on the expertise and experience of his or her staff to accomplish the details of the institutional vision.

For most presidents their power is derived through their influence with the various campus and community constituents. In working with the curriculum and other components of the educational programs, the president typically encourages faculty to take the lead and reserves specific input for those items that are absolutely critical for the fulfillment of the institution's vision. As the college or university representative, the president's views typically carry significant weight. This significance allows for the opinion of the president to steer decisions in a manner perceived as beneficial to the college or university.

From the vision comes the task of strategic planning to enable an institution to achieve its goals. The president must look beyond next year's class size, the goal for the upcoming annual fund, and other short-term concerns of the institution to see beyond the horizon and craft a path for the college or university on its way to fulfilling the vision. Crafting a long-range plan constitutes one of the major areas of time spent by a president. He or she must also spend considerable time on and off campus raising money for the institution, visiting with alumni in areas with significant numbers, and meeting with key individuals who may have the ability to support the institution.

See also: BOARD OF TRUSTEES, COLLEGE AND UNIVERSITY; COLLEGES AND UNIVERSITIES, ORGANIZATIONAL STRUCTURE OF; FACULTY SENATES, COLLEGE AND UNIVERSITY; GOVERNANCE AND DECISION-MAKING IN COLLEGES AND UNIVERSITIES.

BIBLIOGRAPHY

COHEN, MICHAEL D., and MARCH, JAMES G. 1974. *Leadership and Ambiguity: The American College President.* New York: McGraw-Hill.

FISHER, JAMES L. 1984. *Power of the Presidency.* New York: Macmillan.

FISHER, JAMES L., and KOCH, JAMES V. 1996. *Presidential Leadership: Making a Difference.* Phoenix, AZ: Oryx Press.

KERR, CLARK, and GADE, MARIAN. L. 1986. *The Many Lives of Academic Presidents: Time, Place and Character.* Washington, DC: Association of Governing Boards.

MURPHY, MARY KAY, ed. 1997. *The Advancement President and the Academy: Profiles in Institutional Leadership.* Phoenix, AZ: Oryx Press.

ROSS, MARLENE, and GREEN, MADELINE F. 2000. *The American College President: 2000 Edition.* Washington, DC: American Council on Education.

ALAN P. DUESTERHAUS

PRESSEY, SIDNEY L. (1888–1979)

Father of the teaching machine, author of the first book on standardized testing, and founder of the Division on Adult Development and Aging of the American Psychological Association, Sidney Leavitt Pressey was an innovator. Although twenty-first century educators and psychologists are constantly rediscovering Pressey's contributions to their fields, few are aware of the range of topics that he explored.

Pressey was born in Brooklyn, New York; his father was a minister in the Congregational Church and his mother was a teacher. Because of his asthma, the family eventually moved to a suburb of St. Paul, Minnesota, where he spent most of his childhood and youth. He received his B.A. from Williams College, his father's alma mater.

Although he majored in American history, a course in social psychology led him to attend graduate school at Harvard University in 1912. At Harvard he studied with several notables, Robert M. Yerkes chief among them. With Yerkes's assistance, Pressey became an intern at Boston Psychopathic Hospital while still in graduate school. During his internship he met Luella Cole who, for fifteen years, would be his wife and collaborator.

After receiving his doctoral degree in 1917, Pressey obtained an appointment as a special research assistant at Indiana University. After four years, he accepted an invitation to Ohio State University as an assistant professor and remained on the faculty of Ohio State for the next thirty-eight years, achieving the rank of full professor in 1926 and retiring from the university in 1959. During his retirement, Pressey remained very productive, authoring eighteen papers between 1959 and 1967.

Pressey was rather unique because he grounded his research in the problems that he encountered on a daily basis, rather than in theory or prior research. This "grounding" was evident very early in his career. While interning at Boston Psychopathic Hospital he studied ways of empirically differentiating among psychotics, alcoholics, and "feebleminded" individuals.

During his four years as a research assistant at Indiana University, he began studying children whom modern psychologists would term as having below normal IQs, but soon became interested in those possessing superior abilities. This research led to the publication of several journal articles and *Introduction to the Use of Standard Tests*. Following World War II, he returned to this line of research and published *Educational Acceleration: Appraisals and Basic Problems*. By "acceleration" Pressey suggests a means of accommodating the needs of academically gifted students.

During his initial years on the faculty at Ohio State University, he was concerned with the quality of graduate education, particularly the teaching of psychology. He investigated the study methods used by superior and failing students in an attempt to identify the most effective and least effective methods. He designed a teacher education program, the central feature of which was a project involving actual work in the school or with young people.

After retirement he would declare:

Now at the age of eighty, I am still battling long-continuing gross faults in our schools which first irked me as a boy in the grades. Trained as a laboratory psychologist, I was soon declaring the laboratory too piddling artificial and psychology either too biological or too theoretical to come helpfully to grips with major human problems. (Pressey 1971, p. 231)

Finally, as he aged, he began to study aging. Initially, he reflected on his experiences with the experiences of those he had studied at the Boston Psychopathic Hospital. Eventually, his writing became more personalized and introspective. He initiated the first American Psychological Association division—on maturity and old age—in 1945 to 1946.

Although Pressey's impact on educational thought and practice was substantial, it could have been even greater had he not been so far ahead of his time in so many respects. Pressey invented and patented the first teaching machine in 1924, fully thirty years before B. F. Skinner's popularization of teaching machines. Skinner based his machine on the behaviorist theory of learning that was prevalent at the time, and Pressey was amazed by the learning theorists' ignorance of the body of research concerning learning in school. He criticized Skinner and his associates for applying concepts derived primarily from rats that had learned to run mazes and students who had memorized pairs of letter combinations. Pressey was a cognitive psychologist who rejected a view of learning as an accumulation of responses governed by environmental stimuli in favor of one governed by meaning, intention, and purpose. In fact, he had been a cognitive psychologist his entire life, well before the "mythical birthday of the cognitive revolution in psychology" (Bruner, p. 780).

In commenting on Pressey's second autobiography, Geraldine Clifford wrote that "despite Pressey's participation in national meetings, his even greater national involvement in work on aging, and his frequent visiting teaching posts at various campuses, the impression persists that his environment was essentially an immediate one: that of his institution, department, his courses, his students, recognized duties." Clifford concluded: "Sidney Pressey probably would be an idol of today's students—clamorously seeking from their professors involvement, dedication to teaching, meaningful guidance, and personal concern—as he indeed was to many among earlier generations of students" (p. 275).

See also: EDUCATIONAL PSYCHOLOGY.

BIBLIOGRAPHY

BRUNER, JEROME S. 1992. "Another Look at New Look 1." *American Psychologist* 47:780–783.

HOBBS, NICHOLAS. 1980. "Obituary: Sidney Leavitt Pressey (1988–1979)." *American Psychologist* 35:669–671.

PRESSEY, SIDNEY L. 1949. *Educational Acceleration: Appraisals and Basic Problems.* Columbus: Ohio State University Press.

PRESSEY, SIDNEY L. 1967. "Autobiography." in *A History of Psychology in Autobiography,* Vol. 5, ed. Edward G. Boring and Gardner Lindzey. New York: Appleton-Century-Crofts.

PRESSEY, SIDNEY L. 1971. "Sidney Leavitt Pressey, Part I: An Autobiography." In *Leaders in American Education,* ed. Robert J. Havighurst. Chicago: University of Chicago Press.

PRESSEY, SIDNEY L., and PRESSEY, LUELLA C. 1922. *Introduction to the Use of Standard Tests.* Yonkers-on-Hudson, NY: World Book.

PRESSEY, SIDNEY L., and PRESSEY, LUELLA C. 1926. *Mental Abnormality and Deficiency.* New York: Macmillan.

LORIN W. ANDERSON

PRINCIPAL, SCHOOL

The school principal is the highest-ranking administrator in an elementary, middle, or high school. Principals typically report directly to the school superintendent, but may report to the superintendent's designee, usually an associate superintendent, in larger school districts. The highest-ranking school level administrator in some private schools is called the head master. Head masters have many of the same responsibilities as principals, but they may engage in additional activities such as fund-raising. In some school districts, a single person functions as superintendent and principal. Principals, head masters, and others who are responsible for the overall operation of a school are often called school leaders. In an era of shared decision-making and site-based management, the term *school leader* may also be used in reference to other school administrators and leaders within the school such as assistant principals, lead teachers, and others who participate in school leadership activities.

Schools have not always had principals. Around the beginning of the twentieth century, as schools grew from one-room schoolhouses into schools with multiple grades and classrooms, the need arose for someone to manage these more complex organizations. This need was filled initially by teachers, who continued to teach while also dealing with their school's management needs. These teachers were called principal teachers. As schools continued to grow, principal teachers became full-time administrators in most schools. Most principals soon stopped teaching because of the many demands their management responsibilities placed on their time. As managers, principals were responsible for financial operations, building maintenance, student scheduling, personnel, public relations, school policy regarding discipline, coordination of the instructional program, and other overall school matters. The management role included some curriculum and instruction supervision, but overall school management was the primary role principals played until the early 1980s. As the accountability movement gained momentum, the role of the principal changed from school manager to school instructional leader and then to the school reform leader. With this shift in role focus, principals retained their management roles. Principals currently play multiple roles: school manager, instructional leader, and the leader of school reform.

The Role of Elementary and Secondary School Principals

Principals are responsible for the overall operation of their schools. Some of their duties and responsibilities are delineated in state statutes. States and school districts have also set expectations for principals through their principal evaluation criteria and procedures. During the latter part of the twentieth century, as schools began to be held more accountable for the performance of their students on national and state assessments, the duties and responsibilities of principals changed. Principals became more responsible for teaching and learning in their schools. In particular, their duty to monitor instruction increased along with their responsibility to help teachers improve their teaching. With this change in responsibilities, principals discovered the need to more effectively evaluate instruction and assist teachers as they worked to improve their instructional techniques. The principal's duty to improve the school instructional program is mandated by legislation in some states. Some state legislation requires the removal of principals when schools are classified as low performing (students do not meet achievement expectations) for a specified period of time.

Principal Duties and Responsibilities

With schools facing increased pressure to improve teaching and learning, the duties and responsibilities of principals expanded further to include the responsibility for leading school reform that would raise student achievement. Success in leading reforms to increase student achievement often hinged upon a principal's ability to create a shared vision within the school community and success in implementing new organizational structures that engage teachers in shared decision-making. Principals have discovered that engaging the entire school staff in making decisions results in more commitment to school reform initiatives.

Principals are also responsible for facilitating their school's interactions with parents and others in the school community. This responsibility includes working with parents when disciplinary issues arise, when students are not succeeding academically, and when parents have concerns. Principals also interact with parents who serve on school advisory boards, parent/teacher organizations, and booster clubs. Principals report that they spent a significant part of their time working with parents of students who have been identified as needing special services through the Individuals with Disabilities Education Act Amendments of 1997 (IDEA).

Principals continue to be responsible for the management of their schools even though their primary responsibility has shifted. One major management responsibility is school safety. This responsibility includes ensuring that facilities and equipment are safe and in good working order, the development of overall school discipline policies and the enforcement of those policies, and the assignment of supervisory responsibilities among school

personnel. At the elementary level, principals are cognizant of their responsibility to ensure constant supervision of the very young children in the school. As students advance into the higher grades, the need for supervision changes as students mature. The responsibility for supervision remains high for older students who are handicapped; who are in areas where the potential for injury is greater such as labs, shops, and athletic facilities; and who are in situations (field trips, athletic events, etc.) where additional caution is required.

Principal Qualifications

A license is required for those who seek employment as principals in most states. Licensure requirements vary from state to state, but the requirements generally include experience as a teacher, graduation from a state accredited principal preparation program, and a passing score on a nationally validated licensure exam. Principal qualifications have been the subject of considerable debate during the 1980s and 1990s as pressure increased to make schools more accountable for student achievement.

The national organizations representing principals and other school administrators have actively engaged in the debate over appropriate qualifications for principals. The National Association of Secondary School Principals (NASSP) took an active role in identifying principal qualifications in the 1980s through the creation of an assessment process. This process focused on the leadership skills that were determined to most significantly impact their ability to effectively lead their schools, and the procedure was based on a task analysis conducted in cooperation with the American Psychological Association (APA). The skills assessed through the NASSP Assessment Center included leadership, sensitivity, organizational ability, judgment, problem analysis, range of interest, motivation, decisiveness, educational values, oral and written communication, and stress tolerance. Later the National Association of Elementary School Principals (NAESP) created an assessment process that assessed similar skills.

In the mid-1990s the National Policy Board for Educational Administration (NPBEA) decided to review principal qualifications. The NPBEA included most of the major national organizations that represent education administrators from state superintendents to principals. The NPBEA also included organizations that represent professors who prepare school administrators. One of the members, the Council of Chief State School Officers (CCSSO), took on the major role of developing a set of standards for school leaders. Working with the member associations and representatives from thirty-seven states, the CCSSO led the effort to identify a new set of standards for principals. This group was known as the Interstate School Leaders Licensure Consortium (ISLLC).

The six standards that were created by ISLLC were designed to influence the preparation of principals, guide states in the development of their own state principal standards, and serve as a tool for licensure or evaluation. The six standards address a principal's need to promote the success of all students through the following:

- The creation and implementation of a shared school vision

- The nurturing and sustaining of a culture and instructional program conducive to learning and staff development

- The ensuring of the management of school operations to produce a safe and effective learning environment

- The collaboration with families and the diverse communities schools serve

- The promotion of integrity, fairness, and ethical behavior

- The interaction with larger political, social, legal, and cultural contexts of schooling

The ISLLC Standards became the basis upon which the Educational Testing Service (ETS) developed a licensure assessment for use by ISLLC member states. A number of states use this ETS-developed School Leaders Licensure Assessment (SLLA) along with other criteria to license principals.

Research on School Leadership

Research has consistently shown that principals play a significant role in school reform efforts. As the accountability movement gained momentum during the 1980s and 1990s, research on school effectiveness, generally referred to as effective schools research, focused on principals and their role. These studies consistently found that the principal was the key to an effective school. Research found that the unique position principals hold, as the one person in a school who is responsible for and empowered to oversee the entire school, places them in a powerful position to coordinate the entire school operation and move it forward. The research further revealed that the most effective principals had a clear vision of how the school could serve its students; had aligned resources and priorities with the vision; and could engage other key players, within and outside the school, in achieving the goals embedded in the vision.

Other studies have supported the key roles principals play in their school's success and point to other leader characteristics as critical to the principal's success. These characteristics include high energy, initiative, tolerance for ambiguity, sense of humor, analytical ability, and common sense. As society grows more diverse, researchers are beginning to look into the principal's role in leading schools that are increasingly diverse.

Research on the principalship is focused on the changing role of school leaders in a changing society. Thus far, research has shown the principal to be a key to a school's successful transition into an institution that will adequately prepare students. This research was based upon an existing system of public and private education. As society continues to change and technological advances change the tools available for teaching, the role of the principal will likely change. Vouchers, charter schools, and technology have the potential to change schooling in fundamental ways. As these changes take place, the role of the principal will also change. The principal of an online school will function in very different ways than the principal of a traditional school.

Demographic Profile of School Principals

Demographics on the principalship are collected and reported by the United States Department of Education. The National Center for Education Statistics collected data on the public and private school principal population in 1987 through 1988, 1990 through 1991, and 1993 through 1994. These data show a 2.2 percent growth in the number of public school principals from 1987 through 1988 to 1993 through 1994. There was no significant change in the number of private school principals over the same period. In 1993 through 1994 the number of public elementary school principals was almost triple the number of secondary school principals (71.9% to 24.4%).

The majority of principals at all three levels of public schooling (elementary, middle, and high school) are males; however, the percentage of female principals increased from 24.5 percent to 34.5 percent from the 1987 through 1988 survey to the 1993 through 1994 survey. The most significant increase in the number of female principals occurred at the elementary level during this period. In 1993 through 1994, 41 percent of public elementary school principals were female. The number of female public school principals will continue to increase in the future based on data showing that 48.1 percent of the new public school principals hired in 1993 through 1994 were female.

Data on the principalship at the private school level shows that the majority of principals are female and the percentage of female principals is increasing. Female elementary principals of private schools outnumber their male colleagues three to one; however, this ratio is reversed at the secondary level. The number of private school female principals has increased from 1987 through 1988 to 1993 through 1994.

Public and private school principals are predominately white non-Hispanics. The 1993 through 1994 survey revealed that 84 percent of public school principals and 92 percent of private school principals were white non-Hispanics. The percentage of minority principals in public schools increased between 1987 and 1988 and 1993 through 1994 from 13 percent to 16 percent. Most minority public school principals (35%) were in central city schools in the 1993 through 1994 survey. There are few minority principals in school districts with less than 1,000 students. The number of minority principals increases as school district size increases. The percentage of private school principals has remained consistent at around 8 percent, and the number of new minority private school principals indicates the percentage is not going to change significantly in the future.

See also: CURRICULUM, SCHOOL; NATIONAL ASSOCIATION OF ELEMENTARY SCHOOL PRINCIPALS; NATIONAL ASSOCIATION OF SECONDARY SCHOOL PRINCIPALS; SCHEDULING; SCHOOL-BASED DECISION-MAKING; SCHOOL FACILITIES; SCHOOL REFORM; SUPERVISION OF INSTRUCTION.

BIBLIOGRAPHY

JENLINK, PATRICK M., ed. 2000. *Marching into a New Millennium.* Lanham, MD: Scarecrow.

SERGIOVANNI, THOMAS J. 2001. *The Principalship: A Reflective Practice Perspective,* 4th edition. Boston: Allyn and Bacon.

SEYFARTH, JOHN T. 1999. *The Principalship: New Leadership for New Challenges.* Upper Saddle River, NJ: Merrill.

UBBEN, GERALD C.; HUGHES, LARRY W.; and NORRIS, CYNTHIA J. 2001. *The Principal: Creative Leadership for Effective Schools,* 4th edition. Boston: Allyn and Bacon.

INTERNET RESOURCE

NATIONAL CENTER FOR EDUCATION STATISTICS. "Public and Private School Principals in the United States: A Statistical Profile, 1987–1988 to 1993–1994." <http://nces.ed.gov/pubs/ppsp/97455-2.html>.

KERMIT G. BUCKNER JR.

PRIVATE SCHOOLING

Considerable diversity was evident among the 27,223 private elementary and secondary schools that existed in the United States in the autumn of 1999. "Other religious schools" were the most numerous at 49 percent; followed by Catholic schools, at 30 percent; and then nonsectarian schools, accounting for 22 percent of all private schools. Parochial (parish) schools were the most numerous among Catholic schools, followed by diocesan and then private religious order schools. There were more conservative Christian or unaffiliated schools than affiliated ones (those affiliated with a specific denomination) in the "other religious" category. Regular schools, followed by special emphasis and then special education schools, were the most numerous among the schools not affiliated with a denomination or religious association.

The region with the most private schools, but not necessarily with the highest enrollment, was the South (30%); the West had the fewest (20%). Most private schools (82%) maintained a regular elementary/secondary program.

Private school students numbered 5,162,684 in the fall of 1999, representing approximately 10 to 11 percent of the total elementary and secondary enrollment in the United States. Approximately 49 percent of these students were in Catholic schools, about 36 percent were in other religious schools, and about 16 percent were in schools not affiliated with any religious denomination. Approximately 77 percent of private school students were white, non-Hispanic; 9 percent were black, non-Hispanic; 8 percent were Hispanic; 4 percent were Native American/Native Alaskan; and 5 percent were Asian/Pacific Islander. About half (49%) attended schools that were in urban areas, approximately 40 percent attended schools that were located in an urban fringe or a large town, while only 11 percent attended schools in rural America.

These students were taught by 395,317 full-time equivalent (FTE) teachers. Catholic schools employed 38 percent and other religious schools had 39 percent of FTE teachers. The remainder were in schools that were not affiliated with any religious denomination.

What Is a Private School?

Private schools (sometimes known as nonpublic schools) exist in the United States as corporate entities separate from public schools, which are supported by the government. Though they differ widely in function, geographical location, size, organizational pattern, and means of control, these schools have two features in common—they are ordinarily under the immediate control of a private corporation (religious or nonaffiliated), not of a government agency or board; and they are supported primarily by private funds. They are characterized by a process of double selection because the schools select their teachers and students and the parents select the schools for their children.

History of Private Schools in the United States

Private schools date back to the schools opened by Catholic missionaries in Florida and Louisiana in the sixteenth century, which predated the beginning of formal education in Massachusetts. These Catholic schools were the offspring of missionary zeal. The distinction between public and private, of such importance during the second half of the nineteenth century and throughout the twentieth century, was not an issue in colonial North America. Schools quite frequently were the products of combined efforts of ecclesiastical and civil authorities, along with parental support, the latter often constituting the primary factor in the schooling of the young. No one pattern existed across the colonies; the government had no de facto monopoly in the operation of schools anywhere. Some schools were free, some were supported by a combination of financial sources, and some relied solely on tuition. There were "old field" schools (schools that existed in abandoned fields in the South), and proprietary schools, which taught trades. In New England there were town schools, which existed alongside private schools; there were dame schools (taught by literate women in their homes) and writing schools. The Latin Grammar School, such as the one in Boston, often was the crown of the schools. In some places denominational schools were, in effect, public schools, operating under civil and religious supervision, with the goals of inculcating the essentials of faith and knowledge and making good citizens of the church and commonwealth. By the end of the colonial period the institution of school was firmly rooted on the American continent. But nothing resembled the modern concept of secular, free, compulsory, universal schooling.

The national period. Men such as Benjamin Franklin, Thomas Jefferson, Benjamin Rush, George Washington, and Noah Webster were among the leaders of the new nation who saw the need for intelligent leadership, an informed citizenry, and an educated professional class. Their proposals, however, had little impact on schooling arrangements. Quasi-public town schools, charity schools for the poor, and a variety of private schools for those who could afford them existed. As the nineteenth century opened, schooling was widely available without a government mandate. The line between public and private remained blurred; diversity of schooling persisted.

The common school period—the age of the academies. The combination of industrialization, urbanization, and immigration (mainly Irish) into the northeast, complemented by the civil disarray in Europe, led Horace Mann, Henry Barnard, and others to push for a "common school" that would forge an American identity. Private schools, especially those of a religious nature, were looked upon as divisive, even un-American. The universal, free, compulsory primary school, open to all, allegedly religiously neutral (but in practice Protestant) was the result. Meanwhile, the academies, both in the North and South, functioned as the major educational institutions at the "middle" level. Ranging from boarding schools for the upper class to institutions that barely surpassed, if at all, the common schools, the academies reached their peak about 1850 when they numbered approximately 6,000. As was the case with the colonial schools, the distinction between "public" and "private" was largely meaningless then. Often popular, local, and with a rural character, the academies overlapped curricular levels, offered a variety of subjects, were flexible with regard to the individual student, and served as an "opener-upper" for girls for formal schooling beyond the elementary level. They often received tax and land subsidies, and sometimes tuition assistance, from local and state governments. They were to succumb in popularity, with some exceptions, to the rise of the public high school that accompanied the growing industrialization and urbanization following the Civil War (1861–1865).

In the wake of the Civil War. Following the Civil War, universal public schooling, separate by race and unequal, began at the primary level in the South. In the North, government regulatory activity increased. Private schools, especially those religiously affiliated, were often looked upon as being "un-American." This allegation was hurled at Roman Catholic schools, in particular, founded as a defense against first the pan-Protestant nature of public schools, and second the secular, "Americanizing" school, each of which was perceived as a threat to the faith of a poor, besieged, immigrant population. Despite the widespread poverty of its members, the Catholic Church continued to found and operate parish elementary schools, able to do so because of the dedication of a teaching corps of vowed religious women, commitment from its members, the drive of its leaders, and ethnic concerns. The sometimes violent activities of the Know-Nothing Party, the American Protective Association, and the Masons that were directed against Catholics testified to the depth and breadth of anti-Catholic prejudice in American society, prejudice that was fanned by some statements of Catholic leaders, for example, the *Syllabus of Errors* by Pope Pius IX in 1864. Other denominations had also established private elementary schools. The Old School Presbyterians, for example, established almost 300 schools in the mid-nineteenth century, mainly because of concern over the alleged secularism of the common schools. For the most part, with the exception of the Lutheran Church-Missouri Synod, the schools founded by Protestant denominations did not endure.

Statistics for the percentage of enrollment in American K–12 private schools in the latter part of the nineteenth century reveal that in 1879 private secondary enrollment made up 73.3 percent of the total; by 1889–1890, in the wake of the growth of public secondary education, that figure had dropped to 31.9 percent. By 1900, 7.6 percent of the total school enrollment was in private schools.

In the latter years of the nineteenth century, government regulatory activity in educational affairs increased. Doubts were cast on the ability and desire of some private schools, especially those with an "old-world" connection, to foster citizenship among their pupils. Laws were passed, as in Wisconsin and Illinois, that attempted to control or perhaps eliminate private schools. In 1889, for instance, Wisconsin passed the Bennett Law, which defined a school as a place where the subjects were taught in the English language and which required students to attend a school in the public school district within which they resided. Following a bitter political campaign, the law was repealed, in large measure because of the efforts of a Catholic-Lutheran alliance, many of whose schools were threatened because of their adherence to the German language and customs.

The impact of World War I. World War I (1914–1918) provided a major impetus to patriotism and an espousal of all things "American." The nation looked to its schools to instill loyalty and civic virtue in its youth. The decade following the war witnessed a startling rise of membership in the Ku Klux Klan, a "Red Scare," and vitriolic anti-Catholicism in the presidential campaign of 1928. Private schools, especially those connected with anything foreign, in particular German, were under suspicion of being disloyal. Government regulation of these schools grew; parental rights in the schooling of their children were under duress. Three U.S. Supreme Court decisions in the 1920s stand as testimony to the struggles that engulfed private schools and parental rights in those years, struggles against the allegations of some in government and their allies, who attempted to eradicate or at least minimize them. The first decision (*Meyer v. Nebraska*) was issued in 1923 as a result of a Nebraska law that forbade the teaching of a foreign language to any student prior to the ninth grade. Robert Meyer, a teacher in a Lutheran school, disregarded the law and tutored a boy in German. The Court upheld Meyer's right to teach and the parents' right to engage him, maintaining that the allegation by the state that a given practice endangered it was not sufficient to limit Meyer's and the parents' rights; Nebraska had not shown proof of any such danger.

The second decision, even more crucial for the rights of parents in education and of private schools came in Oregon as a result of *Pierce v. Society of Sisters* in 1925. Following a referendum, Oregon enacted a statute that required all Oregonians between the ages of eight and sixteen to attend a public school while such was in session, on the grounds that such attendance was necessary to produce good citizens (private schools were, obviously, socially divisive under this interpretation). The Court struck down the Oregon law on the basis of the Fourteenth Amendment, because the law's enforcement might have resulted in the closure of the appellee's primary schools, thus violating their due process rights. In interesting further comments, the Court declared that parents have the right to send their children to private schools that provide religious as well as secular education. The child, the Court held, "is not the mere creature of the state."

The third decision was issued in 1927 in *Farrington v. Tokushige*. This decision again limited the rights of the government and protected the rights of parents and private schools, this time Japanese-language schools in Hawaii. The decision was based on the Fifth Amendment. The court held that the law would have violated the due process property interests of the parents and schools that might have led to the schools' closure.

The mid-twentieth century. Private schools experienced phenomenal growth in the years during and following World War II (1939–1945), increasing by 118 percent, compared with 36 percent in the public sector, and enrolling 13.6 percent of the total elementary-secondary school population in 1959–1960, up from 9.3 percent in 1939–1940 and 11.9 percent in 1949–1950. Assuming an average cost of $500 per pupil in the 1960s in public schools, private schools saved state and local governments roughly $31 billion during that decade. Private schools also became embroiled in a number of legal struggles during that period, struggles that focused on religiously affiliated private schools. In the next several decades the Supreme Court upheld public bus transportation to private schools and the loan of secular textbooks to the schools, and forbade most other kinds of aid on the grounds that such aid violated the establishment clause of the First Amendment that requires the separation of church and state. The basic legal principles on which the Court based its

decisions were that: (1) the legislation must have a secular legislative purpose; (2) the principal or primary effect of the legislation could not violate religious neutrality; and (3) the legislation could not foster "excessive entanglement" between church and state (these were collectively known as the "Lemon Test," because of *Lemon v. Kurtzman,* 1979). The Court also invoked the "child benefit" principle, which identifies the child as the principle beneficiary of government aid. Indirect aid that flowed to the parents and through them to the schools had a better fate than direct aid to the private schools themselves.

In the midst of the debate regarding the legality of government aid to nonpublic or private schools, Catholic schools reached their all-time enrollment high in 1965–1966 with 5.6 million pupils, constituting 87 percent of private school enrollment. Catholic enrollment plummeted in the years following, stabilizing some years later. Meanwhile, Christian Day Schools, founded by evangelical and fundamentalist Christians, were established and proliferated. The number of these private school institutions founded between the mid-1960s and the early 1980s has been calculated at between 4,000 and 18,000, with an enrollment range from 250,000 to more than 1.5 million. The best estimates seem to be between 9,000 and 11,000 schools with a student population of around 1 million.

The charge of elitism. One of the most serious charges leveled at private schools of all types by their opponents is that they are "elitist." Several major studies were conducted in the 1980s that would seem to belie that accusation. One of these was *Inner-City Private Elementary Schools,* conducted in 1982, which was sponsored by the Catholic League for Religious and Civil Rights. Using a randomly selected sample of sixty-four schools in eight cities, fifty-four of which were Title I recipients, and with a minority population of at least 70 percent, this study found strong support for these schools by their patrons. Residing in rundown facilities, beset with financial problems, the majority operated under Catholic auspices, but with a third of the student body Protestant, these schools provided a safe environment, emphasized basic learning skills, and fostered moral values in their pupils. The academic achievement of minority students in Catholic secondary schools, which surpassed that of minority students in their public counterparts, was reported by the priest-sociologist Andrew Greeley. Further, the overall minority enrollment (African American, Hispanic

American, Asian American, and Native American) had grown from 4 percent of the total private school population in 1970 to 11.2 percent in 1987.

But it was two controversial studies headed by the noted sociologist James S. Coleman that occupied center stage for private schools in the 1980s. The first, *High School Achievement: Public, Catholic, and Private Schools Compared,* which was published in 1982 and which Coleman cowrote with Thomas Hoffer and Sally Kilgore, produced results indicating not only that students in Catholic high schools and possibly other private secondary schools academically outperformed those in public schools, but also that these schools were more integrated racially than were their public counterparts. Coleman, Hoffer, and Kilgore claimed to have controlled for "selection bias" in this study; they also maintained that private schools provided a safer, more disciplined, and orderly environment than public schools. The second book, *Public and Private High Schools: The Impact of Communities,* which was published in 1987 and written by Coleman and Hoffer, continued the line of reasoning present in the 1982 work. In this second report the authors stated that the goals of education are determined by the social organization of schools, their communities, and the families that they serve. In "functional communities," in which the parents, teachers, and students know one another, schools—whether public or private—are more likely to be successful. "Social capital," the relationships that exist among parents, and the parents' relations with the institutions of the community that result promote high levels of academic achievement, particularly among students most at risk of school failure.

Types of Private Schools at the Dawn of the Third Millennium

As noted in the beginning of this entry, the private sector includes Catholic, "other religious," and independent private schools. There are three types of Catholic schools: parochial (parish), diocesan, and private (operated by a religious order). Other religious schools are those operated by other denominations, including various Protestant, Islamic, and Jewish organizations. Independent schools are conducted by groups that are not affiliated with any religious body. In addition, the nation witnessed the advent of proprietary "for-profit" schools in the 1990s. The Edison Company, for example, operated seventy-nine charter schools (which are nonreligious public schools) under several models with 37,000 students at the end of 2001. Other firms have joined Edison; some have predicted that by 2010 for-profit schools' share of spending on K–12 education will increase considerably. Oftentimes these commercial firms seek out schools with academic problems. Sylvan Learning Center, for instance, looks to contract with Title I schools to raise the reading achievement of low-achieving students. Teacher unions have been in the forefront of the opposition to this "privatization" move.

Another form of schooling, a direct result of parental choice, is home schooling. While home schooling is not an institution of schooling per se, it is the direct result of parental choice and a consequence of parental rights in schooling. Home schooling has been a rapidly growing phenomenon since the 1970s, and estimates put the number of youngsters who were home schooled in 1998 at 750,000 to 1.7 million.

Current Trends and Controversial Issues

Private, as well as public, schools were all but engulfed with controversy at the beginning of the twenty-first century. Among the debated issues were accreditation, minority enrollment, privatization, and school choice and vouchers.

Accreditation. States are responsible for the licensing or chartering of all educational institutions within their borders. A license is an authorization to operate, while accreditation certifies that a school meets minimum standards of quality adopted by the accrediting agency. Licensing and accrediting are means of controlling or regulating private schools; hence, they may become the source of conflict between government and private schools. Some private schools, for instance, operate without seeking government licensure of personnel or accreditation of programs. Where state approval is necessary to operate, the private school may not legally open until officially approved, and noncompliance may be a misdemeanor. States may exempt private schools from certain provisions, for example, because they are operated by a church. States may also offer tax exemptions to private schools because they perform a public service, are not operated for profit, or are conducted by a religious organization. Current accountability measures enacted by states may pose a threat to private schools via required curricular content, standards of measurement, and tests.

The most widely recognized accreditation of private nonprofit schools is conducted by six regional accrediting associations, founded between 1885 and 1924. The first of these was the New England Association of College and Secondary Schools, the last the Western Association of Schools and Colleges. A more recent organization, the National Council for Private School Accreditation, was founded specifically for the purpose of accrediting private schools. In 2002 it consisted of fourteen state and national accrediting organizations representing more than 2,500 accredited schools with more than 650,000 students. It was recognized, or was in the process of being recognized, by as many as fifteen states.

Minority enrollment. In the autumn of 1999, private school enrollment was approximately 9 percent African American, 8 percent Hispanic, 4 percent American Indian/Alaskan Native, and 5 percent Asian/Pacific Islander. Of the students enrolled in Catholic schools in 1999–2000, 24.9 percent were minorities; in inner-city and urban areas, that percentage was significantly larger. Urban Christian schools, which like the Catholic schools were founded to better meet the needs of students in urban centers, experienced an ever-increasing enrollment in the 1990s; the Association of Christian Schools International has a goal of establishing Christ-centered schools in each of the approximately 600 urban school districts in the United States. Minority parents, African American and Hispanic/Latino, are increasingly embracing school choice, thus confounding the contention that private schools are the haven of upper and upper-middle class whites seeking elitist schooling opportunities for their children. Furthermore, Jay Greene's studies suggest that private schools, on average, are more racially integrated than public schools.

Privatization. Some people fear that a trend toward privatization in education may have harmful effects on civic participation. Writing in 1999, the North Carolina sociologists Christian Smith and David Sikkink pointed out, however, that such is not necessarily the case. While private education and home schooling are not panaceas, these researchers suggested that private school families are considerably more involved in the public square than are their public school counterparts. If Smith and Sikkink are correct, then, private schooling will help renew participation in public affairs and advance, rather than harm, the public weal.

School choice and vouchers. School choice, both within and without the public school structure, has become a major issue since the 1990s. Vouchers, especially publicly funded ones, are the most controversial issue in American education. The controversy is said to be a struggle over America's educational future. Basically, a voucher means that the government issues a credit for education of children to their parents, who then take that credit to the school of their choice.

The concept of vouchers is not new. Catholic leaders, upholding the primary rights of parents in the education of their children, argued in the latter half of the nineteenth century that it was the responsibility of the state in distributive justice, the concept of giving to everyone what is their due, to support parents in the choice of schooling for their offspring. Under anti-Catholic attacks from Nativists and their allies, the Catholic bishops soft-pedaled their advocacy. There were other pre-1990 movements to have government acknowledge the primacy of parents (or in the case of adults as in the G.I. Bill, the adults themselves) in the education of their children. In the 1950s, basing his argument on the free market approach, the Nobel laureate economist Milton Friedman argued for the voucher. In the 1970s John Coons and Stephen Sugarman lent their support to the movement on social justice grounds. Others, such as Charles Glenn, emphasized parental liberty in their advocacy for the voucher. The publication of *A Nation at Risk* in 1983, followed by reforms such as site-based management, contributed to the growing sentiment that, at least in some instances, especially in inner cities, public schools were failing, and that enabling parents to have the means to be able to choose the appropriate school for their children would truly reform American K–12 education. The very system, which was publicized in the late nineteenth and early twentieth centuries as guaranteeing educational success to all students who sought it, was being criticized as an inept, cumbersome bureaucracy that contributed to student failure and, in the case of inner-city schools, often to their neglect and personal danger. John Chubb and Terry Moe called for implementation of the voucher in 1990, under the auspices of the free market.

It is well to note that school choice options exist within the public school system, namely, charter schools, magnet schools, and open enrollment. In addition to publicly funded vouchers, school choice options include privately funded schools, where individuals and corporations provide scholarships to children from low-income families. Deductions, tuition tax credits, and "child-care certificates" are other public means of aiding students in private schools. Such programs are most notably operating in Indianapolis, New York City, and San Antonio.

Also worth noting is that not all private school groups are in favor of vouchers. Some are concerned that vouchers may make the private school subject to excessive government regulation and control and thereby negate the unique quality of their private school.

Advocates advance a number of arguments in support of the voucher. Dale McDonald noted in 2001 that the United States is the only Western democracy that does not provide parents with a share of their education tax dollars that would enable them to choose the school for their children. Some argue for the voucher (or other aid) on the basis of the value of competition in a free market. Others contend that the voucher would recognize the primacy of parents in the schooling of their children. Some maintain that the voucher is called for by distributive justice. Yet others hold that government should not have a de facto monopoly of pre-K–12 schooling. The call for vouchers (or other means of school choice) is especially strong in situations where poverty is widespread and where urban public schools are in serious trouble. Other school choice programs, such as those available in Illinois and Minnesota, tend to favor tax credits for educational expenses, which lessen the threat of government entanglement and regulation.

Opponents to the voucher advance a variety of reasons for their opposition. Some aver that the voucher would destroy the public school system, privatizing it. Others contend that in the case of religiously affiliated private schools the voucher would violate the establishment clause of the First Amendment. Some say that in the cases of the urban poor, the voucher does not cover the entire cost of schooling and so the very poor are eliminated from participation, while yet others hold that the voucher helps only a select few in those cities and ignores the plight of the majority of the poor. Some say the voucher would result in the balkanization of education and of the United States. Finally, some contend that the practice of vouchers does not make their adherents accountable to the public in the use of tax dollars as is the case with public education.

Proponents and opponents disagree as to the effect of the vouchers on the school achievement of children. Some scholars hold that research on the effects of voucher programs in Milwaukee and Cleveland is inconclusive. Others point to high levels of parental satisfaction with voucher schools and to the improving test scores of their students. In June 2002 the U.S. Supreme Court, which in effect upheld the constitutionality of the Milwaukee plan by not reviewing a lower court decision, ruled that Cleveland program is constitutional, thereby upholding the use of public funds for religious school tuition. It is interesting to note that the Black Alliance for Educational Options, headed by Howard Fuller, former superintendent of schools in Milwaukee, filed a brief on behalf of the parents who were participating in the program. Seventy percent of the students were minorities; 73.4 percent came from homes that were headed by a single mother, whose average annual income was $18,750.

Conclusion

Private education in the United States is undergirded by parental choice. That choice has been an essential, though not always respected, feature of the educational landscape since colonial times. Indeed, for a considerable time the concept of parental rights in the schooling of their young was all but submerged under the rising tide of public school bureaucracy. This often led to a conflict between the professional authority of the school and the moral authority of parents. The relationship between parents and school authorities became adversarial in many instances; in others, parents were allowed to participate in the education of their children in a way and at a level determined by school authorities. The balance of power between government officials and parents may, however, be changing. Parents in the early twenty-first century may choose from an increasing variety of educational options. Regardless of their economic status, parents may be able to choose from a growing number of institutions for the education of their children and for the accomplishment of public purposes such as preparation for citizenship. If such is the case, the line between public and private schooling may become blurred, as it was in the colonial period, and the focus of public policy in education may shift from public education to the education of the public.

See also: CATHOLIC SCHOOLS; HOME SCHOOLING; PROTESTANT SCHOOL SYSTEMS; SUPREME COURT OF THE UNITED STATES AND EDUCATION.

BIBLIOGRAPHY

ARCHER, JEFF. 2000. "A Private Choice." In *Lessons of a Century: A Nation's Schools Come of Age,* ed. Virginia B. Edwards et al. Bethesda, MD: Editorial Project in Education.

ASSOCIATION OF CHRISTIAN SCHOOLS INTERNATIONAL. 2001. "Urban School Services." Washington, DC: Association of Christian Schools International.

BUETOW, HAROLD A. 1970. *Of Singular Benefit: The Story of Catholic Education in the United States.* New York: Macmillan.

"The Business of Education." 2001. *Business Week* December 14:1–2.

CARNOY, MARTIN. 2000. "School Choice: Or Is It Privatization?" *Educational Researcher* 29(7):15–30.

CARPER, JAMES C. 1984. "The Christian Day School." In *Religious Schooling in America,* ed. James C. Carper and Thomas C. Hunt. Birmingham, AL: Religious Education Press.

CARPER, JAMES C. 2000. "Pluralism to Establishment to Dissent." *Peabody Journal of Education* 75(1 and 2):8–19.

CARPER, JAMES C. 2001. "The Changing Landscape of U.S. Education." *Kappa Delta Pi Record* 37(3):106–111.

CARPER, JAMES C., and LAYMAN, JACK. 1997. "Black Flight Academies: The New Christian Day Schools." *Educational Forum* 61(2):114–121.

CHUBB, JOHN E., and MOE, TERRY M. 1990. *Politics, Markets, and America's Schools.* Washington, DC: Brookings Institution.

CIBULKA, JAMES C.; O'BRIEN, TIMOTHY J.; and ZEWE, DONALD. 1982. *Inner-City Private Elementary Schools: A Study.* Milwaukee, WI: Marquette University Press.

COLEMAN, JAMES S., and HOFFER, THOMAS. 1987. *Public and Private High Schools: The Impact of Communities.* New York: Basic.

COLEMAN, JAMES S.; HOFFER, THOMAS; and KILGORE, SALLY. 1982. *High School Achievement: Public, Catholic, and Private Schools Compared.* New York: Basic.

COONS, JOHN E., and SUGARMAN, STEPHEN D. 1991. *Education by Choice: The Case for Family Control.* Berkeley: University of California Press.

CREMIN, LAWRENCE A. 1977. *Traditions of American Education.* New York: Basic.

CURRAN, FRANCIS X. 1954. *The Churches and the Schools: American Protestantism and Popular Education.* Chicago: Loyola University Press.

CUTLER, WILLIAM W., III. 2000. *Parents and Schools: The 150 Year Struggle for Control in American Education.* Chicago: University of Chicago Press.

Farrington v. Tokushige, 273 U.S. 284 (1927).

FRIEDMAN, MILTON B. 1955. "The Role of Government in Education." In *Economics and the Public Interest,* ed. Robert A. Solo. New Brunswick, NJ: Rutgers University Press.

FRIEDMAN, MILTON B. 1960. *Capitalism and Freedom.* Chicago: University of Chicago Press.

GLENN, CHARLES L. 1997. "The History and Future of Private Education in the United States." In *Private Schools: Partners in American Education,* ed. Thomas C. Hunt. Dayton, OH: Peter Li Publishing.

GREELEY, ANDREW M. 1982. *Catholic High Schools and Minority Students.* New Brunswick, NJ: Transaction Books.

GREELEY, ANDREW M. 1989. "My Research on Catholic Schools." *Chicago Studies* 28:245–263.

GREENE, JAY P. 2000. "Why School Choice Can Promote Integration." *Education Week* 19(31):72, 52.

HUNT, THOMAS C. 1981. "The Bennett Law: Focus of Conflict between Church and State." *Journal of Church and State* 23(1):69–94.

HUNT, THOMAS C. 2000. "The History of Catholic Schools in the United States: An Overview." In *Catholic School Leadership: An Invitation to Lead,* ed. Thomas C. Hunt, Thomas A. Oldenski, and Theodore J. Wallace. New York and London: Falmer Press.

JORGENSEN, LLOYD P. 1987. *The State and the Non-Public School, 1825–1925.* Columbia: University of Missouri Press.

KOBER, NANCY. 1996. *Private School Vouchers: What Are the Real Choices?* Arlington, VA: American Association of School Administrators.

KRAUSHAAR, OTTO F. 1972. *American Nonpublic Schools: Patterns of Diversity.* Baltimore: Johns Hopkins University Press.

Lemon v. Kurtzman, 403 U.S. 602 (1971).

McCLUSKEY, NEIL G. 1959. *Catholic Viewpoint on Education.* Garden City, NY: Hanover House.

McDonald, Dale. 2001. "Pluralism and Policy: Catholic Schools in the United States." In *Handbook of Research on Catholic Education,* ed. Thomas C. Hunt, Ellis A. Joseph, and Ronald J. Nuzzi. Westport, CT: Greenwood Press.

McLachlan, James. 1970. *American Boarding Schools: A Historical Study.* New York: Scribner.

Meyer v. Nebraska, 262 U.S. 390 (1923).

Moe, Terry M. 2001. *Schools, Vouchers, and the American Public.* Washington, DC: Brookings Institution Press.

National Center for Educational Statistics. 2001. *Private School Universe Study, 1991–2000.* Washington, DC: U.S. Department of Education, Office of Educational Research and Improvement, National Center for Education Statistics.

Pierce v. Society of Sisters, 268 U.S. 510 (1925).

Powell, Arthur G. 1976. *Lessons from Privilege: The American Prep School Tradition.* Cambridge, MA: Harvard University Press.

Reid, Karla Scoon. 2001. "Minority Parents Quietly Embrace School Choice." *Education Week* 21(14):1, 20.

Ross, William G. 1994. *Forging New Freedoms: Nativism, Education, and the Constitution, 1917–1927.* Lincoln: University of Nebraska Press.

Russo, Charles J. 2002. "O'Connor, Breyer Likely to Swing Supreme Court in Favor of Vouchers." *Dayton (Ohio) Daily News* January 3.

Sherrill, Lewis J. 1932. *Presbyterian Parochial Schools, 1846–1870.* New Haven, CT: Yale University Press.

Sizer, Theodore R. 1964. *The Age of the Academies.* New York: Teachers College Press.

Slaughter, Diane T., and Johnson, Deborah J., eds. 1988. *Visible Now: Blacks in Private Schools.* New York: Greenwood Press.

Smith, Christian, and Sikkink, David. 1999. "Is Private Schooling Privatizing?" *First Things* 92(April):16–20.

INTERNET RESOURCES

American Federation of Teachers. 2002. "AFT on the Issues: Vouchers." <www.aft.org/Edissues/schoolchoice/Index.htm>.

Learning Exchange Charter School Partnership. 2002. "Edison Schools." <www.lx.org/csp/edison.html>.

Thomas C. Hunt
James C. Carper

PROFESSIONAL DEVELOPMENT SCHOOLS

Professional development schools (PDSs) are innovative institutions formed through partnerships between teacher education programs and pre-K–12 schools. Their mission, like that of a teaching hospital in the field of medicine, is complex, consisting of strong professional preparation through intensive clinical experience, enhanced learning opportunities and outcomes for pre-K–12 students, and continuing education and development for experienced professionals. Their strategy for achieving this complex mission is also analogous to that used by teaching hospitals: professional education in the context of practice.

Unique demands are made on partners in a PDS. They are called upon to share responsibility for adult and children's learning, to commit and reallocate their resources to a new setting and new kinds of work, and to be accountable professionally and publicly for outcomes for all participants. Like their medical counterparts in teaching hospitals, PDS partners believe that by working together in these ways, the learning outcomes will be better for teacher candidates, faculty, and students.

Children's learning is at the core of all PDS work. Candidates and school and university faculty engage together in identifying and meeting children's learning needs. It is through this inquiry and implementation process that adult learning occurs and children's needs are met. Research thus becomes a tool for improving outcomes.

PDSs look different than traditional schools with student teachers. The use of alternative staffing patterns that incorporate candidates into instructional teams provides both unique learning opportunities for candidates and release time for school faculty to work as teacher educators that observe, mentor, and assess novice teachers. Faculty are selected and trained for their roles as mentors and supervisors. They meet high standards for professional practice and they uphold high standards for candidates and pre-K–12 students. University faculty spend most of their time in the school setting working with candidates, supporting staff development, engaging in collaborative research with school faculty, and participating in the planning, instruction, and problem-solving activities of the school.

The Creation of Professional Development Schools

Professional development schools grew out of efforts in the 1980s and 1990s to reform teacher education and to restructure schools. The Holmes Group, an organization of the deans of schools of education in research universities committed to the reform of teacher education, recommended in 1990 the creation of professional development schools to provide intensive clinical preparation to teacher candidates and create a bridge between academia and the schools.

At about the same time, school reformers called for students in the nation's schools to learn more and for teachers to teach for understanding. Educators realized that this would require a different kind of teaching and a new approach to teacher preparation. Professional teachers needed to be well prepared in their subject areas, but they also needed clinical experiences to reinforce the desired dimensions of professional practice. This included knowledge-based decision-making, work with colleagues, an orientation to problem solving and inquiry, and accountability for enhanced learning outcomes. PDS partnerships were developed, in part, to create clinical experiences grounded in these values and designed to provide the kinds of learning experiences associated with developing expertise in professional practice.

The second impetus for the creation of professional development schools originated from a desire to bridge the long-standing gap between universities and schools. Educators in both sectors pointed to the distance between research and practice, and to the lack of fit between professional preparation and the real world of schools. University educators believed that teacher education needed to be informed by practice. School faculty sought ways to make university-generated knowledge more accessible to teachers, and PDSs created a needed link between the sectors.

The Impact of Professional Development Schools

Several hundred PDSs have been developed since the Holmes Group recommendations in 1990. The National Network for Education Renewal, organized by John Goodlad, was formed to support these partnerships, and they were endorsed by the National Commission on Teaching and America's Future as an approach to quality teacher education. The American Federation of Teachers and the National Education Association have supported major PDS projects, and the National Council for Accreditation of Teacher Education (NCATE) developed standards and an assessment process for PDS partnerships. In 2001 approximately 30 percent of the 525 institutions accredited by NCATE reported having PDS partnerships. PDS partnerships may involve elementary, middle, and secondary schools in urban, suburban, and rural communities. Public and private universities are involved in PDSs, as are large and small institutions, four- and five-year teacher education programs, and one-year certification or master's degree programs. In 2001 thirty-one states had school/university partnership initiatives supported by various federal higher education grants.

Early research on PDS partnerships consisted mostly of self-reports or case studies. In the late 1990s research on PDS effectiveness began appearing in the literature. Studies conducted in various partnerships using observational data, teacher competency test scores, and teacher attrition data suggest that teacher learning and retention are enhanced in PDS partnership schools. Similarly, studies have begun to indicate that student achievement, using a variety of measures, goes up in PDSs over a period of time.

Trends, Issues, and Controversies

Standards. In 1996 NCATE initiated a project to develop PDS standards. Working with PDS practitioners, researchers, and policymakers, NCATE developed and field-tested standards in eighteen representative partnerships. The standards were endorsed by NCATE and are being used by many PDS partnerships and several states across the country.

Institutional support. Gaining institutional support can be a challenge for PDS partnerships. It is critical that leaders of universities, schools, and teacher's unions be committed to the innovation. Changes in roles and responsibilities require institutional support and incentives, and often require the removal of cultural and policy barriers. For example, universities must address promotion and tenure requirements, ensuring that they value clinical work and research. Schools, on the other hand, must restructure their programs to include teacher education as part of the responsibility of the school.

Policy issues. PDSs are part of the long-term teacher quality agenda. The standards movement of the 1990s introduced a new level of professional and public accountability to teacher education, and PDS partnerships have a critical role to play in that arena. For PDSs to be sustainable, teacher quality initiatives in teacher testing, licensing, mentoring, and induction must be consistent with the underlying vision of the PDS—teaching as professional practice.

The greatest opportunity for PDS development, however, may occur as states and school districts seek to address a growing teacher shortage. PDSs may be able to provide a viable alternative to placing underprepared individuals in classrooms. When PDSs are established in high-needs schools where shortages are most acutely felt, they can bring cadres of candidates into the school under the expert supervision of university and school faculty members.

Controversies. Because PDS partnerships require major restructuring in both the university and school, they often meet with opposition. The selection of PDS sites, in particular, can be contentious.

PDSs remain somewhat controversial within the teacher education community. The requirement of a full-year internship as part of professional preparation introduces an additional cost to teacher candidates, many of whom are already beginning low-paying careers with significant debt. The added value of the full-year internship in terms of teacher competency and retention is beginning to be documented, and salaried internships or stipends (supported by school districts) may be a way of addressing this issue in the future, particularly in the context of teacher shortages.

In the early part of the twentieth century, the education of doctors, the practice of medicine, and the hospital as an institution were all radically reformed by the creation of a new institution: the teaching hospital. PDSs have the potential for playing a similar role in the preparation of teachers, the practice of teaching, and the school as an institution that supports both professional and pre-K–12 student learning.

See also: EARLY CHILDHOOD EDUCATION, *subentry on* PREPARATION OF TEACHERS; NATIONAL COUNCIL FOR ACCREDITATION OF TEACHER EDUCATION; SCHOOL REFORM; TEACHER LEARNING COMMUNITIES.

BIBLIOGRAPHY

ABDAL-HAQQ, ISMAT. 1997. *Professional Development Schools: Weighing the Evidence.* Thousand Oaks, CA: Corwin.

BYRD, DAVID M., and MCINTYRE, D. JOHN, eds. 1999. *Research on Professional Development Schools. Teacher Education Yearbook VII.* Thousand Oaks, CA: Corwin.

DARLING-HAMMOND, LINDA, ed. 1994. *Professional Development Schools: Schools for Developing a Profession.* New York: Teachers College Press.

FISHCHETTI, JOHN; HOVDA, RIC; KYLE, DIANE W.; and STROBLE, BETH, eds. 1999. "Professional Development Schools: Historical Context, Changing Practices, and Emerging Issues." *Peabody Journal of Education* 74(3,4):85–94.

GOODLAD, JOHN. 1990. *Teachers for Our Nation's Schools.* San Francisco: Jossey-Bass.

HOLMES GROUP. 1990. *Tomorrow's Schools: Principles for the Design of Professional Development Schools.* East Lansing, MI: Holmes Group.

LEVINE, MARSHA, ed. 1992. *Professional Practice Schools: Linking Teacher Education and School Reform.* New York: Teachers College Press.

LEVINE, MARSHA, ed. 1998. *Designing Standards that Work for Professional Development Schools.* Washington DC: National Council for Accreditation of Teacher Education.

LEVINE, MARSHA, and TRACHTMAN, ROBERTA, eds. 1997. *Making Professional Development Schools Work: Politics, Practice and Policy.* New York: Teachers College Press.

MURRELL, PETER. 1998. *Like Stone Soup: The Role of the Professional Development School in the Renewal of Urban Schools.* Washington DC: American Association of Colleges of Teacher Education.

NATIONAL COUNCIL FOR ACCREDITATION OF TEACHER EDUCATION. 2001. *Standards for Professional Development Schools.* Washington, DC: National Council for Accreditation of Teacher Education.

NATIONAL COUNCIL FOR ACCREDITATION OF TEACHER EDUCATION. 2001. *Handbook for the*

Assessment of Professional Development Schools. Washington, DC: National Council for Accreditation of Teacher Education.

OSGUTHORPE, RUSSELL T.; HARRIS, CARL R.; HARRIS, MELANIE; and BLACK, SHARON, eds. 1995. *Partner Schools: Centers for Educational Renewal.* San Francisco: Jossey-Bass.

PETRIE, HUGH G., ed. 1995. *Professionalization, Partnership, and Power: Building Professional Development Schools.* Albany: State University of New York Press.

TEITEL, LEE. 2001. *How Professional Development Schools Make a Difference: A Review of Research.* Washington DC: National Council for Accreditation of Teacher Education.

TEITEL, LEE, and ABDAL-HAQQ, ISMAT. 2000. *Assessing the Impacts of Professional Development Schools.* Washington DC: American Association of Colleges for Teacher Education.

MARSHA LEVINE

PROGRESSIVE EDUCATION

Historians have debated whether a unified progressive reform movement existed during the decades surrounding the turn of the twentieth century. While some scholars have doubted the development of a cohesive progressive project, others have argued that while Progressive Era reformers did not march in lockstep, they did draw from a common reform discourse that connected their separate agendas in spirit, if not in kind. Despite these scholarly debates, historians of education have reached a consensus on the central importance of the Progressive Era and the educational reformers who shaped it during the early twentieth century. This is not to say that historians of education do not disagree—in fact, they disagree intensely—on the legacy of Progressive educational experiments. What they do agree on is that during the Progressive Era (1890–1919) the philosophical, pedagogical, and administrative underpinnings of what is, in the early twenty-first century, associated with modern schooling, coalesced and transformed, for better or worse, the trajectory of twentieth-century American education.

Philosophical Foundations

The Progressive education movement was an integral part of the early twentieth-century reform impulse directed toward the reconstruction of American democracy through social, as well as cultural, uplift. When done correctly, these reformers contended, education promised to ease the tensions created by the immense social, economic, and political turmoil wrought by the forces of modernity characteristic of fin-de-siècle America. In short, the altered landscape of American life, Progressive reformers believed, provided the school with a new opportunity—indeed, a new responsibility—to play a leading role in preparing American citizens for active civic participation in a democratic society.

John Dewey (1859–1952), who would later be remembered as the "father of Progressive education," was the most eloquent and arguably most influential figure in educational Progressivism. A noted philosopher, psychologist, and educational reformer, Dewey graduated from the University of Vermont in 1879, taught high school briefly, and then earned his doctorate in philosophy at the newly formed Johns Hopkins University in 1884. Dewey taught at the University of Michigan from 1884 to 1888, the University of Minnesota from 1888 to 1889, again at Michigan from 1889 to 1894, then at the University of Chicago from 1894 to 1904, and, finally, at Columbia University from 1904 until his retirement in 1931.

During his long and distinguished career, Dewey generated over 1,000 books and articles on topics ranging from politics to art. For all his scholarly eclecticism, however, none of his work ever strayed too far from his primary intellectual interest: education. Through such works as *The School and Society* (1899), *The Child and the Curriculum* (1902), and *Democracy and Education* (1916), Dewey articulated a unique, indeed revolutionary, reformulation of educational theory and practice based upon the core relationship he believed existed between democratic life and education. Namely, Dewey's vision for the school was inextricably tied to his larger vision of the *good society,* wherein education—as a deliberately conducted practice of investigation, of problem solving, and of both personal and community growth—was the wellspring of democracy itself. Because each classroom represented a microcosm of the human relationships that constituted the larger community, Dewey believed that the school, as a "little democracy," could create a "more lovely society."

Dewey's emphasis on the importance of democratic relationships in the classroom setting necessarily shifted the focus of educational theory from the institution of the school to the needs of the school's students. This dramatic change in American pedagogy, however, was not alone the work of John Dewey. To be sure, Dewey's attraction to child-centered educational practices was shared by other Progressive educators and researchers—such as Ella Flagg Young (1845–1918), Dewey's colleague and kindred spirit at the University of Chicago, and Granville Stanley Hall (1844–1924), the iconoclastic Clark University psychologist and avowed leader of the child study movement—who collectively derived their understanding of child-centeredness from reading and studying a diverse array of nineteenth and twentieth-century European and American philosophical schools. In general, the received philosophical traditions employed by Dewey and his fellow Progressives at once deified childhood and advanced ideas of social and intellectual interdependence. First, in their writings about childhood, Frenchman Jean Jacques Rousseau (1712–1778) emphasized its organic and natural dimensions; while English literary romantics such as William Wordsworth (1770–1850) and William Blake (1757–1827) celebrated its innate purity and piety, a characterization later shared by American transcendentalist philosophers Ralph Waldo Emerson (1803–1882) and Henry David Thoreau (1817–1862). For these thinkers, childhood was a period of innocence, goodness, and piety that was in every way morally superior to the polluted lives led by most adults. It was the very sanctity of childhood that convinced the romantics and transcendentalists that the idea of childhood should be preserved and cultivated through educational instruction.

Second, and more important, Dewey and his fellow educational Progressives drew from the work of the German philosopher Friedrich Froebel (1782–1852) and Swiss educator Johann Pestalozzi (1746–1827). Froebel and Pestalozzi were among the first to articulate the process of educating the "whole child," wherein learning moved beyond the subject matter and ultimately rested upon the needs and interests of the child. Tending to both the pupil's head and heart, they believed, was the real business of schooling, and they searched for an empirical and rational science of education that would incorporate these foundational principles. Froebel drew upon the garden metaphor of cultivating young children toward maturity, and he provided the European foundations for the late-nineteenth-century kinder-

garten movement in the United States. Similarly, Pestalozzi popularized the pedagogical method of object teaching, wherein a teacher began with an object related to the child's world in order to initiate the child into the world of the educator.

Finally, Dewey drew inspiration from the ideas of philosopher and psychologist William James (1842–1910). Dewey's interpretation of James's philosophical pragmatism, which was similar to the ideas underpinning Pestalozzi's object teaching, joined *thinking* and *doing* as two seamlessly connected halves of the learning process. By focusing on the relationship between thinking and doing, Dewey believed his educational philosophy could equip each child with the problem-solving skills required to overcome obstacles between a given and desired set of circumstances. According to Dewey, education was not simply a means to a future life, but instead represented a full life unto itself.

Taken together, then, these European and American philosophical traditions helped Progressives connect childhood and democracy with education: Children, if taught to understand the relationship between thinking and doing, would be fully equipped for active participation in a democratic society. It was for these reasons that the Progressive education movement broke from pedagogical traditionalists organized around the seemingly outmoded and antidemocratic ideas of drill, discipline, and didactic exercises.

Pedagogical Progressivism

The pedagogical Progressives who embraced this child-centered pedagogy favored education built upon an experience-based curriculum developed by both students and teachers. Teachers played a special role in the Progressive formulation for education as they merged their deep knowledge of, and affection for, children with the intellectual demands of the subject matter. Contrary to his detractors, then and now, Dewey, while admittedly antiauthoritarian, did not take child-centered curriculum and pedagogy to mean the complete abandonment of traditional subject matter or instructional guidance and control. In fact, Dewey criticized derivations of those theories that treated education as a mere source of amusement or as a justification for rote vocationalism. Rather, stirred by his desire to reaffirm American democracy, Dewey's time- and resource-exhaustive educational program depended on close student–teacher interactions that, Dewey argued, required nothing less than the utter reorganization of traditional subject matter.

Although the practice of pure Deweyism was rare, his educational ideas were implemented in private and public school systems alike. During his time as head of the Department of Philosophy at the University of Chicago (which also included the fields of psychology and pedagogy), Dewey and his wife Alice established a University Laboratory School. An institutional center for educational experimentation, the Lab School sought to make experience and hands-on learning the heart of the educational enterprise, and Dewey carved out a special place for teachers. Dewey was interested in obtaining psychological insight into the child's individual capacities and interests. Education was ultimately about growth, Dewey argued, and the school played a crucial role in creating an environment that was responsive to the child's interests and needs, and would allow the child to flourish.

Similarly, Colonel Francis W. Parker, a contemporary of Dewey and devout Emersonian, embraced an abiding respect for the beauty and wonder of nature, privileged the happiness of the individual over all else, and linked education and experience in pedagogical practice. During his time as superintendent of schools in Quincy, Massachusetts, and later as the head of the Cook Country Normal School in Chicago, Parker rejected discipline, authority, regimentation, and traditional pedagogical techniques and emphasized warmth, spontaneity, and the joy of learning. Both Dewey and Parker believed in learning by doing, arguing that genuine delight, rather than drudgery, should be the by-product of manual work. By linking the home and school, and viewing both as integral parts of a larger community, Progressive educators sought to create an educational environment wherein children could see that the hands-on work they did had some bearing on society.

While Progressive education has most often been associated with private independent schools such as Dewey's Laboratory School, Margaret Naumberg's Walden School, and Lincoln School of Teacher's College, Progressive ideas were also implemented in large school systems, the most well known being those in Winnetka, Illinois, and Gary, Indiana. Located some twenty miles north of Chicago on its affluent North Shore, the Winnetka schools, under the leadership of superintendent Carleton Washburne, rejected traditional classroom practice in favor of individualized instruction that let children learn at their own pace. Washburne and his staff in the Winnetka schools believed that all children had a right to be happy and live natural and full lives, and they yoked the needs of the individual to those of the community. They used the child's natural curiosity as the point of departure in the classroom and developed a teacher education program at the Graduate Teachers College of Winnetka to train teachers in this philosophy; in short, the Winnetka schools balanced Progressive ideals with basic skills and academic rigor.

Like the Winnetka schools, the Gary school system was another Progressive school system, led by superintendent William A. Wirt, who studied with Dewey at the University of Chicago. The Gary school system attracted national attention for its *platoon* and *work-study-play* systems, which increased the capacity of the schools at the same time that they allowed children to spend considerable time doing hands-on work in laboratories, shops, and on the playground. The schools also stayed open well into the evening hours and offered community-based adult education courses. In short, by focusing on learning-by-doing and adopting an educational program that focused on larger social and community needs, the Winnetka and Gary schools closely mirrored Dewey's own Progressive educational theories.

Administrative Progressivism

While Dewey was the most well known and influential Progressive educator and philosopher, he by no means represented all that Progressive education ultimately became. In the whirlwind of turn-of-the-century educational reform, the idea of educational Progressivism took on multiple, and often contradictory, definitions. Thus, at the same time that Dewey and his followers rejected traditional methods of instruction and developed a "new education" based on the interests and needs of the child, a new cadre of professionally trained school administrators likewise justified their own reforms in the name of Progressive education.

Administrative Progressives shared Dewey's distaste for nineteenth-century education, but they differed markedly with Dewey in their prescription for its reform: administrative Progressives wanted to overthrow "bookish" and rigid schooling by creating what they believed to be more useful, efficient, and centralized systems of public education based on vertically integrated bureaucracies, curricular differentiation, and mass testing.

Professional school administrators relied on managerial expertise in order to efficiently supervise increasingly large public school systems. Significantly, the new administrators, borrowing the language and practice of efficiency experts like Frederick W. Taylor, attempted to rationalize disparate school districts within one hierarchically arranged system of primary, middle, and high school institutions. Powerful school boards—often comprising elite business and civic leaders—hired professionally trained school superintendents to implement policies and to oversee the day-to-day operations of these vast educational systems. The superintendent, often a male, distanced himself from the mostly female corps of teachers, not to mention the students the school was intended to serve. In the name of efficiency, superintendents relied on "scientific," if often sterile, personnel management techniques, which had been developed by and for private industry and imported to the school setting by way of business-friendly school boards and through graduate training at the newly developed schools of education.

The school's turn toward bureaucratic efficiency directly shaped curricular construction. In particular, the idea of *differentiation* became a new watchword in administrative Progressive circles, reflecting the burgeoning economic and status markers signified by the attainment of educational credentials. By differentiating the curriculum along academic and vocational tracks, school administrators sought to meet the needs of different classes and calibers of students, and to more tightly couple educational training with educational outcomes. While administrators justified this curricular innovation (which was most often used in the high schools) on the basis of equal opportunity for all students based on ability, it reflected a larger, more significant shift in the basic aims and objectives of American education. Where the school once provided intellectual and moral training, in the face of an increasingly diverse student population, Progressive administrators took their chief professional administrative responsibility to be the preparation of students for their future lives as workers in the American labor force.

For many contemporary observers, however, curricular differentiation was little more than a euphemism for "social control," which critics suggested curtailed liberal education in order to meet the labor demands of America's budding industrial soci-

ety. While this is a cynical view of the Progressive administrative drive, there is much justification for it. Founded in 1906 by a committee of educators and business and industrial leaders, the National Society for the Promotion of Industrial Education (NSPIE) helped organize vocational education programs in high schools around the country during the first several decades of the twentieth century. Vocational education, which critics conveniently, if incorrectly, linked to Progressive education, was expressly designed to train students for immediate employment following, and often in lieu of, graduation.

On the other hand, administrative Progressives justified the rise of vocational tracks by pointing to the relatively miniscule college-going population and by proclaiming it as an effective means of assimilating newly arrived immigrants into American life and institutions. That these students' high school education was essentially terminated before it ever started was of little concern, for in the face of rapid social upheaval, which reformers believed eroded the traditional institutions of church and family, the school was the last best hope to inculcate immigrants with American values, while simultaneously providing industry with a consistent influx of trained workers.

The interest in the efficient management of bureaucratic school systems and students was strengthened further by developments in educational psychology and intelligence testing. Among the twentieth century's prominent educational psychologists, E. L. Thorndike (1874–1949)—who studied under William James at Harvard, and taught at Columbia University's Teachers College during Dewey's tenure—was undoubtedly the most influential. Presaging the rise of post–World War I mass intelligence testing by relying on intelligence tests in his own studies as early as 1903, Thorndike's research advanced a narrowly focused stimulus-response definition of intelligence that justified the spread of worker training through vocational education at the same time that his mechanistic conception of intelligence corrupted Dewey's own ideas about the organic connection between thinking and doing. Thorndike, relying on data gathered from his study of 8,564 high school students in the early 1920s, labeled his theory of intelligence *psychological connectionism*. Thorndike likened the mind to a "switchboard" where neural bonds (or connections) were created between stimuli and responses. He believed that students of higher intellect formed more and better bonds more quickly than students of lower intellect.

For the administrative Progressives, Thorndike's findings were nothing short of revolutionary: By emphasizing the preponderant role of native intelligence through the statistical analysis of mass-administered intelligence tests, Thorndike and his fellow testers—H. H. Goodard, Lewis H. Terman, and Robert M. Yerkes, among them—provided school officials and policymakers with scientifically incontrovertible evidence in favor of increased psychometric testing and pupil sorting. In comparison with Dewey's more human and material-intensive approach to education, which required individualized student attention and creative pedagogy, Thorndike's conception helped reify separate curricula and perpetuate patterns of unequal access. Precisely (if paradoxically) because of the malleability of the idea of Progressive educational reform, it was possible for both pedagogical and administrative Progressives to advance their radically different agendas in the name of democracy during the first several decades of the twentieth century.

Life-Adjustment Progressivism

Yet the internal contradictions and ideological inconsistencies of the pedagogical and administrative Progressives in many ways forecast the demise of the Progressive education movement. A system of education that championed both child-centeredness and individuated attention on the one hand, and explicit curricular differentiation through intelligence testing on the other, was perhaps destined to collapse; and with the introduction of life-adjustment education during the 1940s and 1950s, the Progressive education movement did just that.

Life-adjustment education emerged on the scene during the 1940s and witnessed its heyday during the early days of the cold war. The cause of life-adjustment education was advanced by leaders of the vocational education movement like Charles Prosser, who helped pass the monumental 1917 Smith-Hughes National Vocational Education Act, who believed that the school's main function should be to prepare students for the work world. To this end, the life adjusters borrowed generously from the pedagogical and administrative Progressive lexicon by advocating that schools should test and track students at the same time that they should improve students' physical and emotional well-being. Ultimately, the United States Office of Education's

Commission on Life Adjustment Education for Youth co-opted the mantel of Progressive education. Using commission reports published in 1951 and 1954 as its blueprint for action, the life adjustment movement succeeded in instituting its therapeutic curricula—geared toward the development of personal hygiene, sociability and personality, and industrious habits of mind—at thousands of schools around the country.

Critics denounced the public school's shift toward an overtly custodial function as both anti-American, anti-intellectual, and, ironically, antidemocratic. In the shadow of Joseph McCarthy's communist witch hunt, the Progressive's sponsorship of international understanding through education, the perceived penchant for feel-good classroom instruction, and the alleged liberal political orientation of Progressive educators cut against the grain of 1950s conservative America. The alleged anti-intellectualism of adjustment pedagogy, however, fueled even more criticism. Among others, the historian Arthur Bestor led the charge against life adjustment's anti-intellectualism. In his *Educational Wastelands* (1953) and *The Restoration of Learning* (1955), Bestor argued that life adjustment's emphasis on vocational instruction and life management skills marginalized the place of traditional core subjects. According to Bestor, it was impossible to be a fully educated person in the absence of at least some exposure to traditional liberal studies.

In this traditional view, most similar to the nineteenth century concept of education as mental discipline, Bestor was joined by other neotraditionalist educational luminaries, including Robert Maynard Hutchins, president of the University of Chicago and advocate of the great books curriculum, and James Bryant Conant, the highly respected and influential president of Harvard University. All three men agreed on the fundamental aimlessness and futility of life adjustment education in particular, and American high school education in general. Thanks to these men's efforts, the tenor of the national conversation on education changed dramatically, as more educators and public officials came to believe that it was once again time to think anew about the direction of American education.

Not surprisingly, in the midst of intense neotraditionalist scrutiny and growing public dissatisfaction with life-adjustment education, the Progressive Education Association, the principal administrative organ of the Progressive education movement, closed its doors in 1955; two years later, following the Soviet Union's successful launch of *Sputnik I,* the general orientation of American education shunned life adjustment pedagogy and embraced traditional academic studies in the liberal arts, mathematics, and the hard sciences. With the communist threat looming ever larger, the neotraditionalists believed the future of American democracy depended on a return to traditional academic studies.

Progressive education did not entirely disappear, however. The fundamental tenants of Progressive education's pedagogical and administrative functions continue to inform contemporary educational debates. What is the relationship between education and democratic citizenship, between teachers and students? Are school districts too large? To what extent is the school responsible for the emotional as well as intellectual development of its pupils? Do achievement tests provide valid and reliable measures of student learning? Is the core curriculum sacrosanct or amenable to change? These are just some of the questions Progressive educators attempted to ask and answer, and they are questions that educators still wrestle with at the beginning of the twenty-first century.

See also: CURRICULUM, SCHOOL; DEWEY, JOHN; ELEMENTARY EDUCATION, *subentry on* HISTORY OF; GARY SCHOOLS; PHILOSOPHY OF EDUCATION; PROSSER, CHARLES; SECONDARY EDUCATION, *subentry on* HISTORY OF; THORNDIKE, EDWARD L.; WASHBURNE, CARLTON.

BIBLIOGRAPHY

ANGUS, DAVID, and MIREL, JEFFREY. 1999. *The Failed Promise of the American High School, 1890–1995.* New York: Teacher's College Press.

CALLAHAN, RAYMOND E. 1962. *Education and the Cult of Efficiency: A Study of the Forces That Have Shaped the Administration of Public Schools.* Chicago: University of Chicago Press.

CREMIN, LAWRENCE. 1961. *The Transformation of the School: Progressivism in American Education.* New York: Knopf.

DEWEY, JOHN. 1899. *The School and Society.* Chicago: University of Chicago Press.

DEWEY, JOHN. 1902. *The Child and the Curriculum.* Chicago: University of Chicago Press.

DEWEY, JOHN. 1916. *Democracy and Education.* New York: Macmillan.

FILENE, PETER. 1970. "An Obituary for the Progressive Movement." *American Quarterly* 22(1):20–34.

KLIEBARD, HERBERT. 1995. *The Struggle for the American Curriculum, 1893–1958,* 2nd edition. New York: Routledge.

RAVITCH, DIANE. 1984. *The Troubled Crusade: American Education, 1945–1980.* New York: Basic Books.

RAVITCH, DIANE. 2001. *Left Back: A Century of Failed Education Reform.* New York: Simon and Schuster.

REESE, WILLIAM. 2001. "The Origins of Progressive Education." *History of Education Quarterly* 41:1–24.

ROGERS, DANIEL T. 1982. "In Search of Progressivism." *Reviews in American History* 10(4):113–132.

TYACK, DAVID. 1974. *The One Best System: A History of American Urban Education.* Cambridge, MA: Harvard University Press.

WESTBROOK, ROBERT B. 1991. *John Dewey and American Democracy.* Ithaca, NY: Cornell University Press.

ZILVERSMIT, ARTHUR. 1993. *Changing Schools: Progressive Education Theory and Practice, 1930–1960.* Chicago: University of Chicago Press.

CATHERINE GAVIN LOSS
CHRISTOPHER P. LOSS

PROJECT METHOD

The project method is an educational enterprise in which children solve a practical problem over a period of several days or weeks. It may involve building a rocket, designing a playground, or publishing a class newspaper. The projects may be suggested by the teacher, but they are planned and executed as far as possible by the students themselves, individually or in groups. Project work focuses on applying, not imparting, specific knowledge or skills, and on improving student involvement and motivation in order to foster independent thinking, self-confidence, and social responsibility.

According to traditional historiography, the project idea is a genuine product of the American

Progressive education movement. The idea was thought to have originally been introduced in 1908 as a new method of teaching agriculture, but educator William H. Kilpatrick elaborated the concept and popularized it worldwide in his famous article, "The Project Method" (1918). More recently, Michael Knoll has traced the project method to architectural education in sixteenth-century Italy and to engineering education in eighteenth-century France. This illustrates that the project of the architect—like the experiment of the scientist, the sandbox exercise of the staff officer, and the case study of the jurist—originated in the professionalization of an occupation.

The project method was first introduced into colleges and schools when graduating students had to apply on their own the skills and knowledge they had learned in the course of their studies to problems they had to solve as practicians of their trade. With some simplification, five phases in the history of the project method can be differentiated:

- 1590–1765: At the academies of architecture in Rome and Paris, advanced students work on a given problem, such as designing a monument, fountain, or palace.

- 1765–1880: The project becomes a regular teaching method; newly established schools of engineering in France, Germany, and Switzerland adopt the idea. In 1865, the project is introduced by William B. Rogers at the Massachusetts Institute of Technology into the United States.

- 1880–1918: Calvin M. Woodward adapts the project concept to schoolwork. At his Manual Training School students actually produce the projects they designed. Gradually the idea spreads from manual training (Charles R. Richards) to vocational education (David. S. Snedden, Rufus W. Stimson) and general science (John F. Woodhull).

- 1918–1965: Kilpatrick conceives the project broadly as "whole-hearted purposeful activity proceeding in a social environment." After being criticized by Boyd H. Bode, John Dewey, and other leading American Progressive educators, Kilpatrick's approach loses its attraction in the United States, yet receives general approval in Europe, India, and the Soviet Union.

- The 1970s: Kilpatrick's project method, now taken as the only adequate method of teaching

in a democratic society, is rediscovered in Germany, the Netherlands, and other European countries. Under the influence of British primary school education, U.S. educators attempt to redefine the project, viewing it as an important supplement to the traditional teacher-oriented, subject-centered curriculum.

There are two basic approaches for implementing the project method. According to the historically older approach, the students take two steps: initially, they are taught in a systematic course of study certain skills and facts, then they apply these skills and knowledge, creatively and self-directed to suitable projects. According to the second approach, the instruction by the teacher does not precede the project but is integrated in it. In other words the students first choose the project, then they discuss what they need to know for solving the problem and learn the required techniques and concepts. Finally they execute the chosen project by themselves. In both approaches, time for reflection should be provided during all phases of project learning, giving students the opportunity to evaluate their progress. Many teachers—especially vocational and industrial arts educators—use a series of small-scale projects to help students develop continuously increasing competence in practical problem solving.

See also: KILPATRICK, WILLIAM H.

BIBLIOGRAPHY

GRUBB, W. NORTON, ed. 1995. *Education through Occupations in American High Schools,* Vol. 1: *Approaches to Integrating Academic and Vocational Education.* New York: Teachers College Press.

HELM, JUDY H., and KATZ, LILIAN G. 2001. *Young Investigators: The Project Approach in the Early Years.* New York: Teachers College Press.

KATZ, LILIAN G., and CHARD, SYLVIA C. 1989. *Engaging Children's Minds: The Project Approach.* Norwood, NJ: Ablex Publishing.

KNOLL, MICHAEL. 1995. "The Project Method: Its Origin and International Influence." In *Progressive Education across the Continents. A Handbook,* ed. Volker Lenhart and Hermann Röhrs. New York: Lang.

MICHAEL KNOLL

PROSSER, CHARLES (1871–1952)

An important figure in the vocational education movement, Charles Allen Prosser is particularly known as the architect of the 1917 Smith-Hughes Act and as the figurehead of the 1945 campaign for life adjustment education.

Prosser, born as a steelworker's son in New Albany, Indiana, received B.A. (1897) and M.A. (1906) degrees from DePauw University, the LL.B. (1899) from the University of Louisville, and a Ph.D. (1915) from Teachers College, Columbia University. He worked as superintendent in the post office, practiced as lawyer in Missouri, served as teacher, principal, and superintendent in Indiana, went to New York for doctoral studies, became, under David S. Snedden, assistant commissioner of education in Massachusetts (1910–1912), and acted as executive secretary of the National Society for the Promotion of Industrial Education (1912–1915). From 1915 to 1945, the rest of his professional life, he served as director of the William H. Dunwoody Institute in Minneapolis, interrupted only by a short but crucial period as the first executive director of the Federal Board for Vocational Education (1917–1919).

Beginning in 1903 Prosser, like all Progressive educators, criticized the high school curriculum with its traditional emphasis on scholarship and college preparation. After the sixth grade, he argued, education should be differentiated because of marked difference in interests, aptitudes, and occupational opportunities that were open to the young. What the great majority of pupils needed was vocational education, that is, "real vocational education" and explicitly not manual training, homemaking, or industrial arts, since the traditional practical subjects had failed to help children "to get a job, to hold it, and to advance to a better one."

Like Edward Thorndike, Prosser believed that knowledge could not be transferred from one field of learning to another; like David Snedden, he maintained that learning, to be effective, had to be specific and directed to immediate ends; and following Georg Kerschensteiner, he pled for separate secondary schools which—apart from the traditional high school—offered as many specific vocational courses or groups of courses as there were occupations. In 1911 Prosser began campaigning for federal funds to provide social and economic opportunities for practically inclined children above fourteen years of age through the creation of specific vocational schools and programs. From his view, the duties, tasks, and problems of shop, home, and farmwork had to be learned in practical ways, preferable by the activity and project method. Pointing to the German model, he propagated a system of "dual control," that is, the vocational schools and courses were to be administered not by the general boards of education which already existed, but by separate boards of vocational education, which had to be newly established. For the most part, Prosser wrote the influential *Report of the National Commission on Aid to Vocational Education* (1914), and many of the ideas and proposals he expressed there were included into the Smith-Lever Act of 1914 and the Smith-Hughes Act of 1917—federal laws that he shepherded through Congress. At Dunwoody, the school for workers he directed, Prosser made sure that the students carried out their exercises and projects under conditions as much like those of real work in industry as possible. Since he was convinced that specific industrial methods changed rapidly in the face of changing science and technology, he institutionalized in his school short-term courses for retraining and updating skills and knowledge.

In the "Prosser Resolution" of 1945 he once again accused the secondary schools of failing to prepare the great majority of children to take their place in adult society. He claimed that 20 percent of the high school population was receiving an appropriate college-entrance education and another 20 percent was being well served by vocational programs, but that the remaining 60 percent desperately needed "life adjustment education"—they needed practical training that included personality, etiquette, health, home, and family living. In essence, the resolution revived Prosser's old idea that the principal function of schooling should be the adjustment of individuals to the social and occupational circumstances in which they live. In the long run, most of Prosser's initiatives did not prevail; nevertheless, more than any other single person, he was responsible for the fact that vocational education in the United States became the most successful curricular innovation of the twentieth century.

See also: KERSCHENSTEINER, GEORG; SECONDARY EDUCATION, *subentry on* HISTORY OF; SNEDDEN, DAVID; VOCATIONAL AND TECHNICAL EDUCATION.

BIBLIOGRAPHY

GADELL, JOHN. 1972. "Charles Allen Prosser: His Work in Vocational and General Education." Ph.D. diss., Washington University.

GREENWOOD, KATY L. B. 1978. "A Philosophical Rationale for Vocational Education: Contributions of Charles A. Prosser and His Contemporaries, 1900–1917." Ph.D. diss., University of Minnesota.

KLIEBARD, HERBERT M. 1986. *The Struggle for the American Curriculum, 1893–1958.* New York: Routledge and Kegan Paul.

PROSSER, CHARLES A. 1939. *Secondary Education and Life.* Cambridge, MA: Harvard University Press.

PROSSER, CHARLES A., and ALLEN, CHARLES R. 1925. *Vocational Education in a Democracy.* New York: Century.

PROSSER, CHARLES A., and ALLEN, CHARLES R. 1929. *Have We Kept the Faith? America at the Cross-Roads in Education.* New York: Century.

PROSSER, CHARLES A.; HAWKINS, LAYTON S.; and WRIGHT, JOHN C. 1951. *Development of Vocational Education.* Chicago: American Technological Society.

PROSSER, CHARLES A., and LOCKWOOD, GEORGE B. 1905. *The New Harmony Movement.* New York: Appleton.

WIRTH, ARTHUR G. 1972. *Education in the Technological Society. The Vocational-Liberal Studies Controversy in the Early Twentieth Century.* Scranton, PA: Intext.

MICHAEL KNOLL

PROTESTANT SCHOOL SYSTEMS

Protestant schools are a small but dynamic and diverse part of the landscape of education in the United States. These institutions, which are usually much smaller than their state-controlled counterparts and depend heavily on private financing, enroll about 3 percent of all K–12 students. In 2000 approximately 1.6 million students attended nearly 12,400 elementary and secondary Protestant schools (excluding pre-kindergarten and kindergarten-only schools) operated by churches affiliated with more than twenty denominations, institutions of higher learning, or groups of individuals committed to particular Protestant belief systems. These figures represent about 30 percent of the 5.2 million students in K–12 nonpublic schools and 45 percent of the nearly 27,400 private schools in the United States.

Colonial and Nineteenth-Century Protestant Schooling

Protestant schooling is not new to education in the United States. Prior to the advent of state school systems in the middle decades of the nineteenth century, the rich religious diversity that characterized overwhelmingly Protestant colonial and early national America was manifested in an equally rich diversity of Protestant schools. Throughout these years, Lutherans, Quakers, Presbyterians, Moravians, Mennonites, German and Dutch Reformed, Baptists, Methodists, and Anglicans established elementary schools and academies. Even the so-called town schools of colonial New England and the quasi-public district schools and charity schools of the early 1800s were de facto Protestant schools.

The mid-1800s marked an era of intense debate and reform focusing on issues of control, finance, and curriculum that led to major changes in education in the United States. By the 1850s in the North and the 1870s in the South, states had established public or common school systems. Student enrollment shifted significantly to the free common schools, the earlier practice of distributing tax dollars to schools under private control for the accomplishment of public purposes was sharply curtailed, and nonpublic schools were increasingly cast as un-American and divisive. During the period several Protestant denominations, such as the Methodist and Episcopalian, considered establishing alternative school systems, and in the case of the latter, a number dioceses, mostly in the South, encouraged the establishment of schools. In the 1840s and 1850s, the Old School Presbyterians attempted to establish a system of schools to transmit orthodox beliefs. Although nearly 300 schools were founded, a schism bred by intersectional strife ended the experiment by the time of the Civil War. Individual churches continued to maintain schools, but with the exception of the Lutheran Church–Missouri Synod, Protestant denominations and most of their members accepted state provision of elementary schooling, though not without occasional expressions of concern about secularization of public education. They did so in large measure because nineteenth-century public schools were general Protestant schools and were thought to be a principal means to creating and maintaining a moral, disciplined, and unified Protestant citizenry. Furthermore, as Roman Catholics asked for tax dollars to support their schools and complained about Protestant practices such as Bible reading in the common schools, a majority of Protestant denominations and their members set aside their denominational differences and supported the purportedly "nonsectarian" common school.

By the end of the nineteenth century, most Protestant denominations no longer discussed the possibility of establishing an alternative to the state school system. Only the Lutheran Church–Missouri Synod (which was founded in 1847 with a strong commitment to Christian education and by 1897 boasted 1,603 schools with an enrollment of 89,202); the Wisconsin Evangelical Lutheran Synod (which operated eighty-five elementary schools in 1875, twenty-five years after its creation); the Seventh-day Adventist Church (which committed itself to a system of elementary schools in the 1890s and by 1900 claimed more than 200 schools with an enrollment of about 5,000); and the Christian Reformed Church (whose commitment to Christian schools in the Calvinist tradition was only slowly realized—fourteen schools by 1900) maintained a significant denominational emphasis on Christian schooling to preserve or protect confessional and/or cultural distinctives. Though most denominations decided not to construct alternative systems, individuals, churches, and parishes sponsored Protestant schools, including a significant number of secondary institutions. Exact enrollment figures for Protestant-oriented schools in the late 1800s are not available. A 1985 study by the scholar Thomas Hunt, however, used the U.S. census of 1890 to arrive at the following figures: Lutheran, 151,651; Methodist, 58,546; Presbyterian, 37,965; Baptist, 29,869; Congregational, 27,453; and Episcopal, 21,650.

Early Twentieth-Century Protestant Schooling

Compared to public school figures, enrollment in Protestant schools had declined markedly in the 1800s as tax-supported education became more widely available and a growing number of Protestants claimed the public schools as "theirs" and even asserted that all children, Protestant and Catholic alike, attend them. By 1900, 15,503,000, or about 92 percent of the 16,855,000 elementary and secondary students in the United States, were enrolled in public schools, while 1,352,000, or approximately 8 percent, attended private institutions. About 854,000, or 63 percent of these students, were enrolled in the burgeoning Roman Catholic institutions. Most of the rest, about 3 percent of the total K–12 enrollment, attended Protestant schools, according to Otto Kraushaar's 1972 study.

Charges that nonpublic schools were undemocratic and assertions that all children should attend schools run by the state, which had been voiced since the 1840s, as well as a rising tide of nativism in the late 1800s and early 1900s led to several efforts to restrict or eliminate Catholic and Protestant schools. In 1889, for example, Wisconsin and Illinois passed the Edwards and Bennett laws. Directed primarily at Catholic and Lutheran schools, which were heavily populated by children of German-speaking parents, the Edwards law defined a school as a place where subjects were taught in English and required children to attend school in the district in which they resided. The Bennett law mandated that all children between the ages of seven and fourteen attend a public school in the district in which they resided for at least sixteen weeks (eight of which had to be consecutive) per year. Catholics, Lutherans, and other religions joined forces to bring about the repeal of both laws within two years. The gravest threat came in Oregon in 1922 with a referendum-based law that required children between the ages of eight and sixteen to attend a public school. Three years later, the U.S. Supreme Court in *Pierce v. Society of Sisters* struck down the law, affirming the right of private schools to exist and right of parents to "direct the upbringing and education" of their children.

Spurred by the Pierce decision (often called the Magna Carta of private schools), a brief period of prosperity, and a gradual softening of the xenophobia of the 1910s and early 1920s, nonpublic school enrollment began to rise slowly from about 7 percent of all K–12 students in 1920 to 9.4 percent in 1930, declining only slightly to 9.3 percent in 1940. During the interwar years, however, Protestant school enrollment accounted for between only 1 and 2 percent of all K–12 students.

While enrollment remained fairly stable throughout the 1920s and 1930s, reforms were underway that brought many Protestant schools closer to the public school model. For example, the Lutheran Church–Missouri Synod, the Seventh-day Adventist Church, and the National Union of Christian Schools (renamed Christian Schools International in

1979), founded in 1920 to represent parent-governed Calvinist Christian schools, undertook efforts to upgrade teacher preparation and curriculum as well as prepare their schools for accreditation. In Missouri Synod schools, English replaced German as the primary language of instruction. Some critics, however, asserted that their schools were becoming too much like their public counterparts.

Post–World War II Protestant Schooling

Private school enrollment increased significantly between the end of World War II and 1960, the year that nonpublic school enrollment reached a twentieth-century high of 13.6 percent of all K–12 students. Although the lion's share of the growth occurred in the Roman Catholic system, enrollments in most Protestant school groups grew during these years and, in some cases, beyond. By 1961, for example, the Lutheran Church–Missouri Synod (LCMS), which at that time operated the largest "system" of Protestant schools, claimed 1,323 schools with an enrollment of 150,440. (The term *system* is used loosely here as the control of most Protestant schools is very decentralized with local churches or boards owning the buildings and setting policy with denominations or national and regional associations providing services, resources, and accreditation.) According to Jon Diefenthaler's 1984 study, by 1983, LCMS figures had increased to 1,603 schools and 198,061 students. During the 1990s, however, K–12 enrollments have fluctuated between 165,000 and 172,000.

The much smaller, more conservative Wisconsin Evangelical Lutheran Synod also has maintained its historic commitment to Lutheran education. Its schools and enrollment have grown slowly from 239 and 27,448 in 1965 to an estimated 375 and 36,656 in 1999. On the other end of the theological spectrum, the congregations of the 5.1 million member Evangelical Lutheran Church in America, which was formed from a merger of three North American Lutheran bodies in 1988, operated an estimated 122 schools with an enrollment of 18,000 students in 1999. Like LCMS schools, ELCA institutions enrolled a significant minority of non-Lutheran children at the beginning of the twenty-first century.

Episcopal schools operated by parishes, independent corporations, or dioceses have increased rapidly since World War II. In 1951 approximately 100 Episcopal schools existed in the United States, more than half of which were long-established

boarding institutions. As a result of the increase in parish elementary schools, by 1966, 347 Episcopal schools enrolled 59,437 students. By 1981, 320 schools enrolled 76,888 students, and in 1999, 346 schools enrolled 92,466 students. Like their Quaker (Society of Friends) counterparts whose 76 broadly inclusive schools enrolled almost 19,000 students in 1999 (up from about 11,000 in 1966 and 13,000 in 1989), many Episcopal schools identify closely with the more secular, academically oriented independent school sector. More than two hundred members of the National Association of Episcopal Schools, a voluntary organization that provides support and services, also hold membership in the National Association of Independent Schools or one of its regional associations.

According to George Knight, though a relatively small denomination, the Seventh-day Adventist Church operated more than 5,500 schools worldwide in 1999. Following a century-long trend, enrollment in U.S. Adventist schools, which stress cooperation rather than competition and a biblical worldview, increased from 64,252 in 884 schools in 1966 to 81,507 in 1,324 schools in 1983. Since the mid-1980s, however, enrollment has declined. In 1999 the church operated approximately 1,013 schools with an enrollment of about 64,000.

Christian Schools International (CSI), which claims the Bible as explained in Reformed creeds as its organizational basis, provides services and support to Calvinist Christian schools. These schools have their roots in the Netherlands and emphasize the development of students who are capable of applying Christian principles to all realms of life. Once populated by students of Dutch descent, member schools now enroll students from a variety of ethnic and theological backgrounds. According to Peter DeBoer, though enrollment remained around 50,000 in the 1960s and 1970s, it increased significantly in the 1980s. Between 1981 and 1989 CSI membership grew from 217 schools with 51,849 students to 295 schools with 87,215 students. In 1999, 395 member schools enrolled approximately 88,000 elementary and secondary students.

Though Amish and Mennonites share a common Anabaptist heritage from the Protestant Reformation, their education philosophies differ. The education of Amish children is limited to elementary schooling in basic subjects, excluding science and physical education, followed by vocational training (an approach that brought persecution until the

Yoder decision of 1972 granted the Amish relief from laws that required schooling beyond the eighth grade). It is designed to prepare them for participation in a separate, nonconformist life in the Amish community. Most Mennonites, on the other hand, look to elementary and secondary schools to promote academic excellence as well as Mennonite distinctives such as peacemaking and service to the wider community. Until around 1900 Amish and most Mennonites sent their children to local public schools within their community that reflected their beliefs. Enforcement of compulsory attendance laws, increasing secularization, and consolidation prompted them to found their own schools in the 1920s through the 1940s. The National Center for Education Statistics estimated that in 1999, 414 Mennonite schools enrolled around 24,262 students, while 709 Amish schools enrolled 26,473 students.

Since the mid-1960s, when Lutheran, Calvinist, Episcopal, and Seventh-day Adventist schools dominated this segment of private education, fundamentalist and evangelical Protestants and their churches, few of which are members of "mainline" denominations, have been establishing alternatives to public education that are often referred to as independent Christian day schools. As many as 150 of these institutions were founded between 1920 and 1960. It was not until the 1960s, however, that disenchantment with the ongoing secularization of state schools, a resurgent evangelical faith, and, in some cases, fears related to desegregation sparked the rapid increase in the number of these schools, all of which profess centrality of Jesus Christ and the Bible in their educational endeavors and attempt to inculcate a Christian worldview, but are quite diverse in facilities, size, and ethos. The National Center for Education Statistics reports that approximately 10,000 Christian day schools were founded between the 1960s and 1990s, most of which were racially integrated by the end of the century. Furthermore, in the 1980s and 1990s a small but growing number of these schools were established by and for African Americans. In 2000 enrollment in Christian day schools, most of which are affiliated with either the Association of Christian Schools International or the more conservative American Association of Christian Schools, exceeded 1 million.

As is the case with Christian day schools, Protestant schooling as a whole is a diverse segment of education in the United States. Some schools endeavor to transmit orthodox beliefs, some to evangelize students, some to promote academic excellence, and some to craft Christian citizens. Despite their differences, however, most Protestant schools face at least three questions in the early twenty-first century. First, how will they remain affordable to their middle-class clienteles, not to mention poor families? Second, how religiously pluralistic can schools rooted in particular theological traditions become before they lose their identity? Finally, how will Protestant schools respond to the availability of tax dollars for private education expenses? Given the nature of Protestant schooling, responses will likely be many and varied.

See also: CATHOLIC SCHOOLS; ELEMENTARY EDUCATION, *subentry on* HISTORY OF; ISLAM; JEWISH EDUCATION, UNITED STATES; NATIONAL ASSOCIATION OF INDEPENDENT SCHOOLS; PRIVATE SCHOOLING; SECONDARY EDUCATION, *subentry on* HISTORY OF.

BIBLIOGRAPHY

CARPER, JAMES C. 2001. "The Changing Landscape of U.S. Education." *Kappa Delta Pi Record* 37(3):106–110.

CARPER, JAMES C., and LAYMAN, JACK. 1995. "Independent Christian Day Schools: Past, Present, and Prognosis." *Journal of Research on Christian Education* 4(1):7–19.

CARPER, JAMES C., and LAYMAN, JACK. 1997. "Black Flight Academies: The New Christian Day Schools." *Educational Forum* 61(2):114–121.

COOPER, BRUCE S., and DONDERO, GRACE. 1991. "Survival, Change and Demands on America's Private Schools: Trends and Policies." *Educational Foundations* 5(1):51–72.

CURRAN, FRANCIS X. 1954. *The Churches and the Schools: American Protestantism and Popular Elementary Education.* Chicago: Loyola University Press.

DEBOER, PETER P. 1993. "North American Calvinist Day Schools." In *Religious Schools in the United States, K–12: A Source Book,* ed. Thomas C. Hunt and James C. Carper. New York: Garland.

DIEFENTHALER, JON. 1984. "Lutheran Schools in America." In *Religious Schooling in America,* ed. James C. Carper and Thomas C. Hunt. Birmingham, AL: Religious Education Press.

FORBES, DAVID R. 1993. "Episcopal Schools." In *Religious Schools in the United States, K–12: A Source Book,* ed. Thomas C. Hunt and James C. Carper. New York: Garland.

HUNT, THOMAS C. 1985. "Episcopal Schooling: A Time for Reconsideration." *NAES Journal* 1(2):11–21.

JORGENSON, LLOYD P. 1987. *The State and the Non-Public School, 1825–1925.* Columbia: University of Missouri Press.

KAESTLE, CARL F. 1983. *Pillars of the Republic: Common Schools in American Society, 1780–1860.* New York: Hill and Wang.

KASHATUS, WILLIAM C. 1993. "Seeking the Light and Nurturing the Intellect: A Brief History of Quaker Education in America." In *Religious Schools in the United States, K–12: A Source Book,* ed. Thomas C. Hunt and James C. Carper. New York: Garland.

KNIGHT, GEORGE R. 1993. "Seventh-day Adventist Schooling in the United States." In *Religious Schools in the United States, K–12: A Source Book,* ed. Thomas C. Hunt and James C. Carper. New York: Garland.

KRAUSHAAR, OTTO F. 1972. *American Nonpublic Schools: Patterns of Diversity.* Baltimore: Johns Hopkins University Press.

NATIONAL CENTER FOR EDUCATION STATISTICS. 2001. *Private School Universe Survey, 1999–2000.* Washington, DC: U. S. Department of Education.

Pierce v. Society of Sisters. 1925. 268 U.S. 510.

SHERRILL, LEWIS J. 1932. *Presbyterian Parochial Schools, 1846–1870.* New Haven, CT: Yale University Press.

STEINER, DONOVAN D., and MULLET, JUDY H. 1993. "Amish/Mennonite Schools." In *Religious Schools in the United States, K–12: A Source Book,* ed. Thomas C. Hunt and James C. Carper. New York: Garland.

JAMES C. CARPER

PSYCHOLOGIST, SCHOOL

School psychology is the application of psychological principles and techniques to the education of children. Drawing upon its own knowledge base and that of related fields, including clinical and educational psychology, school psychology focuses on the individual study of children's learning and adjustment primarily in educational settings.

School psychology originated in the late nineteenth century. Its origins are closely connected to those of special education, clinical and educational psychology, the rise of psychological science, the development of psychoeducational tests, and the implementation of special education programs in response to the needs of atypical children required to attend school under state compulsory attendance laws.

Roles and Functions

The major roles and functions of practicing school psychologists include psychoeducational assessment, consultation, interventions, research and evaluation, in-service education, and administration.

Psychoeducational assessment. School psychologists spend at least 50 percent of their time administering psychological and educational tests, conducting observations and interviews, and gathering relevant information in the assessment of students experiencing learning and adjustment problems. The assessment often includes tests of cognitive ability, school achievement, psychomotor skills, adaptive behavior, social skills, and personal-social adjustment. Such assessments also involve interviews with parents and teachers, observations in school, and inspection of school records. Each case study is summarized in a written report.

Consultation. School psychologists spend about 20 percent of their time in consultation. This is an indirect method of providing services in which the psychologist works to alter the attitudes and behaviors of others (usually parents and teachers) to affect changes in student behavior, school curriculum, or school system policies.

Interventions. Practitioners spend about 20 percent of their time in direct interventions, including remediation and therapy, that involve referred children. Conducted individually or in groups, these services are intended to alleviate academic and behavior problems.

Research and evaluation. About 3 percent of practitioner time is devoted to research and evaluation. Although this is an important role for school psychologists, other priorities preclude much involvement in the design of research and evaluation projects that might better assess the efficacy of referral methods, assessment techniques, therapeutic outcomes, and the evaluation of district programs.

In-service education. Less than 3 percent of practitioner time is devoted to in-service education of district personnel or parents. This activity may be directed at many topics, including reducing systemic problems in child study and improving teaching or parenting skills.

Administration. Modern-day services require an unusual amount of record keeping, accounting, and administrative tasks. This role may account for 5 percent of practitioner time.

Employment Settings

Most school psychologists are employed in schools, colleges and universities, or private practice.

Schools. Surveys have consistently shown that at least 80 percent of school psychologists are employed in public school settings. Perhaps an additional 5 percent are employed in related settings such as private schools, correctional schools, residential treatment centers, and boarding schools.

Colleges and universities. About 4 percent of school psychologists have their primary employment in academic settings, usually as faculty members assigned to the training programs for school psychologists. Some hold positions in the institution's psychological services center or agency for assisting students with disabilities.

Private practice. About 4 to 5 percent of school psychologists work in private practice, many on a part-time basis. Some are independent practitioners, whereas others work within a group practice with pediatricians, psychiatrists, social workers, and other psychologists.

Relationship to Special Education

School psychology practice is closely linked to special education programs. The need for psychologists to help determine student eligibility for placement and to recommend subsequent educational programs and interventions is formalized in federal and state regulations (e.g., the Individuals with Disabilities Education Act Amendments of 1997). Practitioners spend about two-thirds of their time in activities related to special education; these activities may include any of the roles mentioned above.

Relationship to Other Pupil Personnel Workers

In most school districts, the school psychologist works with a pupil personnel services team. Other team members may be school counselors, social workers, nurses, and speech and language therapists. The team works with teachers, parents, and adminis-

trators to try to alleviate specific problems, and it consults with school personnel on district-wide prevention programs.

Training

School psychologists are prepared in programs leading to master's (M.A., M.S., M.Ed.), specialist (Ed.S.), or doctoral (Ph.D., Ed.D., Psy.D) degrees. Approximately 220 institutions provide school psychology training in about 90 doctoral and 200 nondoctoral programs.

The National Association of School Psychologists (NASP) considers the specialist degree or its equivalent (a graduate program of at least sixty semester hours including internship) as the appropriate entry-level training for school psychology practice. The American Psychological Association (APA) considers the doctoral degree as the appropriate entry-level training for school psychology practice. The department of education in the program's home state typically approves programs. The NASP approves programs according to its standards at the specialist and doctoral levels and participates in the accreditation process of the National Council for Accreditation of Teacher Education. The APA has an accreditation office that accredits professional psychology programs at the doctoral level only.

Credentialing

Practice credentials are available in every state, usually from two separate agencies. Credentials offered through the state's department of education are almost always required for employment in the settings under its jurisdiction, typically all public educational facilities in the state and often private schools as well. Each state's board of examiners in psychology offers a credential for practice in the settings under its jurisdiction, typically all nonschool settings. In some states these two agencies have overlapping authority to issue credentials. These agencies issue either a certificate or a license to practice.

Growth and Current Status

The rapid development of the field is observed in the growth in the number of practitioners, organizational developments and memberships, expansion of professional literature, and the importance of professional regulation through accreditation and credentialing.

Number of school psychologists. School psychology has seen enormous growth since the 1950s.

Whereas there were only 1,000 people in the field in 1950, the number of practitioners grew to 5,000 by 1970, 22,000 by 1990, and to at least 25,000 by the early twenty-first century. Female representation among school psychologists rose from about 50 percent in the 1960s to 70 percent in the early twenty-first century. Minorities comprise less than 10 percent of the work force.

Organizational representation. The field of school psychology is represented at the national level by the NASP and by the Division of School Psychology within the APA. The NASP's membership is approximately 22,000, whereas that of APA's Division of School Psychology is about 2,500. Each group holds an annual convention, provides products and literature for its members, and advocates for school psychology according to its policies. Each state has a NASP-affiliated association that provides similar services. These associations are generally independent of the state's APA-affiliated psychology association, although in some states the school psychology association is a part of the state psychology group. There may also be local and regional groups of school psychologists that affiliate with the state groups.

Literature. Two journals specifically for school psychologists were founded in the 1960s: *Journal of School Psychology* and *Psychology in the Schools*. Additional journals for school psychologists in North America include *School Psychology Review, School Psychology Quarterly, Canadian Journal of School Psychology,* and *School Psychology International*. School psychologists also subscribe to related journals (e.g., *Journal of Psychoeducational Assessment, Journal of Clinical and Consulting Psychology, Exceptional Children*). State and national associations provide newsletters and other publications. Books specific to school psychology date to 1930, but most have been published since 1960.

Employment and salaries. There is a shortage of practitioners in almost every state. Opportunities for employment are greatest in urban and rural school districts, as well as in academic settings. Suburban school districts also have many job opportunities.

Salaries have followed inflation for several decades. According to Daniel J. Reschly, the median salary of NASP members was in the $35,000 to $40,000 range in 1990 and in the $48,000 to $50,000 range by the late 1990s.

Future perspectives. Demand for school psychologists is expected to outweigh supply indefinitely.

School settings will continue to be the primary practice locale, though job opportunities will be plentiful in other settings. Employment opportunities in training programs for persons holding doctoral degrees will be very attractive. Salaries will continue to increase at a gradual but steady rate.

Traditional practice roles will persist although the technical adequacy of test and intervention techniques will improve. The specialist level of training will continue to be the entry level for practice in school settings, but doctoral training will increasingly be expected in other settings. The number of training programs is not likely to rise by any significant extent, but more doctoral programs are expected to be established, especially in freestanding schools of professional psychology.

Credentialing for school-based practice will continue to be regulated by the state departments of education, most of which will continue to require nondoctoral training. Credentialing for nonschool practice will continue to be regulated by state boards of psychology, granting credentials mainly at the doctoral level, with increasing expectations for postdoctoral training.

The importance of diversity in school psychology training and practice will be a priority. Female representation among school psychologists may grow to 80 percent. The recruitment of males and minorities of either gender will become increasingly important.

See also: EDUCATIONAL PSYCHOLOGY; GUIDANCE AND COUNSELING, SCHOOL; PERSONAL AND PSYCHOLOGICAL COUNSELING AT COLLEGES AND UNIVERSITIES; SCHOOL-LINKED SERVICES, *subentry on* TYPES OF SERVICES AND ORGANIZATIONAL FORMS; SPECIAL EDUCATION, *subentries on* CURRENT TRENDS, HISTORY OF.

BIBLIOGRAPHY

CURTIS, MICHAEL J.; HUNLEY, SAWYER A.; and PRUS, JOSEPH R., eds. 1998. *Credentialing Requirements for School Psychologists.* Bethesda, MD: National Association of School Psychologists.

CUTTS, NORMA E., ed. 1955. *School Psychologists at Mid-Century.* Washington, DC: American Psychological Association.

FAGAN, THOMAS K., and WARDEN, PAUL G., eds. 1996. *Historical Encyclopedia of School Psychology.* Westport, CT: Greenwood Press.

FAGAN, THOMAS K., and WISE, PAULA S. 2000. *School Psychology: Past, Present, and Future.* Bethesda, MD: National Association of School Psychologists.

HILDRETH, GERTRUDE H. 1930. *Psychological Service for School Problems.* Yonkers-on-Hudson, NY: World Book.

Individuals with Disabilities Education Act Amendments of 1997. U.S. Public Law 105-17. *U.S. Code.* Vol. 20, secs. 1400 et seq.

MAGARY, JAMES F., ed. 1967. *School Psychological Services in Theory and Practice: A Handbook.* Englewood Cliffs, NJ: Prentice-Hall.

RESCHLY, DANIEL J. 2000. "The Present and Future Status of School Psychology in the United States." *School Psychology Review* 29:507–522.

REYNOLDS, CECIL R., and GUTKIN, TERRY B., eds. 1999. *Handbook of School Psychology,* 3rd edition. New York: Wiley.

THOMAS, ALEX, ed. 1998. *Directory of School Psychology Training Programs.* Bethesda, MD: National Association of School Psychologists.

YSSELDYKE, JAMES; DAWSON, PEG; LEHR, CAMILLA; RESCHLY, DANIEL; REYNOLDS, MAYNARD; and TELZROW, CATHY. 1997. *School Psychology: A Blueprint for Training and Practice II.* Bethesda, MD: National Association of School Psychologists.

THOMAS K. FAGAN

PTA

See: NATIONAL PTA.

PUBLIC EDUCATION, CRITICISM OF

Despite several decades of reform, public education in the United States is criticized by some as not teaching all children effectively. Consistently poor test results and low graduation rates attest to this. As a result, many taxpayers criticize public schools and demand better results. At the same time, many Americans express a deep faith in the ability of public education to address the needs of the greater society.

There are five issues that cloud the public's perception of the public schools and fuel criticism.

While more than five issues could be identified by the public—who consistently rate the performance of schools as less than optimal—these are central issues found in schools across the country. Two of these issues are long-standing characteristics of the public education system: inequality of opportunity and the burden of bureaucracy. Two are highly debated, more recent movements that attempt to address these characteristics: achievement-based outcomes and school choice. The fifth issue concerns how these movements contribute to American public education reform.

Inequality of Opportunity

Public education in the United States has long promised quality education for all children, regardless of ethnicity, race, or income. However, critics of public education argue that many children do not have equal opportunities to learn and are not likely to attend a quality school. In fact, critics suggest that the education system perpetuates poverty and disadvantage, providing rich and poor schools with stark contrasts in learning environments and physical surroundings. Impoverished neighborhoods typically house run-down schools with less money and poor conditions, while affluent neighborhoods house newer and safer schools providing better learning environments. Furthermore, ethnic minority students are more likely to attend the lower-quality urban schools. While there have been many efforts to improve this inequality of opportunity, such efforts are only the first step in achieving equity, even with millions of dollars invested in federal programs.

Since the 1950s, federal compensatory education efforts have tried to achieve equity in education with programs such as Head Start, giving preschoolers from low-income families a chance to start kindergarten at the same level as their middle- and upper-class peers. Other major federal policy efforts created categorical programs—such as Title I, bilingual education, and special education initiatives—to promote equity for children with economic disadvantages, language barriers, and physical or mental disabilities.

A groundbreaking federal commitment, the Elementary and Secondary Education Act of 1965, and subsequent amendments, supports education achievement and equity by providing federal funds to states and school districts. The Bilingual Education Act (1968), the Education for All Handicapped Children Act (1975), and Title IX (1972), which removed barriers to women in education institutions, also serve as examples of early and sustained commitments by the federal government to achieve equity in schools.

Data from the National Assessment of Educational Progress (NAEP) reports that 63 percent of fourth graders perform at only basic, or below basic, levels in reading. Sixty-nine percent perform at these levels in mathematics. African-American, Hispanic, and Native American fourth graders perform consistently lower than their white counterparts. Furthermore, schools in the United States fail to teach higher-order skills to about half of the student population. And once again, this "bottom half" comprises primarily the poor and ethnic minorities.

The inequalities of access to quality schools and achievement of children in public schools have been the source of years of debate and millions of dollars in programs attempting to achieve equity for all students. Yet, as shown above, critics of public education cite ample evidence that inequality and inequity exists and that little has been done to level the playing field. NAEP data, however, does show that the gap in reading and mathematics between white students and their African-American and Hispanic counterparts narrowed between 1973 and 1999 at all grade levels.

Highly Bureaucratic Systems

Critics of American public education argue that the United States is unable to educate all children effectively, partly because of the highly bureaucratic nature of its governance structure. Attached to most federal government funding are layers of rules burdened by paperwork and regulation; thus, federal programs become difficult to implement or change. This institutionalized problem of excessive bureaucracy shuffles funds and responsibility around to various bodies and, in the case of public education, shifts the responsibility of academic achievement onto parents, administrators, teachers, and students. The result of public education being tied to the agendas of so many stakeholders—voters, politicians, school boards, administrators, teachers, unions, parents, and students—has been fragmentation and lack of control, leaving the public to wonder who has the authority in the system.

The same burden of bureaucracy also exists at the state, district, and school level. Critics assert that oversight of public schools is unnecessarily heavy.

The state boards of education and administrative regulation by state departments of education add yet another layer to the policymaking process. Locally, elected school boards attempt to maintain the mission and vision of the district, yet they are often accused of micromanaging and adding layers of bureaucracy. District administrations, with central authority over the schools, are often fighting for control with the school boards.

One way to decrease bureaucracy is to decentralize control to the district or site level, known as *site-based management*. Not only will bureaucracy decrease when control is local, say proponents, but administrators, teachers, and the community will have a greater influence on the needs of their children, as well as strategies to serve those needs. Another way to lessen bureaucratic weight is to add competition and choice in public schools through charters and vouchers. Advocates of school choice believe, among other things, that some of the bureaucratic burden causing inefficiency and ineffectiveness will be lifted when schools are run more like businesses and parents can choose their children's schools—more like consumers. Yet, these ideas of choice and localized control meet resistance from the education establishment, who often argue that maintaining and adding to current practices is the best bet for improving public education. This resistance to change also fuels criticism from the public.

Achievement-Based Outcomes

To ensure students are mastering the skills necessary to successfully enter either the workforce or institutions of higher learning, measures of academic success have emerged. Most indicators come in the form of standardized tests, administered at several grades throughout elementary and secondary school. NAEP state performance indicators have confirmed that students are not learning and succeeding at the level expected by parents, taxpayers, and policymakers. In addition, some critics regard these high-stakes tests as unfair, citing data showing cultural bias against students from low-income families and racial/ethnic minorities, who often perform lower in these measures. However, most racial and ethnic subgroups of children have improved their scores over time, performing better on mathematics, reading, and science measures. Nevertheless, the gap in achievement, measured by these widely used tests, causes critics to blame the public education for failing to teach students.

Indicators of achievement on mathematics and science, such as the Third International Mathematics and Science Study (TIMSS) comparison of students in the fourth and eighth grades from forty nations (and twelfth-grade students from twenty nations), have revealed that the overall achievement of students in the United States is low compared to students in other industrialized nations. Twelfth graders in the United States were outperformed by fourteen of twenty nations in mathematics and science, according to TIMSS results, initiating a flurry of debate and concern nationwide about public education. Others have debunked criticisms of achievement in the United States based on TIMSS data since cross-national comparisons do not consider the dramatically different student diversity and pluralism in America and the varying governance serving its diverse population. Still, the aftermath of TIMSS resulted in government pressure on students to enroll in more difficult math and science classes, and also forced the nation to reevaluate its place among competing nations in the global economy. Despite all of this concern about students and their ability to perform in the economy of the early twenty-first century, data from 1990 to 2000 showed steady economic growth in the United States, the strongest in several decades, in fact.

State-level accountability systems have emerged across the country during the 1980s and 1990s. These systems include rules for state-administered standardized tests and curriculum standards for all grade levels. In these accountability systems, some states reward students, teachers, and school and district leaders for improving academic achievement. Part of the criticisms came when leaders had difficulty implementing these systems of accountability, often due to having standards not aligned with tests and curriculum not aligned with standards. Efforts to improve these disparities and ultimately improve achievement outcomes have been slow to show results. For example, experts continue to change the measures themselves, putting teaching strategies and curriculum used to teach them in constant flux. In addition, where schools are consistently performing very poorly on high-stakes tests, the state intervenes by way of sanctions or takeover of the school or district. Critics say these interventions and accountability systems are presented with little evidence of their likelihood to positively change the system. Seldom are these changes backed with research-based rationale.

School Choice

Many believe competition among schools can solve the problems of poor student achievement, inequity, and government bureaucracy. Since the 1990s, school choice has gained enormous momentum, providing a variety of enrollment options for children, such as charter schools, voucher programs, district/school open enrollment, and tax credits/deductions. Advocates of school choice feel that when parents become consumers of education, schools will compete, forcing public schools to improve student academic performance or risk closure. They also believe that public schools are unable to reform successfully because of too much government oversight. Critics of school choice argue the lack of a monitoring mechanism will mean far less accountability with no guarantee that all children are learning basic skills. Others challenge the constitutionality of some choice programs, arguing that including religious schools in a choice program—particularly when vouchers with public funds are involved—violates the separation of church and state. A brief description of each of the various school choice options follows.

Charter schools. Charter schools are independent public schools formed by communities, and they are therefore relatively free from state and local laws and regulations. The school operates under the framework of a contract, or *charter,* established by the parents, businesses, and the community the school serves. Less controversial than vouchers, charter schools and their enrollment have grown tremendously since 1994 when Congress authorized the Public Charter School Program through Title X of the Elementary and Secondary Education Act. Since 1991, thirty-seven states have passed charter school legislation. Although there is some evidence that charters may improve academic achievement, the research is mixed. Early studies cited higher achievement for some groups in some grades when compared to conventional schools, as well as lower achievement for others.

Vouchers. Vouchers are public funds given to families and organizations to provide tuition for children at any public, private, or parochial school they choose. Advocates of voucher programs say they expand options for low-income parents. Critics claim that vouchers divert public funds away from already ailing public schools and into private and religious institutions. Furthermore, they argue that vouchers "skim" off the best students, thereby further stratifying and segregating schools. Moreover, legal disputes related to the constitutionality of vouchers pervade state and federal courts. Capacity and cost are two major barriers to the implementing of a sound voucher program. While there is a demand for school choice, the supply of schools and their capacity to enroll additional students depend on their ability to expand, which adds to teaching staff, class size, and administrative faculty. In addition, private schools vary widely in their tuition costs. Because vouchers are given based on state per-pupil expenditures, many families may still have to pay significant costs to send their children to the school of their choice, and many families will be unable to afford to send their children to the school of their choice.

District/school open enrollment. Sometimes referred to as intradistrict/interdistrict choice, District/school open enrollment allows families to choose a school in their area other than the one the student was assigned, dependent on availability of space. Open enrollment laws can be either mandatory or voluntary.

Tax credits/deductions. Tax credits and deductions allow families to recoup money on their taxes spent on private education costs, including tuition, textbooks, transportation, and other direct school expenses. Since these deductions can only be taken after the money is spent, through deductions of taxes owed, many low-income families are not able to participate.

A strongly debated issue, criticisms of school choice come from many angles. Some criticisms have been aimed at the idea of competition among schools in general, while others criticize those in the system who are opposed to this promising effort to improve education for many American children.

Reform after Reform

As educators and legislators continue to believe in the power of change through education reform, dollars will be spent on one innovative idea after another to improve academic performance, efficiency, or other structural characteristics of the schools. American public education has, since 1980, endured reform after reform, with few reforms sustained over the long-term, and little to show for the effort except frustration and lack of clarity in the mission of the reforms. Instructional reforms (e.g., whole language vs. phonics instruction in reading), pedagogical reforms (e.g., constructivist vs. direct instruction), and

management reforms (e.g., centralized decision making vs. site-based control) create a *reform build-up* in schools and districts. Even after years of reforms, some assert that classroom practices have changed very little. Yet, states, districts, schools, and classrooms have periodically seen positive outcomes from their reforms. This often results in countless efforts to replicate success stories when the context may not be conducive to the same effects. Research shows that effective reforms are gradual and incremental, suggesting that change and reform is a step toward progress, not progress itself. Educators and reformers are then charged with the task of asking the public to be patient in seeing results. Too often, this reform build-up creates doubt and mistrust among those inside and outside of the system.

Public education in the United States has historically been both the panacea for societal ills and the target for criticism and disapproval. For every critic pointing out the failures of the system, there's a success story to be told that outlines the progress public education has made. Given the many failed reforms and less than successful attempts to create a more equal and fair system, there is no evidence that eliminating the entire system would improve the system or halt any criticisms. Instead, like every other institution in America, educators, policymakers, and reformers learn from the mistakes of the past and continue to pave new ways of helping students learn and succeed.

See also: ASSESSMENT; INTERNATIONAL ASSESSMENTS; SCHOOL-BASED DECISION-MAKING; SCHOOL REFORM; TESTING.

BIBLIOGRAPHY

CAMPBELL, JAY R.; HOMBO, CATHERINE M.; and MAZZEO, JOHN. 2000. *NAEP 1999 Trends in Academic Progress: Three Decades of Student Performance.* Washington, DC: National Center for Education Statistics.

CHALL, JEANNE S. 2000. *The Academic Achievement Challenge: What Really Works in the Classroom.* New York: Guilford Press.

CHUBB, JOHN E., and MOE, TERRY M. 1990. *Politics, Markets, and America's Schools.* Washington, DC: Brookings Institution Press.

CUBAN, LARRY, and TYACK, DAVID. 1995. *Tinkering Toward Utopia: A Century of Public School Reform.* Cambridge, MA: Harvard University Press.

ELMORE, RICHARD F. 1997. "Education Policy and Practice in the Aftermath of TIMSS." In *Learning from TIMSS: Results of the Third International Mathematics and Science Study,* ed. Alexandra Beatty. Washington, DC: National Academy Press.

GILL, BRIAN P.; TIMPANE, P. MICHAEL; ROSS, KAREN; and BREWER, DOMINIC J. 2001. *Rhetoric Versus Reality: What We Know and What We Need to Know About Vouchers and Charter Schools.* Santa Monica, CA: RAND.

KIRST, MICHAEL. 1993. "Strengths and Weaknesses of American Education." In *The State of the Nation's Public Schools: A Conference Report,* ed. Stanley Elam. Bloomington, IN: Phi Delta Kappa.

KOZAL, JONATHAN. 1992. *Savage Inequalities: Children in America's Schools.* New York: Perennial Publishers.

WESTED REGIONAL EDUCATION LABORATORY. 1999. *What We Know About Vouchers: The Facts Behind the Rhetoric.* San Francisco: WestEd.

WESTED REGIONAL EDUCATION LABORATORY. 2000. *Analysis and Implications of California Proposition 38: Will Vouchers Improve Student Access to Private Schools?* San Francisco: WestEd.

INTERNET RESOURCES

RILEY, RICHARD. 1998. "Secretary of Education's Remarks on TIMSS Results Impact for Our Economic Future and Individual Opportunities." <www.ed.gov/inits/TIMSS>.

U.S. DEPARTMENT OF COMMERCE. 2002. <http://home.doc.gov>.

PAUL KOEHLER
JOY W. LEWIS

PUBLIC SCHOOL BUDGETING, ACCOUNTING, AND AUDITING

The three major financial functions in education—budgeting, accounting, and auditing—are separate, discrete operations, but they are nonetheless closely interrelated. They are required activities in providing reliable fiscal information, guidance, and accountability in the use of the $365 billion raised and expended in 2001 on preschool through grade twelve public education in the United States. Budgeting is a process and plan for determining how money is to be raised and spent, as well as a document—the budget—developed and approved during the budgeting process.

Money is organized and spent according to an accounting system, using a general ledger that standardizes each spending category and accounts for its use. The National Center for Education Statistics published the *Financial Accounting for Local and State School Systems,* commonly called *Handbook II, Revised* (1990), by William J. Fowler. *Handbook II, Revised* is an accounting system with line codes for each category and function to make it easier for external agencies to analyze and audit school spending to ensure the legal and appropriate use of public funds.

Budgeting

William Hartman, author of *School District Budgeting* (1999), defines education budgeting as a "working tool" for the successful operation of states and local school districts, and as a "significant opportunity to plan the mission, improve their operations, and achieve their education objectives" (p. 1). As such, the budgeting process allows various levels of government to "make better financial and program decisions, improve operations, and enhance relations with citizens and other stakeholders" (National Advisory Council on State and Local Budgeting, p. 2).

In more technical terms, a budget is a statement of the total educational program for a given unit, as well as an estimate of resources necessary to carry out the program and the revenues needed to cover those expenditures. A *vertical budget* includes the various income and expenditure estimates (by line item, function, object, and cost center) in a given fiscal year, while a *horizontal budget* will include current estimates for a given fiscal year, compared to prior audited income and expenditures, and a projection of costs into the future. Hence, the budget is a statement of purpose and a review of income and expenditures by function—with a timeline to explain past, current, and future financial practices.

Education agencies, like businesses and other enterprises, have experimented with various forms of budget organization: line-item and function/object budgeting are basic to all systems; and planning-programming-budgeting systems, zero-based budgeting, and site-based budgeting are attempts to link the budget to goals and objectives while devolving the budgeting process to the school level.

Line-item budgeting. Barry Mundt et al. define line-item, or "traditional," budgeting as "a technique in which line items, or objects of expenditures—e.g., personnel, supplies, contractual services, and capital outlays—are the focus of analysis, authorization, and control" (p. 36). While helpful in tracking costs, line-item budgeting is virtually useless for planning or management, since the functions of the expenditures are not explained and the particular need, school site, and type of students being served are lost in spending aggregated by "line." Thus, *teachers' salaries,* for example, is a budget line-item; but which teachers, at which schools, teaching which types of students (e.g., bilingual special needs) is not explained.

Function/object budgeting. Most districts use function/object budgeting, since it organizes spending around the basic functions of the system, such as instruction, student support, operations, administration, and transportation. In addition, functions are subdivided (e.g., into elementary instruction, high school operations), while the object being purchased (e.g., elementary textbooks, high school cleaning equipment) is also specified. Personnel services or salaries and benefits may be handled by function; that is, for instructional, support, or plant maintenance staff, for example.

While these broad categories, objects, and processes are generally the same for education budgeting across the country, a strategic attempt has also been made to determine the most effective and efficient uses of resources. These efforts have led to such innovations as zero-based, program-planning, and site-based budgeting, which attempt to be more mission-driven and constituent-friendly than traditional types of budgeting in education.

Zero-based budgeting (ZBB). Popular in the 1950s and 1960s, ZBB began with the assumption that the school system starts out yearly with a "clean slate." Thus, each function, program, and agency has to justify its expenditures annually, relating all costs to system goals and objectives to avoid habitual spending. Because so many costs, such as tenured teachers' salaries and benefits, are "fixed" across annual budgets, and because the programs are so complex, zero-based budgeting becomes more an exercise

than a practical reality. As Hartman explains, "ZBB . . . forces comparisons of and choices among programs and activities that are often difficult to compare adequately" (p. 49). In addition, most programs are not "up for grabs" on an annual basis, since, for example, schools cannot eliminate their elementary school classes, making such a requirement difficult to justify.

Program-planning-budgeting systems (PPBS). Used by the U.S. Defense Department during the Vietnam War, PPBS seek greater efficiency by attaching spending to particular programs (e.g., the development of a new multipurpose fighter jet aircraft that might be used jointly by the Army, Navy, and Air Force—thus saving costs, but failing, in fact, to meet the needs of any of the armed services very well). While rarely used in education, PPBS would require school districts to spell out their mission and goals, lay out alternatives to reach these objectives, attribute costs to each choice, analyze the costs, select the best option, and then build the budget around this outcome, and finally feed data back to adjust the costs to the results. While this method sounds ideal, it often becomes so complex, and the programs so numerous, that school districts and states cannot readily sustain this approach.

Site-based (school-site) budgeting (SBB). SBB is concerned with who will do the budgeting and where in the organizational hierarchy the decisions will be made. In attempts to bring the budgeting process closer to "end-users"—the teachers, parents, and school administrators—SBB encourages, if not requires, decision-makers in each school to examine their programs and to set their budgets to meet their particular needs as part of the process of shared decision-making. Allan Odden et al. explain that school reform may require greater decentralization, a step "in which teams of individuals who actually provide the services are given decision-making authority and held accountable for results" (p. 5). Under site-based budgeting, districts must determine who will serve on SBB committees; which decisions and resources are devolved to schools—and using what formulas; how much autonomy is granted to spend for local school needs; exactly how to analyze the budget at each school; and what training and support are needed to make SBB work effectively.

In practice, school districts or divisions thereof will utilize variations of many, if not all, of the above methods in compiling their budgets. For example, a school principal may require teachers to justify their individual budget requests (zero-based) in the development of a school (site-based) budget. A component of the district's budget may include a proposal for a new educational program, including all anticipated expenditures, revenues, and cost savings (program-planning budget). The entire district budget may be compiled onto a state-mandated format that requires line items to be categorized by fund, function, program, and object (function/object budgeting). Once the fiscal year begins, the budget is transformed from a financial plan into the initial baseline data for a working, dynamic financial accounting system.

Accounting

Related to budgeting is the accounting system. If a school district's budget is a financial reflection of its educational mission, goals, and philosophies, then the accounting system becomes the method by which a district can assess the overall effectiveness of the financial plan. In fact, the accounting structure (line items, spending categories, costing and spending procedures) is reflected in the budget, and will later be used in auditing the system for legal, appropriate, and responsible spending.

David Thompson and Craig Wood explain five purposes for the use of accounting in schools. The first purpose is to "set up a procedure by which all fiscal activities in a district can be accumulated, categorized, reported, and controlled" (p. 111). The second function is to assess the alignment of the district's financial plan (budget) with the district's educational programs. An accounting system allows the district's management to assess whether a district has the financial resources to meet the needs of its programs.

The third function relates to the state and federal reporting requirements to which school districts must adhere. States have the constitutional authority for the provision of education, and, as such, they bear the final responsibility for fiscal accountability. Likewise, federal funds are distributed to local districts—through the states—and require adequate accounting and reporting procedures. These reporting requirements have led to the development and adoption of uniform budgeting procedures and accounting standards. The Governmental Accounting Standards Board (GASB), operating under the auspices of the Financial Accounting Foundation (FAF), is responsible for the establishment and revision of Generally Accepted Accounting Principles (GAAP) for local and state governments.

One significant difference in the utilization of GAAP for school districts and GAAP for private business is that school districts utilize fund accounting that classifies spending into three broad fund categories: governmental, proprietary, and fiduciary. Governmental funds represent those activities typical of district operations such as instruction, special revenues (grants), and debt service funds. Proprietary funds include those activities that are similar to private enterprise, such as food service and transportation funds. Fiduciary funds are utilized when the district is acting directly for a third party, including private trusts (scholarships), pension trusts, investment trusts, and agency (payroll) funds.

Budget preparation is the fourth purpose of accounting. By accumulating accurate baseline data, accounting provides the budget with the information necessary for a horizontal comparison (prior year, current year, and future annual revenues) of actual vertical (line-item) expenditures and budget performance. The fifth and final purpose of accounting, as proposed by Thompson and Wood, is to provide proper fiscal controls and accountability, which, in turn, build public trust and confidence.

Critics of the current system of accounting utilized in public schools have claimed that the collection and reporting of financial data no longer provides adequate information to policymakers. Jay G. Chambers asserts that the desire for programmatic cost information, the need for data compatibility, and the importance of understanding the relationship between educational inputs and outputs all point to the need for improving the standards for organizing and reporting educational resource data. To measure resources adequately in education, Chambers proposes a system that is related more to economics rather than accounting.

The *resource cost model,* which Chambers recommends, "places paramount importance on measuring productivity and the cost-effectiveness analysis, the economist's stock in trade" (p. 26). Several states, including Hawaii, South Carolina, and Rhode Island, have adopted another reporting tool that integrates with the existing GAAP accounting systems utilized at the school and district level. This financial analysis model allows expenditure data to be reported on a school-by-school basis and actually tracks dollars spent on the classroom for "classroom instruction." The reporting program allows policy-makers to "explore the equity, efficiency, and effectiveness of spending"(Cooper et al. 2001, p. 28) between schools as opposed to school districts.

Accounting is thus the tool by which school district management can structure, organize, and operationalize the district's financial plan (the budget). Accounting also provides the roadmap by which fiduciary entities, such as board of education members, public citizens, and state government officials can evaluate a school's financial status. In addition, school district accounting provides the necessary procedures and data to enable an independent, certified public accountant to conduct the district's annual financial audit.

Auditing

Since schools are public agencies, their raising and spending of money must be reviewed and audited on a yearly basis—and on an as-needed basis, as determined by the governing body. In addition, an effective management system would include internal reviews and audits on a continuous basis to ensure accuracy and prevent fraud. Thus, two broad categories of audits—external and internal—are important in holding schools accountable for the use of public funds.

An external audit is an objective, systematic review of resources and operations, followed by a written or oral report of findings. Robert E. Everett et al. (1995) define three basic types of external audits. *Financial compliance audits* address the "fairness of presentation of basic financial statements in conformity with Generally Accepted Accounting Principles (GAAP)" (p. 4). This type of audit is most commonly associated with the annual independent audit that most states require: namely, a Comprehensive Annual Financial Report (CAFR) to be prepared by the school district that conforms to standards developed by the Governmental Accounting Standards Board and state reporting requirements. It is the auditor's responsibility to render an opinion of the financial statements contained in the CAFR, based on their audit of district records.

A *program compliance audit* is a review of a local education agency's (LEA) adherence to the educational and financial requirements of a specific funding source, such as a discretionary federal grant. The third type of audit is a *performance audit,* which addresses the "economy and efficiency of the LEA"

(Everett et al., p. 4), examining an LEA's internal controls for weaknesses, which would expose possible mismanagement or fraud.

Internal audits, on the other hand, are usually incorporated into a district's internal control procedures, a system of checks and balances designed to ensure ongoing accountability by requiring certain members of the organization to perform a financial audit on an individual or department. For example, board of education members perform an audit each month on the financial statements submitted to them for their approval. The requirement of multiple signatures for the approval of a purchase order constitutes an internal audit of purchasing. The accounting or bookkeeping department may also perform an audit on the general ledger prior to closing the financial statements at the end of each month.

Future Trends

The school finance system, with its budgeting, accounting, and auditing sub-systems, was designed to support the operation and improvement of public education. When a public budget is aligned to the needs and programs of the nation, state, district, or school; when the accounting structure is clear and well constructed to reflect the way money is collected and spent; and when the auditing process determines that money was managed legally and appropriately, then school should have the tools to use funds effectively, efficiently, and productively. With new technologies, a popular drive to improve the funding of education, greater interest in schools as the decision-making unit, increased privatization of education, and the growing influence of federal agencies in determining accounting and budgeting principles, the nation faces an interesting and challenging future in school finance. There are four key issues facing school finance: changing federal-state-local dynamics; privatization, expanding technology; and a move to funnel resources to students.

Changing federal-state-local dynamics. The drive to standardize accounting practices in education across the nation can lead to some interesting future develops. For example, in 1999 the General Accounting Standards Board (GASB), issued Statement 34, which requires, among other changes, that districts and states combine all funds that would account for their debt against the value of their monetary assets and fixed assets (e.g., land, buildings, and equipment). In some states, the balance between district assets and district debt is negative, although presumably the ability of districts to borrow funds (backed by the relevant cities and state) will not allow school systems to go bankrupt. However, this subtle change in accounting requirements may have far-reaching effects for school districts, as their bond ratings may be affected negatively, thus limiting the amount of funds they may borrow for capital improvements. Future developments in budgeting, accounting, and auditing will see greater standardization as the levels of government work together to improve school spending, accountability, and performance.

Increasing privatization of school provision. Private provision of education, with public tax support, appears to be increasing. The number of charter schools, for example, has grown exponentially and U.S. President George W. Bush's national policies place "parental choice" and private provision as keys to school reform. As more and more public dollars are diverted to private providers—as a result of national, state, and local political decisions—the money will be placed into the hands of private organizations unaccustomed to the budgeting, accounting, and auditing in which public schools have developed expertise.

Further, the mingling of public funding and private (even for-profit) management will make budgeting-accounting-auditing systems even more complex, blurring the lines between public and private provision, funding, and accountability. As budgets are being approved by local school boards, for example, and funding is reaching individually-managed schools (i.e., charter schools), more profit-making corporations, such as the Edison Schools or Knowledge Is Power Program, will become part of the education budgeting-accounting-auditing process.

Expanding technology and public awareness. *Sunshine laws,* requiring that all official meetings in publication education be announced in advance and to open to the public, are converging with advances in technology, heightening the possibility of financial information becoming real-time data for public inspection. With computers, Internet accessibility, and growing public interest, one can assume that budgeting-accounting-auditing procedures will become more systematic, accessible, and transparent to stakeholders of education nationwide.

Funneling resources to students. The future will also include an increasing interest in school-site and student-centered budgeting and accounting. Driven by interest in such devices as vouchers, whereby funding would be awarded to each student (family), future systems will include revising current budget and accounting models that link resources to students. Agencies as different as the State of Hawaii and the New York City Public Schools now account for spending by individual school, function, and program, creating greater interest in equity and productivity at the school and classroom levels. Whatever future financial structures U.S. schools adopt, the budgeting-accounting-auditing system will be required to plan, allocate, and hold decision-makers accountable for the enormous resources of the nation's largest public service: education.

See also: ACCOUNTING SYSTEMS IN HIGHER EDUCATION.

BIBLIOGRAPHY

CHAMBERS, JAY G. 2000. "Measuring Resources in Education: A Comparison of Accounting and the Resource Cost Model Approach." *School Business Affairs* 66(11):26–34.

COOPER, BRUCE S., and RANDALL, E. VANCE. 1998. "From Transactional to Transformational Accounting." *School Business Affairs* 64(4):4–16.

COOPER, BRUCE S.; NISONOFF, PHILIP H.; and SPEAKMAN, SHEREE T. 2001. "Advanced Budget Technology in Education: The Future Is Now." *School Business Affairs* 67(2):27–32.

COOPER, BRUCE S., and SPEAKMAN, SHEREE T. 1997. "The Three R's of Education Finance Reform: Re-Thinking, Re-Tooling, and Re-Evaluating School-Site Information." *Journal of Education Finance* 22 (4):337–367.

EVERETT, ROBERT E.; LOWS, RAYMOND L.; and JOHNSON, DONALD R. 1995. *Financial and Managerial Accounting for School Administrators.* Reston, VA: Association of School Business Officials International.

FOWLER, WILLIAM J., JR. 1990. *Financial Accounting for Local and State School Systems.* NCES 90096. Washington, DC: National Center for Education Statistics.

GLICK, PAUL E. 1999. *New Jersey ASBO Intermediate Governmental Accounting. Session 1: Introduction and Overview.* (Workshop Manual.) Bordentown: New Jersey Association of School Business Officials.

HACK, WALTER, et al. 1994. *School Business Administration: A Planning Approach.* Boston: Allyn and Bacon.

HARTMAN, WILLIAM T. 1999. *School District Budgeting.* Reston, VA: Association of School Business Officials International.

HIGA, MARION M. 2000. *Fiscal Accountability Audit of the Department of Education: Analysis of Selected School Expenditures. A Report to the Governor and the Legislature of the State of Hawaii.* Report No. 00-14. Honolulu: Office of the Auditor, State of Hawaii.

KIRST, MICHAEL W. 1975. "The Rise and Fall of PPBS in California." *Phi Delta Kappan* 56:535–538.

MUNDT, BARRY M.; OLSEN, RAYMOND T.; and STEINBERG, HAROLD I. 1982. *Managing Public Resources.* New York: Peat Marwick International.

NATIONAL ADVISORY COUNCIL ON STATE AND LOCAL BUDGETING. 1995. *A Framework for Improved State and Local Budgeting and Recommended Budgeting Practices.* Chicago: Government Finance Officers Association.

NEW JERSEY DEPARTMENT OF EDUCATION. DIVISION OF FINANCE. 2001. *Financial Accounting for New Jersey School Districts: The Audit Program.* Trenton: New Jersey Department of Education.

ODDEN, ALLAN; WOHLSTETTER, PRISCILLA; and ODDEN, ELEANOR. 1995. "Key Issues in Site-Based Management." *School Business Affairs* 61(5):2–11.

THOMPSON, DAVID C., and WOOD, CRAIG R. 2001. *Money and Schools.* Larchmont, NY: Eye on Education, Inc.

BRUCE S. COOPER
PHILIP H. NISONOFF

PUTNAM, ALICE (1841–1919)

A leader in the American kindergarten movement, Alice Putnam was a Progressive educator who trained many teachers and helped establish public kindergartens in Chicago. The daughter of Chicago Board of Trade founding member William Loring Whiting and Mary Starr, she was educated privately in a school run by her mother and sister, and at the Dearborn Seminary. She married Joseph Robie Putnam, a businessman, on May 20, 1868, and became a Swedenborgian (members of a church basing its theology on the work of the philosopher and theologian Emanuel Swedenborg), like her husband. The mother of four children, she started a parents' group to discuss Friedrich Froebel's kindergarten pedagogy. Putnam then began a home kindergarten, a kindergarten organization, and a training school, and became involved in kindergarten and educational reform in Chicago and nationally. Although little known because of her self-effacing humor, Putnam was a major figure within the group of Progressive educators and social reformers whose radical ideas were the force behind child-centered education.

Putnam came by her interest in the kindergarten, one of the most successful and lasting of all Progressive reforms, through her concerns about the education of her two eldest children. The parents' group, which she began in her home in 1874, was made up of a dozen or so of her friends, including three men, and focused on Froebel's *Mother Play and Songs,* a book of finger plays, games, and songs intended for the home education of young children. Putnam then trained as a kindergarten teacher herself, at a school run in Columbus, Ohio, by Anna J. Ogden. In 1880, Putnam took over the training class Ogden had started in Chicago. Other influential kindergarten leaders, such as Anna Bryan (who revolutionized American kindergarten methods by including more activities based on children's actual lives) were trained by Putnam, who ran the class until 1910.

A model of the maternalistic, social housekeeping ideal in which women extended the private sphere of domestic caring to public good works, Putnam moved her training class to Hull-House, at the request of Jane Addams—the founder of the settlement that was the seedbed for so many progressive reforms. For seven years, Putnam commuted between her home on Chicago's suburban West Side to the South Side slum where Hull-House was located, and did fundraising to support the Children's Building at Hull-House. John Dewey was a frequent guest lecturer at Putnam's training school, and gained some of his knowledge about educational methods from her.

In 1880 Putnam's original parents' group became the Chicago Froebel Association, which further promoted the kindergarten cause. By this time the kindergarten movement was becoming factionalized into a conservative Froebelian, a progressive American, and a more radical scientific wing. Although she received training from Susan Blow in St. Louis and from Maria Kraus-Boelte in New York City, both traditional Froebelians, Putnam's pragmatic attention to the needs of her own children and those of other parents from different backgrounds had a liberalizing, stabilizing effect. Later, in 1901, Putnam became president of the International Kindergarten Union, the group that tried to mediate dissension within the kindergarten movement.

A strong believer in civic pride and stewardship, Putnam expanded her kindergarten work to serve the city of Chicago as a whole. In 1886, under Putnam's auspices and with the permission of the Chicago Board of Education, the Chicago Froebel Association began a kindergarten housed in a public school. By 1892, when the association successfully petitioned the school board to adopt the kindergarten, there were twelve private kindergartens in public schools. These classes were incorporated into the public system, as was usual in the transition from charity to public kindergartens. This evolution of private good work into public services, through the advocacy and support of energetic individual leaders or private foundations, was a hallmark of the establishment of social welfare programs in the United States, an endeavor in which Putnam played a major role in the city of Chicago.

Like many Progressives, Putnam was influenced by the growth of the new science of child psychology. In 1894, Putnam, along with a number of other charity, or "free kindergarten," directors, attended G. Stanley Hall's Clark Summer School of Higher Pedagogy and Psychology in Worcester, Massachusetts. There she was introduced to Hall's experimental child study methods and participated in educational research. Hall asked Putnam and her former student, Anna Bryan, to design a special kindergarten survey, or *topical syllabus,* that was sent out to kindergarten teachers' to find out their views on subjects such as hygiene, music, and stories. Putnam's and Bryan's questions about whether teachers felt free to deviate from Froebel's formal educational routines showed how American kindergarten teachers were beginning to modify his sequenced educational materials, or "gifts," and handwork "occupations." Unlike younger modern kindergarten leaders such as Patty Smith Hill, who became closely allied with developmental psychology, Putnam continued to focus on children primarily from the perspective of family life.

Putnam's personal, practical motivation and lack of dogmatism won her great respect within the kindergarten movement. She worked especially closely with Elizabeth Harrison, who shared Putnam's interest in parent education and was also a moderate within the kindergarten movement. In 1883 Putnam and Harrison started the Chicago Kindergarten Club, which many affluent mothers joined along with their children.

In addition to her kindergarten leadership, Putnam was a key member of the group of educational Progressives who made turn-of-the-twentieth-century Chicago a hotbed of social reform. Putnam was directly responsible for getting Francis Parker, one of the main architects of child-centered progressivism, appointed to the principalship of the Cook County Normal School. Eagerly open to new educational ideas, Putnam had attended a summer school that Parker had held on Martha's Vineyard, where she learned about Parker's Quincy Method, in which reading and language arts were integrated with other subjects. Always seeking to combine her private and public life, Putnam moved her family to a house near Cook County Normal School, so that her three daughters could attend the laboratory school attached to the school. Putnam herself taught a kindergarten class at Cook County Normal School for some years and was the kindergarten trainer there. She joined with other pedagogical progressives, such as John Dewey and Ella Flagg Young, who clustered around Parker and helped spread Dewey's child-centered educational philosophy. Dewey was a frequent lecturer in Putnam's training classes.

A woman of affluence and intelligence with little formal education, Alice Putnam had a great impact on the kindergarten movement and on Progressive education through her own ideas and work and through the way she supported and connected other educators with differing views and backgrounds. She wrote articles, some of which appeared in the *Kindergarten Review* and other kindergarten publications; gave speeches, some of which were published in *National Education Association Proceedings*; and maintained a voluminous correspondence. In 1906 she began teaching two correspondence courses at the University of Chicago, "The Training of Children (A Course for Mothers)" and "Introduction to Kindergarten Theory and Practice." Putnam designed this coursework to inform parents and teachers about how children's learning could be integrated with children's lives, the central theme in Putnam's educational thinking. Putnam's work as a parent educator and kindergarten teacher, trainer, and leader and her involvement with Progressive education in Chicago had an important impact on the shift from subject-centered to child-centered pedagogy that was, and remains, the central dividing issue in American educational philosophy and methods.

See also: EARLY CHILDHOOD EDUCATION; FROEBEL, FRIEDRICH.

BIBLIOGRAPHY

BEATTY, BARBARA. 1995. *Preschool Education in America: The Culture of Young Children from the Colonial Era to the Present.* New Haven, CT: Yale University Press.

SHAPIRO, MICHAEL STEVEN. 1983. *Child's Garden: The Kindergarten Movement from Froebel to Dewey.* University Park: Pennsylvania State University Press.

WEBER, EVELYN. 1969. *The Kindergarten: Its Encounter with Educational Thought in America.* New York: Teachers College Press.

BARBARA BEATTY

ISBN 0-02-865599-0

90000